MANAGERIAL ECONOMICS

Robert E. McCormick

Clemson University

Prentice Hall, Englewood Cliffs, NJ 07632

McCormick, Robert E.
    Managerial economics / Robert E. McCormick.
        p.   cm.
    Includes bibliographical references and index.
    ISBN 0-13-544750-X
    1. Managerial economics.   I. Title.
HD30.22.M394   1992
338.5'024658—dc20   91-25797
                                              CIP

For Emily, Exley, and Jesse

Acquisition Editor: Stephen Dietrich
Editorial/production: Joanne Palmer
Cover design: Ray Lundgren Graphics
Cover art: Marvy!
Prepress buyer: Trudy Pisciotti
Manufacturing buyer: Patrice Fraccio
Editorial Assistant: Liz Becker

© 1993 by Prentice-Hall, Inc.
A Simon and Schuster Company
Englewood Cliffs, New Jersey 07632

Printed in the United States of America
10 9 8 7 6 5 4 3 2 1

ISBN 0-13-544750-X

Prentice-Hall International (UK) Limited, London
Prentice-Hall of Australia Pty. Limited, Sydney
Prentice-Hall Canada Inc., Toronto
Prentice-Hall Hispanoamericana, S.A., Mexico
Prentice-Hall of India Private Limited, New Delhi
Prentice-Hall of Japan, Inc., Tokyo
Simon & Schuster Asia Pte. Ltd., Singapore
Editora Prentice-Hall do Brasil, Ltda, Rio de Janeiro

CONTENTS

iii

CHAPTER 3   TOPICS IN CONSUMER BEHAVIOR   115

CHAPTER 4   ESTIMATING DEMAND FUNCTIONS   173

CHAPTER 5   TIMING, INTEREST, DISCOUNTING AND ARBITRAGE   241

CHAPTER 8   MONOPOLY, SEARCHING FOR THE BEST PRICE   393

CHAPTER
13

TEAM PRODUCTION, COORDINATION, AND CONTROL 599

CHAPTER
14

ADDITIONAL TOPICS IN PROPERTY RIGHTS AND THE ECONOMICS OF INFORMATION 589

CHAPTER 17

PLANT LOCATION DECISION MAKING: A CASE STUDY   689

PREFACE

The purpose of this book is rather simple and straightforward. I want to acquaint the student, the future manager, with the power of economic thinking. As a social science, economics has grown to be a broad-based paradigm for analyzing choices at many different levels. Government leaders confer with economists. Economists are important consultants to virtually every leading company in the world. Lawyers in firms large and small use economists as experts in a wide variety of litigation. On top of this, economic analysis, properly applied, is sufficiently powerful to address a large number of personal and private decisions, including work choice, educational decisions, simple consumption determinations, and more esoteric questions involving marriage and family matters. In a nutshell, economics is a way of thinking, a potent way of thinking, that can be useful to just about any manager regardless of his or her job or company.

There are a number of good managerial economics texts already in the field. What makes this book different or better? First, most of the existing books are a bit mechanical. Economics can be like that sometimes. In many ways this is not a flaw. The exactness required of many problems mandates precision that is difficult or impossible to make lively and entertaining. Like so much of life, it's just hard work. However, on occasion economists seem to go out of their way to make their ideas seem dull and lifeless. As Ronald Coase said in his Nobel Address, "What is studied is a system which lives in the minds of economists but not on earth. I have called the result 'blackboard economics.' The firm and the market appear by name but they lack any substance. The firm in mainstream economic theory has often been described as a 'black box.'"[1] I do not claim that I have made economic concepts funny, but I have tried to incorporate real world examples

---

[1] Ronald Coase, "The Institutional Structure of Production," *American Economic Review,* 82(4), September 1992, 714.

whenever possible to demonstrate that economics is far more than an academic game best played in an ivory tower. One thing that differentiates this text from some of the others, then, is the idea that economics is about real life.

In addition, it often seems that traditional texts in this area fail to observe and accommodate the crucial distinction between traditional microeconomics and managerial economics. This book is different from the field because of its orientation. Over the past fifteen to twenty-five years an important change has taken place in economic analysis of the firm, what some now call the revolution in industrial economics or the new institutional economics. Recent advances in areas such as information and uncertainty, pricing issues, transaction costs, game theory, and agency theory have truly altered the playing field. The analytical structure that has emerged from this body of work is extraordinarily powerful. Moreover, the tools and concepts seem to have direct implications for managers. The framework can actually be put to use down at the production level and in the corporate board room. In a sense sad, this intellectual breakthrough has not yet been reflected in the managerial economics textbooks available to senior under-graduates and first year MBA students.[2] Heretofore, in order to teach students this material, it was necessary for a teacher to put together a price theory book with a collection of journal articles, not particularly written for students at this level. What I have tried to do with this book is change this state of affairs by merging the best points of microeconomic theory applicable to managers with the property rights theory of the firm and the new industrial organization. This text is designed to have the traditional microeconomic material necessary to give students a feel, in the abstract, for how economies work. There is also new material that allows the instructor to pursue more detailed issues such as pricing, organizational design (for example, vertical integration), incentive compensa-tion, and contracting.

I spent several years teaching at the Graduate School of Management at the University of Rochester, now the William B. Simon Graduate School of Business. There I routinely taught two courses. One we called applied price theory, and the other was named property rights. In many ways this book is the end product that combines those two courses into one. Naturally you, the teachers and students, are the best judges of how well I have accomplished this goal.

The book can be divided into five sections—(1) introductory material, (2) consumer behavior, (3) finance-related matter, (4) the firm and its external rela-tions with markets and customers, and (5) the internal organization of firms. The introductory section has three parts. Besides a description of the concept of managerial economics, Chapter 2 and its appendix review, in turn, the basics of supply and demand and markets and mathematical analysis. Chapter 2 should be read by all students, even those with a recent and strong background in econom-ics. For one reason, it lists many terms and notations used throughout the rest of the book. For another, it is a quick way to learn my writing style and meth-

---

[2] The new book by Paul Milgrom and John Roberts, *Economics, Organization & Management* (Englewood Cliffs: Prentice Hall, 1992), is a good example of a higher level text that is filling this void.

odological approach to economics. Moreover, it contains a long section on elasticity.

Chapter 2 has an appendix on mathematics. Students with a weak background here should apply themselves with diligence. Others will find it a convenient review. It is possible to teach managerial economics using this book without reading the appendix to Chapter 2, but quite a few problems will be a lot easier if the student can use some basic mathematical techniques.

Section two incorporates the theory of the consumer. Here there are two chapters, 3 and 4. Chapter 3 lays out the theory of consumer behavior and contains many related topics. Chapter 4 is devoted to statistical analysis of consumer demand functions.

Section three includes Chapters 5 and 16. Chapter 5 supplies a transition from consumer behavior to intertemporal decision making. Interest rates, discounting and the like are introduced. Chapter 16 stands alone as a tool for understanding linear programming.

I do not think it is bold or pompous to say that this text is unique. The next two sections reflect this fact. The fourth section has six chapters, 6-11, which characterize the firm and its external relations with customers, markets, and input suppliers. Issues in information and contracting are addressed here as well. Portions of Chapter 15 also fit in here.

Chapters 12-14, in many ways the heart of the volume, stand out in the text. Public goods and common access goods are introduced and then are shown to be a major part of managerial decision making. Team production is shown to be a potent machine for unraveling the mysteries of the firm. The shroud is removed from the firm, and the student is forced to look inside the black box and try and understand why it does what it does. The fiction that firms make decisions is discarded.

Here is how the textbook works. I presume that the students are well motivated. Most senior undergraduate business students and virtually all MBAs are well aware of the opportunity cost of education and naturally are inclined to try and get as much as they can out of the course, the teacher, and the text. Because I believe this to be true, the book takes a definite approach. Problems are presented to students. These are either in text and called "hypothetical business problems," or they are included at the end of each chapter as "study problems." These are far more than normal homework. They are living proof that the principles being presented apply to the day-to-day chores of managers, and as such, are intended to get the student excited about the material. As a natural consequence, a simple reading of the book is insufficient. The student has to work the problems, either alone or in a study group. And then the teacher has to cover some of them in class to show how they apply to the lessons. Precisely for this reason I have tried to answer many of the problems in the text. At first blush this would seem to make it somewhat difficult for the teacher to use the study problems as test questions. But actually that probably is not true. If the students can work the problems in or at the end of the chapters, then they have really learned the material. And hence, the questions become a valuable tool for judging the learning level of the students. I cannot say it more strongly—the problems are a vital part of the book. Not using them leaves a lot of the value of the text on the table.

The book contains more material than most teachers will want to cover in a one-semester course or a two-quarter sequence. This approach is designed to give the instructor flexibility to exploit his or her strengths and interests in this field. Let me propose several different approaches to deal with the variety of material. First, in virtually all cases, Chapters 1 and 2 should be employed with the appendix to Chapter 2 included for those students with a weak mathematical background. These are introductory and necessary. At this point two different paths emerge. One is to concentrate on consumer or pricing issues. This route next studies Chapters 3 and 4. For programs with a strong econometric orientation, the material in Chapter 4 might be redundant and can be skipped without loss of orientation.

An alternative course would shift to chapters 5 and 16 after the introductory material. The matter here focuses on nuts and bolts managerial economics, discounting, project evaluation, and linear programming.

Whether the instructor chooses the first or second of these plans, the material in Chapters 6-11 and then Chapters 12-14 should be covered next. This deals with the theory of the firm, both externally and internally. The coverage here is fundamental.

At this point there are two chapters remaining, Chapter 15 on regulation and Chapter 17, a case study on plant location decisions. Either or both of these can be incorporated regardless of the previous orientation. They are both self-contained.

It is almost immoral for me to place my name on this book alone, so many other people have contributed. Let me name just a few of them by placing them in several different groups. First, beginning while in school, many teachers, Bob Basmann, Ray Battalio, Bob Ekelund, Chuck Maurice, Tom Saving, Bruce Yandle, and particularly Bob Tollison, to name a few, had an especially powerful influence on me and the way I think about managerial economics. The second group, my colleagues at the University of Rochester and Clemson University, have nurtured and aided me too many times to count. If you the reader wouldn't think I was being silly I would list virtually all of them by name. That's how important they have been to me. Surely a few stand out and bear notation. The influence of Mike Jensen, Bill Meckling, Gregg Jarrell, Mike Bradley, Ken French, Cliff Smith, Jerry Zimmerman, Ross Watts, John Long, Ron Hansen, Bill Schwert, Jim Ferguson, and Marty Geisel at Rochester pervades this book whether they want to admit it or not. In addition, I taught a number of classes jointly with Mike Jensen, Bill Meckling, Ken French, Dennis Sheehan, Anne Coughlan, and Mel Jameson that help prepare the notes on which this manuscript is based. At Clemson a number of people worked hard directly on this book to help it come to fruition. Dan Benjamin, Taufiq Choudhry, Robert Clement, Charley Diamond, Mason Gerety, Kim Knight, and Curtis Simon made valuable contributions and deserve a giant thanks. Indirectly, the daily counsel of Matt Lindsay and my other colleagues at Clemson is duly noted.

The third group includes the large number of dedicated, professional economists upon whose back almost all of the work here rests, those people who helped shape and mold modern managerial economics, industrial economics, and the theory of the firm.

Next, undergraduate and MBA students at Clemson have suffered through numerous photocopied versions of this text full of typing errors, errors of analysis, and oversights over the five years this project has been developing. They deserved better, and hopefully the end product somehow justifies their ordeal. I also forced a provisional version of the text on students at the Universidad Francisco Marroquin in Guatemala while visiting there in the winter semester of 1990. In addition, a number of other faculty have used provisional copies of the text in their undergraduate and graduate classes in managerial economics at Clemson and other schools. Many helpful ideas and suggestions emerged from that process. To all of you, your comments and patience are appreciated, y muchas gracias.

Several people at Prentice Hall deserve recognition. First, to Marty McDonald who prodded me to write this book and Bill Webber who convinced me to do it, thanks. Second, to Whitney Blake and especially to Dianne deCastro, Garret White, and Stephen Dietrich who provided the finishing touches, thank you. For those of you who might be considering writing a text, I hope that your editor serves you as well as Stephen has me. Fifteen anonymous readers, contracted by Prentice Hall, made a profound contribution to this project. They carefully and critically read the entire text, made detailed suggestions which were so sharp and to the point that I incorporated virtually all of them. They should feel proud of the work they did. I am in their debt. They encouraged me, and they made the book a lot better.

Two special people in my life warrant particular notice. My colleague, coauthor, and counselor, Mike Maloney, always willing to listen to my questions, to hold my hand, to set my head on straight, is all that a friend can be. I would never have finished this task without him. I will not try to thank him.

My wife, Emily Wood, on top of being my friend, edited, read, and reread so many versions of this text, that she probably deserves to be listed as a coauthor. Her suggestions for improvement of verse and analysis are literally found on every page of text. I would never have finished this task without her either. She and my son Exley gave up a husband and father for far too long in order that this book could be written. I hope enough of you like this book so that I can pay them back.

When I started this project, I had little idea how much work goes into the technical aspects of publishing a book. Two people at Prentice Hall worked very hard to make this book a success. I owe Joanne Palmer and Linda Pawelchak an enormous pat on the back for a job well done, far beyond the call of duty. Thanks. You both served me well.

It is customary and obligatory at this point to hold all these parties blameless for the errors remaining in this book. Perhaps one of the lessons contained here is that my name on the cover sort of takes care of that problem. Let it be. I hope you enjoy the book and the lessons in it.

Robert E. McCormick
Clemson University

CHAPTER

1

INTRODUCTION TO MANAGERIAL ECONOMICS

- Introduction
- The Methodology of Economic Analysis
- Topics
- Analysis
- The Methodology of the Book
- Topics to Review
- Study Problems
- Suggested Readings
- Suggested Solutions to Selected Study Problems

INTRODUCTION

The area of study called **managerial economics** has many facets. It is primarily the application of economic principles to managerial decision making. It is a way of thinking, but it is not the only way to think—it is the way an economist thinks. In this text, it is the author's vision of the way an economist thinks. Over the years, from the time of Adam Smith until today, economists have developed a set of tools, a bag of tricks if you will, that they use to describe, analyze, and understand a wide range of problems. For the purpose of managerial decision making, only a small subset of these tools is employed. For example, it is common for economists to divide their work into two broad camps: macroeconomics and micro-economics. **Macroeconomics** is the study of aggregate phenomena such as inflation, unemployment, and gross national product. Macroeconomics is concerned with the bulk of the items on economics that you read about in the paper or see on television all the time: "Today the government announced that unemployment was down three-quarters of a percent for the month of June. Many economists interpret this to mean that the recent recession has bottomed out." **Micro-economics,** on the other hand, is the application of economic paradigms to the study of the individual, the firm, or the family. For example, microeconomics is used to understand why companies use different pricing schemes. Many of you have visited Disneyland or Disney World and have paid a fee to get in the gates. Once inside, however, you did not have to pay to enter most attractions. By contrast, the county fairs that many of you have attended charged an admission fee, but you also often paid an additional fee for each attraction that you visited or rode. Most telephone companies charge a fixed monthly fee for local service, independent of the number of local calls, but they charge individually for each long-distance call. Electric and water utilities almost never have a fixed fee system like the telephone company. Why do these similar enterprises price differently? This is the type of question we answer with microeconomic analysis. Managerial economics, at least according to this author's vision, is almost exclusively micro-economics. This means that we do not, to any important degree, concern ourselves with unemployment, inflation, or the value of the dollar versus international currencies. Instead, we concentrate on individual firm behavior, individual consumer prices, and the like. These other topics are important, and no self-respecting economist or manager would be foolish enough to treat them lightly. However, no text can cover all topics, and some subjects are left for other classes. So it is with macroeconomics here.

Managerial economics is supposed to teach you how to deal with the nature of the firm, how and why it is organized the way it is, in order to make you a better, more efficient, and more highly rewarded executive. To this end, managerial economics is application oriented. It is designed to be put to direct use. Many of the courses you take in college provide background information and theory. Others are truly applied. This course fits somewhere in between. You will be taught a lot of theory here, but you will also be shown how to use theory to make day-to-day decisions. This is not a cookbook or a success manual, but rather a guidebook pointing your way to beautiful vistas while helping you avoid the dark alleys.

THE METHODOLOGY OF ECONOMIC ANALYSIS

Economic analysis is divided into two distinctly different areas. First, there is optimality analysis, or what is more commonly called **normative analysis.** The normative branch of economics seeks to find the *best* solution to a particular problem. In order to accomplish this goal, some *objective function* describing the desired outcome must be assumed or assigned, and hence the phrase *normative analysis* is often employed. An **objective function** describes goals. It picks and chooses among various alternative outcomes. For instance, the objective function of most major league baseball teams is to win the World Series. Thus normative economics is used to sort among various policies and objectives. In the area of managerial economics, normative analysis addresses questions such as, What should the company's goal be? Should the company maximize profit and value, or should the company also concern itself with social issues such as minority hiring, environmental decay, and individual liberty? It is easy to see how reasonable people can disagree on these issues because, to some degree, each of us has a different set of values or mores. Hence, normative analysis is subjective and argumentative. Indeed, many if not most managerial disagreements arise because parties have different goals in mind, not because they disagree about the facts. Worse yet, the goals themselves never seem to surface in the discussion; they remain unspoken, hinder discussion, and cloud the issues. Consequently, it is often wise during a heated discussion to take stock and ensure that all parties have the same objective in mind or that they all agree to debate the appropriate objective. Otherwise, one group will be arguing about the facts and another group will be debating whether some situation is good or bad. *This is an unjoined debate and should be avoided at all costs.* It is fruitless, distracting, and unproductive. Consider a simple scenario. Suppose a company sells a product, say ether, that has many uses, but one of them is illegal—the production of cocaine. A management committee has been formed to investigate the situation and make a recommendation to the CEO. One faction on the committee reports that if ether production is terminated, lost sales will cost the company $565,000 per year, and the firm will have to lay off 125 workers. Another group on the committee strongly contends that the company has a moral commitment to stop production of ether because so much of it ends up being used to produce cocaine and crack, which are consumed by young people. Is this a joined debate? No. The first group has made a factual forecast about the future that may turn out to be right or wrong. The second group has *not* disputed those facts but instead has presented what it thinks the moral position of the company should be. The first group has not presented an alternative to the second group either. It did not, for example, say that the objective of the company should be to make as much money as it legally could, which *would* have been a counterproposal to the position held by the second group. Much futility is in store for managers who do not distinguish between objective principles and factual statements.

Contrasted with normative analysis is another branch of economic methodology dealing with facts, which is called positive or scientific analysis. **Positive analysis** focuses attention on what *is*, rather than what should be. The approach here is to find out what is going on in the world and explain why it is that way.

Questions include, If the price of labor in the automobile industry increases by 12 percent, how much will the price of cars rise? Or, what will happen to the number of firms in the domestic textile industry if the U.S. Congress imposes a quota on foreign textile goods? Of course, these questions are also arguable, but, unlike normative analysis, reasonable people will not disagree on the issues if they are given enough facts.

The purpose of positive analysis is prediction. Managers find it useful to have educated guesses about events likely to occur in the future. What will happen to sales if we raise the price by 15 percent? Positive analysis is only concerned with the correct answer to that question. In that sense, it is amoral or scientific. That sounds easy enough until we get involved in the solution of real-world problems, and then it is easy to get tangled between the empirical truth and our own values. Many hours are lost in meetings when one person is arguing a positive position and another is defending what appears to be the opposite position, when in fact the two are actually debating the appropriate objective. Science has no objectives. It is simply correct or it is not. For example, the issue of abortion is so controversial and heated that many people get confused between the normative and scientific prongs of the problem. Many people believe that women should have the right to choose whether or not to stop an unwanted pregnancy, while others take the position that abortion is murder. This is a normative debate. At the same time, there is scientific evidence on the number of abortions performed in the United States since the Supreme Court's famous *Roe v. Wade* decision. The issue of how many abortions have been performed is scientific and is not arguable given enough information. The question of whether abortion should be legal or not is individually moralistic and unresolvable with science. Thus, little headway is gained in a discussion in which one person is talking about the growth in the number of abortions since 1972 and the other is taking a moral stance.

It is difficult but important to separate normative from positive analysis. It is imprudent of managers to think something will happen just because they want it to, or because it should. For example, even though you think people should not steal or murder, the crime rate in this country is not zero. The wise analyst can make the distinction.

In August 1990, armed forces from Iraq invaded Kuwait and threatened Turkey and Saudi Arabia. As a direct response, the spot and future delivery price of crude oil went up a great deal, 25 percent or more in some cases. About the same time, the price of gasoline in the United States also increased. There was a great outcry from consumers, politicians, oil industry analysts and managers, and others over whether the public was being gouged at the gas pump. Many questions were asked. Few were answered. Why had the price of gas risen so much? Would the price of gas have decreased by the same amount if crude oil prices had fallen instead of risen? Should oil companies have held the line on gas prices to keep from hurting the economy at a time when many people feared a recession was near at hand? Should the government investigate situations like this? Should the government intervene as it had in the 1970s to regulate the flow and price of oil and gas? Should the United States have a governmentally mandated comprehensive energy plan?

Oil company profits went up dramatically as the price of crude rose. Should the companies have raised the price of gas in this circumstance? Obviously, the answer to that question is a moral one, and each of us has an opinion. Some would say no. It is unconscionable for companies to raise prices in this situation. Others would say that the managers had a fiduciary responsibility to the shareholders of the company to make as much money as possible. Although it is important and necessary, this debate has no end. The original question still remains, Why did the price of oil go up by the amount it did? Was it due to monopoly forces in the oil industry? Was it because the owners and managers of oil companies were compelled by the forces of competition to increase prices? Did the price of gas increase in this situation more than the price of bread would have increased if the price of flour had gone up by 25 percent? These latter questions can be resolved by scientific inquiry, but that does not mean they are more or less important. It simply means that a correct answer can be pursued.

Which types of questions do you find most interesting, the moral or scientific ones? As a general rule, most people find it more enjoyable to discuss the moral issues of a problem. Why that is so (assuming it is) is an interesting question in its own right, but one that must wait for another course or book. What you need to do to be successful in this course is to retrain your way of thinking. What this course will try to teach you is why the price of gas rose as much as it did. This will not be an apology for the oil companies or a battle cry for consumer activists. It will be a hard-edged, refutable, explanation for the events at hand. This process will require some patience and diligence on your part, but if you want to be successful in this area, you will make the effort. One of the main purposes of this book and course is to make this job easier for you. In the end, perhaps you will find it slightly less onerous to probe into the reasons why gas prices rose the way they did.

TOPICS

This book covers a lot of material, and you are not likely to read all of it. The next chapter reviews the simple analytics of supply and demand. Included is a basic explanation of the way markets work. This is a general overview and review of the principles of economics. We discuss the determinants of demand and supply and the way prices are set in competitive markets. We also review the important topic of elasticity. You are introduced to a number of analytical and numerical problems. Virtually all of you should explore this chapter. Even those of you with an extensive background in economics will find it useful, for you can become acquainted with this author's question-and-answer method. You will see a general approach. A question is asked, some techniques are taught to address the question, and then a solution is presented. Chapter 2 contains an appendix for those of you who need to review the basic principles of mathematics and calculus. Not all students need this material. For those unfamiliar with the rules of mathematical optimization or differential calculus, this chapter provides a basic review. Here again, many students will find this material redundant.

The next group of three chapters is devoted to analysis of consumer behavior and the economist's view of how people make spending decisions. Chapter 3 provides the economic theory of consumer behavior. At first this may seem out of place to you in a course on managerial economics; however, those of you who end up in marketing or pricing positions will find this material very useful. The chapter also has applications that are designed to prove useful in dealing with employees, who after all work so they can consume. Chapter 4 is devoted to econometric (statistical) analysis of consumer demand, estimating the actual numerical relation between price and quantity. This chapter is especially useful for those of you interested in marketing or pricing strategies. It is heavily oriented toward applications. It requires that you master some elementary statistical concepts, but sufficient material is presented to guide the way for those students who have little or no formal training in this area. This chapter will be your introduction to the relation between managerial economics and computers. Depending upon the orientation of your instructor, you could spend a great deal of time here learning to use computers and statistical software. Chapter 5 is an analysis of interest rates, discounting, and present values—and their importance for managerial decision making. As in most of the chapters in this book, some theory and some applications are presented. The theory is taught not for its own sake, but so that you can solve the problems you might eventually encounter as a manager on the job, as well as the ones presented in the text.

The third section in the book examines the theory of the firm. There are actually two distinctly different ways to analyze this theory. The first, commonly referred to as the **neoclassical theory of the firm,** treats the firm itself as the unit of study; it focuses on the firm's decisions about what to produce, how much to produce, and what price to sell it for. This material is presented in Chapter 6. The theoretical problems of cost minimization and profit maximization are explored, and the managerial implications of these economic concepts are developed. Chapter 7 covers the behavior of the firm in a competitive market. This is especially useful for an overview of markets and as a foundation for understanding the firm as a greater part of markets and society.

Chapter 8 continues the focus on the firm as a whole and covers the monopoly firm. The material introduced here is broader than you might first think. Many firms have some control over the prices they charge. First, there is a discussion of the sources of pricing or monopoly power. Then the general theoretical problem of the optimal price is presented. Applications of this principle follow with Chapter 9, which is devoted to an understanding of price discrimination and pricing in general. Chapter 10 is oriented toward market structures that lie somewhere between competition and monopoly. The chapter also contains a discussion of game theory, cooperation, and cartels between rival firms in the economy. Chapter 11 examines related issues concerning topics in information economics and industrial organization.

The second way to analyze firms is called **property rights theory;** it emphasizes organizational aspects within the firm. Chapters 12 and 13 lay a strong theoretical foundation for studying organization structure. Then applied business problems are addressed. For instance, managerial compensation is studied, and the reasons for different structures within firms are investigated. A great deal of attention is paid here to rules and regulations within firms. You will be exposed to theory and applications in this section. The theory is necessary to provide structure. The applications are designed to help you gain experience. For example, in large multidivisional companies, goods are often transferred between component parts within the organization. For accounting and economic purposes, it is imperative to assign value to these goods when they change divisions. These values are called transfer prices, and a part of Chapter 14 is devoted to a basic understanding of them.

Chapter 12 begins with a theoretical discussion on public goods, private goods, common access, and private access goods. This discussion is used in Chapter 13 to explore the notion of team production, a fundamental building block in the theory of the firm. When a good is common access property, when it is available for all to use, a set of problems develops. These problems create opportunities for managers to reveal their abilities, and substantial portions of Chapters 13 and 14 are devoted to an in-depth understanding of the many problems associated with team production and common access property.

Chapter 15 is a discussion of the relation between firms and government. It is not meant to be exhaustive, but it is designed to be practical. The new economic theory of regulation is developed in detail, along with the concept of rent seeking and how it applies to the firm. Different regulations and regulatory agencies are discussed. Although some theory is presented, there is a great deal of reference to the facts of regulation as they are contained in modern economics literature. Chapter 16 on linear programming follows the regulation chapter. It provides the essential elements of linear programming and then examples of the principles in practice. Linear programming is a valuable tool used by a wide range of companies and managers. At a minimum, an aspiring corporate executive has to be familiar with the strengths and weaknesses of this technique. Chapter 16 is intended to provide the necessary background. Some theory is presented, but the chapter is primarily application oriented.

Chapter 17 is a case study on plant location decision making. It is neither necessary nor sufficient for training as a manager. However, it is a real case problem faced by managers, and as such, it gives you the opportunity to acquire a keener understanding of the types of problems faced by those ahead of you.

ANALYSIS

At its most esoteric level, **economic analysis** is the ability to recognize a problem, carve out the substance for the situation at hand, and create a solution or a course of action. Milton Friedman says, "Economics as a positive science is a body of tentatively accepted generalizations about economic phenomena that can be used to predict the consequences of changes in circumstances."[1] This is something far more than memorizing a litany of definitions, formulas, and jargon. A parrot can be taught to say, "Supply and Demand." When I was a young boy, my father and I visited the site of a large train derailment near our home. Walking around the accident scene, we encountered a railroad security guard, and my father asked about the cause of the accident. The guard replied, "Mechanical failure." I was amazed at the guard's perception, but I was too embarrassed to admit in his

---

[1] Milton Friedman, *Essays in Positive Economics.* (Chicago: University of Chicago Press, 1953), p. 42.

presence that I did not understand, instead choosing to mutter, "Oh yeah. That's too bad." As we walked away, I turned to my pop and asked him what mechanical failure meant. His reply has been etched in my mind for a lifetime, "It means he doesn't know what caused the wreck."

Suppose you are outside one summer evening at 11:30 P.M. and a friend turns to you and says, "Why is it dark now?" There are basically two ways to approach this query. One is to offer a definition without analysis, to wit, "Because it's nighttime, silly." By contrast, the analytical approach is much more profound. Your response begins with a discussion of the sun's production of light, the nature of light waves, and the apparent fact that they travel in a straight line but cannot pass through the earth and includes a discussion about the absence of a reflector such as the moon. More complete analysis would include talk about electric lights and why they were not installed or turned on. Do not misunderstand: Definitions and taxonomy are useful, but they are not substitutes for analysis. Suppose your boss repeatedly observes one of your underlings acting strangely and inquires about the nature and cause of this behavior. As a manager, it will not suffice for you to respond, "He is weird." For you to *explain* this behavior on grounds that the person is weird is merely a tautology, a truth offering no substance. By definition, a *weirdo* is a person who does odd sorts of things. Hence, to say that the *reason* a person acts strangely is that he is weird amounts to saying that he acts strangely because he is strange. People who offer tautologies and definitions in lieu of analysis do not usually climb many rungs on the corporate ladder. The best managers, and the ones most highly paid, generally hold mere taxonomists in low regard. There are few substitutes for rock hard analysis. At least, that is the theory underlying this book.[2]

Constructing Theories, Evaluating Theories, and the Scientific Methodology

What are the essential elements of analysis? In the paradigm of economics, there are basically three components. First, there is the construction of a theory. Next, there is the construction of an alternative hypothesis, and third, there is the evaluation of the theory. Let's discuss each of these components in turn.

A **theory** is actually quite a simple thing. It is a set of assumptions followed by a series of conclusions deduced using certain rules. The primary canon in the construction of a theory is that the analysis must be free of all contradictions. A contradiction is the inclusion of a statement and its opposite. Thus, theories cannot assume (1) that it is raining outside and (2) it is not raining outside. Aside from this cardinal rule, a theory has few restrictions. The author or creator of the theory is basically free to choose any assumptions deemed appropriate. Of course, others are free to make different, perhaps conflicting assumptions. This necessarily pits theories against each other, and it is the competition between

---

[2] The student who wishes to pursue this line of inquiry is recommended to Robert Pirsig, *Zen and the Art of Motorcycle Maintenance: An Inquiry into Values* (New York: Morrow, 1974).

theories that gives rise to debate requiring some method for choosing between the alternatives. But before we discuss these methods, let's first discuss the role of assumptions in more detail.

What is an assumption, and what is its purpose? An **assumption** is an abstraction from reality. For instance, when we travel in our car, we assume that the shortest distance between two points is a straight line, and for relatively short distances, that assumption usually serves us well. However, air travel over great distances would be far more expensive if carriers used this approach. When traveling around a sphere, the shortest distance between two points is an arc, called a great circle.

Assumptions are made for the sake of analytical simplicity. Many problems are far too complicated to cope with unless some aspects of the puzzle are ignored. Thus we make assumptions that are conscious deviations from reality for the purpose of dealing with a difficult, multifaceted question. Naturally this means that many assumptions, by their very nature, are wrong or unrealistic *on purpose*.

The implication of this line of reasoning is profound. To summarize, a theory is an abstraction from reality. Assumptions are made to simplify an otherwise overly complex problem. The very nature of the assumptions renders the theory incorrect, for some (preferably minor or insignificant) aspect of reality has been ignored. We are left with the inescapable conclusion that in order to be useful, any and all theories must be wrong, at least in some dimension. Thus, assumptions must be chosen with care, for they define the purpose and usefulness of a theory. The aspects of a problem that are assumed away cannot, by construction, be analyzed with the theory. Thus, different parts of a large, complex problem may require different assumptions and different theories. We are left with the conclusion that all theories are somewhat in error, and it brings into question the idea of judging a theory on the basis of the reasonableness of its assumptions. Given this dilemma, economists acting as scientists have, for the most part, chosen the approach that the assumptions do not matter, only the conclusions do.

In turn, this implies that alternative theories, using competing and contradictory sets of assumptions, will be judged less on the subjective quality of the assumptions and more on the ability of their conclusions to predict outcomes. A simple example may help to enlighten.

Suppose a carpenter comes to your house to add an extra bedroom. One of the first tasks accomplished will be the layout of the foundation. A transit or level typically will be used to lay the foundation level. This device will be used on the assumption that the earth is flat, an assumption destroyed in the minds of most many years back, at least as far back as 1492. Does this unrealistic, flat-earth assumption mean that the carpenter is incompetent? In fact, quite the opposite. Over the range of 10–30 feet, the assumption, although incorrect, is so innocuous that the errors made are trivial compared to the cost of calculating the curvature of the earth over such a short span. Thus, the assumption that the earth is flat, although wrong, is very useful, for the theories built upon it work. That is, they predict well. Houses built on foundations made level using the flat-earth assumption are constructed daily.

Naturally, this assumption falls on hard times when it comes to planning earth orbits for the space shuttle. But the point here is that the assumption is abandoned for space travel, not because it is unrealistic, but rather because the conclusions of theories built with that assumption do not predict the path of space ships with any degree of accuracy. In spite of all the advances in physics over the past century, most of which have destroyed the classical Newtonian notions of molecular motion, Newton's laws are still used to plan and model satellite motion about the earth. Even though we know that Newtonian ideas of molecular motion are wrong and that the principles of quantum mechanics are far better tools for understanding the behavior of physical bodies, Newtonian theories still work sufficiently well to be the primary tool for guiding astronauts around the earth. The theories are used not because their assumptions are good, but rather because their conclusions are accurate *for the purposes at hand.*

Because a theory by definition cannot be right, there will always be alternative theories competing for attention. It is this competition that gives rise to the development of new ideas and the progress of knowledge. A theory is developed. Another theory challenges some of the conclusions of the first theory. Some facts are brought to bear on the issue, and one theory or the other wins the battle, but the war is not over. Either more facts emerge or another theory surfaces to dispute the winner of the first battle. Then, even more facts are brought to light. The process of analysis is continuous and evolutionary. At some point, one particular theory may have so much evidence on its side that people no longer construct alternatives nor collect additional information to confirm or deny the theory. At this point the theory has become a **law.** The law of gravity immediately comes to mind. But even then one never knows when some person will uncover a new insight or a rare fact that defies the accepted wisdom. Knowledge is always in a tenuous state.

Mathematical Analysis

Mathematical analysis scares a lot of people. However, some problems are so much easier to solve with the insight of mathematical analysis that few students can afford the luxury of ignoring algebra and calculus. Chapter 2 has an appendix that presents a brief review of all the mathematical principles required in this book. Moreover, virtually every problem that is presented mathematically is also analyzed with words or graphs. You are almost never left alone with math. The world around us is becoming more quantitative. Computers, electronic scanners, and other data collection devices make it increasingly important for managers to have a solid grasp of mathematical methods and numerical analysis. There are fewer and fewer places for the mathematically ignorant manager to hide. But mathematics is a tool, not an end unto itself. It is only used here to solve managerial problems. Use it when it serves you, discard it otherwise. From time to time, you will see equations and Greek letters scattered throughout the text. *Do not* let these symbols scare you. They are not essential to your learning, and you should never waste time trying to memorize them. They are analytical shortcuts that can, when used properly, provide a level of rigor more cheaply than the alternatives. Virtually everything of substance in this book can be learned without reading one line of equations or one Greek symbol. This does *not* mean that you can pretend that the mathematics is irrelevant. Indeed there is quite a bit of analysis in the book using the mathematical techniques. This material is important, and those of you who want to excel as managers will learn to use the methods of mathematics.

THE METHODOLOGY OF THE BOOK

This book employs an empirical approach to managerial decision making. What does this mean? First, a problem presents itself. Sometimes it is obvious; other times it is shrouded by irrelevancies. Next, a theory is applied to the problem. Often multiple theories compete for attention. Facts or data are then brought to bear to resolve the competition between theories. That is, an empirical resolution is sought. Finally, once you are armed with some facts, a solution presents itself.

But the process is continuous. New facts are immediately collected to determine if the solution was correct. New theories develop. More facts are collected. Managerial decision making is a dynamic and ongoing process. Consider a simple example. The managers of the local cable television company fear that some customers are illegally capturing the coded signals of specialty channels such as ESPN and HBO. One group says that it is too costly to correct the problem while another faction argues that too much revenue is being lost to the pirates. The empirical approach to resolving this problem is straightforward. The cable television company investigates a sample of homes to determine what fraction of its consumers have illegal descramblers. Next, it computes the cost of switching to a new scrambling technique. Then it becomes obvious to both groups which solution is better: keep the status quo or fight the pirates. Facts have resolved the debate. Naturally, as time passes, it is necessary to reexamine the facts to ensure that the previous position remains the correct course of action.

As a pedagogical tool, so-called hypothetical business problems are presented throughout the book. Typically, theory is then developed and analysis presented to address the problem at hand. Data are often presented to resolve the issues. In most cases, the data are actual numbers from real situations; the view taken here is that in the mass of interesting managerial situations, facts resolve arguments. Sources are also cited if the data are in the public domain. The conscientious student is urged to (1) reproduce the data and (2) replicate the numerical analysis presented. In most cases, this analysis is not the only solution, merely a viable one. The examples are pedagogical; they are designed to acquaint the student with the power of economic analysis. To learn the method, the student must persevere and practice, problem after problem. There is no alternative.

This book is about analysis. The person who learns analysis can apply it to any problem that presents itself. The student who attempts to memorize, categorize, or create a taxonomy out of every problem will likely be successful if and only if the same or similar problem is encountered in the future. Since there is virtually no way that this book or your teacher can present an example of every problem that you might face once you are on the job, developing analytical tools that can be applied to the actual problems you will face is the route to success. You must learn to think. After that, it all seems easy. I hope you enjoy the material presented here and find it worth the cost.

TOPICS TO REVIEW

These are topics that you should feel comfortable with before you leave this chapter. If you cannot write out a clear and concise sentence or paragraph explaining the topic after you have worked on the study problems, you should reread the relevant section of the text.

Positive Analysis

Normative Analysis

Microeconomics

Macroeconomics

Role of Assumptions in Theories

Scientific Methodology

STUDY PROBLEMS

The study problems in this book are intended to be an integral part of the learning process. Reading the material in each chapter is only the first step. After that you must practice putting the principles into action. This is the only way to master the concepts discussed in the text. In a way, the study problems are the heart of the material. Unless you attack them with vigor, you will not get full value from the book. You should *write* out the answers, working with others if you wish. Study groups are advised. It is probably a mistake to read the problem and then presume that you know the answer without writing out your proposed solution. Students who do this usually trick themselves into believing that they would have analyzed the problem in much the same manner as the proposed solution. Put it in writing.

1. Why do economists and others often make a distinction between science and art? What is the value of each approach? What are some of the advantages and disadvantages of each? Why do some people feel it is important to make theories value free? When is it important to make theories value free?

2. What does it mean to say, "That is good in theory, but it doesn't work in reality"?

3. Which of the following statements, hypotheses, or theories are value free and which are not? Why so?

   a. Unemployed people should receive income compensation from the state because they are deserving.

   b. If people want to ride Amtrak, they should pay the full price of that service.

   c. On average, women earn about 62 percent as much as men.

    d. Because women often earn less than men for the same or seemingly the same work, they must be the victims of wage discrimination.

    e. Because women earn less than men, often for the same work effort, it is important to pass equal pay for equal work laws or equal rights for women laws.

    f. Textile quotas and tariffs are the only long-run salvation of the domestic textile industry in the United States.

    g. If it is true that textile quotas and tariffs are the only way for the domestic textile industry to survive, it is important to pass such laws now.

    h. Pacific Gas & Electric has a monopoly in the sale of electricity in certain parts of California.

    i. Monopolies charge a higher price and sell less output than comparable competitive firms.

    j. For the most part, it is not legal in the United States for people to "truck and barter" with each other.

4. A ballet company in Cleveland believes the demand for its performances is closely approximated by the following function:

$$q = 10,000 - 1000 \cdot p$$

where q is the number of patrons purchasing tickets and p is the price per ticket. The current price is $5. At a recent board meeting, some members felt the price should be lowered to encourage more attendance. Others argued a higher price was necessary to raise more revenues. Reconcile these two different points of view. What might you say if you were involved in the discussion?

SUGGESTED READINGS

Friedman, Milton. *Essays in Positive Economics.* Chicago: University of Chicago Press, 1953, pp. 3–43.

Pirsig, Robert. *Zen and the Art of Motorcycle Maintenance: An Inquiry into Values.* New York: Morrow, 1974.

SUGGESTED SOLUTIONS TO SELECTED STUDY PROBLEMS

The following are only *suggested* solutions to the study problems presented at the end of this chapter. In all cases, the suggestions here put heavy emphasis on analysis rather than a single correct answer. Since most managerial problems do not fall into neat little boxes, the individual characteristics of the problems that you will encounter on the job will typically mandate a solution using the principles developed here and in other courses. Memorizing these solutions will not make you a good manager; learning the *principles* detailed here will help make you a better manager.

1. People make a distinction between science and art because the two have different objectives and applications. Science is designed to explain and understand objective reality. Art's role is to make reality more creative and

enjoyable and to formulate and change opinion. Science is truth and the search for reality. Art is beauty and the cultivation of tastes and preferences. Science is amoral. Art has character. The advantage to making a theory value free is that it allows for a termination to an argument. You and I can disagree forever about whether abortion is good or bad, but we must ultimately agree whether a light bulb is on or off. It is important to make theories value free when the objective is prediction and explanation rather than creating and converting opinion.

2. I have no idea what it means to say "That is good in theory, but it doesn't work in reality." According to the scientific paradigm, a theory is only as good as its predictive content.

3. a. Not value free, includes reference to "should" which is necessarily tied to some particular person's value system.
    b. Same as a.
    c. This is science. It purports to be a statement about reality. It might be correct or wrong, but it contains no reference to a particular set of morals or values.
    d. This is a scientific statement. It could be shown to be incorrect once the author defines, in objective terms, the economic concept of *discrimination*. No person's ethics are being referenced.
    e. The statement "it is important" refers to someone's idea of good, bad, and important. This is not a statement of science; it is normative.
    f. This is a scientific statement. Either the industry requires tariffs and quotas to survive or it does not. Objective facts could solve this argument.
    g. See e. above. This is art.
    h. This statement addresses objective facts. It is either correct or incorrect without reference to any person's value system.
    i. Same as h. above.
    j. Same as h. above.

4. The purpose of this problem is to get you to differentiate between positive and normative analysis. The two different statements in the problem *do not* contradict each other. The first group, those arguing that the price "should be lowered to encourage more attendance" is making a statement about what the objectives of the ballet company should be. The second group has *not* taken up a contrary position. Instead it has simply said that a "higher price was necessary to raise more revenues." Although the first group can neither be right or wrong because it is stating its values, the second statement would be incorrect if the price elasticity of demand was elastic. The first statement is subjective, arguing that the goal of the ballet is to encourage attendance, while the second statement is scientific, contending that the price elasticity of demand is inelastic. Debates like this often are heated when in fact there is no disagreement between the two groups. One is arguing policy; the other is making a prediction. This is an unjoined debate, and the point is that it should be avoided.

CHAPTER

2

THE WAY MARKETS WORK

- Introduction
- Hypothetical Business Problem 2.1
- Demand
- Elasticity
- Hypothetical Business Problem 2.2
- Suggested Solution to Problem 2.2
- Opportunity Cost
- Supply
- Demand and Supply Together
- Suggested Solution to Problem 2.1
- Comparative Statics
- Hypothetical Business Problem 2.3
- An Application of the Supply and Demand Model to Sales Taxes
- Hypothetical Business Problem 2.4
- An Economist's View of Price Gouging
- Suggested Solution to Problem 2.3
- Suggested Solution to Problem 2.4
- Topics to Review
- Study Problems
- Suggested Readings
- Suggested Solutions to Selected Study Problems
- Appendix—Mathematical Review

INTRODUCTION

This chapter is a detailed review of the principles of supply and demand. It begins with the development of the individual demand function and its determinants. This framework is used to show how market demand is the sum of a collection of individual demands. Elasticity, an important and powerful tool, is studied next. After that, the supply side is introduced, and the two forces, demand and supply, are put together to show how markets work.

Several other important economic concepts are studied in this chapter. One of the most critical of these is opportunity cost, a tool no successful manager can do without. The remainder of the chapter is devoted to diagnosing shocks in markets, including the examination of commodity or excise taxes. There is an appendix at the end of the chapter that reviews a number of important mathematical principles. The chapter closes with a number of study problems that are essential to the learning process. We also start with an interesting problem for you to consider.

Hypothetical Business Problem 2.1

Suppose the minimum wage is $3.65 per hour, and at that wage rate there are 10 million people in the United States who would like to work. Further, suppose that over a wide range of wages that if the wage rate goes up by 10 percent, the number of people who would be willing to work goes up by 10 percent. Next, suppose that 6 million of these people actually have jobs. That is, at $3.65 per hour, the quantity demanded of unskilled labor is 6 million workers. Assume that a 10 percent increase in the wages paid to workers reduces the number of workers hired by 20 percent. First, what is the unemployment rate? Suppose the minimum wage were reduced to $3.50 per hour. What would happen to the unemployment rate in the U.S. labor force?

DEMAND

Demand is one of the most important and fundamental concepts in all economic analysis. **Demand** is a relation between the quantity purchased of some good and a variety of variables that affect this quantity. These variables include the price of the good, the prices of related goods, the income of the purchaser, consumer expectations about the future, and the taste and preferences of the buyer. Mathematically, we represent demand with the following shorthand notation:

$$q = q(p, p_r, y, e, u)$$

where q = the quantity purchased per unit time
p = the price per unit of the good
p_r = the price(s) of related goods

y = income
e = expectations of the future
u = tastes and preferences

everything else is constant

It is confusing to allow a lot of things to change simultaneously; therefore, economic analysis typically allows only one of the many independent variables to change at a time. The independent variables are the factors that influence or determine the quantity demanded. For example, we ask what happens to quantity demanded if price changes, or if income changes, but we do not ask what happens to the quantity demanded if both income and price change at the same time. The analytical exercise is too confusing unless we examine only one change at a time. If we want to address a complicated problem with many variables changing, we generally analyze them sequentially, not simultaneously. This technique of examining the relation between quantity demanded and one independent variable at a time involves the use of the *ceteris paribus* assumption—all other things remaining constant.

Price plays such an important role in determining quantity that economic analysis separates its effect from the others. For example, consider a particular person, Annabelle. She makes $500 per week; she is 23 years old, a college graduate, living in Austin, Texas. When the price of gasoline is $1.45 per gallon, she purchases 15 gallons per week (on average). She commutes to work and to her gym. She also likes to drive in the country on weekends. Suppose that recent declines in the price of crude have resulted in lower prices at the pump. Gas now costs $1.15 per gallon. As a direct consequence of the lower price, Annabelle spends additional time driving in the country, and when she runs into the 7-11 for a soda, she occasionally leaves her car running with the air conditioning on, so she will not be hot upon returning. On average, she now purchases 18 gallons of gas a week. Further declines in the price of crude reduce the price of regular unleaded gas to $0.79 per gallon. For similar reasons, suppose that Annabelle now buys 21 gallons of gas per week.

Figure 2.1 graphs Annabelle's demand for gas, given her income, expectations, and tastes. The demand curve is labeled D.[1] Notice that as price falls, *quantity demanded* increases. This is known as the **first law of demand.** Price and quantity are inversely related. Insofar as economists can tell, there has never been an exception to this law. It is not an overstatement to argue that this is the most important concept in all economic analysis. The first law of demand is the essence of economics and is so strongly nurtured by its followers that any researcher who discovered an exception to the rule would almost surely believe that a mistake had been made. In the next chapter, considerable attention is devoted to explain-

---

[1] Technically speaking the demand function is the entire relation between quantity consumed and *all* the other relevant variables. However, one of the main features of economics is its focus on price, and consequently, we often hold everything but price constant and call the remaining relation between price and quantity the demand curve.

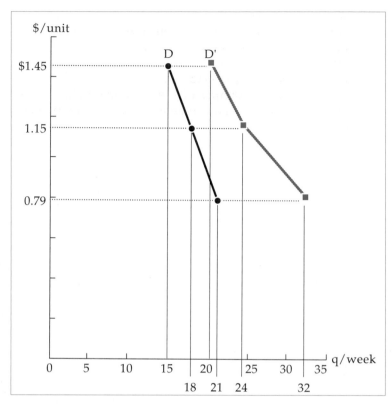

FIGURE 2.1
The Demand Relation

ing and expanding on this important economic principle. At this point, it suffices to say the law is broad in scope and general in application.[2]

Now suppose that Annabelle gets a big raise to $750 per week. As a consequence, she buys a new car, a Nissan 300ZX Turbo. It gets 10 miles less per gallon than her old Honda Accord. This changes her demand for gasoline. At $0.79 per gallon she now buys 32 gallons per week. Observe her behavior as the price changes. At $1.15 she buys 24 gallons, and at $1.45 she purchases 20 gallons. Figure 2.1 also graphs this new relation between price and quantity, labeled D'. The new demand curve lies to the right of the old one. This is called an *increase in demand*.

It is important to distinguish between a *change in demand* and a *change in quantity demanded*. When Annabelle's income went up, her *demand* for gasoline increased. However, when the price of gas declined, she increased her *quantity*

---

[2] Raymond C. Battalio, John H. Kagel, and Carl A. Kogut, "Experimental Confirmation of the Existence of a Giffen Good," *American Economic Review*, 81(4), September 1991, 961–969 report research that finds a positively sloped demand curve for rats in an experimental setting. They conclude, "From a methodological point of view, we note that determining that the class of Giffen goods is not empty would have been very difficult without using experimental methods or if we had been restricted to using human consumers" (p. 969).

demanded of gas. This may sound like a trivial semantic distinction, but the wording allows us to separate outcomes due to price changes and effects due to all other fluctuations. Hence, a *shift* of a demand curve is called a **change in demand,** and a *movement along* a demand curve (due solely to a price change) is called a **change in quantity demanded.**

Here is an example of how the inability to make a distinction between changes in demand and changes in quantity demanded can cause a great deal of confusion:

> Recent medical evidence has drawn a link between a high fiber diet and reduced risks of intestinal cancers. Based on these findings, the demand for whole grains has grown tremendously, driving up their prices. However, the higher prices have caused a lot of people to purchase less. This reduced consumption has hurt the midwest farming states, and some politicians are calling for federal government intervention to alleviate the crisis.

In this hypothetical example, changes in demand and changes in quantity demanded are confused. When demand grows, and nothing else changes, consumption cannot decrease. To be sure, price will rise, but *more* will be purchased at the higher price, not less. Do not be confused; this is not a violation of the first law of demand. The first law of demand says the quantity purchased declines when the price increases, *and nothing else changes*. Here consumption has increased because there has been a change in information available to consumers. At every price, some people now want to buy more grain as a way of reducing the risk of cancer. Since more people now believe that grains impede cancer, demand for grain is higher. Therefore, in the example, the price rise was a consequence of the demand change, not the other way around. Increased demand caused the price to go up, and since people want to buy more, it is wrong to conclude that consumption could actually decrease. Even though the price has risen, the quantity produced and consumed has also increased. It is imperative that you make a careful distinction between a change in demand and a change in quantity demanded.

Effects Due to the Prices of Related Goods

Related goods fall into two camps: **substitutes** and **complements.** Goods are substitutes when price increases for one cause demand increases for the other. Suppose that chicken and beef are substitutes. When the price of chicken goes up, the demand for beef increases. Conversely, when the price of beef falls, the demand for chicken declines. This means that at every price, people now consume less chicken than before. When goods are substitutes, higher prices for one make the alternative relatively cheaper, and people are inclined to shift some of their consumption. The more nearly the two goods are alike, the closer they are substitutes, and the more the demand for one shifts when the other experiences a price change.

Complements are the opposite. When two goods are complements, price increases for one lead to demand declines for the other. Suppose that personal computers and software are complements. Price increases for PCs cause the demand for software to decrease. Similarly, if automobiles and tires are complements, increasing car prices reduces the demand for tires. Since complements are used together, when the price of either one goes up by itself, the overall cost of using the package of the two rises, and hence, some people also buy less of the good that has not had a price change. The more any two goods are indispensable to each other, the closer they are complements, and the larger is the demand change for one when the price of the other fluctuates.

Goods are not substitutes or complements on the basis of logic. For example, consider bacon and eggs. Many people eat these together for breakfast; logically then one is inclined to say they are complements. If the price of bacon increases, the demand for eggs would decline, and surely it would for some folks. On the other hand, when the price of pork rises, others may simply eschew bacon and supplement their breakfast diet with *additional* eggs, or perhaps with more toast or fruit. In the second scenario, eggs and bacon are not complements, but they are substitutes. Of course, intuition can be used to classify goods as substitutes or complements, but ultimately facts must be brought to bear to answer the question. For now, we generally allow intuition to rule. Later, in Chapter 4, methods are presented for statistically divining the relation, if any, between goods with similar characteristics.

Effects Due to Changes in Income

Income affects the consumption of commodities in a number of different ways. In the example of Annabelle's demand for gasoline, the rise in her income led to an increase in demand. This makes a good such as gasoline **normal**—an increase in income leads to larger consumption and a decline in income causes a decrease in demand. Most goods are normal, but they need not be. For some goods or people, income increases can reduce consumption. For many, diet is closely linked to income. Income increases lead to a reduction in the consumption of fast food, pizza, and the like, and an increase in the consumption of gourmet-style foods. In this case, fast foods are **inferior** goods, and gourmet foods are normal. Calling goods inferior is only labeling. It is not meant to imply that they are low quality, although they may be, but only that people buy less of them when their income goes up.

There is a third category of goods. **Superior** or **luxury** goods are ones whose demand increases disproportionately with income. If a 10 percent increase in income leads to a 25 percent increase in the consumption of compact disks, we label compact disks superior goods. Again, no judgment is implied. Superior goods are a special case of normal goods in which small increases in income lead to large increases in demand.

Expectations

Expectations about the future change. Imagine that a severe drought like the one the United States experienced in 1988 hits the midwestern states, ruining most of the wheat and corn crops. Insightfully, you predict that beef and hog prices will

Syw think that p will increase → *4 gu dem now*

rise, and consequently you purchase a side of beef for your freezer to avoid the future price increase. You *now* want to buy *more* beef even though the price has not changed because beef will be more expensive in the future. This is an increase in demand based on changing expectations. Likewise, a story in the *Wall Street Journal* about poor sales for IBM PCs could lead you to anticipate a price decline in the near future. Hence, your demand (in the current period) declines. That is, at each price, you are willing to buy less now, waiting instead for lower prices in the future.

Computer software manufacturers seem to be acutely aware of this type of consumer behavior. Some of them cut the price for their current version when the introduction of a significant product upgrade is imminent. Others, in order to maintain sales in the period just preceding the introduction of the upgrade, offer a free or inexpensive upgrade option to anyone who purchases the current, soon-to-be-outdated version. Presumably they do this because consumers' revised expectations about the new product make demand fall for the current version.

Tastes and Preferences

Economists have a peculiar way of coping with tastes and preferences. Given the current state of technology, it is impossible to measure tastes and preferences. Admittedly we can measure the trappings of tastes and preferences, for example, Mercedes versus VW, but not the actual taste or preference. Suppose in 1984 a person bought an Audi after carefully examining several other cars such as the Peugeot and the Saab. Further imagine that in 1986 the same person crashed the Audi and replaced it with a Cadillac. Have this person's tastes changed? We have no way of knowing for certain because too many other factors could have changed over time. A person's inherent preferences are immeasurable without a mind-reading machine, and we eschew analysis of the relation between tastes and preferences and demand because we never know whether tastes and preferences have changed. Since we cannot actually measure tastes, it is impossible to refute the contention that a change in consumption was caused by a change in tastes and preferences. Consider again the person who bought the Cadillac to replace the Audi. Maybe the relative prices of the cars were different or she had a child or maybe a new job. And, even if we knew all these things we could never be certain of her actual tastes. To the economist, the inner workings of the individual mind are unobservable and sacrosanct. We cannot observe its computations, only its output. Until we are capable of actually observing the human brain in motion, we must settle for this lamentable state of affairs; tastes and preferences are unknowable. This does not mean that tastes and preferences do not change, but instead that economists go to great lengths to find alternative explanations for differences or changes in behavior.[3]

In sum, in economics we take tastes as given. Marketing science is the discipline devoted to understanding and measuring preferences across individu-

---

[3] For further elaboration on this point, you may wish to consult George J. Stigler and Gary S. Becker, "De Gustibus Non Est Disputandum," *American Economic Review,* March 1977, pp. 76–90.

als. And thus it is best if we leave the issues of tastes and preferences for the methods and practices of the experts there. We include tastes and preferences in the demand equation although, at present, we have little capacity to measure this determinant of consumer behavior. Having said all that, economists often incorporate taste-related variables into the quantitative models. Examples include age, religion, sex, race, and demographic variables capturing seasonal changes and geographic locations. In Chapter 4, several methods are presented for incorporating these factors into the estimation of empirical demand equations.

The Aggregation of Individual Demands to Market Demand

Each of us individually demands many products. However, in most cases, it is the collection of all of us together that creates a market. Rare is the circumstance in which one buyer makes a market, but all of the principles that apply to individual demand also pertain to market demand. The process of creating a market demand curve out of individual demands is thus quite simple.

Consider the set of individual demands denoted in Table 2.1. There we have three individuals, Jacob, Juan, and Addie. Each of these people likes the movies. The left-hand column, (1), of the table lists various prices; columns (2)–(4) list the number of tickets that each of these three people would purchase each month at those prices. Column (5) is the sum of the individual demands at each price. For instance, when the price of tickets is $7, Jacob would see 2 movies each month, Juan 4, and Addie 6; the total is 12. Were tickets free, the individual quantities demanded would increase to 5, 8, and 10, respectively. Then, the total number of movies consumed would be 23.

Figure 2.2 demonstrates the creation of market demand as the sum of individual demands. The three separate demands of Jacob, Juan, and Addie are shown in the figure. The sum of the individual demands, total demand, is also depicted as the line *ABCD*. Notice how the total demand curve is kinked at points *B* and *C*. When the price is $15 or higher, only Addie has effective demand, and hence total demand is the same as her demand. When the price falls below $15, Juan begins to purchase tickets, and thus the total demand curve is the sum of the two individual

TABLE 2.1 THE AGGREGATION OF INDIVIDUAL DEMAND INTO MARKET DEMAND				
PRICE OF MOVIE TICKETS	JACOB'S DEMAND	JUAN'S DEMAND	ADDIE'S DEMAND	TOTAL DEMAND
(1)	(2)	(3)	(4)	(5)
$18	0	0	0	0
15	0	0	2	2
12	0	2	3	5
7	2	4	6	12
0	5	8	10	23

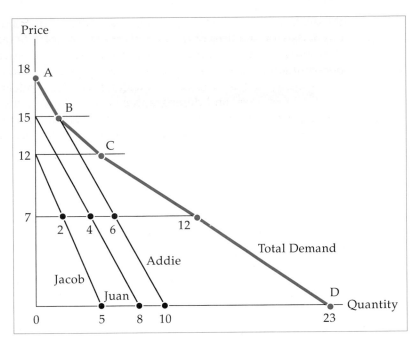

FIGURE 2.2
The Aggregation of Individual Demands

demands. This is why the demand curve changes slope at point *B* in the figure. Similarly, there is another kink at point *C*. When the price falls below $12, the maximum price that Jacob is willing to pay for any tickets, the total demand curve includes the sum of three different buyers, and again the slope changes. At the other end, the demand curve intersects the quantity axis at 23 movies (point *D*), the total number of movies that Jacob, Juan, and Addie would attend monthly if the price were zero.

The market demand curve is simply the horizontal sum of the individual demand curves of all the people who value the good. The market demand curve has all the same properties as the individual demand curves. Namely, there is an inverse relation between price and quantity. In addition, for normal goods the market demand curve shifts to the right as the income of the individual demanders increases. The market demand curve, by its very nature, has one additional element, the number of demanders. As the table and figure demonstrate, as the number of demanders increases, the market demand curve shifts to the right. By contrast, when the number of demanders decreases, the market curve naturally shifts left.

ELASTICITY

The previous discussions about demand have all been qualitative. Even though we have said that a price decline causes an increase in quantity demanded, we have not been specific about how much quantity changes when price changes.

Elasticity is a quantitative concept that fills in this gap. Elasticity measures sensitivity to change. For example, consider the price elasticity of demand, represented by the Greek symbol η. Then

$$\eta = \frac{\%\ change\ in\ quantity\ demanded}{\%\ change\ in\ price}.$$

Also,

$$\eta \equiv (dq/q)/(dp/p), \tag{2.1}$$

or

$$\eta \equiv (dq/dp)\bullet(p/q), \tag{2.2}$$

or

$$\eta \equiv d\ log(q)/d\ log(p), \tag{2.3}$$

where d is the **derivative** (a *derivative* measures the rate of change in one variable as another changes), q is quantity, and p is price.[4] Each of the three expressions, (2.1)–(2.3), is a different way of saying the same thing; **price elasticity**—sometimes called the own price elasticity of demand—is the percentage change in quantity demanded for a percentage change in price. Suppose that the price elasticity of demand for residential electricity consumption is -1.2. Examine the formula for the price elasticity of demand:

$$\frac{\%\ change\ in\ quantity\ demanded}{\%\ change\ in\ price} = -1.2,$$

but if we multiply both sides of the expression by the percentage change in price, then we can see that

$$\%\ change\ in\ quantity\ demanded\ =\ -1.2\bullet\%\ change\ in\ price.$$

When we write the elasticity formula this way, it makes it easy to see why the concept is so useful. For any given price change, the percentage change in consumption is simply the value of the elasticity times the percentage change in price. For instance, a 20 percent increase in the price of electricity leads to a $(-1.2\bullet20\%)$ = 24 percent decline in the consumption of electricity.

If the price elasticity of demand is less than 1 in absolute value, $|\eta| < 1$, we say that demand is inelastic (because quantity demanded is relatively insensitive to price changes). When the absolute value of the elasticity is greater than 1, we say

---

[4] An appendix to this chapter explores derivatives in detail and lists some of the rules of differentiation.

OWN PRICE ELASTICITY OF DEMAND

Numerical Value of Elasticity	Definition
$|\eta| < 1$	Inelastic
$|\eta| = 1$	Unitary Elastic
$|\eta| > 1$	Elastic

---

that demand is elastic. Unit or unitary elasticity is the cusp between elastic and inelastic demand, when $\eta = -1$.

There are two extremes to the value of the price elasticity of demand. First, there is the limiting case of inelasticity, when consumption does not respond to price. In this case the percentage change in consumption, for any change in price, is zero, and the price elasticity of demand is also zero. We say that demand is perfectly inelastic. At the other limiting extreme, when even the smallest change in price leads to an extremely large change in consumption, the change in quantity for even the least price change tends to be infinitely large. We define this situation as perfectly elastic demand and assign the elasticity a value of minus infinity, $-\infty$.

Elasticity is a simple but powerful idea. Conceptually, it is simply the ratio of two percentage changes, and accordingly we can compute the elasticity of just about any quantifiable relation as you will see throughout the book.

The Total Revenue Test

The value of elasticity as a managerial tool is made transparent with a simple analytical exercise. Consider a firm selling one good to everyone at the same price. Revenues are the price of the good times the quantity sold. According to the economic theory of demand, higher prices reduce the amount sold. This means that revenues change as the firm adjusts its price. For the sake of example, suppose the firm raises its price. Divide the change in revenues into two parts. First, the price of all units will be higher, and on this count revenues will increase. But, at the same time, people will buy less. On this second count, revenues will be lower. Which effect will dominate? If the price increases more than the quantity decreases, then revenues will increase, but if the quantity declines a lot when the price increases a little, then revenues will fall. Elasticity offers us a handy way to summarize this simple, yet powerful result.

When demand is inelastic, the reduction in quantity demanded is smaller (in absolute value) than the increase in price. This means that for any given price increase, there will be a relatively smaller reduction in quantity demanded. In this case, the firm raises price a lot, but quantity demand only declines by a small amount. The net effect is that revenues increase. On the other hand, when demand is elastic, the absolute change in quantity demanded is larger than the change in price. This means that a relatively small increase in price will lead to a

THE TOTAL REVENUE TEST

To a firm selling one good at a single price, total revenue is price times quantity. That is, letting R stand for revenue, p stand for price, and q represent quantity,

$$R = p \bullet q.$$

However, according to the first law of demand, quantity is a function of price, and so we write that q is a function of p:

$$q = q(p).$$

Therefore, by substitution of the demand function into the revenue function, we obtain

$$R = p \bullet q(p).$$

When we take a derivative of a function we evaluate the change in the dependent variable (the one on the left-hand side) as the independent variable (the one on the right-hand side) changes by a very small amount. Taking the first derivative of revenue with respect to price yields

$$dR/dp = q(p) + p \bullet dq/dp.$$

If we multiply the second term on the right-hand side by q/q, preserving the term, then

$$dR/dp = q + q \bullet [(dq/dp) \bullet (p/q)], \tag{i}$$

and since

$$\eta = dq/dp \bullet (p/q), \tag{ii}$$

we can write the expression for the impact on total revenue for a change in price as

$$dR/dp = q \bullet (1 + \eta). \tag{iii}$$

Expression (iii) says the change in revenue associated with any price change equals the current quantity sold times 1 plus the price elasticity of demand. Hence, very simply, if demand is inelastic, $|\eta| < 1$, then $dR/dp > 0$, and a price increase will raise total revenue. Similarly, if demand is elastic, $|\eta| > 1$, price decreases will raise total revenue.

---

substantial reduction in sales. In this case, even though each unit sold commands a higher price, this effect is overwhelmed by the reduction in quantity sold. Revenues will fall. A simple principle emerges: When demand is elastic, price decreases lead to higher revenues, and price increases lead to lower revenues; when demand is inelastic, price increases lead to higher revenues, and price decreases lead to lower revenues. The accompanying box summarizes these findings.

The ability to project changes in revenues based on elasticity is a powerful tool. A manager who knows the price elasticity of demand for a product can instantly forecast what would happen to the company's revenues if the product price were raised or lowered. In Chapter 4, methods for estimating the elasticity of demand are discussed. As a management tool, it is one of the simplest and easiest to implement.

Consider the following example: You are the manager of a small chain of delicatessens in a city. Among other things you sell submarine sandwiches. You currently charge $3.79 for a regular size sub with two meats and one cheese. At that price, your sales each day are 1000 sandwiches. Suppose that the price elasticity of demand has (somehow) been measured to be -0.80. What would happen to your sales, cost, and profits if you raised the price of these sub sandwiches to $3.99? Interestingly, knowing the elasticity is just about all we need to draw some useful inferences about these three important aspects of your business.

First compute your total revenue at the present. You are selling 1000 units at $3.79, and so

$$R = 1000 \cdot \$3.79 = \$3790.$$

Raising the price to $3.99 would be a 5.28 percent increase in price:

$$\$0.20/\$3.79 = 0.05277 = 5.28\%.$$

ELASTICITY, PRICE CHANGES, AND REVENUES

TOTAL REVENUE AND ELASTICITY

ELASTICITY	PRICE CHANGE	IMPACT ON REVENUES
Inelastic	Increase	Increase
	Decrease	Decrease
Elastic	Increase	Decrease
	Decrease	Increase
Unitary Elastic	Either	No change

According to the formula for the price elasticity of demand, this price increase would translate into a 4.22 percent reduction in sales:[5]

$$\eta = -0.8 = (\%\Delta\text{sales})/(\%\Delta\text{price});$$

therefore, by rearranging terms

$$(\%\Delta\text{sales}) = -0.8\bullet(\%\Delta\text{price}),$$

or

$$(\%\Delta\text{sales}) = -0.8\bullet+5.28\% = -0.04224 = -4.22\%.$$

So, your prices have increased by 5.28 percent to $3.99, but your sales have only declined by 4.22 percent to 958 sandwiches per day:

$$(1 - 0.0422)\bullet1000 = 958.$$

What has happened to your revenues? The new higher price, $3.99, times the new lower quantity, 958, is actually a higher revenue than before:

$$\$3.99\bullet958 = \$3822.$$

Your revenues have increased by $32 per day ($3822 − $3790 = $32). When demand is inelastic, when $|\eta| < 1$, price increases lead to higher revenues.

What impact does the price increase have on costs and profits? At the old price of $3.79, you were selling 1000 sandwiches. Now, at the higher price, your sales are only 958. Your costs are almost surely lower, and in the worst case scenario, they are no higher than before. Selling 42 fewer sandwiches saves materials, cleaning, and labor costs. Thus, under virtually any scenario, you save money on the cost side by raising the price and producing less. In turn then, profits must necessarily be higher. Your revenues increased while your costs decreased. And this is why economists say that no reputable manager would ever allow his or her company to set a price in the inelastic portion of the product's demand curve.[6] When demand is inelastic, a profit opportunity is available, and it persists until price is raised into the elastic portion of the product demand function.

---

[5] The symbol delta, Δ, is often used to denote "the change in" a variable.

[6] This whole discussion is predicated on the assumption that the manager *can* set price where he or she would like. Many businesses have little or no control over the price at which they sell. This is determined by market forces outside their control. This point is covered in more detail in Chapters 7 and 8. In addition, in extreme cases, such as a temporary crisis or a natural disaster, some sellers when faced with an extremely inelastic demand curve may rationally choose not to exploit their position to generate good will with their customers. These sellers may opt to forgo the short-term profits and price increases in exchange for loyal customers in the future.

Elasticity and Linear Demand

Consider the formula for the price elasticity of demand:

$$\eta = dq/dp \bullet (p/q).$$

The first term in the formula, dq/dp, is the slope of the demand curve. For the special case of a linear demand curve, the slope is a constant; it does not change as we move along the demand curve. Hence, for a linear demand curve, the elasticity is a constant (the slope of the curve) times the price of the good divided by the quantity demanded. Consider Figure 2.3. At price p_1, the quantity demanded is q_1. The elasticity at this point, η_1, is

$$\eta_1 = dq/dp \bullet (p_1/q_1).$$

When the price is higher, we move up the demand curve to, say, price p_2. At this higher price, the quantity demanded decreases to q_2, and the elasticity, η_2, is

$$\eta_2 = dq/dp \bullet (p_2/q_2).$$

Since the demand curve is linear, the slope, dq/dp, is constant and hence equal in the two elasticity formulas. Thus the relative value of η_1 compared to η_2 depends

FIGURE 2.3
Elasticity Along a Linear Demand Curve

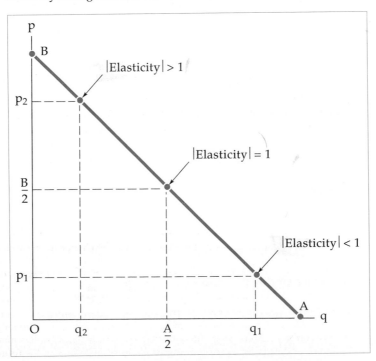

solely on the values of price and quantity. At the point denoted by (p_2, q_2), price is higher and quantity is lower than the original point, (p_1, q_1). Thus, the second term of η_2 has a larger numerator and smaller denominator than the comparable term in η_1. This means that η_2 is larger in absolute value than η_1. In other words, as we move up the demand curve from a point with a low price and high quantity to a point with a high price and low quantity, the elasticity increases; demand becomes more elastic as we move up a linear demand curve.

It turns out that the midpoint of a linear demand curve has an elasticity equal to -1. So the point $(B/2, A/2)$ in Figure 2.3 has unitary elasticity, and at this point small price changes in either direction do not disturb total revenue. Moreover, maximum revenue occurs at this point. Any other price-quantity combination would necessarily lower total revenue. Do not be confused. This does not by itself mean that a company would want to price at this point. Even higher prices, although they would lead to lower revenues (because demand is elastic), would also reduce costs, implying that profits *could* be higher at prices above the revenue maximizing level.

Other Forms of Elasticity

It is possible to compute an elasticity for just about any relation. Consider the impact of income on consumption. The **income elasticity of demand,** η_y, is the percentage change in demand divided by the percentage change in income. A good is labeled *inferior* if the percentage change in demand divided by the percentage change in income is negative. A good is *normal* if the percentage change in demand divided by the percentage change in income is positive. A special case of the normal good is the *superior* or *luxury* commodity. These are goods where the percentage change in demand divided by the percentage change in income is greater than one, in other words, when the percentage change in demand is greater than the percentage change in income.

The **cross elasticity of demand** computes the change in demand for one good, A, as the price of some second good, B, changes. It is the percentage of change in demand for good A divided by the percentage change in the price of good B:

$$\eta_{AB} \equiv (dq_A/dp_B) \bullet (p_B/q_A).$$

THE INCOME ELASTICITY OF DEMAND

The **income elasticity of demand** is defined as

$$\eta_y \equiv (dq/q)/(dy/y) = (dq/dy) \bullet (y/q) = d \log(q)/d \log(y).$$

A good is *inferior* if $\eta_y < 0$, *normal* if $\eta_y > 0$, and *superior* or *luxury* if $\eta_y > 1$.

For substitutes, since price increases for good B lead to demand increases for good A $(dq_A/dp_B > 0)$, the cross elasticity of demand is positive. In the case of complementary goods, price increases for B reduce the demand for A $(dq_A/dp_B < 0)$, and the cross elasticity is negative.

More on Elasticity

Except in special cases, price elasticity varies along a demand curve. We have just discussed how demand becomes more elastic as we move up a linear demand curve. By contrast, it should be noted that nonlinear demand functions of the form $q = a \cdot p^b$ have constant elasticity along the entire demand curve.[7] Except in this special exponential case, when price changes, the price elasticity of demand also changes. This is not a problem when price changes are small, because the elasticity change will also be small, but when the price change is substantial, we need to take into account the changing elasticity.

When price does change substantially, the **arc elasticity** concept is used to correct for the changing elasticity. Consider Figure 2.4, in which price decreases from p_1 to p_2. When price is p_1, quantity is q_1. See point A in the figure. When the price changes to p_2, quantity increases from q_1 to q_2, point B in the figure. At price p_1 the **point elasticity** is

$$\eta_1 = (dq/dp) \cdot (p_1/q_1),$$

but at p_2 the *point elasticity* is

$$\eta_2 = (dq/dp) \cdot (p_2/q_2).$$

Whatever the elasticity is at the point (p_1, q_1), A, it is less at the second point, B. Why is this true? First, at p_1, the price is higher than at p_2. Second, the quantity q_1 is less than q_2. On both counts, the second term on the right-hand side of the elasticity formula is larger when price is p_1 than it is when price is p_2. For instance, if $|\eta_1| = 1.0$ then $|\eta_2| < 1.0$. Any calculations based on p_1 as the starting point will give *different* answers from calculations based on p_2 as the starting point. Arc elasticity simply takes the *average* of these two starting points so that the answer is invariant to the starting point. *No* technique will give precisely the correct answer unless the exact form of the demand function is known. The arc elasticity concept is nevertheless useful especially when the change in price or quantity is large. The average or arc elasticity formula is

$$\eta_a = \frac{dq}{dp} \times \frac{\dfrac{(p_1 + p_2)}{2}}{\dfrac{(q_1 + q_2)}{2}} = \frac{dq}{dp} \times \frac{(p_1 + p_2)}{(q_1 + q_2)}.$$

---

[7] To see why this is true, take the logs of both sides of the expression. Then

$$\log(q) = \log(a) + b \cdot \log(p).$$

The elasticity is the derivative of $\log(q)$ with respect to $\log(p)$, $d \log(q)/d \log(p)$, and in this special case the derivative and the elasticity are b, a constant.

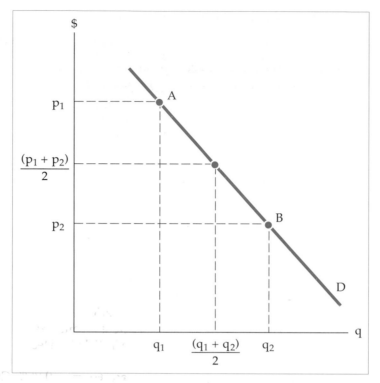

FIGURE 2.4
Arc Elasticity

In effect, arc elasticity is equivalent to treating price and quantity as though both were midway between the starting and ending points and then employing the point elasticity at this midpoint. Equal movements away from this midpoint in opposite directions give the same answer, and the starting point problem is mitigated.

To see how the concept of elasticity can be used, consider the following problem.

Hypothetical Business Problem 2.2

For many years the Citrus Bowl stadium in Orlando, Florida, could seat only some 55,000 fans. For the Forty-Second Annual game on January 1, 1988, between Clemson and Penn State, the posted ticket price was $27.50. However, the black market or after market price commanded by scalpers was about $50. First, assuming that the price elasticity of demand for tickets to that game was -0.75, how many tickets could the Citrus Bowl Committee have sold at the posted price of $27.50 if they had had sufficient seating to accommodate all persons demanding a ticket? Since that game in 1988, the stadium has expanded to 70,000 seats. Second, suppose ticket demand for the 1992 game between Clemson and Cal-Berkeley were the same as it was in 1988, predict the price of tickets being sold outside the stadium by scalpers at the 1992 game.

Suggested Solution to Problem 2.2

To address this question examine Figure 2.5. The demand for tickets to the bowl game is drawn. For the 1988 game, the posted price was $27.50, and 55,000 tickets were available. This is point *D* in the figure. However, at that price, there was excess demand, and the scalpers were able to obtain $50 per ticket (point B in the figure). In other words, the quantity demanded at $50 was 55,000 tickets. If there had been no stadium capacity constraint, at a price of $27.50 the bowl officials could have sold what is labeled *q** tickets. This is point *A* in the figure. To compute the number of tickets Citrus Bowl officials could have sold, we employ the formula for the price elasticity of demand and the assumption that this elasticity is −0.75:

$$\eta = \frac{\% \ Change \ in \ Quantity \ Demanded}{\% \ Change \ in \ Price} = -0.75.$$

What we want to know is the percentage change in quantity demand associated with a price decrease from $50 to $27.50. This is a ($27.50 − $50)/$50 or −45 percent price decline. This is the movement in the figure from point *B* to point *A*. Therefore, from the formula for the price elasticity of demand, the increase in tickets sales is

% Change in Quantity Demanded = −0.75% Change in Price = −0.75•(−45%) = +33.75%.

We compute that the percentage change in quantity demanded is −0.75•(−45%) = +33.75%. A 33.75 percent increase from 55,000 is 1.3375•55,000 or 73,563. If the stadium had had sufficient capacity, and if

FIGURE 2.5
The Demand for Citrus Bowl Tickets

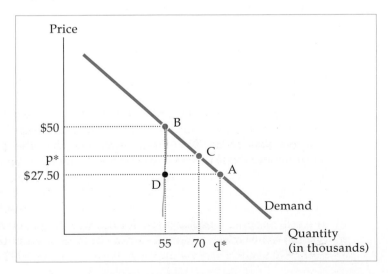

the price elasticity of demand for tickets truly was -0.75, then the Citrus Bowl officials could have sold approximately 73,500 tickets to the 1988 game at the posted price of $27.50. This point is represented as $q*$ in Figure 2.5. As the stadium capacity allows for more patrons, the price falls to the point A in the figure.

We use the same approach to answer the second part of the question. Here we want to know the price that will induce 70,000 people to purchase tickets to the game. We know that at a price of $50, 55,000 will buy tickets. Increasing the quantity demanded to 70,000 is a (70,000 − 55,000)/55,000 = 27% increase. Again, using the formula for the price elasticity of demand and inserting a 27 percent increase in quantity demanded into the formula, we can compute the percentage change in price required:

$$+27\% = -0.75\% \text{ Change in Price.}$$

Therefore, by manipulation, the percentage change in price is $+27\%/(-0.75)$ or -36 percent. A 36 percent decline in price from $50 is $(1 - 0.36) \cdot \$50$ yielding a price of $31.82. Again examine Figure 2.5. In this case, we know the quantity is 70,000. We must compute the price $p*$ that will induce 70,000 people to come to the game. This increase in quantity from the old capacity of 55,000 is a shift from point B in the figure to the point C. In other words, with the new stadium capacity, and assuming that demand is the same in 1992 as it was in 1988, and assuming that the price elasticity of demand is -0.75, then, if the Citrus Bowl officials expected to have a sell out of their newly enlarged facility the ticket price should have been about $32. In fact, the posted ticket price was $30.[8]

OPPORTUNITY COST

Price means many things to many people, but to the economist it means **opportunity cost.** The price of something is what is given up to get it—the highest valued forgone alternative. In that sense of the word, almost everything has its price. The economic paradigm holds that people base decisions on opportunity cost, not posted price or any other notion of cost. Consider the following example: According to reports, tickets to Super Bowl XXVIII in New Orleans cost approximately $500 on the open market. Suppose you had won two tickets to the game in a radio contest. The posted price on the tickets is $75. What would it have cost you to attend the game? One view says the game is free—you were given the tickets. Another view, the opportunity cost approach, says that you easily could have sold the pair of tickets for $1000. Hence, in terms of your *alternatives*, if you walk into the stadium with those tickets you have just given up $1000 in cash that you could

---

[8] These price and quantity changes are sufficiently large to make one wonder if the arc elasticity formula may not be more appropriate. How would the answer change if we had used the arc elasticity?

have had in your pocket. To the economist, the tickets cost $500 apiece whether you bought them, stole them, found them, or received them as a gift.[9] To be sure, it matters to your total wealth whether you had to pay for the tickets or not; you are richer if someone gives you the tickets. But the important lesson here is that the decision to use the tickets or sell them does not hinge on their source. This is what economists mean when they say that people base their decisions on opportunity cost. However, it remains an empirical issue, not a philosophical one, whether the economic paradigm is valid or not. This means it does little good to argue philosophically over the notion that people act according to opportunity cost; instead, we must examine the facts to answer the question.

SUPPLY

The essentials of supply involve many of the same fundamentals as demand. We specify a **supply function,** very much like a demand function, where quantity supplied is some function of price and the cost of production (input prices). Although the weather, natural forces, and acts of God also impact supply, pedagogically, we treat them simply as input prices, at least in our simple models of supply. The functional relation between prices and quantity is determined by physical laws, human ingenuity, and the state of technology. In general, the higher the price, the larger the quantity supplied. Let the symbol w represent a set or vector of input prices. Then, the supply function is mathematically represented in shorthand form by the equation

$$q_s = q_s(p,w).$$

The relation between quantity supplied and input prices is straightforward. The more costly the things used in production, the less the firm is willing to supply. Put another way, when input prices go up, supply goes down. In some important sense, this is all we need to define the supply curve.

Stochastic or Random Events in Supply

Consider an agricultural example. Obviously, the weather is important in the production of most agricultural goods. Why then is the weather left out of the supply function? There is no technological reason that farmers cannot affect the weather in their fields just as you control the weather inside your house. Heaters, air conditioners, lamps, shades, insulation, and humidifiers are all ways of controlling the environment. When citrus growers or peach farmers expect very cold weather, they light smudge pots, spray water, and move air using large fans to prevent freezing of their fruit. This suggests an alternative way to think about the weather. For the fruit producer, cold weather is just a price increase for heating. It is reasonable to talk about weather affecting agriculture; it is also very sensible to characterize weather problems as just one of many different inputs.

---

[9] The National Football League now has a policy that it will not have the Superbowl in a city that does *not* have an antiscalping law. Why do you think they have this rule?

In addition, flooding is an increase in the cost of drainage, and drought is an increase in the price of irrigation. A pest infestation is an increase in the cost of fumigation. Analyzing supply this way makes its study quite simple and avoids confusion. Random or stochastic events over which the firm has little direct control are treated as inputs. A company with a traveling sales staff may not have control over some kinds of automobile accidents, but it does have control over their effects. Efforts aimed at educating drivers, purchasing insurance, mandating the wearing of seat belts, or installing protective devices around parked vehicles all work to mitigate the impact of stochastic events in this situation.

The Impact of Technology on Supply

Technology, the state of affairs in the world, impacts the firm's ability to produce. Advances in technology mean that for a given set of input prices at a given price of output, the firm is willing to supply more. Mathematically, a change in technology is a change in the relation between output price and input prices and in quantity supplied. That is, when technology changes, the supply function, q_s, changes.

The Slope of Supply

It is a general proposition, but not necessarily a universal rule, that higher price implies higher quantity supplied. This is a loose analog to the first law of demand. Be cautioned that in Chapter 6 we discuss market situations in which this law of supply is relaxed. There are many circumstances in which increases in output do not have to come with higher prices, at least in the long run. However, as a general rule, in supply we specify a relation between price and quantity that is the opposite of the relation between price and quantity in demand. This implies a supply curve that slopes upward.

Figure 2.6 illustrates the **first law of supply**—increases in price lead to increases in quantity supplied. Consider the curve labeled S. Movements along this locus, from point A with a low price, p_1, and low quantity supplied, q_1, to point B with a higher price, p_2, increase the quantity supplied to q_2. Consider an example that is easy to visualize. Would you be willing to work for your neighbor next Saturday for a dollar an hour, watching her cat to ensure he does not scratch the furniture? What if the wage rate were $5 per hour, or $25 per hour, or $100 per hour? As the wage rate increases, the willingness to work increases (at least over this range of wages).[10] As a general phenomenon, the more you pay people, the harder and longer they work. This positive relation between wages and work generalizes to many sorts of supply situations. For instance, the higher the price of crude oil, the deeper drillers seem willing to explore.

Just as it was critical to distinguish between changes in *quantity demanded* and changes in *demand*, it is also important to differentiate changes in *quantity supplied*

---

[10] In Chapter 3 we discuss the possibility that labor is one of those commodities that violates the maintained supply relation; at high wages, for some people, wage increases may reduce the willingness to work.

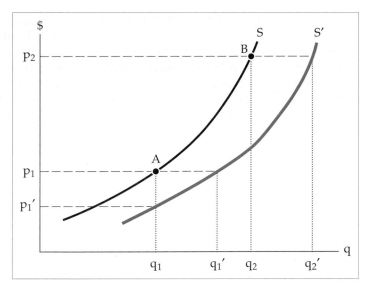

FIGURE 2.6
The Supply Relation

from changes in *supply*. **Changes in supply** are shifts of the supply function. An increase in supply refers to a rightward (or a downward) shift in the supply curve and can be due to one of two things: a cost-reducing improvement in technology or an input price reduction. Lower input prices allow firms to supply larger quantities at the same output price; or put another way, for the same quantity produced, they are now willing to accept a lower price. This shift is shown in Figure 2.6 and is conceived in either of two ways. At the old price, p_1, firms are willing to supply quantity q_1. However, with a reduction in input prices, they are now willing to supply a larger quantity, q'_1. Alternatively, how much must the firm get paid in order to supply q_1 at the lower input price? The answer is a lower price, p'_1. Either way, the answer is the same: The supply curve is shifted to the right or down. Similarly, an increase in input prices shifts the supply curve up or to the left. Higher input prices raise the cost of production, thereby reducing supply.

The Elasticity of Supply

The **price elasticity of supply** is calculated in much the same way as the price elasticity of demand. Let the Greek letter σ represent the price elasticity of supply, or the percentage change in quantity supplied in response to a given percentage change in price. That is,

$$\sigma = \frac{\frac{dq_s}{q_s}}{\frac{dp}{p}} = \frac{dq_s}{dp} \times \frac{p}{q_s} = \frac{d\log(q_s)}{q\log p}.$$

Supply is said to be **elastic** when the reaction in quantity supplied, in percentage terms, to a particular percentage change in price is *greater* than one. If quantity supplied is sensitive to price changes, then a small price change invokes a large quantity change; therefore, the ratio of percentage change in quantity supplied to percentage change in price is larger than one. If quantity supplied is *not sensitive* to price changes, then $\sigma < 1$, and we say that supply is **inelastic.**

Consider the case of land, and forget for a moment that it is possible to make more land as the Dutch do from the sea or as bulldozers do when they flatten hills. In this special case, the percentage change in quantity supplied is zero, even when price changes by a large amount. By construction, the amount of land is constant; the supply curve is vertical. Hence, regardless of the price change, the change in quantity supplied is zero. In this case $\sigma = 0$, and we say that supply is **perfectly inelastic.** At the other extreme, imagine you just walked into your neighborhood grocery and you started purchasing hamburger meat. You can probably buy as little as eight ounces or as much as 25 pounds at the same price. In this situation as far as you are concerned, the supply curve is horizontal, since at the posted price the store will sell you as much as you want. In this limiting case $\sigma = \infty$, and we say that supply is **perfectly elastic.**

Consider now the perfectly elastic supply curve S_1 in Figure 2.7. As the supply curve is rotated in the counterclockwise direction (as shown by the arrow), it becomes increasingly inelastic until the perfectly inelastic, vertical supply curve is reached. S_2 is more inelastic than S_1; S_3 is more inelastic than S_2; and S_4 is perfectly inelastic. Put differently, S_1 is more elastic than S_2; S_2 is more elastic than S_3; and S_3 is more elastic than S_4.[11]

DEMAND AND SUPPLY TOGETHER

It is time to put the demand side of the market with the supply side. With the demand and supply model, there are basically three things to consider: price determination, quantity determination, and the concept of **comparative statics**— a method for analyzing the impact on price and quantity when the parameters in

---

THE ELASTICITY OF SUPPLY

Numerical Value of Elasticity	Definition
$\sigma < 1$	Inelastic
$\sigma = 1$	Unitary Elastic
$\sigma > 1$	Elastic

---

[11] Conversely, as a demand curve is rotated counterclockwise, demand becomes more elastic at every price.

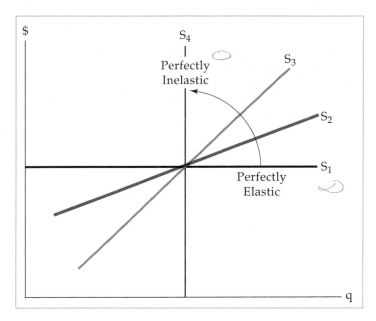

FIGURE 2.7
Relative Elasticity of Supply

the demand and supply functions change. Consider the market represented in Figure 2.8. Generically, demand is D, and supply is S.

Shortages

Suppose price in this market is p_1. Correspondingly, the quantity supplied is q_{S_1} (point A in the figure), but at that price, quantity demanded is q_{D_1} (point B in the figure). Consumers want to purchase more than producers offer for sale. At price p_1, the quantity supplied is less than the quantity demanded—$q_{S_1} < q_{D_1}$, and a number of things are expected to occur. First, let's define the situation. When quantity demanded exceeds quantity supplied at price p_1, there is **a shortage** (a synonym for shortage is **excess demand**). Put another way, price is too low, and quantity demanded exceeds quantity supplied.

It is critical to note that we economists do not say that "a shortage occurs when demand is greater than supply." Demand is a relation between price and quantity. It is the entire locus of points labeled D. Supply is the connection between production and price, the entire line S. It makes little economic sense to say that one line is bigger than another. Therefore, we do not say that demand is bigger than supply. Instead, we emphasize that price is too low, and a shortage occurs when *quantity demanded is greater than quantity supplied*.

This may sound like a semantic distinction, but it forces attention on the critical variable in analysis: price. For example, it is meaningless to talk about an oil shortage as a technological state of the world, or of a food shortage, a water shortage, or a housing shortage that is not responsive to price. *A shortage is a state of affairs due to a price that is too low and is not allowed to respond.*

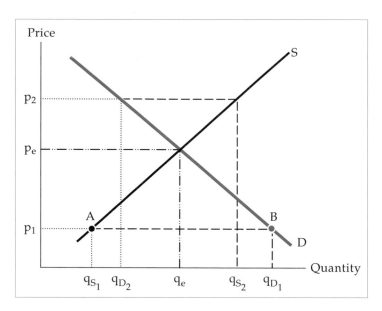

FIGURE 2.8
The Demand-Supply Model

Suppose the quantity demanded of shoes exceeds the quantity supplied at the current price. Observe a shoe store where people are trying to buy more shoes than are currently available for sale. The shelves are depleted. The stockrooms are almost bare. Customers are often told, "I'm sorry we don't have that style shoe in your size. We have had them on order now for several weeks, but we just can't seem to get enough of them in." If there is no restriction on the movement of price in a free-market economy, the store manager or supervisor will, over time, seize the opportunity to make more money by raising prices. Moreover, some demanders put pressure on price also, offering bonuses or side payments to the seller who can deliver the goods. In this environment, the shortage situation will not persist indefinitely. When a shortage exists, natural pressures brought about by demanders and suppliers raise price, and that process continues until there is no excess demand. This does not necessarily happen instantly, but there is a natural tendency for price to increase.

Two things happen when price increases. Quantity supplied increases and quantity demanded declines. Since both these effects tend to mitigate the shortage, price adjustments help eliminate shortages. When the quantities supplied and demanded are equal, we say there is an **equilibrium.** At this point, no forces within the market exist to raise or lower price. We also say the **market clears** or the **market clearing price** has been attained.

What happened to the shortage? There was no government intervention, nor any technological change. Nothing changed but price, and the shortage was eliminated. In sum, shortages are not technological phenomena. They are economic ones. They are created by markets when price does not act to equate quantity supplied and quantity demanded, or at least that is what the demand and supply model says.

In August 1990, Iraq's army invaded Kuwait. Almost instantly, the price of crude oil jumped substantially. This was followed by a surge in gasoline prices. Almost as swiftly, politicians, reporters, and others complained about price gouging by oil companies, and many a cry was heard for price regulation or some other form of control. What would happen if price controls were implemented? For one view, read the accompanying story reported in the *Los Angeles Times*.

ABOUT GASOLINE SHORTAGES
BLAMING THE BAD NEWS BEARER

John R. Lott, Jr.

Politicians are again out to kill the messenger who brings bad news. Oil companies are doing exactly what they should be doing by raising gasoline prices. If political threats of antitrust litigation, price controls and increased regulation prevent prices from rising now, it is the consumers who will suffer in the long run.

The free advice offered by political commentators is that since it takes six weeks for oil to travel from the Persian Gulf to refineries in the Gulf of Mexico, it is improper for prices to rise today. Waiting six weeks to raise prices means that consumers will end up paying even higher prices when a reduced oil flow out of the Persian Gulf is finally felt. Higher prices today reduce consumption and increase inventories and thus reduce how much prices will rise tomorrow.

The American oil industry is no more concentrated today than it was two weeks ago, and oil companies possess no sudden increase in monopoly power. Neither have they suddenly become greedier in the past two weeks. While Iraq and Kuwait have accounted for 8.2% of world oil output, the threat of war between Saudi Arabia and Iraq also places Saudi oil fields in jeopardy of at least temporarily being disabled. . . .

Many have called for new price controls. They seem to believe that controls did not work last time, simply because past administrations (apparently both Republican and Democratic) failed to administer them properly.

Economists may not agree on a lot of things, but one thing they do agree on is that controls create shortages.* Trying to stop real prices from rising is an impossible task. Controls and quotas can only change the form that the price increase takes. Instead of higher dollar prices, consumers still pay a higher price for gasoline with their time. They will be forced to wait again for odd-numbered days if their license plates are even-numbered, and then they will be forced to wait some more in the long queues at the gas station.

The gasoline shortage of the 1970s would never have occurred without price controls. . . .

---

*(italics added)

Los Angeles Times, Monday August 13, 1990, p. B5.

Surpluses

Look again at Figure 2.7. Let price be p_2; the quantity demanded at that price, q_{D_2}, is less than the quantity supplied, q_{S_2}. A **surplus** or an **excess supply** is said to exist. The shelves in the shoe store are no longer empty. In fact, now the opposite is true. Inventories accumulate; people are consuming less than current production. In this situation, most shop owners have a sale or some other promotion to stimulate buyers. Some demanders may suggest to store owners that they will buy more if the price is lowered. That is, both buyers and sellers put downward pressure on price, and this continues until the surplus is eliminated at p_e and q_e.

This is an **equilibrium** theory of price determination; natural market forces continuously push price in the correct direction to eliminate shortages or surpluses, even though equilibrium might never be reached because the world is dynamic. Notice that when the market is at equilibrium, there is a seller for every buyer. Everyone who wishes to purchase at this price finds a seller, and each producer locates a buyer. It makes little sense to talk about a great wave of selling at this price, unless you simultaneously talk about a great wave of buying. That is the concept of equilibrium.

You have now been exposed to the basic principles of supply, demand, and elasticity. With these you should now be able to construct a solution to Hypothetical Business Problem 2.1, which was presented at the beginning of this chapter. Try to work this problem, and then compare your solution to the following analysis.

Suggested Solution to Problem 2.1

There are 10 million people seeking work, and 6 million are employed.

Therefore, the unemployment rate is $(10 - 6)/10$ or $4/10$ or 40 percent.

First, on the demand side, the change in the law reduces the price of labor by 0.041 or -4.1 percent.

Since the price elasticity of demand is -2.0, the percentage change in quantity demanded of labor is -2 times the percentage change in price. Therefore, the percentage change in the quantity demanded of labor is $-2 \bullet (-4.1\%) = +8.2$ percent.

An additional 8.2 percent or 492,000 workers will be hired.

On the supply side, if the supply elasticity is assumed to be 1.0, 4.1 percent or 410,000 less people will want to work.

The new unemployment rate is $(9,590,000 - 6,492,000)/9,590,000$ or 32.3 percent.[12]

---

[12] The diligent student will rework this problem in arc elasticity terms and compare the results to the point elasticity estimates.

COMPARATIVE STATICS

Hypothetical Business Problem 2.3

Consider two different countries. They are otherwise the same except the price of beef is regulated in country *A* (the price cannot change) and unregulated in country *B*. Assume that beef and chicken are substitutes in consumption. The price of *chicken* is unregulated in *both* countries. Suppose the supply of *chicken* increases in both countries by the same amount, but, because the price of *beef* is regulated in country *A*, it (the price of beef) cannot respond as much or as rapidly as in country *B*. Other things the same, in which country does the quantity demanded of *chicken* change more? Put another way, which country has the more elastic demand for chicken?

In this book, we do very little dynamic analysis.[13] This is clearly a shortcoming, but the simplicity is deemed a bargain. Most experimentation involves comparative statics. We let the model parameters change one at a time, and we observe what happens to the variables in the theory.

Demand Shifts

Consider a computer center at a large university or inside a corporation. The organization demands computing services, the mainframe, disk drives, terminals, tapes, printers, and software. This demand is represented in Figure 2.9 by *D*. Suppose the supply of these services is *S*. Assume that none of the assets is priced for use within the organization; anyone within the company may use the computer at no charge. At this price, users would like to consume q_{D_0} computer services. But nobody wants to work for free; the computer center has no interest in supplying that quantity unless the president or the CEO gives the computer center a budget. From a cost point of view, it makes little sense to supply all the computer services that people want for free, q_{D_0}. The cost of that much computing, C_0, is relatively large compared to its value.[14] The computer center is being used for many purposes, some of which are not very valuable but are quite expensive to deliver. As this problem is set up, the computer center is constrained not to charge a price at all; the pricing system previously discussed is not allowed to work. That is, company policy does not let the market reach equilibrium.

How would the market work if the money price were actually set to zero? Suppose the computer center could supply all the services demanded, but this would make it broke (violate its budget). It must do something. One way is to cut

---

[13] Dynamic analysis is the time study of economic phenomena. The temperature changes incessantly throughout the day. Understanding that process is dynamic analysis. Studying the perpetual forces continuously affecting economic variables is likewise dynamic analysis. Here, we opt for the alternative approach, static analysis, examining one shock to the system at a time.

[14] How do we know this? What is the nature of demand that reveals this truth?

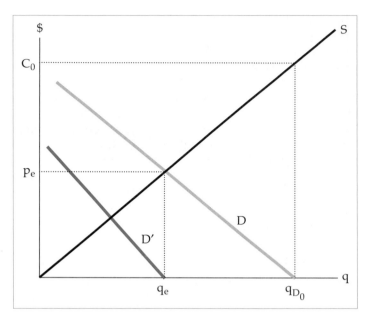

FIGURE 2.9
The Demand and Supply of Computer Services

back on the amount of services available. When this course is chosen, users find they have to wait to use the system. Their batch jobs wait in queues sometimes for hours, and they must wait for printouts. Others discover they cannot store data on disk because there is no space available. At the help desk and in the various computer services, lines ebb and flow in length and are longest when demand is at its peak, say between 10 A.M. and 3 P.M.

The computer center is rationing without pricing. Lines impose a time cost on users that reduces the demand for services, D' in Figure 2.9. There are other ways to reduce demand: Users can be assigned priorities; they might be required to make written requests for data disk storage space; or they can be made to request a specific time slot for using the system. These rules help eliminate lines, but they impose the cost of filling out forms and so on. Like a pricing scheme, a waiting list also rations. Analytically, the use restrictions reduce the demand for computer services. If the managers of the computer center are not charging the market clearing price, then they must restrict the use of their services in order to reduce demand or ration supply. Reservations are used by restaurants in much the same way. Appointments at the doctor's office are another example of non-price rationing.

Contrast the price rationing mechanism versus the alternative. First, a big advantage of the market mechanism is that the individuals using the service make their own determination of the value of the service. This is a critical feature of the market approach to the rationing problem. If the cost of disk storage is two cents per track per day, you decide for yourself if it is worth two cents or not. If, however, the computer center imposes no cost on the user, the officials there must determine whether, in their judgment, it is worth two cents to store your information on disk. Typically, the computer center bureaucrats are not in as good a position to decide the value of data storage services to the end user. Therein lies one advantage of the market system; the people with the best information make the use decision.

Second, the market often works for free. Compare the price mechanism with the priority assignments, written requests, or waiting list system. All of those involve costs. Administrators must determine the priority assignments; they must inform people of the rules and enforce them. The same is true of waiting lists, plus the obvious cost of standing around waiting in line is time lost that users cannot recover. There are also costs associated with the market mechanism. The seller and the buyer must exchange. There must be some enforcement of those rights; if not, the market will collapse. People will not voluntarily exchange unless they get to keep the bounty. Contract enforcement accompanying exchange in a market is not free, but the other services, the matching of buyers and sellers, and the assignment of resources and priorities are provided by the market cheaply.

Price and waiting lists are not the only ways to ration limited computer resources. Peer pressure can be used. The president of the university might send out a memo to all users saying:

> There is enormous waste going on in our computer center. Students and faculty must make every effort to curb use, purge files, and become more efficient. If something does not happen soon, it will become necessary to cut back on the services offered.

That plea works better at a small junior college than at a large university with 20,000 students. In the latter case, when the president sends a mimeographed letter to everyone at the university, most people do not even read it. But at the smaller college many might take heed. Pressure to follow the rules is most effective when the number of peers is small. In a large environment, each individual feels more isolated and is thus less willing to accede to the president's request. However, in the small numbers situation, when one person is observed adhering to the president's warning, others feel more inclined to conserve computer use also; they know the system will collapse unless most behave in the desired fashion, and most important, they feel their behavior can prevent breakdown.[15]

As the previous scenario suggests, the ability of nonprice rationing systems to adjust behavior depends on the number of people involved. The extreme cases make the point obvious. Families do not typically use price rationing to allocate the use of cars, telephones, the dining table, and the like. Instead, a set of loose rules or informal agreements is employed. Each of us has eaten in restaurants where ketchup is served in small plastic packages. One advantage of this packaging is that it reduces demand. Having to open small packages taxes the customer,

---

[15] This is just the introduction to a complex economic and management problem covered in far more detail in Chapter 12.

reducing his or her demand for the condiment, thereby effectively reducing consumption. Of course, the store could charge for ketchup (McDonald's did this early on in some of its restaurants), but presumably the cost of enforcing the rights, contracting, and collecting the money price that scheme out of the market. Other restaurants offer ketchup in bottles or bowls free of charge. Customers take as much as they like, where the demand curve intersects the quantity axis. We expect this situation in the small restaurant or diner where the customers are well known or easily observed and, hence, less likely to waste large portions of ketchup. Of course, there are other cost-based reasons why some restaurants use large bottles in lieu of small packages. Small restaurants with frequent idle periods may find it cheaper to refill large bottles, an option that is costly to the large, routinely busy establishment. But the point remains: Small packages reduce the demand for ketchup.

So, rules can be used to reduce demand. This shift has two impacts. It lowers both the equilibrium price and the quantity. In Figure 2.9, this change is depicted by the new demand curve D'. If the appropriate rules are chosen, the demand curve will shift back to a point where the quantity demanded for free is equal to q_e, the same quantity that would exist if the computer center charged the market clearing price, p_e.[16] A general result follows: Demand decreases lead to reduced quantity and lower price. Conversely, demand increases raise market clearing price and quantity.

Supply Shifts

Supply shifts also affect the market price and quantity. Increases in supply lower the equilibrium price and raise the market clearing quantity bought and sold. In Figure 2.10, let the original supply of some commodity be the curve labeled S. What happens when the price of one of the inputs used in the production process falls? Since the costs of production have decreased, the manufacturers are now willing to sell their wares at lower prices; the supply shifts down to S' as a consequence of lower production costs. The net result is that price falls from p_1 to p_2. At the same time, quantity increases from q_1 to q_2. In contrast, input price increases raise production costs and reduce supply, shifting the curve from S to S''. In this case, price increases to p_3, and quantity falls to q_3.

Notice that if both demand and supply curves shift simultaneously, either the market clearing price or quantity is indeterminate. That is, when we try to analyze a concurrent demand and supply shift, we will only be able to predict one of the two variables, not both. If demand and supply increase at the same time, then both effects increase quantity. However, since demand increases put upward pressure on price and supply increases act to reduce price, the net effect on price depends on the relative magnitudes of the two shifts, an empirical issue. Sim-

---

[16] In reality, well-managed universities or companies typically charge users through a budget. Each user gets accounting dollars to pay the computer center fees. In the ideal situation, the budget funds can also be spent on travel, telephone, office furniture, and the like. We say ideally because, for a budget to work effectively, there must be opportunities that pose costs when forsaken.

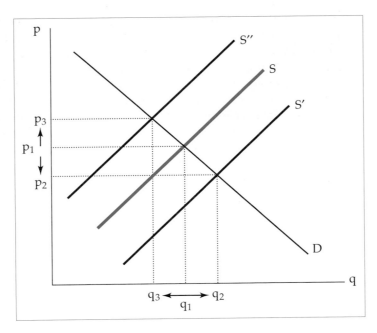

FIGURE 2.10
Comparative Statics

ilarly, if demand and supply decrease, downward pressure on price from the demand change is mitigated by the supply shift and the net effect on price is ambiguous. Notice here though that both shifts put downward pressure on the market clearing quantity; therefore, it declines in either case.

Consider the so-called war on drugs currently underway in the United States. The program has two aspects. The first is an attempt to reduce demand. On this side of the market, police have become considerably more strict in the enforcement of the law. At the same time, the "Just Say No" crusade has tried to persuade people to reduce their consumption of marijuana, cocaine, and such commodities. The net effect of this two-pronged attack has been to reduce the demand for such drugs (at least for the purpose of this discussion).

At the same time, the federal government through the Drug Enforcement Agency has mounted a forceful attack on drug suppliers. At least they say they have. Let us presume that this effort has met with some success. The cost of selling drugs has increased, and the supply of these drugs has decreased. Together, then, we have a reduction in demand and a reduction in supply. What is the net effect of these two simultaneous shifts on the market for illegal drugs?

Let us consider one such drug, cocaine. Examine Figure 2.11. The original demand for coke is D, and the original supply is S. Prior to the war, the black market price of coke is p_0 while consumption is q_0. The war, to the extent that it is effective, decreases both the demand and supply to D' and S' respectively. We can say one thing unambiguously: There is a decrease in consumption from q_0 to q_1. However, the overall effect of the two curves shifting at the same time leaves the theoretical question of the new price ambiguous. Suppose the war has a greater

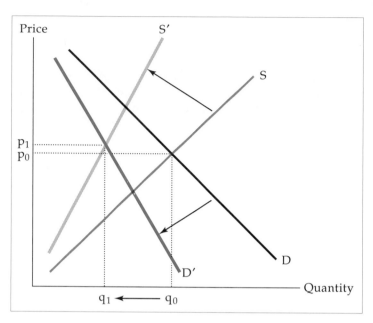

FIGURE 2.11
The War on Drugs

impact on demand than supply. Then the relative decrease in demand dominates the reduction in supply, and the black market price decreases. On the other hand, if supply side interdiction is relatively more effective, then supply will decrease more than demand, and market price will be higher after the war than before. Figure 2.11 presumes that there is a greater impact on supply than demand, and hence, price is higher: $p_1 > p_0$. However, the main point of this exercise is that the new price could turn out to be lower than the prewar price if the shift in demand were just a bit greater.

AN APPLICATION OF THE SUPPLY AND DEMAND MODEL TO SALES TAXES

Hypothetical Business Problem 2.4

Suppose that econometricians have estimated that the price elasticity of demand for whiskey is approximately -0.8. Current consumption is approximately 10 quarts per person per year in the United States. Imagine that the price elasticity of supply is quite elastic; it is about 2.5, and for the sake of this problem let's assume that all domestic consumption is produced in this country and that U.S. producers do not export. The average price of a quart of whiskey in the United States is $10. There is talk in Washington of raising the tax on distilled spirits an additional $2 per quart. If that law passes:

1. What will be the average price paid for whiskey?

2. How much whiskey will the average American consume?

3. How much additional revenue will the U.S. government collect?

The supply and demand model can be used to answer some interesting questions. On April 1, 1983, the federal government added a nickel per gallon to the road use tax on gasoline. What does the model predict happened to the price of gasoline as a result of this tax increase? Possible answers are (1) nothing, (2) it went up by five cents, (3) it went up by more than five cents, (4) it went up by less than five cents, and (5) it went down. Without thinking, many people will answer that the price goes up by five cents. In general, this is not right. It could be argued that in order for companies to stay in business, they have to recover their costs. Because cost went up by five cents, price has to rise by five cents in the long run. In order to see the error in this line of reasoning, make the following simplifying assumptions: (1) The tax is imposed on the seller, (2) the tax imposes no other cost on the seller, and (3) the tax is enforced on all sellers.

In Figure 2.12, D is the demand for gasoline and S is the supply. The sellers will only supply quantity q_1 if they are paid p_1 dollars per gallon. This means they must be paid p_1 plus t dollars per gallon for quantity q_1 after the tax is levied, where t is the dollar amount of the tax per unit. The same is true at all other prices and quantities. Put simply, the supply curve shifts *vertically* by an amount exactly equal to the per unit tax. Supply decreases because of the tax, or we say there is an upward shift of the supply curve; the new supply curve is shown by the line $S + t$.

FIGURE 2.12
The 5¢/Gallon Gas Tax

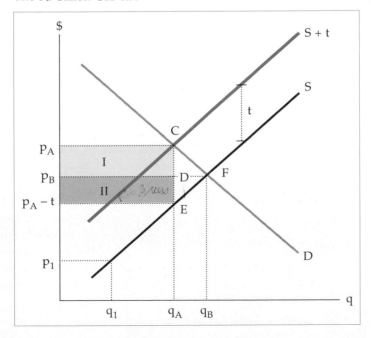

At every price, firms are willing to sell less. The tax has reduced supply. For example, suppose the market was willing to sell 500 million gallons of gasoline per day at $0.75 per gallon. With the introduction of the five-cent tax, the sellers will now require $0.80 before they are willing to sell the same 500 million gallons.

The pretax price, p_B, and quantity, q_B, are shown in Figure 2.12. When the tax causes supply to decrease or shift to the left, two things happen. Market price goes up, and market quantity goes down. The new price is determined by the intersection of the old demand curve, D (the tax has *no* impact on demand), and the new supply curve, $S + t$.[17] The new higher price is p_A, and the new quantity is lower, q_A. As discussed in the last section, any time the supply function decreases (shifts up), market price rises and market quantity falls. That is a general phenomenon, and it refers to any change in supply, whether caused by a tax or some other factor.

We are now in the position to answer the question, How much does the price go up? Obviously from the graph, the price goes up less than the tax. The old price p_B, plus the tax t, is greater than the new price p_A (the new supply curve is vertically above the old by the amount of the tax). The after-tax price is less than the price before tax plus the tax. Why is this true?

An upward sloping supply curve describes an industry in which costs are higher when output is higher. When an industry expands, it buys more of some inputs, and eventually, increased demand for inputs usually raises some of its prices. When the gasoline refining industry increases production, additional amounts of crude are demanded. To satisfy this extra demand, crude oil producers explore and drill deeper. This raises the price of crude. When the refining industry contracts, crude oil prices fall. The two prices move in concert. Rising input prices explain the upward sloping supply curve.[18]

In turn, we see why the price of gasoline does not go up as much as the tax. The increase in the price of gas causes a decrease in quantity demanded. As a consequence, the amount produced falls, keeping the market in equilibrium. The reduction in production causes input prices to fall. The cost of production per unit falls from p_B to $p_A - t$, because less gas is being refined.

Who pays the $0.05 per gallon tax then? Since there are higher prices for gasoline, buyers are paying part of the tax, but since the price rose by less then $0.05, they are not paying all of it. Suppose the original price, p_B, was $1 per gallon. The net price *received* by the refiners after the tax is $p_A - t$, *which is less than the pretax price*, $1. Therefore, even though price has gone up, the net price received by the seller has gone down. And, of course, the after-tax price paid by the buyer is more than $1. The tax raises the price to the buyer and lowers it to the seller; therefore, it is correct to say that the tax burden is shared by both buyer and seller.

How much of the tax is paid by the buyers? The rectangle denoted by $P_A CDP_B$ in Figure 2.12 is the increase in price multiplied by the number of gallons bought,

---

[17] Why doesn't the tax affect demand?

[18] We discuss this concept in more detail in Chapter 7.

and hence it is the burden of the tax paid by the buyers. But the government also collects from the seller the difference between p_B and $p_A - t$ on every gallon sold; the net price received by the seller has fallen by the amount $p_B - p_A - t$. Since the price received by the sellers is lower after the tax, and the price paid by the buyers is higher, the total tax collection, $t \cdot q_A$, is borne partly by buyers and partly by sellers. This helps us understand why tobacco farmers and cigarette manufacturers are big opponents to excise taxes on cigarettes, and why brewers are opposed to increased taxes on beer. Not all of the tax increase is passed on to customers.

In sum, a per unit commodity tax shifts the supply curve vertically above the old one a distance equal to the amount of the per unit tax. The intersection of the new supply curve with the old demand curve determines the new price and quantity. Subtracting the tax from the new price determines the new net price received by the seller. Divide the new net price by the price before the tax, and you have the producer's share of the tax in percentage terms. The remainder is paid by consumers. In dollar terms, the burden of the tax paid by consumers is given in Figure 2.12 by the area of rectangle I, and the weight or incidence of the tax that falls on producers is equal to the area of rectangle II.

Welfare Economics of Taxes

Welfare economics is normative economics. It refers to the social value and consequences of economic phenomena and policies. Although most of managerial economics generally avoids normative economics, the welfare consequences of tax policies are especially useful in understanding the operation of markets. Therefore, in this section we decompose the effect of a commodity tax into its component parts.

We have seen that, in general, commodity taxes affect both consumers and producers. Taxes paid to the government come out of consumers' and producers' pockets. Yet on top of these taxes, there is also a triangle of wealth, *CEF* in Figure 2.12, that vanishes after the tax is imposed; it goes to no one. This is called the **deadweight loss** of the tax or the **excess burden** of the tax. At the new market clearing quantity, the price that buyers are willing to pay for gasoline, p_A, is more than the sellers have to be paid in order to sell it voluntarily, $p_A - t$. In general, when one party is willing to pay more for something than the current owners are willing to sell it for, they trade. But these parties cannot trade; government has effectively outlawed some exchanges via the tax. The tax drives a wedge between the buyer's demand price and the seller's supply price, creating an economic inefficiency called the excess burden of the tax. People who *would* trade, cannot. The price that buyers must pay now exceeds the price received by the sellers; buyers who used to trade at the pretax price, but who now find the price too high, cannot legally do business with sellers, who used to produce, but now find the net price too low. The gains from trade that these parties used to enjoy are erased by the tax, and in economics we call this the deadweight loss of the tax since these gains simply vanish.

For example, suppose a neighborhood teenager cuts your grass once a week for $10. Suppose that he would be willing to do the work for $9, and you would be willing to pay him $11. Splitting the difference, you settle on $10. The activity creates two dollars of consumer and producer surplus, one dollar each. The work costs the boy $9, and he gets paid $10, leaving $1. Similarly, the fresh lawn, worth $11 to you, only costs you $10 out of pocket. You are also better off by $1. Now suppose the city government imposes a tax on lawn cutters of $3 per lawn. When the teenager cuts your grass, he must pay the city treasurer $3. His costs increase from $9 to $12. Since you are only willing to pay $11, no market transaction takes place now. Instead you cut your own law or plant some other ground cover. As a consequence of the tax, trade between you and the boy stops, and $2 of economic gain, $1 to the lawn cutter and $1 to you, disappear. This is what we mean by the deadweight loss of the tax.[19]

Computing Tax Revenues

Returning to our gasoline tax example, if we know the posttax quantity, q_A, we can calculate the tax revenues created by the tax of $t per unit. It is important to note that tax revenues are not simply the quantity purchased before the tax multiplied by the amount of the tax. Remember the first law of demand: When price increases, quantity bought declines. The imposition of the tax causes price to go up, and hence consumption to decrease. This means that the quantity of gasoline purchased before the tax increase does not accurately predict the ultimate tax revenues to the federal government. What one must also know is the price elasticity of demand and the price elasticity of supply in order to forecast consumers' responses to the price increase correctly.

For example, assume that just prior to the tax increase, 9 million barrels of gasoline were consumed per day and that the pretax price of gasoline was $1 per gallon. The tax is $0.05 per gallon. Can we predict the change in price or the change in quantity? From Figure 2.12, it is clear that it is necessary to know the elasticities of both demand and supply before we can make a quantitative prediction. The more inelastic is demand, the greater is the price increase for a given tax, and the less is the quantity change. Conversely, the more inelastic is supply, the less is the price increase, *ceteris paribus*, and the smaller is the quantity change as well. If supply is perfectly inelastic, there is no change in price paid or quantity. The net price received by the sellers is lower by the total amount of the tax.

In order to make this problem simple, let us begin by making a slightly unrealistic assumption. Presume that supply is perfectly elastic, horizontal. Imagine that the price elasticity of demand for gasoline is -0.8. Calculate the tax revenue received by the government as a result of the additional $0.05 road use tax on gas.

In most actual cases, supply is not, in fact, perfectly elastic. When supply is

---

[19] People have obvious incentives to cheat on the tax arrangement. For instance, the teenager could appear to cut your lawn for free in exchange for your paying him in cash rather than by check. Economists classify black market transactions such as this as "participating in an underground economy." This type of behavior has been studied extensively particularly with reference to Latin America where the practice is said to be pervasive.

CALCULATING THE TAX REVENUE

$\eta = [\%$ change in $q]/[\%$ change in $p] = -0.8$, and hence the $\%$ change in $q = -0.8\bullet[\%$ change in $p]$

Since supply is perfectly elastic, price increases by the amount of the tax, \$0.05. The new supply curve is vertically above the old supply curve by five cents.

Therefore, the [$\%$ change in p] = \$0.05/\$1.00 = 5\%.

Consequently, the [$\%$ change in q] = $-0.8\bullet5\% = -4\%$.

Assume the pretax quantity was 9 million barrels per day. Hence, the posttax q is $(1-4\%)\bullet9$ or $0.96\bullet9$ million or 8.64 barrels.

A barrel is 42 gallons.

Therefore, the posttax revenue is $42\bullet8.64\bullet\$0.05 = \$18.144$ million per day.

If you had naively predicted that tax revenues would be the tax times the pretax quantity, your calculation would have been \$0.05\bullet9\bullet42, or \$18.9 million. This is \$756,000 per day more than calculated, taking into account the reactions of consumers to the higher price.

---

less than perfectly elastic, that is, when the supply curve is upward sloping rather than horizontal, the quantity reduction is less pronounced than calculated here; therefore, the ultimate tax revenues will be more than the \$18.144 million calculated in the accompanying box. In the problems at the end of the chapter, you are asked to compute the tax revenue based on a supply elasticity of 1.0.

Finally, consider the changes in the burden of the tax as the elasticities of demand and supply change. The price increase is higher for any given tax increase as supply becomes elastic or demand becomes more inelastic. In either case, the consumer bears a larger burden of the tax. As we have noted, as supply becomes more inelastic or demand becomes more elastic, the burden shifts to the supplier.[20]

AN ECONOMIST'S VIEW OF PRICE GOUGING

On Thursday, September 21, 1989, Hurricane Hugo hit the U.S. coast at Charleston, South Carolina. Advance warnings led most residents to evacuate the area, and loss of life was minimal. However, large segments of the region were totally devastated. Damage to homes and businesses was estimated in the billions of dollars. By late Friday and Saturday, residents began to trickle back into the

---

[20] More specifically, the burden shifts to the resource whose price increases as industry output expands. A more detailed discussion of this effect is contained in Chapter 6 when we discuss the concept of economic rent.

HURRICANE HUGO AND FOOD SUPPLIES

"There's no bread, there's no meat," Harold Washington said at a supermarket that had doughnuts and peanut butter but lacked staples. "You can't survive like that. Things just aren't working fast enough."

Greenville News, September 25, 1989, p. 1.

---

disaster area. To prevent looting and pilfering, state troopers and National Guard soldiers stopped most people except residents from venturing into the storm damage area. In fact, some residents were not even allowed to return to their own homes. Telephone service was nonexistent, and the lack of electricity made food storage and preparation a nightmare. Tap water was unpotable. Basic supplies such as ice and gasoline were difficult if not impossible to locate.

Stories abound about so-called price gouging in the area. There were newspaper reports of gasoline selling for $5.00 and $10.95 per gallon in a couple of cases where stations had bought emergency generators to operate pumps. Most food stores were open only a couple of hours per day, and they only allowed a few customers in at a time, creating extremely long lines outside as people waited for the chance to shop. As you might expect from the demand and supply model, all of this led to extremely high prices for virtually anything available for sale: "Police said there was a report of a company charging $3000 to cut down five trees."[21] Chain saws were selling for $600 on the street, while ice commanded $10 per bag. There were reports of generators normally selling for $500 bringing $2000 on the street. By late Saturday night, an emergency law was enacted to prevent *profiteers*, as they were called in the press, from charging such high prices.

Let us examine this situation from an economic perspective to determine what is going on and just what the impact of such a law might be. In Figure 2.13,

---

HURRICANE HUGO AND THE PROFITEERS

Tempers flared at one location where people sought ice to keep their food fresh.

"People were . . . begging for ice," said Staff Sgt. Bill Petty of the SC National Guard. "There were fistfights in line."

At stores that managed to reopen Saturday, people waited in lines for up to four hours.

Greenville News, September 25, 1989, p. 5a.

---

[21] *Greenville News*, September 25, 1989, p. 1a.

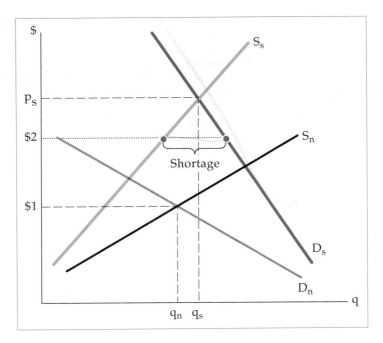

FIGURE 2.13
Demand and Supply Analysis of Profiteering

the normal supply and demand functions, S_n and D_n, are drawn. The normal price of ice, for example, is \$1 per bag, and q_n bags are bought and sold daily in the area. What happens when the hurricane hits, destroying the electrical network in the area? A substitute for ice, refrigeration, ceases to exist in most homes. This necessarily increases the demand for ice and *makes that demand more inelastic.* (Why is it more inelastic?) In Figure 2.13, demand shifts to D_s. At the same time, supplying ice becomes a great deal more expensive. Electricity is not available to suppliers either, except by the use of more expensive emergency generators. In addition, outside suppliers are not legally allowed into the area. On both these counts, supply also shifts left and becomes more inelastic, S_s. The natural economic consequence is for price to shoot up dramatically to try to clear the market. Even this process takes time, as the long lines described in newspaper and television reports attest. Let the storm equilibrium price and quantity be p_s and q_s respectively.

What happens now if the government enacts a regulation against the so-called profiteering? Suppose the law only lets the price double, and say that \$2 is much less than p_s. What will happen? On the demand side, the quantity demanded will be higher than it would without the price ceiling because the legal price is lower than the market clearing price. With the price regulation, people will want more ice; they will be less frugal with it when they get it, and they will be less inclined to substitute coolers and the like for ice. On the supply side, the legal price of \$2 is much lower than the storm equilibrium price, p_s, naturally muting the sellers' incentives to find ways to get ice to the market. The bottom line is that people are trying to buy more ice while businesspeople are willing to sell less. The law makes the crisis worse, or so it would seem. Lawmakers and reporters can call these high price sellers price gougers or profiteers, but in actuality the high prices they charge are the result of natural economic forces. Any other response only makes for a greater shortage, creating a crisis on top of a crisis.

If this model is correct, why then does government enact such a law? The answer is beyond the scope of this chapter, but by the time we reach Chapter 15, The Economic Theory of Regulation, we will be in a position to discuss this matter. For now consider the following questions: Who benefits from the enactment of the profiteering law? What about the local business establishments? Do people who own and work in businesses already in place, such as K-Mart, Walmart, and Ace Hardware, who must care for their own damaged homes and stores, make more money if fewer chain saws are sold in the first few hours after such a disaster hits? Does closing the market to all sellers actually only close the market to itinerant, out-of-town suppliers? Does the law not, in effect, make demanders wait until the existing business establishments in the area can get back on their feet to supply the goods?

The economic principles of supply and demand analysis, elasticity, and comparative statics have been sufficiently developed for you to answer Hypothetical Business Problems 2.3 and 2.4. Always remember, the solutions that follow are just one way of dealing with the issue. What counts is analysis and methodology.

Suggested Solution to Problem 2.3

When the supply of chicken increases in the two countries, a difference emerges because in the A country the price of beef cannot adjust to the change. Since beef and chicken are assumed to be substitutes, when the supply of chicken increases in country B, the price of chicken falls, *and the falling price of chicken impacts the beef market.* When the price of chicken falls, the demand for beef is reduced because the two goods are substitutes. The demand for beef falls because the price of a substitute, chicken, has gone down. The reduction in the demand for beef will cause its price to decline somewhat. Thus, the impact of the increase in the supply of chicken is spread across two markets. This secondary impact is foreclosed in country A by regulation; therefore, the price of beef will not fall in country A. In the B country, lower prices for chicken *reduce* the demand for beef, ultimately causing the price of beef to decline. So, in country B, the price of both chicken and beef falls when the supply of chicken increases. By contrast, in country A, only the price of chicken decreases. The lower price of beef in country B has a reverberation effect on the demand for chicken. Lower beef prices reduce the demand for chicken in country B. Therefore, the demand for chicken is less responsive in country B. Although the price of chicken is lower in country B, the demand is less; and the overall impact of the price change is a smaller increase in quantity demanded than if the price of beef had not adjusted. In effect, when the price of chicken falls in the *B* country, the impact is distributed over two markets, making the response in the chicken market less dramatic.

Suggested Solution to Problem 2.4

1. What do we know from the statement of the problem? The price elasticity of demand, η, is -0.8. Therefore,

$$(dQ_d/dp_d)(p_d/Q_d) = -0.8.$$

We also know that before the additional tax, $Q_d = 10$, and that $p_d = \$10$. Therefore,

$$(dQ_d/dp_d)(10/10) = -0.8.$$

Hence,

$$dQ_d = dp_d(1)(-0.8).$$

On the supply side, the elasticity is 2.5, and consequently,

$$(dQ_s/dp_s)(p_s/Q_s) = 2.5.$$

We also know that the quantity supplied is 10 and the supply price is \$10 before the additional tax, and hence we can write

$$dQ_s = dp_s(1)(2.5).$$

However, the change in the supply price must equal the change in the demand price less the amount of the tax, \$2; therefore,

$$dp_s = dp_d - 2.$$

By substitution then we observe that

$$dQ_s = (dp_d - 2)(2.5).$$

For the market to clear after the tax is imposed, the change in quantity demanded must equal the change in quantity supplied, or $dq_s = dq_d$. Therefore, by substitution,

$$(dp_d - 2)(2.5) = dp_d(-0.8).$$

Hence, the change in the price paid by demanders is

$$dp_d = 5/3.3 = \$1.52.$$

The price to buyers increases by \$1.52. The price received by sellers, which is the price paid by the buyers less the tax paid to the government, is \$1.52 − \$2.00, or \$−0.48. The seller's price falls by 48 cents.

2. What is the new quantity? The answer can be found working on either the demand or the supply side. Let's do it here on the supply side and you can work it out for yourself on the demand side. From manipulation of the supply elasticity, we know that

$$dQ_s = (dp_d - 2)(2.5).$$

And we know the change in demand price is +\$1.52. Therefore,

$$dQ_s = (1.52 - 2)(2.5) = -1.2.$$

Production will fall by 1.2 quarts per person per year. Naturally, by the notion of equilibrium, consumption falls by a like amount. Thus the new level of consumption and production is

$$10 - 1.2 = 8.8 \text{ quarts per year per person.}$$

Examine Figure 2.14. The demand for whiskey is D. The original supply of whiskey is S. After the new tax is levied, the supply curve shifts up vertically and parallel by exactly \$2 (forgetting any administrative costs of paying the tax). The original price is p_0 and the quantity is q_0. The new demand price is p_d, while the new quantity is q_n. Note that the supply price, the price received by the sellers, is equal to the demand price less \$2. In Figure 2.14, $\Delta p_d = \$1.52$, and $\Delta q = -1.2$.

3. How much additional revenue will the government collect? The tax per unit is \$2, and 8.8 units are consumed per person. So the total tax revenues from the new tax are \$2•8.8 times the population. However, to know the actual change in tax collections, we must know how much tax was being collected originally, because there is a decrease in consumption after the tax is increased. Hence, some of the revenue that was being collected is now lost because there is less consumption. The change in consumption is −1.2 quarts per person per year. So the lost revenue on this count is just the old tax rate times 1.2 times the population. The sum of the tax increase from the new \$2 tax and the tax collection decrease from the decline in consumption gives us the new total tax collections.

TOPICS TO REVIEW

These are topics that you should feel comfortable with before you leave this chapter. If you cannot write out a clear and concise sentence or paragraph explaining the topic after you have worked on the study problems, you should reread the relevant section of the text.

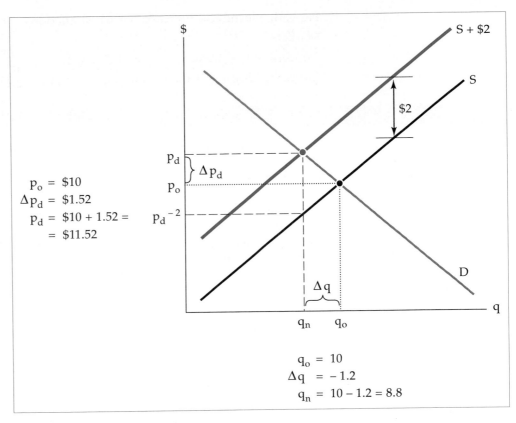

$$p_o = \$10$$
$$\Delta p_d = \$1.52$$
$$p_d = \$10 + 1.52 =$$
$$= \$11.52$$

$$q_o = 10$$
$$\Delta q = -1.2$$
$$q_n = 10 - 1.2 = 8.8$$

FIGURE 2.14
The Whiskey Tax

Individual Demand Function

Change in Demand Versus Change in Quantity Demanded

First Law of Demand

Normal Good

Inferior Good

Superior or Luxury Good

Substitutes

Complements

Market Demand Function

Price Elasticity of Demand

Relation Between Elasticity and Total Revenue

Opportunity or Alternative Cost

Supply Function

Role of Input Prices in Supply

Elasticity of Supply

Perfectly Elastic and Perfectly Inelastic Functions

Markets

Concept of Equilibrium Price and Quantity

Impact of Shifting Demand and Supply Curves on Market Equilibrium

STUDY PROBLEMS

The study problems in this book are intended to be an integral part of the learning process. Reading the material in each chapter is only the first step. After that you must practice putting the principles into action. This is the only way to master the concepts discussed in the text. In a way, the study problems are the heart of the material. Unless you attack them with vigor, you will not get full value from the book. You should *write* out the answers, working with others if you wish. Study groups are advised. It is probably a mistake to read the problem and then presume that you know the answer without writing out your proposed solution. Students who do this usually trick themselves into believing that they would have analyzed the problem in much the same manner as the proposed solution. Put it in writing.

1. Japan has a total ban on the importation of foreign rice. Japanese rice consumption is completely dependent on domestic production. The Japanese government claims this policy protects its national security. Assume that Japanese domestic consumption of rice is 1 billion pounds per year and that the current price is $2 per pound. Further assume that the world price of rice is $0.25 per pound (delivered to Japan). It is estimated that the price elasticity of demand for rice in Japan is −1.0 while the domestic price elasticity of supply in Japan is 0.5. Suppose that years of international pressure and trade negotiations lead the Japanese to open their markets to foreign producers of rice. Given the large volume of rice production in the world, assume that the world supply of rice available to the Japanese market is perfectly elastic. The Japanese can buy all the rice they desire at the delivered price of $0.25 per pound. What will happen to the consumption of rice in Japan? Specifically,
    a. What is the free trade level of rice consumption in Japan?
    b. How much rice do domestic farmers produce in Japan?
    c. How much rice is imported into the Japanese market?

2. Recall the $0.05 per gallon tax problem from the text section, Computing Tax Revenues. Rework that problem assuming that the initial quantity of gasoline consumed is 5 million barrels per day, the initial price is $0.89 per gallon, the demand elasticity is −1.0, and the elasticity of supply is 1.0. Specifically,
    a. What is the price after the tax is imposed?
    b. How much gasoline is consumed?
    c. How much tax revenues are raised?

3. The federal government has a complicated price support system in place to raise the income of peanut farmers. One of the impacts of these regulations is to raise price. Without going into the intricate details of the system, simply suppose a support (minimum legal) price is tied to input costs, and the

current price is $15 per bushel. At that price, total farm sales of peanuts are 2 million bushels to the private market. Farmers produce 35 percent more peanuts than this, and the government buys the surplus. Econometric studies estimate that the price elasticity of demand for peanuts is -1.5, and the supply elasticity is estimated at 1.0.

   a. What is the total quantity supplied of peanuts at the support price of $15 per bushel?
   b. Some farmers are lobbying for an increase in the support price to $17.50 per bushel. Suppose the price is raised.
      (1)   How many peanuts (in total) will be produced?
      (2)   Of the total peanuts produced, how many will the private market buy, and how many will the government purchase?
      (3)   How much will the $2.50 per bushel increase in price supports cost the government?

4. According to some reports, more than 40 percent of the American servicemen sent to Vietnam experimented with heroin. Of these, 57 percent became addicts in Vietnam. Upon their return, however, only 10 percent remained addicts. Sociologists claim this reduction is due to different social mores in the United States compared to Vietnam. As an economist, what do you say?

5. On Monday, October 26, 1987, the stock market had its largest one day decline in history. On Tuesday, the following conversation was overheard, "For the first time in several weeks, I didn't wake up this morning feeling stupid." When asked why, the person responded, "Because I haven't bought any stock in the past few months." Presumably, he was happy because he had not lost any money in the crash. By contrast, if he had bought a lot of stock late Monday afternoon when the market was very depressed, he could have made a lot of money Tuesday or Wednesday because stock prices went way up on those days. Is there any reason for this person to feel any smarter late Monday than on Tuesday or Wednesday afternoon?

6. Suppose the government enacts a price support system to raise the price of almonds. The price support is tied to input prices, and the current price is $20 per bushel. At that price, total farm sales of almonds are 10 million bushels to the private market. Farmers produce 50 percent more almonds than this, and the government buys the surplus. Econometric studies estimate that the own price elasticity of demand for almonds is -2.0, and the supply elasticity is estimated at 1.5.

   a. What is the total quantity supplied of almonds at the support price of $20 per bushel?
   b. Some consumers are lobbying for a decrease in the support price to $18 per bushel. Suppose the price is lowered. How many almonds (in total) will be produced?
   c. Of the new total amount of almonds produced, how much will the private market buy, and how much will the government purchase?
   d. How much will the $2 per bushel decrease in price supports save the government?

7. The sale of some drugs, heroin and cocaine for example, is illegal in the United States. Simple possession of these substances is also banned. Suppose these laws were repealed, and neither sale nor possession was against the law. What do you predict would happen to the price of these drugs and the quantity bought and sold?

8. Analyze the following: In many regions of the country, dairy farmers are losing a lot of money because their costs of production exceed the price they receive for their goods. Unless the federal government does something to correct this situation—for example, increase price through a price support system or give subsidies to cover costs—then all these dairy farmers will be forced out of business, and Americans will be left with little or no fresh whole milk to drink.

9. The average price for cars bought and sold in the United States is currently about $15,000. Say that sales for 1992 were expected to total approximately 20 million units. Suppose regulations put in place in Washington call for mandatory airbags in 1994 cars. These bags add about $800 to the *price* of cars. Based on relatively accurate econometric studies, the supply elasticity of cars is 1.5 and the demand elasticity is −1.25.

   a. After the regulations go into effect, how many cars will be sold in the United States? How many will be bought?

   b. Interest rates have a big impact on the sales of cars. The interest rate elasticity of the demand for cars is estimated to be −2.5. The 1992 interest rate on car loans was about 15 percent. If the interest rate fell to 12 percent in 1994 on top of the airbag price increase, what would happen to the number of cars bought and sold, *compared to the number incorporating the airbag price increase?*

10. Just suppose that the federal government decides to raise the price of gasoline. As you probably know, the state of Texas suffers now and then because the price of gas (actually crude) gets too low. For the sake of this problem, say the current price of crude oil is $15 per barrel. At that price, the prevailing quantity produced and consumed is 16 million barrels per day. Imports comprise one-half of this production. The plan being considered in Congress forces the price to be 25 percent higher than whatever the current market price is and allocates funds to buy any *domestically* produced or legally imported surplus. The plan affords existing importers a license to continue their *current* levels of importation. Suppose the price elasticity of demand is −1.0 and the domestic elasticity of supply is 1.6.

   a. What is the U.S. price after the law goes into effect?
   b. How much crude is consumed domestically?
   c. How much crude is produced domestically?
   d. How much crude is imported?
   e. How much crude does the U.S. government purchase daily?
   f. How much money does the U.S. government spend daily?
   g. Now suppose that this program simply costs too much, and the Feds decide just to outlaw imports *rather than impose a price floor.* What is the new equilibrium? Specifically,

(1)   What is the U.S. price after the law goes into effect?

(2)   How much crude is consumed domestically?

(3)   How much crude is produced domestically?

11. On October 17, 1989, the San Francisco Bay Area was struck by the second largest earthquake in U.S. history. As a consequence, utility service was severely interrupted. Let's assume that the price elasticity of demand for flashlights in this region is −0.5. Suppose that at the preearthquake price of $5, a total of 500 flashlights were bought and sold weekly in the region. Say the aftermath of the earthquake increases demand by 100-fold, so that after the disaster, if the price had not changed, the quantity demanded would have been 500•100 or 50,000 bought. Suppose that only 10,000 flashlights are available for sale during that first week after the devastation, and for the sake of simplicity assume that the price elasticity of demand does *not* change. What price will clear the market? Put another way, what price will ensure that all 10,000 flashlights get sold such that no one who wishes to purchase at that price goes without a flashlight?

12. Many sellers, especially sellers of tickets for rock concerts, routinely underprice their product, in the sense that long lines commonly form to purchase tickets. For instance, in the 1989 Rolling Stones tour, people were known to camp out in line for five days in order to buy tickets. For their appearance in Clemson, South Carolina, on November 26, 1989, some 63,000 tickets were made available at a price of $31.50 each. On the day tickets went on sale via telephone, the telephone system in upstate South Carolina went dead for brief periods due to the heavy volume of calls, indicating the extent of demand. Let's make some not so heroic assumptions. Based on the existing price of $31.50, presume that the Stones could have sold 100,000 tickets for their appearance at Clemson. Also presume that the price elasticity of demand for the tickets is −1.

a.   What price would have cleared the market so that every individual who wanted a ticket could have purchased one?

b.   If the Stones had charged the price you computed in part a, how much revenue would they have collected at the gate?

c.   Since they actually sold 63,000 tickets at $31.50 for the concert, realized gate receipts were $1,984,500. How much money did they forgo by undercharging at the gate?

d.   What did the Stones expect to get in return for the substantial investment that you have just computed in part c that they made by undercharging at the gate?

13. Consider the oil market. In early August 1990, the price of gasoline in the United States was about $0.90 a gallon, and consumption was about 10 million barrels or 420 million gallons. The events in the Persian Gulf altered that situation dramatically. Gasoline prices rose to more than $1.20 per gallon in a very short time. Let us suppose that the heightened cost of crude oil reduced the supply of gasoline by 25 percent. Furthermore, let us assume that the short-term price elasticity of demand for gasoline is −0.75. Similarly, the short-term elasticity of supply is +0.75.

Now many people feel that the price increases for gasoline were unwarranted, that the public was being gouged by the oil companies. Here is the question: Suppose that the supply of gasoline did actually decline by 25 percent, and demand did not change. Furthermore, suppose that oil companies had "acted with restraint" in raising prices and only raised the price of gasoline to $1 per gallon. Describe the situation in the retail market for gasoline. Be specific.

a. What would the quantity demanded be?

b. What would the quantity supplied be?

c. Would the market be in equilibrium? If not, how would the market look? What would be the repercussions?

14. There is a great deal of talk in Washington about raising income tax rates for certain people. For instance, one proposal would increase the income tax rate from 28 to 31 percent for those people earning more than $100,000. How much will that increase the tax bill for persons earning over that amount? In other words, will people facing higher income tax rates cheat more or less on their taxes under the new law? Put another way, when the government reduces income tax rates, does it simultaneously change the amount of resources it devotes to auditing income tax returns?

15. Say the average car bought and sold in the United States is priced at $15,000. Suppose that domestic production is 5 million units per year. For the sake of this problem, let us assume that the price elasticity of demand for cars is −1.5, while the domestic supply elasticity is +1. Also assume that foreign production, imported into the United States, is currently the same volume as domestic production. Let us presume that the foreign elasticity of cars supplied into the United States is 0.8. Pretend that foreign and domestic cars are perfect substitutes in the eyes of consumers. Now imagine that we go into a recession and the demand for cars falls by 25 percent.

a. What is the price of cars after the recession hits?

b. How many cars are bought in the United States after demand declines?

c. How many cars are manufactured in the United States? How many are imported?

There is a great cry made by domestic auto manufacturers that foreigners are killing their market. The U.S. Congress responds by restricting foreign imports to 3 million cars per year.

d. Given the import restriction, what is the price of cars?

e. Given the import restriction, how many cars are produced domestically?

f. Given the import restriction, what is the total sales of cars in the United States?

16. American textile producers have complained for many years that foreign imports are driving them out of business. Congress has responded with a number of proposed laws, but the bills always seem to get vetoed by the president. Let's suppose that the next president is more sensitive to the plight of the U.S. domestic textile industry and does not veto the annual textile protection bill. Suppose the average American currently purchases 10 shirts

per year at a price of $25. Assume that the price elasticity of demand is -1.5. Of these 10 shirts, let's say that 6 were made in the United States and 4 were imported (on average) from various foreign countries. Suppose the domestic elasticity of supply is $+1.0$. Assuming there are 250 million people in the United States, the current consumption of shirts is 2.5 billion per year. Suppose the new law restricts foreign imports to 500 million shirts.

a.   What will happen to the price of shirts in the United States? Be precise.
b.   How many shirts will domestic producers manufacture?
c.   How many shirts will be imported from foreign countries?

17. The following sentence began a story in *The News* (Greenville, SC), "Greenville Tech to Raise Tuition," September 4, 1991, p. 1A:

Despite three straight years of record-setting enrollments, Greenville Technical College will impose a 20 percent tuition hike next quarter.

The sentence is flawed from an economic perspective.

a.   What is the flaw in the sentence?
b.   Correct the sentence to erase the flaw.
c.   What sort of logic must the authors, Mathew Burns and Lucy May, have been using when they wrote the sentence?

18. The following paragraph began a story in the *Wall Street Journal* on September 30, 1991:

Robust spending, the effects of the Gulf War and a spectacular banking bust are increasing the pressure on the oil sheiks of Saudi Arabia and the Persian Gulf to raise revenues. And in the economics ruling the Organization of Petroleum Exporting Countries, that means downward pressure on international oil prices.[22]

The story makes a direct statement about the price elasticity of demand. What is it?

19. Read the accompanying story from *Running Journal*. Estimate the price elasticity of demand for running in races. Based on your estimate of the elasticity, do you see how it is possible to have predicted the impact on revenues from the change in entry fee based on your estimate of the price elasticity of demand?

SUGGESTED READINGS

The volume of books and articles on markets is huge. The following titles hardly scratch the surface.

Alchian, Armen A. and Allen, William. *University Economics*. Belmont, CA: Wadsworth Publishing Co., 1964.

---

[22] Peter Truell, "The Outlook: OPEC Sheiks Seem To Be Over a Barrel," *Wall Street Journal*, September 30, 1991, p. A1. Reprinted by permission of *The Wall Street Journal*, © 1991 Dow Jones & Co., Inc. All Rights Reserved Worldwide.

ENTRY FEES

Would you pay $20 to run a road race—even if it was one of your favorites?

Those were the questions that aroused such controversy in Macon, GA, over the weeks preceding the 15th Macon Labor Day Road Race 5K/10K Sept. 2. When the *Macon Telegraph* newspaper, the race's principal sponsor, announced that the entry fee would be raised from $12 in 1990 to $20 this year, runners spoke up loud and clear.

"There's a limit" was the title of an editorial by Jackie Phillips in the Columbus (GA) Track Club's newsletter. . . .

Liddel Rimes was the beleaguered *Telegraph* promotions manager in charge of coordinating the race. Contacted after the race, she admitted that the numbers in the two events fell drastically—from around 1,600 in 1990 to about 900 this year. A little math reveals that the paper's strategy backfired—they received less money from entry fees this year than last.

Margaret Chivers, "They Voted With Their Feet: How Much Is Too Much for a Race Entry Fee?" *Running Journal,* October 1991, pp. 1–2.

Case, Karl E. and Fair, Ray C. *Principles of Economics*, 2d ed. Englewood Cliffs: Prentice Hall, 1992.

Ekelund, Robert and Tollison, Robert. *Economics.* Boston: Little, Brown, 1989.

Marshall, Alfred. *Principles of Economics,* Vol. I, 5th ed. London: Macmillan, 1907.

Smith, Adam. *An Inquiry into the Nature and Causes of the Wealth of Nations.* New York: The Modern Library, 1937. (Originally published 1776)

Stigler, George J. and Becker, Gary S. "De Gustibus Non Est Disputandum." *American Economic Review* 67(2) (March 1977):76–90.

SUGGESTED SOLUTIONS TO SELECTED STUDY PROBLEMS

The following are only *suggested* solutions to the study problems presented at the end of this chapter. In all cases, the suggestions here put heavy emphasis on analysis rather than a single correct answer. Since most managerial problems do not fall into neat little boxes, the individual characteristics of the problems that you will encounter on the job will typically mandate a solution using the principles developed here and in other courses. Memorizing these solutions will not make you a good manager; learning the *principles* detailed here will help make you a better manager.

2. From the problem we know the demand and supply price elasticities and the original price and quantity. From these we see that

$$\eta = [dq_D/dp_D] \bullet (0.89/5) = -1 \tag{i}$$

and

$$\sigma = [dq_S/dq_S] \bullet (0.89/5) = +1. \tag{ii}$$

Therefore,

$$dq_D \bullet (0.89/5) = -dp_D \tag{iii}$$

and

$$dq_S \bullet (0.89/5) = dp_S. \tag{iv}$$

But the tax is 0.05, which means that the new demand price is 5 cents higher than the new supply price. Thus,

$$dp_S = dp_D - 0.05. \tag{v}$$

By substitution of equation (v) into equation (iv), we see that

$$dq_S \bullet (0.89/5) = dp_D - 0.05. \tag{vi}$$

If the market is to be in equilibrium after the tax is imposed, then the quantity demanded after the tax must equal the quantity supplied. Therefore,

$$dq_S = dq_D. \tag{vii}$$

Moreover, from equation (vi) we observe that

$$dp_D = 0.05 + dq_s \bullet (0.89/5). \tag{viii}$$

Therefore, by substitution of equations (vii) and (viii) into equation (iii), we find that

$$dq_S = -0.14044. \tag{ix}$$

Necessarily then the change in quantity demanded is also -0.14044. The new equilibrium quantity bought and sold of petroleum is $5 - 0.14 = 4.86$. From equation (i) we can compute the increase in the demand price as $+0.025$ (or 2.5 cents). Thus the buyer's price rises to $0.915 per gallon, and the seller's price falls to $0.865 per gallon.

3.   a.   Production is 35 percent more than consumption. Consumption is 2 million. Therefore production is $1.35 \bullet 2 = 2.7$ million.

       b.   (1) If the price increases to $17.50 from $15, that is a $2.50/$15 or 16.67 percent increase. The elasticity of supply is $+1$. Therefore, since

$$\% \Delta q_s / \% \Delta p = +1,$$

then

$$\% \Delta q_s = \% \Delta p,$$

and since the percentage change in price is $+16.67$ percent, the percentage change in production is the same. A 16.67 percent increase in production over the current level, 2.7, is $1.1667 \bullet 2.7 = 3.15$ million bushels.

           (2) When the price increases to $17.50 the quantity demanded will decrease. The price elasticity of demand is -1.5. Therefore,

$$\Delta q_d / \Delta p = -1.5, \text{ or }$$

$$\Delta q_d = \Delta p \bullet (-1.5) = +16.67\% \bullet (-1.5) = -25\%.$$

A 25 percent reduction in consumption reduces the quantity demanded from 2 to $0.75(2) = 1.5$ million bushels.

(3) The private market buys 1.5 million, but consumption is 3.15. There-fore the government must purchase $3.15 - 1.5 = 1.65$ million bushels at $17.50. Thus, new government expenditures on peanuts will be 1.65•$17.50 or $28.875 million. However, the *cost* of the price *increase* is only the difference between this new number and the old support figure, whatever that was.

4. Casual evidence suggests that the price of heroin is considerably higher in the United States than it was in Southeast Asia. Therefore, according to the first law of demand and without regard for the notion of addiction, economic principles argue that lower heroin consumption upon return to the United States is due to the higher price of the good. At the end of Chapter 5, after discounting is discussed, this question is explored in more detail with particular reference to life expectancy.

5. The concept of *opportunity cost* tells us that we do not lose any more money when we buy stock whose price subsequently falls than we do when we *fail to buy stock whose price subsequently increases*. In both cases, a mistake was made.

6. a. 50 percent more than 10 million bushels is 15 million.
    b. A price decline to $18 is a $-2/20$ or -10 percent change in price. The price elasticity of supply is 1.5. Therefore, the new quantity supplied (using the point elasticity) is -10%•1.5 or 15 percent. Thus the new quantity supplied is $(1 - 0.15)$•15 or 12.75 million bushels.
    c. When the price falls by 10 percent the quantity demanded will increase by -10%•(-2.0) since the own price elasticity of demand is -2.0. Thus the increase in private consumption is $+20$ percent. The old level of consumption was 10 million; therefore, 12 million bushels are now consumed by the private market. The government purchases the difference between private consumption and production or 0.75 million bushels.
    d. At a price of $20 per bushel, the government spends $20•5 = $100 million. At a price of $18 the government only spends $18•0.75 = $13.5 million. The savings to the government is the difference or $100 - 13.5 = $86.5 million.

7. Since possession and sale are illegal, both demand and supply are reduced because buyers and sellers are taxed (punished) by the law. This is true even if some are not caught. First, there is an expected cost, some probability of being detected prior to engaging in an illegal transaction. Thus, the bribes paid to public officials, or the fees paid to lawyers increase the cost of buying and selling. The legal sanctions thus shift both demand and supply to the left. This absolutely reduces the quantity bought and sold. However, price can be higher or lower than in a legal market depending on whether supply or demand shifts more. If the probability of detection and conviction and fines is the same for buyer and seller, then both curves shift the same, and there is no impact on price. However, it is common for sellers to face stiffer penalties than buyers, in which case, the law reduces supply more than demand. Thus,

legalization would shift supply out more than demand and price would fall. In all cases, quantity bought and sold would increase.

8. This statement is probably wrong. If many farmers are losing money, then eventually some of them will quit. The exit of farmers from the production side of the market will reduce supply to the market, raising price and making it more likely that the remaining farmers can make enough money to stay in business. Naturally, it is always possible that even when most farmers have exited the market, the price is still not high enough to keep a few farmers in business. What this means of course is that people do not demand enough milk to keep the industry in business.

10. First let's lay out the parameters of the problem. Total domestic consumption is 16 million barrels per day. Domestic production is half this amount or 8 million barrels per day.
    a. The current price is $15 and the plan raises the price by 25 percent to $1.25 \cdot \$15 = \$18.75$.
    b. The price is 25 percent higher and the price elasticity of demand is -1. Therefore, domestic consumption will decrease by 25 percent. The current level is 16 million. The new level is $(1 - 0.25) \cdot 16 = 12$ million barrels.
    c. The price elasticity of supply is 1.6 and the price increase is 25 percent. Therefore, domestic supply will increase by $1.6 \cdot 25\% = 40\%$. The current level of domestic production is 8. Therefore, the new level of domestic production will be $1.4 \cdot 8 = 11.2$ million barrels.
    d. Crude imports are pegged at 8 million barrels by the law.
    e. The government purchases the surplus. Total production (domestic and foreign) is $11.2 + 8 = 19.2$. Consumption is 12. Therefore, the surplus is $19.2 - 12 = 7.2$.
    f. The surplus purchased is 7.2. The price is $18.75. Therefore, the expenditure is $7.2 \cdot \$18.75 = \$135$ million.
    g. To answer this part of the question, we have to equate domestic demand with domestic supply. Consult Figure 2.15. We know that when the price is $15, domestic supply is 8. We also know that domestic demand at that price is 16. After the foreign imports are restricted, the new price and quantity will be determined by the intersection of domestic supply and demand. Call the new price p^* and the new quantity q^*. To compute these we have to take advantage of three pieces of information: the price elasticity of demand, the price elasticity of supply, and the fact that the total change in the market is divided between an increase in production and a decrease in consumption.
        (1) The change in quantity supplied is Δq_S and the change in quantity demanded is Δq_D. The change in price is Δp. This means that we have three unknowns that we must determine. However, we can see from Figure 2.15 that the increase in the quantity supplied plus the decrease in the quantity demanded has to equal the amount of foreign production no longer imported. That is,

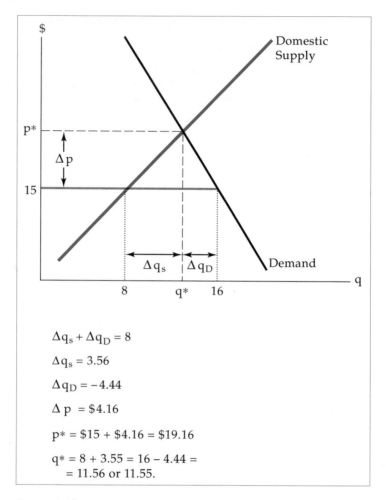

$\Delta q_s + \Delta q_D = 8$

$\Delta q_s = 3.56$

$\Delta q_D = -4.44$

$\Delta p = \$4.16$

$p^* = \$15 + \$4.16 = \$19.16$

$q^* = 8 + 3.55 = 16 - 4.44 =$
    $= 11.56 \text{ or } 11.55.$

FIGURE 2.15
Study Problem 10

$$\Delta q_S - \Delta q_D = 8,^{23}$$

or

$$\Delta q_S = 8 + \Delta q_D.$$

From the formulas for the price elasticities of supply and demand, we can get two more equations that allow us to solve for the three unknowns. From the price elasticity of demand we know that

$$(\Delta q_D / q_D)/(\Delta p / p) = -1.$$

---

[23] Since the change in quantity demanded is negative, we have to subtract it to get the correct sum. In effect, we are adding the decrease, which is subtracting.

From the price elasticity of supply we know that

$(\Delta q_S/q_S)/(\Delta p/p) = 1.6.$

All together then we have these two equations plus the equation reflecting the market clearing adjustment after the loss of foreign imports. We can solve by the use of substitution. We know that $q_S = 8$, that $q_D = 16$, and that $p = 15$. We can use the first equation to eliminate the change in quantity supplied. Making these substitutions into the two elasticity formulas leaves two equations and two unknowns, the change in price and the change in quantity demanded:

$(\Delta q_D/16)/(\Delta p/15) = -1.$

$[(8+\Delta q_D)/8]/(\Delta p/15) = 1.6.$

By manipulation of the first equation,

$\Delta q_D = -(16/15) \bullet \Delta p.$

By manipulation of the second equation,

$\Delta p = (15 \bullet [8+\Delta q_D])/(8 \bullet 1.6) = 1.17 \bullet (8+\Delta q_D).$

We can eliminate the change in price term, substituting the latter into the former:

$\Delta p = 1.17 \bullet (8+[-16/15] \bullet \Delta p).$

This means that

$\Delta p = 9.36/2.248 = +4.16.$

The old price was \$15. The new price is \$15 + \$4.16 or \$19.16.
(2) We know that $\Delta q_D = (-16/15) \bullet \Delta p$. Therefore, the change in quantity demanded is $(-16/15) \bullet 4.16 = -4.44$. The old quantity demanded was 16. Therefore the new quantity demanded, q^*, is $16 - 4.44 = 11.56$.
(3) The new domestic production has to equal domestic consumption by construction. No imports are allowed. Therefore, domestic production has to increase from 8 to 11.56 barrels per day. This can be verified by insertion of the price change into the supply elasticity formula:

$(\Delta q_S/8)/(4.16/15) = 1.6$

implies that $\Delta q_S = 1.6 \bullet (4.16/15) \bullet 8 = 3.55$. Since the old quantity supplied domestically was 8, the new level of domestic production is $8 + 3.55 = 11.55$, which is the same as consumption (accounting for rounding error in computations).

11. To start this problem, observe that the price elasticity of demand is -0.5. This implies that

$(dq/dp)(p/q) = -0.5.$

From the problem we know that after the quake, if the price is $5 then the quantity demanded is 50,000. So

$p = \$5$ and

$q = 50,000.$

We also know that only 10,000 flashlights are available for sale. Normally, 50,000 flashlights would be bought and sold were they available. Hence, the change in quantity necessary to clear the market is

$dq = 10,000 - 50,000 = -40,000.$

The price must increase sufficiently to choke off sales by 40,000 units. Thus, from the formula for the price elasticity of demand, we know all the variables except the change in price. By substitution then,

$(-40,000/dp)(5/50,000) = -0.5.$

Therefore,

$dp = [(-40,000)(5)]/[(-0.5)(50,000)] = +\$8.$

The price must increase by $8, and so the price must increase to $5 + $8 or $13 to clear the market.

13. a.   Examine Figure 2.16. Originally, demand is D, and supply is S. Market price is $0.90 per gallon while production and consumption are 10 million barrels. A 25 percent reduction in supply shifts that curve to the left to S'. At the current price of $0.90 production is 75 percent of 10 or 7.5 million. So the new supply curve, S', passes through the point $p = 0.90$ and $q = 7.5$. We assume the shift is parallel. Now we can compute what would have happened if the price had only risen to $1. First, on the demand side, a price increase from $0.90 to $1.00 is a 0.10/0.90 or 11.1 percent increase. Thus, with a short-term elasticity of demand equal to -0.75, we have

$\%\Delta q_d / \%\Delta p = -0.75$, or

$\%\Delta q_d = (-0.75) \bullet (\%\Delta p) = (-0.75) \bullet (+11.1\%) = -8.33\%$, or

in terms of barrels, this amounts to

$(1 - 0.083) \bullet (10) = 9.167.$

Thus, at a price of $1, the quantity demanded would be 9.167 million barrels.

b.   On the supply side, the current quantity is 75 percent of 10 or 7.5 million barrels at a price of $0.90. The supply elasticity is $+0.75$. The price increase to $1 is an 11.1 percent jump. Therefore, from the elasticity formula

$\%\Delta q_s / \%\Delta p = +0.75$, or

$\%\Delta q_s = 0.75 \bullet (\%\Delta p) = 0.75 \bullet (+11.1\%) = +8.325\%.$

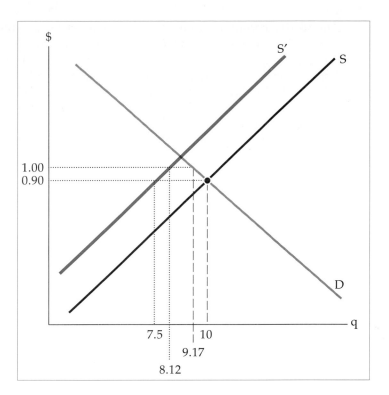

FIGURE 2.16
Study Problem 13

Thus, the new quantity supplied, after the supply shock and the price increase, is

(1 + 0.08325)•(7.5) = 8.12 million barrels.

c.   The market would not be in equilibrium. The quantity demanded, 9.167 million barrels, exceeds the quantity supplied, 8.12 million. A shortage exists. Lines would form or other rationing devices would come into place such as even-odd days for consumption based on license plate numbers or other such schemes that were used in the early 1970s when President Nixon imposed retail price controls on gasoline.

14. Start this problem with the following approach: What happens to the price of cheating on taxes when the tax rate increases? Next, consider the incentives of the government to detect cheating given that the tax rate is higher. The answer to the first part is straightforward. Suppose a person is considering taking an illegal deduction of $100. Under the old law this illegal deduction would save the taxpayer 0.28•$100 or $28. With the new higher rates the savings would be $31. So, assuming the penalties are the same for making the illegal deduction, say a $100 fine (plus the extra tax of course), the payoff to cheating has gone up after the tax rates increased. Thus we expect that some people so inclined will now cheat, and those already cheating will cheat a bit

more. Cognizant of this incentive, we expect the IRS will find it expedient to hire additional agents and search for tax fraud more diligently.

15. This problem is a bit tricky. To start with, let's first concentrate on the demand side. Before the recession, the quantity demanded at $15,000 was 10 million units. During the recession, demand falls by 25 percent. Therefore, recession demand is 75 percent of the original. In other words, at each price the level of consumption is only 75 percent of what it was before the recession. For instance, at the price of $15,000, the original quantity demanded was 10 million units. Thus, the new quantity demanded is 7.5 million units. Consult Figure 2.17. The original demand curve is D. The recession demand curve is D_R. On the supply side, the original quantity supplied by domestic manufacturers at $15,000 was 5 million cars. Label this supply S^D. Foreigners supplied

FIGURE 2.17
Study Problem 15

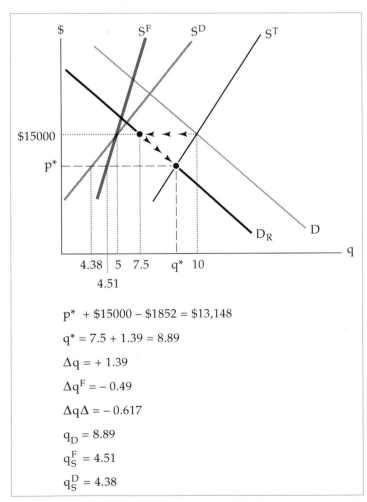

$$p^* + \$15000 - \$1852 = \$13,148$$

$$q^* = 7.5 + 1.39 = 8.89$$

$$\Delta q = +1.39$$

$$\Delta q^F = -0.49$$

$$\Delta q \Delta = -0.617$$

$$q_D = 8.89$$

$$q_S^F = 4.51$$

$$q_S^D = 4.38$$

a like amount for a total of 10. The foreign supply curve is labeled S^F. The total supply curve is labeled S^T. Note that the foreign supply curve is more inelastic than the domestic supply curve. When the recession hits, the quantity demanded at $15,000 is 7.5 units, but the total quantity supplied is 10, 5 by foreigners and 5 by domestic producers. The intersection of the new demand curve, D_R, and the old supply curve, S^T, is the new equilibrium. The new price is p^*, and the new quantity is q^*. The new price is lower than the old; the quantity demanded will increase *from the recession level of 7.5*. This may sound odd. After all demand has decreased. Won't consumers buy less? Yes they will buy less at every price. Demand has decreased. But decreased demand puts downward pressure on price, and when price falls quantity demanded increases. Follow the arrows in the figure. The recession caused demand to decline by 25 percent or 2.5 million units. The market responds in two ways. First producers will manufacture less, and when they do, price is lower. On the second count, because price is lower, the demanders will react by buying more than they would have at the old price. Quantity demanded responds down the new demand curve. This secondary change in quantity demanded (from the point $p = \$15,000$ and $q_D = 7.5$) to the new equilibrium *plus* the reduction in quantity supplied by the domestic and foreign producers has to offset the overall reduction in demand, 2.5 million units.

In sequence, demand decreases by 2.5 million units; the change in the market clearing quantity is -2.5. Lower foreign and domestic production takes up some of this reduction. Part of it is recaptured by an increased quantity demanded as price moves lower. The total effect is a decrease of 2.5 million units. So, we can write

$$\Delta q_D + \Delta q^F + \Delta qD = 2.5.$$

From the formulas for the respective price elasticities of demand, we have

$$(\Delta q_D/\Delta p)\bullet(p/q_D) = -1.5,$$

$$(\Delta q_S^F/\Delta p)\bullet(p/q_S^F) = +0.8,$$

and

$$(\Delta q_S^D/\Delta p)\bullet(p/q_S^D) = +1.0.$$

In addition, we know that $p = \$15,000$, that $q_D = 7.5$, and that $q_S^D = q_S^F = 5$. Substituting these terms and using the four equations to solve for the four unknowns, the change in price, the change in quantity demanded, the change in domestic quantity supplied, and the change in foreign quantity supplied, yields the solution to the problem. From the formula for the price elasticity of demand we see that

$$(\Delta q_D/\Delta p)\bullet(p/q_D) = -1.5.$$

Substituting for price and quantity reveals that

$$(\Delta q_D/\Delta p)\bullet(15000/7.5) = -1.5.$$

Manipulation allows us to state this equation in terms of the change in quantity demanded:

$$\Delta q_D = -0.00075 \cdot \Delta p.$$

Similarly, from the supply elasticities, we see that

$$\Delta q_S^F = 0.000267 \cdot \Delta p$$

and

$$\Delta q_S^D = 0.000333 \cdot \Delta p.$$

Substituting each of these three changes into the expression for the total change yields an equation for the change in price:

$$-0.00075 \cdot \Delta p - 0.000267 \cdot \Delta p - 0.000333 \cdot \Delta p = 2.5.$$

Therefore,

$$\Delta p = \$-1851.85$$

which we can round off to $1852. The new price is $15,000 less $1852 or $13,148. Using this we can compute the respective changes in quantities.

$$\Delta q_D = -0.00075 \cdot (-1852) = 1.389.$$

Thus, the new level of consumption is $7.5 + 1.389 = 8.889$. This is divided between foreign and domestic producers.

$$\Delta q_S^F = 0.000267 \cdot (-1852) = -0.49.$$

Foreign producers sell 0.49 million units less than they did before the recession, which is $5 - 0.49 = 4.51$ million units. Domestic producers sell the rest:

$$\Delta q_S^D = 0.000333 \cdot (-1852) = -0.617.$$

Domestic producers make $5 - 0.617 = 4.38$ million units. Total production, foreign plus domestic, is $4.51 + 4.38 = 8.89$ million units, which is the same as the new level of consumption.

To answer the second part of the question, we need to recognize that foreigners are currently selling 4.51 million units. After the restriction, they will only sell 3 million units. The difference, 1.51 million units, must be made up in one of two ways, a reduction in consumption and/or an increase in domestic production. Domestic producers will make up for some of this shortfall, demanders the difference. Therefore, the increase in production less the reduction in consumption equals the shortfall:

$$\Delta q_S^D - \Delta q_D = 1.51.$$

The original (postrecession) equilibrium was

$p = \$13,148,$
$q_D = 8.89,$

and

$q_S^D = 4.38.$

The problem can now be solved using the elasticity formulas. On the demand side,

$$(\Delta q_D / \Delta p)(p/q_D) = -1.5.$$

On the supply side,

$$(\Delta q_S^D / \Delta p)(p/q_S^D) = +1.0.$$

Making the substitutions for the price and quantities gives us two equations and three unknowns, but we know that the sum of the changes in quantities has to equal -1.51. Thus we have three equations and three unknowns. Solving these yields the solution:

$$\Delta p = \$1111.$$

The new price is $\$13{,}148 + \$1111 = \$14{,}259$. The change in quantity demanded is -1.14. Thus, the new level of consumption is $8.89 - 1.14 = 7.75$ million units. The change in quantity supplied is

$$\Delta q_S^D = 1.51 - 1.14 = 0.37.$$

Domestic production increases by 0.37 million units from 4.38 to 4.75. Imports are 3. Thus total production is $4.75 + 3 = 7.75$, which is the same as domestic consumption. We can check the production figures by using the domestic elasticity of supply. The percentage increase in price is $+1111/13{,}148 = +8.4\%$. The original level of domestic supply was 4.38, and since the elasticity is $+1$, the increase in production will be the same percentage as the increase in price, or 8.4 percent. Multiplying 1.084 times 4.38 yields the new domestic production level of 4.75 million units, and the answer is confirmed.

17. **a.** The flaw occurs in the misinterpretation of a change in demand. Given that the school has had three straight years of increasing enrollment, we must expect that demand has been increasing. When demand is increasing and other things are not changing, we expect higher prices as we move up the supply curve. In this situation, the 20 percent tuition hike is hardly surprising.

   b. One easy way to fix the sentence is to replace the first word *Despite* with the word *Given*, which would suggest that the price increase is the result of the increase in demand.

   c. Perhaps the authors were presuming that the supply was downward sloping, or that the school would only raise revenues if it did not have many students.

A P P E N D I X

MATHMATICS REVIEW

- Functions
- Slopes
- Limits and Derivatives
- Advanced Differentiation
- Applications of Derivatives
- Integration
- Multivariate Calculus
- Level Curves
- Homogeneous and Homothetic Functions and Euler's Theorem
- Applications of Multivariate Calculus
- Matrix Algebra
- The Envelope Theorem
- Summary
- Topics to Review
- Study Problems
- Suggested Readings
- Suggested Solutions to Selected Study Problems

This appendix is intended as a review. It contains the mathematics necessary for understanding and modeling some of the economic problems presented in this book. It is not meant to be exhaustive or complete, but rather a primer on some if not most of the tools you might need to handle the concepts in managerial economics. The appendix begins with a fundamental mathematical concept, the function. The notions of limits and derivatives are also discussed. For most of you, this will be the most important section. After that, the reverse process to derivation—integration—is explored.

Mathematical optimization is the next topic, and you will find that this technique pervades economic analysis. The notions of first and second order conditions are explained. The appendix also contains some matrix algebra and a brief discussion of the envelope theorem. There are a few study problems. However, their purpose here is fundamentally different from that of the problems at the end of the chapters. In this course and book, mathematics is a tool for learning, not an end unto itself. Therefore, mastering the mathematical concepts here is neither necessary nor sufficient for an understanding of the major material in managerial economics. It is background and is only presented to help you better learn the substantive material presented elsewhere.

FUNCTIONS

A **function** is a relation between variables. It tells how, for example, the quantity of apples you consume, Q, varies when the price of apples, P, changes. It can be written in shorthand as

$$Q = f(P).$$

This should be read as "Q, the quantity of apples, *is a function of P*, the price of apples." The letter f is meant to represent any functional relation between Q and P. One such relation is shown in Figure A2.1. Given any P, such as P_0, the function tells the one Q, in this case, Q_0, that is consumed. It bears noting that economists draw the functional relation between P and Q in a nonstandard way. As a general rule, the independent variable is plotted on the horizontal axis, while the dependent variable is graphed vertically. The reason that economists do this is that it used to be common to specify the demand function in the inverse to the form stated here—that is, with price a function of quantity. This is called the Marshallian demand curve and is analytically equivalent to the form being used here. The difference is that the price customers are willing to pay is determined by the quantity they buy. Stated this way, price is dependent on quantity and plots on the vertical axis, and that is how economics came to plot price vertically.

One of the common functions used in economics is the logarithm. Suppose there exists a relation between two variables, x and y, such that

$$A^x = y$$

where A is some number. We define a **logarithm** such that

$$x = \log_A y$$

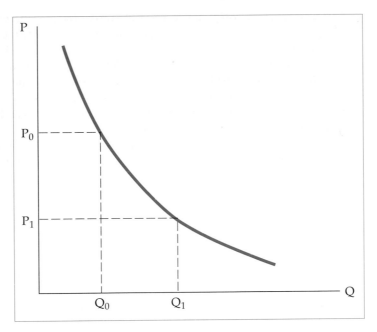

FIGURE 2.1
The Slope of a Function

where A is called the **base of the logarithm.** The base most commonly used in economics is the base e ($e = 2.71828$), which is called the **natural log.** The number e is sometimes called the natural number. Some students may find it useful to substitute the word exponent or power when they encounter the log notation. The natural log is usually abbreviated as "ln."

There are three common manipulations of the logarithm function that are very useful. The first has to do with the log of a product. The log of a product is the sum of the logs, or

$$\ln(p \cdot q) = \ln(p) + \ln(q). \tag{A.1}$$

The second manipulation involves the logarithm of a variable raised to a power. This relation is

$$\ln(p^q) = q \cdot \ln(p). \tag{A.2}$$

The third involves the logarithm of the ratio of two variables,

$$\ln(p/q) = \ln(p) - \ln(q). \tag{A.3}$$

SLOPES

One of the most important things about a function, at least for the economist, is the **slope.** Consider the demand function identified earlier, $Q = f(P)$. The slope tells something about how much Q changes when P changes. If the price of apples falls to P_1, it is obvious from looking at Figure A2.1 that the consumption of apples increases to, Q_1. The change in consumption is $Q_1 - Q_0$. The slope of a straight line connecting (P_0,Q_0) and (P_1,Q_1) is defined as[1]

$$\text{slope} \equiv (P_0 - P_1)/(Q_0 - Q_1). \tag{A.4}$$

You may remember this as "rise over run." Take note that the slope of the straight line connecting points (P_0,Q_0) and (P_1,Q_1) is different from the slope of the function at the point (P_0,Q_0). As a result, if we wanted to know the slope of the function at (P_0,Q_0), we would have to make (P_1,Q_1) very close to the original point, very close indeed. In fact, to have an accurate description of the slope, the second point would have to lie exactly on top of the first point. This would make the division in equation A.4 very difficult since division by zero is not possible or defined. Calculus helps overcome this handicap.

LIMITS AND DERIVATIVES

Examine Figure A2.2. From equation A.4 we know the slope of the straight line connecting points A and B is given by

$$\text{slope} \equiv [f(x_0 + \Delta x) - f(x_0)]/\Delta x \tag{A.5}$$

where Δx is the change in x. Examine what happens as Δx gets very small, as B gets closer to A. We can define an operator called the **limit,** represented by the shorthand notation "lim,"

$$\text{Lim} \atop \Delta x \to 0$$

which is the value that the formula approaches as Δx gets very small, or as mathematicians say, as Δx approaches zero. The limit operator helps us understand what happens to some value as a part of that value gets close to a specific number, usually zero.

Applying the limit operator to the slope formula defines the **derivative** of $f(\mathrm{x})$ as

$$dy/dy = \lim_{\Delta x \to 0} [f(x_0 + \Delta x) - f(x_0)]/\Delta x.$$

Thus, the derivative describes the slope of a function at a particular point, x.

Consider the example $y = x^2$. Apply the slope formula to determine how y changes when x changes by a small amount—that is, find the derivative of y with respect to x.

---

[1] The symbol $\equiv$ is called the identity, and it is quite like the equals sign but more. Logically, $C \equiv D$ means C implies D, and D implies C. Some people prefer to say that the identity represents a definitional relation between C and D; the things on each side of the identity are the same thing.

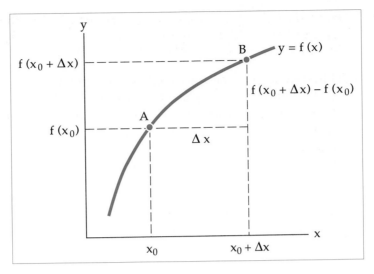

FIGURE A2.2
Limits

$$dy/dx = \lim_{\Delta x \to 0} [(x + \Delta x)^2 - x^2]/\Delta x.$$

Squaring and collecting terms we find that

$$dy/dx = \lim_{\Delta x \to 0} [(x^2 + 2x\Delta x + \Delta x^2 - x^2)]/\Delta x.$$

Simplifying,

$$dy/dx = \lim_{\Delta x \to 0} (2x + \Delta x).$$

Using the limit operator, it is obvious that when the change in x is very small, the term Δx is zero, and therefore

$$dy/dx = 2x.$$

Now the only question that remains is, What does this mean? Simply speaking, the slope of the function $y = x^2$ is equal to two times the value of x at which the function is evaluated. For example, at $x = 4$, $y = 16$ and the slope of the function, dy/dx, is 8.

The function $y = x^2$ is a member of a class of functions that is common in the world of economics, exponential functions. The rule for finding the derivative of a general exponential function

$$y = ax^n$$

is

$$dy/dx = nax^{n-1}. \tag{A.6}$$

This is something the conscientious student will memorize.

The derivatives of exponential and log functions are somewhat special. If

$$y = e^{ax},$$

then

$$dy/dx = ae^{ax},$$

and for

$$y = \ln(x),$$

the derivative is

$$dy/dx = 1/x.$$

Second derivatives are just the derivatives of derivatives. A second derivative gives the rate of change of the slope of a function. It is written as

$$d^2y/dx^2.$$

For the function $y = ax^n$,

$$d^2y/dx^2 = (n-1)nax^{n-2}.$$

For simplicity's sake, we often adopt a shorthand for functions like these; we write dy/dx as $f'(x)$. Similarly, $d^2y/dx^2 \equiv f''(x)$.

ADVANCED DIFFERENTIATION

A composite function is made up of two functions. For example, suppose y is determined by x, but x is determined by t, then we write

$$y = h(x) = h[g(t)]$$

where $x = g(t)$. Suppose the amount of corn harvested on a farm is a function of the amount on the field at harvest time, and the amount on the field at harvest time is a function of the rainfall during the growing season. We could write

$$c = g(f) \text{ and } f = h(r)$$

where c = harvested corn, f = corn in the field, and r = rain. The function g maps the amount of corn in the field into the amount of corn that will be harvested, and the function h maps the amount of rainfall into the amount of corn in the field. Or alternatively, putting these two functions together we get,

$$c = g[h(r)].$$

We could then ask the question, How does the amount harvested change with changes in rainfall? This can be written as

$$dc/dr = (dc/df)(df/dr) = g'(f) \bullet h'(r). \tag{A.7}$$

This is called the **chain rule,** probably because the derivatives are just chained together by multiplication.

A short example may help to enlighten. Let $y = \ln(x)$ and $x = t^3$. There are two ways we can find the derivative of y with respect to t, direct substitution and the chain rule.

By substitution, we can write

$$y = \ln(t^3)$$

and directly find the derivative y'. Using our knowledge of logs, we write this as

$$y = 3\ln(t).$$

Then using the formula developed in equation A.5, we find the derivative of y with respect to t as

$$y' = 3/t.$$

Alternatively we can employ the chain rule. We know that

$$dy/dx = 1/x \text{ and } dx/dt = 3t^2.$$

Therefore,

$$y' = (1/x) \bullet (3t^2),$$

but $x = t^3$. Substituting, we find that

$$y' = (1/t^3) \bullet (3t^2) = 3/t.$$

We get the same answer both ways.

Another set of functions that economists run into often are those of the form

$$y = f(x) \bullet g(x)$$

where there are two or more functions multiplied together. For example, suppose

$$y = 3x^2 \cdot \ln(x).$$

To find the derivative of this function, we employ the **product rule.** The product rule says that

y' = the first function times the derivative of the second function plus the second function times the derivative of the first function:

$$dy/dx \equiv y' = f(x) \cdot g'(x) + g(x) \cdot f'(x). \tag{A.8}$$

Again, this is a formula the dutiful student will commit to memory. In our example, then,

$$y' = 6x\ln(x) + (3x^2)/x = 6x\ln(x) + 3x.$$

A rule for fractions of functions of the class

$$y = g(x)/f(x)$$

can be derived from the product rule, and it is called the **quotient rule.** Consider the function

$$y = [\ln(x)]/x^2.$$

This is convertible to

$$y = [\ln(x)] \cdot x^{-2}$$

and then the product rule can be used, but instead we offer the following rule to be memorized:

y' = the denominator function times the derivative of the numerator function minus the numerator function times the derivative of the denominator function all divided by the denominator function squared:

$$dy/dx \equiv y' = [f(x) \cdot g'(x) - g(x) \cdot f'(x)]/[f(x)]^2. \tag{A.9}$$

In the specific example,

$$y' = [(x^2)(1/x) - (\ln x)(2x)]/(x^2)^2.$$

This can be simplified to

$$y' = (1 - 2\ln x)/x^3.$$

Some common derivatives are given in Table A2.1.[2]

---

[2] The *Standard Math Tables* (Cleveland OH: CRC Press) lists many pages of derivatives.

TABLE A2.1   SOME COMMON DERIVATIVES

FUNCTION	DERIVATIVE
$f(x)$	$f'(x)$
$y = a$	$y' = 0$
$y = ax^b$	$y' = bax^{b-1}$
$y = ae^{bx}$	$y' = abe^{bx}$
$y = a\ln(x)$	$y' = a/x$
$y = f(x) \cdot g(x)$	$y' = f'(x) \cdot g(x) + f(x) \cdot g'(x)$
$y = f(x)/g(x)$	$y' = (gf' - fg')/g^2$
$y = a^{f(x)}$	$y' = f(x) \cdot [\ln(a)] \cdot f'(x)$

APPLICATIONS OF DERIVATIVES

Elasticity

The concept of elasticity of the demand curve was presented earlier in Chapter 2. The formula for elasticity was given as $(\%\Delta q/\%\Delta p)$, or $(\Delta q/q)/(\Delta p/p)$. Taking the limit of this formula as Δp goes to zero yields

$$\lim_{\Delta p \to 0} (\Delta q/q)/(\Delta p/p) = (dq/q)(dp/p) = (dq/dp)(p/q).$$

This is simply the inverse of the slope of the demand curve times the ratio of price to quantity.

For example, examine Figure A2.3. Here the demand curve

$$q = 10 - 2p$$

is graphed.

Now we ask, What is the elasticity of the demand curve at a particular price?[3] Since the derivative of q with respect to p, dq/dp, is

$$dq/dp = -2,$$

the elasticity of the demand curve is

$$(-2)(p/q)$$

for any particular p. For instance, when price is zero, quantity is 10:

$p=0$, $q=10$, and therefore the elasticity $= (-2)(0/10) = 0$.

---

[3] We say at a particular price because, except in the special case of the constant elasticity demand curve discussed earlier in Chapter 2, elasticity varies along the demand curve.

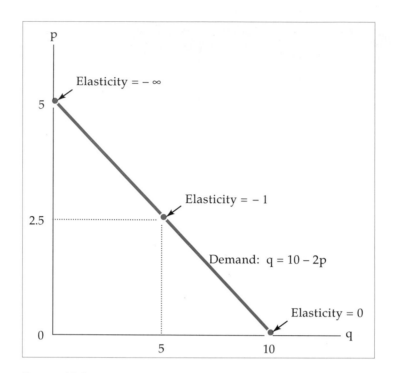

FIGURE A2.3
The Elasticity of Demand

Similarly, when

$$p=5, q=0, \text{ and the elasticity } = (-2)(5/0) \equiv -\infty.$$

And last, when

$$p=2.5, q=5, \text{ the elasticity } = (-2)(2.5/5) = -1.$$

These particular points were picked to illustrate a concept about straight line demand curves. At the quantity intercept (when $p = 0$), the elasticity is zero. At the price where quantity is zero, the elasticity is $-\infty$. Halfway along the demand curve, the elasticity is -1.[4] Along a straight line demand curve the elasticity varies from 0 when price is zero to $-\infty$ when quantity is zero.

Logarithms can be used to help interpret percentage changes and thus are useful in the understanding of elasticities. The change in the logarithm of a variable is equivalent to the change in the level of the variable divided by the level of the variable. In other words, the change in the logarithm of a variable measures

---

[4] The midpoint is calculated in three steps: (1) Find the price that makes quantity equal zero (set q equal to 0 and solve for p), (2) divide this price by 2 and call it p_m, and (3) determine the quantity demanded at p_m (evaluate the demand function at p_m).

the proportional change in the variable and the percentage change in the variable when multiplied by 100. For instance,

$$d \ln(q) = dq/q.$$

Thus, with particular reference to elasticities, which are defined as the percentage change in one variable divided by the percentage change in a second variable, the elasticity can be expressed as the ratio of the changes in the logarithms of the two variables. This yields an important result. For the own price elasticity of demand then, the elasticity is

$$[d \ln(q)]/[d \ln(p)].$$

Extremes, Maxima, and Minima

Another common application of derivatives in economics is to find an **extremum,** either a **maximum** or a **minimum** of a function. Figure A2.4 shows two functions, one with a minimum and one with a maximum. Note that at either the minimum or the maximum, the slope of the function is zero; it is flat (however briefly). To find the maximum or minimum value of a function, all one has to do is locate the point where the function has a slope of zero. To do this, take the first derivative, set it equal to zero, and solve the function. For example, consider the relation

$$y = x^2 - 2x + 4.$$

FIGURE A2.4
Extrema

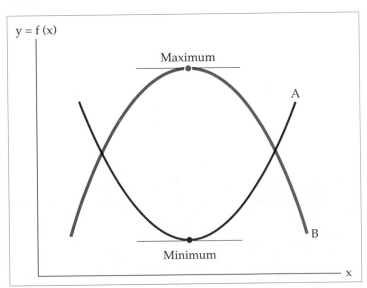

First find the derivative of y with respect to x,

$$y' = 2x - 2.$$

Now set the derivative equal to zero:

$$y' = 2x - 2 = 0.$$

This is called a **first order condition** because it is a prerequisite for the function to be at a local extreme, either a maximum or a minimum. Now solve the equation for x:

$$x = 1.$$

At $x = 1$, the slope of the original function, $y = x^2 - 2x + 4$, is zero. But is this extremum a maximum or a minimum? Examine Figure A2.4 again. For the function with a minimum, the one labeled A, the slope is negative before the minimum and positive after the minimum. The slope is rising as the function passes through the minimum. Therefore, the second derivative, the rate of change of the slope, must be *positive* for the function to have a minimum. The reverse situation is true for a maximum, function B in Figure A2.4. The slope falls as the function passes through the maximum (goes from positive to zero to negative), and as a result the second derivative must be *negative*. These two opposite rules constitute the so-called **second order conditions.** When the first order condition is satisfied, the first derivative is equal to zero, and the second derivative is negative, a local extreme exists and it is a peak or maximum. When the first order condition is met, and the second derivative is positive, the local extreme is a minimum.

Looking back at our example,

$$y'' = 2 > 0,$$

since the first derivative is zero, $y' = 0$, and $y'' > 0$ at $x = 1$; therefore, we have a minimum at $x = 1$ [and $y = 1^2 - 2 \bullet (1) + 4 = 3$]. The student is encouraged to select other values of x in the neighborhood of $x = 1$ to satisfy himself or herself that $x = 1$ does yield a local minimum of the function.

INTEGRATION

Examine Figure A2.5. Suppose you were interested in the area under the curve and above the x axis between $x = a$ and $x = b$. We could get an approximation of this area curve by dividing it into rectangles and adding up their respective areas. The area of the rectangle labeled 1 on Figure A2.5 is equal to the height, $f(a)$, times the width, which we will call Δx. Area 1 is thus calculated as

$$\text{Area}(1) = f(a) \bullet \Delta x.$$

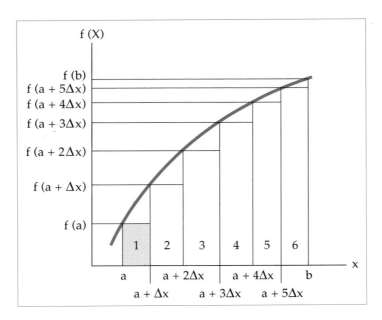

FIGURE A2.5
The Integral

Likewise, the area of rectangle 2 is

$$\text{Area}(2) = f(a + \Delta x) \cdot \Delta x.$$

An approximation of the area under the curve is just the sum of these areas, or

$$f(a) \cdot \Delta x + f(a + \Delta x) \cdot \Delta x + f(a + 2\Delta x) \cdot \Delta x + \ldots + f(a + 5\Delta x) \cdot \Delta x$$

or

$$\sum_{i=0}^{n} f(a + i\Delta x)\Delta x$$

where Σ stands for summation and $n = (b - a)/\Delta x$. The smaller is Δx, the more accurate is the approximation.

We define the area as being exactly equal to

$$Area = \lim_{\Delta x \to 0} \sum_{i=0}^{n} f(a + i\Delta x)\Delta x.$$

This area is called an **integral** and is written as

$$Area = \int_{a}^{b} f(x)dx.$$

There is an interesting relation between integrals and derivatives. Suppose the derivative of some function is known to be $2x$. The integral of $2x$ is $x^2 + C$ where C is some unknown constant; take the derivative of $x^2 + C$. It is $2x$. Integrals and derivatives are inexorably linked in this way.

For simplicity, denote

$$\int f(x) \cdot dx \text{ as } F(x);$$

then

$$F(x) \equiv \int f(x) \cdot dx.$$

To evaluate $F(x)$ between two points, say a and b—that is, to find the area under the function $f(x)$ between the points a and b, you simply calculate

$$F(b) - F(a).$$

That is, you compute the value of the integral at point b and you subtract the value of the integral at point a.

Consider an example. Let $f(x) = 2x$, as graphed on Figure A2.6. The area under the line from $x = 1$ to $x = 2$ is

$$Area = \int_{1}^{2} 2x \, dx.$$

We know that $F(x) = x^2 + C$; therefore, the area is

$$Area = F(2) - F(1) = (2^2 + C) - (1^2 + C)$$

$$= 4 - 1 = 3.$$

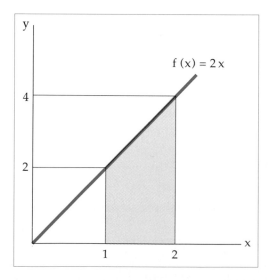

FIGURE A2.6
Computing Definite Integrals

Consequently, the area under the function $y = 2x$ from 1 to 2 is 3. Table A2.2 gives some general rules for integration.

MULTIVARIATE CALCULUS

So far we have dealt with functions of one variable; y is a **univariate function** of x. Many problems encountered in economics are **multivariate;** one variable depends on many other factors. Utility depends on the levels of all goods consumed. Quantity demanded depends on price, income, prices of other goods, and so forth. Hence it is necessary to examine functions of the form

$$y = f(x,z).$$

Of course the two-variable case usually generalizes to any finite number. For simplicity here, we will only deal with the simplest multivariate case.

The first concept is the derivative, or slope, of the function. Examine Figure A2.7. Here we have a three-dimensional graph with y on the vertical axis and x and z on the other two axes. Given a point x_0 and z_0, the function defines y_0:

$$y_0 = f(x_0,z_0).$$

Now consider the slope of the function at (x_0,z_0). The slope of the function depends on the direction we move: (1) We could increase x and hold z constant or (2) increase z holding the level of x constant. The concept of the *partial derivative* addresses this problem.

Partial Derivatives

A **partial derivative** is the slope of a function in a particular direction. In general, the partial derivative (represented by the symbol ∂) of the function f with respect to x is denoted by the expression $\partial y/\partial x \equiv f_x$, and the partial derivative with respect

TABLE A2.2   COMMON INTEGRALS

FUNCTION	INTEGRAL
$\int a\,dx$	ax
$\int af(x)dx$	$a \int f(x)dx$
$\int [f(x) + g(x)]dx$	$\int f(x)dx + \int g(x)dx$
$\int f(x)g'(x)dx$	$f(x)g(x) - \int g(x)f'(x)$
$\int x^n dx$	$x^{n+1}/(n + 1)$ unless $n = -1$
$\int e^x dx$	e^x
$\int e^{ax}dx$	e^{ax}/a
$\int 1/x\,dx$	$\ln(x)$
$\int \ln(x)\,dx$	$x\bullet\ln(x) - x$
$\int a^x\bullet\ln(a)\,dx$	a^x $(a>0)$

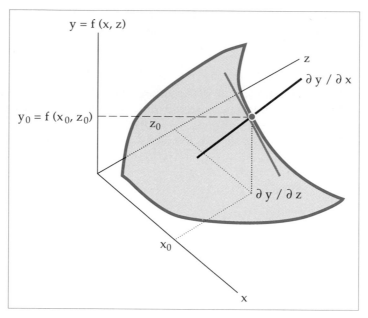

FIGURE A2.7
Multivariate Functions

to z is $\partial y/\partial z \equiv f_z$. Respectively, the partial derivatives are the change in y for a small change in x, holding z constant, and the change in y for a small change in z, not letting x change.

Consider the particular function

$$y = x^a z^b$$

where a and b are constants. The partial derivative of y with respect to x is

$$\partial y/\partial x = ax^{a-1}z^b.$$

What we did was apply the rules of differentiation developed earlier to the function, while forcing z to be a constant, just what the definition mandates. Thus the partial derivative is just the slope of a function in a particular direction. Similarly,

$$\partial y/\partial z = bx^a z^{b-1}$$

tells us the slope of the function when we change z holding x constant.

The rule for computing second partial derivatives is analogous to the one-variable case; just take the derivative of the partial derivative:

$$\partial^2 y/\partial x^2 = a(a-1)x^{a-2}z^b$$

and

$$\partial^2 y / \partial z^2 = b(b-1)x^a z^{b-2}.$$

Note once again that the variable being held constant, z in the first case and x in the second, is treated just like any other constant. There is one other complication here that does not appear in the one-variable case, that of the **cross derivative.** The partial derivative examines the change in y for a small change in one of the functional variables. The cross derivative explores the change in a partial derivative given a small change in some other functional variable. In essence, when we take the second derivative, we take it with respect to the other functional variable. For example, taking the partial derivative of $y = x^a z^b$ with respect to x yields

$$\partial y / \partial x = ax^{a-1}z^b.$$

Now take the derivative of $\partial y / \partial x$ with respect to z. This is written

$$\partial^2 y / \partial x \partial z = bax^{a-1}z^{b-1}. \tag{A.10}$$

Similarly,

$$\partial^2 y / \partial z \partial x = abx^{a-1}z^{b-1}. \tag{A.11}$$

The cross partial derivatives in equations A.10 and A.11 describe the rate of change in the slope of y in a three-dimensional sense. These two cross derivatives are equal. This is true of all twice differentiable functions and is called Young's Theorem. Formally, **Young's Theorem** states that the cross derivatives of a function are invariant of the order of differentiation. In English, this means that it does not matter if we differentiate with respect to x and then z or first z and then x, the result is the same.

For ease of exposition, we will adopt a shorthand for partial derivatives. For the general case of

$$y = f(x,z),$$

we will let $\partial y / \partial x \equiv f_x$ and $\partial y / \partial z \equiv f_z$. Similarly, the second derivatives will be f_{xx}, f_{zz}, f_{xz}, and by Young's Theorem, $f_{zx} = f_{xz}$.

LEVEL CURVES

One of the interesting aspects of multivariate functions for economics is **level curves.** Take for example the function

$$y = f(x,z).$$

Suppose we were interested in the various combinations of x and z that map into a particular value of y, say y_0. Define

$$y_0 = f(x,z)$$

to be a level curve. Figure A2.8 gives one such level curve, plotted in the (x,z) plane. All combinations of x and z on the line map into, or yield the value, y_0 when plugged into the function $y = f(x,z)$. Since y is constant along a level curve at y_0, the function depicting a level curve has only two variables, not three. Indifference curves are examples of level curves. Indifference curves describe various combinations of goods that yield a constant amount of utility for a consumer.

Let f_x and f_z be the first partial derivatives of y. The slope of a level curve is dz/dx, as shown on Figure A2.8. Since y does not change along a level curve, when x changes z must change. Therefore, z is a function of x *along any particular level curve:*

$$z = z(x).$$

Hence, we can rewrite the level curve as

$$y_0 = f[x,z(x)]$$

FIGURE A2.8
Level Curves

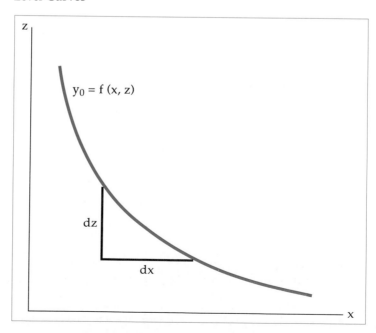

$y_0 = f(x, z)$

dz

dx

substituting the function $z(x)$ for z. Taking the derivative of both sides of the level curve with respect to x, we get

$$0 = f_x(dx/dx) + f_z(dz/dx) \qquad (A.12)$$

using the chain rule.[5] The slope of the level curve is the change in x for a small change in z, dz/dx. Solving equation A.12 for the slope, we get

$$dz/dx = -f_x/f_z$$

as long as f_z is not equal to 0 (note: $dx/dx = 1$).

Many problems in economics require level curves to have a specific shape, namely convex to, or bent inward toward, the origin. This means that the slope of the curve must get closer to zero as x increases; the level curve must get flatter as we move out the x axis. Because the slope of this curve is negative, recall $dz/dx = -f_x/f_z$, and when describing a utility function both f_x and f_y are positive, then the slope must increase (get closer to zero) as x increases. This translates into

$$d^2z/dx^2 > 0.$$

Remembering that

$$dz/dx = -f_x[x,z(x)]/f_z[x,z(x)], \qquad (A.13)$$

the second derivative, the rate of change of the slope, is found by differentiating again with respect to x. Applying the chain rule and the quotient rule to equation A.13, we find

$$d^2z/dx^2 = -[f_z f_{xx}(dx/dx) + f_z f_{xz}(dz/dx) - f_x f_{zx}(dx/dx) - f_x f_{zz}(dz/dx)](1/f_z^2)$$
$$= -[f_z(f_{xx} + f_{xz}(dx/dz)] - f_x[f_{zx} + f_{zz}(dz/dx)](1/f_z^2).$$

Remembering that $dz/dx = -f_x/f_z$ and $f_{xz} = f_{zx}$, then

$$d^2z/dx^2 = -[f_z(f_{xx} + f_{xz}(-f_x/f_z)] - f_x[f_{zx} + f_{zz}(-f_x/f_z)](1/f_z^2)$$
$$= -[f_z f_{xx} - 2f_x f_{xz} + (f_x^2 f_{zz}/f_z)](1/f_z^2)$$
$$= (-f_z^2 f_{xx} + 2f_x f_{xz} - f_x^2 f_{zz})(1/f_z^3). \qquad (A.14)$$

The second derivative, equation A.14, is greater than zero only if

$$f_z^2 f_{xx} - 2f_x f_{xz} + f_x^2 f_{zz} < 0.$$

As abstract as this may seem, it does come up quite a bit in the utility maximization and profit maximization problems encountered in economics.

---

[5] $\partial y_0/\partial x = 0$ because y is not allowed to change along the level curve.

HOMOGENEOUS AND HOMOTHETIC FUNCTIONS AND EULER'S THEOREM

There is a special set of functional forms with properties that simplify economic analysis immensely—the homothetic function. A **homothetic function** is an *increasing monotonic transformation of a homogeneous function.* A function is **homogeneous** if

$$f(t \bullet x, t \bullet z) = t^r f(x,z).$$

In words, a function is **homogenous of degree r** if multiplying all of variables in the function by an arbitrary constant t is equivalent to multiplying the function by t^r. Functions homogeneous of degree one and zero are the most commonly used in economics.

Consider the function

$$y = x^a z^{1-a}.$$

Multiply both x and z by a constant t, resulting in

$$y(t \bullet x, t \bullet z) = (t \bullet x)^a (t \bullet z)^{1-a}$$
$$= t^a x^a t^{1-a} z^{1-a}$$
$$= t \bullet (a + 1 - a) x^a z^{1-a}$$
$$= t \bullet y.$$

Since y times t raised to the first power is $t \bullet y$, this function is homogeneous of degree one.

Demand curves are homogeneous of degree zero. Absolute prices do not affect the choice of quantity consumed; only relative prices matter. If all prices and the individual's income are doubled, there is no change in demand. This is exactly the same as saying that the demand curve is homogeneous of degree zero.

A function is homogeneous of degree zero if multiplication of the variables by a constant t results in no change in the function. For example, a demand curve may have the form

$$q_x = (a \bullet p_y I)/(b \bullet p_x^2)$$

where q_x is the quantity demanded of x,
p_x is the price of x,
p_y is the price of some other good y, and
I is income.

Multiplying p_x, p_y and I by a constant t,

$$q_x(t \bullet p_x, t \bullet p_y, t \bullet I) = (a \bullet t \bullet p_y t \bullet I)/[b \bullet (t \bullet p_x)^2]$$
$$= t^2 (a \bullet p_y I)/(t^2 p_x^2)$$
$$= a \bullet p_y I / p_x^2.$$

Even though each variable was multiplied by a number, t, there was no change in q_x; therefore, the demand curve is homogeneous of degree zero.

If a function is homogeneous of degree r, then the first partial derivatives are homogeneous of degree $r-1$. This leads us to one of the most convenient uses of homogeneous functions. Take a function

$$y = f(x,z),$$

and let it be homogeneous of degree r. Remember that the level curves are defined as

$$y_0 = f(x,z),$$

and the slope of the level curves is $-f_x/f_z$. Multiply both x and z by some arbitrary constant, t:

$$dz/dx = -f_x(tx,tz)/f_z(tx,tz) = -t^{r-1}f_x/t^{r-1}f_z = -f_x/f_z.$$

Therefore, for homogeneous functions, the slopes of the level curves are constant along a ray from the origin. This is shown in Figure A2.9. Along the ray labeled A,

FIGURE A2.9
Homogeneous Functions

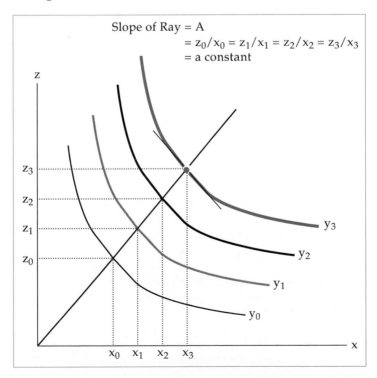

the ratio of x to z is constant. When both x and z are multiplied by a constant, the ratio of x to z is unchanged—the point just moves along this ray. Along this ray the slopes of the level curves are constant.

One other important implication of homogeneous functions is **Euler's Theorem.**[6] Let $f(x,z)$ be homogeneous of degree r. We know that

$$f(tx,tz) = t^r f(x,z).$$

If we differentiate with respect to t, we get,

$$[\partial f/(\partial tx)] \bullet (dtx/dt) + [\partial f/(\partial tz)] \bullet [d(t \bullet z)/dt] = r \bullet t^{r-1} f(x,z),$$

but $d(tx)/dt = x$ and $d(tz)/dt = z$. Therefore,

$$[\partial f/\partial(t \bullet x)] \bullet x + [\partial f/(\partial t \bullet z)] \bullet z = r \bullet t^{r-1} f(x,z).$$

Since t can be any arbitrary constant, let it be 1. Then

$$f_x x + f_z z = r f(x,z).$$

This is Euler's Theorem. If a function is homogeneous of degree r, the sum of the first partial derivatives multiplied by the respective variable of differentiation equals the degree of homogeneity of the function multiplied by the function itself.

We started this section off by saying that homogeneous functions are a subset of a broader class of functions, homothetic functions. An increasing monotonic transformation alters the original function by applying another function that is always rising. For example, $y = f(x)$ is a function. Let $g(u)$ be some other function that has a positive slope for all values of u, $g_u > 0$. Then $t = g[f(x)]$ is an increasing monotonic transformation of the original function $f(x)$. For example, let

$$y = 1 + x \text{ for } x > 0,$$

and let $g(u)$ be the squared function. Then $t = (1 + x)^2$ is an increasing monotonic transformation of $y = 1 + x$. Note the transformation is increasing because the first derivative, $g' = 2u$, is positive for all values of $u > 0$.

All homogeneous functions are homothetic, but not all homothetic functions are homogeneous. Consider the function used before,

$$y = x^a z^{1-a}, \tag{A.15}$$

which we have shown to be homogeneous of degree one. The natural log function is an increasing monotonic function in the positive domain of x because its first

---

[6] *Euler* is pronounced as though it were spelled *oiler.*

derivative, $1/x$, is greater than zero when x is positive. Apply the log transformation to both sides of the original function in equation A.15:

$$\ln(y) = a \bullet \ln(x) + (1-a)\ln(z)$$

is the resulting transformation. This function has level curves with equal slopes along a ray from the origin, but it is not homogeneous. Homothetic functions are often used in utility maximization because the shape of the level curve is important, but the spacing of the level curves is not.

APPLICATIONS OF MULTIVARIATE CALCULUS

Unconstrained Maxima and Minima

Just as single-variable functions may have extreme values, either maximums or minimums, it is possible to locate extremes of multivariate functions. Examine Figure A2.10. There the function $y = f(x,z)$ is drawn. The function has a maximum at (y_0, x_0, z_0). At the maximum, both the slope in the x direction holding z constant and the slope in the z direction holding x constant are zero. This condition defines the first order conditions

$$f_x = 0 \text{ and } f_z = 0$$

for an extreme.

FIGURE A2.10
Extrema of Multivariate Functions

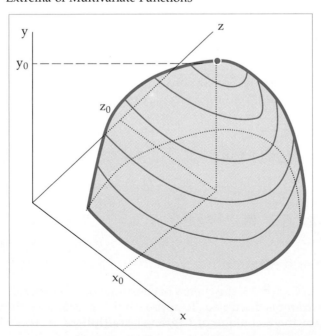

The second order conditions sufficient to ensure that the extreme is a maximum and not a minimum are not so intuitively obvious. Suffice it to say at this point that for the function to have a maximum, it is sufficient for

$$f_{xx} < 0, f_{zz} < 0, \text{ and } f_{xx}f_{zz} - (f_{xx})^2 > 0.$$

Likewise for a minimum,

$$f_{xx} > 0, f_{zz} > 0, \text{ and } f_{xx}f_{zz} - (f_{xx})^2 > 0.$$

Let us work through an example. Suppose a firm wishes to maximize the profit from producing some good, y, manufactured using inputs x and z; $y = f(x,z)$ is called the **production function.** The firm buys inputs x and z at prices w_x and w_z, respectively. The output, y, is sold at price p. What is the maximum profit available to the firm, where profit, π, is revenue (production times price) minus costs, or

$$\pi = p \bullet f(x,z) - w_x x - w_z z?$$

The first term is just price times quantity, or revenues, and the last two terms are the costs of the inputs. The first order conditions necessary to ensure maximum profits are found by taking the first partial derivative of the profit function with respect to first x and then z, setting each equation equal to zero, and solving. The results are

$$\pi_x = p \bullet f_x - w_x = 0 \tag{A.16}$$

and

$$\pi_z = p \bullet f_z - w_z = 0. \tag{A.17}$$

The second order conditions sufficient to guarantee that the extreme found in equations A.16 and A.17 is a maximum and not a minimum are

$$\pi_{xx} = p \bullet f_{xx} < 0, \tag{A.18}$$
$$\pi_{zz} = p \bullet f_{zz} < 0, \tag{A.19}$$

and

$$\pi_{xx}\pi_{zz} - (\pi_{xz})^2 = p^2[f_{xx}f_{zz} - (f_{xz})^2] > 0. \tag{A.20}$$

Constrained Maximum and Minimum

In Chapter 3, the theory of consumer utility maximization subject to a budget constraint is discussed. To approach this problem mathematically, it is necessary to use the technique of **Lagrange multipliers.** In this method, you the analyst introduce an extraneous variable called a Lagrange multiplier and form a new function called a **Lagrangian** from the old objective function, the utility function.

In general, suppose the original objective function to be maximized is

$$y = f(x,z),$$

but there is a constraint of the form

$$g(x,z) = 0.$$

The general principle of the Lagrange technique is to incorporate the constraint into the objective function. Actually this is quite simple. Since the value of the constraint is zero by definition, adding it to the objective function does not change the objective. But before we add the constraint, we multiply it by a constant of our choice, called the Lagrange multiplier. Then we simply take the normal derivatives of the modified objective function, now called the Lagrangian, and set them equal to zero to find the conditions necessary for a maximum. In addition, we must determine the value of our constant, the Lagrange multiplier, and so we also take the derivative of the Lagrange function with respect to the multiplier and set it equal to zero. This adds one equation and one unknown to the system of first order conditions. In sum, since $g(x,z) = 0$, the value of the Lagrangian function, $\mathcal{L}$, is the same as the value of the original function y, regardless of the value of λ, the Lagrange multiplier. Therefore, maximizing

$$\mathcal{L} = f(x,z) + \lambda g(x,z) \tag{A.21}$$

is deductively equivalent to maximizing $y = f(x,z)$. In effect, creating the Lagrange function incorporates the constraint into the objective function. The first order conditions necessary to maximize the Lagrangian, equation A.21, are found by taking the first partial derivatives of $\mathcal{L}$ with respect to x and z and setting them both to zero. This yields:

$$\mathcal{L}_x = 0 = f_x + \lambda g_x, \tag{A.22}$$

$$\mathcal{L}_z = 0 = f_z + \lambda g_z, \tag{A.23}$$

plus we must also differentiate with respect to the Lagrange multiplier, λ,

$$\mathcal{L}_\lambda = 0 = g(x,z). \tag{A.24}$$

These three first order conditions, equations A.22–A.24, can, in general, be solved for the values of x, z, and λ that maximize $f(x,z)$ subject to the constraint $g(x,z) = 0$.

The proof of the second order conditions sufficient to ensure a maximum is beyond the scope of this appendix, but one important result for our use is the condition that

$$\mathcal{L}_{xx}(\lambda_z)^2 - 2\mathcal{L}_{xz}\lambda_x\lambda_z + \mathcal{L}_{zz}(\lambda_x)^2 < 0.$$

This corresponds closely to the condition that the level curves of $f(x,z)$ be convex to the origin. In the case of a linear constraint, $g_x = 0$ and $g_z = 0$, this is exactly the condition that the level curves be convex.

To put this technique to work, we examine the utility maximization problem that is put forth in Chapter 3. There is a consumer with a utility function, U, over two goods, x and z. Thus, the objective function to be maximized is

$U(x,z)$,

but the consumer only has \$$M$ to spend on the two goods. Therefore, there is a budget constraint of the form:

$$p_x x + p_z z = M$$

where p_x is the price of x,
p_z is the price of z, and
M is money income.

The Lagrangian is formed by adding the constraint (zero) multiplied times some constant to be determined, λ, to the objective function U. This yields the Lagrangian function:

$$\mathcal{L} = U(x,z) + \lambda(M - p_x x - p_z z).$$

The first order conditions necessary to maximize this modified objective function are

$$\mathcal{L}_x = U_x - \lambda p_x = 0,$$
$$\mathcal{L}_z = U_z - \lambda p_z = 0, \text{ and}$$
$$\mathcal{L}_\lambda = M - p_x x - p_z z = 0.$$

The first two of these conditions can be combined to yield the now familiar tangency conditions

$$U_x/U_z = p_x/p_z.$$

The ratio of the marginal utilities (the marginal rate of substitution) must equal the ratio of the prices. The third of the first order conditions just forces the consumer to be on the budget constraint.

MATRIX ALGEBRA

A **matrix** is a mathematician's device for simplifying large quantities of information, a form of shorthand. As such, it is useful to learn the techniques of matrix manipulation. Consider the following example: Suppose there are two possible amounts of rainfall a farmer might have during the growing season, lots and little.

Likewise, there are two types of temperatures, hot and cold. If it rains and it is cold, the farmer harvests 30 bushels, but if it rains and it is hot, the output is 50 bushels. When it is dry and cold, the yield is 40 bushels, and last, when dry and hot, only 20 bushels are produced. This information can be summarized in a matrix and presented in a much shorter format. Let the matrix be called **A,** then

$$
\begin{array}{c}
& & & \textit{TEMPERATURE} \\
& & & \text{HOT} \quad\quad \text{COLD} \\
R & \text{LOTS} & 50 \quad\quad 30 \\
A & & \\
\mathbf{A} = \quad I & & \\
N & \text{LITTLE} & 20 \quad\quad\quad 40
\end{array}
$$

The temperature is in **columns,** the rain in **rows.** Each entry in a matrix is called an **element.** In general, if a matrix is named **A,** we denote the elements of the matrix as a_{ij} where i is the row and j is the column locating the element. In this example, $a_{11} = 50$, $a_{12} = 30$, $a_{21} = 20$, and $a_{22} = 40$.

Addition

The **rank of a matrix** is a measure of its size. It is denoted as $m \times n$, where m is the number of rows and n is the number of columns. If matrices have the same size, they can be added together. For example, to add two matrices **A** and **B,**

$$
\mathbf{A} + \mathbf{B} = \begin{bmatrix} a_{11} + b_{11} & a_{12} + b_{12} \\ a_{21} + b_{21} & a_{22} + b_{22} \end{bmatrix}
$$

simply add the elements from the two matrices.

Determinants

The **order of a matrix** is determined by the number of rows and columns. A matrix has an order equal to the lesser of the number of rows or columns. The **determinant of a matrix** is a single number dependent on the elements in the matrix. It is written as det(**A**). Determinants are only defined for matrices of **full order.** A matrix is full order if it has just as many rows as it does columns—that is, if it is square. If a matrix, **A,** has one element, a, then the determinant of the matrix is that element,

det(**A**) = a.

The determinant of a matrix of order two is calculated as

$$
\det(\mathbf{A}) = \det \begin{bmatrix} a_{11} & a_{12} \\ a_{22} & a_{22} \end{bmatrix} = a_{11}a_{22} - a_{21}a_{12}.
$$

To compute the determinant of matrices of higher order, say n, we expand the matrix along *a row or a column*, calculating

$$\det(A) = \sum_{j=1}^{n} a_{ij}\mathbf{A}_{ij}$$

where

$$\mathbf{A}_{ij} = (-1)^{i+j} \bullet \det(m_{ij})$$

and m_{ij} is the **minor** of a_{ij}, and where i is *one of the rows or columns*. **A** minor is the matrix that is left over when the original matrix has row i and column j crossed out. For example, define the matrix **A** as

$$\mathbf{A} = \begin{bmatrix} a_{11} & a_{12} & a_{13} \\ a_{21} & a_{22} & a_{23} \\ a_{31} & a_{32} & a_{33} \end{bmatrix}.$$

The minor of element (1,1), m_{11}, is the 2×2 matrix found by deleting the first row and first column of matrix **A**,

$$m_{11} = \begin{bmatrix} a_{22} & a_{23} \\ a_{32} & a_{33} \end{bmatrix}.$$

Thus, the determinant of a 3×3 matrix has 3 terms. Consider the determinant of the matrix, **B**, where

$$\mathbf{B} = \begin{bmatrix} 1 & 2 & 3 \\ 2 & 2 & 2 \\ 0 & 2 & 1 \end{bmatrix}.$$

Expanding the determinant down the first column:

The first term is $(-1)^{(1+1)} \bullet (2 \bullet 1 - 2 \bullet 2) = +1 \bullet (-2) = -2$.

The second term is $(-1)^{(2+1)} \bullet (2 \bullet 1 - 2 \bullet 3) = (-1) \bullet (-4) = +4$.

The third term is $(0)^{(3+1)} \bullet (2 \bullet 2 - 2 \bullet 3) = 0 \bullet (-2) = 0$.

Therefore, the determinant, the sum of the three terms, is $-2 + 4 + 0 = 2$.

The calculation of the third term points out the economy of expanding the determinant along a row or column with zeros for elements.

Multiplication and Cramer's Rule

Matrices can be multiplied. First, the order of multiplication is important. The product of two matrices, **A** and **B, A•B,** will not, in general, equal the product **B•A.** Second, the matrices for multiplication must **conform;** the number of *columns* in the first matrix (sometimes called the premultiplying matrix) must equal the number of *rows* in the second (postmultiplying matrix). Let matrix **C** be the product **A•B**. Then

$$\mathbf{AB} = \begin{bmatrix} a_{11}b_{11} + a_{12}b_{21} & a_{11}b_{12} + a_{12}b_{22} \\ a_{21}b_{11} + a_{22}b_{21} & a_{21}b_{12} + a_{22}b_{22} \end{bmatrix} = \mathbf{C}.$$

To compute element $\mathbf{C}_{ij}$, add together the product of respective ith row elements in **A** times the respective jth column elements in **B**. That is,

$$\mathbf{C}_{ij} = \sum_{k=1}^{n} a_{ij} \times b_{kj}$$

where n is the number of columns in the **A** matrix or the number of rows in the **B** matrix.

Matrix multiplication has a very practical purpose for the economist. As shown in the last section, in the utility maximization model, a system of equations must be solved for the amounts demanded. These theoretical demand equations take the form

$$a_{11}x + a_{12}z = b_1 \tag{A.25}$$

$$a_{21}x + a_{22}z = b_2 \tag{A.26}$$

for two goods x and z. We can solve this system of equations for x and z using substitution combined with multiplication and subtraction, or we can write them out in matrix form and use **Cramer's Rule.** In matrix form, equations A.25 and A.26 are written

$$\begin{bmatrix} a_{11} & a_{12} \\ a_{21} & a_{22} \end{bmatrix} \cdot \begin{bmatrix} x \\ z \end{bmatrix} = \begin{bmatrix} b_1 \\ b_2 \end{bmatrix}.$$

Note that the number of columns in the **matrix of coefficients, A,** 2, equals the number of rows in the x matrix, 2.

Cramer's Rule can be used to solve for the two unknowns in the system of equations, x and z. Each solution is the ratio of two determinants. For x, replace the first column of the matrix of coefficients, the **A** matrix, with the **solution vector,** the matrix on the right-hand side of the equals, and take its determinant. Then divide this determinant by the determinant of the matrix of coefficients:

$$x = \frac{\det \begin{bmatrix} b_1 & a_{12} \\ b_2 & a_{22} \end{bmatrix}}{\det \begin{bmatrix} a_{11} & a_{12} \\ a_{21} & a_{22} \end{bmatrix}} = (a_{22}b_1 - a_{12}b_2)/(a_{11}a_{22} - a_{21}a_{12}).$$

Likewise for z: You place the solution vector in the *second* column and the matrix of coefficients, **A,** take the determinant, and divide by the determinant of **A.**

THE ENVELOPE THEOREM

How do choice variables change when a parameter changes? For instance, how does the consumer's choice over goods respond to a change in income? It turns out that there is an easy way to deal with this theoretical problem—the use of the envelope theorem. The **envelope theorem** allows us to easily derive comparative statics results from the objective function.

The Unconstrained Case

Consider the problem of profit maximization for a firm—a case in which the objective function, maximize profit, is unconstrained. Profit is revenue minus costs, or

$$\Pi = p \bullet f(x_1, x_2) - w_1 \bullet x_1$$

where $f(x_1, x_2)$ is the production function relating the levels of inputs x_1 and x_2 to output, and w_1 and w_2 are their respective prices. We know that the first order conditions necessary to maximize profit are

$$\frac{\partial \Pi}{\partial x_i} = p \bullet \frac{\partial f}{\partial x_i} - w_i = 0 \text{ (for } i = 1,2),$$

or value of the marginal product of each input must equal its wage rate. These two equations can be solved to yield the values of x_1 and x_2 that maximize profit:

$$x_i = x_i^*(w_1, w_2) \qquad (i = 1,2).$$

These are the input demand functions, and they relate the prices of the two inputs into the quantity demanded of the two inputs. Given the current set of prices, w_1 and w_2, the profit maximizing firm hires x_1^* of the first input and x_2^* of the second. If we insert these two values back into the profit function, we can determine the level for this firm. This procedure, of inserting the solution back into the objective function, creates an *indirect objective function*, which in this case is the indirect profit function:

$$\Pi^* = p \bullet f[x_1^*(w_1, w_2), x_2^*(w_1, w_2)] - w_1 \bullet x_1^*(w_1, w_2) - w_2 \bullet x_2^*(w_1, w_2). \qquad \text{(A.27)}$$

This indirect profit function, equation A.27, can be used to answer the question, How do profits change when one of the parameters, either w_1 or w_2, changes? Let us ask how profits change when the price of the first input, w_1, changes. The envelope theorem says that all we have to do is to take the derivative of the indirect profit function with respect to w_1 and evaluate it to find the answer. In this case,

$$\frac{\partial \Pi^*}{\partial w_1} = p \bullet \frac{\partial f}{\partial x_1^*} \bullet \frac{\partial x_1^*}{\partial w_1} + p \bullet \frac{\partial f}{\partial x_2^*} \bullet \frac{\partial x_2^*}{\partial w_1} - w_1 \bullet \frac{\partial x_1^*}{\partial w_1} - w_2 \bullet \frac{\partial x_2^*}{\partial w_1} - x_1^*.$$

By the rearrangement of terms

$$\frac{\partial \Pi^*}{\partial w_1} = (p \bullet \frac{\partial f}{\partial x_1^*} - w_1) \bullet \frac{\partial x_1^*}{\partial w_1} + (p \bullet \frac{\partial f}{\partial x_2^*} - w_2) \bullet \frac{\partial x_2^*}{\partial w_1} - x_1^*.$$

By the first order conditions of this problem, the first two terms disappear because they are equal to zero. This leaves us with

$$\frac{\partial \Pi^*}{\partial w_1} = - x_1^*.$$

This equation says that profit falls by the amount of the first input used when its price increases, and profit rises by a like amount when the price of the first input falls. The same result holds true for the second input, x_2, so that the first derivative of the objective function evaluated at the optimum levels of input usage with respect to the change in a price of that input is just the input demand functions. This leads us to a set of so-called **reciprocity conditions:**

$$\overset{*}{\Pi}_{wjwi} = \frac{- \partial x_i^*}{\partial w_1} = \frac{- \partial x_i^*}{\partial w_j} = \overset{*}{\Pi}_{wiwj}.$$

These reciprocity conditions say that the cross price effects for the firm's input demand functions are symmetric, or that change in demand for the ith input when the jth input price changes is the same as the change in demand for the jth input when the ith input changes.

The envelope theorem is a powerful tool in the development of economic theory. Its use allows the theoretical economist to bypass many tedious mathematical steps, because it turns out that the comparative static of a particular problem has the same sign as the derivative of the original objective function. The fact that this is only true at the solution values of the maximization (or minimization) problem must be kept at the forefront. The student must remember that by use of the envelope theorem, the assumption of optimization is "built-in" to the problem.

The Constrained Case

The previous discussion maps directly to the constrained case. Remember that with the constrained case, such as the maximization of utility by the consumer, the mathematical device to be employed is the method of Lagrange multipliers. For example, suppose the individual wished to maximize utility subject to a budget constraint. Then the problem is

Maximize $U(x_1, x_2)$ subject to $p_1 \bullet x_1 + p_2 \bullet x_2 = I.$

The Lagrangian then becomes

$$\mathcal{L} = U(x_1, x_2) + \lambda \bullet (p_1 \bullet x_1 + p_2 \bullet x_2 - I).$$

Again by taking the first order conditions of the model (with respect to x_1, x_2, and λ), solving the set of simultaneous equations, and substituting back into the Lagrangian, the decomposition of demand into the income and substitution terms can be derived.

SUMMARY

This appendix started with the simple algebra of slopes of functions and progressed rapidly to more complex notions of multivariate functions. The material in this appendix is a review to some, partially a review and partially new to others, and brand new to many. The only way to learn to use mathematical skills is by practice. It is suggested that those students who encountered new material in this appendix should attempt to use their new knowledge in the problems at the end. But always keep in mind that in economics, mathematics is a tool, not an end unto itself. Use math when it serves you, and discard it otherwise.

TOPICS TO REVIEW

These are topics that you should feel comfortable with before you leave this appendix. If you cannot write out a clear and concise sentence or paragraph explaining the topic after you have worked on the study problems, you should reread the relevant section of the text.

Function

Logarithm

Base of the Logarithm

Natural Logarithm

Slope of a Function

Limits

Derivatives

Integrals

Definite Integrals

Partial Derivative

Chain Rule

Product Rule

Quotient Rule

Extremum

Maximum

Minimum

First Order Conditions
Second Order Conditions
Multivariate Function
Cross Derivative
Young's Theorem
Level Curve
Homothetic Function
Homogeneous of Degree r
Euler's Theorem
Lagrange Multipliers
Lagrange Function
Matrix Addition
Matrix Multiplication
Order of a Matrix
Determinant of a Matrix
Expanding a Matrix
Minor of a Matrix
Cramer's Rule
Matrix of Coefficients
Solution Vector
Envelope Theorem
Indirect Objective Function
Reciprocity Conditions

STUDY PROBLEMS

1. Find the derivatives:

    a. $y = 4\ln(x)$
    b. $y = \ln(xe^x)$
    c. $y = x^2 - 4x$
    d. $y = x^3\ln(xe^{3x})$

2. Find the elasticity of the demand curve

    $$q = p^{-2}$$

    at $q = 3$, $q = 5$, and $q = 7$.

3. Find the extremes of the following functions and determine if they are maximums or minimums:

    a. $y = 3x^2 - 4x - 4$
    b. $y = -6x^2 + 5x + 6$
    c. $y = 3x^3 + 5x^2 + 6x + 7$

4. Suppose a firm produces output according to the production function $y = x^{0.5}z$. The firm is a price taker in both the input and the output markets; the prices of x and z are p_x and p_z respectively. Find the profit maximizing levels of the input x and z, and the profit maximizing levels of the output. Prove that the demand curves for x and z as a function of the wages and prices are homogeneous of degree zero.

5. Given the utility function $U = x^a z^b$, find the consumer's demand curves assuming that prices and money income are given. Under what conditions is the utility function homothetic? What are the price elasticities of demand for the demand functions? What is the income elasticity of demand if the utility function is homothetic?

6. Suppose that

$$\mathbf{A} = \begin{bmatrix} 2 & -6 \\ -4 & 5 \end{bmatrix} \text{ and } \mathbf{B} = \begin{bmatrix} 4 & -4 \\ 3 & 8 \end{bmatrix}$$

   a. Find $\mathbf{A} + \mathbf{B}$
   b. Find $\mathbf{B} + \mathbf{A}$
   c. Does $\mathbf{A} + \mathbf{B} = \mathbf{B} + \mathbf{A}$? Explain.
   d. Find $\mathbf{AB}$.
   e. Find $\mathbf{BA}$.
   f. Does $\mathbf{AB} = \mathbf{BA}$? Explain.

7. Solve the following system of equations for x, y, and z using Cramer's Rule.

   $2x + 4y + 7z = 12$

   $3x - 6y - 4z = 10$

   $4x + 4y + 10z = 4$

8. a. Integrate the function x^2 and find the value of the integral from $x = 1$ to $x = 6$.
   b. Integrate the function $\ln(x)$ and find the value of the integral from $x = 3$ to $x = 5$.
   c. Integrate the function $x^2 - 2x + 4$ and compute the value of the integral from $x = 3$ to $x = 9$.
   d. Integrate the function $x^3 + 4x$ and compute the value from $x = 6$ to $x = 12$.

9. Finding the present value of a project involves evaluating the function

$$\int_0^T f(t)e^{-rt}dt$$

where T is the terminal date of the project and r is the interest rate. Suppose a project generates a net revenue equal to

$R(t) = t^2 - 2t.$

If the project lasts 10 years and the annual rate of interest is 10 percent, what is the present value of the project?

SUGGESTED READINGS

A number of decent personal computer programs exist to help students learn algebra and calculus. These include several programs from True BaSIC Software in West Lebanon, NH: *Algebra, Pre-Calculus, Calculus,* and *Discrete Math, Probability, and Statistics.* In addition, there are a number of well-written texts in mathematical economics. Two that have stood the test of time are

Chiang, Alpha C. *Fundamental Methods of Mathematical Economics,* 3rd ed. New York: McGraw-Hill, 1984.

Silberberg, Eugene. *The Structure of Economics: A Mathematical Analysis,* 2nd ed. New York: McGraw-Hill, 1990.

SUGGESTED SOLUTIONS TO SELECTED STUDY PROBLEMS

1. a. $dy/dx = 4/x$
    b.
    c. $dy/dx = 2x - 4$
    d.

2. $\ln(q) = -2 \bullet \ln(p)$, therefore, $d \ln(q)/d \ln(p) = -2$. Hence,
    a. -2
    b. -2
    c. -2

3. a. $dy/dx = 6x - 4 = 0$ and $d^2y/dx^2 = 6$ implies that y is a minimum at $x = 2/3$.
    b.

C H A P T E R

3

TOPICS
IN CONSUMER
BEHAVIOR

INTRODUCTION

It is reasonable to ask, Is it important to study consumer behavior in a managerial economics course? The answer is, yes—for several reasons. First, many managers deal with the public directly and indirectly most prominently in their pricing policy. A basic understanding of consumer behavior is essential for competent managerial decisions regarding product lines and price. Second, the economic theory of the consumer helps managers understand human beings, and to a certain extent, what else is there to being a good manager? Coping with employee problems, choosing the appropriate compensation package, and understanding labor supply are critical managerial prerogatives. Last, many components of the theory of the consumer can be applied to a host of seemingly unrelated problems. The principles of consumer utility maximization are nearly identical to those of cost minimization and profit maximization. In addition, by focusing your attention on consumer behavior, you are far better able to understand the economist's approach to demand. Specifically, when you study consumer behavior you gain an understanding of the demand function itself—why it makes sense and why we describe it the way we do. Armed with a basic understanding of the economic approach to consumer behavior, you can see why economists talk about the determinants of demand—those factors that we think influence consumption. It also makes the demand construction seem reasonable and intuitively pleasing. All things considered, it is an investment that seems worth its cost. The position taken here is that a good manager is one who is qualified to model and understand consumer behavior.

This chapter begins with the characterization of the consumer as viewed in the economic paradigm. The notion of a utility function is introduced. This construction is then used to demonstrate the consumer's response to a price change. In effect, the theoretical underpinnings of the individual demand curve are derived. Next, opportunity cost is explored in some detail. After that, the first law of demand is investigated in several different dimensions, particularly as it pertains to quality.

Your attention is next directed to human capital and household production, the economist's attempt to understand the make-or-buy decision at the consumer level. This framework is a rich one for understanding a number of interesting managerial problems, such as self-service bank machines and the like. The chapter closes with analysis of the supply of labor. As is customary, there are a number of problems for your consideration. Work them—they form a fundamental part of the learning process.

THEORETICAL MICRO FOUNDATIONS OF DEMAND

Homo Economicus

Although there is some debate, most people say that *homo economicus* was discovered in 1776 by the famous Scottish economist Adam Smith with the publication of his classic, *An Inquiry into the Nature and Causes of the Wealth of Nations*. **Homo economicus** as an economic being is a rational, evaluating, maximizing person.

Rationality to the economist means something precise and slightly different from the dictionary definition. A rational person is one who does not make the same mistakes in judgment time after time. To be sure, people make mistakes and errors; they are often wrong, but in economics we argue that there is no pattern to these errors. This does not just mean they learn; instead, this definition of rationality is couched in terms of forecasting the future. People are not always on the wrong side of the coin toss. Sometimes they overestimate what is going to happen, and other times they underestimate the effect of future events. A rational individual can have a run of bad luck and underestimate an outcome for a long time, but eventually the person compensates so that, on average, the same mistakes in judgment are not repeated consistently. Rationality in economics means the mistakes that people make are random and not consistent over time. To put it formally, the series of errors that people make is not correlated in time. A word of caution is in order here. We all know a person who is always late to class and meetings. Is this person irrational by the economist's definition? The answer is no. The concept of rationality is couched in terms of judgment, not actions. A person who is habitually late may, in fact, be acting quite rationally. On the one hand, only she knows the value of her time. On the other hand, there may be a power advantage to arriving late at meetings. We should not conclude that routine tardiness is a sign of irrationality. In sum, the rational economic consumer has the capacity to make unbiased forecasts.

The second component to *homo economicus* is the capacity to evaluate. A person who **evaluates**, reasons. The person weighs the pros and cons of decisions. He evaluates the benefits and costs of his actions, choosing those avenues that make him better off, at least as seen through his own eyes. This means that people can and do make judgments. They ponder, wonder, worry, and weigh the consequences before they act. This means that people do not act capriciously and reflexively. Again, this does *not* mean that they are foolproof, only that they try to be. To help you understand, think about your PC. Most of the time, when the machine is working properly, it evaluates the signals you send it via the keyboard and mouse. In a loose manner of speaking, the machine thinks. We believe that people are the same. When people receive signals, they evaluate them. Just as various computers interpret inputs differently and/or more quickly than others, so do people. Some people evaluate with expert precision; others appear to need to reboot.

The third element to *homo economicus* is **maximization**. The economic paradigm says that people attempt to maximize their own welfare. This means that they do not settle for just getting by. Instead, they leave no profit on the table. If an opportunity presents itself that will make someone better off, she will take advantage of it. This means that at any moment, whatever an economic person is doing, she thinks the chosen path is the best one. Again, be cautioned that just because a person thinks she has made the right decision does not mean that she has done so. When a person optimizes, she exploits any opportunity to improve. This helps us understand why economists are known to utter, "To say that a situation is hopeless is to say that it is ideal." When a situation is hopeless, there is nothing that can be done to make it better. Therefore, by definition, no opportunities remain for improvement. The person, although miserable, has maximized for there is *nothing* she can do to make matters get better.

In the economic approach to human action, people think and reason. They learn from their mistakes, and they exploit any situation to improve. It is important to recognize that these are assumptions about human behavior, not conclusions. Just because we say that people act this way, it does not automatically follow that they actually do. It remains an open issue, a question worthy of investigation, whether the economic approach is a good one. The remainder of this text is designed to convince you that the economic approach, although less than perfect, is an excellent tool for understanding human action.

Axioms of Behavior

Three basic principles, based on simple postulates of human behavior, are the foundation of consumer demand theory. The first is **insatiability**: People prefer more to less; they are never satisfied. Second, people are rational. As we have said, **rationality** to the economist means that people do not consistently make the same mistakes. The third principle of consumer demand is that people's choices are **transitive**. This principle is related to the axiom of rationality. Given the choice between two bundles of goods, the consumer prefers one over the other or is indifferent to each. We postulate that people do not say "I simply cannot compare these two bundles." The fact that choices are transitive implies that the individual who prefers commodity or situation A to B and B to C will also prefer A to C.

Taken together, these three principles—insatiability, rationality, and transitivity—provide the essentials necessary to deduce all the postulates of consumer behavior in the marketplace. In essence, the basic principles of this model assume that people are not insane and that they prefer more things to less. Critics of the economic approach to consumer behavior sometimes argue that drug addiction is proof that consumers are irrational. However, upon close inspection, it turns out that drug addicts, people declared criminally insane, and others outside the mainstream of life appear to respond to economic signals in much the same ways that other people do. There is abundant evidence that heavy drug users and institutionalized people will work harder when paid higher wages. There is also compelling evidence that when faced with higher costs for the drug of choice, drug addicts resort to alternatives, including coming clean. To put the argument another way, even if drug addiction is irrational, drug addicts seem to behave rationally, in the economic sense, in other aspects of their lives.[1]

With these axioms in the background, it is appropriate to characterize an individual's preferences as represented by a utility function. A **utility function** is simply a convenience, a mathematical representation of an individual's tastes,

---

[1] You may wish to consult George J. Stigler and Gary Becker, "De Gustibus Non Est Disputandum," *American Economic Review,* 67(2), March 1977, 76–90; John H. Kagel, Raymond Battalio, and C. G. Miles, "Marihuana and Work Performance: Results from an Experiment," *Journal of Human Resources,* 15(3), Summer 1980, 373–95; or Raymond C. Battalio, John H. Kagel, and Morgan O. Reynolds, "Income Distributions in Two Experimental Economics," *Journal of Political Economy,* 77, December 1977, 1259–71.

preferences, and morals. An individual utility function takes the form $U = U(x_1, x_2, \ldots, x_n)$; the amount of utility that a person has is some function of the level of goods, $x_1, \ldots, x_n$, consumed. Like a thermometer, the more x_1 or x_2 there is, the higher is the utility indicator. As with all thermometers, the utility numbers are meaningless unless the scale is known. For example, 70 degrees is extremely cold on the absolute scale but very hot on Celsius thermometers. A utility function is the same. The scale is only meaningful in a relative sense; as the number gets larger, the greater is the level of happiness.

The utility indicator is not cardinal; it is only ordinal. The level of the numbers does not indicate quantitative amounts of happiness. Instead, it only compares two states and indicates whether one is better than the other. It is impossible to say that a person enjoys one thing a lot more than something else. All we can say is that a person prefers one bundle or situation to another. If a person is given an extra five pounds of sugar, his utility indicator goes up by some amount, but it is impossible to say by how much. All we can say is that utility has increased—the consumer is happier with more sugar. If this is a drawback, it is not a serious one. All the important conclusions of consumer demand can be deduced without comparing utility states quantitatively. The trouble only comes when we would like to compare my extra happiness from five pounds of sugar to your extra happiness associated with the gift of five pounds of sugar. It would be nice if utility theory would permit us to make this comparison, but the current state of affairs does not allow it.[2]

In sum, the higher the utility indicator, the happier the individual. The more things a person has in the house or the bank account, the higher the utility indicator. It is important, however, to remember that this formulation of consumer preferences does not allow for interpersonal utility comparison, nor does it permit cardinal quantification.

Maximizing Utility

Economic theory assumes the consumer's objective is to maximize utility. People want to be as happy as possible. This is equivalent to saying that people behave according to the three axioms outlined before.[3] However, limited income restricts the ability to achieve maximum happiness or satiation. In other words, income constrains the choice of goods. As a mathematical problem, the consumer maximizes a utility function, $U(x_1, \ldots, x_n)$, subject to the constraint that total expenditures on goods do not exceed the amount of income or money available, M. Expenditures on the first good are

$$E_1 = p_1 {\bullet} x_1,$$

---

[2] Note carefully that this does not prevent the *dollar* comparison of one person's willingness to pay for sugar with another's. Only the utility comparison, being unobservable, is impossible.

[3] Subtle and sophisticated analysis is required to demonstrate this equivalence. The interested student should consult Vivian Walsh, *Introduction to Contemporary Microeconomics* (New York: McGraw-Hill, 1970); or Kenneth Arrow, *Social Choice and Individual Values* (New Haven: Yale University Press, 1951) for the proof.

and similarly for all other goods. Hence, the budget constraint is

$$M = E_1 + E_2 + \ldots + E_n \text{ or,}$$

using the Greek symbol Σ to stand for the summation over a sequence,

$$M = \sum_{i=1}^{n} x_i p_i.$$

Formally then, the economic approach to consumer behavior assumes the consumer maximizes

$$U = U(x_1, \ldots, x_n)$$

subject to the constraint that

$$M = \sum_{i=1}^{n} x_i p_i.$$

This is a straightforward and simple mathematical problem to solve using a technique called **LaGrange multipliers**.[4] Solving this problem is equivalent to finding the appropriate levels of each x_i to maximize happiness given the prices of the goods and the amount of money available. In simple terms, the consumer has a fixed amount of money to allocate among many different goods in a way that gets the greatest level of happiness from the expenditures.

The mathematical conditions necessary to maximize U, subject to the budget constraint, M, are

$$U_i/U_j = p_i/p_j \text{ for all } i \text{ and } j$$

where U_i is $\partial U/\partial x_i$, the **marginal utility** of the ith good. The marginal utility of every good divided by the marginal utility of each other good is equal to the relative price ratio of the goods. Alternatively, we write

$$U_i/p_i = U_j/p_j$$

by dividing both sides by p_i and multiplying both sides by U_j. The second expression is analytically equivalent to the first, but the interpretation is slightly different; the extra happiness a consumer gets from each dollar spent must be the same for all goods. Either of these interpretations is an appropriate characterization of the consumer's equilibrium. Moreover, they tell us something about how much of each good the consumer purchases.

---

[4] See the Appendix to Chapter 2 for the details of this mathematical technique.

Regardless of which equation we use, to maximize utility subject to a budget constraint, the consumer purchases an amount of each good such that the ratio of her marginal utilities is equal to the ratio of their prices. Marginal utility is the increment in utility caused by a change in the amount of a good consumed, the extra happiness a person receives from a small additional quantity of a particular good. The incremental pleasure from drinking one more draft is the marginal utility of beer. The ratio of the marginal utilities of the two goods is the consumer's personal evaluation of one good versus the other, the consumer's own feelings about the merits of one good compared to the other. The price of the first good, p_1, divided by the price of the second, p_2, is the price of the first good in the marketplace in terms of the second good. It represents the *seller's* relative evaluation of one good versus the other. Since the consumer can choose the quantities to buy, equilibrium is only achieved when the consumer chooses goods in proportions that make his own personal evaluation equal to the seller's posted evaluation. The ratio of the marginal utilities of the two goods must equal the ratio of the prices. In essence, to maximize utility the consumer must select goods from a limited budget in such a way that his personal evaluation of the goods is the same as the market's evaluation. Otherwise, there is a profit opportunity, a chance for the buyer to improve his happiness.

The ratio of the marginal utilities of any two goods is called the **marginal rate of substitution**. Utility maximization requires that the consumer arrange expenditures so the marginal rate of substitution is equal to the ratio of prices for all goods.

Consider the preceding discussion in graphic form. In order to make the problem manageable, consider a situation with only two goods. In other words, envision a utility function of the form

$$U = U(x_1, x_2).$$

Examine the three dimensional picture, Figure 3.1. In a southeasterly direction, plot consumption levels of the first good, x_1. To the northeast, plot increasing levels of consumption of the second good, x_2, and vertically plot the utility of x_1 and x_2. The utility function is characterized by the following considerations: Suppose you, the consumer, do not have any x_2, but you increase your consumption of x_1. The theory says your utility increases as the consumption of one good goes up, holding constant the level of the other good. The same is true of x_2; utility increases as consumption of x_2 increases. Therefore, holding constant either x_i, increases in the other good lead to higher utility. At the origin, where the consumption of both goods is zero, there is no happiness, no utility. Standing at the origin and looking out into x_1 and x_2 space, you see a mountainlike object projecting. In fact, call it utility mountain. The height of this mountain at any point represents the level of utility achieved by the individual.

Passing a plane through this mountain at a particular height creates a plateau. Associated with this height or plateau is a particular level of happiness. All along the edge of the plateau, the height is the same distance above the ground. At every point along the edge of a specific plateau, call it I_1, the utility level is the same. This edge is called an **iso-utility line** because each point on it has the same

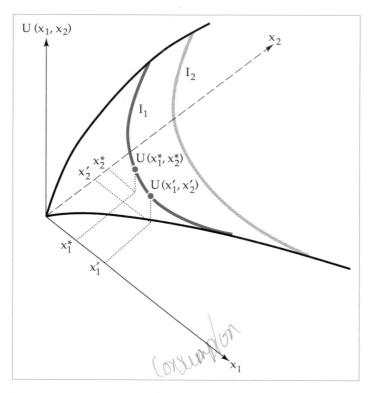

FIGURE 3.1
Utility Analysis

level of utility. Associated with x_2^*, for example, of the good x_2 and x_1^* of the good x_1 is the utility level $U(x_1^*, x_2^*)$ and a certain amount of happiness. If the consumer had less of the second good, x_2', but more of the first, x_1', enough to compensate her for the loss of x_2, she would be willing to trade; she is no worse off. In our terminology, she is indifferent between the combination x_1^* and x_2^* and the pair x_1' and x_2', and for that reason the locus of points is called an **indifference curve.** Along the indifference curve, various combinations of x_1 and x_2 yield the same amount of happiness, and consequently, the consumer is indifferent between them. In Figure 3.1, the first combination of x_1 and x_2 represented by the point (x_1^*, x_2^*) has the same utility for this consumer as the second combination (x_1', x_2'), and that is why we say the consumer is indifferent. The loss of utility from having less of the second good, x_2', as we move from the first point, is *precisely* made up for in the extra utility from having more of the first good, x_1'.

Of course, there are an infinite number of plateaus or levels that can be scribed in the utility mountain at different heights; there is a family of indifference curves. In Figure 3.1, lines I_1 and I_2 are two of the indifference curves or iso-utility lines. This family creates a contour map that is visualized most easily in two dimensions in the same way that topographic maps chart elevation. Consider Figure 3.2, where the utility mountain has been compressed. The family of indifference curves in (x_1, x_2) space represents higher utility farther from the

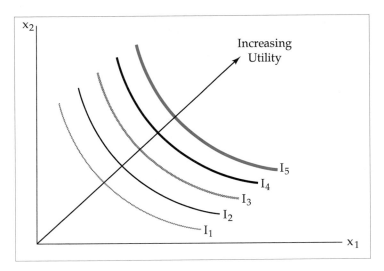

FIGURE 3.2
Increasing Utility

origin, in the direction of the arrow. That is, the utility linked with indifference curve I_1 is less than the utility of I_2, and so forth. Drawing indifference curves in two dimensions facilitates graphic analysis and avoids confusion so long as the student recognizes that indifference curves represent higher utility the farther they are from the origin in a northeasterly direction.

Within this indifference map, it is impossible for indifference curves to cross each other because that would violate the axiom of transitivity. Consider what crossing indifference curves would mean. At the point where the curves intersected, the consumer would achieve two different levels of happiness. Movements along an indifference curve describe the consumer's willingness to trade one good for another. If any two indifference curves were to intersect, it would mean that the consumer had two different valuations of two goods simultaneously. This suggests a type of schizophrenia in consumption that economic theory labels as *intransitive preferences* and does not allow. This nonintersection property is one of the characteristics of indifference curves.

In addition, indifference curves must always have negative slope. Imagine what a positive slope implies. In Figure 3.3, a positively sloped indifference curve is drawn. Consider the combination x_1^* and x_2^*. At this point the consumer has $U(x_1^*, x_2^*)$ utility, but, by construction, the consumer is indifferent between this point and the point x_1^{**} and x_2^*. This means that additional amounts of x_1 do *not* increase the utility of the consumer, a result that violates the more is preferred to less axiom. Hence, positively sloped indifference curves are not consistent with the rational consumer characterized in the opening section of this chapter.

Indifference curves, then, have three characteristics: (1) There are an infinity of them; (2) they cannot cross; and (3) they always have negative slope in (x_1, x_2) space. It is important to note that these are the only constraints imposed on the utility function or indifference map by the postulated axioms of behavior. The

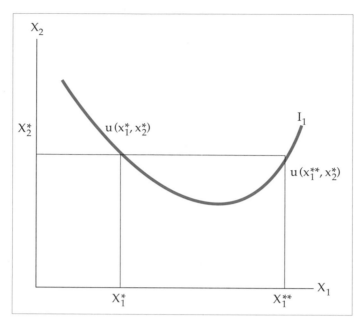

FIGURE 3.3
Positively Sloped Indifference Curves

indifference curves do not have to be parallel, nor do they have to take any particular shape.[5]

What this means is that each consumer has a preference ranking over goods summarized by his indifference map or utility function. The consumer also faces a choice set defined by his income and the prices of commodities he values. This approach allows us to characterize the consumption choices made by buyers. We have a consumer with a fixed amount of income, say M dollars of income. In the store or market, there are two goods available, x_1 and x_2. These two commodities have prices, p_1 and p_2. The consumer must decide how to allocate his limited resources, M, in such a way as to get the maximum pleasure from his expenditure. That is, he must choose the optimal bundle of x_1 and x_2. Figure 3.4 presents the problem graphically.

First we construct the **choice set**, sometimes called the *opportunity set*. The maximum amount of x_2 that could be purchased when the price is p_2 and income is M, is M/p_2. M divided by p_2 is the upper bound on the choice set of good x_2. Similarly, M divided by p_1 is the upper bound on the choice set in good x_1. Connecting those two points describes the choice set for all combinations of x_1 and x_2 that could be purchased. To say this another way, the consumer can choose any combination of x_1 and x_2 defined by the triangle created by the two axes and

---

[5] For some problems in economics, we impose a convexity restriction that requires diminishing marginal rate of substitution between goods. This condition makes indifference curves convex to the origin. The indifference curves in Figure 3.2 are all drawn convex to the origin.

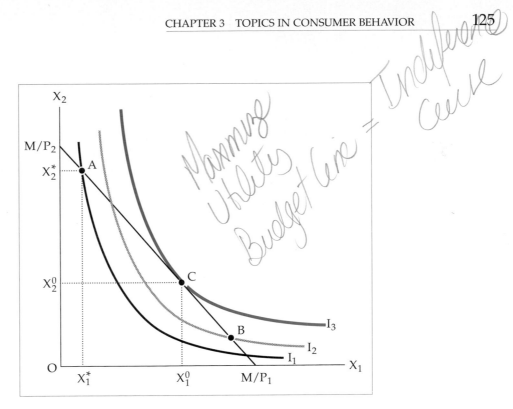

FIGURE 3.4
The Consumer's Choice

the budget line, $M = p_1 \bullet x_1 + p_2 \bullet x_2$. Then the question becomes, Which point gives the highest utility?

Consider point A on indifference curve I_1 in Figure 3.4. Associated with that point are the consumption choices of x_2^* and x_1^*. Notice that the purchase of x_1^* of the first good and x_2^* of the second good exhausts all income. But spending all the money does *not* necessarily mean maximum utility. The consumer might be able to rearrange consumption and be happier. Suppose this person chooses an alternative consumption bundle, moving along the budget constraint to point B, purchasing less x_2 and more x_1. Since indifference curve I_2 is farther away from the origin, and thus higher on utility mountain, the consumer is happier at point B even though total expenditures are constant.

What combination exhausts the opportunity to improve? By construction, the **slope of the indifference curve** is the ratio of the marginal utilities of the two goods, the negative of the marginal rate of substitution, $-U_1/U_2$. At the same time, the slope of the budget constraint is $-p_1/p_2$. Recall the condition we established earlier in this chapter that the marginal rate of substitution must equal the ratio of the prices, $U_i/U_j = p_i/p_j$, which in the two good case requires that $U_1/U_2 = p_1/p_2$. This condition does not hold at point A, and this means that at point A, the marginal utility of one compared to two is not equal to the relative prices. Indeed, the condition does not hold at B either, but the two ratios are more nearly equal.

Point C, where the indifference curve is tangent to the budget constraint, maximizes consumer utility. In fact, there can only be one such tangency. At point

C, the ratio of the marginal utilities of the two goods is equal to the relative price ratio. Hence, this consumer chooses x_1^0 and x_2^0, given the relative prices p_1 and p_2 and money income M.

In a nutshell, the economic theory of consumer choice is straightforward. Consumers maximize utility, a transitive ranking over their idiosyncratic preferences. More is always preferred to less. Optimization requires that the consumer choose among the myriad of goods in a way that the marginal utility per dollar spent on each good is the same for all commodities. Graphically, the consumer tries to advance up utility mountain, but income constrains the climb. Optimal choice involves finding a tangency between the highest possible indifference curve and the income or budget constraint. This tangency maps into a specific amount of each good in the choice set, and therein lies the economic theory of consumer choice at its basic level.

CONSUMER'S RESPONSE TO A PRICE CHANGE

Hypothetical Business Problem 3.1

You are the manager of a large amusement park. You currently charge adults $10 per day to enter the park. Children under 12 are only charged $7. Once inside the park, there is no additional fee for any event or ride. The average adult takes 4 rides, while the typical child enjoys 14 events. Ignore for the moment the money spent at the concession stands. On average, then, adults pay $2.50 for each event they enjoy, and kids pay $0.50. Suppose you changed your pricing policy. First, you let everyone in free, regardless of age. Second, you charge adults $2.50 for each event they choose and kids $0.50 for each ride or event. What will happen to your total revenue?

One of the most interesting and important problems in all economics is the consumer's response to a price change. Consider the initial consumer choice represented in Figure 3.5. For clarity in analysis, we again consider the simple two good case involving the consumer choice over goods x_1 and x_2. Let the original relative prices of these two goods be p_1 and p_2, and suppose income is M dollars. The indifference curves I_1 and I_2 reflect the consumer's tastes and preferences over the two goods. The choice set is depicted by the budget constraint drawn from the vertical intercept (M/p_2) and the horizontal intercept (M/p_1). Based on the previous discussion, we know that under these conditions the consumer optimizes by choosing the quantities x_1^0 and x_2^0, respectively. These selections are represented by point A in the figure. Now let us change the situation and observe what happens.

Suppose the price of x_1 decreases from p_1 to p_1'. How will this consumer react? First, analyze the situation. The choice set has expanded because the price of x_1 has decreased. This shifts the budget constraint out along the x_1 axis to the new intercept, M/p_1'. With a lower price for x_1, the consumer can purchase the original quantity of x_1 and an additional quantity of the second good x_2. Of course, with a lower price for x_1 the consumer could simply purchase an extra quantity of x_1. A

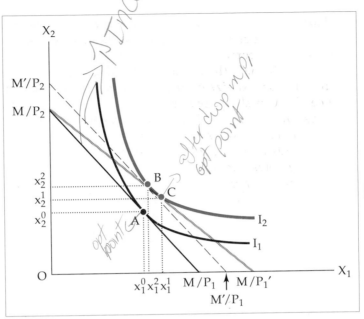

FIGURE 3.5
The Decomposition of Demand

third option would be to purchase additional quantities of both x_1 and x_2. The actual choice hinges on the preferences of the individual.

In Figure 3.5, one of these choices is depicted, the one where the consumption of both goods increases. The new consumer choice, given this person's indifference map, is the combination x_1^1 and x_2^1. This is shown by point C in the figure. At this point, the indifference curve I_2 is tangent to the new budget constraint. This particular consumer has chosen to increase the consumption of both goods. Correspondingly, he has achieved greater happiness witnessed by the higher level of utility at I_2. The lower price of x_1 has increased the consumption of x_1, a reflection of the first law of demand. Although we have also shown an increase in the consumption of the second good, x_2, it need not have turned out this way, although it usually does.

To further understand this shift in consumption, consider this hypothetical situation: If instead of reducing the price of x_1 to p_1', some magic despot had intervened, keeping the price of x_1 constant at p_1, but *giving the consumer an amount of cash that would make him equally as happy as the price decline to p_1'*. How much money would be required? Put another way, we know that lower prices make consumers happier. What we are trying to find here is the precise amount in money terms—the income equivalent to the price change.

We know that in order to make the customer just as happy as the price decline, we must get her to the level of happiness denoted by I_2. To do this without changing the price of x_1 or x_2, we must shift the budget constraint out parallel to the original, until it is just tangent to I_2 (point B in Figure 3.5). Let M' be the new level of income that increases the consumer's level of utility out to I_2 without changing the prices of either good. Then, $(M' - M)$ is the additional money we must give this person to make her as happy as the price decline to p_1'; $(M' - M)$ is the extra amount of money it would take to shift this person's budget constraint out far enough to attain the level of utility denoted by indifference curve I_2. This additional amount of money is one measure of the **consumer surplus** associated with the price decline.

Consumer surplus is the inframarginal or unrequited joy a person gets from consumption above and beyond the amount paid for the goods purchased. Each of us has bought an attractive shirt, enjoyed a nice lunch, or viewed a movie where we would gladly have paid more for the item than the posted price. This additional pleasure is called consumer surplus. It is the object of much envy, and astute managers are always on the lookout for ways to prevent customers from departing their store with it intact.

But to return to our discussion, we are going to shift the budget constraint out by an additional amount of income, $M' - M$, without changing the price of x_1 until we push the consumer to the same level of happiness she obtains when the price of x_1 falls. This theoretical construction helps us to divide the impact of a price change into two parts. The first is the **income effect**, the change in consumption due to an apparent change in income. Although our money income does not change when prices change, our consumption opportunities do. Thus, economists say that **real income** changes when prices change. In economics, real income is denominated in terms of tangible consumption items, not dollars. When a person's real income increases, he or she has more things—food, clothes, and the like—to enjoy. The income effect is the equivalent of the hypothetical experiment we perform by artificially shifting the budget constraint out by an amount that generates the same change in happiness as the change in price.

The second effect is called the *substitution effect,* and we will discuss it in more detail later, but before we do that, first consider the implications of the income effect. Compare consumption bundles under the two scenarios: (1) the price change, money income constant (the movement from point A to point C); and (2) the income change, price constant (the movement from point A to point B). Under the price change scenario, the consumer chooses x_1^1 and x_2^1; but under the income change scenario, the choices are x_1^2 and x_2^2. This is an important result. Even though the consumer is *indifferent* between income M and relative prices p_1' and p_2 on the one hand and income M' and relative prices p_1 and p_2 on the other, her ultimate choices for consumption are *not* the same. According to the way the figure is drawn, when only income changes, the consumer moves to point B. But, when prices change, she chooses the combination at point C which has more x_1 (and less x_2) than in the situation when only income changes (point B).

To better understand this important result, let us examine the income effect in more detail. When income increased to M', this consumer chose to buy more x_1 because x_1 is a normal good. If, alternatively, x_1 was inferior, then the new consumption level of x_1, x_1^2, at prices p_1 and p_2 and income M' (point B in Figure 3.5) would have fallen to the *left* of the original consumption point, x_1^0. In this latter case, the boost in income would have induced the consumer to buy less of the first good. In either case, the change in consumption is due singly to the change in income, not a change in prices, and hence this component of the overall price change is called the income effect.

Relative price changes necessarily cause income effects. When the price of x_1 falls to p'_1, the consumer is effectively richer. The income component of the price change is analytically equivalent to the change in consumption induced by the hypothetical change in income to M' as represented by the movement from A to B. Since the total or overall effect of the price reduction is the movement from point A to point C, the remainder, B to C, is commonly called the **substitution effect**. The buyer is induced to buy more of x_1 because the price is cheaper, even if there were no income effect. That is, holding utility constant, a decrease in prices moves the consumer along the indifference curve to higher consumption of the cheaper good.

The substitution effect exists because a higher relative price for x_1, holding real income constant, increases the opportunity cost of consuming it when measured in terms of the other good, x_2. When the price of x_1 increases, each unit of it chosen now represents additional units of x_2 that must be left on the shelf. This induces substitution out of x_1 and into x_2 above and beyond any effects due to changes in income. Think of the problem this way: The substitution effect is the consumer's response to a price change holding utility constant. This is nothing more than a movement along a particular indifference curve, and since indifference curves must have negative slope, it follows that the substitution effect of a price change is also always negative. When the price of a good increases, all other goods now appear cheaper, and the optimal consumption bundle now includes less of the relatively more expensive good. In the reverse, when the price of a good decreases, it appears cheaper when measured against all other consumption opportunities, and the optimal bundle now includes more of it.

In sum, a price change can be decomposed into two distinctly different parts, an income effect and a substitution effect. The income component of a price change can be of the same sign as the price change (when the good is inferior) or opposite to the price movement (when the good is normal). The second effect, the substitution-only effect, is always of the opposite sign to the price change. The overall effect of a price change is the sum of the parts, and it provides the theoretical basis for the first law of demand. For normal goods, price changes have a substitution effect that is opposite in sign to the price change and an income effect that reinforces the substitution term. For inferior goods, the substitution effect remains opposite in sign, but the income effect mitigates. Hence, for the first law of demand to be universal, in the case of inferior goods, the substitution effect must dominate. This is the basis for the theorem. It remains an empirical issue whether the law is relevant or not, but the evidence is abundant. Scholars have been searching for decades to find an exception to the rule, and to say that success has been limited is to understate the truth. *It is the absence of any empirical evidence to the contrary that turns the price change theorem into the first law of demand.*

A simple numerical example might help you understand the distinction between the income and substitution effects. Suppose there is a consumer named Hector. He has $174 per week of income. For the sake of our example, say he buys two things, pizza and beer. (Hector is sort of weird.) Pizzas cost $10 apiece, and beers cost $1 each. He buys 15 pizzas and a case of beer a week, which exhausts his income. Imagine that Iraq invades Nebraska, causing the price of wheat to increase substantially. As a result, the price of a pizza increases by 10 percent to $11. Hector is worse off. His real income has decreased. With his weekly income of $174, he cannot continue to purchase 15 pizzas and a case of beer. He must reduce his consumption of one or the other or both goods. Suppose that he decides to buy 14 pizzas ($154 of his income) and 20 cans of beer (the remaining $20 of his weekly income). (Naturally, this is the opposite situation to a price decrease, but the analytical division of a price change into income and substitution effects works for price declines as well as price increases.) The original consumption bundle was (15, 24). The new bundle chosen is (14, 20). What are the income and substitution effects?

To answer this question, we must know the amount of money that we would have to take away from Hector to make him just as sad as the increased price of pizza made him. Let us suppose that $10 is the correct amount. Then Hector is indifferent between the situation in which pizza prices are higher (pizzas cost $11, beers cost $1, while income is $174) and the second scenario with lower income (he has $10 less, $164, and the prices of pizza and beer do not change). Now consider the imaginary situation in which prices do not change, but Hector has only $164. What consumption bundle would he choose? We cannot know exactly without observing him, but imagine that he would buy 14.5 pizzas for $145 and 19 beers for $19. The total expenditure ($145 + $19 = $164) would exhaust his hypothetical income of $164. Note that these changes in consumption are due solely to our thought experiment that artificially changes Hector's income down from $174 to $164 per week; we have held the prices of pizza and beer constant. Thus, the changes in consumption are pure income effects. They represent the shock brought about by the income equivalent to the price change.

When the price of pizza increased from $10 to $11, the total change in Hector's consumption of pizza was a decrease of one per week, $15 - 14 = 1$. The income effect is the change in consumption due to the change in real income. We know that when only income changes Hector reduces his consumption of pizza from 15 down to 14.5. The income effect is 0.5 pizza, or $15 - 14.5 = 0.5$. The remainder of the total effect is the substitution effect, $1 - 0.5 = 0.5$. In sum, when the price of pizza increased, Hector was poorer. This reduction in his real income led him to buy 0.5 less pizza each week.[6] At the same time, the price of pizza got more expensive relative to beer, making beer appear more attractive, relatively speaking. For this reason, Hector further reduced his consumption of pizza by 0.5 per week. The total decrease becomes one pizza.

If a picture is worth a thousand words, then maybe a graph will help you understand this example. Consider Figure 3.6. The quantity of pizzas consumed is represented along the horizontal axis, the quantity of beers up the vertical. The original budget constraint is given by the curve labeled M. The pizza axis intercept for the budget constraint is determined by the maximum number of

---

[6] The fact that the income and substitution effects are equal here is purely a coincidence and an artifact of the example.

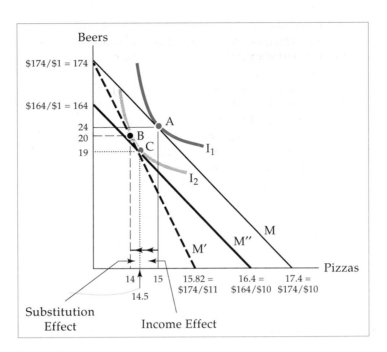

FIGURE 3.6

The Income and Substitution Effects of a Change in the Price of Pizza

pizzas that Hector could consume if he spent all of his money on pizzas. This is his total income, $174, divided by the price of pizzas, $10, or 17.4 pizzas. Similarly, the beer axis intercept is $174/$1 or 174 beers. Given Hector's indifference curve I_1, his optimal consumption bundle is 15 pizzas and 24 beers, point A in the figure.

When the price of pizza increases to $11, the budget constraint rotates in to M' to represent Hector's diminished consumption opportunities. The beer axis intercept remains constant because the price of beer has not changed, but the pizza axis intercept moves inward to 15.82 which is the new maximum number of pizzas that he could purchase at $11 ($174/$11 = 15.82). The new choice bundle is 14 pizzas and 20 beers. This point is labeled B in the figure.

To construct the income effect we artificially subtract the $10 wealth loss from Hector's income, leaving him with $164. This budget constraint, labeled M'', is parallel to the original budget constraint, M, because we have not changed the price of either pizza or beer. The pizza and beer intercepts are given by the reduced income level, $164, divided by the relevant prices, $10 and $1, respectively. The pizza axis intercept is 16.4, while the beer axis intercept is 164. Hector's hypothetical choices given this income adjustment are 14.5 pizzas and 19 beers, point C in the figure.

The overall adjustment to the price change is the movement from point A to point B. The income effect is the movement from point A to point C. The substitution effect is the remainder, the movement from point C to point B. The economist's technique of decomposing the effects of a price change into income and substitution effects is far more than a technical exercise. This methodology helps us understand a wide variety of interesting and important managerial problems. You are now equipped with the skills sufficient to solve Hypothetical Business Problem 3.1, which deals with income and substitution effects. Recall the problem from the beginning of the section Consumer's Response to a Price Change and consider the following analysis.

Suggested Solution to Problem 3.1

In the original scenario, the price of each ride, once inside, is zero. In the second case, the price, $2.50 per ride for adults and $0.50 per ride for kids, is the same as the average revenue ($10/4 = $2.50 and $7/14 = $0.50) under the first case, but the effective price per ride to the consumer is more, $2.50 for adults and $0.50 for kids. The difference between the two pricing schemes hinges on the substitution effect. With the fixed or entry fee system and no charge per ride, rides are effectively cheaper (on the inside) than when each commands a fee of $2.50 or $0.50. Relatively speaking then, rides are cheaper under the fixed-fee system, and more are consumed by people inside the park. The $2.50 and $0.50 charges induce adults and children to substitute away from rides into other consumption items. This effect is absent when there is no charge for each ride. In effect, the fixed-fee system is like a tax or a loss of income that shifts the consumer's budget constraint in parallel toward the origin. If the amusement park is a normal good, this acts to reduce overall visits, but the fixed fee imposes no substitution effect. The consumer can ride to his heart's content without giving up any other commodities. Since the substitution effect is necessarily negative, we conclude that a fee-per-ride system will reduce the number of overall rides, and that total revenue will *fall* if the amusement park begins to charge for each ride individually *if the individual prices are set to equal current average revenue per ride*. However, there is an offsetting effect. Fewer people will visit the park when there is an admission fee. Hence, switching from a fixed entry fee to a fee-per-ride pricing scheme has two opposing effects. More patrons are attracted to the park with a zero entry fee, but each rides fewer rides while there. The ultimate effect on revenues depends on the relative elasticities of demand.

THE CONCEPT OF OPPORTUNITY COST

Hypothetical Business Problem 3.2

You are a seller of college textbooks. Of course, sales are directly tied to college enrollment. Consequently, you spend a great deal of time fore-casting enrollment. Based on numerous reports, you are more or less convinced that the next 15 months (three semesters) will be associated with a substantial business recession. In fact, some people forecast the economic downturn will last even longer. What do you expect will happen to college applications and enrollments (and hence your sales) over the next couple of years?

One of the simplest but most important concepts in the economic paradigm is the principle of **opportunity cost**. Economic theory holds that decision makers choose on the basis of forgone alternatives. That is, decision makers do not concern themselves with expenditures made in the past, nor do they care about the original price of an item, but rather they concentrate on the options precluded by the current decision. In this view, sunk costs, accounting costs, price tags, out-of-pocket costs, and the like do not motivate behavior, but instead people consider their options and behave accordingly. For example, suppose you are going shopping, and along the way, you find $20 in the street. When you get to the store, you find the exact shirt you want for $25. Given that just moments before you found $20, how much does the shirt cost you? One school of thought says the $20 was free, and hence the shirt actually costs you only $5 out-of-pocket. However, according to the economic paradigm, it costs $25. You could have bought a belt, a pair of pants, a hat, or many other things with the money you found, but *you gave up all these things when you spent the money on the shirt,* regardless of where you got the money. The shirt cost you what you gave up to get it, and the money value of the lost option is $25.

This distinction is more than a semantic one. The economic model holds that people base their decisions on opportunity cost; therefore, without any effects due to increased income (income effects), the lucky person who found $20 in the street is no more likely to buy the $25 shirt than if she had not found the money. The cost of the shirt is the same in the two circumstances, and, hence, behavior is the same (again, we are assuming that the extra $20 did not change the demand for shirts).[7] Consider another example. You hear that Neil Diamond is coming to town to give a concert. Tickets are $35 apiece. After much deliberation, you decide that three CDs of his are preferred to a live performance; you do not buy a ticket. Knowing that you are the consummate Neil Diamond fan, your grandmother who lives in Europe arranges for you to have a free ticket. You are fully aware of the resale or scalper's market in tickets and know that with almost no effort you can legally sell your ticket for the face price, $35. Moreover, since your grandmother lives so far away, she will never know you sold the ticket. Will you attend the concert? The economist says no. You have previously decided that the concert was not worth $35. You always had the option of attending the concert or having $35, and the free gift of the ticket changes nothing so long as there are no income effects of the gift.[8] This is the principle of alternative or opportunity cost. We will

---

[7] The demand for shirts will change *only* if the $20 is an important part of the consumer's budget. In general, we expect the $20 will be disbursed across many goods and that the wealth or income effect of finding the money has little if any impact on the demand for any one particular good.

[8] Think of income or wealth effects the following way: Suppose grandmother sent a check for $35, totally oblivious of the concert. Many people would choose to spend the gift on varied and sundry items, not the concert tickets; they simply are not worth it to these people. However, there may be someone who would buy tickets now exactly because of the extra money, *someone who was not so inclined before the check arrived.* The extra income has boosted this person's demand for the concert, the concert is a normal good, and suddenly the consumer is willing to pay the market price to attend.

use it extensively throughout the rest of the book. Make it part of your working knowledge of economics. Few concepts are more important.

Hypothetical Business Problem 3.2 deals with opportunity cost. With the material just presented, you should now be able to address that question. Recall the problem from the beginning of this section and consider the following analysis.

Suggested Solution to Problem 3.2

The cost of attending college has several components. There are the direct costs of tuition, room and board, and books. In addition to these, the opportunity cost of time can be substantial. For instance, consider a person with a summer job upon graduation from high school. Suppose this person is paid $5 per hour for a 40-hour work week. The weekly income is $200 less taxes. Say the net income after deductions is $150. At the end of the summer, imagine that this person has the option of continuing to work or going off to college. If college is the choice, then the wages stop and college costs not only tuition and fees but also the $150 a week that was being earned at work. When the student matriculates, the wages stop and become a cost, in the opportunity sense, of going to college.

The lost income can constitute a significant portion of the total cost of a college education. For a 16-week semester, the lost income is 16•$150 or $2400. At many schools the lost income can even be more than the direct costs of tuition, fees, room and board, and books. This makes it easy to see why some people, especially those with good job opportunities out of high school, stay away from college.

When a recession comes, some people temporarily or permanently lose their jobs. For these people, the opportunity cost of college is lower. When they enroll in school, they are not giving up as much income as they would have had they been working. For them, the opportunity cost of school has decreased, and this increases their desire to enroll. Based on the concept of opportunity cost, the demand for education should increase during business recessions and depressions. By contrast, when economic times are good, some people are inclined to work, making high wages, postponing their college education until a recession or weak economy reduces the opportunity cost of their time. For this reason, the age composition of college student bodies may change slightly during a recession. During normal times, the average freshman is just out of high school, about 18 years old. During a recession, a larger fraction of first-time students may be somewhat older—those who have lost their jobs or had their paychecks cut and found college a relatively cheap option.

Consult the accompanying story from the *New York Times* which details how some college students are dealing with the recession of 1991. It is interesting to note that applications at the largest graduate schools in the country increased by 20 percent. It would seem that college students are well aware of the concept of opportunity cost whether they studied economics formally or not.

THE OPPORTUNITY COST OF COLLEGE DURING A RECESSION

From the beginning of the academic year, Dana M. Lew, a senior majoring in economics at Northwestern University in Evanston, Ill., knew that finding a job after graduation would be a nightmare. *So she, like a record number of this year's seniors, kept her options open by applying to graduate school.*

As the term progressed, Miss Lew, who was reared in Metairie, La., regularly checked the job listings at Northwestern's placement office but did not come across anything hopeful. She spoke to several corporate recruiters who said they would be hiring half as many people as they had first expected.

. . . Finally, she received a letter of acceptance from the University of Illinois at Urbana, for its master's degree program in business administration. "I decided that this was the way to go," she said.

So many members of the Class of '91 at colleges and universities around the country applied to graduate school this year that applications rose by as much as 20 percent at the 430 largest institutions, according to the Council of Graduate Schools, a national organization. Nearly 1 million foreign and American students applied to graduate school in the United States this year as against more than 830,000 last year. . . .

Victor R. Lindquist, the director of placement at Northwestern, who wrote the Lindquist-Endicott Reports, an annual survey of employment trends for college graduates, said that *in a bad economy it is common for applications to graduate school to increase.*

Anthony DePalma, "With Jobs Scarce, Many Turn to Graduate School," *New York Times,* July 3, 1991, p. A17. Copyright © 1991 by The New York Times Company. Reprinted by permission. Emphasis added.

THE EMPIRICAL BASIS FOR THE FIRST LAW OF DEMAND

The previous sections in this chapter discuss the theoretical justification for asserting the first law of demand. However, the first law of demand is actually an empirical proposition.[9] That is, the first law of demand is employed because people (and other living things) actually behave that way.[10] Moreover, they behave that way universally; there are no exceptions to the first law of demand in nature. Any statement that strong is almost surely incorrect in some cases, but the point is, there simply are virtually no documented cases of the law being violated.[11] To say the rule is widely accepted is an understatement.

---

[9] Indeed, for goods that are sufficiently inferior, the first law of demand does not even hold theoretically. This curiosum is often referred to as a Giffen good. Here, the income effect of the price change dominates the substitution effect and quantity moves with price.

[10] Sociobiologists and economic biologists have uncovered a wealth of applications of the first law of demand to nonhuman species, including trees, earthworms, and bees.

[11] You may wish to consult Raymond C. Battalio, John H. Kagel, and Carl A. Kogut, "Experimental Confirmation of the Existence of a Giffen Good," *American Economic Review,* 81(4), September 1991, 961–69, who uncover the Giffen good in an experimental setting using rats as subjects.

In the summer of 1991, the State of Iowa enacted very stringent laws concerning cigarette smoking. No one under the age of 18 is allowed to purchase or possess tobacco products. In the accompanying newspaper account of the law, one teenager remarks that the imposition of the law will not affect her behavior—after all she is an "addict." Do you agree that laws do not alter behavior? In the opportunity sense, adhering to the law imposes a cost. What does the first law of demand say about this?

As a principle of management, the law has profound implications. Regardless of the situation, who is involved, or the circumstances, when the price of some activity or good increases, the people currently pursuing the activity or consuming the good will do less or buy fewer units. And the opposite is also true: When price goes down, more will be consumed. This result is true not only for humans, but for rats, pigeons, fish, worms, and the like. Research reveals that rats reduce their consumption of food and beverage, shifting to alternatives, when they must pay a higher price. In experiments, when the number of lever presses required to obtain a cup of sweet liquid is increased, rats consumed less of it and switch to other things. The weight of the evidence suggests that regardless of what you believe, what you have been previously taught, or what you have heard on "60 Minutes," when the price of cigarettes goes up, people smoke less. When the price of electricity falls, people buy more. Does this mean that the application of the death penalty will reduce the murder rate?

It is important to note that these results are not based on economic intuition; rather, they are based on scientific fact and analysis. You may dislike the law of gravity when you jump to dunk a basketball. However, the first law of demand, like the law of gravity, works whether you like it or not.[12] The student finding an exception to the first law of demand will surely become famous, and it is this incentive that ensures that people will continue to look for the exceptions. It is the absence of data refuting the law that gives us confidence that the statement "there are no exceptions to the first law of demand" is not likely to be challenged soon.

THE OPPORTUNITY COST OF ILLEGAL SMOKING

Anyone under 18 caught smoking, chewing or even possessing tobacco in Iowa is subject to fines of up to $100 or a spell of community service. Teen-age smoking becomes illegal today, and Iowa becomes probably the toughest anti-tobacco state in the union.

"I think it's a bunch of garbage," [Sara] Meeker said. "I've been smoking since I was in fifth grade, when I was 11 years old. *This new law ain't going to change a thing. I smoke, I'm addicted and that isn't going to change.*"

"Iowa Lights Up Toughest Smoking Ban in Nation," *The Post-Standard* (Syracuse, NY), July 1, 1991, p. A–1. Emphasis added.

---

[12] Naturally, you may question the data and methods of any of the scientific papers that have found a negative relation between price and quantity.

THE DEMAND FOR ABORTIONS

According to research by Marshall H. Medoff, professor of economics, California State–Long Beach, the first law of demand holds for abortions.[a] He examined the abortion rate of women of childbearing age in 1980 and estimated that the price elasticity of demand was inelastic, about -0.8, and that abortions are a normal good. The income elasticity was estimated to be about $+0.8$. It is interesting that religious preference did not seem to impact the demand for abortions, nor did educational level seem to be important.

---

[a] Marshall H. Medoff, "An Economic Analysis of the Demand for Abortions," *Economic Inquiry*, 26(2), April 1988, 353– 60.

In management, the empirical richness of the first law of demand can be very useful. When anyone from marketing or accounting or any division under your employ claims that higher prices or lower quality will not reduce sales, you can summarily send that person back to his or her office to rethink the project.

THE SELF-INTERESTED INDIVIDUAL

The role of self-interest is critical in analyzing human behavior. For a variety of reasons, this seems to be a difficult concept to get across to students. Perhaps the reason is that so much of our religious and ethical training teaches us to be charitable and to care for our neighbor, and, of course, each of us has friends and family whom we love. So it seems antithetical to argue that people behave only according to their own self-interest.

The bulk of the problem here is a failure to make a distinction between positive and normative analysis. Whether it is good or bad for people to behave selfishly is an issue far removed from the context of this book. It requires introspection and moral guidance well beyond the capacity of economics to resolve. What the economic paradigm holds is something completely different: People behave selfishly. It is an empirical proposition devoid of moral implications, and the student is advised to treat it as such or otherwise become very lost in a philosophical quagmire. This means that it is appropriate to predict how people will behave by assuming they are selfish, *without assigning any moral sanction to that assumption.* Absolutely nothing here is meant to imply that some people are not altruistic. Instead, as an analytical tool, since we can never know, ex ante, whether people behave charitably or selfishly, the history of economic research suggests it is empirically richer to first assume that people act in their own interests, and if that approach fails, then we resort to the altruistic paradigm.[13]

---

[13] A word of caution is in order here. Economic analysis of intrafamily behavior does rely, in part, on altruism to explain conduct, but, for business purposes, the self-interest axiom seems to predict better.

POLITICIANS AND THEIR INTERESTS—ONE VIEW

The interest-group approach to politics implies that the behavior of political actors within given political institutions can be usefully analyzed by following the guideline that individual economic agents obey the postulates of self-interest generally, whether they are participating in a market or nonmarket setting. Put in so many words, politicians are not different from anyone else. They are economic agents who respond to their institutional environment in predictable ways, and their actions can be analyzed in much the same way as economists analyze the actions of participants in market processes. The important differences between a market and a political setting thus do not consist of the motivations of individual actors. The point is that there is no bifurcation of personality as between our "political" and "private" selves. We do not seek to satisfy the "public interest" when we vote and the "private interest" when we buy groceries. We seek our "self-interests" in both cases. While the story of Dr. Jekyll and Mr. Hyde may make for good cinema, it is a poor basis on which to analyze political behavior.

Robert E. McCormick and Robert D. Tollison, *Politicians, Legislation, and the Economy: An Inquiry into the Interest Group Theory of Government.* Boston: Martinus-Nijhoff Co., 1981, p. 5.

The reason for this approach is straightforward. It works better than any other method of analysis. For example, it is common to think about politicians as serving the public interest. This is contrary to the self-interest approach.

We have all seen movies in which the detective starts a murder investigation by asking the question, Who was made better off by this crime? That is the essence of the economic approach. At the beginning of each and every problem, regardless of the moral implications, the self-interest axiom is introduced. To put the problem in perspective, address for yourself each of the following queries, using the self-interest approach:

1. Why does the United States have minimum wage laws?
2. Why does Budweiser spend money to win the America's Cup?
3. Why do farmers plant wheat?
4. Why does General Motors voluntarily recall sick automobiles?
5. Why does your teacher come to class and give lectures?

APPLICATIONS OF THE FIRST LAW OF DEMAND

Hypothetical Business Problem 3.3

Your company owns a chain of grocery stores from Maine to Florida. Your company is vertically integrated into the production of some of its fruit, oranges and apples specifically. Oranges are grown in your groves in southcentral Florida. Apples are grown in your orchards in central, upstate New York. You ship apples from the New York orchards to all your stores, and similarly with the oranges. Shipping costs are substantial. After the fruit is picked, each is sorted into two grades, which for simplicity we will call high and low quality. Where do you sell the greatest volume of apples and oranges? Where do you sell the greatest volume of high-quality apples and oranges? Put differently, do you have greater shelf space devoted to high-quality apples in the store in Manhattan or the one in Palm Beach?

The first law of demand can be used in a variety of ways to solve a wide range of interesting business problems. Good managers learn to use the law of demand in settings that at first glance do not seem amenable to its application. Consider the case of quality. According to the strongest version of the first law of demand, the principle applies in all cases. Therefore, it should apply to decisions consumers make about quality. When the price of quality declines, we expect consumers to buy more of it.

In the midst of a serious financial crisis, the State of New York increased the sales tax on petroleum products by five cents effective July 1, 1991. According to the accompanying newspaper story, this tax hike has increased the cost of gasoline by about four cents, and one service station attendant claims that this will induce customers to purchase less of the high octane premium grades of gasoline, switching instead to low octane gasoline. Is this line of reasoning consistent with the first law of demand? Let's answer this question and problem 3.3 at the same time with a general theoretical approach.

Suggested Solution to Problem 3.3

Suppose each of the two grades of apples, high quality and low quality, has a price in upstate New York where they are grown. This price ratio is p_h/p_l. Further suppose there is a fixed transportation charge that does

---

GASOLINE TAXES AND THE DEMAND FOR PREMIUM GASOLINE

A new [New York] state business tax of 5 cents a gallon on petroleum products took effect Monday [July 2, 1991]. And most gas stations wasted no time passing on the increase with higher prices at the gasoline pumps. . . .

At Don's Hess station, the price of a gallon of regular unleaded rose from $1.159 to $1.199. Manager Karl Fallace blamed it on the new state tax.

"We're just passing it on," he said.

Fallace said he expects customers to switch to lower octanes from the more expensive middle and premium grades.

Miriam Schulte and Rick Moriarty, "New Tax Drives Gas Prices Up," *The Post-Standard* (Syracuse, NY), July 2, 1991, p. B–5. Emphasis added.

upstate NY
good $10
Good $5
Ratio 2:1

NY city
good $15
Good $10
Ratio 3:2

3 unopened bag
bags for 1
good bag

1.5 bad
for 1 good

NY city purchase
a lot more good apple
because cheaper

nothing to either apple except move it from upstate New York to New York City. Transportation does not make it worse; it does not make it better; it just moves it. The consumer goes to an orchard in upstate New York, and there are some nice, big, firm apples without any scratches on them. They cost $10 per bag. The orchard also sells grungy apples that may have worms. They certainly are not as pretty. Perhaps they are dirty. They cost $5 per bag. The consumer can choose one really nice bag of apples or two not-so-nice bags of apples for the same amount of money. The relative price ratio at the orchard is 2:1. Suppose the fixed charge to transport either type of apple to the Big Apple is $5 per bag. In New York City, high-quality apples cost $10 for the apples plus $5 for the shipping. The low-quality apples cost $5 for the apples plus $5 for the shipping. Now, in relative price terms, the price ratio is $15/$10 or 3:2. In upstate New York, the consumer gives up two bags of crummy apples to get one bag of good apples. In New York City, the buyer only gives up 1.5 bags of crummy apples to get one bag of good apples. Because of shipping, the choice of a bag of high-quality apples in New York City leaves *fewer* low-quality apples on the shelf than it does at the point of production. The first law of demand predicts that when price goes up, quantity demanded goes down. Therefore, since high quality is relatively cheaper in New York City, we expect two things. First, apples are more expensive in New York City due to transportation costs, so people buy fewer of them, other things being the same. But high quality is cheaper in New York City, so when people buy apples they purchase relatively more of the nice ones. Comparing two grocery stores, one in New York City and the other in Seneca (in the middle of the apple-growing region where shipping costs are quite a bit less) in similar neighborhoods, we expect to find relatively large bins of apples in Seneca because more apples are bought there (holding other things constant). However, of the apples for sale, the proportion of high-quality apples will be larger in the New York City store. This proposition, named after its originators, Armen Alchian and William Allen, is also known as "Shipping the Good Apples Out." Let's extend the analysis to the new gasoline tax in New York.

According to the accompanying newspaper story, the price of regular unleaded gasoline at Don's Hess station was $1.159 before the tax increase and $1.199 afterwards, an increase of $0.04. The story does not report the price of premium unleaded, but let's suppose that it was $1.299 before the tax hike, and it too rose $0.04 higher when the new tax was imposed. This makes the new price of premium unleaded $1.339. Compare the relative prices of regular to premium gasoline before and after the tax. Before the tax a gallon of regular cost $1.159, a gallon of premium, $1.299. The ratio was 0.892. Regular gas cost 89.2 percent as much per gallon as premium. After the tax hike, the regular to premium relative price ratio *increases* to $1.199/$1.339 or 0.895. The relative price of regular gasoline has increased a small amount, from 89.2 percent to 89.5 percent of the price of a gallon of premium. If the demand for grades of gasoline obeys the first law of demand, then there should be a small decrease in

unleaded gas before tax 1.159
after tax 1.199

premium   before 1.299
           after   1.339

Ratio $\frac{1.159}{1.299}$ = .892
before

after $\frac{1.199}{1.339}$ = .895

switch to relatively
cheaper one premium

the relative consumption of regular fuel as consumers switch to the relatively cheaper premium quality. At the same time and by the same logic, the relative price of premium fuel fell. Naturally, since the price of all grades of gasoline increased, the overall consumption of gasoline should decline, but as a proportion of total gasoline consumed, premium should be a higher share. Indeed, even though there will be a decline in the overall consumption of gasoline, there is no reason to believe that the consumption of premium gasoline could not actually increase. According to the Alchian and Allen theorem, Mr. Fallace is guilty of fallacious logic.

Consider two families. Identical twin brothers are married to identical twin sisters. The brothers work for one company, the sisters for another, and the incomes are all the same. They live next door to each other in identical houses. The only difference between them is that one couple has children and the other does not. Which family goes out for dinner more? Which family is more likely to go out to a movie? The family with young kids has to hire a baby-sitter, increasing its cost of going out. Hence, the first law of demand says the childless couple will eat out more often and will go to the movies more often. However, when the family with kids does go out, the added cost of the sitter *reduces* the relative cost of a high-quality evening. Therefore, they are more likely to visit an expensive or high-quality restaurant and less likely to visit a low-quality eatery, say the local pizza parlor. If concert tickets cost $50 each and movie tickets cost $5 each, then each concert costs the childless couple 10 visits to the movies. But for the family who hires a baby-sitter for $20 per night, the relative cost of the concert is only *four* visits to the movies. Consider the mathematics of the problem. Let p_c be the price of concert tickets and p_m the cost of a movie admission. For the childless couple, the relative price of concerts to movies is

$$p_c/p_m = 2 \cdot \$50/2 \cdot \$5 = 10.$$

On the other hand, the family with children must purchase a sitter for a fee, F, of $20. For this couple, the relative price of concerts and movies is

$$(p_c + F)/(p_m + F) = (2 \cdot \$50 + \$20)/(2 \cdot \$5 + \$20) = \$120/30 = 4.$$

For the family with the baby-sitting expense, the relative cost of the high-quality evening is considerably lower, only 4:1, than the relative cost of the same high-quality evening for the childless couple, 10:1. Put another way, the family with kids is not likely to hire a baby-sitter so the parents can go to McDonald's.

There is, then, more than one way to ship the good apples out. The apples can be shipped to the people or the people to the apples. Thus, another implication of the theorem is that when out-of-towners visit Boston, they are more likely to choose the nice, big lobsters than people of the same income, age, tastes, and preferences who live in Boston. Since visitors have borne the fixed charge of traveling to Boston, they find the relative price of high-quality goods lower than the natives.

Rochester, New York, experiences long, gray winters. It often snows more than 120 inches per year. It is cold, and the highway department uses a lot of salt on the roads to melt ice. Salt rusts automobiles. By contrast, Los Angeles and San Diego do not suffer that problem. All other things being equal, which place has nicer cars? If by high quality we mean power windows, leather interior, cruise control, and the like, then we expect a greater fraction of the cars in Rochester to have these features when compared to the cars in Southern California. In New York, rust coating or the consequences of rust impose an added charge on the purchasers of cars. Therefore, we predict that fewer people in New York will have cars, but of the cars there, a larger fraction will have convenience options, if other things such as income are accounted for.

The bottom line is simple and straightforward. Think of the most isolated places in the world: Barrow, Alaska, for example. We do not expect to find people drinking Mad Dog 22 or Thunderbird wine there or watching black-and-white television. If people there go to the expense of bringing in wine or television, they will bring in the best.

There are two islands off the coast of South Carolina just south of Charleston, Kiawah and Edisto.[14] They are very close; you can see one from the other. They are almost exactly the same in terms of the location and the quality of the water and air. Land costs quite a bit more on Kiawah than on Edisto Island; Edisto was developed long before Kiawah and Kiawah has other services and restrictions. Will lots be larger or smaller at Kiawah than at Edisto? A beach-front lot on Edisto might cost $75,000–$100,000; on Kiawah, the same lot costs about 50 percent more per square foot. The land cost is like a fixed charge. It does nothing except provide a base for a home. The *relative* price of a high-quality dwelling compared to a low-quality home is lower at Kiawah than it is at Edisto. We expect smaller lots on Kiawah but nicer homes on those lots. In fact, this is the case. The homes on Kiawah Island are very much like the ones at nearby expensive Hilton Head, while the homes at Edisto Beach are simple and modest beach houses. This is especially evident because many of the homes on Kiawah are condominiums that have virtually no land associated with them. We can also predict the inside furnishings of the homes on the two islands. Again, the higher price of land on Kiawah reduces the relative price of high quality there. Therefore, on Kiawah homes have dishwashers, carpeting, microwave ovens, air conditioning, cable TV, and so on. On Kiawah, the average home will be nicer in every dimension of quality because the land is more expensive. People do not put a $0.99 house on a $300,000 lot.[15]

---

[14] Kiawah Island was host to the 1991 Ryder Cup golf tournament.

[15] Naturally, since the islands are very close and similar, land prices are converging over time. As a consequence, the new homes being built on the few remaining lots at Edisto are more expensive than the existing dwellings. They include the conveniences—carpeting, dishwashers, air conditioning, and the like—found in nearly all the homes at nearby Kiawah.

HOUSEHOLD PRODUCTION FUNCTIONS

Hypothetical Business Problem 3.4

The role of women in society is undergoing radical change. Yet we do not see any wholesale change in the proportion of women attending college. Does that make any sense? Given the increase in female labor force participation and the increasing length of stay in the labor force by women, shouldn't an increasing fraction of females attend college?

The methodology of **household production functions** is an approach to consumer behavior that allows us to address a broad range of new problems. Consider the following: How does a consumer decide whether or not to pump his own gas or have a service station attendant do it? How does a consumer decide whether to use an automatic teller machine or to go inside the bank to the human teller? How does a person decide whether to change the oil in his own car or take the car to a filling station? How does a person make a decision whether to buy toothpaste from the 7-11, where he knows the price is going to be high but the time spent is going to be relatively low, a minute or two at most, compared to K-Mart, where the price is relatively low but it often takes as many as five minutes to check out and another five minutes to get in and out of the parking lot?

Here is the framework. Rather than analyzing the consumer's purchase of *goods*, think about people purchasing *flows of services*. Do not consider a person buying a car; think about a person acquiring transportation. Instead of analyzing a person consuming a pound of hamburger meat, envision a person enjoying a meal. In lieu of studying a person renting a videotape, consider a person being entertained at home for two-and-a-half hours. Instead of thinking about a person buying a coat, think about a person not being cold. In this framework, people do not buy shoes, they want to keep their feet dry. In sum, people do not really want a car; they often just do not want to be where they are.

Formally, the consumer's utility function is determined not by the goods, x, consumed, but rather the flow of services, z, yielded by the goods and the time, t, necessary to convert the goods into services. Each one of the z's, say z_i, is produced by a set of goods, x_i, and times, t_i. So z_i is the ith service and x_i is a vector of n goods used in the production of z_i. Also t_i is a vector of n amounts of time used in the production of z_i.

Let z_i be dessert. Most consumers have no intrinsic demand for cream, or sugar, or vanilla, or eggs, or mint, or even chocolate chips, but after a meal of flounder sauteed in garlic butter, mint chocolate chip ice cream can be truly exquisite. Hence, utility is derived not from the individual ingredients but the end product. Z is dessert, and the x's are the ingredients for ice cream—a bowl, a measuring cup, a churn, ice, salt, and an electric outlet. The t_i's are the time necessary to travel to the store and buy the ingredients, churn the ice cream, and finally, wash the dishes when finished. In addition to all this, a recipe or knowledge is required. All together these constitute the inputs to the production of dessert. Of course, instead of making your own ice cream, you can go to Baskin and Robbins or Ben and Jerry's and purchase theirs already made. Even then you go to the store, and gas, a cab, or a runner is required. In sum:

$$z_i = z_i(x_i, t_i).$$

The z_i just described is the household production function for each good i, such as ice cream. Similarly, there are production functions for each other z_i thing a person might enjoy. The exact functional form of the relation between inputs, time, and pleasure varies across people and goods. One person can make tasty ice cream quickly while another just does not seem to have the knack. And this person can change the oil filter in a flash while the first thinks oil is so greasy it could not possibly be helped by filtering.

In the household production framework, the consumer faces two budget constraints. The first is the restriction that the consumer spend no more than his income; this means that $M = \Sigma p_i x_i$. The consumer also faces a time constraint. The amount of time spent on each of the n household activities plus the amount of time spent working, t_w, must equal the total allotted time, T.[16] If the consumer works, he earns a wage of, say, w dollars per hour. Then income is the wage rate times the time spent working plus any other sources of income, such as gifts from grandmother or stock dividends. In total, the consumer has income of $w\bullet t_w + g = M$, where g is all nonwage earned sources of funds and M is total income. Wage income plus outside sources of income yield total income. The consumer buys his own time, in the opportunity cost sense, when cooking his own meals, washing his own car, or painting his own house.

For simplicity, assume fixed proportions in production. This means, for example, that each nine-inch layer cake requires three eggs. Six eggs would not yield more cake unless there were twice as much flour and all the other ingredients for a cake. When there is a link between the inputs and the outputs that does not vary as other inputs change, we say there are **fixed proportions**, and there is no trade-off between the inputs. In other words, and this is an assumption we make for analytical simplicity and not necessarily as a statement of reality, when a recipe calls for three eggs and you only have two, putting in a cup of buttermilk is not going to make it taste the same. You cannot substitute inputs and produce the same level of output. For now, we assume there is no substitutability in inputs.

Fixed proportions between inputs and outputs specify a production function for each of the z goods:

$$z_i = \alpha_i x_i \tag{3.1}$$

and

$$z_i = \beta_i t_i. \tag{3.2}$$

---

[16] Now you say, what about sleeping or sitting on the couch, activities that require time and furniture? In the household production framework, these are recreational activities producing their own z's.

α_i and β_i are the technical coefficients mapping inputs into consumable goods valued by the buyer. These parameters are determined by physical laws of nature and human capabilities. The time coefficient is partly determined by the individual's stock of human capital; the smarter or more competent the person, the higher is β_i. Since production is income directly consumed, total household income is wages earned, nonwage cash income, and household income:

$$M = w \bullet t + g. \tag{3.3}$$

Expenditures are made on goods,

$$\sum_{i=1}^{n} p_i x_i,$$

and time is spent on household production,

$$\sum_{i=1}^{n} wt_i.$$

By the conservation of energy, income equals expenditures. Therefore,

$$\sum_{i=1}^{n} p_i x_i + \sum_{i=1}^{n} wt_i = wt + g = M. \tag{3.4}$$

We can rewrite equations (3.1) and (3.2) in terms of x_i and t_i:

$$x_i = [1/\alpha_i] \bullet z_i \tag{3.1}'$$

and

$$t_i = [1/\beta_i] \bullet z_i. \tag{3.2}'$$

Let $a_i = 1/\alpha_i$ and $b_i = 1/\beta_i$. Substitution of (3.1)' and (3.2)' into (3.4) yields the so-called full-price model of consumer goods:

$$\sum_{i=1}^{n} a_i p_i z_i + \sum_{i=1}^{n} b_i w z_i = \pi_i. \tag{3.5}$$

The full price of any consumer choice, π_i, has two parts: a money price, $a_i \bullet p_i$, and a time cost, $b_i \bullet w$. The full price to any customer hinges on her particular skills, the b_i. A person with a great capacity or ability, a large stock of human capital, is technically proficient (β_i is large; therefore, $1/\beta_i = b_i$ is small), and the time cost component of price is reduced for this individual, *unless her opportunity cost of time, w, is large.* This latter prospect raises a host of interesting queries.

Intuitively, a smart person is rich, unless she is otherwise impaired by bad luck, accidents, or laziness. As a person's technical ability increases, her wage rate will often, but not always, increase as well. Therefore, as a generalization, higher-income persons can do things fast and well, but their time is valuable, and it is not possible, a priori, to determine if the time cost component of price is high or low. In special cases, results are obvious. Many college students are skilled and possess large stocks of human capital potential, but their current wage rates and the value of their time are low: For them, the term $b_i \bullet w$ is relatively low. Compared to the student with similar skills just out of school with a high-pressure, time-consuming job, their time cost is low. By this argument, college students are more likely to wash their own clothes and cars and mow their own lawns than their recently graduated counterparts. In the spirit of this discussion, would you expect to find the bulk of self-service gas stations in poor or rich neighborhoods? Put another way, do rich people pump their own gas?

Suppose a person is rich because she has a high-paying job. For her, the wage rate, w, is large. Another person has a low-paying job, so his w is low. The price of the gas is the same for both people at the pump; the money price is identically the same. The cost of time is high for a rich person, but *some* rich people are smart (technically proficient), and even though their time is valuable, they can pump gas quickly. By contrast, if the poor person has low income because he is technically incompetent, it takes him a long time to figure out how to use the gas pump, and it *can* be true that the total time cost of self-pumping is higher for the poor person than the rich one. In sum, it depends on both the technical abilities of the individual and the time cost.

Compare two people. One person is physically handicapped; the other is not. They are otherwise the same. They work at the same job; they buy their goods at the same store. They have the same wage income. Who is more likely to bake a cake? The physically handicapped person, by definition, has low technical abilities in certain dimensions. He walks slower or takes longer to get from house to car to store. This raises the time cost to him of self-service and induces him to eat out and purchase ready-made commodities, frozen pies and cakes for example. Likewise, he is more likely to have an elaborate home entertainment center and library, as going out is relatively expensive.

Automatic bank teller machines (ATMs) are a relatively recent phenomenon. In many cases, banks offer customers the choice between ATMs and personal service. Some banks even have both side-by-side in the bank. What type of person is most likely to use the ATM versus the personal teller? A business executive with a computer terminal by the desk next to a push button phone is usually well acquainted with electronic machinery, digital display, and all the peripherals. Her technical abilities with respect to using an automatic bank teller machine are high relative to those of an artist or musician who has rarely associated with electronic machinery of that type, especially not on a daily basis. The person with the technical skills to deal with those computerlike machines faces a low time cost even if her wage rate is high, when compared with that of the technically uninitiated.

Not all poor people are dumb. Not all rich people are smart. Consider a person who is rich, not because he earns high hourly wages, but because he has a large inheritance—his parents had a large bequest motive and the wherewithal to satisfy it. He has never worked or been concerned about wealth or income; it was always there in more than sufficient amounts. Suppose for such a person, the opportunity cost of time is high (because of all the consumption options) and his technical abilities are low; other things being the same, his ability to work with machinery is not very good. This rich person demands personal service, more so than his counterpart with the same income derived from wages.

As we mentioned before, most college students are young, physically capable, and accustomed to machinery and computers. Their b_i's are technically proficient in many dimensions, physically as well as mentally. They have wage potential but they do not yet draw paychecks. The college student is the epitome of a person with low time costs; her wage rates are low, but her technical abilities are high. Around a college community, you expect to find self-service gas stations, salad bars, automatic bank teller machines, and laundromats. College students repair their own cars; they serve their own meals in cafeterias; and they do more of their own banking and laundry relative to people in the same age group who do not go to college.

Using the framework of household productions, you can construct a solution to Hypothetical Business Problem 3.4. Recall that problem from the beginning of this section, and consider the following analysis.

Suggested Solution to Problem 3.4

According to the human capital model of consumer choice, the full price of a commodity is

$$\sum_{i=1}^{n} a_i p_i z_i + \sum_{i=1}^{n} b_i w z_i = \pi_i.$$

The full price has two components, the money price and the time price. Now consider the two parts of the time price. The first term is the technical proficiency and the second term is the wage rate. The accumulation of human capital via a college education can affect either or both of these terms. For instance, when women were working primarily in the home, they were concentrating their studies on improving their technical proficiency for home production. That is, they were learning the skills necessary to raise and educate children. Learning literature, art, science, and math skills makes it easier and cheaper to raise children properly. In those days, the males worked in the market and the females worked in the home. Husbands wanted intelligent wives as companions and as managers of their households. College was one way for women to develop the requisite skills for household production within the home.

Today, more women are going outside the home to market their human capital. In this environment, they too need to go to college, but now for a different reason. The purpose of college now is to acquire human capital in order to garner high wages in the outside labor market. A college education can also improve wage-earning skills, the second component of the time price term. If this argument is correct, women today are

---

THE INVESTMENT IN HUMAN CAPITAL

"[S]ome people think it's mandatory to get their sons educated and their daughters can take what's left, but I'm the opposite. A boy can work his way through school if he really wants to. I don't care if a one of my girls never draws a paycheck; I'm going to see that they all finish college. *If a woman is educated, she's a better wife, a better mother, and she's going to raise better children. Every woman who gets educated . . . is an investment in the future.*"

Ferrol Sams, *The Whisper of the River.* New York: Penguin Books, 1984, p. 474. Emphasis added.

---

majoring in subjects different from those their mothers and grand-mothers studied, for they are now selling their human capital skills in the marketplace rather than using their human capital for household production.

Thus, the number of women attending college has not grown drastically as women increasingly enter the work force because the demand for human capital is not different now from what it used to be. Women have always demanded human capital, and hence, they have always demanded college. Now they demand a different type of education, but not more of it. In the accompanying quotation from *The Whisper of the River,* a father passes to his son his 1940s vision of the role that education played for most women in that period—that is, those who were not planning to enter the labor market, but instead were preparing themselves for household production. Whether it be to prepare for market or home production, human capital is valuable.

LABOR SUPPLY: THE DEMAND FOR LEISURE AND INCOME

People work different amounts, and the response to a wage change is not uniform across laborers. To understand the differences, start with the presumption that work is not fun. Why then do people work? Employment provides income that is convertible to housing, clothing, food, and recreation. These are pleasing; people work so they can play and enjoy life. This suggests a simple trade-off: leisure for income. The longer and harder a person works, the less free time she has, but the more income.

The 24 hours in a day are divisible into labor hours, L, or leisure time, P:

$$L + P = 24.$$

Leisure yields utility; labor provides income at the wage rate of w dollars per hour. The workaholic could conceptually spend all 24 hours earning money (at least for a day or so) for a total income of $24 \cdot w$ dollars and no leisure time. At the other extreme, all play and no work provides zero monetary income and 24 hours of leisure. These two end point combinations are plotted in Figure 3.7. Connecting

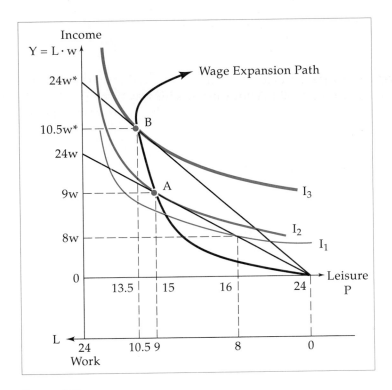

FIGURE 3.7
Labor-Leisure Decisions

them constructs the opportunity set facing the worker. He can choose any combination along the line, selecting the appropriate amount of leisure or work.

Each combination of leisure and income has its reward: utility, $U = U(Y,P)$, where $Y = L•w$. Suppose our hypothetical employee, call her Hannah, works 8 hours per day, she earns $8•w$ dollars, and she has 16 hours for pleasure, household chores, and the like. From this combination, she derives utility $U(8•w, 16)$, which puts her on indifference curve I_1 in the figure.

As drawn, this combination is not utility maximizing. Optimally, Hannah works 9 hours and takes the remaining 15 hours as leisure, point A in the figure. Consumer optimality requires that the marginal rate of substitution of leisure for income equal the opportunity cost of leisure, the wage rate. Each hour playing costs w dollars in lost income. Point A in the figure satisfies the condition.

The Impact of Wage Changes on the Supply of Labor

Hypothetical Business Problem 3.5

You manage a pizza parlor in a college community. Several local students are employed part-time for home delivery. The store usually closes at 12 A.M., but during peak periods, final exam week and the like, the store is kept open until 2 A.M. for extra business. Normally, the delivery drivers

paid $4/hr
peak time $6/hr

are paid $4 per hour. During peak periods, the part-time workers are offered the opportunity to work extra hours at time-and-a-half wages. Consider two of the employees. The first receives $100 per month allowance from home. The second gets none. Which employee is more likely to volunteer for overtime delivery work?

How do employees react to a wage increase? Analysis of labor's response to a wage change is a straightforward application of utility theory remarkably similar to the consumer's reaction to a price shift; there are income and substitution effects. When wages increase, leisure becomes more expensive. Each hour not working costs more in lost income. For this reason, employees are inclined to work more. However, higher wages make laborers richer, *even if they do not work any more hours*. If leisure is a normal good, which it typically is, richer workers will demand more free time. On this count, less labor is supplied at higher wage rates. Thus, the overall impact of the wage change turns on the relative magnitudes of the substitution and income effects.

Figure 3.7 also depicts the choice, the one after wages have risen. The new opportunity set is plotted with an increased wage, w^*. The set expands; it is now possible to earn as much as $24 \cdot w^*$ dollars income by working the entire day. Utility maximization requires a tangency between the new budget constraint and an indifference curve, I_3, point B in the figure. At the higher wage, Hannah works an extra 1.5 hours per day for a total of 10.5 hours. Her income is $10.5 \cdot w^*$, and she has 13.5 hours for leisure. For Hannah, the substitution effect of higher wages dominates the income effect, and she works more at higher wages.

A wage expansion path is drawn in the figure. This locus traces all tangencies between indifference curves and the opportunity set as the wage rate increases, and it forecasts the worker's response to changing wages. Although the path can take any shape, as a general rule the slope is positive but increasing. At high incomes, there is a tendency for the curve to bend back. Here the income effect of wage increases begins to dominate the substitution effect. In this region, workers are sufficiently rich that further wage increases encourage large shifts into leisure. The empirical validity of the backward bending supply of labor hinges on the income elasticity of demand for leisure. As the elasticity becomes greater, the chances increase that future wage increases will lead the worker to supply less labor. People who demand larger quantities of leisure as their incomes grow will have a more inelastic supply of labor.

The Impact of Nonwage Income on the Supply of Labor

Consider now the person who has supplementary nonwage income. Parents often subsidize their children. Many people have investments yielding substantial income. Others receive royalties from previous work. Many others still in the work force have retired from previous jobs and draw Social Security or retirement pay. How do these people respond to a wage change? If the income elasticity of demand for leisure gets larger as income grows, the worker with nonwage income experiences a greater income effect due to a wage increase than a similar worker with no nonwage income. Even if the substitution effect of the wage change is comparable between the two people, the richer person's demand for leisure increases more than the relatively poorer worker. Other things being the same, the employee with nonwage income is more likely to refuse the opportunity to work overtime. Managerially, this means that wages may not be the most effective way to motivate employees with substantial income outside the job.[17]

Eight-Hour Work Days

Many people are faced with the constraint that they must either work eight hours per day five days per week or not at all. When these people experience a wage change, strange things can happen. Examine Figure 3.8. The vertical line at 16 hours leisure is the mandated eight-hour work day. Our representative worker, call him Tyrone, must work eight hours, although if unconstrained, he would chose to work only seven hours per day. The restriction forces Tyrone to have more income, $8 \cdot w$, than he would prefer and less leisure. Even if the wage were raised to w^*, Tyrone has no interest in working more hours. Here the supply of labor is not responsive to the wage because of the constraint imposed by the eight-hour per day rule.

By contrast, some people like to work more than eight hours per day. Faced with an obligatory eight hours work, they can suffer the consequences or moonlight. How do these people respond to a wage change? The wage increase can

FIGURE 3.8
The Eight-Hour Work Day

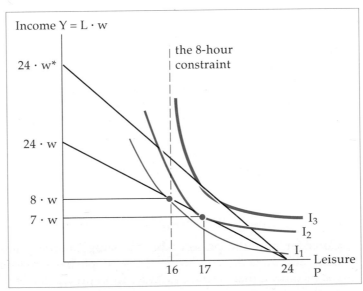

---

[17] The analysis of this section puts you in position to answer Hypothetical Business Problem 3.5. Can you see how the two problems fit together?

reduce their desire to work a second job. In fact, if the wage increase is sufficiently high, it can lead them to abandon extra jobs. See Figure 3.9. At the original wage rate w dollars, our person prefers to work 12 hours per day. Therefore, he gets a part-time job after his regular eight-hour day job. However, when the wage rises to w^*, his demand for leisure has increased, and he now wants to work eight hours per day; he quits moonlighting. Naturally, if the income effect of the wage increase is less dramatic, the employee might desire to work more hours.

INTERTEMPORAL DECISIONS

Consumption does not take place instantaneously. The purchase of a car, a house, or an appliance yields benefits for years. Vacations are usually taken only once or twice per year even though they are valuable year-round. Commodities like these are **intertemporally substitutable**. Most people do not care whether they go to Jamaica the second week in January or the third week in February, just as long as they get to go sometime in the middle of winter.

Analysis of consumer decisions across time requires an understanding of interest rates and discounting, concepts covered in detail in Chapter 5. Suffice to say, in most cases, a bird in the hand is worth two in the bush; consumption today yields higher utility than postponed consumption. People sacrifice consumption only if there are positive rewards. Interest on savings is one inducement. Saving today (not consuming) pays interest, allowing expanded consumption opportunities in the future. Imagine the consumer has a preference ranking, a utility function, over consumption today, C_c, and consumption in the next period, C_t:

FIGURE 3.9
Moonlighting

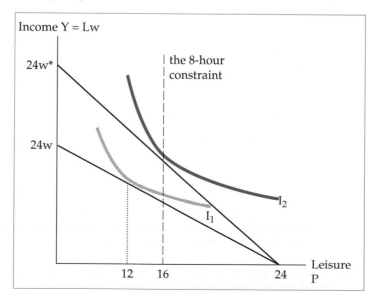

$$U = U(C_c, C_t).$$

[handwritten: today Next period]

Current income is M. Investment yields r percent per dollar invested. Therefore, the consumer could spend M dollars today, $(1+r) \cdot M$ dollars tomorrow, or any combination in between.[18] Optimal intertemporal allocation of the budget requires that the marginal rate of substitution between current and future consumption equal one plus the interest rate:

$$(\partial U/\partial C_c)/(\partial U/\partial C_t) = 1 + r.$$

[handwritten: Interest rate → Opportunity cost of consuming today]

The left-hand side of the expression is called the **personal discount rate**. The right-hand side is the opportunity cost of consuming today. Utility maximization means the consumer adjusts consumption across time until the personal discount rate equals the rate of return on investment opportunities. An increase in the market rate of return, r, makes the consumer forgo current consumption; its price has increased, in favor of future consumption. Adjusting future consumption for the rate of interest is called **discounting**.[19]

Consider an example. You attend a company-sponsored luncheon or a cocktail party at the home of a friend of a friend, or win two tickets to dinner at a restaurant offering all you can eat. In each case, a meal or drinks are offered to you at no personal expense, not even indirectly. Compare consumption under this limited circumstance with your behavior were you required to pay. You are inclined to say you would eat and drink more in the first scenario, because the items are free. But just how much more will you consume? Intuition suggests you consume until the marginal utility of continued consumption is zero, but that may not be correct. Intertemporal equilibrium requires that the discounted (interest rate adjusted) utility of consumption be equal for all time periods. If you stopped consuming when the marginal utility was zero, then intertemporal equilibrium is not established because consumption tomorrow or next week is not free. Therefore, for the food and drink you buy and consume in the future, the marginal utility is *not zero*, $\partial U/\partial C_t > 0$. How then does the consumer behave? The marginal utility of current consumption *per dollar spent* must be positive, and the only way that is possible is for the value of consumption to be *negative*. You get a hangover, overeating and drinking to the point where the *pain* from overindulgence equals the price (discounted to today) the *same* meal would cost you tomorrow. When the anticipated gastric distress and the hangover costs make up for the absence of a tariff, the consumer has properly allocated the budget across time. Even hangovers follow rational economic analysis. In other words, when offered a free meal, the consumer indulges to the point where the overconsumption pain equals the normal cost of the meal.

---

[18] For the moment, exclude the possibility of borrowing, which would allow current consumption to exceed M. It needlessly complicates the analysis.

[19] This brief analysis does little justice to the important topics of discounting and intertemporal substitution. However, the bulk of Chapter 5 is devoted to these and related topics.

THE SECOND LAW OF DEMAND

The **second law of demand** addresses changes in the price elasticity of demand. In certain circumstances, individuals respond very rapidly to price movements—for example, on the floor of the Chicago Board of Trade or the New York Stock Exchange. For several reasons, a typical consumer's response to a price change is generally not so swift. Information is not free, nor is it distributed simultaneously to all consumers. Second, some people have precommitted or prepaid consumption plans. Third, the characteristics of some durable consumer goods cannot be altered cheaply; in the short term, it is difficult to adjust the fuel consumption of a large, gas-guzzling car. However, over time, higher gas prices induce car buyers to shift toward smaller, more fuel efficient means of transportation.

The second law of demand says the longer the consumer has to adjust to a price change, the more elastic the response will be; demand curves become flatter (more elastic) the more persistent is a price change. Longer time periods allow for multidimensional consumer adjustments in behavior. Suppose compact disk players fell in price by 25 percent. Some people who already own a player and many disks might immediately buy a second player for their party room. Others, learning of the price decline, might visit a friend's home to listen and learn the mechanics of compact disks; then after a week or two of contemplation, they make a purchase. Finally, when compact disks have become ubiquitous, some music fans dedicated to records discover they must purchase a CD player because some new music is only available on the new medium. The response to the price fall in the first week was a small increase in quantity demanded. However, over the first two months, the increase in purchases was considerably more substantial, and the jump in purchases over a year was even greater. This is the second law of demand.

CONSUMER'S SURPLUS

The concept of **consumer's surplus** was introduced earlier in the context of the consumer's response to a price change. The principle is sufficiently important that we expand the discussion here. Consumer's surplus is the extra utility a buyer gets from a product, net of the purchase price. Often, people purchase a good, say a dress or a suit, and the price they must pay is lower than the amount they were prepared to pay. This excess is consumer's surplus. It is the demand price for a good minus its purchase price. Equivalently, it is the lump sum amount a consumer would be willing to pay in order to be able to buy some good at a lower price. Reconsider Figure 3.5 on page 127. Originally, the price of x_1 is p_1, the consumer has income of $\$M$, and the price of the second good, x_2, is p_2. The buyer chooses x_1^0 of the first good. How much better off would this person be if the price of x_1 fell from p_1 to p_1'? The increase in utility the consumer gets from the price reduction is I_1 to I_2, *which the buyer could get without the price falling, if she had $\$M'$ income instead of $\$M$.* In other words, this person's wealth increases by the amount $\$M' - \$M$ when the price of x_1 falls to p_1'. Originally, the consumer chooses point A in Figure 3.5 and achieves a utility level denoted by indifference curve I_1. When the price of x_1 falls, the consumer shifts to point C and gets a higher level of utility,

I_2. The amount of money necessary to get to the new, higher level of utility *at the old prices* is \$$M'$. \$$M'$ is found by shifting the old budget constraint out until it is just tangent to the new indifference curve, at point B. The new x_2 axis intercept yields the increase in income necessary to provide the extra utility without changing prices. Hence, \$$M' - $$M$ is the extra utility or *consumer's surplus* associated with the price decline from p_1 to p'_1. The dollar magnitude of consumer's surplus measured this way is the amount the buyer would be willing to pay for the price to be lower.

Theoretically, this is only one measure of consumer's surplus. An alternative, equally appropriate way to measure consumer's surplus is uncovered by asking the question, Given the new low price, how much wealthier is the consumer at the new lower price? That is, what is the amount the consumer would be willing to pay once at point C in Figure 3.5 to avoid a price increase from p'_1 back to p_1? As a general proposition, the dollar amount the consumer would be willing to pay here, to avoid a return to the original price, does not have to be equal to the first measure. The first technique captures the increased welfare of a lower price from a starting point of a high price. The second approach measures the increased welfare of the lower price, *assuming that we have it to begin with.*

Suppose we begin the exercise at point C in Figure 3.5, and we propose a price *increase* from p'_1 back to the original price, p_1. This *reduces* consumer utility from I_2 to I_1. How much would this person pay to avoid the price increase? At price p'_1, if the consumer had a certain amount less income, the utility level achieved would be the same as the one caused by a price decline from p_1 to p'_1. If we shift the budget constraint at point C back in parallel until it is tangent with the indifference curve I_1, we can determine the amount that the consumer would be willing to pay to avoid the price increase from p'_1 to p_1.[20] Without making some restrictive assumption about the shape of the consumer's indifference map, there is no reason at all for the two income shifts to be equal.[21] Why are the two measures of consumer's surplus not necessarily equal? In the first case, when the price is high, the consumer has less real income than in the second situation when the price of x_1 is lower at p'_1. It is this change in real income that creates the potential disparity between the two measures of consumer's surplus. When prices fall, consumers are effectively richer, and given the presence of income effects, this can alter their valuations and demands for goods.

We are left with the general principle: There is no unique way to measure consumer's surplus. However, we have one salvation: Most managerial problems

---

[20] See E. J. Mishan, *Cost-Benefit Analysis* (New York: Praeger, 1976), for a much more detailed discussion. Additional discussion is provided by Arnold C. Harberger, "Three Basic Postulates for Applied Welfare Economics: An Interpretive Essay," *Journal of Economic Literature*, 9(3), September 1971, 785–97.

[21] For the two measures of consumer's surplus to be equal, the slopes of the indifference curves must be constant along a ray drawn from the origin. Economists call this condition **homotheticity,** but it is not vital for managerial purposes, unless you have some reason to suspect your buyers have this characteristic, an unlikely prospect. In-depth knowledge of consumer indifference curves typically requires enormous investment in experimentation far past its value to managers.

are properly solved employing the first measurement technique. Before we demonstrate why this is true, we consider one special class of problems in which multiple measures of consumer's surplus present the greatest dilemmas.

Consider the following problem often encountered by analysts trying to estimate the value of some public project, say a new bridge or an impounded lake. To determine the worthiness of the venture, the costs and the benefits must be calculated. One way to assess the benefits of a new bridge is to compute the amount people would be willing to pay to have the bridge built. Another way to address the problem is to estimate how much people would pay not to have an existing bridge removed. There is no particular theoretical reason to prefer one measure over the other, and different cost-benefit analysts need not realize the same estimate of the worthiness of any particular project.

Most private business managers do not face this, for usually the only relevant question is, What will the buyer pay for this good? The issue of how much will they pay not to take it away rarely comes up. Of course, any victim of extortion, blackmail, or mugging has encountered the latter problem, but let us leave that aside. Just suppose you, as a manager, could magically know how much each customer would be willing to pay to face a lower price for each quantity of every good you sell. You would then be able to charge the buyer these amounts, effectively extracting all the consumer's surplus. Alternatively, without some of this information, you set prices too low and customers retain some residual utility (and willingness to pay), or at the other extreme, when prices are too high, your customers do not buy from you at all. In many pricing situations, it is very important for the manager to have an accurate measure of consumer's surplus. Otherwise, profits suffer. As a practical matter, notwithstanding the theoretical problem previously discussed, since the private firm is *selling* additional quantities, not removing them, the appropriate estimate of consumer's surplus is the area below the ordinary demand curve above price. Why is this true? As a general problem, managers are only concerned with the following question: What will my customers do if I raise (lower) prices? The correct answer is given by the ordinary demand curve, the one drawn holding consumer income constant. In the simplest terms, the ordinary demand curve depicts actual consumer response to changing prices. For the vast majority of managerial purposes, that is sufficient, but occasionally problems present themselves in which alternative measures of consumer's surplus must be considered. The point is only raised here to alert the student to the problem.

A NOTE ON CONSUMER TASTES

As we close this chapter, one additional point is worthy of mention. There is a notable lack of discussion here on the importance of consumer tastes and preferences. This is not an oversight. Economists generally eschew analysis of tastes for one simple reason: They are not measurable. To be sure, we can observe the trappings of tastes—for example, the colors you actually choose to wear—but these are not your tastes per se. Instead, the color or style choice is influenced by price and income. The current state of our knowledge of cell physiology does not allow us to measure tastes. Since we cannot know when tastes have changed, economists are inclined to avoid explanations of behavior based on speculation. This does not mean that tastes and preferences are not important, or that they do not change, only that theories based on unquantifiable conjectures are not refutable. Basically, economics as a science treats tastes the same way it does a lot of other interesting problems—it leaves them for other disciplines. This is not to say that economists totally ignore tastes. In empirical models of demand, the technique of dummy variables can be used to account for seasonal variations in consumption. This methodology is explored in Chapter 4.

TOPICS TO REVIEW

These are topics that you should feel comfortable with before you leave this chapter. If you cannot write out a clear and concise sentence or paragraph explaining the topic after you have worked on the study problems, you should reread the relevant section of the text.

Insatiability, Rationality, and Transitivity

Utility Function

Cardinal Utility and Ordinal Utility

Conditions for Consumer Utility Maximization

Budget Constraint and Choice Set

Marginal Rate of Substitution

Iso-Utility Lines and Indifference Curves

Income and Substitution Effects

First Law of Demand

Consumer's Surplus

Opportunity Cost

Self-Interested Individual

Alchian and Allen Theorem

Household Production Functions

Human Capital

Full Price and Time Price

Supply of Labor as an Exercise in Labor–Leisure Exchange

Personal Discount Rate

Second Law of Demand

STUDY PROBLEMS

Consider each of the following queries or statements. Ensure that your answer offers an explanation of the circumstances, not just a restatement of the question. Be analytical.

1. Comment on the following: The U.S. Congress has forced the states to raise the drinking age to 21 under threat of losing highway funding. It is expected

that this change will have little or no impact on the number of people drinking and the amount of alcohol consumed. Those who want to drink will find a way regardless of the law. Anyway, fake IDs are easy to come by.

2. In England, among other countries, there are public programs for drug addicts. For example, heroin users who declare themselves addicts receive treatment in government centers and are given methadone, a heroin substitute. Other things being the same, does England have a smaller, equal, or larger fraction of its population addicted to heroin than it would without this law?

3. Massachusetts has engaged in something called tax amnesty. Previous tax evaders can declare themselves and simply pay the tax on the correct income with no penalty or threat of jail. (Public libraries sometimes do the same thing for overdue books.) Compare the effective tax rates, the tax collected per dollar of tax levied in states such as Massachusetts with states that have never engaged in tax amnesty programs.

4. Clemson University currently does not charge for the right to park on campus. However, there are plans to implement a fee system for the coming school year. In 1989 the school collected about $301,000 in fines for illegal parking. What do you predict will happen to *parking fine revenue* at Clemson after the parking fee system is installed?

5. Stanford University is a large, high-quality, private university south of San Francisco. Tuition is high, in the neighborhood of $20,000 per year, and the student body is high caliber. The school prides itself on the diversity of student background. Other things being the same, a student from far away, say Vermont, has an easier time entering Stanford than a student from California. But, *adjusting for SAT scores and other background factors,* who has the higher starting salary upon graduation, the average student from California or the average student from far away?

6. Empirical studies strongly suggest that corn and wheat are substitutes in consumption. Suppose that a virus attacks the wheat harvest in the midwestern United States. What will happen to
    a. the demand and supply of wheat
    b. the demand and supply of corn
    c. the market price and quantity of wheat
    d. the market price and quantity of corn

7. Most college football teams run the ball slightly more often than they pass. But suppose there was a meeting of two teams, one that ran the ball 75 percent of the time and one that passed the ball 60 percent of the time. The first team runs the ball more than the average team, and the second runs it less than the average team. What are these two teams inclined to do in inclement weather? Will they run or pass more than usual? On fourth down and short yardage situations, which team is more likely to punt or try a field goal or try to make a first down? (Hint: Suppose inclement weather negatively affects both running and passing.)

8. Ranzino currently consumes (on average) one case of beer per month. The

average price she pays is $15 per case. Consider two scenarios. In the first, the price of beer falls to $12 per case. In the second, Ranzino's godparents give her $36 per year [$3•(1 case per month)•(12 months)]. In which case does her consumption of beer increase more?

9. Each fall, the government changes the time from daylight savings to standard. According to the radio, television, and newspapers, this allows us to sleep an extra hour to catch up for the hour we lost in the spring. Characterize the kind of person who spends the extra hour sleeping.

10. The price elasticity of demand for cars is relatively elastic. Does this mean that cars are a superior good? According to car salespeople, small changes in the interest rate have a big impact on the demand for autos. Does this mean that cars are a superior good?

11. Forget for a moment that personal computers can be used to play games. That is, assume that PCs are used only for production, problem solving, record keeping, word processing, and the like. What type person buys and uses a PC at home? We imagine that rich people like to have accountants do these things for them, so we expect that relatively poor people are the ones who buy PCs, right? Are married people or single people more likely to have a PC?

12. When some people go out to eat, they spend a lot of time in the restaurant. They ponder the menu and converse a great deal. By contrast, others are in a hurry. They seldom order drinks or appetizers, and they do not talk a lot. Can you explain this phenomenon? That is, are there characteristics of each class of people that, on average, allow you to predict whether a particular person will spend a little or a lot of time in a restaurant?

13. What type person is more likely to have a fine wine cellar: the rich retired person or the comparably rich, but hard-working, no–free-time yuppie? (Be cautious—look before you leap here.)

14. Casual empiricism suggests that satellite television dishes are more prominent in rural areas than they are in urban sections. Presuming that is true, why is it so? Second, further casual research suggests that more dishes are seen outside mobile homes than brick houses. Can you explain this?

15. In 1979, 66 percent of all applicants to medical school were admitted, but 75 percent of the sons and daughters of physicians who applied were admitted (the difference is statistically significant at any reasonable level). Is this evidence of some form of discrimination or collusion on the part of doctors? Is there any reason to think that children of doctors might be better prepared for medical school?

16. Some states have laws requiring child restraint seats for youngsters under a certain age (usually four years or less). First, how do you think accident rates per mile driven compare across states with and without this law, holding other things the same. Second, analyze what would happen to the number of accidents per mile driven in a state after it passed such a law. Be specific. Will people who did not use the child restraint seats before the law was enacted drive slower or faster now that they must use the seats? Will there be a long-run change in the type of cars used to transport children?

17. You are the manager at a company employing a number of people. Each employee is required by the firm to work five days a week, eight hours per day. The hourly pay is $7. Some employees would prefer to work just six hours per day at this wage, but they have no choice, and under the circumstances they prefer eight hours work to none at all. For other employees, an eight-hour day is the exact shift they would like to work at $7 per hour. Your state has a policy that allows disgruntled employees to quit work and draw unemployment compensation of $150 per week for six weeks while they seek alternative employment. If the state raises unemployment compensation to $175 per week, will a greater fraction of the first group of employees quit, or the second, *ceteris paribus*?

18. Many business schools offer two interchangeable MBA programs. There is the regular or daytime curriculum and the night (or part-time) program for working students. Tuition and fees are the same and students are not restricted in the classes they may take. Degree requirements are the same. Can you analyze which group has higher grades and starting salaries upon completion, the day or night students?

19. The price elasticity of demand for gasoline was estimated using three different sets of data:

    a. The price of gasoline cycles in four-week intervals during gasoline price wars from $1.00 to $1.20.
    b. The price of gasoline varies across cities from $1.00 to $1.20 due to differential gasoline taxes.
    c. The price of gasoline increases from $1.00 to $1.20 due to foreign supply interruptions.

    Do you expect the elasticity estimates to differ? If so, rank them according to which is the most elastic.

20. Christmas, "tis the season to be jolly," or so the saying goes. But from an economics point of view, Christmas makes little sense. People often buy things for other people that, by definition, the other people do not want. If they wanted them, they would already have purchased them. Put another way, people buy gifts for their friends and relations that they know will be valued *less* than the full price of the gift. In spite of this, Christmas survives as an institution. Therefore, it must offer something. Can you construct a *refutable* economic explanation of gift giving that rescues Christmas from the grinches?

21. Suppose the first-class fare from St. Louis to Tokyo is $4269 (round trip), while regular coach costs $2180, a 49 percent premium. A first-class ticket from St. Louis to Minneapolis costs $734 (round trip), and the regular coach fare is $490, a 33 percent surcharge. For the sake of analysis, assume passengers on the two flights are more or less the same. On which flight do you expect a greater portion of the passengers to fly first class?

22. Consider two consumers, exactly the same except one owns a car and makes house payments taking approximately 50 percent of his income. The other owns no car, lives with his parents, and pays no rent. Compare the average

own price elasticity of demand for other goods, such as soap, theater tickets, and clothes, across the two persons.

23. Consider two families. One has purchased a two-week vacation in the Virgin Islands. The other has won a similar but *free* two-week vacation to the Virgin Islands that provides air transportation and hotel accommodations only. The families are comparable in age and income. Describe and compare the spending patterns of the two families on vacation. Specifically,

   a. Who spends more money on meals, entertainment, night-life, and recreation, or do they spend the same amounts?
   b. Who takes more luggage?
   c. Who leaves larger tips?
   d. Who spends more money on souvenirs?

24. Prior to 1988, the National Basketball Association used two referees in each game to monitor violations of the rules such as walking, double dribbling, out of bounds, and personal fouls. However, for the 1988–1989 season, a third official was added to each game to monitor these same rules. The three officials all work in concert.

   a. Do you expect the number of fouls called per game to be higher, lower, or the same as in the previous years now that there is a third referee?
   b. What do you predict happened to the average points scored in NBA games after the addition of the third referee?

25. Say the current price of gasoline is $0.90 per gallon. The demand elasticity is -0.8, and the supply elasticity is approximately 0.75. Current consumption is 45 million gallons per day. Suppose OPEC successfully raises the price to $1.10 per gallon. What will happen to daily consumption of gasoline?

26. Assume that all college students have the same tastes for work, leisure, and consumption. Some students pursue advanced degrees; some do not. Compare and contrast the behavior of three types of people: those who do not go on for advanced degrees; those who go on at their own expense; and those who go on but receive a scholarship.

27. The price elasticity of demand for beer is more than one in absolute value; it is elastic. Suppose that beer and wine are substitutes in consumption; further imagine that beer and peanuts are complements in consumption. If the price of beer increases by 10 percent, but the prices of peanuts and wine are not affected, can you determine whether the consumption of peanuts or wine will change more?

28. North Carolina raised its gasoline road use tax from $0.15 to $0.20 per gallon effective August 1, 1989, making it the second highest in the country. (The federal road use tax adds an additional $0.10 per gallon to the cost in every state.)

   a. Predict what happened to the average price of gasoline in North Carolina on August 1, 1989.
   b. Compare the change in consumption of regular unleaded gas to the change in consumption of premium unleaded after the tax change.

   c. Predict what will happen to the sales of gasoline in North Carolina during August 1989 compared to sales in August 1988.

   d. Compare gasoline consumption in North Carolina in December 1989 to consumption of December 1988, and then compare the December 1988–1989 adjustment to the August 1988–1989 adaptation to the price change.

29. Seattle, Washington, may be a great place but it certainly is not a sunny place to live. It is cloudy and rainy perhaps as much as any American city. So let's talk about wardrobes. Do residents of Seattle have more extensive rain gear than residents of Los Angeles, or Houston, or Denver, towns with a lot less rainfall? Can you speak about the quality of rain gear in Seattle compared to the other towns? Put succinctly, who spends more on the average raincoat or umbrella, a resident of Seattle or someone who lives in Los Angeles?

30. The federal government issues food stamps that can be used to buy certain types of food, excluding particular items such as cigarettes. Do people using these stamps have a different elasticity of demand for food items than people using money? Put another way, do stores serving a large number of food stamp recipients have the same number, fewer, or more promotional sales than grocery stores serving customers who primarily use cash?

31. Zoos, art museums, community theaters, and the like sometimes have memberships. These memberships allow the patron to visit the facility as many times as she would like at a reduced cost, sometimes for nothing. Suppose the average visitor to one of these places goes 10 times per year. Now imagine that the zoo alters its pricing plan. Instead of issuing a membership card that allows free admission, it sends members 10 tickets good for free entry. The tickets are not numbered or pictured and thus can be transferred from the patron to any other person. What will happen to the number of memberships to the zoo?

32. Most word-processing programs today, such as WordPerfect, Word, and others, have built-in spell checkers. Most of these have to be executed. That is, the computer does not beep when the typist has misspelled a word. Instead, the operator presses a key stroke sequence to make the program check the document for spelling errors. Compare the average document typed today using one of these modern word processors with similar documents typed 15 years ago on a typewriter. Which one will have more grammatical, as distinct from spelling, errors?

33. The price of personal computers has fallen dramatically over the past 10 years. You can now buy for less than $500 what used to cost $4000. As I am sure you know, PCs come with color or monochrome displays. Color cards and monitors add about $300 to $400 to the cost of a system. Do you expect that more or fewer of these low-end computers that now sell for about $500 have monochrome or color monitors than the *same* systems used to have back when they cost about $4000? Put another way, is the typical low-end system now sold with a greater or lesser proportion of color monitors compared to five years ago?

34. Read the accompanying story about running and road races during the 1991 economic recession. During a recession, per capita income decreases. Read

the story as if the author had used the words "lower income" each time he writes "recession." Which of the points in the story make the most economic sense? Are there flaws in the recommendations? Are the recommendations consistent?

35. Clemson University charges undergraduate students by the semester, not the course. The current tuition per semester for an in-state student is about $1200 per semester. The average student takes about 15 credit hours per semester for an implicit charge of $1200/15 = $80 per credit hour. Suppose the university changed its method of charging tuition from the semester technique to the credit hour method, and charged each student $80 per hour instead of $1200 per semester. The average Clemson student now takes about 4.5 years to graduate. What would happen to the average length of time to graduation if Clemson switched pricing methods?

SUGGESTED READINGS

Alchian, Armen and Allen, William. *Exchange and Production: Competition, Coordination, and Control,* 3rd ed. Belmont, CA: Wadsworth, 1983.

Battalio, Raymond C., Kagel, John H., and Reynolds, Morgan O. "Income Distributions in Two Experimental Economies." *Journal of Political Economy* 77 (December 1977): 1259–71.

RUNNING IN A RECESSION

What effect, if any, will a recession in the U.S. economy have on road racing? . . .

As one who makes a living from road races, biathlons, and triathlons, I think that recession will bring the following changes in 1991:

1. I do not expect the number of runners to decline; in general, running is an inexpensive sport and may even become more popular in a recession.

2. Some events, faced with reduced sponsorship dollars, may seek to cut budgets. One of the easiest items to trim is the size of the purse. Reducing a purse affects the least number of runners in a race; and while it may cause an event to lose some of its luster, most races will not suffer a loss of entries. Few of those "back in the pack" know, or even care, who wins a road race or how much they win.

3. Other events will increase entry fees, especially the late fee. This would be the most palatable way of charging runners more. The only ones penalized would be those who enter after the cut-off.

4. While the number of people running might increase, the average number of races that each of those runners enters may decrease. Higher entry fees, higher costs of fuel for traveling to races, and higher unemployment could limit the number of events a runner would enter in a year.

Jim Young, "Running in a Recession," *Running Journal,* January 1991, p. 1.

Becker, Gary. *Economic Theory*, pp. 45–59. New York: Alfred Knopf, 1971.

Borcherding, Thomas E. and Silberberg, Eugene. "Shipping the Good Apples Out: The Alchian and Allen Theorem Reconsidered." *Journal of Political Economy* 86 (February 1978):131–38.

Friedman, Milton. "The Methodology of Positive Economics." In *Essays in Positive Economics*, pp. 3–45. Chicago: University of Chicago Press, 1935.

Kagel, John H., Battalio, Raymond, and Miles, C. G. "Marihuana and Work Performance: Results from an Experiment." *Journal of Human Resources* 15(3) (Summer 1980):373–95.

Lancaster, Kelvin. *Consumer Demand: A New Approach.* New York and London: Columbia University Press, 1971.

Stigler, George J. and Becker, Gary S. "De Gustubus Non Est Disputandum." *American Economic Review* 67(2) (March 1977):76–90.

Umbeck, John R. "Shipping the Good Apples Out: Some Ambiguities in the Interpretation of 'Fixed Charge.'" *Journal of Political Economy* 88 (February 1980):199–208.

SUGGESTED SOLUTIONS TO SELECTED STUDY PROBLEMS

The following are only *suggested* solutions to the study problems presented at the end of this chapter. In all cases, the suggestions here put heavy emphasis on analysis rather than a single correct answer. Since most managerial problems do not fall into neat little boxes, the individual characteristics of the problems that you encounter on the job will typically mandate a solution using the principles developed here and in other courses. Memorizing these solutions will not make you a good manager; learning the *principles* detailed here will help make you a better manager.

1. According to the first law of demand, higher prices reduce consumption. Acquiring fake IDs, evading the law, and masquerading as 21 impose costs. Therefore, the number of people drinking and the amount of alcohol consumed will decline.

2. England subsidizes the cost of purchasing heroin. Part of the cost, the so-called addiction expenses, is borne by the English taxpayers. According to the first law of demand, more heroin will be consumed in England, other things being the same.

4. The answer hinges on facts not presented in the question. First, what will happen to the number of parking tickets issued? If the parking for fee system charges a small price, then some people who currently park illegally will purchase a legal parking pass and park without fear of paying fines. In this case, parking fines will decline. However, if the cost to park on campus is very high, few people will purchase parking decals. Indeed, some people who legally park for free under the current system may be inclined to switch completely to the black market—that is, not register their vehicles and take their chances with the meter attendant. In this case, parking fines may increase. In the limit, if the legal parking fee is exorbitant, all parking might become illegal, and parking fine revenues could grow considerably.

5. The student from far-away Vermont faces travel and related costs unborne by the local Californian. Therefore, according to the Alchian-Allen theorem, he is inclined to consume a higher-quality product. The Vermont student has

to purchase airplane tickets to travel back and forth, and his long-distance phone bill is higher, *ceteris paribus*. Thus, the relative price of a high-quality education is relatively cheaper for him than the local student. He will take the harder courses, study more, and go the extra mile, which on average will map into a higher starting salary upon graduation.

6. a.   Demand for wheat unchanged, supply decreases.
   b.   Supply of corn unchanged, demand for corn increases because the price of wheat increases in response to supply decrease (this assumes no substitution in the production of corn and wheat).
   c.   Price of wheat increases because supply has declined and quantity declines.
   d.   Price of corn increases in response to demand increase. Similarly, the quantity goes up.

7. Think of this problem in terms of the Alchian and Allen theorem. A team that passes a lot must find the relative value of running compared to passing expensive, and vice versa for a team that runs a great deal more than average. The relative value of passing compared to running is expensive. Presume that bad weather adds an equal cost to the value of both type plays. A running play is less valuable because of the wet field and the chances of a fumble. A passing play is less valuable because of the decreased chance of catching the thrown ball. In other words, the inclement weather adds a fixed cost to each type play and the expected yardage gained on both plays falls by the same *absolute* amount. Now consider the relative value ratios. For the passing team, running is relatively expensive, but in inclement weather, both running and passing are more expensive by the same amount. This *reduces* the difference in the relative values. Thus, a passing team will pass *less often* in inclement weather than it will on average. By contrast, for the running team, passing is relatively expensive, and the inclement weather costs affect running and passing by the same fixed amount (by assumption), and so again, the relative values converge. The running team passes more often in bad weather than it does on average under good field conditions. Think of the problem this way: The bad weather partially erases the advantage that running has over passing. The superiority of running for the running team is muted by the bad weather, and vice versa for the passing team. Naturally, if foul weather has an asymmetric effect on the two plays, that is, it affects passing more than running or vice versa, then these results may not hold.

9. Imagine a utility function with two arguments, time spent sleeping and time spent doing all other things. Both of these are goods. The typical day has 24 hours that can be divided between sleeping and all other activities. On the day in the fall when the clocks are set back, the budget constraint shifts out by one hour, but the trade-off remains; time spent sleeping can not be used for other activities and vice versa. Thus, the person who spends the entire hour sleeping has a zero income elasticity for time spent in all activities except sleeping, a rare person indeed.

10. The price elasticity of demand is composed of two parts, the substitution effect elasticity and the income effect elasticity. When the overall elasticity is

elastic, one or the other or both of the two separate effects must also be elastic. Thus, it is reasonable to conjecture that when a good is elastic, one of the reasons might be that it is income elastic, that is, superior.

11. According to the model of human capital and household production developed in the chapter, people with a lot of computer-type skills and those with relatively low time cost will do their own home computing and management of personal finance. Others will let the bank or accountant or financial services adviser do this chore for them. If rich people are rich because they have a lot of ingenuity and expertise, then for them, the cost of using the PC will be lower than for less intelligent, less qualified persons. Even though poor people have a low cost of time, they may not be technically proficient. Thus it is hard to tell on the surface whether a poor or a rich person will use the PC most. Married persons may be less inclined to have a PC, but only if one of the marriage partners does not work outside the home. When one does not work, she or he is left home to run the household affairs, be it child rearing, cleaning, cooking, shopping, or financial management. Thus, the family with only one working parent is more inclined to do things for itself. Whether this maps into a higher or lower demand for computers remains an open question and depends on the opportunity cost of time for the partner working in the home.

14. Again, in the context of human capital and household production, people with little human capital are inclined to watch a lot of television. Why? It requires little expertise, and it is time consuming. At the same time, these people do not make a lot of money. Why not? Because they have little human capital. It is a relatively simple matter to switch channels and find something the viewer likes; inconsequential human capital is required. By contrast, reading books, playing card games, engaging in conversation, and other such activities are more common in households with larger stocks of human capital, in homes where incomes are higher.

16. Laws that force people to constrain their children in seats, when they would not otherwise do so, *decrease* the costs of being involved in an accident. When a wreck occurs, the occupants are less likely to be seriously injured. This reduces the cost of careless or reckless driving. Accordingly, when people are forced to buckle up against their will, they are inclined to drive a bit faster, slightly more carelessly, with less attention, and in poor conditions that they might otherwise avoid. All this implies a *higher* accident rate in states with mandatory laws. By similar argument, since children are now safer, some people might choose slightly less safe cars that are more cheaply built and priced. The death rate of children will probably go down as the seat restraints protect children involved in accidents, but nevertheless, there should be an increase in the number of accidents per mile driven and the use of less safe cars will mitigate some of the effect of safety seats. We expect a relative shift in the types of accidents. There should be a decrease in bodily harm (the children are wearing the safety seats) but an increase in physical damage to cars, that is, more minor and less serious accidents. The implication is that

safe conditions lead drivers to be less cautious, and hence, in the reverse, poor road conditions lead to more careful driving.[22]

17. Those employees preferring to work only six hours suffer a smaller loss of utility when they quit than those who voluntarily choose to work eight hours. The first group is not equating the marginal value of income to the marginal value of leisure. That is, they are not on their desired consumption expansion path. Thus they give up less when they quit than those who are maximizing their utility and are thereby more inclined to quit when unemployment compensation increases than those content with the eight-hour work day.

18. The answer to this question is not straightforward. On the one hand, the day students have a lower opportunity cost of time, *ceteris paribus*. Thus, study costs them less, and they should study more than working students. However, at the same time, working students have by the virtue of their choices revealed that they are well motivated and driven. To compensate for their higher time cost, they should study more intensively when they do study. Their study groups should take fewer breaks and should have fewer distractions than comparable full-time students. Since the cost of their time is higher, they will study less, but when they study, they will study hard.

19. Employ the second law of demand to answer this question. The greater time the market has to adjust to a price change, the more elastic is demand. Scenario B has the most permanent price change and thus is the most elastic. Case C is the most unanticipated and thus is the most inelastic. Situation A fits somewhere in between the other two.

20. This question addresses basically two issues. The first is survivorship and the second is full pricing. Since Christmas has survived for so many years, it must be a valuable institution. Thus, the fact that people buy gifts for others knowing that they value them less than the purchase price does *not* make Christmas dumb. Quite the contrary. Second, what people want to do in this case is find a gift that the recipient would purchase if the choice were available. So children purchase socks, underwear, shirts, and ties for their parents—things they *know* are valued by revealed preference. Alternatively, because they have low time costs they fabricate a gift that conveys love and generosity. Aunts, uncles, and grandparents living far away with little knowledge of a child's preferences can mute the problem by giving cash or securities. Parents try to buy gifts for their children that they suppose the

---

[22] A recent article in *Economic Inquiry* by Christopher Garbacz, "Impact of the New Zealand Seat Belt Law," April 1991, pp. 310–16 offers additional empirical evidence in support of the economic view of driving, and he also carries a number of additional citations that those of you who are having trouble adopting the economic line of reasoning here might want to consult. Garbacz reports "that the favorable effect on automobile occupants may be offset partially, or in some models completely, by deaths among cyclists and pedestrians that may be caused by more dangerous driving by drivers who feel safer" (p. 310). In addition, see the piece by Patrick S. McCarthy, "Highway Safety and the 65-mph Speed Limit," *Contemporary Policy Issues*, 9(4), October 1991, 82–92. McCarthy finds that raising the speed limit to 65 mph actually saves lives because drivers use the safer interstate highway system more and the two-lane regular highway system less when the speed limit is higher.

child would purchase, *if he or she had the money.* Put another way, parents buy things for their children that they think the children would buy if they gave them the monetary equivalent. They may also buy them educational toys as a means of developing their human capital. There are other ways to overcome this problem. Consider person A who has lots of shopping skills and low time cost who buys gifts for person B that require a lot of search time, that is, the total cost to person A is less than the total cost to person B. Then it is possible for the full price of the good to person A to be sufficiently low that person B would buy the good if he faced the price paid by person A. Gifts from trips abroad nicely fit into this category and help us understand the custom of bringing souvenirs home to friends and family.

21. According to the first law of demand, when price is low, quantity is high. Since the price of first class is lower on the St. Louis–Minneapolis trip than it is on the St. Louis–Tokyo trip, and since we have no other information about the income or personal characteristics of the travelers, we must project that the St. Louis–Minneapolis route will have more first-class passengers.

22. For any given change in price, the consumer who owns a car and makes house payments experiences a greater change in income, in percentage terms, than the comparable consumer living at home who avoids these expenses. Thus, assuming equal substitution effects of any price change, the income effect will be greater for the person with the lower disposable income. Accordingly, for normal goods the price elasticity will be greater, more elastic, and more inelastic for inferior goods.

23. There are two tacks to take on this question. First, suppose that the family who won the vacation could liquidate it. Then when they go, they bear the same cost, in opportunity terms, as the family who pays. In this case, there is no difference between the two. More realistically, it will be hard for the family who won the trip to sell it for the same price as paid by the first group. Thus, the trip is cheaper, even if not free, for the lucky family. In this case the Alchian and Allen theorem applies. The fixed travel costs are less for the family who won the trip, and thereby, they will be less inclined to take a high-quality vacation. They are not as likely to take tuxedos and evening gowns as the paying family. They will not spend as much money on souvenirs, and they will not go to the fanciest restaurants. The family who pays will do the nicer things. Why else would they spend their money going if they were not going to have a nice trip? By contrast, the trip is more or less free to the family who won the prize.

24. The third official is in position to detect some crimes that previously had been ignored or unobserved. Hence, the probability of detection increases with the third official. Naturally, players adjust to this increased chance of being caught breaking the rules. In sum, any foul committed is more likely detected, but fewer fouls should be committed; therefore, in total we cannot say whether there will be more or fewer fouls after the third official is added.[23]

---

[23] For an empirical investigation of this problem in the context of college basketball, see Robert E. McCormick and Robert D. Tollison, "Crime on the Court," *Journal of Political Economy,* 92, April 1984, 223–35.

Since there is less crime committed with three officials, the quality of play should increase. Players will spend less time practicing fouling techniques, pretending to be fouled techniques, and the like and spend greater time on offensive and defensive skills. With a higher-quality game, one is inclined to expect higher points, but that is arguable since defense is such an integral part of the sport.

25. The information on the supply elasticity is irrelevant and thrown in simply to make you think. On the demand side the only thing that matters is price, and we know what that is, $1.10. With current consumption at 45 million gallons, price at $0.90, and a price elasticity of demand equal to -0.8, a price increase of $0.20 to $1.10 will reduce quantity demanded to

$$(\Delta q/\Delta p)(p/q) \ = \ -0.8,$$

$$(\Delta q/+0.2)(0.9/45) \ = \ -0.8,$$

and so

$$\Delta q \ = \ (-0.8) \bullet (+0.2) \bullet (45/0.9) \ = \ -8.0.$$

Thus, the new level of consumption will be 45 less 8 or 37 million gallons.

27. Since the demand for beer is elastic, when the price of beer increases by 10 percent, expenditures on beer will *decrease*. The consumption of wine will increase and the consumption of nuts will decline. In both cases, there are income and substitution effects. However, they work in opposite directions. Since there are *less* expenditures on beer, there is an increase in effective income. Being complements, the higher price of beer reduces the consumption of peanuts, but the income effect works in the opposite direction (assuming that nuts are normal). Wine, being a substitute, will increase in consumption on both income and substitution effect grounds. So relative to its baseline level, the change in wine will be greater. Indeed, it could turn out that the consumption of nuts will change very little, even zero were the income and substitution effects equal.

28. a.   The price of gasoline should increase, but less than the amount of the tax increase.

   b.   Assume that regular unleaded and premium unleaded increased by the same dollar amount. Then, the price of the more expensive premium fuel has decreased, relative to regular unleaded. Say the price of premium was $1.29 and the price of regular was $1.09, a ratio of 1.183. Suppose both grades increase by four cents per gallon. The new prices are $1.33 and $1.13, a ratio of only 1.177. The price of quality has decreased, and according to the first law of demand, we expect a shift out of regular gas toward premium.

   c.   By the first law of demand, gasoline sales should be lower; price is higher.

   d.   According to the second law of demand the greater time that consumers have to respond to a change, the greater is the change. Therefore, given the extra time to respond, to find alternative ways of dealing with the higher price, we expect a greater response over the longer time window.

30. The trick here is to separate the food stamp customers into two groups, those

spending some of their own money on food, and those eating solely off food stamps. For the first group, a dollar spent on food has the same opportunity cost as for people who do not use food stamps at all. For those who do not spend any of their own money on groceries, the substitution effect of a price increase is different from that for regular customers. These people can only migrate to other grocery items, while cash-paying customers can shift to any commodity, not just groceries. Therefore, the food stamp recipients will have more inelastic demand for food stuffs. Techniques other than price will have to be used to motivate them.

32. Caution is in order here. This problem is like the advent of seat belts and other safety devices such as football helmets and auto insurance. It tends to lower the cost of carelessness. Thus the advent of word processors and spell checkers reduces our demand to proofread. In spite of the fact that the spell checker will catch most spelling errors, it cannot discern between "two," "too," and "to" mistakes, which are thus more likely today than in the past. We proofread less because the machinery makes it less valuable, and, at the same time, some other errors slip through the cracks. In addition, the expansion of word processors means that many nonsecretaries are now doing their own typing, bolstered by the security of spell checkers and the like. Thus many less proficient typists are now in the pool. This too acts to make for more mistakes. In total then we cannot say which effect dominates. We do expect less straightforward spelling errors, but more grammatical and syntactical errors in all likelihood. Writing style probably suffers a bit as well in the sense that some poor sentence structures do not catch the eye of the proofreader who is less inclined to be as careful with the spell checker in place. The headline from a small, weekly paper in South Carolina would seem to be evidence on this point: "Wreck Breaks Car Into."[24] The author probably meant to write, "Accident Breaks Car in Two."

34. The first statement suggests that running is neither an inferior nor a superior good. If income changes, as it does during a recession, and demand does not change, then the good has a zero income elasticity of demand. (This prediction does not seem consistent with the casual view that running is a yuppie-type phenomena mostly enjoyed by relatively high-income persons.)

The second statement argues that the number of runners is not sensitive to the prize money being offered, and although that statement may be correct, it suggests that the supply of runners is not positively sloped. Moreover, the statement is inconsistent with the first statement, which argued that the number of runners would not decrease because of the recession. If the number of runners is not decreasing during a recession, then there is little cash crunch for race directors. So what is the problem that they face?

The third statement seems to be built on the premise that races are facing financial difficulty. But, again this contradicts the first statement. If the number of racers is not expected to decline, then why are races facing a financial problem?

---

[24] *The Travelers Rest Monitor,* October 23, 1991, p. 1.

The fourth statement suggests that the runners will enter fewer races, a direct contradiction to the first statement. But it probably is correct. Assuming that racing is a normal or superior good, then a recession that lowers income will probably reduce the demand for running in road races.

35. Currently, once a Clemson student has matriculated, the cost of a course is zero. With the new plan, the price increases to $80 per hour, *but there is no income effect* because the net payment effect is zero. That is, the total cost of 15 credit hours under either system is the same, $1200. Therefore, all we have to analyze is the substitution effect, which of course is negative. This will make students take *lighter* loads. Consequently, they will take longer to graduate. For casual empirical confirmation of this result, it does appear that Clemson students take lighter loads during summer school when they must pay for courses on a credit hour basis.

CHAPTER

4

ESTIMATING DEMAND FUNCTIONS

- Introduction
- Hypothetical Business Problem 4.1
- Statistical Concepts
- Regression Analysis
- Quality of the Estimates
- Managing Econometric Studies
- Summary
- Suggested Solution to Problem 4.1
- Topics to Review
- Study Problems
- Suggested Readings
- Suggested Solutions to Study Problems

INTRODUCTION

This chapter is about regression analysis. It begins with a review of some basic notions from statistics—random variables, probability distributions, and sampling. After that, the details of regression analysis are explored. Then various pitfalls in the econometric modeling process are scrutinized. We end with a number of study problems to consider. Regression analysis is one of those topics that is only learned through repeated trial and error. Practice and study are essential. We start with a problem for you to consider. By the time you get to the end of this chapter, you should be able to construct a reasonable answer to this problem.

Hypothetical Business Problem 4.1

Consult Table 4.1. The data there are the actual accounting figures compiled at a real restaurant in a large midwestern city. AV. REV., SALES, and ADS are, respectively, the average revenue per customer, total revenue, and advertising expenditures per month, all denominated in dollars. CUS is the number of customers who visited the restaurant each month. FCA is the number of people who visited an amusement park near the restaurant. Could this restaurant have made more money by raising or lowering prices, or are prices set to maximize profits?

STATISTICAL CONCEPTS

Knowing what customers are willing to pay for products is one of the manager's most important functions. The process of unraveling this mystery begins with the estimation of the product demand curve. The techniques employed are built upon standard statistical methods, especially something called regression analysis. The purpose of this chapter is to acquaint you with the rudiments of these powerful analytical devices. However, the student is cautioned: Demand estimation is very tricky business. Successful completion of this chapter is not sufficient preparation. Additional courses, study, and practice are definitely in order before the student puts the principles discussed here to work.

One of the basic notions in statistics is the **random variable**. A random variable is a quantity that can take on any one of a set of values. Random variables can be **discrete** or **continuous**. Continuous random variables can take any numeric value. The weight or height of people is a continuous variable. Continuous variables are divisible into infinitely small units of measure. By contrast, discrete random variables can only take specific values. The number of people in a room or a family is restricted to integers. The number of tests in a course must be a whole number. Discrete random variables need not be integers however. U.S. currency denominations, for example, come in fractions of a dollar; 1/100 of a dollar is a penny, making it impossible to have $0.372 in your pockets. You can only have fractions that are a multiple of one cent.

Random or stochastic variables are observed with different values, that is, they are not constants. Random variables are assigned values that, at least in part, are determined by chance. Suppose you weighed yourself each morning for two months. In all likelihood, these measurements would not all be the same. Your weight is a random variable. Other examples include the temperature outside, the amount of rainfall per year, the price of some particular common stock, the number of customers in a store at a particular time, and the like. Random variables are summarized and organized using probability density and cumulative distribution functions. These mathematical concepts are ledgers that give the relative frequency of each value of the random variable. Consider the data in Table 4.2, which contains data on the heights of a sample of professors at Hypothetical University. The heights have been classified into intervals that are four inches wide.

Figure 4.1 plots the proportion of professors in each interval as a function of height. Figure 4.2 plots the cumulative number of professors who are at a given height or less. The former is called the **probability density function** and the latter is the **cumulative distribution function**. The first describes the proportion of people at each height while the second characterizes the number who are that tall *or shorter*. Both graphs paint a picture of the relative frequency of height, but some questions are answered better with one than the other. For example, Figure 4.1 reveals that the most frequently occurring height is the 5'8"–6'0" range; it occurs 44 percent of the time. On the other hand, Figure 4.2 shows that 84 percent of the professors are 6'0" or less in height.

Things in nature tend to follow their own particular distribution. Although there are an infinite number of distributions, several are used frequently in statistical analysis because they have been found to describe a wide variety of phenomena. These include the **Poisson distribution**, the *F* **distribution**, the *t* **distribution**, the X^2 **distribution**, and the **normal** or **Gaussian distribution**, which is not called normal because the others are abnormal. Tables delineating the characteristics of these distributions, in much the same way as Table 4.2 does, are found in most statistics textbooks or mathematics handbooks.

Moments

Probability density functions have **moments**. Moments summarize characteristics of distributions. The first moment is called the **mean**, and it is a measure of central tendency. The second is the **variance**, and it is a measure of dispersion. The third is referred to as the **skewness**, which describes the symmetry of the distribution. The fourth is named the **kurtosis**; it measures the relative frequency of observations near the mean versus those far away, what statisticians call the **tails** of the distribution. The kth moment, m_k, of a discrete distribution is defined as

$$m_k = \sum_{i=1}^{n} x_i^k f(x_i)$$

where $f(x_i)$ is the value of the probability density function for the ith observation and n is the number of observations in the sample. The moments of an empirical

TABLE 4.1   RESTAURANT DATA

YEAR	MONTH	AV.REV.	SALES	CUS	ADS	FCA
1982	1	$8.99	$143211	15923	$1158.78	1140
1982	2	9.05	154503	17068	1102.34	890
1982	3	8.87	190791	21499	0.00	4430
1982	4	10.19	194339	19065	76.13	5660
1982	5	9.68	164610	17003	925.45	3970
1982	6	9.89	155868	15753	2593.07	4130
1982	7	9.55	140513	14709	1060.48	4510
1982	8	9.35	142034	15198	2356.11	3870
1982	9	9.83	125615	12785	1751.87	2490
1982	10	10.30	149436	14513	2219.11	4690
1982	11	9.74	124105	12748	2958.79	4650
1982	12	10.13	145700	14383	3234.41	2930
1983	1	9.51	124155	13051	216.00	2490
1983	2	8.98	127215	14170	2429.00	4980
1983	3	9.14	177022	19375	3629.00	10730
1983	4	9.48	174488	18415	1508.00	17020
1983	5	10.51	159284	15152	1935.00	9510
1983	6	10.72	173617	16192	1782.00	9570
1983	7	10.54	165743	15728	2179.00	11000
1983	8	10.38	161401	15543	2157.00	10050
1983	9	10.43	139267	13357	2093.00	6010
1983	10	10.37	151759	14639	1865.00	29750
1983	11	10.64	138461	13016	2843.00	5490
1983	12	10.41	142568	13695	3090.00	4170
1984	1	10.49	140844	13425	2442.00	3760
1984	2	11.29	135740	12024	1766.00	5280
1984	3	10.61	215121	20275	1670.00	11440
1984	4	10.47	195878	18708	1347.00	10440

distribution can be estimated using a sample drawn from a distribution. For example, the mean of a sample, often represented by the symbol $\bar{x}$, is

$$\bar{x} = \sum_{i=1}^{n} x_i/n,$$

where n is the number of observations on the sample of x_i's. The mean is often called the average of the sample. The variance of a sample, σ^2, is the average squared deviation from the mean:

$$\sigma^2 = \sum_{i=1}^{n} (x_i - \bar{x})^2/(n - 1).$$

The standard deviation, σ, is simply the square root of the variance.

TABLE 4.1	(continued)					

YEAR	MONTH	AV.REV.	SALES	CUS	ADS	FCA
1984	5	10.22	176125	17233	1427.00	8710
1984	6	9.96	192887	19375	1354.00	12440
1984	7	10.68	173090	16204	1214.00	13070
1984	8	10.72	166872	15573	3083.00	10170
1984	9	10.24	144980	14164	1464.00	6150
1984	10	10.23	144512	14131	1425.00	7080
1984	11	10.75	132379	12314	1587.00	5680
1984	12	10.74	154566	14390	720.00	6400
1985	1	9.92	136016	13710	1043.00	3320
1985	2	9.49	137962	14542	403.00	5550
1985	3	9.63	193890	20136	394.00	11630
1985	4	9.70	167892	17304	54.00	10430
1985	5	9.67	177153	18317	915.00	10190
1985	6	9.97	161297	16180	3746.00	12310
1985	7	9.24	138096	14950	2544.00	12840
1985	8	9.58	134279	14013	2537.00	9260
1985	9	9.61	128725	13390	722.00	510
1985	10	9.93	134404	13539	2705.00	6670
1985	11	9.29	120847	13004	3507.00	5860
1985	12	10.46	142441	13621	2009.00	4070
1986	1	9.85	138663	14082	4816.00	4380
1986	2	9.17	152899	16671	4797.00	6810
1986	3	9.32	182387	19576	5413.00	12780
1986	4	10.18	175936	17286	3497.00	12210
1986	5	10.05	168122	16721	4289.00	9130
1986	6	9.60	167511	17447	3322.00	10790
1986	7	9.19	138796	15110	3874.00	10120

TABLE 4.2	HEIGHTS OF PROFESSORS AT HYPOTHETICAL U.			

HEIGHT	NUMBER OF PROFESSORS	PROPORTION OF TOTAL	CUMULATIVE NUMBER OF PROFESSORS	CUMULATIVE PROPORTION OF TOTAL
<5'0"	1	0.04	1	0.04
5'0"–5'4"	3	0.12	4	0.16
5'4"–5'8"	6	0.24	10	0.40
5'8"–6'0"	11	0.44	21	0.84
6'0"–6'4"	3	0.12	24	0.96
6'4"–6'8"	1	0.04	25	1.00
>6'8"	0			

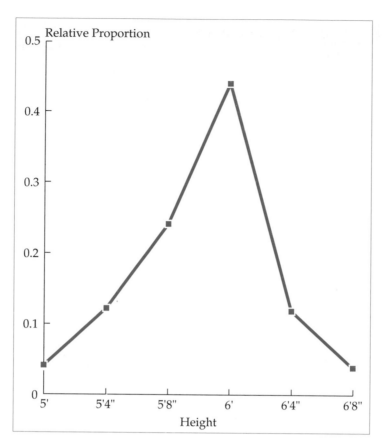

FIGURE 4.1
Probability Density Function

The moments of a probability density function are used to draw inferences about the world and to separate hypotheses. But the true moments of a probability distribution, the physical constants in nature that generate or describe the random variables, are almost always unknown to the investigator. Since the true underlying distribution of most random variables of interest to managers cannot be known, the investigator resorts to a sample of data available to measure or estimate the relevant moments. This means that the sample mean, variance, and standard deviation must be used instead of the true moments. Thus, the way samples are chosen and their size become important managerial prerogatives, a point to which we will return.

Hypothesis Testing

Distributions are used to test statistical hypotheses. We begin this process by asserting a **null hypothesis** (sometimes called the **maintained hypothesis**) that claims a random variable is equal to, greater than, or less than some value chosen by the investigator. For example, consider the hypothesis that the height of the

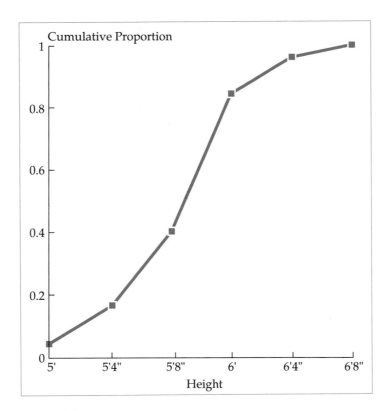

FIGURE 4.2
Cumulative Distribution Function

average professor at Hypothetical U. is less than 5′7½″. In order to investigate this null hypothesis, we must formulate an **alternate hypothesis**. In this case, the alternate hypothesis is that the average height is greater than or equal to 5′7½″. This means that if the actual height is *either* greater than 5′7½″ or equal to 5′7½″, we reject the null hypothesis and accept the alternate. Remember this simple dictum: It takes a hypothesis to beat one. Suppose we simply compare the sample mean with the height proposed under our null hypothesis. The actual sample mean is 5′10″. Should we then reject the maintained hypothesis? On the surface, you might be inclined to say yes. However, the problem is that we collected only a *sample* of the population. We did not measure the heights of all the professors at H.U. If we had chosen a different sample of teachers, perhaps we would have obtained a different sample mean height. How then do we reject or accept the null hypothesis with confidence that our results are not purely a function of the sample we selected?

In order to test the null hypothesis, a number of choices must be made. First, we must decide upon the appropriate statistical distribution of the data in question. There is no rule here. Typically, the investigator has some familiarity with similar data and some feeling or prior knowledge on which to make an educated prediction about the correct functional form, but one can never be sure. When the stakes are high, it usually pays to investigate the distribution empirically. For the problem at hand, let us suppose that heights of human beings are distributed according to the normal distribution.[1]

Given that we have chosen a distribution, we must collect the data. We could measure the heights of all the professors at the school. For most managerial problems, this course is too costly, and we resort to a sample of information from the data in question. Table 4.2 has 25 observations on height. We can use these data to test the null hypothesis. Without going into the details, if the heights of professors are truly distributed according to the normal distribution but the true mean and variance of the distribution are unknown to the investigator, then the mean of the *sample* divided by the *sample* standard deviation is distributed according to the t distribution with parameter value equal to one less than the number of sample observations. In other words, in statistical terms we write

$$\bar{x}/\sigma_{\bar{x}} \sim t_{n-1}.$$

In statistics, the symbol, $\sim$, means that the ratio $\bar{x}/\sigma_{\bar{x}}$, the mean of a sample divided by its standard deviation, is described by a t distribution with a parameter value of $n-1$. The t distribution has a bell shape similar to the normal but with slightly fatter tails; compared to the normal distribution, the mass of the probability in the t distribution is shifted toward the extreme values and away from the mean. The probability values of the t distribution for different parameter values are found in most statistics handbooks. This parameter value, $n-1$, is commonly called the **degrees of freedom**. For most managerial purposes, you can think of degrees of freedom as the number of observations in the sample, corrected for calculations of sample moments. For example, we do not know the true mean or variance of the heights in our population. Therefore, these are approximated by computing the mean and variance from our sample of heights. In each case, the degrees of freedom are the sample size less one for the moment we are estimating. In our example, we have data on the heights of 25 professors. Our degrees of freedom for the mean and variance are each 24.

In this specific case, the average height of the sample, $\bar{x}$, is 5.833' (5'10"), and the standard deviation of the mean, $\sigma_{\bar{x}}$, is $0.569/\sqrt{25} = 0.1138$.[2] To test the null hypothesis, compute the **t statistic** by first subtracting the null value from the sample average, and then second, dividing the result by the standard deviation of the mean. In this case, the t statistic is

$$t = (5'10'' - 5'7\frac{1}{2}'')/0.1138' \text{ (or } [5.833' - 5.625']/0.1138') = 0.208'/0.1138' = 1.828.$$

---

[1] The normal distribution has the famous bell shape so familiar to students wishing their grades to be curved.

[2] The standard deviation of the mean of a sample is the standard deviation of the sample divided by the square root of the sample size. That is, if the standard deviation of a sample is σ, then the standard deviation of the mean of the sample, $\sigma_{\bar{x}}$, is $\sigma/\sqrt{n}$, where n is the number of observations in the sample.

If we investigate a table of probabilities for the t distribution, we see that a value of 1.828 does not occur with great frequency when there are 24 degrees of freedom. Most of the time, 95.998 percent to be precise, the t statistic will be smaller than 1.828 when the null hypothesis is true. This means that a t statistic as large as 1.828 only occurs about 4 percent of the time by chance alone. Consequently, since the chances are small that the t statistic could be so large by chance alone under the null hypothesis, we are inclined to search for an alternate explanation for the facts at hand. Namely, we are led to conclude that the null hypothesis is false, and the alternate is correct, at least based on this sample of information. Therefore, the sample of information contains some evidence to reject the null hypothesis, and with some likelihood the average height of professors at H.U. is more than 5'7½" based on the sample of information in Table 4.2.

Intuitively, the t statistic compares the sample mean with the height proposed under our null hypothesis, *relative to the standard deviation* of heights in our sample. For a given value of the null hypothesis, a larger variance leads to a smaller t statistic. The larger the variance, the less confidence there is that our sample mean is truly different from the value maintained under the null hypothesis. On the other hand, for a given value of the null hypothesis and sample mean, the bigger the t statistic, the greater is our confidence that the sample mean is truly different from the value maintained under the null hypothesis.

Samples

Samples are very important in economic research. In the preceding example, suppose we had, by chance, collected our sample of data solely from women, and 95 percent of the faculty were men. We could easily have drawn the wrong inference about the *population* of professors from the calculated t statistic. Since our t statistic is based on our sample, and our sample is not representative of the overall population, our conclusions might mislead us. Alternatively, suppose all the people in the sample were full professors (older than average). Again, we could have drawn an inaccurate inference, if older people are, on average, shorter than younger people. For these reasons, care is to be taken in selecting data samples. Other things being the same, larger samples are better than smaller samples. In almost all cases, a randomly selected sample is preferred to one that is drawn based on specific criteria.

An apocryphal story best illustrates the importance of samples. Several years ago, Coca-Cola introduced New Coke; the syrup formula used in the making of Coke was changed. Apparently, a great deal of market research went into the decision-making process. Thousands of people were sampled in blind taste tests, and sufficient numbers preferred the taste of New Coke to Coke. As most of you are aware, New Coke was not the resounding success the random sample of tasters suggested it should be. Coke Classic was reintroduced and dominates New Coke in sales. What went wrong? It turns out that the people tested were *not* about to purchase a soft drink. The problem with the random sample in this case is that people typically consume sodas when they are thirsty, and *when people are thirsty or about to drink a soda on their own volition, they prefer the old formula.* Market research failed because the researchers did not carefully select the sample of taste testers. As the owners of Coca-Cola stock can attest, mistakes like this can be very expensive.

The Coke example highlights a general situation called **selection bias** that is important in all types of analysis. Selection bias is the collection of data from a sample that does not represent the population under consideration. For instance, suppose your company is selling life or automobile insurance. You have set your rates competitively based on the average mortality or probability of an accident, but *you do not screen your applicants.* What will happen? Over the long run, you will be the victim of a selection bias—the sickest patients and the worst drivers, being different from the average, will find your rates attractive. Thus, your clientele will consist of an abnormally large group of sick people or bad drivers, and because these people are prone to sickness and accidents, their claims will be above average. Worse yet, if you raise your rates, you will lose the best customers that you have, leaving you with an ever-deteriorating situation.

Errors

Two errors are possible when testing hypotheses. First, the null hypothesis can be rejected when it is true; in this case, we are led to conclude the alternate is true when in fact it is false. This is commonly called a **Type I error**. Alternatively, the null hypothesis is accepted (the alternate is rejected) when the null is false, and the alternate is true. This is called **Type II error**. Sadly, reducing one error type increases the other. Investigators vary in their opinion as to which error is more important to minimize. Typically, the problem at hand suggests its own preference, but you should be aware that most analysts focus almost exclusively on Type I error.

It is common for analysts to report the probability of Type I error, the probability that they have rejected a null hypothesis when, in fact, it is true. Curiously, it is just as uncommon for an investigator to report the probability that a Type II error has been committed, accepting the null when it is false.[3]

REGRESSION ANALYSIS

The Demand Function

Regression analysis is the primary technique used by econometricians (economic statisticians) to estimate demand curves. The process begins with the construction of a theory. This corresponds to the discussions presented in Chapters 2 and 3 concerning the determinants of demand. The commodity in question is defined, and then the factors that are presumed to influence its consumption are delineated. A model develops. Typically, the theory is specified in individual terms. Of course, in most cases, the manager is not interested in the individual demand, but rather the market demand. This means that the individual demands

---

[3] This is primarily due to the fact that the distributions of the errors are not well known.

have to be aggregated. As a general rule, this is accomplished by assuming that the individual demands are the same across the demanders. Thus, market demand is simply the sum of the individual demands.[4]

For instance, consider the individual demand for electricity. We assume that the consumption of electricity is a function of its price, the income of the consumer, and the price of related commodities:

$$q_d = q(P, Y, P_r).$$

If there are n such individual demanders, then the total or market demand is

$$n{\bullet}q_d = Q_d,$$

where Q_d represents total or market demand. Thus by inference, the total or market demand is a function of price, income, related prices, *and the number of individual demanders*:

$$Q_d = Q(P, Y, P_r, n).$$

The exact structural form of the relation between consumption and price or income depends on the theory of individual demand and remains an open question at this point in the econometric inquiry. However, experience is a good guide here, and previous research is often used as a beacon. Later in the chapter we will expand on the importance of selecting the appropriate structural form of the relation between variables.

Let us explore the demand for electricity. Consider the data in Table 4.3. Column (1) is the average income per capita by state in 1977; column (2) is the state population; column (3) is the total sales of electricity in millions of kilowatt hours; column (4) is the number of electricity customers; column (5) is the average price of electricity in the state in cents per kilowatt hour; and column (6) is the average price per thousand cubic feet of a related good, natural gas.

Figure 4.3 is a scatter plot of average price versus sales per capita [column (3) in Table 4.3 divided by column (2)] for each of the 50 states (several of the individual states are annotated). Regression analysis is a statistical technique that finds the vertical intercept and the slope of a line in order to minimize the squared deviations of the actual values from that line. The slope is the rise of the function over the run. Two of the deviations are marked in Figure 4.3. These are a and b. These deviations of actual values from the line are called **error terms** or the **residuals of the regression**. The technique of regression is simply the application of a set of statistical formulas that estimate the intercept and slope by minimizing the sum of the squared deviations (a^2 and b^2 plus all the others). Finding a combination of intercept and slope that minimizes the sum of the squared values of the error terms has certain pleasing statistical properties, namely that the predicted parameters of the regression, α and β, are the statistician's best guess

---

[4] See the discussion in Chapter 2 on demand aggregation.

TABLE 4.3   ELECTRICITY DATA BY STATES, 1977

STATE	YPC (1)	POP(× 1000) (2)	SALES (3)	CUSTOMERS (4)	ELEC. PRICE (5)	GAS PRICE (6)
AK	10586	413	2471	129280	3.85	1.048
AL	5622	3691	49200	1550337	2.80	1.654
AR	5540	2152	19977	923679	3.19	1.237
AZ	6509	2305	22720	902580	3.82	1.677
CA	7911	21887	155707	8932768	3.61	1.929
CO	7160	2625	18193	1131997	2.88	1.429
CT	8061	3107	20119	1188308	4.23	3.780
DE	7697	582	5467	229443	4.22	2.595
FL	6684	8466	78724	3987529	3.69	1.618
GA	6014	5041	47617	2032381	3.24	1.776
HI	7677	891	5795	275402	4.62	6.989
IA	6878	2888	22688	1211063	3.47	1.606
ID	5980	856	13987	372248	1.65	2.293
IL	7768	11228	93073	4310310	3.38	2.071
IN	6921	5350	54466	2112394	2.95	1.775
KS	7134	2320	20263	1000288	3.26	1.254
KY	5945	3468	54189	1388250	2.06	1.685
LA	5913	3930	50583	1517295	2.21	1.464
MA	7258	5777	31350	2116593	4.90	3.678
MD	7572	4137	37892	1591020	3.80	2.785
ME	5734	1084	7301	504364	3.29	3.980
MI	7619	9148	69845	3548461	3.64	2.062
MN	7129	3980	28697	1562770	3.32	1.806
MO	6654	4822	36702	2016596	3.30	1.808
MS	5030	2386	22407	955070	3.20	1.634

about the true relation between sales per customer and price. The technique of minimizing the squared deviations of actual from predicted values is named after itself, **ordinary-least-squares regression**, or **OLS** as it is commonly abbreviated.

Consider one particular demand function for electricity:

$$q = \alpha + \beta_1 \cdot p + \beta_2 \cdot y + \beta_3 \cdot c + \beta_4 \cdot g + \varepsilon$$

where q is the quantity consumed of electricity; p is the price; y is the income of the customers; c is the number of customers; g is the price of a related good, natural gas; and ε is the error term. The parameters, α and β_1–β_4, describe the demand relation between the independent variables—price, income, customers, and gas price—and the dependent variable, consumption. For example, according to the first law of demand, we can formulate one null hypothesis, specifically that $\beta_1 \geq$

TABLE 4.3   (continued)

State	YPC (1)	POP($\times$1000) (2)	SALES (3)	CUSTOMERS (4)	ELEC. PRICE (5)	GAS PRICE (6)
MT	6125	766	10036	338291	1.38	1.573
NC	5935	5515	57611	2306428	3.01	2.604
ND	6190	650	4460	264817	3.11	1.808
NE	6720	1555	12898	672948	2.80	1.397
NH	6536	850	5453	383993	4.30	3.084
NJ	7994	7338	46399	2757876	5.01	3.139
NM	5857	1196	8270	449405	3.19	1.570
NV	7988	637	7974	283284	2.98	1.854
NY	7537	17932	101555	6279676	4.92	2.963
OH	7084	10696	120693	4145089	2.90	2.115
OK	6346	2817	26898	1258254	2.88	1.452
OR	7007	2385	34874	1053837	1.61	2.482
PA	7011	11796	95988	4522854	3.68	2.343
RI	6775	937	4825	356689	4.78	3.676
SC	5628	2878	34363	1160166	2.88	1.688
SD	5957	688	4305	286158	3.10	1.530
TN	5785	4292	73496	1774623	2.09	1.597
TX	6803	12806	152036	4877782	2.86	1.889
UT	5923	1270	8881	451558	2.83	1.311
VA	6865	5095	44183	1853331	3.61	2.524
VT	5823	482	3321	218863	3.61	2.678
WA	7528	3681	64203	1591668	0.99	2.366
WI	6890	4644	34218	1870932	3.26	2.134
WV	5986	1853	19079	752717	2.79	1.874
WY	7562	406	5339	188547	1.81	1.279

Source: Statistical Yearbook of the Electric Utility Industry 1982 (Washington, DC: Edison Electric Institute, 1983), pp. 10, 24, 33, 35, and 92.

0. We form the null hypothesis that when the price of electricity increases, the quantity consumed will also increase. Notice that we form the null hypothesis in a way that we believe is *incorrect*.[5] We start from the position that we will *not* find what we expect. The alternate hypothesis is that $\beta_1 < 0$. In words, the alternate hypothesis says that electricity prices and consumption vary inversely; higher prices lead to lower consumption. We expect the data to reject the null in favor of the alternate.

---

[5] You may note that the American system of jurisprudence uses a similar approach when it starts from the presumption of innocence. Framing a null hypothesis with the assertion that there is no relation between the two variables is the statistician's way of saying that a relation is "innocent until proven guilty."

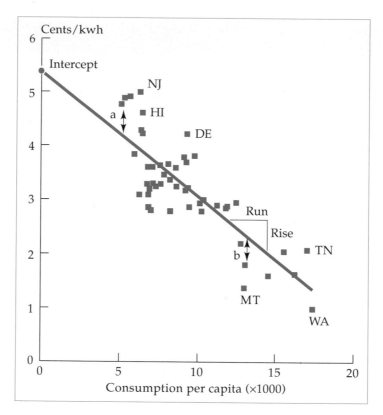

FIGURE 4.3
Electricity Consumption, 1977

Similarly, we can formulate a hypothesis about the relation between income and electricity consumption. The null hypothesis here is that $\beta_2 = 0$. Creating a null hypothesis such that a coefficient equals zero is useful because, if the null is correct, then we believe there is *no* relation between the independent variable and the dependent variable. That is, the independent variable does not affect the variable in question. Our second maintained hypothesis is that a consumer's level of income does not affect her consumption of electricity. Again we have stated a hypothesis that we do not believe to be correct. The alternate hypothesis is that the level of income is related to the consumption of electricity. That is, that $\beta_2 \neq 0$. In the simple case, when we do not specify a sign for the alternative hypothesis, the test is called a **two-tailed test**. We could formulate a more complex test. For instance, if we had prior knowledge or theoretical suspicion that electricity was a normal good, then our alternate hypothesis would be that $\beta_2 > 0$. In this case, our null hypothesis would be that $\beta_2 \leq 0$. This is called a **one-tailed test**. We formulate tests for all the parameters in a similar fashion. There is one test for each parameter in the model.

Table 4.4 presents the ordinary-least-squares regression estimates of α and

> TABLE 4.4   ESTIMATES OF REGRESSION PARAMETERS—MODEL 1

Dependent Variable: Sales of Electricity (q)

ANALYSIS OF VARIANCE

SOURCE	DF[a]	SUM OF SQUARES	MEAN SQUARE	F RATIO	PROB $>F$
Model	4	62128583110	15532145777	110.954	0.0001
Error	45	6299423836	139987196		
Total	49	68428006945			
Root MSE = 11831.62			R^2 = 0.9079		

A

PARAMETER ESTIMATES

VARIABLE	PARAMETER ESTIMATE	STANDARD ERROR	t RATIO	PROB $>|t|$
Intercept	36136.2339	12370.3053	2.9212	0.0054
Price of Electricity (p)	-9956.6134	2344.0804	-4.2476	0.0001
Income per Capita (y)	-0.8656	1.9213	-0.4505	0.6545
Customers (c)	0.0210	0.0010	20.7393	0.0001
Price of Natural Gas (g)	2221.7663	1997.5252	1.1123	0.2719

B   *C*

[a] Degrees of Freedom

β_1–β_4 using the data in Table 4.3, a PC, and the statistical software package, SAS©.[6]

Three areas of interest on this output are labeled: *A*, *B*, and *C*. Area *A* contains the analysis of variance and summary information on the entire regression, and *B* reports the independent variables and their respective parameter estimates, while *C* reports tests of hypotheses concerning these parameter estimates.

In area *A*, we find the analysis of variance, which decomposes the variation in the dependent variable, electricity consumption, into the part explained by the independent variables and the part left unexplained. The **sum of squares for the model** (sometimes called the sums of squares for the regression) is 62,128,583,110, a number that, by itself, has little meaning.[7] If we divide this sum by the **model degrees of freedom** (abbreviated DF in Table 4.4), 4, we obtain the model mean square or 15,532,145,777. The model degrees of freedom is the number of independent variables in the regression. We have four: price of electricity, income, the number of customers, and the price of natural gas. The **error sum of squares** comes next. This is the sum of the squared deviations of the predicted values of

---

[6] SAS is available from the SAS Institute Inc., Box 8000, Cary, North Carolina 27511.

[7] The formulas for computing the model sums of squares is somewhat complicated and beyond the scope of this text. The topic is covered in detail in standard econometric textbooks.

the regression from the actual data points. These deviations correspond to the distances marked as *a* and *b* in Figure 4.3. The sum of the squared residuals is 6,299,423,836. We divide the sum by the **degrees of freedom for error** to compute **mean squared error**, which in this case is 139,987,196.

The model and error mean squares are used to compute the F ratio, which is just the model mean square divided by the error mean square, or

$$F = 15,532,145,777/139,987,196 = 110.954.$$

The F ratio or F statistic tests the hypothesis that *all* the independent variables jointly affect the dependent variable. That is, the null hypothesis here is that

$$\beta_1 = \beta_2 = \beta_3 = \beta_4 = 0.$$

Higher F statistics suggest a smaller probability that there is no relation between the dependent variable and the entire set of explanatory variables. The F ratio of 110.954 is quite large. *If the null hypothesis were true* and there were no relation between the independent variables and consumption, then we would not expect to obtain such a high F statistic. The table also reports the probability of obtaining an F statistic as high as 110.954 with four independent variables and 50 observations. This is labeled *Prob > F*. In this case the probability that we would obtain an F statistic as large as 110.954 by chance alone is 0.0001.[8] How do we interpret this? The F statistic is computed assuming that the null hypothesis is true. However, if the null is true, the probability is scant, less than 0.0001, that we would obtain a statistic as high as 110.954. There is a very small chance, almost none, that we could obtain an F statistic of 110.954 with four independent variables and 50 observations if the null hypothesis were true. Thus, we are inclined to search for an alternative explanation of this statistical finding, and of course this means that there is almost surely some relation between the independent variables and consumption. In terms of hypothesis testing, there is massive evidence that the null hypothesis of no relation is to be rejected in favor of the alternate hypothesis that there is some kind of relation. That is, at least one of the β_i's is not equal to zero. Since the F statistic is so high, we are led to believe that the null hypothesis is wrong. Note carefully that this does not mean that *all* of the coefficients are probably different from zero, only that at least one probably is.

Area A of Table 4.4 also reports R^2 and the root mean squared error. R^2 is the proportion of the dependent variable explained by the model.[9] It is the fraction of the variation in the consumption of electricity accounted for by the four independent variables: the price of electricity, income, the number of customers, and the price of natural gas. When the model does a poor job explaining the variation in the dependent variable (when the unexplained variation in the dependent vari-

---

[8] In fact, the probability is likely smaller than 0.0001. The smallest probability that SAS reports is 0.0001.

[9] Some people refer to R^2 as the coefficient of determination.

able is high), then R^2 is small. By contrast, when the model describes the variation in the dependent variable with accuracy, then R^2 is large, and we say the model has good fit. R^2 ranges from a low of zero to a high of one. R^2 values close to zero signal a model that explains a small proportion of the variability in the dependent variable, regardless of the significance of the coefficients in the model. This situation is lamentable but unavoidable if alternative models have lower probabilities of being associated with the dependent variable (the probability of a Type I error is larger than the existing model). In this case, the analyst must be resigned to a model that, even though better than the alternatives, is itself rather poor in its predictive capacity. Table 4.4 reports an R^2 of 0.9079. This means that 90.8 percent of the variation in the dependent variable, total consumption of electricity across states in the United States, is explained by variation in the four independent variables—price, income, customers, and the price of natural gas.

The **root mean squared error** (labeled *Root MSE*) is the estimated standard deviation of the residuals. Faithful to its name, it is the square root of the mean squared error. In this case, it is

$$\sqrt{139,987,196} = 11,831.62.$$

By construction of the regression, the average residual must be zero. The root mean squared error measures the dispersion of the residuals.

Area *B* of Table 4.4 contains the estimated model parameters. First the estimate of α, the intercept, is reported as 36,136.2339. Next, the estimates of β_1 through β_4 are reported in turn. For example, the estimate of the relation between price and consumption is -9956.6134, which says as price goes up one cent per kilowatt hour, total state consumption declines by 9956.6134 million kilowatt hours per year. After the estimates of the model parameters, estimates of the **standard errors of the parameters** are reported. These measure the dispersion of the parameter estimates. When a standard error is large relative to the estimated coefficient, then the researcher does not hold the estimate in high confidence. By contrast, when the standard error is small relative to the parameter estimate, then faith is high that the estimate is accurate. The parameter estimate and its standard error are used to compute the t ratio. The t ratio tests the null hypothesis that the individual parameter is equal to zero, that is, that $\beta_i = 0$. The t ratio is the parameter estimate divided by its standard error. For instance, the estimate of β_1, the coefficient on price, is -9956.6134, and the estimated standard error is 2344.0804. Thus, the t statistic for the price parameter is $-9956.6134/2344.0804 = -4.2476$. The other t ratios are computed in the same way.

Area *C* reports the tests of five different null hypotheses using the t ratio. In turn, they are that α and β_1 through β_4 are each separately equal to zero. If the null hypothesis is correct, then the t ratio is centered on zero. As the calculated t ratio differs from zero, the researcher gains confidence that the null hypothesis is incorrect, and in fact, there is some sort of a relation between the independent variable and the dependent variable. When the absolute value of the t ratio (or t statistic) is large (in general, above 2), the suggestion is that the null hypothesis is not valid. For example, if in truth there is no relation between the price of electricity and the consumption of electricity, then there is an incredibly small chance, less than 0.01 percent, that we would have found a t statistic as low as -4.2476 by chance alone in our sample across the 50 states in 1977. In probabilistic terms, there is a great deal of evidence that the parameter estimate, -9956, is smaller than zero. Indeed, we have little choice but to conclude that the first law of demand holds for the consumption of electricity across states (at least in 1977).

As we examine the other t ratios in area C of Table 4.4, we see that there is little evidence to reject the null hypothesis that electricity consumption is independent of income. The t ratio is -0.4505, and the probability of obtaining a value that high when the null is true is quite large, 0.6545 to be exact. In this case, we say there is little evidence of any relation between income and the consumption of electricity. This result is somewhat surprising and deserves more attention than we can afford to give it here. It suffices to say that electricity is demanded by residential, commercial, and industrial customers, and in all likelihood, these demands are not homogeneous. Thus, part of the reason that we have not found a relation between income and the consumption of electricity may be due to the fact that we have improperly aggregated residential demand with business demand. It is possible to obtain the different classes of data from the Edison Electric Institute's *Statistical Yearbook*. This might prove to be a worthwhile project.

The t ratio on the coefficient for number of customers is very large at 20.7393. The probability of measuring a t ratio this large by chance alone when there is no relation between the two variables is virtually nonexistent. Thus, we have a great deal of confidence that the estimated parameter, 0.0210, is significantly different from zero. The t ratio testing the null hypothesis that the coefficient on the price of natural gas is zero is 1.1123. If the null were true, we would obtain a t statistic this high by chance alone about 27 percent of the time. Thus we say there is some very weak evidence that natural gas and electricity are substitutes, but our confidence here is very shaky. Were we to conclude that there is a substitute relation between natural gas and electricity, there is a 27 percent chance that we would be wrong. For most analysts, this is too much of a margin of error. In your own work, you will have to make that decision for yourself. The economist as scientist would typically say that there is not enough evidence to conclude that there is a substitute relation.

Estimating Elasticities

It is possible from the parameter estimates in Table 4.4 to derive an estimate of the price elasticity of demand. Recall that the price elasticity of demand is the percentage of change in quantity demanded divided by the percentage of change in price, or $(\partial q/\partial p) \cdot (p/q)$. The first term in the formula, $\partial q/\partial p$, is the slope of the relation between price and consumption. According to the results in Table 4.4, this is estimated by β_1 as -9956.6134. In order to compute the elasticity, we must answer the question, What values do we use for p and q? The correct answer depends on our interest. If we wanted to make a statement about the price elasticity of demand across the whole country, then the best choice is the average across our sample. Simple averages for some of the variables listed in Table 4.3 are reported in Table 4.5.

The average price across the 50 states was 3.219, and the average consumption

TABLE 4.5 SIMPLE AVERAGES—ELECTRICITY DATA					
VARIABLE	NUMBER OF OBSERVATIONS	MEAN	STANDARD DEVIATION	MINIMUM VALUE	MAXIMUM VALUE
Price of Electricity (p)	50	3.219	0.896	0.994	5.013
Income per Capita (y)	50	6777.020	953.844	5030.000	10586.000
Price of Natural Gas (g)	50	2.172	0.999	1.048	6.989
Customers (c)	50	1711804.240	1749370.855	129280.000	8932768.000
Population ($\times 10^3$)	50	4313.980	4520.516	406.000	21887.000
Sales (q) ($\times 10^6$)	50	39015.820	37369.639	2471.000	155707.000
Sales per Customer (spc)	50	23124.070	7177.810	13527.190	41414.990

was 39015.820. Hence, using the average p and q, the estimate of the price elasticity of the demand for electricity in 1977 is $-9956.6134 \cdot (3.219/39015.820) = -0.821$. According to this estimate, a 10 percent increase in electricity rates is, on average, associated with a 8.21 percent decline in electricity consumption.

Similarly, it is possible to estimate the income elasticity, the customer elasticity, and the natural gas price elasticity. You should do this yourself as an exercise. The absence of a relation between the consumption of electricity and the price of natural gas is puzzling and counterintuitive, and the result reported here may be due to a model misspecification. For instance, as we discussed in reference to the income elasticity of demand, the total consumption of electricity is comprised of residential, commercial, and industrial uses, and these three separate consumer groups may have radically different demand functions. Put another way, it may be inappropriate to estimate a single demand equation for electricity. The alternative—of estimating different equations for each consumer class—may be superior. Again, if you wish to pursue this line of inquiry, the data source listed in Table 4.3 reports consumption and price data for each separate consumer class.

Note that in Table 4.4 the t statistic on the estimated coefficient for income is close to zero, and accordingly the probability of obtaining a t statistic that close to zero by chance is large, 0.6545; there is little evidence to reject the null hypothesis of no relation between income and consumption (so we conclude that $\beta_2 = 0$). Therefore, even though the estimate of the income elasticity is $-0.8656 \cdot (6777.02/39015.82) = -0.136$, there is little factual basis to believe the true elasticity is different from zero.[10] The customer elasticity is 0.0210 times the average number of customers divided by the average consumption. The average number of customers per state in 1977 was 1,711,804, and so the customer elasticity estimate is $0.0210 \cdot 1711804/39015 = 0.92$. A 10 percent increase in electricity customers is associated with a 9.2 percent increase in electricity consumption.

Although we have estimated these elasticities at the means of all the variables, other values could have been used, such as the values for any particular state. For example, in 1977 the average price of electricity in the state of Wash-

[10] Table 4.5 reports the average income per capita in the United States in 1977 as $6777.

ington was 0.99 cents per kwh (operation of large-scale hydroelectric generators is mainly responsible for the low price). Consumption was 64,203 million kwh, and income per capita was \$7528. Using these figures, the price elasticity of demand in Washington is $-9956.6134 \cdot (0.99/64203) = -0.153$.[11]

The estimate is considerably more inelastic than at the average, a not-so-surprising finding, considering the low price.[12] The estimate of the income elasticity is $-0.865 \cdot (7528/64203) = -0.103$, which, again, is not statistically significantly different from zero. There were 1,591,668 electricity customers in Washington in 1977; thus, the customer elasticity is $0.021 \cdot (1591668/64203) = 0.5206$, more inelastic than the average state.[13]

Model Specification

The theoretical demand curve used to derive the preceding estimates was not divined from the gods. The linear model used, Model 1,

$$q = \alpha + \beta_1 \cdot p + \beta_2 \cdot y + \beta_3 \cdot c + \beta_4 \cdot g + \varepsilon,$$

is not necessarily the correct one. The functional form could be wrong. Important variables could be omitted, or other flaws could be inherent. This model is just one of many possibilities. For example, there was no variable measuring the effect of weather. If weather affects electricity consumption, then the preceding model is **misspecified**; something is left out.

The model uses total state consumption of electricity as the dependent variable and includes the number of customers as an independent variable to control for the extent of the market. That is, it is the aggregate demand curve for electricity in a state. An alternative is to presume that the individual demands are all the same and compute a consumption per customer variable (labeled *spc*), which is q/c, and estimate the individual demand function. In other words, rather than estimating the total electricity consumed in each state per year, we could specify a model of individual electricity consumption per year. The consumption per customer model, Model 2, is:

$$spc = \alpha + \beta_1 \cdot p + \beta_2 \cdot y + \beta_3 \cdot g + \varepsilon$$

where *spc* is sales per customer or the annual consumption of electricity per

---

[11] A different way, and arguably a better way, to compute the elasticity for an individual state is to *predict* the level of consumption rather than use the actual value.

[12] Recall the discussion in Chapter 3 on changing elasticity along the demand curve.

[13] Econometric studies using this approach commonly estimate the price elasticity of demand for a host of consumer products. For example, it has been estimated that the elasticity of the basic subscription fee for cable television differs between urban and rural systems. See Patricia L. Pacey, "Cable Television in a Less Regulated Market," *Journal of Industrial Economics*, 34(1), September 1985, 81–91. In addition, it has been estimated that the elasticity of demand for medical care is about -0.2. See Willard G. Manning et al., "Health Insurance and the Demand for Medical Care: Evidence from a Randomized Experiment," *American Economic Review*, 77(3), June 1987, 251–77.

customer, and all other variables are the same as before. Table 4.6 reports the OLS estimates of this model.

Comparing Model 2 (Table 4.6) to Model 1 (Table 4.4; see p. 187), we see several things. First, the overall F ratio is higher for Model 1, even though in probabilistic terms the difference is small; both models are significant at the 0.01 percent level. In addition, the R^2 is higher for Model 1. However, you are strongly cautioned that it is not strictly valid to compare the R^2's directly unless the dependent variables are the same. In this situation, we have two different dependent variables, total consumption and consumption per customer, and the two R^2's should only be used as a rough guide. Do not base policy on the difference in R^2's when models have different dependent variables. However, the preferred method is more complicated. It involves the prediction of the dependent variable in comparable terms and the use of sophisticated statistical tests. Comparing the individual t ratios, the only important difference is that the coefficient on the price of natural gas, g, is significantly different from zero at the 10 percent **confidence level**, $\alpha = 0.10$, in Model 2, but not in Model 1. Using Model 1, there is slight evidence that gas and electricity are substitutes. Using Model 2, however, there is more evidence that the demand for electricity increases when the price of gas goes up. Which model is correct? In truth there is no way to know. The analyst has to use experience and judgment. In this case, both models fit the data well and both should be considered. A wise manager would look at both projections, perhaps weighting the estimates of Model 1 slightly higher.[14]

How do other estimates of the two models compare? Computing the price elasticity from Model 2, we multiply the coefficient on price, -6924.1518, times the average price, 3.219, divided by the average consumption per customer, 23,124.07. The result is

$$(\partial q/\partial p)/(p/q) = -6924.1518 \cdot (3.219/23124.07) = -0.964.$$

TABLE 4.6   ESTIMATES OF REGRESSION PARAMETERS—MODEL 2

Dependent Variable: Sales per Customer (*spc*)

F Ratio	Prob $>F$	Root Mean Squared Error	R^2
21.820	0.0001	4759.1865	0.5873

VARIABLE	PARAMETER ESTIMATE	STANDARD ERROR	t RATIO	PROB $>|t|$
Intercept	39194.0000	4947.3237	7.922	0.0001
Price of Electricity (*p*)	-6924.1518	924.9108	-7.486	0.0001
Income per Capita (*y*)	0.4848	0.7614	0.637	0.5275
Price of Natural Gas (*g*)	1350.9594	794.7378	1.700	0.0959

---

[14] For a more sophisticated discussion on functional form see Damodar Gujarti, *Basic Econometrics*, 2d ed. (New York: McGraw-Hill, 1988), pp. 147, 183–84.

Recall that the estimate of the price elasticity of demand from Model 1 was -0.821. How then do we choose between the models? Using the notion of confidence limits, we can investigate the statistical difference between these two estimates.

Confidence limits are statistical bounds placed on parameter estimates. Confidence limits place upper and lower limits that surround the actual value of a parameter with a certain degree of probability. For example, we may wish to know the upper and lower bounds of an estimated coefficient, such that the true (but unobserved) coefficient lies within these bounds with probability 95 percent. Calculating the limits requires the investigator to make an assertion about the correct distribution of the sample estimate. In the case of regression parameter estimates, the t distribution is used. The upper and lower confidence limits are given by the following formulas:

$$U_{\alpha,n} = \beta + s_{\beta} \cdot t_{(\alpha/2, n-m-2)}$$

$$L_{\alpha,n} = \beta - s_{\beta} \cdot t_{(\alpha/2, n-m-2)}$$

where β is the regression parameter, α is the chosen probability of a Type I error, n is the number of observations in the regression sample, s_{α} is the standard error of the estimated coefficient β, m is the number of independent variables in the model (excluding the intercept), and $t_{(\alpha/2, n-m-2)}$ is the value of the t statistic with $n - m - 2$ degrees of freedom and with $\alpha/2$ probability in each tail of the distribution. In this case, β from Model 1 is -9956.6, and s_{β} is 2344.1. The value of β from Model 2 is -6924.1518, and its standard error is 924.9108. With $n = 50$ and $\alpha = 0.05$, $t_{(\alpha/2, n-m-2)} = 2.0$. However, we do not want to test the equality of the β's but rather the two elasticities. Hence, we must adjust the formulas for U and L. To do this, we substitute the elasticity estimate for β, and we calculate the standard error of the elasticity estimate as follows: The standard error of β is s_{β}. The elasticity *at the mean of the data* is $\beta \cdot$ (average price/average consumption). Hence, the standard error of the elasticity estimate is $s_{\beta} \cdot$ (average price/average consumption). Correspondingly, Table 4.7 reports the calculations of U and L for both elasticity estimates.

α, the probability of a Type I error, was chosen as 0.05. This means the probability that the actual value of the parameter lies outside the bounds defined by the upper and lower limits is 0.05. In the case of Model 1, U is -0.435, and L is -1.207. There is only a 5 percent chance that the true value of the elasticity using Model 1 is smaller in absolute value than 0.435 or larger than 1.207. In the case of Model 2, the bounds are closer together. Notice that s_{β} is smaller in Model 2, relative to the price coefficient, than it is in Model 1. This is confirmed by the larger t ratio on price in Model 2 than in Model 1. The upper limit is -0.706, and the lower limit is -1.222. Figure 4.4 plots the densities of the two elasticities. Both are assumed to be distributed according to the t distribution. Inspection reveals that there is considerable overlap between the two.[15] If the effort to predict the

---

[15] It is possible to test the equality of the two elasticities directly using a t statistic. See Jan Kmenta, *Elements of Econometrics* (New York: Macmillan Publishing Co., 1971), pp. 235–39 for the details.

| TABLE 4.7   CONFIDENCE LIMITS ON ELASTICITY ESTIMATES | |

	MODEL 1	MODEL 2

$$\beta = -9956 \qquad s_\beta = 2344 \qquad \qquad \beta = -6924 \qquad s_\beta = 924.9$$
$$\eta = -9956 \cdot (3.219/39105.8) \qquad \qquad \eta = -6924 \cdot (3.219/23124)$$
$$= -0.821 \qquad \qquad = -0.964$$
$$s_\eta = 2344 \cdot (3.219/39105.8) \qquad \qquad s_\eta = 924.9 \cdot (3.219/23124)$$
$$= 0.193 \qquad \qquad = 0.129$$
$$U = -0.821 + 2.0 \cdot 0.193 \qquad \qquad U = -0.964 + 2.0 \cdot 0.129$$
$$= -0.435 \qquad \qquad = -0.706$$
$$L = -0.821 - 2.0 \cdot 0.193 \qquad \qquad L = -0.964 - 2.0 \cdot 0.129$$
$$= -1.207 \qquad \qquad = -1.222$$

elasticity were to stop here, the analyst would conclude with a great deal of probability that the elasticity lies between -0.435 and -1.222. More exactly, the point estimate of the elasticity lies between -0.821 and -0.964. If more apparent precision were required (without the benefit of additional information), the average of -0.821 and -0.964 suggests a prediction of -0.893. The appropriate question to ask now is, What other information can be obtained cheaply?

Consider the exponential form of the demand function:

$$q = \alpha \cdot p^{\beta_1} \cdot y^{\beta_2} \cdot c^{\beta_3} \cdot g^{\beta_4} \cdot \varepsilon.$$

The function can be rewritten by taking the natural logarithm of each side of the equation. This functional form is called an **exponential** or a log model and is written:

$$\ln q = \ln \alpha + \beta_1 \cdot (\ln p) + \beta_2 \cdot (\ln y) + \beta_3 \cdot (\ln c) + \beta_4 \cdot (\ln g) + \ln \varepsilon.$$

FIGURE 4.4
Elasticity Densities

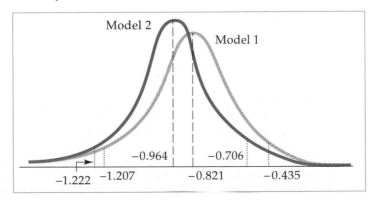

Figure 4.4

This transformed model of demand can be estimated using OLS just like Models 1 and 2. All that is necessary is for the observations on q, p, y, c, and g to be positive. If any one of these data points is negative, then the natural log does not exist, and the corresponding observations must be discarded. In this particular analysis, however, all observations have positive values. Consequently, all that is required to investigate the quality of this model specification is to take the natural logarithm of each independent variable and the dependent variable, substitute each of these respectively, and reestimate the model parameters using ordinary-least-squares. The OLS estimates of Model 3 are reported in Table 4.8.

The logarithmic specification performs well in comparison to Models 1 and 2. The F statistic and the R^2 are both higher.[16] This suggests that we also investigate the exponential version of Model 2:[17]

$$\ln spc = \ln \alpha + \beta_1 \bullet (\ln p) + \beta_2 \bullet (\ln y) + \beta_3 \bullet (\ln g) + \ln \varepsilon.$$

The OLS estimates of α and β_1–β_3 for this model are reported in Table 4.9.

Model 4, although better than its counterpart, Model 2, does not perform as well as Model 3. However, all may not be as it seems. Models 2 and 4 are not strictly comparable with Models 1 and 3. The first and third models predict total state demand. Models 2 and 4 predict consumption per customer. The chores, although comparable, are not exact, and the appropriate model actually depends upon the question at hand.

Compare the elasticity estimates derived from Models 2 and 4 with the ones computed for Models 1 and 3. In the log specification, computing elasticities is

---

TABLE 4.8   REGRESSION ESTIMATES OF PARAMETERS—MODEL 3

Dependent Variable: Log of Sales (ln q)

F Ratio	Prob $>F$	Root Mean Squared Error	R^2
362.039	0.0001	0.19708	0.9699

VARIABLE	PARAMETER ESTIMATE	STANDARD ERROR	t RATIO	PROB $>|t|$
Intercept	-3.8185	1.9216	-1.9870	0.0530
Log of Price of Electricity (ln p)	-0.6918	0.0962	-7.1902	0.0001
Log of Income per Capita (ln y)	-0.0007	0.2184	-0.0030	0.9976
Log of Customers (ln c)	1.0563	0.0279	37.8760	0.0001
Log of Price of Natural Gas (ln g)	0.0137	0.0840	0.1624	0.8717

---

[16] It is not strictly valid to compare the R^2's directly. However, the preferred method is more complicated. It involves the prediction of the dependent variable in levels using the log coefficient, and thus we employ the shortcut method of direct comparison.

[17] The notation ln and log are used interchangeably, both referring to the natural logarithm.

TABLE 4.9   REGRESSION ESTIMATES OF PARAMETERS—MODEL 4

Dependent Variable: Log of Sales per Customer (ln *spc*)

F Ratio	Prob >F	Root Mean Squared Error	R^2
18.558	0.0001	0.20355	0.5476

VARIABLE	PARAMETER ESTIMATE	STANDARD ERROR	t RATIO	PROB $> |t|$
Intercept	10.6188	1.9590	5.420	0.0001
Log of Price of Electricity (ln *p*)	−0.6730	0.0989	−6.805	0.0001
Log of Income per Capita (ln *y*)	0.0150	0.2254	0.066	0.9473
Log of Price of Natural Gas (ln *g*)	0.0148	0.0868	0.170	0.8656

much easier. Recall that elasticity is the percentage of change in quantity demanded for the percentage of change in price. Therefore, since the coefficient on price in the log model is $\partial \log(q)/\partial \log(p)$ by construction, the elasticity is read directly from the regression output; the estimated coefficient is the estimated elasticity. In the case of Model 3, the estimate is -0.6918, and in Model 4 it is -0.6730. Using the formulas for confidence limits, we can calculate the interval that contains the true elasticity with probability of error 5 percent. The standard error in Model 3 is 0.0962, and it is 0.0989 in the case of Model 4. Correspondingly, the upper bound for the estimate of the elasticity in Model 3 is

$$-0.6918 + s_\beta \bullet t_{(\alpha/2, n-m-2)} = -0.6918 + 0.0962 \bullet 2.0 = -0.499.$$

LOG EQUATIONS AND ELASTICITY

Mathematically,

(% change q)/(% change p) $\equiv (\partial q/q)/(\partial p/p)$

or

$= (\partial q/\partial p) \bullet (p/q),$

but this is also equal to

$\partial \log(q)/\partial \log(p).$

Therefore, the estimated β coefficient is the estimated value of the elasticity directly.

The lower bound is $-0.6918 - 0.0962 \bullet 2.0 = -0.8842$. Similarly, the upper and lower bounds for the Model 4 estimate of the price elasticity of demand for electricity are $-0.6730 + 0.0989 \bullet 2.0 = -0.4752$ and $-0.6730 - 0.0989 \bullet 2.0 = -0.8708$.

Comparing these estimates with the earlier estimates from the linear model, we observe that the elasticity estimates from the log specifications are slightly smaller in absolute value, but all told the results are remarkably similar. This gives us added confidence that our estimate of the price elasticity of demand is not very sensitive to the choice of model specification.

Forecasting

One of the uses of econometric models is forecasting. **Forecasting** is the art and science of predicting the course of the future. Naturally this is dangerous business, and most forecasters are well aware of the limitations of their business. For instance, reconsider the model of electricity demand, Model 1:

$$q = 36136.2339 - 9956.6134 \bullet p - 0.8656 \bullet y + 0.0210 \bullet c + 2221.7663 \bullet g.$$

Suppose you were working for the Office of the Governor of the State of Michigan in 1978, and you were given the job of forecasting the level of electricity demand in 1980. You decided to use Model 1 to create your prognostication. What would you do? First, reexamine Table 4.3 on page 184. There you can observe that the price of electricity in Michigan in 1977 was 3.64 cents per kwh. The income per capita was $7619; the number of customers was 3,548,461, and the price of natural gas was $2.062.

You have estimated that Michigan's population will be 1 percent higher in 1980 than it was in 1977. Also, officials at the Public Service Commission have led you to believe that the price of electricity will not increase much over the next three years, perhaps only 2 percent. They have also predicted that the price of natural gas will actually decline by as much as 5 percent. Colleagues in your office have predicted that income will grow 4 percent per year for two years, and hence the cumulative growth in income is 8 percent over two years.[18] Based on these numbers, how much electricity do you forecast that Michigan will consume in 1980?

First, if the population increases by 1 percent, we can reasonably expect the number of electricity consumers to increase by a similar number. Thus we project that the number of consumers will also increase by 1 percent. The number of customers in 1977 was 3,548,461. Therefore, the forecast for the number of customers in 1980 is $1.01 \bullet 3,548,461 = 3,583,945$. The price of electricity is expected to be 2 percent higher, or $1.02 \bullet 3.64 = 3.713$. We expect that income will be 8 percent higher or $8229. A 5 percent decline in the price of natural gas predicts a price of $0.95 \bullet 2.062 = 1.959$ in the year 1980. We now have all the tools necessary to forecast

---

[18] Actually the growth will be $4\% + 4\% + 4\% \bullet 4\% = 8.16\%$, but the proof of that proposition must wait until next chapter, and for now we simply assume that income is 8 percent higher.

electricity consumption in Michigan in 1980. We have a model and the predicted parameters, and we have forecasts for values of all the independent variables. The next step is simply to insert the values for the independent variables into the formula:

$q = 36136.2339 - 9956.6134 \bullet p - 0.8656 \bullet y + 0.0210 \bullet c + 2221.7663 \bullet g.$

Price (1980) $= 1.02 \bullet 3.64 = 3.713$

Income (1980) $= 1.08 \bullet 7619 = 8229$

Customers (1980) $= 1.01 \bullet 3,548,461 = 3,583,945$

Gas Price (1980) $= 0.95 \bullet 2.62 = 1.959$

Therefore,

q (1980) $= 36136.2339 - 9956.6134 \bullet 3.713 - 0.8656 \bullet 8229 + 0.0210 \bullet 3583945 +$ 2221.7663 \bullet 1.959,

or

q (1980) $= 71,760$ million kwh of electricity.

You have probably heard the old expression "garbage in, garbage out." That idiom was probably created by forecasters. The prediction we have made is based on the guesses of experts in several different fields, precisely the estimates of price, income, population, and natural gas price in 1980, and the forecast is no better or more accurate than those projections. One way to deal with this inherent uncertainty is to construct confidence limits on the forecast.

To better understand the nature of this forecast and the confidence limits surrounding it, let us examine the forecast in more detail. The forecast can deviate from the actual value for two reasons. First, there is some inherent randomness in the consumption of electricity. Notice that our model only explains about 90 percent of the variation in consumption across states. There are factors not included in our model that affect consumption; the model is not perfect. We have noted that the weather is not included. Furthermore, even if we had data over many years, we would still have some error in our forecasts due to randomness and omitted variables. Second, any one forecast can deviate from the actual value because of **sampling error**. Sampling error occurs when the estimated coefficient differs from the true value because we have estimated the parameter using a sample of information, not the entire population of data. The first problem has no direct solution, but the second obstacle can be overcome, or at least mitigated, by increasing the number of observations. All together this means that the variance of the forecast error will be higher when

1. The sample size is smaller.
2. The independent variables are not dispersed very much.
3. The specific values of the independent variables for the forecast in question are distant from their sample means.

In order to create a small confidence interval, it is necessary to use a large sample with disperse independent variables near their means.

The upper and lower confidence limits on the forecast are computed using the following formulas:

UPPER LIMIT: Forecast $+ s_F{\bullet}t_{(n-m-2,\ \alpha/2)})$

LOWER LIMIT: Forecast $- s_F{\bullet}t_{(n-m-2,\ \alpha/2)}.$

The forecast is the number we have computed, s_F is the standard error of the forecast, $t_{(n-m-2,\ \alpha/2)}$ is the value of the t distribution with $n-m-2$ degrees of freedom, and α is the probability of Type I error, the significance level chosen by you, the investigator. The formula for the standard error of the forecast is slightly complicated, but most computer software packages will cipher it for you. In the case of just one right-hand side independent variable, the formula is:

$$s_F = \sigma^2 \times (1 + \frac{1}{n} + \frac{x_i - \overline{x}}{\sum\limits_{i=1}^{n} x_i^2})$$

where σ^2 is the variance of dependent variable, consumption per state in this case; and $\overline{x}$ is the mean of the independent variable.[19]

Econometricians also forecast using time series of data. The analysis here is sophisticated and powerful. Indeed most undergraduate and MBA curriculums offer whole courses on the topic.[20] Univariate time series analysis of data can be very revealing and rewarding, but the subject is simply too complex to be covered here and necessarily must be left for other courses and books.

The Technique of Dummy Variables

All of the models presented so far have employed continuous variables. However, a lot of economic problems involve discrete variables. The seasonality of consumption immediately comes to mind. For instance, the enormous increase in retail sales that takes place around Christmas or the big jump in student-age population occurring in Ft. Lauderdale around spring break are two examples of highly seasonal demand conditions. When examining a time series of sales that includes such periods, the technique of **dummy variables** can be quite useful. A dummy variable is simply a variable that normally takes the value 0 or 1 in the regression. Again, think of Christmas sales. To control for the Christmas effect in a demand equation, a December dummy variable can be inserted. This dummy variable takes the value 0 for all observations except those in December, and it

---

[19] The variance of the dependent variable is estimated by the mean square error from the regression.

[20] For a vision of this field, consult Charles R. Nelson, *Applied Time Series Analysis for Managerial Forecasting* (San Francisco: Holden-Day Inc., 1973).

takes the value 1 for any data during the month of December. The coefficient on the dummy variable then captures the change in sales due to the Christmas crunch.

Consider the following model of demand:

$$q = \alpha + \beta p + \delta D + \varepsilon$$

where q is the quantity demanded, p is the price of the good, D is a 0,1 dummy variable taking the value 1 for December and 0 for all other months, α is the intercept, β is the slope coefficient on price, and δ is the dummy coefficient. Since the dummy variable takes the value 0 in all months but December, the model is equivalent to one *without* the dummy for the first eleven months of the year. However, for any observation during December, the intercept, α, shifts by an amount equal to δ, the coefficient on the dummy. Dummy variables are simply intercept shift parameters that capture idiosyncratic characteristics of specific data points in the analysis.

Dummy variables can be used effectively to improve the reliability of parameter estimates because they can reduce residual variance. At the same time, the technique can be abused when the researcher uses them indiscriminately without adequate theoretical guidance or in lieu of collecting data on the true underlying structural variable that the dummy represents. For example, in a model of electricity consumption, you may be inclined to use a dummy variable for the states west of the Mississippi River in place of population or population density. Because most of those states have low population densities, your dummy variable would likely be significant. The better method is to use the underlying structural variables, population and density. If the dummy remains significant after these variables are included, it would be wise to search for the economic characteristics of the western population that affect consumption. The cost of using dummy variables is that they mask the true model of consumption, and they should only be used with caution and after careful examination has failed to reveal the underlying causal variable that is being dummied.

Summary

What is regression analysis? Imagine you have drawn some circles of different circumferences. Now suppose you measure the circumference and the diameter of each circle. Call these C and D respectively. This creates a database of C_i's and D_i's with the same number of observations as circles you have drawn. Now, specify a linear function relating circumference to diameter of the form $C = \alpha + \beta \bullet D$. Next, using regression analysis, estimate the coefficients α and β. What do you expect to find? First, if you have measured the circumferences and diameters very accurately then the estimated α is 0 and the estimated β is 3.1416. Why is this so? In this case we know the true relation between the circumference of a circle and its diameter, $C = 3.1416 \bullet D$. The t ratios on the coefficients are a function of accuracy in measurement. Since α truly is 0, the expected t ratio on this coefficient is 0; there should be no evidence to reject the null hypothesis that $\alpha = 0$. By contrast, when measurement is accurate, the t ratio on β is high because we know there truly is a relation between diameter and circumference, leading us to reject the null hypothesis that $\beta = 0$.

In this example, there is an exact relation between C and D (we expect most of the error terms to be very close to 0); however, there remains a single source of error, our ability to draw and measure correctly. Therefore, unless measurement is perfect, R^2, gauging goodness of fit, will be less than 1. With careful and accurate measurement, R^2 approaches 1. Sloppy measurement reduces R^2. Even then, unless the same mistake is made repeatedly, the coefficient on β is expected to be the famous constant π. Many constants in nature are discovered via trial-and-error techniques remarkably similar to regression analysis, that is, looking at the association between one number and another. The economic problems dealt with in this text, such as discovering a particular demand function, are no different.

THE QUALITY OF THE ESTIMATES

In order for OLS estimation to have the desirable statistical characteristics and for the appropriate economic interpretation to be reliable, certain criteria must be met. Notably, (1) the error terms must be uncorrelated with any of the independent variables or any linear combination of the independent variables; (2) if the independent variables are not fixed, they must be uncorrelated with each other; (3) the variance of the error term must be constant across observations; and (4) the individual errors must be uncorrelated across observations. If any of these four criteria is not met, then OLS can produce unreliable results. In most cases, the investigator can determine the seriousness of the problem, if he or she is willing to bear the costs of examining the underlying characteristics of the OLS output.

Simultaneous Equation Bias

The first of these four problems is most serious, and the solution to the problem is typically expensive. The problem generally occurs when the researcher is trying to explain one dependent variable, but one of the independent variables is a function of the dependent variable under scrutiny. This problem is referred to as an endogeniety problem or a **simultaneous equation bias**. The dependent variable is sometimes called the endogenous variable; its value is determined inside the model. When there is a simultaneous equation bias, the model has more than one endogenous variable.

Consider the typical demand and supply model. Suppose the specified demand equation is

$$q = \alpha + \beta_1 p + \beta_2 y + \beta_3 z + \varepsilon$$

where p is price, y is income, and z is other things.

This model argues that quantity demanded is a function of price. However, when a market is in equilibrium, quantity demanded is the same as quantity supplied. Thus, when we measure quantity demanded, we also measure quantity supplied, and what makes this a problem is the fact that quantity supplied can also respond to price. Thus, price moves about in a marketplace because both demand and supply curves shift about. If we do not take this knowledge into account, we can be in for serious errors in analysis. Examine Figure 4.5. There we show the case where demand is shifting at the same time as supply. The data points that would be observed are (p_1, q_1), (p_2, q_2), (p_3, q_3), and (p_4, q_4). In this case, the model generating q is also generating p. OLS estimates of the parameters α and β_1, through movements in y and z, might lead to seriously flawed conclusions. To correct this problem, the investigator must also specify a second equation, the supply function:

$$p = \alpha' + \beta'_1 q + \beta'_2 w + \varepsilon'$$

where w represents the appropriate factor or input prices and q is endogenous and jointly estimate α, β_1 through β_3, α', and β'_1 through β'_2 at the same time.[21] Only then will the estimates of the hypothesized demand function have the desired economic interpretation.

FIGURE 4.5
Simultaneous Equation Bias

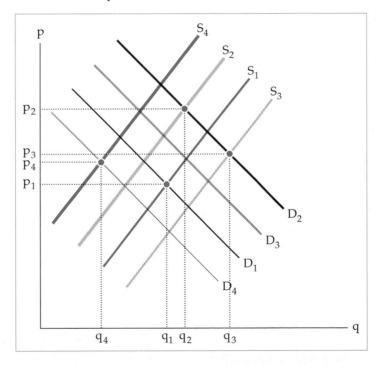

---

[21] This is accomplished using techniques such as two-stage-least-squares, three-stage-least-squares, seemingly unrelated regressions, or instrumental variables technique. Modern econometric texts detail which one of these is appropriate for a given circumstance. See for example Jan Kmenta, *Elements of Econometrics* (New York: Macmillan, 1971); John Johnston, *Econometric Methods* (New York: McGraw-Hill, 1972); or Michael Intriligator, *Econometric Model, Techniques, and Applications* (Englewood Cliffs, NJ: Prentice Hall, 1978).

Multicollinearity

Another of the problems encountered in demand estimation is **multicollinearity**. Here, the independent variables in the selected sample are not fixed or independent of each other. However, the resulting estimates are generally not seriously flawed. The only real problem is that the estimates of the standard errors on the coefficients are inflated, which may incorrectly lead us to believe that an independent variable is unrelated to the dependent variable when it truly is. Multicollinearity is a property of the sample collected, and hence a common cure is to collect more data. Alternatively, we could delete one of the variables in the model.

For example, multicollinearity can be a problem in regressions when both income and education are used as independent variables. Suppose we were estimating the demand for pianos, and we hypothesized that income and education both affect consumption; richer and more educated people have a higher demand for pianos. Since people with a lot of education often have high incomes, there stands to be a correlation between the two independent variables, and in small samples this can cloud our OLS results. Typically, one or both of the independent variables, income and education in this case, will be insignificant. Indeed, one might even take the wrong sign, and this is usually a clue that multicollinearity is affecting the sample.

Detecting multicollinearity is sometimes difficult, particularly when the number of explanatory variables is greater than three or four. One can never be sure that some combination of the independent variables is not related to some other linear combination of the independent variables. Most analysts do two things to check for multicollinearity. First, they look for insignificant variables when prior research or theory strongly suggests a significant relation. Second, by examining the simple correlation among the independent variables, they can sometimes spot the problem. Third, when the model F statistic and R^2 are high, but the individual t statistics are low, multicollinearity may be present.

Heteroskedasticity

A third problem that arises in econometric analysis is called **heteroskedasticity**. When it exists, the variance of the error term for some observations is different from the variance of the error term for others. This can happen in cross-sectional data analysis when, for example, states or households with high income have low variance, and states or households with low income have high variance. When the variance of the residuals is not constant across observations, the residuals typically present a pattern similar to the one depicted in Figure 4.6. When this problem is present, the OLS estimates under heteroskedasticity are unbiased, but the sampling variance is higher than it should be. The OLS formulas for computing the standard errors of the coefficients are biased. To correct this problem, the **weighted-least-squares** methodology is employed to homogenize the variance of the errors. The first step is to identify the variable linked to heteroskedasticity, say income in a cross-sectional regression. Then you must determine if the residual variance increases or decreases with the variable linked to the heteroskedasticity. If residual variance declines, then the appropriate weighted-least-squares meth-

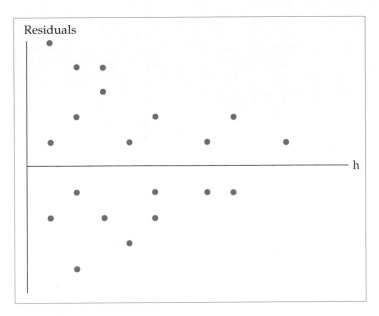

Residuals

h

FIGURE 4.6
Heteroskedasticity

odology is to multiply each data point, all the y's and the x's, by the inverse of the root of the respective variable. Let w_i be the weighting device for the ith observation, then

$$w_i = 1/(\sqrt{h_i})$$

where h_i is the variable linked to the heteroskedasticity of variance. If the residual variance *increases* with the linked variable, then the weighting device is simply the square root of the linked variable:

$$w_i = \sqrt{h_i}$$

In either case, to compute weighted-least-squares estimates of the coefficients, simply run ordinary-least-squares on the original model, multiplying each data point by its respective w_i.

There are other ways to detect and correct for heteroskedasticity. For instance, it is possible to discover patterns in the residuals or error terms. These patterns can then be used to readjust the estimates of the standard errors used to compute t ratios about coefficients. This technique is especially useful when the economic analyst has little prior intuition or knowledge about the structure of the heteroskedasticity.[22]

---

[22] See Halbert White, "A Heteroskedasticity-Consistent Covariance Matrix Estimator and a Direct Test for Heteroskedasticity," *Econometrics*, 48, 1980, 817–38 for more details.

Autocorrelation

In time series analysis, it is common for the error terms to be **autocorrelated**. When this happens, the error in one period is related to errors in the past. When the actual form of the correlation between errors can be deduced from the data, the problem is correctable. If autocorrelation is present, serious, and not corrected, the standard errors of the coefficient on the independent variables are biased downward, causing the *t* ratios to be too high. As a consequence, the investigator is led to believe that independent variables are related to the dependent variable when, in fact, they are not.

Autocorrelation can be easy or difficult to detect. When the structure of the autocorrelation is uncomplicated, say of the first order (meaning that the error in one period is related to the error in the previous period), then a simple correlation coefficient is an easy gauge of the problem.[23] At the same time, a test called the Durbin-Watson test exists and is useful. When the structure is more complicated, autocorrelation is more difficult to detect and requires more diligence and sophistication.

Examining the Residuals

The residuals or error terms from OLS can provide clues as to whether any of these problems exists. Moreover, they help to determine if important independent variables have been left out of a model. Table 4.10 lists the residuals from OLS estimation of Model 2.

Notice the extreme values of the residuals. These are sometimes referred to as outliers. They can be a valuable source of information, helping you to identify a misspecified model. Look for patterns in the residuals. For instance, are the residuals from the New England states all of the same sign? Are the largest residuals in the largest states, or the smallest ones, or are they randomly distributed by size of state? Notice that the model does an excellent job of predicting the consumption in Alaska and West Virginia; the errors are almost nil. At the same time, the model does a weak job predicting consumption in Maine and Tennessee. The model grossly overestimates consumption in Maine, while it predicts far less than actual consumption in Tennessee, but, on the surface, these do not seem to suggest a pattern.

The residuals are plotted against income per capita in Figure 4.7. A number of the states are annotated. Although the picture is less than definitive, it suggests that the residuals are smaller as income increases. This prospect can be investigated with regression analysis. Each error term is used to form a separate estimate of the variance of the residuals. First, square the error terms; call this **squared error**. Then determine if there is a systematic relation between any of the independent variables and the squared errors. The common way to do this is to take the natural logarithm of the squared errors and the variables that might logically

---

[23] Second order correlation means the residuals are correlated with the errors two time periods in the past and so on.

TABLE 4.10	OLS Residuals from Model 2						
State	Actual Consumption per Customer	Prediction of Model 2	Residual (Actual–Prediction)	State	Actual Consumption per Customer	Prediction of Model 2	Residual (Actual–Prediction)
AK	19114	19101	13	MT	29667	34754	−5087
AL	31735	24800	6935	NC	24978	24751	228
AR	21628	21475	152	ND	16842	23084	−6242
AZ	25172	18199	6974	NE	19166	24923	−5757
CA	17431	20616	−3185	NH	14201	16782	−2581
CO	16072	24676	−8604	NJ	16824	12596	4228
CT	16931	18928	−1997	NM	18402	22047	−3645
DE	23827	17180	6648	NV	28148	24941	3207
FL	19743	19061	682	NY	16172	12753	3419
GA	23429	22087	1343	OH	29117	25378	3740
HI	21042	20335	707	OK	21377	24322	−2945
IA	18734	20704	−1971	OR	33092	34807	−1715
ID	37574	33794	3780	PA	21223	20304	919
IL	21593	22349	−756	RI	13527	14344	−817
IN	25784	24537	1247	SC	29619	24293	5326
KS	20257	21751	−1494	SD	15044	22654	−7610
KY	39034	30116	8918	TN	41415	29687	11728
LA	33338	28735	4602	TX	31169	25244	5925
MA	14812	13719	1093	UT	19667	24222	−4554
MD	23816	20338	3478	VA	23840	20967	2873
ME	14476	24557	−10081	VT	15174	20655	−5481
MI	19683	20436	−753	WA	40337	39154	1183
MN	18363	22136	−3773	WI	18289	22856	−4566
MO	18200	22014	−3814	WV	25347	25283	64
MS	23461	21679	1782	WY	28317	32081	−3765

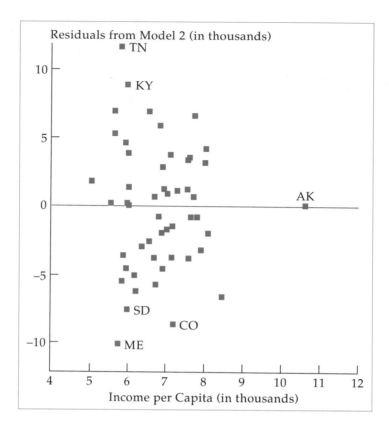

FIGURE 4.7
Residuals from Model 2

be linked with heteroskedasticity. For example, Table 4.11 reports the OLS regression of ln (e_i^2) from Model 2 on the natural log of (1) state income per capita (ln y), (2) the number of customers in the state (ln c), and (3) the state population (ln pop).

From Table 4.11 observe that there is no statistically credible relation between the estimated residual variance [ln (e_i^2)] and the log of customers or the log of population. In each case, the F ratio and t ratio are insignificant, signaling no relation between residual variance and customers or population. This suggests that residual variance is not a function of any of these two things. However, in the case of income per capita, the F statistic and t ratio suggest a negative relation between income per capita and the estimated variance. Recall that we suspected this from the plot in Figure 4.7. It seems that variance is smaller when income is larger. The chances are small, less than 3 percent, that we could have obtained an F or t statistic this high by chance alone. We conclude that insofar as we have gone, there may be a problem of heteroskedasticity that is linked with income per capita, and weighted-least-squares estimation of Model 2 is in order.

Most statistical software packages will perform weighted-least-squares regression automatically, that is, without you, the investigator, having to create the weighting variable. However, you should always be aware of what the software is doing to prevent misinterpretation of the results. Since the estimated

TABLE 4.11 EXAMINATION OF ERROR VARIANCE—TESTING FOR HETEROSKEDASTICITY

Dependent Variable: Log of Squared Residuals ($\ln e_t^2$)

F Ratio	Prob $>F$	Root Mean Squared Error	R^2
5.626	0.0218	2.49973	0.1049

VARIABLE	PARAMETER ESTIMATE	STANDARD ERROR	t RATIO	PROB $>|t|$
Intercept	70.8861	23.3775	3.032	0.0039
Log of Income per Capita ($\ln y$)	−6.2915	2.6526	−2.372	0.0218

F Ratio	Prob $>F$	Root Mean Squared Error	R^2
0.043	0.8368	2.64098	0.0009

Intercept	14.3781	5.1628	2.785	0.0076
Log of Customers ($\ln c$)	0.0768	0.3708	0.207	0.8368

F Ratio	Prob $>F$	Root Mean Squared Error	R^2
0.000	0.9856	2.64215	0.0000

Intercept	15.3920	2.9174	5.276	0.0001
Log of Population ($\ln pop$)	0.00670	0.3668	0.018	0.9856

residual variance is assumed to be increasing with income per capita, the appropriate weighting technique is to multiply all the variables used in the estimation of Model 2 by the square root of income per capita. Table 4.12 reports the weighted-least-squares estimates, and you can compare them with the ordinary-least-squares estimates in Table 4.6. They do not differ dramatically. The differences are minor, and were you to test them, you would not find any of the

TABLE 4.12 WEIGHTED-LEAST-SQUARES ESTIMATES OF MODEL 2

Dependent Variable: Sales per Customer (*spc*)—Weighted by the Square Root of Income per Capita

F Ratio	Prob $>F$	Root Mean Squared Error	R^2
20.974	0.0001	59.95967	0.5777

VARIABLE (All weighted by $\sqrt{y}$)	PARAMETER ESTIMATE	STANDARD ERROR	t RATIO	PROB $>|t|$
Intercept	40026.0000	5267.8511	7.598	0.0001
Price of Electricity (p)	−7065.3964	965.4676	−7.318	0.0001
Income per Capita (y)	0.4609	0.8304	0.555	0.5816
Price of Natural Gas (g)	1251.6548	849.2346	1.474	0.1473

differences to be statistically significant. Nevertheless, given the link between residual variance and income per capita we have uncovered, the weighted estimates are deemed superior.

MANAGING ECONOMETRIC STUDIES

The management of econometric studies presents a variety of challenges. An essential ingredient to any quality econometric study is variance in the dependent and independent variables. For example, suppose you are trying to estimate the price elasticity of demand for one of your company's products; let's say it is a computer modem. If the price is the same week in and week out, you have no way of estimating the relation between price and sales. Similarly, if you are trying to determine the relation between the frequency and size of magazine ads for the modem and their sales, but the ads are always in the same magazine, the copy is always the same, and the location in the magazine does not vary, then it is practically impossible to do econometric analysis. It is essential to find ways to adjust price, to change advertising copy, to shift ad location, and to manipulate the price of related products, or econometric analysis will be valueless or, worse, extremely misleading.[24] This helps us understand why companies have sales, why they offer discounts, and why they proffer coupons. Each of these is a way of cutting price, which in turn allows the company to measure the sales response. The company can take advantage of variation in sales to estimate the demand curve for its product.

Take a simple one variable case of y regressed on x. The standard error of the estimated coefficient is

$$s_{\hat{\beta}} = \sqrt{\frac{\frac{\sum_{i=1}^{n} e_i^2}{(n-2)}}{\sum_{i=1}^{n} x_i^2}}$$

Notice that as the sum of the x_i^2's increases, holding constant the sum of the squared errors, the standard error of the coefficient decreases because the denominator of the expression is larger. Also, as sample size increases, the standard error of the coefficient decreases because the numerator is smaller. That is, as the variation in the independent variable increases and the sample size gets larger, other things being the same, the standard error of the coefficient is smaller.

---

[24] For a slightly different view of the problems associated with estimating demand, consult the article by F. William Barnett, "Four Steps to Forecast Total Market Demand," *Harvard Business Review*, 88(4), July–August 1988, 28–38.

SUMMARY

Econometric or quantitative analysis is indispensable for helping to solve a host of managerial problems. Among these are pricing and output decisions. Typically, demand estimation is fundamental to planning for the future, determining product prices, and scheduling output. The basic tool used is regression analysis—curve fitting. A number of statistical concepts help the manager quantify his or her intuition. These include F and t ratios, R^2, and residual analysis. No textbook can ever hope to provide the prospective manager with the sufficient skills to master all the nuances of econometrics. Hands-on work and practical skills learned through many hours of trial and error are the only way to master demand estimation. Only the rudiments have been presented in this chapter.

Hypothetical Business Problem 4.1 was presented at the beginning of this chapter. The question asks whether the restaurant whose sales figures are reported there has properly set its prices. Using the tools of regression analysis, you should now be able to construct a solution to that problem by estimating a demand equation for meals in that establishment and then inspecting the price elasticity of demand.

Suggested Solution to Problem 4.1

One way to attack this problem is to ask the question, What is the price elasticity of demand? Is it inelastic or elastic? For instance, if it turns out that demand is estimated to be inelastic, the suggestion is that price is too low (see the discussion in Chapter 2, page 26, on the relation between elasticity and total revenue). Consider the following linear model of restaurant demand:

$$CUS = \beta_0 + \beta_1 AVREV + \beta_2 FCA + \beta_3 ADS + \beta_4 MONTH + \beta_5 YEAR + \beta_i ADSLAGi \ (i=1 \text{ to } 4).$$

The model speculates that the quantity of customers (CUS) is a function of price as measured by average revenue ($AVREV$), the attendance at the proximate amusement park (FCA), the month and year, the size of the advertising budget (ADS), and the size of the advertising expenditures in each of the previous four months all entered separately ($ADSLAG1$–$ADSLAG4$). The model was estimated by ordinary-least-squares using the software package SAS©. The specific procedure is SAS's PROC GLM. This procedure in SAS allows for the automatic creation of a sequence of dummy variables in a situation like this one when we wish to investigate whether there are monthly, yearly, or other seasonal variations in demand. SAS calls this technique a CLASS variable. When using this method, the dummy coefficients are all interpreted relative to one level of the class variable. In this case, the dummy coefficients on month are all relative to December, while the year coefficients are all relative to 1986. We will explain this in a bit more detail later in the solution.

First, examine Table 4.13. The R^2 for the linear model is 0.917; approximately 92 percent of the variation in customers is explained by the model. This is fairly good in absolute terms but ultimately must be compared to alternative model specifications to determine whether better models do not exist. The F ratio is 16.02, and it is significant at the 0.0001 level. In general, these are quite decent summary statistics. Thus,

TABLE 4.13   SUGGESTED SOLUTION TO PROBLEM 4.1

Dependent Variable: Number of Customers (*CUS*)

	F Ratio 16.02	Prob >F 0.0001	Root Mean Squared Error 863.305	R^2 0.9168

VARIABLE	PARAMETER ESTIMATE	STANDARD ERROR	t RATIO	PROB $>|t|$
Intercept[a]	24130.36	3557.059	6.78	0.0001
Average Revenue (*AVREV*)	−659.86	330.987	−1.99	0.0548
Attendance at Amusement Park Nearby (*FCA*)	0.05	0.043	1.14	0.2616
Advertising Expenses (*ADS*)	−0.29	0.160	−1.81	0.0802
Month[b] 1	−758.43	669.913	−1.13	0.2660
2	52.68	707.818	0.07	0.9411
3	4904.04	738.098	6.64	0.0001
4	2988.86	721.432	4.14	0.0001
5	2032.80	713.359	2.85	0.0076
6	2012.79	698.852	2.88	0.0070
7	156.31	672.498	0.23	0.8177
8	932.08	738.421	1.26	0.2160
9	−778.70	686.181	−1.13	0.2649
10	−305.64	771.427	−0.40	0.6946
11	−1283.53	697.149	−1.84	0.0749
Year[c] 1982	−1890.94	971.463	−1.95	0.0604
1983	−1976.59	731.934	−2.70	0.0110
1984	−1431.01	863.651	−1.66	0.1073
1985	−2541.36	867.798	−2.93	0.0062
Advertising Expenses Last Month (*ADSLAG1*)	−0.11	0.157	−0.68	0.4988
Advertising Expenses Two Months Ago (*ADSLAG2*)	−0.32	0.163	−1.99	0.0551
Advertising Expenses Three Months Ago (*ADSLAG3*)	−0.21	0.164	−1.27	0.2134
Advertising Expenses Four Months Ago (*ADSLAG4*)	0.18	0.129	1.37	0.1801

[a] The intercept includes the value for December 1986.
[b] The month coefficients are deviations from December.
[c] All year coefficients are deviations from 1986.

let us turn our attention to the coefficient estimates on the individual independent variables.

Let's skip the discussion of *AVREV* for a moment. We see that there is a positive relation between attendance at the nearby amusement park and customers at the restaurant; the coefficient on *FCA* is positive, 0.05. However, the *t* ratio is only 1.14, and the chance of getting a *t* statistic this high by chance alone when the null hypothesis (that the coefficient is zero) is correct is somewhat high, 0.2616. When the chance is that high, we are generally inclined to reject the alternate hypothesis in favor of the null, and thus, we conclude that there is probably not a relation between the two businesses. Nevertheless, the *point estimate* or best guess says that 100 additional visitors to the amusement park in a month are associated with 5 more customers per month in the restaurant (100•0.05 = 5).

Next observe the five coefficients on advertising activity. The pattern is an odd one and certainly requires additional investigation. If we are to believe these coefficients, advertising is associated with fewer customers. The coefficient on advertising expenses this month, *ADS*, and each of the first three lagged values is negative (even though only three of the five are significant at the 0.10 level). It may be that the restaurant is advertising in months when it does not have many customers, as a way of boosting its business.[25]

Now examine the dummy variable estimates on month and year. For month, recalling that all coefficients are deviations from December, we observe that customers are significantly different from December in five months of the year. Four of these are positive, March, April, May, and June; the number of customers in November is less than in December. Early spring to summer is the best time of the year for this business. Regarding years, each of the years prior to the reference year, 1986, has fewer customers per month, and loosely speaking, each is significant. The business has been growing.

Last, we examine the most important variable for the problem at hand, price. We see that the coefficient is estimated to be -659.86. This means that if the average price per meal were raised by $1, the store would lose about 660 customers per month or 22 per day in round numbers. This coefficient is significant at the 0.10 level. This means that the chances of getting a *t* statistic this low by chance alone when the null hypothesis of no relation is actually true are less than one in ten. Thus, since the odds are slim that we would get a *t* value of -1.99 when the null is true, we are inclined to reject it in favor of the alternate that there is an inverse relation between price and the number of customers. The evidence suggests that

---

[25] You will recall from the discussion on simultaneous equation bias that this means that the expenditures on advertising are what we call endogenous. That is, not only does the number of customers depend on advertising, but advertising also depends on the number of customers. Hence, it might be important to estimate two equations simultaneously, the demand equation and the advertising expenditure equation. We leave that project for another time.

the customers at this restaurant obey the first law of demand. However, the base question is, What is the price elasticity of demand? To compute this using the levels estimates, we must insert values for price and customers into the formula. Table 4.14 reports the means of the variables. It is reasonable to estimate the elasticity at the average of the price and customers. Let's do that. The elasticity formula is

$$\eta = (\partial CUS / \partial AVREV) \bullet (AVREV / CUS).$$

From Table 4.13, we know the coefficient on *AVREV* is the estimated value of the slope. That is, $\partial CUS / \partial AVREV = -659.86$. The average price is 9.94, and the average number of customers per month is 15,643.55. Thus, the estimated price elasticity of demand is

$$\eta = -659.86 \bullet (9.94 / 15,643.55) = -0.419.$$

In this case, since our estimate of η is less than one in absolute value, we are inclined to believe that demand is inelastic. When demand is inelastic, price increases *raise* revenues and *lower* costs. Accordingly, we must conclude, based on these numbers, that price is too low in this establishment.

Many questions must be answered before we categorically conclude that this business should increase its menu prices. First, do we have model misspecification? Is a log model better, and if so does it give different estimates? Second, are there omitted variables? One prominent candidate here includes the prices being charged by competitors. Is the simultaneous equations bias we discussed serious? Third, since we have time series data, is autocorrelation in the residuals a problem? But leaving aside these crucial issues (which no serious manager would ever do), we have some preliminary evidence that this restaurant could make more money if it charged higher prices.

At this point, one is inclined to ask, Are there noneconometric reasons why this conclusion is unwarranted? Without going through a complete litany of explanations, consider this: If total revenues are underreported for any reason, then our data source will incorrectly be telling us that price is lower than it truly is. Why might revenues be underreported? Two answers stand prominently. First, someone may be stealing cash, and second, the managers/owners may be skimming cash illegally to

TABLE 4.14 MEANS OF RESTAURANT VARIABLES	
VARIABLE	MEAN
Average Revenue (*AVREV*)	9.94381
Number of Customers (*CUS*)	15,643.54545

avoid the payment of income taxes. Only the managers of the establishment know the answers to these questions, but the situation points out how econometric analysis can be used in more ways than one.

If the manager took our advice and raised prices, *but his profits fell contrary to our prediction,* and assuming that our model and procedures are correct, what would have to be true? Leaving aside the question of model specification, it could only mean that cash being received at the register was not being reported on the accounting ledger. Theft and/or skimming are the most likely culprits in this situation.

TOPICS TO REVIEW

These are topics that you should feel comfortable with before you leave this chapter. If you cannot write out a clear and concise sentence or paragraph explaining the topic after you have worked on the study problems, you should reread the relevant section of the text.

Discrete and Continuous Random Variable

Probability Density Function

Cumulative Distribution Function

Moments—Mean and Standard Deviation

Null or Maintained Hypothesis

Alternate Hypothesis

t Distribution

Selection Bias

Type I Error

Type II Error

Ordinary-Least-Squares Regression

Residual/Error Term

F Ratio

t Ratio

Degrees of Freedom

R^2

Computing Elasticities from Regression Estimates—Logs and Levels

Confidence Level

Confidence Limits

Simultaneous Equation Bias

Multicollinearity

Heteroskedasticity

Weighted-Least-Squares Regression

Autocorrelation

STUDY PROBLEMS

1. The Federal Highway Administration of the U.S. Department of Transportation publishes monthly data on highway deaths and miles driven for each of the 50 states. Using these data for the years 1980–1982 and additional state-level information on income, population, and area, a regression model of highway deaths per 100,000 miles driven was estimated. Data on arrests are missing for New Mexico in 1981 and Vermont in 1980. We are missing 24 observations on this count. The overall sample has 1776 observations. See Table 4.15. The dependent variable, deaths per 100,000 miles driven, measures the probability of being killed in a highway accident in each state. In this sample the average number of deaths per 100,000 miles driven is 3.1716. According to the economic paradigm of human behavior, people's demand for death prevention should conform to the first law of demand when they drive.

   a. Do the data support this economic view of driving? That is, is the model an accurate description of highway deaths?
   b. Is the prevention of death a normal good?
   c. Is police activity a deterrent to death?
   d. Do educated people demand more death prevention?
   e. Does increasing the legal age of consuming alcohol reduce highway fatalities?

2. Consider again the regression output in Table 4.15.
   a. How does rain affect driving, according to the parameter estimates there?
   b. Offer a theoretical explanation of the relation between rain and highway deaths per mile driven.
   c. Is the probability of being killed in a highway accident higher or lower on rural roads?
   d. Offer a theoretical explanation for the relation between highway deaths and the fraction of miles driven that are driven on rural roads.

3. Tables 4.16, 4.17, 4.18, and 4.19 report some facts about the relation between undergraduate college tuition and enrollment. Table 4.16 reports the raw data on undergraduate enrollment, tuition (for state schools, tuition is the average of in-state and out-of-state tuition), volumes in the library, state personal income (state in which the school is located), and state population. Table 4.17 is the OLS regression output of enrollment on tuition, library, income per capita, and population. All variables are in logs. Table 4.18 reports the means of the variables in levels, and Table 4.19 is the OLS regression output using the levels of the variables rather than the logs.

   a. If tuition in 1976 had been 10 percent higher on average across these schools, how many people would have attended the average college?
   b. What is the probability that the first law of demand does not apply to college education?

TABLE 4.15   OLS REGRESSION ESTIMATES OF HIGHWAY DEATH EQUATION

Dependent Variable: Highway Deaths per 100,000 Miles Driven

F Ratio	Prob >F	Root Mean Squared Error	R^2
69.840	0.0001	0.83161	0.3570

VARIABLE	PARAMETER ESTIMATE	STANDARD ERROR	t RATIO	PROB $>|t|$
Intercept	3.739	0.643	5.808	0.0001
Fraction of Total Miles Driven that Were Driven on Rural Highways	1.927	0.282	6.813	0.0001
Minimum Legal Age for Consumption of Whiskey	−0.017	0.020	−0.849	0.3962
0,1 Dummy Variable for Mandatory Jail Sentence for First DUI	0.050	0.056	0.900	0.3680
State Personal Income per Capita (×10000)	−1.337	0.208	−6.419	0.0001
State Population Density per Square Mile	0.973	0.280	3.473	0.0005
Area of the State in Square Miles (×1000000)	3.156	0.323	9.759	0.0001
Fraction of Population in 1980 with High School Diploma	−0.004	0.004	−0.886	0.3757
Miles Driven on Rural Highways per Mile of Rural Highway in Place	−0.009	0.003	−2.490	0.0129
Miles Driven on Urban Highways per Mile of Urban Highway in Place	−0.000	0.001	−0.014	0.9889
Heating Index—the Higher the Index, the Higher the Average Temperature	0.492	0.043	11.256	0.0001
Sun Index—the Higher the Index, the More Sunny Days	−0.026	0.048	−0.544	0.5866
Rain Index—the Higher the Index, the More Rainfall	−0.281	0.043	−6.523	0.0001
Alcohol Consumption per Capita	0.242	0.030	7.825	0.0001
Arrests for DUI per Mile Driven	−25.271	3.805	−6.641	0.0001

Note: The data are monthly observations per state for the period January 1980–December 1982.

Sources: Highway Statistics (Washington, DC: U.S. Department of Transportation, Federal Highway Administration, 1980–1982); *A Digest of State Alcohol–Highway Safety Related Legislation,* (Washington, DC: U.S. Department of Transportation, Federal Highway Administration, 1983); *Annual Statistical Review 1983/84,* (Washington, DC: Distilled Spirits Council of the United States, Inc., 1984); and *Statistical Abstract of the United States,* (Washington, DC: U.S. Department of Commerce, Bureau of the Census, 1981–1983).

   c. Do schools that have large libraries have large student bodies? What is the impact on enrollment of a 10 percent change in library size?

   d. Do states with a lot of people have large schools?

4. The Distilled Spirits Council of the United States publishes annual data on the amount of alcohol consumed in each of the 50 states. Table 4.20 reports the average annual *total* state consumption of alcohol (measured in thousand

TABLE 4.16   COLLEGE DATA, 1976

SCHOOL	ENROLLMENT	TUITION	LIBRARY	YPC	STATE POP. (×1000)
Adelphi	8000	2670	300000	7019	18084
Agnes Scott	577	2500	140000	5548	4970
Alice Lloyd	248	1600	25000	5379	3428
Amherst	1328	3975	507000	6588	5809
Arizona	24594	450	2165245	5800	2270
Arizona State	28974	450	1240000	5800	2270
Arkansas-LR	10062	400	150000	4935	2109
Arkansas Poly	2111	430	127000	4935	2109
Auburn	18044	732	783515	5106	3665
Baldwin Wallace	2470	2679	174000	6412	10690
Belmont Abbey	698	1630	65000	5453	5469
Bowling Green	15632	798	549985	6412	10690
Butler	4300	2050	135000	6222	5302
Cal Lutheran	1885	2400	79302	7260	21198
Cal State LA	26400	186	700000	7260	21198
Cal St. Long Beach	24500	190	605000	7260	21198
Catholic	5666	3100	969731	6881	4144
Centenary (LA)	793	1400	115000	5405	3841
Chaminade	1678	1200	40000	7141	868
Colby	1628	3300	325000	5365	1070
Colgate	2334	3825	299790	7019	18084
Creighton	4453	4370	347000	5835	1553
Dartmouth	4045	4230	1100000	6012	822
Davidson	1278	2730	215000	5453	5469
Delaware State	1957	356	87000	7031	582
Denison	2243	3375	182255	6412	10690
Duke	8817	3230	2622167	5453	5469
Duluth	7162	630	230895	6183	3965
Eastern Montana	3785	474	96483	5688	753
Fairfield	3972	2700	120318	7356	3117
Fairleigh Dickinson	2828	2250	117000	7382	7336
Fayetteville State	1940	1516	106679	5453	5469
Florida Atlantic	6025	900	367466	6019	8421
George Washington	12118	2632	675000	6881	4144
Georgia	19974	555	1522682	5548	4970
Georgia State	21075	570	512866	5548	4970
Georgia Tech	8500	3053	750000	5548	4970
Grinnell	1183	3575	203000	6245	2870
Gustavus Adolphus	2090	3200	150000	6183	3965
Hendrix	1028	1500	127000	4935	2109
Hillsdale	1050	2700	70000	6754	9104
Idaho State	7147	410	224033	5637	831
Indiana	30080	722	2762582	6222	5302
Indiana Central	1915	2050	80000	6222	5302
Jackson State	6427	432	246698	4530	2354
Jacksonville	2058	1850	115000	6019	8421

TABLE 4.16   (continued)

School	Enrollment	Tuition	Library	YPC	State Pop. ($\times 1000$)
Jefferson (MO)	3890	240	35000	4530	2354
Johns Hopkins	3050	3500	1550000	6881	4144
Kansas State-Pitts.	568	390	196600	6470	2310
Kentucky	21488	480	1568810	5379	3428
Louisiana Tech	8154	358	211059	5405	3841
Loyola (IL)	10813	2480	753389	7347	11229
Manhattan	3917	2780	219022	7019	18084
Maryland	35890	758	1316029	6881	4144
McPherson	448	1820	60364	6470	2310
Metro State	1250	360	130000	6439	2583
Miami (FL)	14588	3300	1173749	6019	8421
Michigan	37505	960	4936472	6754	9104
Michigan-Dearborn	3913	640	175000	6754	9104
Minnesota-Morris	1572	630	85000	6183	3965
Mississippi State	11709	561	43500	4530	2354
Missouri-Rolla	4415	1080	250000	5964	4778
Missouri-Southern	3040	300	95000	5964	4778
Missouri Western	2823	372	88032	5964	4778
Monmouth (IL)	741	2780	155000	7347	1229
Montana State	8565	510	650000	5688	753
Nebraska-Omaha	11092	540	280000	5835	1553
New Haven	4735	2145	87310	7356	3117
North Carolina	19009	256	2125640	5453	5469
Northern Montana	1060	425	75100	5688	753
Northwestern	13423	3840	2474852	7347	11229
Ohio U.	13610	825	797529	6412	10690
Plymouth State	2794	617	160000	6012	822
Princeton	5798	4300	2715458	7382	7336
Purdue	40697	750	1232000	6222	5302
RIT	9513	2649	142149	7019	18084
Santa Clara	5585	2718	282880	7260	21198
Southern Miss.	9611	558	753000	4530	2354
St. Bonaventure	2150	2300	200000	7019	18084
St. Cloud State	3613	550	468434	6183	3965
Stetson	2025	2400	138300	6019	8421
Trenton State	9000	535	350000	7382	7336
Trinity	1700	3570	550000	7356	3117
Tufts	6500	3800	450000	6588	5809
UC-Davis	17231	632	1375359	7260	21198
Vassar	2206	3600	500000	7019	18084
Wake Forest	4226	2400	603733	5453	5469
Wartburg	1186	2230	105000	6245	2870
Wellesley	2004	3300	552467	6588	5809
Wesleyan	2250	3900	740000	7356	3117
Wittenberg	2345	3072	244989	6412	10690
Youngstown State	12677	678	325000	6412	10690

Sources: Peterson's Guide to Four-Year Colleges (Princeton: Peterson's Guides, 1977) and *Statistical Abstract of the United States* (Washington, DC: U.S. Department of Commerce, Bureau of the Census, 1979).

TABLE 4.17   OLS REGRESSION ESTIMATES—LOGS

Dependent Variable: Log of Enrollment

F Ratio 46.158	Prob >F 0.0001	Root Mean Squared Error 0.66161	R^2 0.6797		
VARIABLE	PARAMETER ESTIMATE	STANDARD ERROR		t RATIO	PROB $> \lvert t \rvert$
Intercept	3.5765	5.0414		0.709	0.4800
Log of School Tuition	−0.5463	0.0824		−6.728	0.0001
Log of State Income per Capita	−0.2078	0.6231		−0.333	0.7397
Log of Volumes in School Library	0.6766	0.0619		10.929	0.0001
Log of State Population	0.2428	0.0882		2.751	0.0072

TABLE 4.18   MEANS

VARIABLE	NUMBER OF OBSERVATIONS	MEAN	STANDARD DEVIATION	MINIMUM VALUE	MAXIMUM VALUE
School Enrollment	92	7983.16	9000.60	248	40697
School Tuition	92	1770.26	1287.40	186	4370
Volumes in School Library	92	586390.41	791311.53	250000	4936472
State Income per Capita	92	6234.18	783.56	4530	7382
State Population	92	6496.53	5593.32	582	21198

TABLE 4.19   OLS REGRESSION ESTIMATES—LEVELS

Dependent Variable: Enrollment

F Ratio 38.369	Prob >F 0.0001	Root Mean Squared Error 5536.746	R^2 0.6382		
VARIABLE	PARAMETER ESTIMATE	STANDARD ERROR		t RATIO	PROB $> \lvert t \rvert$
Intercept	5493.241	5184.239		1.060	0.2923
School Tuition	−3.217	0.488		−6.591	0.0001
State Income per Capita	0.316	0.924		0.342	0.7330
Volumes in School Library (x1000)	7.531	0.737		10.220	0.0001
State Population	0.276	0.121		2.281	0.0250

gallons) for the years 1975–1982.[26] Table 4.21 reports demographic data on the individual states, along with the price of a representative bottle of whiskey (all for 1980, except whiskey price is for 1984).

a. Construct a model of the demand for alcohol using these data.
b. What is the price elasticity of demand for alcohol? Construct a 95 percent confidence interval for your estimate.
c. Is alcohol a normal good?

5. Table 4.22 reports OLS estimates of the following model using annual data from 23 National Basketball Association teams' home attendance records from 1981 through 1987:

$$\log(q) = \beta_0 + \beta_1 \log(p) + \beta_2 \log(w) + \beta_3 SEASON + \beta_4 TEAM$$

where q = a team's total season home attendance
         p = average ticket price in \$
         w = number of games won by home team per season
$SEASON$ = a dummy variable for each season of play compared to the 1986–1987 season
   $TEAM$ = a dummy variable for each team in the league compared to the Washington Bullets

a. *Ceteris paribus*, what would happen to revenues if ticket prices were higher?
b. Do teams that win more games have smaller or larger home crowds?
c. Each team in the NBA plays a total of 82 games per season, and hence the average team wins exactly 41 games per season. The average ticket price over the period of this analysis is \$11. Suppose that some average team were to win one additional game, 42 instead of 41. What change in its total annual home gate receipt revenues, assuming that ticket price does not change, does the model forecast?
d. Make suggestions for improving the quality of the model estimates. Specifically, what additional independent variables would you like to see included in the model?
e. The Clippers moved from San Diego to Los Angeles beginning in the 1984–1985 season. The dummy coefficient for the L.A. Lakers is estimated to be 0.495 in the period prior to the arrival of the Clippers, but the dummy coefficient is only 0.273 for the period while the Clippers were in Los Angeles. Can you explain the change in this coefficient?

6. Table 4.23 lists the total and per capita consumption for natural gas by the states for 1977. Recall the state level data on the price of natural gas, income per capita, and the price of electricity in Table 4.3. These data were used to estimate the demand for natural gas. Table 4.24 reports OLS estimates of the demand per capita for natural gas in levels. Table 4.25 reports estimates of the

---

[26] Consumption does not represent actual ingestion by consumers. Stock changes at the wholesale, retail, and consumer level may affect the level of intake in a given year. In addition, tourist trade and cross-border sales may affect the reported level of consumption in some states.

TABLE 4.20   AVERAGE ANNUAL ALCOHOL CONSUMPTION PER CAPITA, 1975–1982

STATE	AVERAGE TOTAL ALCOHOL CONSUMPTION (×1000) 1975–1982	STANDARD DEVIATION 1975–1982	MINIMUM VALUE 1975–1982	MAXIMUM VALUE 1975–1982
Alabama	5627.6	244.81	5994	5395
Alaska	1304.5	79.75	1391	1186
Arizona	4990.8	570.22	5697	4145
Arkansas	2688.8	270.97	2998	2366
California	54960.4	2065.15	57069	52054
Colorado	6792.5	479.67	7336	6084
Connecticut	7338.5	110.08	7569	7195
Delaware	1541.3	59.04	1637	1482
District of Columbia	4093.1	443.65	4828	3503
Florida	24666.5	1727.14	26615	22330
Georgia	10813.3	419.11	11264	9945
Hawaii	2126.8	82.07	2190	1970
Idaho	1274.5	92.33	1391	1135
Illinois	25244.0	1034.63	26826	23404
Indiana	7763.4	447.84	8147	7006
Iowa	3936.6	133.64	4044	3646
Kansas	3019.0	164.97	3294	2808
Kentucky	5086.6	154.04	5283	4857
Louisiana	7650.5	537.05	8107	6700
Maine	2179.5	120.85	2289	1951
Maryland	10889.0	191.15	11086	10516
Massachusetts	12551.5	4504.06	14373	1411
Michigan	17459.3	450.51	17998	16721
Minnesota	8883.8	341.19	9370	8426
Mississippi	3757.9	222.81	3976	3366

demand model in logs. Table 4.26 reports the means of all the variables in question.

a. What is the price elasticity of demand for natural gas?

b. From 1982 to 1987, income per capita in the United States grew by about 20 percent. Forecast the change in the consumption of natural gas over that same period.

c. According to the estimates, what impact on the consumption of natural gas does a 10 percent increase in the price of electricity have?

TABLE 4.20 (continued)				

STATE	AVERAGE TOTAL ALCOHOL CONSUMPTION (×1000) 1975–1982	STANDARD DEVIATION 1975–1982	MINIMUM VALUE 1975–1982	MAXIMUM VALUE 1975–1982
Missouri	7091.3	437.90	7680	6258
Montana	1544.9	38.00	1585	1474
Nebraska	2669.4	64.68	2733	2523
Nevada	4420.5	175.73	4611	4096
New Hampshire	4482.6	110.40	4687	4328
New Jersey	16122.3	411.08	16751	15649
New Mexico	2078.6	90.68	2208	1954
New York	40026.8	1151.61	41740	37897
North Carolina	9132.5	658.47	9889	8292
North Dakota	1399.1	16.18	1424	1384
Ohio	14612.0	506.40	15113	13627
Oklahoma	4500.4	400.34	5041	3905
Oregon	4432.1	301.35	4787	3961
Pennsylvania	16900.4	341.53	17272	16165
Rhode Island	2058.0	62.39	2133	1970
South Carolina	6306.6	214.92	6682	6057
South Dakota	1337.5	57.83	1401	1242
Tennessee	5948.5	345.02	6355	5357
Texas	20784.0	2522.46	23987	17168
Utah	1366.6	119.47	1502	1184
Vermont	1400.0	91.33	1528	1243
Virginia	9094.6	340.48	9451	8621
Washington	7966.8	577.76	8648	7066
West Virginia	2587.1	237.29	2764	2049
Wisconsin	11159.4	239.16	11511	10739
Wyoming	1041.9	105.00	1150	878

Source: Annual Statistical Review 1983/84 (Washington, DC: Distilled Spirits Council of the United States, 1984).

7. Table 4.27 reports hypothetical ordinary-least-squares estimates of the following model:

$$\ln q = \alpha + \beta_1 \ln p + \beta_2 \ln y + \beta_3 \ln s + \varepsilon$$

where q is the quantity demanded of chicken; p is the price; y is the income of the consumers; s is the price of beef; and ε is a random error term.

a. Is chicken a normal good?
b. Which will cause the quantity demanded of chicken to change more, a 10 percent increase in the price of chicken or a 10 percent change in the price of beef?

TABLE 4.21   State Demographic Data for 1980

State	Population	Area in Square Miles	Income per Capita	Percentage of Population with a High School Diploma	Minimum Legal Age of Beer Consumption	Minimum Legal Age of Liquor Consumption	Retail Price of a Representative Bottle of Whiskey[a] (750 ML)
Alabama	3895000	51609	7477	56.7	19	19	$6.85
Alaska	403000	586412	12916	82.8	21	21	9.63
Arizona	2731000	133909	8832	72.3	19	19	7.35
Arkansas	2299000	53104	7166	54.9	21	21	6.73
California	23771000	158693	10920	73.6	21	21	6.26
Colorado	2903000	104247	10042	78.1	18	21	6.46
Connecticut	3114000	5009	11536	70.5	20	20	7.51
Delaware	596000	2057	10066	67.8	21	21	6.02
Florida	9874000	58560	9201	67.2	21	21	6.87
Georgia	5482000	58876	8061	56.5	19	19	6.81
Hawaii	969000	6450	10222	73.4	18	18	7.77
Idaho	947000	83557	8044	72.8	19	19	6.70
Illinois	11433000	56400	10471	65.0	21	21	5.70
Indiana	5489000	36291	8896	65.9	21	21	6.57
Iowa	2913000	56290	9336	71.2	19	19	5.93
Kansas	2367000	82264	9942	72.3	18	21	7.01
Kentucky	3662000	40395	7648	51.9	21	21	6.55
Louisiana	4222000	48523	8525	58.0	18	18	6.82
Maine	1126000	33215	7672	68.5	20	20	6.49
Maryland	4225000	10577	10385	66.7	21	21	5.82
Massachusetts	5743000	8257	10089	72.7	20	20	6.87
Michigan	9255000	58216	9872	68.2	21	21	5.95
Minnesota	4083000	84068	9688	72.4	19	19	6.50
Mississippi	2523000	47716	6680	55.1	18	21	5.96
Missouri	4924000	69686	8720	63.7	21	21	6.13
Montana	788000	147138	8361	75.4	19	19	6.45

TABLE 4.21 (continued)

State	Population	Area in Square Miles	Income per Capita	Percentage of Population with a High School Diploma	Minimum Legal Age of Beer Consumption	Minimum Legal Age of Liquor Consumption	Retail Price of a Representative Bottle of Whiskey[a] (750 ML)
Nebraska	1572000	77227	9137	73.8	20	20	7.20
Nevada	807000	110540	10761	75.5	21	21	6.49
New Hampshire	923000	9304	9010	72.0	20	20	4.90
New Jersey	7377000	7836	10976	67.8	21	21	7.11
New Mexico	1305000	12166	7891	68.2	21	21	6.88
New York	17575000	49576	10283	66.2	19	19	7.00
North Carolina	5888000	52586	7753	55.3	19	21	6.00
North Dakota	654000	70665	8759	66.5	21	21	7.09
Ohio	10800000	41222	9430	67.4	19	21	6.58
Oklahoma	3038000	69919	9187	66.7	21	21	5.55
Oregon	2638000	96981	9356	74.7	21	21	7.05
Pennsylvania	11880000	45333	9389	64.5	21	21	6.51
Rhode Island	949000	1214	9174	60.7	20	20	6.61
South Carolina	3127000	31055	7298	54.0	18	21	7.20
South Dakota	690000	77047	8028	68.5	18	21	7.31
Tennessee	4595000	42244	7662	55.4	19	19	7.22
Texas	14321000	267338	9538	61.4	19	19	6.76
Utah	1472000	84916	7656	80.3	21	21	6.80
Vermont	512000	9609	7832	70.5	18	18	5.90
Virginia	5362000	40817	9357	62.5	19	21	5.85
Washington	4148000	68192	10198	77.0	21	21	7.65
West Virginia	1950000	24181	7665	56.6	19	21	7.23
Wisconsin	4728000	56154	9347	70.0	18	18	6.81
Wyoming	475000	97914	11042	77.8	19	19	6.56

Sources: See Table 4.15

[a] Jim Beam

TABLE 4.22   THE DEMAND FOR NBA GAMES

Dependent Variable: Log of Home Attendance

F Ratio	Prob $>F$	Root Mean Squared Error	R^2
14.38	0.0001	0.14962	0.81998

VARIABLE	PARAMETER ESTIMATE	STANDARD ERROR	t RATIO	PROB $>|t|$
Intercept	11.878	0.397	29.91	0.0001
Ticket Price	−0.262	0.124	−2.09	0.0387
Games Won	0.480	0.061	7.86	0.0001
Season[a]				
8182	−0.307	0.070	4.33	0.0001
8283	−0.326	0.060	−5.35	0.0001
8384	−0.270	0.056	−4.78	0.0001
8485	−0.193	0.050	−3.83	0.0002
8586	−0.102	0.045	−2.23	0.0281
Team[b]				
Atlanta	−0.137	0.086	−1.58	0.1181
Boston	0.325	0.099	3.25	0.0015
Chicago	0.186	0.088	2.11	0.0377
Cleveland	−0.123	0.090	−1.36	0.1770
Dallas	0.380	0.086	4.37	0.0001
Denver	0.240	0.089	2.69	0.0084
Detroit	0.436	0.086	5.03	0.0001
Golden State	0.035	0.087	0.40	0.6916
Houston	0.349	0.087	3.98	0.0001
Indiana	0.172	0.089	1.92	0.0579
Kansas City	−0.119	0.097	−1.22	0.2271
Clippers	0.114	0.112	1.02	0.3106
L.A. Lakers (after Clippers in L.A.)	0.273	0.110	2.48	0.0149
L.A. Lakers (while Clippers in S.D.)	0.495	0.129	3.82	0.0002
Milwaukee	−0.018	0.092	−0.19	0.8501
New Jersey	0.361	0.101	3.57	0.0006
New York	0.433	0.091	4.71	0.0001
Philadelphia	0.322	0.096	3.35	0.0011
Phoenix	0.238	0.087	2.72	0.0077
Portland	0.289	0.087	3.30	0.0014
Sacramento	0.137	0.125	1.09	0.2791
San Antonio	0.007	0.087	0.09	0.9297
San Diego	−0.245	0.111	−2.20	0.0304
Seattle	0.117	0.086	1.35	0.1807
Utah	0.121	0.088	1.37	0.1727

[a] All season coefficients are relative to the 1986–1987 season.
[b] All team coefficients are relative to Washington.

Source: Data for computations were obtained from various editions of *The Sporting News Official NBA Guide* (Saint Louis: The Sporting News).

TABLE 4.23   NATURAL GAS CONSUMPTION DATA

STATE	GAS SALES (IN MILLION CUBIC FEET)	GAS SALES PER CAPITA	STATE	GAS SALES (IN MILLION CUBIC FEET)	GAS SALES PER CAPITA
AK	291000	0.70460	MT	658000	0.85901
AL	2156000	0.58412	NC	790000	0.14325
AR	1958000	0.90985	ND	229000	0.35231
AZ	1377000	0.59740	NE	1540000	0.99035
CA	15959000	0.72915	NH	82000	0.09647
CO	2363000	0.90019	NJ	2594000	0.35350
CT	641000	0.20631	NM	1484000	1.24080
DE	177000	0.30412	NV	650000	1.02041
FL	1403000	0.16572	NY	5785000	0.32261
GA	2610000	0.51775	OH	8717000	0.81498
HI	35000	0.03928	OK	4526000	1.60667
IA	2681000	0.92832	OR	907000	0.38029
ID	499000	0.58294	PA	6416000	0.54391
IL	11341000	1.01006	RI	238000	0.25400
IN	4317000	0.80692	SC	1048000	0.36414
KS	3897000	1.67974	SD	272000	0.39535
KY	1624000	0.46828	TN	1887000	0.43966
LA	4875000	1.24046	TX	19515000	1.52390
MA	1591000	0.27540	UT	1189000	0.93622
MD	1372000	0.33164	VA	1146000	0.22493
ME	20000	0.01845	VT	36000	0.07469
MI	8468000	0.92567	WA	1511000	0.41049
MN	2489000	0.62538	WI	3214000	0.69208
MO	3337000	0.69204	WV	1343000	0.72477
MS	1355000	0.56790	WY	544000	1.33990

Source: Gas Facts 1979, (Arlington, VA: American Gas Association, 1980), p. 85.

TABLE 4.24   NATURAL GAS DEMAND—LEVELS

Dependent Variable: Quantity of Natural Gas Consumed per Capita (in million cubic feet)

F Ratio	Prob $>F$	Root Mean Squared Error	R^2
10.052	0.0001	0.32913	0.3960

VARIABLE	PARAMETER ESTIMATE	STANDARD ERROR	t RATIO	PROB $>|t|$
Intercept	0.79448	0.34214	2.322	0.0247
Price of Natural Gas	−0.23228	0.05496	−4.226	0.0001
State Income per Capita (×1000)	0.08229	0.05266	1.565	0.1243
Price of Electricity	−0.06538	0.06396	−1.022	0.3121

TABLE 4.25   NATURAL GAS DEMAND—LOGS

Dependent Variable: Log of Natural Gas Consumption per Capita (in million cubic feet)

F Ratio	Prob >F	Root Mean Squared Error	R^2
26.033	0.0001	0.576767	0.6293

VARIABLE	PARAMETER ESTIMATE	STANDARD ERROR	t RATIO	PROB >|t|
Intercept	−13.7184	5.5508	−2.471	0.0172
Log of Gas Price	−1.9461	0.2459	−7.913	0.0001
Log of State Income per Capita	1.6573	0.6387	2.595	0.0127
Log of Electricity Price	−0.2311	0.2802	−0.825	0.4139

TABLE 4.26   MEANS OF VARIABLES

VARIABLE	MEAN	STANDARD DEVIATION	MINIMUM VALUE	MAXIMUM VALUE
Natural Gas Consumption per Capita (in millions of cubic feet)	0.6383	0.410	0.0185	1.6797
Income per Capita	6777.0200	953.8439	5030.0000	10586.0000
Price of Natural Gas	2.1712	0.9939	1.0484	6.9891
Price of Electricity	3.2189	0.8962	0.9944	5.0133

TABLE 4.27   OLS ESTIMATES OF THE DEMAND FOR CHICKEN

Dependent Variable: Log of Quantity Demanded ($\ln q$)

F Ratio	Prob >F	Root Mean Squared Error	R^2
215.56	0.0001	12.5674	0.5432

VARIABLE	PARAMETER ESTIMATE	STANDARD ERROR	t RATIO	PROB >|t|
Intercept	0.156	0.028	5.467	0.0001
Log of the Price of Chicken ($\ln p$)	−1.285	0.148	8.693	0.0001
Log of Income per Capita ($\ln y$)	2.234	0.691	3.234	0.0114
Log of the Price of Beef ($\ln s$)	0.126	0.054	2.314	0.0212

8. Use the information in Table 4.27 to answer the following question: The current price of chicken is \$2/pound. Suppose a federal excise tax is enacted that causes the price of chicken to increase by \$0.25 per pound. Will total expenditures in the economy on chicken rise or fall? Will total revenues, net of taxes, from the sale of chicken increase or decrease?

9. Your company has decided to make you the head of a new department that is responsible for monitoring and keeping tabs on the price elasticity of demand for its products. Choose one or more of the goods produced by the company you work for now or would like to work for when you finish school (or make up a company if you prefer). Describe the kinds of data you will require to perform your job. Be very specific, taking into account the characteristics of the good in question and the market being serviced. Discuss the models you will estimate. Anticipate any problems that you might reasonably expect to encounter.

10. Data were collected from approximately 200 different colleges and universities in the United States for the year 1972. Six different model specifications of demand were estimated by OLS (Tables 4.28–4.33). Consider them in order. Variable definitions are TUITION is tuition; LIBRARY is the number of volumes in the library (in thousands); SALARY is the average salary of the full professors at the school; SAT is the average SAT score of the entering freshmen; SPORTS is a 0,1 dummy variable taking the value 1 if the school has a big-time athletic program; FACULTY is the number of faculty on staff; AGE is the number of years the school has been in business in 1972; SEXRATIO is the female/male undergraduate enrollment ratio; LNT is the log of tuition; LNLIB is the log of LIBRARY; LNSAL is the log of SALARY; LNSAT is the log of SAT; and LNFAC is the log of FACULTY.

   a. Of the five linear models, which is the best?
   b. What is the relation between the age of a school and the number of

TABLE 4.28 MODEL 1

Dependent Variable: Undergraduate Enrollment

F Ratio	Prob >F	R^2
61.10	0.0001	0.7110

VARIABLE	PARAMETER ESTIMATE	t RATIO	PROB $>|t|$
INTERCEPT	13409.000	2.309	0.0223
TUITION	−3.457	−3.288	0.0013
LIBRARY	−0.427	−0.628	0.5312
SALARY	0.731	2.711	0.0075
SAT	−17.043	−2.431	0.0162
SPORTS	4983.843	4.137	0.0001
FACULTY	7.199	9.019	0.0001

TABLE 4.29   MODEL 2

Dependent Variable: Undergraduate Enrollment

F Ratio	Prob >F		R^2	
53.75	0.0001		0.7177	

VARIABLE	PARAMETER ESTIMATE	t RATIO	PROB $>|t|$
INTERCEPT	13873.000	2.407	0.0173
TUITION	−3.554	−3.404	0.0009
LIBRARY	−0.125	−0.179	0.8578
SALARY	0.664	2.463	0.0149
SAT	−13.902	−1.944	0.0538
SPORTS	4560.748	3.751	0.0003
FACULTY	7.444	9.279	0.0001
AGE	−24.425	−1.873	0.0630

TABLE 4.30   MODEL 3

Dependent Variable: Undergraduate Enrollment

F Ratio	Prob >F		R^2	
47.94	0.0001		0.7192	

VARIABLE	PARAMETER ESTIMATE	t RATIO	PROB $>|t|$
INTERCEPT	8678.689	1.214	0.2271
TUITION	−4.097	−3.440	0.0008
LIBRARY	−0.620	−0.858	0.3927
SALARY	0.850	2.650	0.0090
SAT	−15.250	−2.045	0.0428
SPORTS	5200.347	3.866	0.0002
FACULTY	7.364	8.624	0.0001
SEXRATIO	4855.440	1.480	0.1413

students? Are older schools bigger? Do schools with big-time sports programs have smaller or larger student bodies?

c. Use the information in Table 4.34 to compute the price elasticities from the various linear models. Compare them to the estimate from Model 6. What is the predicted impact on enrollment of a 10 percent increase in tuition?

d. Now examine the residuals. Consider Figure 4.8 and Figure 4.9. Figure 4.8 plots the errors from Model 5 against the size of the faculty at each school. Figure 4.9 plots the squared errors, the estimated variances,

TABLE 4.31   MODEL 4

Dependent Variable: Undergraduate Enrollment

F Ratio	Prob >F	R^2
27.983	0.0001	0.5598

VARIABLE	PARAMETER ESTIMATE	t RATIO	PROB $> |t|$
INTERCEPT	16585.000	1.875	0.0630
TUITION	−4.203	−2.829	0.0054
LIBRARY	2.930	3.955	0.0001
SALARY	1.514	3.900	0.0002
SAT	−29.648	−3.271	0.0014
SPORTS	5808.748	3.467	0.0007
SEXRATIO	−838.149	−0.209	0.8347

TABLE 4.32   MODEL 5

Dependent Variable: Undergraduate Enrollment

F Ratio	Prob >F	R^2
43.042	0.0001	0.7259

VARIABLE	PARAMETER ESTIMATE	t RATIO	PROB $> |t|$
INTERCEPT	9691.000	1.362	0.1755
TUITION	−4.364	3.666	0.0004
LIBRARY	−0.300	−0.425	0.6714
SALARY	0.777	2.425	0.0167
SAT	−11.608	−1.513	0.1327
SPORTS	4575.072	3.316	0.0012
FACULTY	7.575	8.858	0.0001
AGE	−26.660	−1.780	0.0774

against the size of the faculty. From Figure 4.8, the errors appear to be randomly distributed. From Figure 4.9, the variance does not appear to be constant across various sizes of faculty. What do these two figures suggest?

e. The next regression, reported in Table 4.35, is a test for hetero-skedasticity. It examines whether the error variance is a function of the size of the faculty. Here the log of the squared errors from Model 5 is regressed on the log of faculty size. What does the test reveal? Does it hint that additional work is required?

f. Examine Table 4.36. What does the information reported there reveal? Is

TABLE 4.33   MODEL 6

Dependent Variable: Log of Undergraduate Enrollment

F Ratio	Prob >F		R^2
3.106	0.0001		0.2901

VARIABLE	PARAMETER ESTIMATE	t RATIO	PROB $> |t|$
INTERCEPT	−0.1286	−0.022	0.9825
LNT	−0.1130	−0.877	0.3859
LNLIB	0.2224	2.220	0.0325
LNSAL	0.0340	0.045	0.9641
LNSAT	−0.0014	−0.002	0.9986
LNFAC	0.0861	0.749	0.4583

TABLE 4.34   MEANS

VARIABLE	MEAN
Undergraduate Enrollment	12195
Tuition	1732
Volumes in Library	955021
Salary of Full Professors	20858
Average SAT Score	1116
Number of Faculty	960

TABLE 4.35   TEST FOR HETEROSKEDASTICITY

Dependent Variable: Log of Errors Squared

F Ratio	Prob >F		R^2
18.919	0.0001		0.1213

VARIABLE	PARAMETER ESTIMATE	t RATIO	PROB $> |t|$
INTERCEPT	11.74854	11.653	0.0001
LNFAC	0.65652	4.350	0.0001

TABLE 4.36   CORRELATION

Correlation Coefficients
Between
LIBRARY and FACULTY

Simple Correlation   0.72184

there a strong correlation between the size of the faculty and the size of the library? Based on this information, is multicollinearity likely to be a problem?

11. Using data covering the period May 1988 through October 1990, a graduate student attempted to estimate the demand for meals at a Mexican restaurant in Clemson, South Carolina. The data included the average price per meal (p), the number of customers (q), and advertising expenditures (a). He estimated the following model in levels and logs:

$$q = \beta_0 + \beta_1\, p + \beta_2\, a + \beta_3\, s + \beta_4\, trend + \varepsilon.$$

The s variable measures seasonality and requires a little explanation. Clemson is a small town with big crowds during athletic events and few students in the summer. The graduate student set the season variable equal to one during the regular school months and zero in the summer months and December—the times when there are few students in town. The $trend$ variable captures any time trend and takes the value one for the first month of the data, two for second, and so on. Table 4.37 reports estimates of the model first in levels and then in logs. The table also reports the means of the variables.

a.   What is the price elasticity of demand?
b.   Is the restaurant's advertising program effective?
c.   If you were the manager of the restaurant, would you change the advertising budget?
d.   Is the business in this restaurant stable, getting better, or declining over time?
e.   Is business slower during the months when students are gone from the area?

12. Table 4.38 reports the estimated number of home satellite stations by state for the United States as of early 1990. Suppose you wanted to model the demand for the television receiving devices. What factors do you think would have to be included in the model? How would you go about obtaining the data necessary to construct an economic model of the demand for home satellite stations?

TABLE 4.37   REGRESSION ESTIMATES (LOGS AND LEVELS) AND MEANS

Dependent Variable: Number of Customers—LEVELS

F Ratio	Prob >F		R²	
19.354	0.0001		0.7559	

VARIABLE	PARAMETER ESTIMATE	STANDARD ERROR	t RATIO	PROB > |t|
Intercept	8790.423	1716.784	5.120	0.0001
Price (p)	−505.929	168.451	−3.003	0.0060
Advertising Expenses (a)	0.824	0.593	1.390	0.1767
Season (s)	966.142	178.373	5.416	0.0001
Trend (trend)	25.866	11.076	2.335	0.0279

Dependent Variable: Number of Customers—LOGS

F Ratio	Prob >F		R²	
23.994	0.0001		0.7993	

VARIABLE	PARAMETER ESTIMATE	STANDARD ERROR	t RATIO	PROB > |t|
Intercept	10.018	0.823	12.177	0.0001
Log of Price (ln p)	−0.995	0.316	−3.150	0.0042
Log of Advertising (ln a)	0.097	0.062	1.575	0.1277
Season (s)	0.199	0.032	6.212	0.0001
Trend (trend)	0.005	0.002	2.539	0.0177

MEANS of VARIABLES

VARIABLE	NUMBER OF OBSERVATIONS	MEAN	STANDARD DEVIATION	MINIMUM VALUE	MAXIMUM VALUE
CUSTOMERS	30	5026.73	726.011	3952.00	6610.00
PRICE	30	10.42	0.557	9.25	11.42
ADS	30	602.20	148.227	305.00	970.00

SUGGESTED READINGS

Barnett, F. William. "Four Steps to Forecast Total Market Demand." *Harvard Business Review* 88(4) (July–August 1988):28–38.

Beyer, William H. (ed.). *CRC Standard Probability and Statistics Tables and Formulae.* Boca Raton: CRC Press, 1990.

Gujarti, Damodar. *Basic Econometrics,* 2d ed. New York: McGraw-Hill, 1988.

Hicks, Charles R. *Fundamental Concepts in the Design of Experiments.* New York: Holt, Rhinehart & Winston, 1973.

Intriligator, Michael. *Econometric Model, Techniques, and Applications.* Englewood Cliffs, NJ: Prentice Hall, 1978.

TABLE 4.38   SATELLITE SYSTEMS

STATE	NUMBER OF SATELLITE SYSTEMS INSTALLED	STATE	NUMBER OF SATELLITE SYSTEMS INSTALLED
Alabama	76,700	Montana	38,850
Alaska	5,000	Nebraska	40,800
Arizona	47,000	Nevada	29,800
Arkansas	52,500	New Jersey	20,000
California	325,000	New Hampshire	15,500
Colorado	47,250	New Mexico	21,700
Connecticut	11,000	New York	119,500
Delaware	6,500	North Dakota	14,900
DC	1,600	North Carolina	139,500
Florida	162,500	Ohio	110,000
Georgia	82,250	Oklahoma	56,700
Hawaii	1,100	Oregon	68,000
Idaho	27,200	Pennsylvania	90,700
Illinois	88,400	Rhode Island	3,600
Indiana	82,900	South Carolina	54,400
Iowa	51,800	South Dakota	16,500
Kansas	47,600	Tennessee	113,600
Kentucky	59,200	Texas	265,800
Louisiana	61,000	U.S. Territories	10,400
Maine	17,800	Utah	20,400
Maryland	31,400	Vermont	19,500
Massachusetts	13,000	Virginia	75,000
Michigan	120,000	Washington	68,600
Minnesota	47,000	West Virginia	42,000
Mississippi	49,500	Wisconsin	58,300
Missouri	84,500	Wyoming	14,500

Source: Satellite ORBIT (Vienna, VA: Orbit Publishing, September 1991), p. B3.

Johnston, John. *Econometric Methods*. New York: McGraw-Hill, 1972.

Kmenta, Jan. *Elements of Econometrics*. New York: Macmillan, 1971.

Manning, Williard G., Newhouse, Joseph P., Duan, Naihua, Keeler, Emmett B., Leibowitz, Arleen, and Marquis, Susan M. "Health Insurance and the Demand for Medical Care: Evidence from a Randomized Experiment." *American Economic Review* 77(3) (June 1987):251–77.

Nelson, Charles R. *Applied Time Series Analysis for Managerial Forecasting*. San Francisco: Holden-Day Inc., 1973.

Pacey, Patricia L. "Cable Television in a Less Regulated Market." *Journal of Industrial Economics* 34(1) (September 1985):81–91.

SUGGESTED SOLUTIONS TO STUDY PROBLEMS

The following are only *suggested* solutions to the study problems presented at the end of this chapter. In all cases, the suggestions here put heavy emphasis on analysis rather than a single correct answer. Since most managerial problems do not fall into neat little boxes, the individual characteristics of the problems that you encounter on the job will typically mandate a solution using the principles developed here and in other courses. Memorizing these solutions will not make you a good manager; learning the *principles* detailed here will help make you a better manager.

1. a.   The data do seem to support the economic paradigm in the following sense: People appear to respond to changes in their environment. That is, they are rationally affected by their surroundings. For instance, we observe that as income increases, deaths per mile driven decrease; the coefficient on state personal income per capita is negative and significant.

    b.   For the prevention of death to be a normal good, the number of deaths per mile driven would have to decrease as income increases. As we have just observed, the coefficient on state income is negative and significant.

FIGURE 4.8
Errors from Model 5

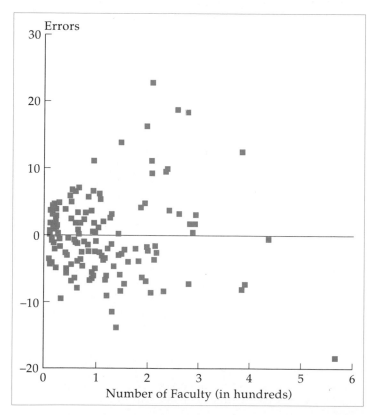

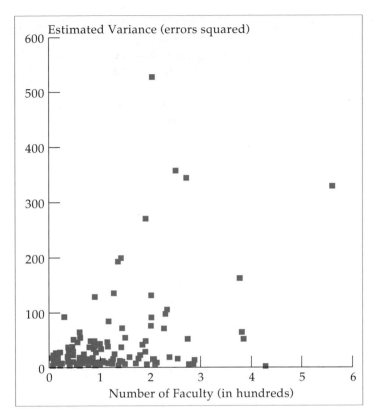

FIGURE 4.9
Estimated Residual Variance

Therefore, as the income per capita of the citizens in a state increases, the deaths per mile driven decrease. Why do you think this is true? Is it because rich people find it more expensive to die because their opportunity costs of being killed are higher?

c. The coefficient on arrests for DUI per mile driven is negative and significant. As such, using this one measure of law enforcement, we conclude that more stringent administration is associated with fewer deaths per mile driven, other things being the same.

d. The coefficient on the fraction of the population with a high school diploma is negative, but not significant; the t ratio is only -0.886. Thus, we have a dilemma. The point estimate suggests that educated people are better drivers, but the statistical confidence that this coefficient is actually different from zero is fairly low. Strictly speaking, the coefficient is not statistically different from zero, and we must conclude that there is little evidence of a relation between education and deaths per mile driven.

e. The coefficient on the minimum age for the legal consumption of whiskey is similar to the coefficient on education. It is negative, but not significant. The t ratio is -0.849 with a probability of 0.3962 that it would have occurred this low by chance alone. So, practically speaking, 40 percent of the time when the null hypothesis of no relation is true you get a *t* ratio this high. For most purposes, this is simply not strong enough to reject the null. Using this line of reasoning, we conclude that there is little evidence to reject the hypothesis that there is no relation between deaths per mile driven and the minimum legal age for the consumption of whiskey.

2. a. The coefficient on the rain index is negative and highly significant. The *t* ratio is -6.523, and the probability of obtaining a *t* ratio this high by chance alone when the null hypothesis of no relation is true is vanishingly small. Almost with certainty we can say there is a negative relation between the amount of rain and accidents per mile driven.

    b. The negative coefficient says there are fewer deaths per mile driven when the rain index increases. This does not mean there are fewer accidents. According to the first law of demand, as price increases quantity demanded decreases. Thus, when weather conditions deteriorate, the cost of driving carelessly, fast, and without due caution goes up. Naturally, people respond by driving more carefully. Presumably this is why there is a negative relation between deaths per mile driven and rain. For instance, in places where it rains a lot, people buy safer cars, check their tires more often, and keep their brakes in good condition. Moreover, when it rains, they drive more slowly and cautiously. Rain may lead to more accidents, but if it does, they are less serious. Maybe people wear their seat belts more frequently when it is raining.

    c. The coefficient on the variable *Fraction of Total Miles Driven that Were Driven on Rural Highways* is positive and significant. This suggests that deaths per mile driven are higher on rural roads.

    d. A number of factors come to mind here: Rural roads may not be lighted; they may be narrower; they may have more curves; drivers may drive faster; the types of cars and drivers who most often use rural roads may be less safe compared to their counterparts on city streets.

5. a. Since the attendance model is in logs, the coefficient on ticket price provides a direct estimate of the price elasticity of demand for NBA attendance. The coefficient is estimated as -0.262, and it is significantly different from zero at the 5 percent level of confidence. Since we estimate that demand is inelastic, the coefficient is less than one in absolute value, we conjecture that revenues would increase if ticket prices were higher. Can you think of a reason why NBA teams might want to set ticket prices below the apparent profit maximizing level?

    b. The coefficient on the number of games won is positive and significant. Teams that win more games have a larger home attendance.

    c. The win elasticity of home attendance is approximately 0.48. Winning one additional game per year at the average (42 instead of 41, a 2.44 percent increase) raises attendance by 0.48 times 2.44 percent or about 1.2 percent. Thus we estimate that total annual home gate receipts would increase by 1.2 percent if some hypothetical average team won one additional game.

e. After the Clippers moved to Los Angeles, there was more competition in the entertainment market for the Lakers—a substitute was available. This should reduce the demand for tickets to Laker games, and this is what the coefficient says. The dummy variable for the Lakers prior to the arrival of the Clippers is 0.495, and it falls to 0.273 after the Clippers moved. You can use a t test to determine if the two coefficients are equal. Recall the discussion in the text concerning the standard error of an estimated coefficient.

6. a. Using the log model, the coefficient on price is the estimated elasticity. It is -1.9461. Using the levels model evaluated at the means of the data, the elasticity is the coefficient on price times the average price all divided by the average quantity:

$(-0.23228) \cdot (2.1712/0.6383) = -0.7901.$

Note that this is considerably less elastic than the estimate provided by the log model.

b. Using the log model the coefficient on income per capita is 1.6573. Since income grew by 20 percent, we expect that the demand for gas grew by $1.6572 \cdot 20\%$ or 33.14 percent over the period.

c. The coefficient on the price of electricity is not significant in either the logs or the levels model. Based on this, we have little confidence that the price of electricity has any impact on the demand for natural gas. This result may be due to the aggregation of residential, commercial, and industrial gas consumers into one group.

8. Since the demand for chicken is elastic (the estimate is -1.285), higher prices will lead to reduced expenditures on chicken. Since total expenditures on chicken will actually decrease, suppliers will sell less chicken at a lower net price. Thus, the total revenues to producers will also decrease. If you are having trouble understanding why the net price to the sellers is lower after the tax, review the section in Chapter 2, An Application of the Supply and Demand Model to Sales Taxes.

10. a. Models 1, 2, 3, and 5 are better than Model 4, but the differences among the four of them are so slight as to be ignored. One wonders what Model 5 would look like if SEXRATIO were included.

b. According to Models 2 and 5, the coefficient on AGE is negative and marginally significant. Thus, according to this evidence, older schools are smaller, *ceteris paribus*. According to the coefficient estimates in Models 1–5, the dummy coefficient on SPORTS is positive and significant. Schools with large-scale sports programs have larger student bodies.

c. The linear estimate of the price elasticity can be evaluated at the means of the data. Of course, you may insert values for any particular school that you wish to estimate the price elasticity at that institution. For Model 1 the estimated coefficient on tuition is -3.457. The average tuition is $1732, and the average enrollment is 12,195. Multiplying the price coefficient times price and dividing by the average enrollment yields the estimated elasticity,

$$-3.457 \bullet 1732/12195 = -0.49.$$

Similar calculations reveal the elasticity estimates for the other linear models. The coefficient from the log model is a direct estimate of the elasticity. From Model 6 this coefficient is estimated to be -0.11, which is more inelastic than the levels estimates. Using the estimated elasticity from Model 5, arguably the best model, the elasticity is

$$-4.364 \bullet 1732/12195 = -0.62.$$

Using this estimate, -0.62, a 10 percent increase in tuition is associated with a $10\% \bullet (-0.62) = -6.2$ percent decline in enrollments. Since the average enrollment is 12,195, a 6.2 percent decrease reduces the average student body by 756 people ($-0.062 \bullet 12195 = -756$). According to this methodology, the average student body would fall to 11,439 people.

d.   The largest residuals seem to occur with the largest schools. This suggests that residual variance is correlated with the number of faculty.

e.   The log of the squared residuals (an estimate of residual variance) is positively related with the log of the number of faculty. This suggests that these data are heteroskedastic, and superior estimates might be obtained by using weighted-least-squares.

f.   There is a strong, positive correlation between the number of faculty and the number of volumes in the library. Multicollinearity may be a problem and may be the reason that none of the coefficients on the library variable are significant unless the size of the faculty variable is deleted. One way to deal with this problem is to enlarge the sample to include more schools or additional years of observations at the existing schools.

12.   A number of factors come to mind. First, there is the price of a system. However, there is little reason to suspect that this differs significantly across the states. In all likelihood, it is a constant. The number and availability of substitutes stands to be important, for instance, the prevalence of cable TV, population density, and the number of over-the-air broadcast stations. Income may matter. The presence or absence of other recreational activities that may substitute for TV is a factor. Climate may matter. Bad weather, which drives people indoors, may increase the demand for high-quality TV. Demographic data on population and income are available from *The Statistical Abstract of the United States*. Climatic data are also available there. Information on the cost of satellite dishes might be obtained from a trade association on satellite TV. If such an organization exists, it probably has an office in Washington, DC. Similarly, the FCC has information on the number of over-the-air broadcast stations by state and city.

INTRODUCTION

This chapter is designed to acquaint you with the topics of intertemporal decision making, interest rates, discounting, and present values. We begin with some theoretical analysis of the consumer faced with choices today versus choices tomorrow. This framework naturally flows into the computation of present values and future values. At this stage, a number of important formulas used in financial and economic analysis are developed. Most of the rest of the chapter involves the application of the principles developed at the outset. For instance, you will be asked to answer the question, When is it time to drink the wine? As is customary, there are quite a number of application-oriented study questions at the end of the chapter. You should study these problems carefully; they are an important part of the learning experience.

INTERTEMPORAL DECISION MAKING

The tools of analysis developed so far have allowed us to consider a host of problems arising from one of the unfortunate circumstances facing the world—scarcity. Scarcity of computer resources makes computer time not free, forcing the owner to allocate this resource among competing users. Scarcity of farmland, fertilizer, and water means that there is a cost associated with satisfying our hunger. Chapter 3 developed a framework for analyzing consumers' demand for goods under this constraint. In this chapter, we consider a unique class of problems deriving from the scarcity of **time.** The scarcity of time arises because consumption is generally time-consuming. At any moment, it is not possible to simultaneously attend a football game and view a movie. Participation in one consumption activity postpones the utility from many other adventures. Even if all other resources were free, current consumption of one thing would cost the *current* consumption of the alternatives.

Utility maximization requires much more than simply allocating income across alternative bundles of goods. Consumption must also be allocated over time. What portion of your salary do you save, and what portion do you spend? Should you mow the grass today or wait until next week? Is it best to spend three extra years in school or go ahead and start working now? In the words of the late Orson Welles, Paul Masson "will sell no wine before its time." How do they know when it is time? Our focus in this chapter is on the development of a framework for answering these and other questions that deal with **intertemporal decision making**, that is, decisions that involve allocating consumption or production across different time periods.

Suppose you won the California state lottery and were offered two alternative payoffs: $1 million per year for 10 years or $10 million today. Which would you choose? Without a doubt, you would choose the second. But why? The total dollar amounts are the same! However, comparing today's dollars to those received 10 years from now makes no more sense than directly comparing dollars to rubles. Current and future dollar amounts alone are insufficient to assess the relative values of current and future consumption possibilities. We need to know the exchange rate. This exchange rate between current and future dollars can be calculated when we know the appropriate **discount rate** or **interest rate**. First, however, we explore the theoretical foundations of intertemporal choice.

Theory of the Consumer Revisited

Why do people value $1 today more than that same dollar one year from now? There are several reasons. To begin, let's recast our theory of the consumer in an intertemporal setting. First, utility is redefined as a function of consumption today, C_0, and consumption in the next period, C_1. Then we say there is a utility function over two goods, C_0 and C_1:

$$U = U(C_0, C_1)$$

assuming, for analytical simplicity, a two-period world. As in the previous utility function of one period and many goods, the marginal utility of current and future consumption, $\partial U / \partial C_i$, is positive. That is, as consumption in the next period increases, holding consumption in the current period constant, utility increases. Furthermore, to hold utility constant, an increase in current consumption must be offset by a reduction in future consumption. This is illustrated by the negatively sloped indifference curve shown in Figure 5.1. Again, indifference curves allow us to determine marginal rates of substitution. Recall that the marginal rate of substitution between two goods is defined by the ratio of the marginal utilities of the two goods and represents how much the consumer values good C_0 relative to good C_1.

FIGURE 5.1

The Consumer's Intertemporal Choice

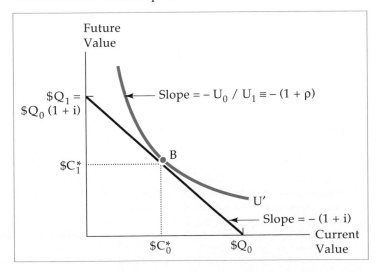

In Figure 5.1, the marginal rate of substitution between C_1 and C_0 is the slope of this indifference curve $(-U_0/U_1)$ and describes the consumer's subjective valuation of current versus future consumption—her time preference. If a consumer is willing to forgo $100 of consumption today to get $110 in period 1, the marginal rate of substitution is -1.1. Where does the -1.1 come from? Each $1 consumed today *costs* $1 consumed tomorrow *plus* the cost, in her eyes, of waiting for the future consumption, $1•0.1.[1] We call the individual's subjective interpretation of the cost of waiting her **personal discount rate**. The total cost is the loss of current consumption plus the cost of waiting, $1 + 0.1•$1 or $1.1. Since the consumer is willing to give up $1.1 next period for $1 in return today, we say the trade-off is -1.1. The minus sign signifies that current consumption is irretrievably *lost* for future consumption. Put differently, the consumer is willing to forgo one unit of consumption today in order to receive a 10 percent increase in consumption next period. The personal cost of waiting, the 0.1 increment in this example, again, is called the consumer's personal discount rate. Thus, the exchange rate for the consumer between current and future consumption is expressed as $(1 + \rho)$, where ρ is the discount rate.

The Budget Constraint

Indifference curves alone do not yield many useful behavioral predictions. Therefore, we must determine the opportunities available to the consumer with respect to multiperiod consumption.

Consider this example. Donnell, owner and sole proprietor of the Great American Worm Farm, has worms worth a total of $10,000; if he sells them all today and spends his money on current consumption, C_0 is $10,000 and C_1 is $0. However, if he waits until next year to sell the worms, and his worms grow in size and number by 10 percent (net of his costs of feeding and caring for them), then after one year, he will have $11,000 available for consumption or other uses. In this latter case, $C_0 = \$0$ and $C_1 = \$11,000$.

Donnell's worms are worth more at the end of the year because worms procreate and multiply at some net rate, say i. Allowing the worms to reproduce and grow rather than selling them today is called **investment**.[2] The rate of return on this particular investment is 10 percent. That is, if Donnell invests $\$Q_0$ worth of worms today, they will be worth $\$Q_0•(1 + i)$ in one year. Call this future amount $\$Q_1$.

To present Donnell's intertemporal consumption choices in familiar terms, suppose Donnell begins with a stock of worms with a current market value of

---

[1] The cost of waiting in this example, $1•0.1, is purely subjective. The number 0.1 was merely presumed for the sake of discussion. This cost varies across people and time and is determined by the preferences of the individual consumer.

[2] This is, of course, only one example of a productive investment. Wealth can be generated through investment in a number of ways that do not require procreation: Fermentation of grape juice yields wine; schooling results in productive work skills; dams and generators built now reduce current consumption opportunities but produce electricity in the future.

Q_0. Donnell's consumption opportunities over the two periods of this example depend on his investment choices in the first period, expressible in terms of the initial stock of worms available. Let Q_{0i} be the value of the worms invested. The value of the stock of worms available at the beginning of the second period, Q_1, is determined by the level of investment and the growth rate i:

$$Q_{0i} \bullet (1 + i) = Q_1.$$

One worm invested today yields $(1 + i)$ worms in one year. Put another way, one worm consumed today costs $(1 + i)$ worms consumed next period. This is an important result: Current consumption costs future consumption.

We can now restate the utility maximizing condition for intertemporal consumption. Utility is maximized when the marginal rate of substitution between current and future consumption, the ratio of the respective marginal utilities, equals the relative opportunity cost of current consumption, Q_1/Q_0, when

$$U_1/U_0 = \$Q_1/\$Q_0.$$

The ratio of the marginal utilities is $(1 + \rho)$, where ρ is the individual's personal discount rate. Therefore, by construction,

$$U_1/U_2 \equiv 1 + \rho.$$

Suppose the entire initial stock is invested and pays a return of i, then

$$\$Q_{0i} = \$Q_0, \text{ and thus}$$
$$\$Q_1 = (1 + i) \bullet \$Q_0.$$

Therefore, and in general,

$$\$Q_1/\$Q_0 = 1 + i.$$

We conclude, at the consumer optimum, that the interest rate (representing the return on investment) equals the personal discount rate,

$$1 + \rho = 1 + i;$$

therefore, when the consumer intertemporally maximizes utility,

$$\rho = i.$$

This is the case at point B in Figure 5.1. When Donnell maximizes utility, current consumption is $\$C_0^*$ in Figure 5.1, and future consumption is $\$C_1^*$. With his allocation of worms and their productivity, Donnell is happiest at these levels of consumption that equate his personal discount rate with the interest rate on investment opportunities available to him.

Summary of Intertemporal Consumption

We make three assertions concerning the allocation of consumption across time periods: (1) The level of utility attainable depends on the individual's original endowment and the investment opportunities available to him; (2) at equilibrium, the personal discount rate always equals the rate of return on investment; and (3) a change in the rate of return on investment induces a change in intertemporal consumption. This third proposition is analytically similar to the price changes considered in Chapter 3. An increase in the rate of return on investment increases the intertemporal exchange rate, $(1 + i)$, and hence increases the price of current consumption in opportunity cost terms. In accordance with the first law of demand, we expect that an increase in the return on investment reduces current consumption and increases future consumption.[3]

INTEREST RATES

In our earlier discussion of the theory of the consumer, we took the prices of the two goods as given—that is, we put them beyond the control of the individual consumer. In the intertemporal formulation of the theory, the relative prices of future and current consumption are determined by the rate of return on Donnell's investment of worms. However, most people do not have an endowment of worms. Instead, they have money, and, unlike worms, money does not procreate. Indeed, when consumers delay consumption, they are not investing but saving. The distinction is more than pedantic. **Saving** is simply the act of delaying consumption. **Investment** is the employment of resources for the purpose of increasing wealth. Thus, the act of saving, which in turn allows investment, pays rewards dependent on the actual investment choice, a decision over which the consumer has some control.

So what is the relevant rate of return that defines the opportunity cost of current consumption? Any consumer making intertemporal consumption decisions faces myriad repositories for her savings, offering different expected rates of return. These opportunities exist because worm farmers and other entrepreneurs are willing to share the rewards of their investments with those who provide the initial investment capital, those willing to forgo current consumption—the savers. For the moment, we assume that there is one best opportunity and, hence, only one interest rate to consider; the consumer has only one investment option. Furthermore, we ignore inflation. The interest rate represents a **real** rate of return on investment—an increase in purchasing power. In a later section, we consider in more detail the determination of interest rates.

CAPITAL GOODS

In the worm farm example, Donnell's utility indirectly derives from his allotment of worms and his ability to convert those worms into other goods (using dollars as

---

[3] This is an empirical, not theoretical, truism. Theoretically, price changes cause substitution *and* income effects, which may compete. Refer back to Chapter 3 for a more complete discussion.

a conduit, of course). As such, the worms are capital goods. A **capital good** is defined as a good that generates benefits (income) in more than one time period. For example, a share of stock, a house, a painting, and a willow tree are all examples of capital goods.[4]

The Concept of Value

The most interesting and important questions about capital goods and the intertemporal choices facing a manager turn on the concept of **value**. Value is a most dangerous concept to consider in a science textbook. Therefore, we must propose a definition that allows us to employ our analysis impartially and precisely, whether or not that definition meets other criteria. Remember, the purpose of a theory is prediction.

What is the value of an original painting by Vincent van Gogh? A 30-year Treasury bond? Your pinkie finger? Many readers of this textbook would never imagine that the first is worth as much as $53 million and that the last is worth perhaps as little as a few hundred dollars. In fact, most people would probably argue that there are no objective criteria for value, or that, like beauty, worth is in the eyes of the beholder. This confusion arises because there are two different ways to discuss value—personal use value and market value. **Personal use value** is the utility you get from some consumption bundle; **market value** is the price you could sell the bundle for. Many of us have mementos or items with sentimental value worth much more to us than we might ever hope to receive in the marketplace. Value in use and market value can, and often do, diverge. Only the market value of a good can be objectively ascertained. An example will elucidate the economic use of the concept of market value.

Suppose you were blind and could not experience the visual sensations produced by a beautiful painting. Would the painting be of no value to you? Be careful. Even to an unsighted person, art can be valuable. This concept of value is closely related to the notion of opportunity cost. Suppose you were also the curator of a museum. Surely then the painting has value to you even though you are blind; it is part of the job. Even though blind people cannot enjoy the visual rewards of art, as creators, owners, or curators, they can certainly appreciate the monetary rewards of art. One of the benefits obtainable from a good is the income received from selling or renting it. As long as someone is willing to buy or rent the painting, the value of the painting to *any owner* is at least as high as the highest bid.[5]

The science of economics is typically unable to explain the pleasure some

---

[4] Some economists do not consider a stock certificate a capital good. Instead, they view the underlying machines or assets giving stock value as the only capital goods. This distinction depends on whether one speaks in the aggregate or individually. For the individual, a share of stock is a capital good; it generates income across time because it is the legal claim to a portion of the underlying assets. If you do not believe it, ask any number of pensioners with stock in their portfolio. In the aggregate, the actual stock certificate or claim to assets produces nothing; only the actual assets themselves do this.

[5] Van Gogh's *Irises* sold for $53 million at auction.

people derive from *looking* at paintings, but value in that dimension is not necessary for our analysis. We hope to be able to predict some behavior by recognizing that the sale of paintings generates utility, albeit indirectly.

Capital Goods, Value, and the Consumer

Consider now another capital asset, a **zero coupon bond**; a zero coupon bond pays no interest. It simply pays a specified amount of money to the bearer on a specific date in the future. Unlike a painting that may have intrinsic consumption value, the benefits to the owner of the bond are solely monetary. Let's consider the value of the zero coupon bond in terms of the theory of the consumer.

Suppose the face value (that is, the dollar amount posted on the face, not the resale value) of the bond, which is the amount of the future payment, is $1000, and the bond matures in one year. What is the value of the bond today? Our theory of intertemporal consumption decisions implies that the consumer allocates consumption across time such that, given her personal discount rate, her own intertemporal exchange rate, say $(1 + \rho)$, she is willing to forgo C_0 today only if she receives at least $C_1 = C_0 \bullet (1 + \rho)$ next period in return. In this case, she will buy this bond only if the forgone current consumption, the price she must pay, is worth less to her than the current value of $1000 to be received in one year. To calculate this amount, we must convert the $1000 future payment into current dollars.

This conversion is called **discounting**; the value of a payment in the future stated in current dollars is the **discounted value** or **present value** of that payment. If the intertemporal allocation of consumption is utility maximizing, the present value of the bond must equal its price. When this condition is met, the consumer is indifferent between giving up the $1000 one year from now and the consumption forgone to pay for the bond, $P. Consequently, $P, the present value, represents the highest possible value of the bond for this consumer.

DISCOUNTING AND PRESENT VALUE

Discounting is straightforward. If an individual's intertemporal exchange rate is $(1 + \rho)$, then to this person the value of future consumption is current consumption times $(1 + \rho)$, or

$$C_1 = C_0 \bullet (1 + \rho),$$

and consequently,

$$C_0 = C_1 / (1 + \rho).$$

In general, the present value of a future receipt, one period from now, is given by

$$P = F / (1 + \rho)$$

where P is the present value, F is the future receipt and ρ is the appropriate discount rate. As was mentioned in the last section, choice of the appropriate discount rate is not simple and straightforward. For the individual, it is the personal discount rate. For the manager allocating firm funds, it is the opportunity cost of capital, but this depends on risk, return, and other factors. For our purposes here, these factors are simply ignored and left to other times and places for discussion. Of course, this is the central topic in many finance courses and texts. For our example, we presume the discount rate is calculable and known. Therefore, from this point on we will use the symbol r to refer to the market interest rate, the discount rate. If the appropriate discount rate is 10 percent, the intertemporal exchange rate in our example is 1.1 and the present value of the bond is $909.09. Discounting can be used in a number of ways to find the value of capital goods.

Future Value

We often know the present value or market price of a capital good and want to know what the item might be worth some time into the future, the **future value** of the asset. For example, if someone asked you for $1000 dollars today in exchange for some future amount, the minimum amount you would demand in repayment is the amount that makes you indifferent between your current payment, $1000, and the future payment to you. To calculate the future payment, F, simply multiply $1000 by $(1 + r)$. If the appropriate interest rate is 10 percent, your future receipt must be $1100 if you are to be just willing to provide $1000 today. A simple algebraic manipulation of the present value formula yields the formula for calculating the future value of a present amount:

$$F = P \bullet (1 + r)$$

when the payment comes in one year.

COMPOUNDING

The preceding discussion of discounting is simplified somewhat by considering only two-period decisions. However, many, if not most, intertemporal decisions involve more than two periods. Consequently, it would be helpful to extend the analysis to the n period case. Since this theoretical leap is cheap, we take it.

The biggest obstacle in this extension of the theory is that interest rates are typically expressed in yearly terms, but the general formulation of the problem involves periods of less or more than one year. For example, suppose a zero coupon bond were due to mature in two years. The original formula is no longer applicable because the discount factor only converts *next* year's consumption into present value.

Consider an investment of $\$I$ that pays a yearly rate of return equal to 8 percent. After one year, the value of the investment is $\$I \bullet (1 + 0.08)$. If the year-end value of the income generated from the investment, $\$I \bullet (1 + 0.08)$, is reinvested at the end of the first year and earns 8 percent for the second year, the value of the original investment will be $\$I\bullet(1+0.08)\bullet(1+0.08)$ after two years. The accrual of interest on the interest earnings of an investment is called **compounding**.

To understand this phenomenon better, suppose $1000 is placed in two types of accounts, one earning 8 percent compounded annually and another earning $80 per year. Table 5.1 shows the end of year values of the two investments, simple and compounding interest, over a five-year period. Clearly, 8 percent per year compounded annually is not the same as 8 percent simple interest or $80 interest per year.

These formulas can be generalized to the n period case when interest is compounded each period. The future value, F, of a present sum of money, P, n years from now at r percent interest is[6]

$$F = P\bullet(1 + r)^n,$$

and thus the present value of some future amount is given by

$$P = F/(1 + r)^n \tag{5.1}$$

where r is the **periodic** interest rate and n is the number of compounding periods. The formula holds for any length period—daily, monthly, quarterly, or yearly. In general, interest rates are expressed in annual terms, but that is not a problem. If the annual interest rate is 10 percent and the interest is compounded monthly, the periodic interest rate is $0.10/12 = 0.0083$ or 0.83 percent. Similar computations can be used to convert annual interest rates into weekly or daily rates.[7] We can rewrite equation 5.1 as

$$P = F\bullet[1/(1 + r)^n].$$

TABLE 5.1   COMPOUNDING AND SIMPLE INTEREST

	COMPOUNDING			SIMPLE INTEREST		
YEAR	PRINCIPAL	INTEREST	TOTAL	PRINCIPAL	INTEREST	TOTAL
1	$1000.00	$ 80.00	$1080.00	$1000	$80	$1080
2	1080.00	86.40	1166.40	1000	80	1160
3	1166.40	93.31	1259.71	1000	80	1240
4	1259.71	100.78	1360.49	1000	80	1320
5	1360.49	108.84	1469.33	1000	80	1400

[6] An appendix at the end of this chapter has a table of compound factors, $F_{n,r}$, for various periods and interest rates.

[7] It is a practice in some financial institutions to pretend that the year has only 360 days. Few people know where this practice originated, but do not be alarmed if you discover that an annual interest rate has been converted to a daily rate by dividing the annual rate by 360 instead of 365 or 366.

Then the term

$$1/(1 + r)^n$$

can be labeled $D_{n,r}$ and called the **discount factor** or the **present value factor**.[8] Thus,

$$D_{n,r} \equiv 1/(1 + r)^n.$$

If, in our example of Donnell and his worms, Donnell sold none of his worms for five years, and they grew at the rate of 10 percent per year for the whole time, then the value of his worm allotment after five years would be $\$10{,}000 \bullet (1 + 0.1)^5$, or $16,105.10. Similarly, at an interest rate of 10 percent, the present value of $16,105.10 to be received five years from now is $10,000.

Notice that r, the interest rate, is expressed here as a yearly rate. However, in many cases, interest on an investment is paid quarterly, daily, or even continuously. Imagine a savings account paying 12 percent per year **compounded quarterly**. In other words, the bank pays 3 percent interest on the account each quarter so the interest earned in the first quarter is added to the balance. Both the principal and interest then earn interest in the second quarter, and so on. When interest is compounded over less than a year, the **effective annual interest rate** will be higher than the stated annual rate. To calculate the effective rate, we employ the formula

$$r_e = (1 + r/n)^n - 1$$

where r_e is the effective annual interest rate, r is the stated annual rate, and n is the number of compounding periods per year. In this example, 12 percent compounded quarterly is an effective rate of 12.55 percent $[= (1 + 0.12/4)^4 - 1 = (1.03)^4 - 1 = 0.1255]$. With interest compounded daily, the effective annual interest rate would be $(1 + 0.12/365)^{365} - 1$, or 12.747 percent. In the most extreme case, interest is compounded continuously. Continuously compounded interest will, of course, yield the highest possible effective annual interest rates. Generally, the effective annual rate under continuous compounding is

$$r_e = e^r - 1$$

where $e = 2.71828$, the base of the system of natural logarithms. If our account earns 12 percent per year compounded continuously, the effective annual rate is 12.75 percent because $e^{0.12} - 1 = 0.1275$. The effective annual rate is often called the **APR**, representing the annual percentage rate. Thus, 12 percent simple interest rate compounded continuously carries an APR of 12.75 percent. The

---

[8] An appendix at the end of this chapter has a table of discount factors for a number of different interest rates and periods of time.

general formulas for converting present and future amounts under continuous compounding are

$$P = F \cdot e^{-rt}$$

and

$$F = P \cdot e^{rt}$$

where t is the number of years. Recall the example of van Gogh's painting that sold for $53 million. Using a continuously compounded real interest rate of 6 percent, van Gogh's *Irises,* worth $53 million today, would have been worth about $150,000 (based on its value today) when it was painted in 1889. Unfortunately for him, Vincent van Gogh was in a mental institution when most of his work was done, and he gave his paintings to his doctors, perhaps testimony to the wages of psychiatrists in the nineteenth century.

It is important, then, to be mindful of the compounding period when calculating present values. Table 5.2 compares the present value of $1 million due in two years under yearly, quarterly, monthly, and continuous compounding at 10 percent annual interest.

These amounts are the initial investments necessary to yield $1 million after two years. Since the effective annual rate is higher the more often interest is compounded, the initial investment required to produce $1 million in the future is lower when compounding is more frequent.

Hypothetical Business Problem 5.1

You are considering a real estate investment that will generate a net income of $20,000 per year for four years and will be sold for $50,000 at the end of the fifth year. Alternative investments are known to produce a rate of return of 8 percent over this time period. What is the most you are willing to pay for this property?

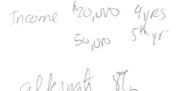

TABLE 5.2 VARIOUS TYPES OF COMPOUNDING		

PRESENT VALUE OF $1,000,000 DUE IN TWO YEARS		
Annual Compounding	$1,000,000/(1 + 0.10)^2	= $826,446.30
Quarterly Compounding	$1,000,000/(1 + 0.10/4)^8	= $820,746.57
Monthly Compounding	$1,000,000/(1 + 0.10/12)^{24}	= $819,409.54
Daily Compounding	$1,000,000/(1 + 0.10/365)^{730}	= $818,753.18
Continuous Compounding	$1,000,000/e^{(0.1) \cdot 2}$	= $818,730.75

Suggested Solution to Problem 5.1

The value of this real estate investment (your highest bid) can be determined using the discounting techniques already developed. For example, the present value of the first year's income is simply \$20,000/1.08 (presuming that the income is received at the end of the year), or \$18,518.52. Similarly, each subsequent year's income, including the resale income, can be converted to present value. The general formula in this case is

$$P = F_1/(1 + r)^1 + F_2/(1 + r)^2 + F_3/(1 + r)^3 + \ldots + F_n/(1 + r)^n. \quad (5.2)$$

Table 5.3 reports the five calculations.

Paying \$100,271.71 for this property initially would return 8 percent per year over the life of the investment. Of course, this example ignores tax considerations. However, the general framework can be used to calculate the present value of virtually any capital good. We explore other valuation techniques later in this chapter.

ANNUITIES

One special case of discounting is called an annuity. An **annuity** is a constant stream of payments made or received over several time periods. Although there are many kinds of annuities, one of the most common types is an installment loan. Suppose you receive a \$25,000, 48-month loan at an annual rate of 10 percent, compounded monthly, for the purchase of a BMW. What are the monthly payments? The \$25,000 is the present value of a stream of equivalent payments, F_i, which will yield a 10 percent annual rate of return for the lender. Equation 5.2 can be rewritten as

$$P = \sum_{i=1}^{n} F_i /(1 + r)^i \quad (5.3)$$

where F_i is the payment in period i, r is the periodic interest rate, and n is the number of periods. Although the discounting tools we have presented are sufficient for solving this problem, a simpler method is applicable.

TABLE 5.3   PRESENT VALUE CALCULATION

YEAR	INCOME	PRESENT VALUE
1	\$20,000	\$18,518.52
2	20,000	17,146.78
3	20,000	15,876.60
4	20,000	14,700.60
5	50,000	34,029.16
Sum of present values		\$100,271.71

Equation 5.3 can be rewritten as

$$P = F \times \sum_{i=1}^{n} 1/(1 + r)^i$$

where, since the F_i's are equal across time, F represents the annuity payment. The right-hand term is equal to F times the sum from 1 to n of the simple discount factors at interest rate r. This sum can be written as[9]

$$A_{n,r} \equiv \frac{1 - (1 + r)^{-n}}{r}$$

and is called the present value of an annuity factor.[10] The general formula for calculating the present value of an annuity is

$$P = F \bullet A_{n,r}. \tag{5.4}$$

Therefore, to determine the periodic annuity payment, F, for a given principal, P, a number of periods, n, and an interest rate, r, we simply solve equation 5.4 for F:

$$F = \frac{P}{\left(\dfrac{1 - (1 + r)^{-n}}{r}\right)}$$

or

$$F = P/A_{n,r}.$$

The monthly payment, F, can be computed using nonlinear solution methods or determined using numbers in a table of annuities. Both methods are commonly employed, although the solution technique is gaining market share due to widespread appearance of desktop computers. Let's employ the tables in the appendix at the end of this chapter to compute the monthly payment, F, for this 48-month, \$25,000 loan at 10 percent annual interest. First, since the annual interest rate is 10 percent, the monthly interest rate is $0.10/12 = 0.83$. If we look in the appendix at the table labeled Present Value of Annuity Factors under the 48 period row and the 0.83 interest rate column, we find the annuity factor 39.431. Inserting this value and the amount of the loan into the formula yields the solution:

$$F = \$25000/39.431 = \$634.02.$$

---

[9] The derivation of this expression is omitted in the interest of brevity. The inquisitive student may wish to explore the algebraic computation.

[10] A schedule of annuity factors for different values of r and n is presented at the end of this chapter.

The monthly payment on this loan would be $634.02, and it represents to the lender a rate of return of 10 percent per year on the $25,000 investment.

The Future Value of an Annuity

It is sometimes necessary to determine the future amount to which a series of equal payments will grow. For example, you might wish to know the future value of your retirement savings if you contribute a certain constant amount per year to the account. Again, the simple future value formula is sufficient for this calculation but unnecessarily tedious. By manipulating the future value equation, we can calculate the future value of an annuity by using the annuity compounding factor, $C_{n,r}$.

Assuming the payments are made at the end of each of n years, the future value of a stream of equal payments can be expressed as

$$S = F_1(1 + r)^{n-1} + F_2(1 + r)^{n-2} + F_3(1 + r)^{n-3} + \ldots + F_n(1 + r)^{n-n}$$

or

$$S = \sum_{i=1}^{n} F_i (1 + r)^{n-i}.$$

In the case of constant payments, this expression can be rewritten as

$$S = F \times \sum_{i=1}^{n} (1 + r)^{n-i}.$$

The right-hand term in this equation, which we call $C_{n,r}$, simplifies to

$$C_{n,r} \equiv \frac{(1 + r)^n - 1}{r}$$

which is called the annuity compound factor.[11] Thus, the general formula for calculating the future amount to which a series of equal payments will grow is

$$S = F \cdot C_{n,r}. \tag{5.5}$$

Hypothetical Business Problem 5.2

You plan to retire in 30 years and would like to generate a monthly income of $500 for a period of 10 years once you reach retirement. The interest rate is 12 percent per year compounded monthly. How much should you save each month?

---

[11] A schedule of these factors is presented in an appendix at the end of this chapter.

Suggested Solution to Problem 5.2

As with any discounting problem, the key to the solution is to convert all dollar amounts into common terms. There are two annuities involved in this problem. You must first determine how much money it will take to supply you with $500 a month for 10 years when you retire. This is the present value of an annuity paying $500 per month for 10 years. Put another way, it is the amount of money you must have in your savings account when you retire in 30 years in order to withdraw $500 a month for 120 months. Second, you must determine how much money to put into savings each month for 360 months starting today so that you will have sufficient funds available in 30 years to withdraw $500 a month for 120 months. The particular algorithm we use converts the two annuities into values corresponding to your retirement date. We note that an annual interest rate of 12 percent converts to a monthly rate of 1 percent.

We use the present value of an annuity equation to determine the future amount of money required to generate the monthly retirement benefits. The present value of an annuity factor is $A_{n,r}$ or

$$\frac{1 - (1 + r)^{-n}}{r}.$$

Since the annuity future amount, call it F_1, is $500, the monthly interest rate is 1 percent, and you wish to withdraw money for 120 months, this formula multiplied times $500 reveals the present value of the annuity,

$$P = \$500 \bullet (1 - 1.01^{-120})/0.01.$$

Solving this equation for P reveals the amount of money that must be available in 30 years in order to withdraw $500 a month for 120 months. Using a calculator we find that $P = \$34,850.26$. Alternatively, we could examine the Present Value of Annuity Factors table in the appendix to determine $A_{120,0.01}$, which is 69.701. Multiplying that figure times $500 yields the same answer except for rounding error. That is, $\$500 \bullet 69.701 = \$34,850.50$. If you deposited $34,850.26 in an account earning 12 percent per year (compounded monthly), you could withdraw $500 each month for 10 years.

Now we must compute the amount of money that you would have to deposit monthly in order to have $34,850.26 available in 30 years assuming that you can earn 12 percent per year on your investment. The compound annuity factor is

$$C_{n,r} \equiv \frac{(1 + r)^n - 1}{r}.$$

Inserting the appropriate values for the interest rate and length of period, and multiplying times F_m which is the monthly deposit, the future value of your monthly savings, S, is

$$S = F_m \bullet (1.01^{360} - 1)/0.01.$$

The problem requires that the compounded value of the monthly investments equal the present value of the annuity, in other words, that $S = P$. Therefore, we can set the two equations equal to each other:

$$\$500 \bullet (1 - 1.01^{-120})/0.01 = \$34{,}850.26 = F_m \bullet (1.01^{360} - 1)/0.01.$$

We can then solve this equation for F_m,

$$F_m = \$500 \bullet [(1 - 1.01^{-120})/0.01]/[(1.01^{360} - 1)/0.01] = \$9.97.$$

This problem can be stated in terms of the annuity compound factor and the present value of an annuity factor. In general, since S must equal P we can write

$$S = F_1 \bullet C_{n_1, r_1} = P = F_2 \bullet A_{n_2, r_2},$$

where F_1 is the amount that must be deposited monthly for n_1 periods earning r_1 interest, and F_2 is the amount that can be withdrawn monthly for n_2 months if the funds are earning r_2 interest. Solving this expression for F_1, the amount of the monthly investment, reveals that

$$F_1 = F_2 \bullet A_{n_2, r_2} / C_{n_1, r_1}.$$

In this example the monthly retirement withdrawal, F_2, is $500. Therefore,

$$F_1 = (\$500) \bullet A_{120, 0.01} / C_{360, 0.01}.$$

You can use the tables in the appendix to this chapter to compute a solution to this problem. The values for $A_{120, 0.01}$ and $C_{360, 0.01}$ are shown in the tables. Using the table labeled Present Value of Annuity Factors and looking in the row for the 120 period and the column for 1.0 percent, we find that the value for $A_{120, 0.01}$ is 69.701. Similarly, in the table labeled Annuity Compound Factors, looking in the row for the 360 period and the column for 1.0 percent, we find the value 3494.96. Inserting these values into the formula gives the result,

$$F = \$500 \bullet 69.701/3494.96 = \$9.97$$

which is the same answer we computed using the earlier method.

PERPETUITIES

An annuity with an infinite number of payments is called a **perpetuity**. Suppose you were offered an annual payment of $100 forever. The present value, P, is

$$P = \sum_{i=1}^{n} \$100(1 + r)^i = \$100 \times \sum_{i=1}^{n} (1 + r)^i.$$

Notice that as the number of periods, n, approaches infinity, the expression becomes simply $1/r$; the limit of

$$\sum_{i=1}^{n} (1 + r)^i$$

as n approaches ∞ is $1/r$. Consequently, the general formula for the present value of a perpetuity is

$$P = F/r,$$

where F is the amount of the periodic payment and r is the interest rate.

An easy way to understand why the present value of an infinite stream of payments is finite is to consider how much you would have to deposit in the bank to withdraw r percent of your deposit each year forever. The withdrawals are the annuity payments. A deposit of $833.33 at 12 percent interest would allow you to withdraw $100 per year forever. Therefore, the present value of $100 in perpetuity at 12 percent is equal to $100/0.12, or $833.33.

INTEREST RATE DETERMINATION—A SIMPLE EXPOSITION

The most important concept in this chapter is that the value of a capital good reflects the discounted value of all the future benefits generated by that good. The price of the capital good, then, depends on (1) the future income, (2) the number of periods, and (3) the discount rate. So far, our analysis has assumed that the interest rate was known. How do we know the appropriate discount rate for valuing a capital good?

Certainty

The market for capital goods works just like other markets. The interaction of suppliers and demanders generates an equilibrium price, an equilibrium interest rate. The appropriate interest rate for discounting, when the income from the capital good (sometimes referred to as the net cash flows) is known with absolute certainty, is the interest rate that makes the marginal consumer indifferent between those cash flows and the current consumption forgone by purchasing

The Refund Anticipation Loan

To encourage you to file your return electronically, the IRS promises to deliver your refund faster—within ten days to two weeks—if you file via modem and have the refund deposited electronically in your bank account.

To create an economic incentive for banks to help taxpayers file electronically, the IRS has agreed to honor an assignment of the refund to a bank. If you assign your refund to a bank, the bank can lend you the amount of your refund with full security. This makes it profitable for a number of banks to offer short-term loans (called refund anticipation loans or RALs) to electronic filers.

How profitable? Suppose you are entitled to a refund of $1000. The preparer's charge for completing a typical return is in the range of $75; add $30 for the electronic filing. Then add, say, another $70 for the RAL, which brings the total cost to $175. The first $105 of that total would get you your refund in ten days to two weeks, but since you're in a hurry, you spring for the extra $70 for the RAL. Not out of pocket, of course. The preparer subtracts all the charges from the refund and, after the IRS's electronic acknowledgement in a day or two, hands you $825.

What did this cost? If it's only $70 to borrow $825, it may sound like you're paying less than 10 percent (or 8.48 percent). But wait! Interest rates are usually quoted as annual rates. And since the lending bank is paid back by the IRS within two weeks, you've borrowed the money for only those two weeks. Seventy dollars for $825 for two weeks is actually an annual rate of 221 percent! Hey, that sounds like the terms I could get from my friendly neighborhood loan shark!

Doesn't a federal Truth in Lending law apply here somewhere? Sure, but under the Truth in Lending law the bank "assumes" the loan is due in one year (although most are written as due on demand) and discloses a rate of interest based on a one-year maturity. So despite the fact that the IRS will pay off your RAL in two weeks, the bank, with a straight and lawful face, recites that the interest rate is 8.5 percent.

About 87 percent of the taxpayers filing electronically last year paid for a RAL. Who would pay nearly 220 percent for a two-week loan? It's tempting to think that only a financially unsophisticated person would do such a thing. On the other hand, perhaps someone who needs the money immediately would swallow hard and put up with the inflated interest rate. That's a decision each individual must make on his or her own, but it should be made with a clear understanding of the actual costs that are involved.

Laura Lou Meadows, "Refund Anticipation Loans: Is the Convenience Worth the Cost?" *PC Magazine,* March 12, 1991, p. 474.

the good. This is equivalent to the determination of the equilibrium price discussed in Chapter 2. In this certainty case, if two capital goods offering the exact same stream of net cash flows are offered, they must have the same present value or market price.

For example, consider two zero coupon bonds offered for sale by the government.[12] Each of the bonds matures in one year and has a face value of $1000. If one is offered for $900 and the other for $950, competitive bidding will cause the prices to converge. Otherwise, a profit opportunity exists that allows an investor to buy the low-priced bond and sell it at the higher price. Profit opportunities in the market for capital goods attract market participants who attempt to exploit disparities between price and value. **Arbitrage** opportunities, simultaneously buying at a low price and selling at a higher price, ensure the movement toward a single equilibrium interest rate.

Uncertainty

The more common interest rate determination process involves capital goods with uncertain cash flows. The cash flows, or dividends, accruing to the owner of a share of common stock are estimable but not certain. General economic conditions, labor market conditions, resource price changes, consumer demand, managerial competency, and many other variables affect the actual dividends paid. In other words, the expected dividend payments are actually the expected values of a probability distribution of payments, the variance of which depends on these factors. Due to these vagaries, the owner of a capital good may receive cash flows that are less or more than expected. There is **risk**.

Risk and Interest Rates

A fundamental assumption we make about consumer behavior is that risk is undesirable. In other words, if two investments offer the same *expected* rate of return, investors prefer the one for which the variance of the cash flows is less; they are **risk averse**. Of course, nothing in the theory of the consumer precludes the desire to gamble. However, the assumption of risk aversion is, in general, empirically more reliable.

One capital good that generally offers uncertain future benefits is an oil well. Geologists are capable of estimating the amount of oil likely to be yielded by a particular well with only a slight degree of precision. Conversely, let us presume that agricultural prognosticators can estimate the yield from an orange grove in Southern California with a great deal of accuracy. If the expected net income streams from both an oil well and an orange grove are the same, risk averse investors must be compensated for investing in the oil well. As a result, the claims to the cash flows from the oil well will have a lower selling price, implying a higher rate of return. Of course, even if the returns to an individual oil well are quite risky, the return to a pool of wells may be much less so. Diversification can reduce risk and the required rate of return.

Generally, the more variable are the expected benefits from a capital good, the higher the discount rate that must be applied to its cash flows. The market for capital goods generates a **risk premium**, an increase in the equilibrium interest rate owing to risk bearing. Of course, the abundance of capital goods and their

---

[12] Recall that zero coupon bonds pay nothing, no interest, to the holder until the maturity date.

varying riskiness give rise to an apparent host of interest rates rather than one single rate. As in the certainty case, however, the market for capital goods ensures a *single* equilibrium rate of return *for any particular level of risk,* as measured by the variance of the probability distribution of cash flows.

Inflation

One of the factors that causes interest rates to differ is a change in the general price level, or inflation. In the United States, most intertemporal contracts are written in so-called **nominal terms**. This means the specified payments are denominated in currency values rather than units of real consumption, cans of peas or gallons of gas for examples. Suppose I agree to pay you $110 in one year if you lend me $100 today. This is a nominally denominated contract. By contrast, a **real** contract specifies payment in consumption terms. For example, I agree to pay you 110 pounds of potatoes in return for the loan of 100 pounds of potatoes today. Of course, it is possible to specify a real contract in dollar terms so long as both parties agree as to the instrument for converting real consumption into currency. Many labor contracts are now written in real purchasing terms using government-generated statistics to adjust the value of currency. Consider a hypothetical example. A local labor union agrees to a three-year contract with a firm. The contract specifies the current wage rate as $20 per hour. There is to be a 5 percent raise *in real terms* at the end of the first and second years, and the so-called GNP implicit price deflator published by the Bureau of Labor Statistics of the U.S. Department of Commerce will be used to adjust the nominal raises to ensure a real 5 percent increase in purchasing power. Suppose there is 10 percent inflation, a 10 percent increase in the general level of prices over the first year according to the GNP implicit price deflator. Then, for the union members to get a real 5 percent increase in purchasing power, they must be able to purchase $21 worth of today's goods next year. Since prices have risen by 10 percent, this means the actual wage rate next year is 1.1•$21 or $23.10 per hour. Now suppose in the second year, the GNP price deflator says that the general level of prices in the economy has actually fallen by 2 percent. Then to get a real 5 percent increase in purchasing power the workers must earn $23.10•1.05•0.98 or $23.77 per hour. In summary, in the current year workers earn $20 per hour, which allows them to purchase many things. A contract calling for a real 5 percent wage increase adjusts pay to account for price level changes that affect the workers' ability to purchase consumption items. By contrast, a nominally denominated contract ignores any changes in the overall level of prices that might occur.

If all prices are expected to increase by 10 percent over the next year, a *nominal* interest rate of 10 percent implies no *real return.* An investment costing $100 today in return for $110 one year from now generates no increase in consumption opportunities for the investor if all prices have increased by 10 percent.

As a practical matter, inflation must be recognized when considering intertemporal problems of more than very short terms. In fact, market interest rates generally include an inflationary adjustment. Since most consumers care only about the amount of cigars and candy they have to smoke and eat, savers must be compensated not only for their willingness to forgo consumption, but also for any expected changes in the overall level of prices. Put differently, it is reasonable to believe that interest rates incorporate the expected level of inflation at any point in time. Of course, at the beginning of the contract period, we can only guess what the *real* interest rates are in these cases; we must wait to see what actually happens to the general level of prices to know the real rate of return with certainty. In sum, it is instructive to be cognizant of inflationary effects on intertemporal decision making, but the basic analysis of discounting and compounding is unaltered by its inclusion.

APPLICATIONS

Hypothetical Business Problem 5.3

Suppose car A costs $10,000 originally, and annual maintenance averages $1000. The car lasts for 10 years, and then, for all practical purposes, is junk. Car B is virtually the same except that it only costs $500 per year for maintenance on average. It too lasts 10 years and then is junk. Presume the automobiles are otherwise the same. What is car B's original selling price?

The Fallacy of Automobile Rates of Depreciation and Value

Automobile buyers often claim that "I bought my BMW [Honda, Audi, Chevrolet, etc.] because BMWs consistently hold their value longer, and so I will benefit from the relatively high resale price of the car. BMWs are a better investment because they depreciate slowly." Is this statement valid?

In fact, this line of reasoning ignores one of the fundamental principles underlying the value of capital goods: The price of a capital good reflects the present value of *all* of the benefits generated by the good. Consider two cars that provide the exact same transportation services each year. Car A is more durable and delivers these services for 10 years, at which time it is of no further value. Car B is the same but lasts only 8 years.

Suppose the stream of benefits produced by the two cars is as given in Table 5.4. Car A is worth $2000 per year to the owner for 10 years; car B is the same except it only lasts for 8 years. Suppose the appropriate discount rate is 10 percent. Columns (3) and (6) are the present values of the succeeding cash flows of the two cars as the buyer stands in the lot contemplating purchase. Both cars provide services each year, but the value of the services in the future is worth less today because the buyer has to wait to get them. We must discount the future services rendered by either car to account for this wait. The sum of the discounted value of services is the value of the car to the prospective buyer and represents the buyer's demand price for the automobile. This amount is computed for car A in column (4) by summing the present value of $2000 each year for 10 years. Thus, we add $2000 (the present value of $2000 this year), plus $1818 (the present value of $2000 in 1 year), plus $1653, and so forth down to $848 (which is the present value of $2000 in 10 years). For a car that yields $2000 of value for 10 years, the sum, which is the present value of the flow at 10 percent interest, is $13,518. The sum of these present

TABLE 5.4   THE PRESENT VALUE OF TWO CARS

YEAR (1)	CAR A FLOW (2)	PRESENT VALUE OF FLOW AT 10% (3)	SUM OF PRESENT VALUES (4)	CAR B FLOW (5)	PRESENT VALUE OF FLOW AT 10% (6)	SUM OF PRESENT VALUES (7)
1	$2000	$2000	$13518	$2000	$2000	$11737
2	2000	1818	11518	2000	1818	9737
3	2000	1653	9700	2000	1653	7919
4	2000	1503	8047	2000	1503	6266
5	2000	1366	6544	2000	1366	4763
6	2000	1242	5178	2000	1242	3397
7	2000	1129	3936	2000	1129	2155
8	2000	1026	2808	2000	1026	1026
9	2000	933	1781	0	0	0
10	2000	848	848	0	0	0

values is the buyer's willingness to pay for the car, the worth of the car to him. Similarly, the present value of the flows to car B and their sum over time are reported in columns (6) and (7) respectively. For simplicity, we have assumed the flows are received at the beginning of the year. Car A is worth $13,518 new, and car B is worth $933 + $848 or $1,781 less because it does not last for the full 10 years. Its new price is $13,518 − $1,781 = $11,737.

The two cars do not have the same original price. Nor do they have the same price at any time during their life. At any discount rate, car A is always more expensive, that is, more valuable. Indeed, car A is a better car, the analog to a BMW in the car buyer's statement. It has a higher resale value at any time. However, the initial price of the BMW is higher by an amount that perfectly offsets its increased durability.

The fallacy of the statement rests on the notion that the slow depreciation rate of BMWs results in a better rate of return on these cars as opposed to similar but less durable cars. This notion is only true if the market for cars consistently ignores or underestimates these future benefits. It is plausible but doubtful that this is the case in the market for automobiles. The price of durable and reliable cars will be bid up until the rate of return on the investment is equal to the rate of return on inferior cars. The original price of car A and its price at any point in time is higher by an amount exactly equal to the increased present value of its durability. Surely, the car manufacturer and any subsequent used car seller will not give these values away. Competition between buyers and across sellers ensures that the car sells for the present value of its expected cash flows at any point in time. Again, arbitrage ensures this result.[13] So, the better car, car A, sells

---

[13] Does this mean that consumers will be indifferent among all cars? If not, can you justify the apparent contradiction?

for more money in the first year, $13,518 as opposed to $11,737 for the *B* car; and this holds for all years. Note that both cars lose $2000 in value from the beginning of the first year to the beginning of the second year. For car *A* this is a decline of $2000/$13,518 or 14.8 percent, but for car *B*, the reduction is $2000/$11,737 or 17.0 percent. The value of car *A* falls more slowly *in percentage terms* than the value of car *B*. Yet, at any point in time the value and price of car *A* exceed the value and price of *B*. Put another way, car *A* is not a better buy because it holds its resale value longer, but instead the car is worth more and has a higher selling price at every point in time because it lasts longer. The fact that the car lasts longer means that holding constant the services rendered by the car, it costs more new than a comparable car that wears out in a shorter time. There is no such thing as a free lunch or a free car.

Interest Rates and Construction Materials

"They just don't make 'em like they used to" is a common refrain heard about cars, houses, appliances, roads, and many other capital goods. The implication is that Americans are now satisfied with inferior products or perhaps manufacturers now take less pride in their work. An alternative and refutable hypothesis is that higher interest rates encourage less durable construction. Many people believe that cars made 20 years ago were typically more durable than cars made today. How might interest rates have generated this change? Consider what happens to the *present* value of a benefit that occurs far into the future as interest rates rise. As interest rates increase, the present value of future benefits is lower. Compare two items—one lasts 12 years, the other 15. When interest rates are high, the value of the extra three years of service provided by the more durable good is lower; the present value of the distant rewards is more heavily discounted. Higher interest rates induce more current consumption and less future consumption. Durability is worth less when interest rates are high, and consumers are willing to pay less for it when interest rates increase, other things being the same. In fact, the real interest rate has apparently risen a good bit from the 1950s until today. The real interest rate on 10-year U.S. Treasury notes averaged 1.66 percent during the decade 1950–1959, while the rate averaged 4.08 percent over the period 1980–1986.[14]

When Is It Time to Drink the Wine?

One of the intertemporal choice paradigms mentioned at the beginning of this chapter concerns the decision about when to drink wine that is aging. This question is actually a special case of a more general problem: the timing of the consumption of capital goods that increase in value over time. In general, the fermentation of grape juice yields a more savory beverage that becomes ever more piquant over time and, hence, more valuable to its consumer. Consequently, the

---

[14] The real rate was computed by subtracting the realized inflation rate in the previous year from the nominal rate in the current year.

question of when to drink the wine is an intertemporal one. The proper time to drink the wine is when the change in its present value is not worth the opportunity cost of lost investment opportunities.

Solving this problem requires two steps. First, the growth function describing the appreciation of the wine must be identified. Second, since the value of the wine will be greater in the future, its current value can be expressed using discounting. The value of the wine at each point in time, t, can be expressed mathematically as

$$V_t = g(t)$$

where g is the growth function. The value of the wine is assumed to increase at a decreasing rate, so $g'(t) > 0$ and $g''(t) < 0$ where g' refers to the first derivative of the growth function with respect to time and g'' is the second derivative. Employing continuous discounting, the present value of the wine is

$$P = g(t) \bullet e^{-rt}.$$

The maximum value for P occurs when the partial derivative of the value function with respect to time is equal to zero:

$$\partial P/\partial t = g(t) \bullet (-re^{-rt}) + g'(t) \bullet e^{-rt} = 0.$$

Therefore,

$$g(t) \bullet (-re^{-rt}) = -[g'(t) \bullet e^{-rt}],$$

and, dividing both sides by the common term, e^{-rt},

$$g(t) \bullet (-r) = -[g'(t)]$$

or

$$r = g'(t)/g(t).$$

Notice that $g'(t)/g(t)$ is the percentage change in the consumption value of the wine. The result demonstrates that the proper time to drink the wine is when the market rate of return (the opportunity cost of investment) is equal to the percentage change in the consumption value of the wine.

Suppose you hold a bottle of wine, the value of which is increasing at a rate of 10 percent while alternative investments offer only 8 percent. Investing in the wine by postponing consumption is utility enhancing. If the market rate of interest were 12 percent, the consumption value of the wine would be increasing at a slower rate than the value of alternative investments. To continue this investment would reduce utility.

It is instructive to recognize that this analysis is valid whether or not the owner of the wine is the ultimate consumer. Even for a teetotaler, the wine is most valuable when $r = g'(t)/g(t)$, if the wine can be sold. The analysis assumes, of course, that $g(t)$ is known. The statement made in the Paul Masson commercial asserts that the vintner knows this function and the consumer of Paul Masson wine can be assured that she is buying the wine when its value is growing no more than the interest rate on alternative investments, presumably when the value of additional fermentation is not worth the wait. Finally, notice that when the return to alternative investments increases, wine gets uncorked sooner; to restore the equality in equation 5.6, the owner of the wine uncorks it when $g'(t)$ is higher and $g(t)$ is lower. Naturally, the reverse is true as well: Lower interest rates on long-term government securities and declining returns to capital investments induce owners to leave wine in the cellar longer.

Manipulating the Price of a Capital Good

A common misconception about capital asset prices is that myopic managers can artificially increase the price of an asset by generating current income at the expense of future income. The standard argument is that a farmer, for example, can boost the current market price of his farm by overusing the soil and producing an abundant harvest this year, while damaging future harvests. This is viewed as a profitable strategy in the short run but a deleterious one for the long-run prospects of the farm.

Let's examine this problem with some numbers. Suppose the equilibrium net cash flow from a farm is $2000 every year, forever. At 10 percent, the farm is always worth $20,000 because the value of the farm is

$$V = \$2{,}000/0.1 = \$20{,}000.$$

Now suppose the farmer plants more intensively so that his harvests in the near future will be abundant, but future harvests will suffer from the use of overextensive farming methods. Overuse of the soil today increases current yields but depresses future yields as nutrients are bled from the soil. The future depletion exceeds the current increase. Can he make the value go up in the *short run* by doing this?

Suppose farm 1 earns a constant $2000 per year. The present value of this flow in perpetuity is $20,000. Farm 2 is abused and overused in the first two years making yields there temporarily higher than for farm 1. Yields are $4900 in the first year and $3500 in the second. Thereafter, because of soil and nutrient depletion in the first two years, the returns are always less in the future, $1500. The net cash flows from the respective yields are reported in Table 5.5. For simplicity, we assume the crops are received at the end of the year. The value of each farm at the beginning of every year is the present discounted value of the net cash flows. At farm 1, $2000 per year in perpetuity at 10 percent interest is worth $20,000. However, at farm 2, the net cash flows vary. They are higher in the first two years, and lower in all subsequent periods. The present value of the net cash flow is $19,743.80 at the beginning of the first year, $18,181.82 in the second year, and $15,000 every year after that.

How did we compute these values for farm 2? The present value of the cash

	FARM 1		FARM 2	
YEAR	NET CASH FLOW FROM YIELD	PRESENT VALUE OF CASH FLOW	NET CASH FLOW FROM YIELD	PRESENT VALUE OF CASH FLOW
1	$2000.00	$20,000.00	$4900.00	$19,743.80
2	2000.00	20,000.00	3500.00	18,181.82
3	2000.00	20,000.00	1500.00	15,000.00
4	2000.00	20,000.00	1500.00	15,000.00
5 − ∞	2000.00	20,000.00	1500.00	15,000.00

TABLE 5.5   MANIPULATING THE PRICE OF A CAPITAL ASSET

flows in the first year is the value of $4900 at the end of the year ($4900/1.1 = $4454.55) plus the value of $3500 two years from now [$3500/(1.1)^2 = $2892.56] plus the value of $1500 forever thereafter. To compute the value of this last term, recognize that beginning in two years (the value of the annuity in perpetuity is computed from the beginning of the period), the owner of the farm will receive a perpetuity of $1500 which, at 10 percent, is worth $1500/0.1 or $15,000. Since he must wait two years to realize this amount, the value now is $15,000/(1.1)^2 or $12,396.69. Therefore, the value of the farm is the sum of these present values, or $4454.55 + $2892.56 + $12,396.69 = $19,743.80. The value of the farm in the second year is computed using the same technique.

The result of this farming strategy is not an increase and then a decrease in the price of the common stock claims to the farm, even though the average net cash flows from the yields for farm 2 over the first five years are greater than the annual average net cash flows from the yields over the same period for farm 1. Farm 1 earns a total of $10,000 in the five-year period, while farm 2 brings in $12,900 in total. Indeed, switching from the efficient use of the land (farm 1) to the more intensive but damaging method (farm 2) *immediately* reduces the value of the second farm. Note, at the end of the first year, the second farm has produced $4900 − $2000 = $2900 more *revenue* through intensive cultivation, but the present value of the flows to this farm is only $19,743.80. Capital values and markets are not myopic. The economic concept of value implies that an action that alters the magnitude and timing of cash flows either increases or decreases value at the moment the action is taken, not later when the results of the action come to fruition.[15] If the expected value of the net cash flows to a project falls, the price of the ownership rights to the flows falls. In sum, present values render meaningless the misleading distinction between so-called *short-run* and *long-run* values. There

---

[15] The numbers in Table 5.5 are fictional. They could have been different. For example, the net cash flows to farm 2 could have fallen only to $1900 in the third and subsequent years, but the point remains. In this latter case, the value of the farm rises due to the change in cultivation methods, but it rises at the outset, not just when the extra crops are cultivated. In either case, it is impossible to intertemporally manipulate the present discounted value of the asset.

is only one value, the net present value. Overproduction in the agricultural example only pays if the farmer can fool investors into believing that current higher yields will persist in the future. In a competitive market, the only way to manipulate the value of an asset is to withhold information or fool people about the actual facts surrounding a particular project.

Recall Hypothetical Business Problem 5.3. Tools and techniques have now been presented so that you can solve this problem. Reread the problem and consider the following analysis.

Suggested Solution to Problem 5.3

The key to answering this problem has two parts. First, recognize that if the cars are identical, then the original selling price must be equal. Car *A* costs $10,000, but the owner must spend $1000 annually on maintenance. Buyers of car *B* only have to spend $500 each year for maintenance. Hence, since car *B* provides the same services as car *A*, it is worth the same amount as car *A*, $10,000, *plus* the value of the maintenance savings. Car *B* is worth *more* because the buyer expects to spend $500 *less* each year on maintenance. So car *B* is worth $10,000 plus the present value of $500 a year for 10 years, the maintenance savings.

The second part of the answer simply involves computing the present discounted value of $500 for 10 years. To do this part, we must make some assumption about the appropriate discount rate. To simplify the computations, assume the expenditures on maintenance are made at the end of the year. Then the present discounted value of the maintenance savings, *P*, is simply

$$P = \sum_{i=1}^{10} \$500/(1 + r)^i.$$

Table 5.6 reports values of *P* for interest rates ranging from 5 to 15 percent. The third column in the table adds the maintenance savings to the price of car *A*, yielding the value and hence the selling or demand price for car *B*.

In sum, the value of car *B* fluctuates with the interest rate, ranging from $13,860 when the interest rate is low—5 percent—to $12,509 when the interest rate is high—15 percent. Why does the relative price of car *B* fall as the interest rate decreases?

PROJECT EVALUATION—CAPITAL BUDGETING

A time-consuming and important managerial responsibility is to evaluate investment projects. In this section, we briefly detail a number of ways this is done. The presentation here is not meant to be exhaustive or complete, but instead it provides an overview. Project evaluation can be divided into three parts. The first is computation of the cash flows. Second comes the choice of discount rates, and the third is the selection of a decision criterion. We will only concern ourselves

TABLE 5.6 THE PRESENT VALUE OF MAINTENANCE SAVINGS		
DISCOUNT RATE	PRESENT VALUE OF DISCOUNTED MAINTENANCE SAVINGS	VALUE OF CAR *B*
0.05	$3860.87	$13,860.87
0.06	3680.04	13,680.04
0.07	3511.79	13,511.79
0.08	3355.04	13,355.04
0.09	3208.83	13,208.83
0.10	3072.28	13,072.28
0.11	2944.62	12,944.62
0.12	2825.11	12,825.11
0.13	2713.12	12,713.12
0.14	2608.06	12,608.06
0.15	2509.38	12,509.38

with the study of the third, that is, how you decide which decision criterion to use.

There are basically three different decision criteria: the **pay-back period**, the **internal rate of return**, and the **net present value computation**. Each has its strengths and weaknesses. The trade-offs involve quickness and simplicity versus precision. More precision requires more time and study. First consider the pay-back period.

The Pay-Back Period

The pay-back period is the quickest and simplest of decision criteria. It can be employed by unsophisticated and inadequately trained employees. It is easy to oversee and implement. Naturally, these are advantages. Sadly, it has serious flaws that dictate that it be used infrequently, prudently, and only when small investments are at stake. The pay-back period is easy to compute. Simply add up the number of periods it takes to get the initial investment back. Consider the sequence of cash flows in Table 5.7. Say the initial investment involves the purchase and installation of a drink machine in the break room. This outlay is $1300. After that, money starts to flow in. In the first month, the net receipt, net of the maintenance, electricity, and purchase of soft drinks, is $50. Net receipts grow for a few months as employees adjust to the new machine. In the sixth and twelfth months, periodic maintenance reduces the net receipts by $100. According to the pay-back period of project evaluation, this investment takes 11 months to restore all of the initial investment. In the tenth month, $125 remains unreturned. In the eleventh month, the machine has repaid the original $1300 with $25 left over. The pay-back period is 11 months.

How, when, and where is the pay-back period used? Since the pay-back

TABLE 5.7	CASH FLOWS FROM INSTALLING A SOFT DRINK MACHINE	

MONTH	NET CASH FLOWS	SUM OF NET CASH FLOWS
0	$-1300	$-1300
1	50	-1250
2	75	-1175
3	100	-1075
4	150	-925
5	150	-775
6	50	-725
7	150	-575
8	150	-425
9	150	-275
10	150	-125
11	150	25
12	50	75

period methodology takes no account of the time value of money, its use is restricted to very few cases. It can be used to give unsophisticated subordinates a rule of thumb in their small purchases, which otherwise would require inspection and oversight of many mundane and routine matters. Supplying these people with a simple, workable rule gives them direction while allowing them freedom to make their own choices and decisions. Thus, it can allow junior employees to make certain decisions without senior consultation.

The Internal Rate of Return

The internal rate of return evaluation technique is more sophisticated than the pay-back period approach, but it is not perfect. The internal rate of return is the discount rate that makes the present value of the sequence of cash flows equal to zero. It computes the present discounted value of all the cash flows to a project and finds the number, called the internal rate of return, that makes the sum zero. Reexamine the sequence of cash flows in Table 5.7. The internal rate of return is found by solving the following equation for r:

$$0 = -1300 + 50/(1 + r)^1 + 75/(1 + r)^2 + 100/(1 + r)^3 + 150/(1 + r)^4 + \ldots + 50/(1 + r)^{12}. \tag{5.7}$$

In this case the solution for r, the internal rate of return on this project, is 0.8197 percent per month or 9.84 percent on an annual basis $(0.008197 \cdot 12 = 0.0984)$.[16]

---

[16] Solving an equation like this by hand is not easy. It requires trial and error. However, virtually all spreadsheets used in personal computers have a function that calculates the internal rate of return automatically. For instance, in the spreadsheet by Lotus, 123, the function @IRR (initial estimate, range of cash flows) computes the internal rate of return for any sequence of cash flows.

The internal rate of return can be useful when comparing mutually exclusive investment alternatives or when deciding whether or not to take a gamble. However, it must be used with caution and care for it is flawed. The technique does take into account the time value of money, but it incorrectly assumes that net cash flows are reinvested at the internal rate of return rather than at the actual opportunity cost. This means that when the internal rate of return is high, cash flows received early are presumed to be reinvested at rates higher than will be possible. This will tend to make the project look more attractive than it actually is. Moreover, there may be more than one solution to a nonlinear equation such as equation 5.7. For any given sequence of cash flows, the computed internal rate of return may not be unique.

As with the pay-back period, the internal rate of return criteria can be used to control and give guidance and direction to subordinate employees. For instance, a manager may make a rule allowing people under her charge to make any investments so long as the internal rate of return is 20 percent or greater. It is important to place a size restriction on the investment for numerous reasons—most prominently because the rule is not perfect. Less than perfect rules have their place, but only when the stakes are relatively small. The best way to see the advantage of using the internal rate of return versus its superior alternative, the net present value computation, is to understand the strengths and weaknesses of the latter. Let us do that now, and then we can summarize all three techniques.

The Net Present Value Technique

The method of net present value computation calculates the present discounted value of each cash flow at the opportunity cost of funds and sums them. It computes the present value of the project using the appropriate discount factor, the risk- adjusted opportunity cost of capital. The sequence of cash flows in Table 5.7 is reproduced in Table 5.8 along with present values computed at two different annual rates, 4 percent and 12 percent (0.33 and 1.0 percent respectively on a monthly basis). The sums of the discounted present values are also reported there, and they are $43.82 at 4 percent per annum and $-15.75 at 12 percent annual interest. The fact that the value of the project depends on the discount rate is characteristic of the net present value computational technique—a strength and weakness at the same time. Since the method takes into account the time value of money, the solution critically depends on the choice of discount rate. Thus, if the annual interest rate is 4 percent, this project adds $43.82 to the value of the company if it takes this venture. But if the rate is 12 percent, this investment lowers the value of the firm by $15.75.

In order for a manager to require his subordinates to use the method of net present value computation in making investment decisions, the appropriate discount rate must either be chosen by the subordinates or mandated from above. This imposes cost. Allowing discretion here can be dangerous, for the subordinates may not be well versed or qualified in the proper methods of determining the correct discount rate. Thus, they must generally be required to justify their choice of discount rates. The problem with specifying a discount rate for all subordinates to utilize is that the project in question itself often impacts the appropriate rate. If the rate is project specific, it is hard to post a unique rate for all

TABLE 5.8 THE NET PRESENT VALUE TECHNIQUE

PERIOD	NET CASH FLOWS	PRESENT VALUE AT 4% ANNUALLY (0.333% MONTHLY)	PRESENT VALUE AT 12% ANNUALLY (1.0% MONTHLY)
0	$-1300.00	$-1300.00	$-1300.00
1	50.00	49.83	49.50
2	75.00	74.50	73.52
3	100.00	99.01	97.06
4	150.00	148.02	144.15
5	150.00	147.52	142.72
6	50.00	49.01	47.10
7	150.00	146.55	139.91
8	150.00	146.06	138.52
9	150.00	145.57	137.15
10	150.00	145.09	135.79
11	150.00	144.61	134.45
12	50.00	48.04	44.37
Sum		$43.82	$-15.75

to use. This naturally makes it costly to delegate responsibility and requires that senior officials be part of the process. This is precisely the reason that other techniques, such as pay-back and internal rate of return, are sometimes used. However, any time substantial sums are being considered for investment, the superiority of the net present value calculation goes unchallenged. In spite of the problems associated with selecting the right rate, the alternatives are simply too dangerous and potentially misleading. No self-respecting manager would use any technique save the net present value for investments of any reasonable magnitude.

Other Considerations

Project evaluation is not simple. In addition to the question of which method to use, several problems still remain. The first of these is the estimation of the net cash flows. In the preceding discussion, the net cash flows at each point in time were assumed to be known. This will not generally be the case. And worse yet, the more unusual the problem, the less data will exist from experience to guide the analyst. Computing the initial costs of investment is often the easiest task here. The price of the project is often known in advance, say for instance, when it is being supplied by other firms that bid or post prices. However, for many projects of large magnitude, such as the construction of the Alaskan Oil Pipeline or a plant to manufacture a new product, it is a complex chore just to calculate costs.

Even when initial outlays can be estimated with confidence, revenue computations are tricky and problematic. It is very hard to know with any degree of certainty what the future will bring. Consumers can be a capricious lot. The easiest case, of course, is when the output creating the income is sold under long-term contract. Then the revenues are known with confidence, leaving aside the financial solvency of the buyer.

The changing level of prices and varying relative prices present problems here as well, for they must be forecast with care in order to have reliable revenue projections. The technique that many managers adopt to deal with this situation is sensitivity analysis, especially given the widespread adoption of spreadsheets and personal computers. **Sensitivity analysis** refers to the act of changing net cash flow projections and observing the resulting change in the present discounted value of the project.[17] When the project appears abnormally sensitive to the revenue or cost forecast, then an extra portion of prudence is required. This can be accomplished by obtaining more careful or sophisticated net cash flow projections or making a more cautious choice of the discount rate.

In summary, there are three methods for evaluating projects, the pay-back period, the internal rate of return, and the net present value method. Each has its costs and benefits. The pay-back method is cheap and easy to use, yet it often renders unreliable results. It is used only when the stakes are small and when it is important to give discretion to subordinates. The internal rate of return method is somewhat more complicated, but it produces more reasonable results. It is flawed by two characteristics. It does not value resources at their opportunity cost, and its computation may not be unique. The net present value method can be costly to put into practice primarily because it can be expensive to administer; the analyst must assign a discount rate. Despite this cost, its superiority is rarely in doubt when substantial sums of money are involved.

Putting the Principles into Practice: An Example Using Light Bulbs

According to the *Wall Street Journal,* low-wattage, fluorescent light bulbs are quickly becoming substitutes for regular, incandescent bulbs: "One of the most popular is a 27-watt Panasonic bulb that substitutes for 60-watt incandescent bulbs."[18] The new fluorescent bulbs are very expensive relative to regular bulbs. A regular 60-watt bulb costs about $0.75 while a fluorescent light counterpart retails for about $15 but lasts about 10 times as long. On top of this, the fluorescent bulb "casts about the same color and intensity of light and uses only 15 watts." Now here is the question, At what interest rate and price for electricity does it pay a consumer to install the fluorescent bulbs in lieu of the more traditional incandescent ones?

How do we solve this problem? Let's compute the present cost of both options and then compare them. First assume that a regular 60-watt bulb will produce

---

[17] This method can also be used to determine how critical the correct choice of discount rate is.

[18] See David Stipp's column, *Environment,* and the story, "Fluorescent-Bulb Sales Become Electrifying," *Wall Street Journal,* August 30, 1990, p. B1.

1000 hours of light. General Electric makes such a claim for many of the incandescent bulbs it sells. Next assume that the light is used 4 hours per day. Thus, one incandescent bulb will last for 250 days. According to the *Wall Street Journal* story, the fluorescent bulb lasts 10 times as long, or 2500 days. The problem amounts to the choice between the purchase of one fluorescent bulb or the sequential purchase of 10 incandescent bulbs. Examine the time chart in Figure 5.2. At the beginning, you either purchase a fluorescent bulb for $15 or one incandescent bulb for $0.75. At the end of 250 days, a second incandescent bulb is purchased for an additional $0.75. The first bulb, now dead, is removed, and the second new bulb is installed. This process repeats itself 9 times. In the end, 10 different incandescent bulbs have been purchased and installed to produce the light of one fluorescent bulb. For the moment let us ignore the costs of removing the old bulb and installing the new one. We will discuss this situation a bit later. What is the present cost of the two alternative investment options? Let B_f and B_i be the respective costs in present value terms of the fluorescent and incandescent investment options. Then,

$$B_f = \$15, \text{ and}$$

$$B_i = \$0.75 \cdot (1 + D_{1,r} + D_{2,r} + D_{3,r} + \ldots + D_{9,r}), \text{ or}$$

$$B_i = \$0.75 \times \sum_{i=0}^{9} D_{i,r}$$

where $D_{i,r}$ is the discount factor for the ith period.[19] For example, since the period of analysis in this problem is 250 days, the life of one incandescent bulb is our period of analysis and in annual terms amounts to 250/365, or 0.685 of a year. Then, assuming a 10 percent annual interest, the appropriate discount rate for

FIGURE 5.2
The Purchase of Light Bulbs

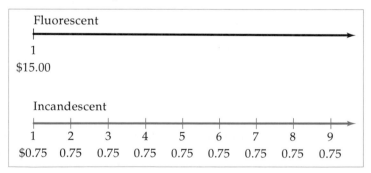

---

[19] Since the bulbs are bought at the beginning of the period, we start with $i = 0$ which implies no discounting on the first purchase, and we stop with the purchase of the tenth bulb at the end of the ninth period.

each period of this problem is 0.1•(250/365) = 6.85 percent. Thus, the present value of the light bulb that must be purchased at the end of the first period is found by computing $D_{1,r}$ = 1/(1 + 0.0685) = 0.936 and multiplying this factor times the purchase price of $0.75. Similarly, the present value of the cost of purchasing the tenth bulb is determined by first computing the discount factor, $D_{9,0.0685}$, which is $1/(1 + 0.0685)^9$ = 1/1.815 = 0.551 and multiplying it times the price.[20] The bulb purchased to replace the ninth bulb will only cost 55.1 cents on the dollar or 0.551•$0.75 = $0.41 in present value terms, because the cash outlay is delayed for nine 250-day periods. Computing all the discount factors and summing them is a way of mapping the future cost of incandescent light bulb purchases into current dollar terms. At 10 percent annual interest, the sum of the discount factors is 7.557, and so we compute that B_i is

($0.75)•(7.557) = $5.67.

Based on this simple calculation, the fluorescent bulb, costing $15 initially, is a very poor investment. The present value of the sequential purchase of 10 incandescent bulbs costs only $5.67, assuming a discount rate of 10 percent, and as the discount rate increases, the cost of the incandescent bulb falls. For example, at a rate of 12 percent, the present cost of the incandescent bulbs is only $0.75•7.19 = $5.39. Of course, the fluorescent bulb offers two advantages that we have yet to incorporate. First, there is the energy savings. Recall from the *Wall Street Journal* story that the fluorescent bulb only uses 15 watts of power as opposed to 60 watts for the incandescent bulb. Thus, there is a lower cost of operation for fluorescent bulbs. To make this adjustment, let us compute the present value of the electricity consumption for an incandescent bulb and then compare it to the fluorescent bulb. In order to make this computation, we must make an assumption about the price of electricity, and this assumption could be very important. Let's start with a price of $0.07 per kilowatt hour. (Electrical engineers call this a *kwh*.) Since a kilowatt is 1000 watts, a 60-watt bulb uses 60/1000 or 0.06 of a kilowatt every hour. Thus, a bulb burning for 4 hours per day uses 4•0.06 or 0.24 of a kilowatt of power daily. At $0.07 per kwh the incandescent bulb costs $0.07•0.24 or $0.0168 each day. What is the present value of this daily expenditure on electricity? We have to compute the cost of electricity for each of the next 2500 days.[21] This is the time that 10 incandescent bulbs will last. In notational form, it is

$$c_e \times \sum_{i=1}^{2500} 1/(1 + r)^i = c_e \times \sum_{i=1}^{2500} D_{i,r}$$

where c_e is the daily cost of electricity. When the price of electricity is $0.07 per kwh and the 60-watt bulb burns for 4 hours per day, the daily cost is $0.0168.

---

[20] These discount values can also be gleaned from the table labeled Discount Factors in the appendix at the end of this chapter.

[21] Assume that electricity is paid for at the end of each day.

Assuming an annual discount rate of 10 percent, which is a daily rate of 0.00027397, the present value of the cost of electricity using incandescent bulbs is

$$\$0.0168 \times \sum_{i=1}^{2500} D_{i,0.00027397} = \$0.0168 \times 1809.772 = \$30.40.$$

The present value of the electricity used by 10 60-watt incandescent bulbs 4 hours each day is $30.40 when the price of electricity is $0.07 per kwh and the cost is discounted at a rate of 10 percent per year. Since the fluorescent bulb uses only 15 watts, its cost is 15/60 or 25 percent of this amount. Thus, the present value of the electricity cost for the fluorescent bulb is 0.25•$30.40 or $7.60. The total cost of the incandescent bulb is the purchase cost of the bulbs, $5.67, plus the electricity cost of $30.40, for a total of $36.07. Similarly, the total cost of the fluorescent bulb is its initial outlay, $15, plus its electricity cost, $7.60, for a total of $22.60. Over the 2,500 days of use, the fluorescent bulb saves a substantial amount, $36.07 − $22.60 = $13.47 or 37 percent. These numbers strongly favor the purchase of the fluorescent bulb and help us understand why, as the *Wall Street Journal* story says, "Sales of energy-saving fluorescent light bulbs are brightening so fast that retailers are having trouble keeping some in stock."

In fact, costs savings of fluorescent bulbs are sufficient to make one wonder why anyone would ever buy another incandescent bulb. However, we have left two things out of our analysis, one of which favors the incandescent bulb, and this may help explain why incandescent bulbs remain viable in the market. First, we have not included the installation costs into the problem. If we did this, the fluorescent bulb would come out even more favorably. Since it is only installed once for each 10 installations of the incandescent bulb, the costs have to be lower for the fluorescent bulb. However, light bulbs are fragile, and this may turn out to be important. Suppose you purchase a bulb and place it in a lamp. The next day the dog grabs the lamp cord, pulling the lamp to the floor and breaking the bulb into pieces. Your original investment is destroyed. In the case of the fluorescent bulb, this is a big setback, but had you installed an incandescent bulb, you would only be out $0.75. Light bulbs are often installed in public places but are rarely stolen. Their value is too small to warrant the trouble. However, a $15 bulb shines a different light on the matter, and theft becomes a real concern. This argues in favor of the cheaper initial investment, the incandescent bulb.

The fluorescent bulb costs a lot initially, but it saves a lot on electricity over time. By contrast, the incandescent bulb has a low starting cost, but it uses relatively more electricity over time. Thus, when the situation is secure, the fluorescent bulb is preferred. When breakage or theft is a strong possibility, the scales can tilt in favor of the incandescent light. In order to compare the two alternatives accurately, we would have to make some assumptions about the probability of breakage and theft, but we can offer two general remarks. As the price of electricity increases, the fluorescent bulb becomes more attractive. Second, as the probability of theft and breakage increases, the incandescent bulb is favored. It is worth noting that the impact of the choice of discount rate is ambiguous. As the interest rate increases, the incandescent bulb becomes the better investment as its original investment costs are delayed. On the other hand, the cost savings from using less electricity with the fluorescent bulb are also delayed. However, based on the relative magnitudes, it does appear that higher interest rates favor the incandescent bulb.

The point of this exercise is simple. It is often possible to use the tools of present value computation and discounting to make what appear to be difficult decisions become rather easy and transparent. No self-respecting manager would ever go to all this trouble if only the purchase of one or two light bulbs were at stake, but some companies buy hundreds if not thousands annually, and moreover, the principles of this problem apply to many business investment decisions. Therein lies the usefulness of the exercise.

MANAGING ARBITRAGE OPPORTUNITIES: A STUDY OF PROFESSIONAL BASKETBALL

The goal here is to quantify the extent of managerial ability to exploit profit opportunities. One school of thought says that intense competition between firms and managers erases all profit opportunities, but what we need to understand is the timing of this process. Are managers required to instantly and constantly monitor all markets to ensure that the risk-adjusted, marginal rate of return on all investments is identical? An option to the zero profit condition asserts that gaps may arise between the returns to alternative investment opportunities that are neither quickly nor easily erased for a number of reasons. It is easy to see why economic forces quickly (instantly?) arbitrage away any profit opportunities that might arise by buying gold in dollars, using the dollars to buy Swiss francs, and then using the Swiss francs to get back to gold. There are literally thousands of traders in the financial markets who would leap at such an opportunity. However and by contrast, managers of firms often have simultaneous investment opportunities *inside* their own organizations available only to them and foreclosed to the general market. Are there forces that make these managers perfectly equate the marginal rates of return on these alternatives; and if so, how fast do these forces work, or alternatively, is the structure of management so organized that some managers need not flawlessly work every margin? Put differently, can you expect to walk into a well-functioning organization and find ways to make more money, or do you expect to just try and keep the ship running as it has been, that is, just keep profits from falling?

The On-Court Alternative Investment Opportunities in Pro Basketball

To touch on this issue, consider professional basketball. For the years 1980–1987 the National Basketball Association (NBA) was composed of 23 teams playing 82 regular games per season. Since the beginning of the 1979–1980 season, NBA teams have had the option of shooting a regular shot for two points or attempting a more difficult shot from outside 23' 9" for three points.[22] Figure 5.3 depicts the shot alternatives available to NBA teams. Data encompassing the 1980–1981 season through the 1986–1987 season on 2- and 3-point rates of return are summarized for the entire league in Table 5.9.

During the seven-year sample period investigated, the 2-point shot is almost always the more profitable option. Consult Table 5.10, which reports the 10 teams with the lowest expected value for a 3-point shot and the 14 teams for which the 3-point shot had a higher expected value than the 2-point alternative.

For the league as a whole, the gap between the marginal rates of return seems to be narrowing over time, and the data in Table 5.9 suggest that this is due to improved 3-point shooting. At first glance, shouldn't teams equate the marginal rates of return on the different types of shots? Yet there is an amazing distribution of differences in expected value of the two investment opportunities over teams and time in the NBA. When we look across all the teams over this time period, at one end of the spectrum, the 1982–1983 Los Angeles Lakers headed by second-year coach Pat Riley scored 1.067 points on average for each 2-point shot they took while they only scored 0.31 points for each 3-point field goal they attempted, a difference of 3/4 of a point. At the other extreme, the 1980–1981 San Diego Clippers coached by Paul Silas perfectly equated the expected values of the two shot opportunities; on average, they earned 0.973 points for each 2- or 3-point shot. It is worth noting that in 1982–1983, the Lakers shot only 96 3-point shots, slightly more than one per game and only 1.3 percent of all shots taken from the floor.

Figure 5.3
The NBA Court

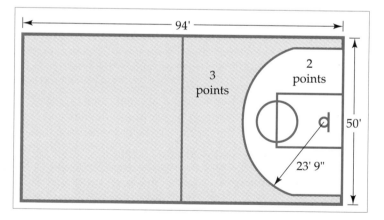

[22] Official Rules of the National Basketball Association, Rule 1, Section Id says "Three-point field goal area which has parallel lines 3 feet from the sidelines, extending from baseline, and an arc of 23 feet 9 inches from the middle of the basket which intersects the parallel lines." Rule 5, Section Ib continues, "A goal from the field counts 2 points unless attempted from beyond the 3pt. line which counts 3 points." Note (4) adds, "For successful 3 point field goal player must have one or both feet on the floor and be beyond the 3 point line when he attempts shot. After release of ball he may land on line or in 2 point area."

| | TABLE 5.9   THE EXPECTED VALUE OF 2- AND 3-POINT SHOTS IN THE NBA—1980–1987 | | | |

SEASON	AVERAGE 2-PT. SHOOTING %	AVERAGE 3-PT. SHOOTING %	AVERAGE VALUE OF 2-PT. SHOT	AVERAGE VALUE OF 3-PT. SHOT
1980–1981	0.4914	0.2293	0.9829	0.6879
1981–1982	0.4971	0.2527	0.9943	0.7580
1982–1983	0.4917	0.2310	0.9833	0.6929
1983–1984	0.4985	0.2482	0.9970	0.7446
1984–1985	0.4988	0.2736	0.9976	0.8209
1985–1986	0.4954	0.2683	0.9908	0.8048
1986–1987	0.4906	0.2902	0.9812	0.8706

TABLE 5.10   TEAMS WITH LOW AND HIGH 3-POINT PAYOFFS

TEAM	YEAR	V_2[a]	V_3[b]
LA Lakers	1982–1983	1.0663	0.3125
Atlanta	1980–1981	0.9670	0.3658
LA Lakers	1981–1982	1.0428	0.4149
Detroit	1980–1981	0.9339	0.4643
Indiana	1985–1986	0.9756	0.4825
Portland	1980–1981	1.0061	0.5068
Chicago	1983–1984	0.9584	0.5128
San Antonio	1980–1981	0.9890	0.5294
Indiana	1980–1981	0.9779	0.5325
Houston	1980–1981	0.9843	0.5339
San Diego	1980–1981	0.9729	0.9729
Seattle	1986–1987	0.9889	1.0035
Boston	1985–1986	1.0348	1.0534
Dallas	1984–1985	0.9969	1.0293
Indiana	1981–1982	0.9430	0.9778
Cleveland	1985–1986	0.9772	1.0127
New York	1986–1987	0.9639	1.0000
Boston	1984–1985	1.0293	1.0679
Boston	1986–1987	1.0601	1.0991
Utah	1984–1985	0.9649	1.0065
LA Lakers	1986–1987	1.0520	1.1006
Dallas	1986–1987	1.0008	1.0612
New York	1985–1986	0.9292	1.0292
Washington	1983–1984	0.9733	1.1703

[a] The average expected value of a 2-point shot.
[b] The average expected value of a 3-point shot.

Interestingly, the 1980–1981 Clippers took 407 3-point shots (almost 5 per game)—5.6 percent of all the shots they took from the field.

A number of explanations come to mind for the conscious decision of a coach not to equate the expected values of the alternative investment options. First, for one reason or another, he may not be risk neutral.[23] Since the 3-point shot is a more risky venture, risk averse coaches will choose to shoot relatively more 2-point shots, risk lovers the opposite. However, as a game comes to its close, the team that is far behind with a remote chance to win faces a bankruptcy type situation; the game is about over and they are about to lose. This has managerial consequences. That is, they are inclined to take high-payoff, high-risk investments—teams are inclined to forsake the higher expected payoff 2-point shot and take more of the higher valued, but riskier, 3-point field goal shots late in a game. Along similar lines, teams far ahead may be less inclined to worry about working every margin, and they too may casually or unwisely invest, taking either too few or too many 3-point shots relatively speaking. Moreover, as each of the first three quarters of a game nears its finish, it may prove wise to launch a long-distance 3-point shot when insufficient time remains to get into position to shoot a 2-point shot. In these cases, there is no option, and looking at the expected values, the team will appear to take too many 3-point shots. In fact, the data suggest this. For the whole league over the time frame we examine, the overall average expected payoff on a 2-point shot exceeds the expected value of a 3-point shot. This fact is consistent with the argument that many 3-point shots are taken in desperation when the 2-point option is technically unavailable. The NBA also has a 24-second shot clock that sometimes forces teams to make an ill-prepared shot. However, there is little reason to suspect that there will be more 3- than 2-point shots in this circumstance.

In addition, the choice of a 2- or 3-point shot may be more complex than it appears on the surface. It may be easier or less expensive for some teams to launch one type shot rather than the other. For example, if a team has very good guards and weak inside people, getting the ball inside to take a 2-point shot may impose costs absent in the decision to take a 3-point shot. Alternatively, since 3-point shots are long range, rebounds may not bounce the same as rebounds from 2-point shots. Thus, teams more proficient in one type rebound versus the other are *not inclined* to equate the expected values of the two shot opportunities. This point obviously generalizes to many different team skills.

If we put aside these potentialities, the inequality of expected values of the two investment opportunities has but two explanations. First, some managers are incompetent and should soon either be replaced or change their behavior. Second, since management encompasses many attributes and qualities, that is, management is lumpy, arbitrage may not work rapidly or even at all to erase the differential in the expected rate of return so long as the existing bundle of

---

[23] As a general principle, this force is probably not powerful in most organizations, but when large stakes of wealth are involved and the coach and owner find it expensive to diversify their portfolios, as they might in a sports franchise, that possibility cannot be ruled out. This is especially true when the ownership claims are not usually divisible into small marketable units.

manager skills dominates the next best alternative. That is, the head coach may not be perfect, but he may be better than anyone else available for the job. However, it still remains true that as long as these arbitrage opportunities are present, we should expect that those managers most capable of spotting and exploiting them will be more successful than those who are less competent (as we have seen from Table 5.9 and the related discussion). What we have is an amazing diversity as we look across the many coaches and teams in the NBA. What is the point of all this? It stands to reason that in at least some of these cases, coaches are not taking advantage of all the profit opportunities available to them.[24] In turn, this implies that better qualified managers, those more capable of taking advantage of these opportunities, might be able to step in and improve the profitability of many business enterprises. Of course, whether that will actually happen or not critically depends on whether the new manager can not only perform some chores better than the existing boss, but also whether he can perform the *overall* management as well.

TOPICS TO REVIEW

These are topics that you should feel comfortable with before you leave this chapter. If you cannot write out a clear and concise sentence or paragraph explaining the topic after you have worked on the study problems, you should reread the relevant section of the text.

Discount Rate

Interest Rate

Personal Discount Rate

Saving

Investment

Capital Goods

Value

Present Value

Discounted Present Value

Future Value

Compounding

Continuous Compounding

Discount Factor

Effective Interest Rate

Annuities

---

[24] For a far more complete discussion on this point, see two related papers in the economics literature: Robert E. McCormick and Robert C. Clement, "Intrafirm Profit Opportunities: Evidence from Professional Basketball," in *Advances in the Economics of Sports*, ed. by Gerald Scully (New York: JAI Press, 1991), and Kevin Grier and Robert Tollison, "Arbitrage in a Basketball Economy," *Kyklos*, FASC 1990, 611–24.

Perpetuities

Risk Premium

Nominal Terms

Real Terms

Depreciation

Pay-Back Period

Internal Rate of Return

The Net Present Value Technique

Sensitivity Analysis

STUDY PROBLEMS

1. Recall the discussion of automobiles and depreciation rates. Some people obviously prefer BMWs to other cars. Is this preference inconsistent with the theory? If not, why do some people buy BMWs? Under what circumstances might a BMW be a good investment? Describe the kinds of car owners who drive BMWs. (Hint: Recall the discussion in Chapter 3 on human capital and the do-it-yourself decision. Also think about accident rates.)

2. Sellers of large appliances, cars, and computers are often accused of exploiting consumers by selling products that break down shortly after the warranty expires, effectively making the warranty worthless. Discuss this accusation.

3. Discounting allows us to assess the value of capital goods objectively . Can the analysis be extended to human life? If so, suggest a method of finding the value of a human life, a hand, a kidney.

4. Your son, Eldon, is one year old today. When he turns 18, he will go to college where we can presume that tuition and other expenses will cost about $15,000 per year. Suppose he will attend for four years. You are contemplating ways to save for his education. Assume the annual interest rate is 8 percent.

    a. How much would you have to deposit in an account each month to have enough in the account on Eldon's eighteenth birthday in order to pay for his education if interest is compounded monthly?

    b. Suppose you wanted to deposit one lump sum today. How much would you have to deposit?

    c. Which of these savings plans is best and why?

5. Suppose you own a garden that is expected to produce a net income of $5000 per year forever. What is the value of the garden at 6 percent? What happens to the value of the garden if the interest rate falls to 3 percent? If the expected net income rises to $10,000? Do you have a preference between the two?

6. According to facts reported in the study problems section of Chapter 2, drug addiction among American servicemen declined after they returned from overseas. Using the concept of present value and interest rates, suggest another explanation for this phenomenon.

7. A disproportionate share of soft drinks is sold during the summer. Con-

sequently, net cash flows for soft drink companies are always highest in June and July. Absent other disturbances in the expected net cash flows over time, is the price of the stock highest during these months? Why or why not? Describe the pattern of these stock prices over time.

8. Consider two people, Henry and Keith, who are alike in every way except that Henry smokes, drinks and does not exercise while Keith is a health nut. Other things being the same, who is more likely to own a cemetery plot? Who is more likely to use credit cards for purchases? Who is more likely to go to college? Who is more likely to invest in stocks?

9. Compute the present value of $100 received today and an additional $100 on this anniversary every year for the next four years at 10 percent interest. Now compute the present value of a similar gift of five $100 payments, but you receive the first payment one year from today (again use a 10 percent interest rate). Now compute the present value of $100 five years from now at 10 percent interest and subtract it from $100. Compare this difference to the difference between the values of the two different receipts.

10. Suppose the market produces two different types of brooms. Broom A lasts exactly one year with certainty. Broom B will sweep for exactly two years.

   a.   How do consumers decide which broom to purchase?
   b.   Suppose some people are richer than others. Can you predict which people will buy the type A brooms and which will buy the B type brooms?

11. Suppose your company has made a big sale on some of its real estate, and the buyer has offered you the following deal. Plan A pays you $1 million now and $5 million each year for five more years. Plan B pays $250,000 now and $6 million for six additional years. Plan C pays $3.5 million now and each year for 10 more years.

   a.   At 10 percent interest, which plan is the best for your company?
   b.   At 12 percent interest, which plan is the best for your company?

12. Your company sells electric motors. Currently the price of a five horsepower model is $100. On average, this motor lasts for five years, and the users typically have to spend $50 per year on maintenance. Your engineering staff has just developed a superior model that requires less maintenance and lasts longer. The new model requires only $25 per year annual maintenance and is expected to last for eight years. What is the selling price of the new, improved electric motor?

13. You are in charge of purchasing a specialized fan for your company. Three different types of fans are available. Brand A originally costs $100 but requires $10 maintenance annually. Brand B costs $120 originally but only requires $8 of maintenance annually. Each of these two fans typically lasts for four years. A third type of fan is available that only lasts one year, but it costs only $40. If the fans are the same performance wise and otherwise, which is the best buy for your company?

14. Suppose your bank bought a five-year municipal bond one year ago. The bond pays $1000 per year interest for each of four years and then returns the

face value at the end of the fifth year, plus another $1000 interest. When you bought the bond the interest rate was 10 percent, and the face value of the bond is $10,000. You have just received your first interest payment, but the interest rate has also just now increased to 12 percent, and you are thinking of selling the bond. What price do you expect to receive? Is it a good idea to sell or should you hold?

15.   Volvo makes cars that last a long time, or at least they claim they do. Suppose that Volvos last, on average, for eight years while Toyotas last for only four years. (*For purposes of this question, assume that the cars, except for the length of time they last, are otherwise the same.*)

a.   If the interest rate is 12 percent, and Toyotas cost $15,000 on average, how much does a Volvo cost?

b.   What happens to the price of Volvos if the interest rate increases to 14 percent?

16.   USAA is a large mutual insurance company based in San Antonio, Texas, offering a variety of insurance and financial services primarily to current and former members of the U.S. Armed Services. The company publishes a magazine, *Aide Magazine,* six times a year. In the October 1990 issue (p. 9),the following question to the editor appeared:

> I am shopping for a home and called my bank about mortgage loan interest rates. They offered a 10 percent rate with no discount points or a 9.5 percent interest rate with two discount points. Which is best?

The magazine responded, in part,

> As a refresher, let's back up and explain that a point, which is paid to the lender, is one percent of the loan amount—i.e. $1000 on a $100,000 loan. If discount points are part of your settlement costs, they reduce your interest rate. On a standard 30-year loan with interest rates around 10 percent, one discount point equals about one-quarter percent in the loan interest rate. By paying two discount points, you lower your interest rate to 9.5 percent.
> Which is better? It depends. If you plan to sell your home in a few years, a loan with no discount points is generally advantageous because you won't have time to recover the cost of the points with lower mortgage payments.
> If you are going to stay in your home indefinitely, it may better to pay the discount points and benefit from the lower interest rate. If you'll be in the house eight to ten years, mortgage loan experts at the USAA Federal Savings Bank say you could go either way.

Now here are the questions:

a.   Evaluate the magazine's analysis. Is it good advice?

b.   How did the experts at the bank determine that staying in a home for eight to ten years was the break-even point on the two decisions?

17.   People who own home satellite dishes can purchase a variety of television programs, movies, and sports entertainment through vendors who bundle various packages of these goods. There a lot of these services. One of them is Netlink of Denver, Colorado. Netlink sells its packages two different ways, a monthly or an annual contract. For instance, they have a package they call 1-

Stop that includes about 16 different channels, ESPN, CNN, Discovery, and others. This package, when coupled with four movie channels, HBO, Cinemax, Showtime, and the Movie Channel, costs $39.95 per month to the home dish owner. However, if the bundle is bought on an annual basis, the price is $439.45, which is the same as payment for 11 months. What is the implicit discount rate that Netlink uses when a subscriber pays for a year in advance in lieu of paying 12 separate monthly installments? If you were a subscriber to this service, which payment option would you choose?

18. National Public Radio has a talk show on Saturday mornings called *Car Talk* featuring the Tappet brothers, Click and Clack (actually Tom and Ray Magliozzi), who answer questions and offer advice about the care of automobiles.[25] During their show on August 24, 1991, one of the brothers offered the following advice (and I am paraphrasing here), "Have you ever noticed how it is that many people take very good care of their cars when the cars are young. They change the oil on schedule. They maintain the tire pressure. They wash the car when it is dirty. They change the spark plugs and keep the car tuned to perfection. However, when the car gets a few miles on it, about 60,000 to 80,000, they curtail the maintenance, *just when the car needs it the most.* Why is it that people stop maintaining their car at a time when the car is most likely to require help?"

   Let's assume the assertion is correct, that people maintain their cars when the cars are new and abandon or reduce the care for them as they get older. Does this make any economic sense? Can you generalize the argument to other capital assets, such as homes, human capital, and the like?

19. Suppose you can hire someone to mow your lawn for $20. Your grass requires cutting 15 times per year. A good riding lawn mower costs $1200. Which option do you prefer?

SUGGESTED READINGS

I have only listed two readings here as most of you have taken or will take at least one course in finance or capital budgeting. There are numerous other well-written articles and books on the topics discussed in this chapter.

Brealey, Richard and Myers, Stewart. *Principles of Corporate Finance.* New York: McGraw-Hill, 1984.

Martin, John D., Cox, Samuel H., and MacMinn, Richard D. *The Theory of Finance: Evidence and Applications.* New York: The Dryden Press, 1988.

SUGGESTED SOLUTIONS TO SELECTED STUDY PROBLEMS

The following are only *suggested* solutions to the study problems presented at the end of this chapter. In all cases, the suggestions here put heavy emphasis on analysis rather than a single correct answer. Since most managerial problems do

---

[25] You may find it interesting that the Tappet Brothers are represented by the famous law firm Dewey, Cheatham, and Howe.

not fall into neat little boxes, the individual characteristics of the problems that you encounter on the job will typically mandate a solution using the principles developed here and in other courses. Memorizing these solutions will not make you a good manager; learning the *principles* detailed here will help make you a better manager.

4. First we compute the sum of money necessary to educate Eldon. In 17 years you will need $15,000, in 18 years another $15,000, in 19 years a third payment of $15,000, and in 20 years you must have $15,000 to pay for Eldon's senior year in college.

a. If interest is compounded monthly then the periodic interest rate is 8 percent per annum divided by 12 or 0.667 percent per month. What we need to compute is an annuity whose future value is $15,000 in 17 years (and similarly for the other 3 years of college). Recall from equation 5.5 that the formula for computing the future amount to which a series of equal payments will grow is

$$S = F \bullet C_{n,r}$$

where

$$C_{n,r} = \frac{(1 + r)^n - 1}{r},$$

and where F is the monthly payment and S is the value of the stream at the end of n periods. In this case $r = 0.667$ percent or 0.00667 and n is the number of months, which in the case of the freshman year is 17 years or 204 months. Therefore, the annuity compound factor, $C_{204,0.00667}$, is

$$C_{204,0.00667} = \frac{(1 + 0.00667)^{204} - 1}{0.00667} = 431.97.$$

The future amount we require, S, is $15,000. So

$$\$15,000 = F \bullet C_{204,0.00667} = F \bullet (431.97).$$

Therefore, the monthly payment required is

$$F = \$15,000/431.97 = \$34.72.$$

As a parent, to provide tuition for your son's *freshman* year of college in 17 years, you must invest $34.72 per month at 8 percent interest per year compounded monthly. By similar calculations you determine the money you must currently set aside to finance the sophomore, junior, and senior years. These numbers compute to $31.23 per month for the second year of college, $28.16 for the third year, and $25.45 for the fourth year. The total monthly payment necessary to pay tuition is $119.57. (These calculations assume you continue to make monthly contributions for the second, third, and fourth years until the actual payment is made.)

b. In 17 years you will need $15,000, in 18 years another $15,000, in 19 years a third payment of $15,000, and in 20 years you must have $15,000 to pay for Eldon's senior year in college. What is the present value of his tuition expenditure? At an interest rate of 8 percent per year, the four payments today require

$$\$15,000\bullet[1/(1+0.08)^{17} + 1/(1+1.08)^{18} + 1/(1.08)^{19} + 1/(1.08)^{20}] =$$

$$\$15,000\bullet(0.270268 + 0.250249 + 0.231712 + 0.214548) =$$

$$\$15,000\bullet(0.966778) = \$14,501.67.$$

The present value of Eldon's educational expenses is $14,501.67, so if you deposited that sum today and it earned 8 percent per year, you would have enough money to withdraw $15,000 per year for 4 years starting 17 years from now.

c. Neither plan is necessarily better. If you have access to $14,501.67 today and you can earn less than 8 percent on that money then the better plan is to invest it now at 8 percent. If you have access to the lump sum now, but it is earning more than 8 percent then it is better to leave it where it is. If you do not have access to the lump sum now, the question is moot. Since the present value of both plans is identical, it really makes little sense to talk about which is better unless your personal opportunity cost of funds differs from the market interest rate.

5. The present value of $5000 per year forever is the principal divided by the interest rate,

$$P = \$5000/0.06 = \$83,333.33.$$

At 3 percent interest the present value increases to

$$P = \$5000/0.03 = \$166,666.66.$$

If the annual net income increases to $10,000 at an interest rate of 6 percent the present value in perpetuity is

$$P = \$10,000/0.06 = \$166,666.66.$$

So long as the interest rate and net income are not expected to change, you should be indifferent between the two alternatives. Both provide an asset value of exactly the same magnitude, $166,666.66. Since your wealth is the same either way, you are indifferent.

6. Economic analysis suggests that higher prices for drugs caused consumption to decline among Vietnam veterans once they returned to the United States. However, there is another factor inducing soldiers to take fewer drugs once they have completed their Vietnam tour. While in Vietnam, life expectancy was reduced. More than 50,000 American soldiers lost their lives prematurely during the war. It is also important to note that many of the adverse side effects and costs of drug addiction do not surface immediately. Rather, they only crop up later in life as hepatitis and other illnesses. Given a reduced life expectancy from dying in the war, some of these costs are not anticipated by the soldiers in harm's way. However, once they return to civilian life, the future costs of current drug addiction are now included in the present value of the net cash flows associated with consuming drugs. Consequently, once

these costs are included, it becomes obvious why so many people in the service weaned themselves from addicting drugs. Put another way, while in Vietnam the value of a soldier's human capital was attenuated by the fact that he might get killed prematurely. Once that threat had passed, when he landed back in the United States, the present value of the cash flows to his human capital, the value of his life, jumped abruptly because many additional years of life expectancy were suddenly added.

Think of the problem another way. Suppose you own a car used in a demolition derby—that is, it gets wrecked quite often, and usually only lasts for about three events. Will you be inclined to grease the bearings, change the oil, and otherwise maintain it very well? Suppose you got out of the demolition derby business with a couple of your old cars intact. Are you not more inclined to do periodic maintenance since the cars now have a much longer life expectancy?

7. Stock prices *should not* be higher in the summer than any other time of the year. The stock price reflects the present discounted value of all future cash flows, regardless of when they accrue. Hence, seasonal sales, if rationally anticipated are expected, imputed, and capitalized into the price of stock long before the summer or peak season.

8. The gentleman who does not smoke can reasonably expect to live longer. Thus his investments that pay off far into the future are more attractive to him than those of his counterpart who does not expect to live quite so long. On this count, the nonsmoker is more likely to go to college. The fruits of investing in college do not pay for a long time. The careless person, the one living the dangerous lifestyle, is less apt to get his original investment back from going to school, and thus he is more prone to go straight from high school to work.

9. The point of this problem is to show you that waiting to get paid until the end of the period is equivalent to lopping off the interest earned on the last payment. The present value of $100 today and each year for the next four years is

$100 \cdot (1 + 1/1.1 + 1/1.1^2 + 1/1.1^3 + 1/1.1^4) =$

$100 \cdot (1 + 0.909 + 0.826 + 0.751 + 0.683) =$

$100 \cdot (4.1699) = \$416.99.$

The present value of five $100 payments starting in one year is given by:

$100(1/1.1 + 1/1.1^2 + 1/1.1^3 + 1/1.1^4 + 1/1.1^5) =$

$100 \cdot (0.909 + 0.826 + 0.751 + 0.683 + 0.621) =$

$100 \cdot (3.7908) = \$379.08.$

The present value of $100 five years from now is

$100/(1.1^5) = \$100/(1.6105) = \$62.09.$

Subtracting this from $100 we have $100 − $62.09 = $37.91. The difference between the two payment schemes is $416.99 − $379.08 = $37.91. They are the same. Getting paid at the end of the period is the same as forgoing the interest earned for the whole period on the periodic payment.

10. a.   The cost of buying two years of sweeping services for Broom B is simply its price, p_B, plus the time cost of going to the store, t. The current cost of buying one Broom A today and another one in two years is

$$(p_A + t) + (p_A + t)/(1 + r).$$

Consumers purchase Broom A if

$$(p_A + t) + (p_A + t)/(1 + r) < (p_B + t), \text{ or if}$$

$$p_A + (p_A + t)/(1 + r)] < p_B.$$

Otherwise they purchase the more durable Broom B.

b.   This is a bit tricky. Notice that the purchase of Broom A requires two different trips to the store. On that grounds, most people are inclined to buy the longer-lasting variety, B. However, the cost of making the product more durable may more than offset the cost of traveling to the store. Moreover, brooms can get lost, stolen, burned, or eaten by the dog. People in harm's way here are inclined to buy the cheaper, less durable variety. Since the cost of going to the store is probably higher for rich people than poor ones (based on the opportunity cost of their time), we expect that rich people are more likely to buy the durable Broom B, *ceteris paribus*. This result generalizes.

11.   At 10 percent the present values of the plans are

A: $1,000,000 + $5,000,000•$(1/1.1 + 1/1.1^2 + 1/1.1^3 + 1/1.1^4 + 1/1.1^5)$ =

$1,000,000 + $5,000,000•$(0.909 + 0.826 + 0.751 + 0.683 + 0.621)$ =

$19,953,933

B: $250,000 + $6,000,000•$(1/1.1 + 1/1.1^2 + 1/1.1^3 + 1/1.1^4 + 1/1.1^5 + 1/1.1^6)$ =

$250,000 + $6,000,000•$(0.909 + 0.826 + 0.751 + 0.683 + 0.621 + 0.564)$ =

$28,381,564

C: $3,500,000•$(1 + 1/1.1 + 1/1.1^2 + \ldots + 1/1.1^{10})$ =

$3,500,000•$(7.144567)$ =

$25,005,984.

Since the present value of the cash flows to Plan B is the highest, it is the best.

14.   The key to answering this problem is first to write out the sequence of cash flows and then to compute their present values. At the end of the first year the bond pays $1000 interest. The same amount is received at the end of the second, third, and fourth years. At the end of the fifth year, the bond returns the face amount, $10,000, plus another $1000 interest. After the first interest

payment has been made, there are four interest payments left plus the return of the principal. The accompanying table lists the cash flows and their present values computed at the new market interest rate, 12 percent. The interest payments on the bond do not change when the interest rate changes. The payments are fixed at the time the bond is sold. Therefore, the value of the bond is now lower because it has to be discounted at a higher rate. The sum of the discounted values of the cash flows using an interest rate of 12 percent is the value of the bond. Given the new market interest rate of 12 percent, it does not matter whether you hold the bond or sell it. It is worth what it is worth, and your decision to buy or hold will depend on other factors, such as your cash position, and not the fact that the value of the bond is now lower. There is nothing you can do to affect the value of the bond. That is determined by the interest rate and the sequence of cash flows.

Payment	Amount	Discount Factor at 12%	Discount at 12%	Present Value at 12%
1	$ 1000	—	—	—
2	1000	$1/(1.12)$	0.89386	$ 892.86
3	1000	$1/(1.12)^2$	0.79719	797.19
4	1000	$1/(1.12)^3$	0.71278	711.78
5	1,000 + 10,000	$1/(1.12)^4$	0.6355	9,392.53

After the first payment is received, four payments are left. When the interest rate is 12 percent, the next payment is discounted by $1/(1.12)$ or 0.89386. Thus, the second interest payment, which will be received in one year is now worth $892.86. Similarly, the other future payments are computed. The sum of them is $9392.53.

15. If the cars are otherwise the same, then any difference in price can only be due to the fact that Volvos last longer. This means that a Volvo is worth the present value of a Toyota purchased today plus the present value of a second Toyota bought in four years:

$$\text{Price}_{\text{Volvo}} = \text{Price}_{\text{Toyota}} \bullet [1 + 1/(1 + r)^4].$$

As can be seen from the formula, the higher the interest rate, the lower is the price of the Volvo. This makes a lot of economic sense. When discount rates are high, the value of a long-lived machine is reduced, for the benefits coming in the future are diminished in value today.

17. Two pay options are available. The yearly option costs $439.45, and of course, that is its present value. What is the present value of the 12 monthly install-ments? Naturally it depends on the discount rate. Let's set up the equation to solve for the interest rate that makes the two payment options equal. Under the monthly installment plan, 12 monthly payments are made and the first one is made up front, at the beginning of the period, and so we do not discount the first payment. The sequence of payments is

Month	Payment	Discount Factor	Present Value at $r = 19.48\%$
0	$39.95	1	$39.95
1	39.95	$1/(1+r)$	$39.31
2	39.95	$1/(1+r)^2$	38.68
3	39.95	$1/(1+r)^3$	38.07
4	39.95	$1/(1+r)^4$	37.46
5	39.95	$1/(1+r)^5$	36.86
6	39.95	$1/(1+r)^6$	36.27
7	39.95	$1/(1+r)^7$	35.69
8	39.95	$1/(1+r)^8$	35.12
9	39.95	$1/(1+r)^9$	34.56
10	39.95	$1/(1+r)^{10}$	34.01
11	39.95	$1/(1+r)^{11}$	33.46
		Sum at 19.48%	$\overline{\$439.45}$

To determine the present value of the monthly installments we sum the discount factors times the payment. This sum is

$$\$39.95 \bullet [1 + 1/(1+r) + 1/(1+r)^2 + 1/(1+r)^3 + 1/(1+r)^4 + 1/(1+r)^5 +$$

$$1/(1+r)^6 + 1/(1+r)^7 + 1/(1+r)^8 + 1/(1+r)^9 + 1/(1+r)^{10} + 1/(1+r)^{11}].$$

Now to solve the problem all we have to do is set this equation equal to the value of the annual payment, $439.45 and solve for r:

$$\$439.45 = \$39.95 \bullet [1 + 1/(1+r) + 1/(1+r)^2 + 1/(1+r)^3 + 1/(1+r)^4 +$$

$$1/(1+r)^5 + 1/(1+r)^6 + 1/(1+r)^7 + 1/(1+r)^8 + 1/(1+r)^9 + 1/(1+r)^{10} +$$

$$1/(1+r)^{11}].$$

Finding the value of r that solves this equation is not simple. One way to do it is through the substitution of different values for r. Spreadsheets and personal computers make this rather easy. I found the solution this way to be 0.1948. (Remember that the value of r in the equation is the *monthly* rate. To compute the annual rate, the monthly rate has to be multiplied by 12.) So the implicit interest rate that equates the value of the two payment options is 19.48 percent. The plan that you should choose depends on the interest rate you are currently paying or receiving. At interest rates above 0.1948, the present value of the monthly payments is *less* than $439.45. At interest rates less than 0.1948, the present value of 12 monthly payments exceeds the upfront annual payment of $439.45. For instance, at an annual interest rate of 8 percent, the present value of the 12 monthly installments is $462.32 or $22.87 more than the single annual payment. So, if you are borrowing or lending money at less than 19.48 percent, then the annual payment is better. Otherwise, the monthly payments are cheaper.

A P P E N D I X

FINANCIAL TABLES

- Discount Factors (*Dn,r*)
- Present Value of Annuity Factors (*An,r*)
- Annuity Compound Factors (*Cn,r*)
- Compound Factors (*Fn,r*)

Discount Factors $(D_{n,r})$
$$D_{n,r} \equiv 1/(1+r)^n$$

Interest Rate

Period	0.50	0.83	1.0	3.0	4.0	5.0	6.0	7.0	8.0	9.0	10.0	11.0	12.0	15.0	20.0
1	0.9950	0.9917	0.9901	0.9709	0.9615	0.9524	0.9434	0.9346	0.9259	0.9174	0.9091	0.9009	0.8929	0.8696	0.8333
2	0.9901	0.9835	0.9803	0.9426	0.9246	0.9070	0.8900	0.8734	0.8573	0.8417	0.8264	0.8116	0.7972	0.7561	0.6944
3	0.9851	0.9754	0.9706	0.9151	0.8890	0.8638	0.8396	0.8163	0.7938	0.7722	0.7513	0.7312	0.7118	0.6575	0.5787
4	0.9802	0.9674	0.9610	0.8885	0.8548	0.8227	0.7921	0.7629	0.7350	0.7084	0.6830	0.6587	0.6355	0.5718	0.4823
5	0.9754	0.9594	0.9515	0.8626	0.8219	0.7835	0.7473	0.7130	0.6806	0.6499	0.6209	0.5935	0.5674	0.4972	0.4019
6	0.9705	0.9514	0.9420	0.8375	0.7903	0.7462	0.7050	0.6663	0.6302	0.5963	0.5645	0.5346	0.5066	0.4323	0.3349
7	0.9657	0.9436	0.9327	0.8131	0.7599	0.7107	0.6651	0.6227	0.5835	0.5470	0.5132	0.4817	0.4523	0.3759	0.2791
8	0.9609	0.9358	0.9235	0.7894	0.7307	0.6768	0.6274	0.5820	0.5403	0.5019	0.4665	0.4339	0.4039	0.3269	0.2326
9	0.9561	0.9281	0.9143	0.7664	0.7026	0.6446	0.5919	0.5439	0.5002	0.4604	0.4241	0.3909	0.3606	0.2843	0.1938
10	0.9513	0.9204	0.9053	0.7441	0.6756	0.6139	0.5584	0.5083	0.4632	0.4224	0.3855	0.3522	0.3220	0.2472	0.1615
11	0.9466	0.9128	0.8963	0.7224	0.6496	0.5847	0.5268	0.4751	0.4289	0.3875	0.3505	0.3173	0.2875	0.2149	0.1346
12	0.9419	0.9052	0.8874	0.7014	0.6246	0.5568	0.4970	0.4440	0.3971	0.3555	0.3186	0.2858	0.2567	0.1869	0.1122
13	0.9372	0.8978	0.8787	0.6810	0.6006	0.5303	0.4688	0.4150	0.3677	0.3262	0.2897	0.2575	0.2292	0.1625	0.0935
14	0.9326	0.8904	0.8700	0.6611	0.5775	0.5051	0.4423	0.3878	0.3405	0.2992	0.2633	0.2320	0.2046	0.1413	0.0779
15	0.9279	0.8830	0.8613	0.6419	0.5553	0.4810	0.4173	0.3624	0.3152	0.2745	0.2394	0.2090	0.1827	0.1229	0.0649
16	0.9233	0.8757	0.8528	0.6232	0.5339	0.4581	0.3936	0.3387	0.2919	0.2519	0.2176	0.1883	0.1631	0.1069	0.0541
17	0.9187	0.8685	0.8444	0.6050	0.5134	0.4363	0.3714	0.3166	0.2703	0.2311	0.1978	0.1696	0.1456	0.0929	0.0451
18	0.9141	0.8613	0.8360	0.5874	0.4936	0.4155	0.3503	0.2959	0.2502	0.2120	0.1799	0.1528	0.1300	0.0808	0.0376
19	0.9096	0.8542	0.8277	0.5703	0.4746	0.3957	0.3305	0.2765	0.2317	0.1945	0.1635	0.1377	0.1161	0.0703	0.0313
20	0.9051	0.8471	0.8195	0.5537	0.4564	0.3769	0.3118	0.2584	0.2145	0.1784	0.1486	0.1240	0.1037	0.0611	0.0261
21	0.9006	0.8401	0.8114	0.5375	0.4388	0.3589	0.2942	0.2415	0.1987	0.1637	0.1351	0.1117	0.0926	0.0531	0.0217
22	0.8961	0.8332	0.8034	0.5219	0.4220	0.3418	0.2775	0.2257	0.1839	0.1502	0.1228	0.1007	0.0826	0.0462	0.0181
23	0.8916	0.8263	0.7954	0.5067	0.4057	0.3256	0.2618	0.2109	0.1703	0.1378	0.1117	0.0907	0.0738	0.0402	0.0151
24	0.8872	0.8195	0.7876	0.4919	0.3901	0.3101	0.2470	0.1971	0.1577	0.1264	0.1015	0.0817	0.0659	0.0349	0.0126
25	0.8828	0.8127	0.7798	0.4776	0.3751	0.2953	0.2330	0.1842	0.1460	0.1160	0.0923	0.0736	0.0588	0.0304	0.0105
26	0.8784	0.8060	0.7720	0.4637	0.3607	0.2812	0.2198	0.1722	0.1352	0.1064	0.0839	0.0663	0.0525	0.0264	0.0087
27	0.8740	0.7993	0.7644	0.4502	0.3468	0.2678	0.2074	0.1609	0.1252	0.0976	0.0763	0.0597	0.0469	0.0230	0.0073
28	0.8697	0.7927	0.7568	0.4371	0.3335	0.2551	0.1956	0.1504	0.1159	0.0895	0.0693	0.0538	0.0419	0.0200	0.0061
29	0.8653	0.7862	0.7493	0.4243	0.3207	0.2429	0.1846	0.1406	0.1073	0.0822	0.0630	0.0485	0.0374	0.0174	0.0051
30	0.8610	0.7797	0.7419	0.4120	0.3083	0.2314	0.1741	0.1314	0.0994	0.0754	0.0573	0.0437	0.0334	0.0151	0.0042
31	0.8567	0.7732	0.7346	0.4000	0.2965	0.2204	0.1643	0.1228	0.0920	0.0691	0.0521	0.0394	0.0298	0.0131	0.0035
32	0.8525	0.7669	0.7273	0.3883	0.2851	0.2099	0.1550	0.1147	0.0852	0.0634	0.0474	0.0355	0.0266	0.0114	0.0029
33	0.8482	0.7605	0.7201	0.3770	0.2741	0.1999	0.1462	0.1072	0.0789	0.0582	0.0431	0.0319	0.0238	0.0099	0.0024
34	0.8440	0.7542	0.7130	0.3660	0.2636	0.1904	0.1379	0.1002	0.0730	0.0534	0.0391	0.0288	0.0212	0.0086	0.0020
35	0.8398	0.7480	0.7059	0.3554	0.2534	0.1813	0.1301	0.0937	0.0676	0.0490	0.0356	0.0259	0.0189	0.0075	0.0017
36	0.8356	0.7418	0.6989	0.3450	0.2437	0.1727	0.1227	0.0875	0.0626	0.0449	0.0323	0.0234	0.0169	0.0065	0.0014
48	0.7871	0.6715	0.6203	0.2420	0.1522	0.0961	0.0610	0.0389	0.0249	0.0160	0.0103	0.0067	0.0043	0.0012	0.0002
60	0.7414	0.6079	0.5504	0.1697	0.0951	0.0535	0.0303	0.0173	0.0099	0.0057	0.0033	0.0019	0.0011	0.0002	0.0000
120	0.5496	0.3696	0.3030	0.0288	0.0090	0.0029	0.0009	0.0003	0.0001	0.0000	0.0000	0.0000	0.0000	0.0000	0.0000
360	0.1660	0.0505	0.0278	0.0000	0.0000	0.0000	0.0000	0.0000	0.0000	0.0000	0.0000	0.0000	0.0000	0.0000	0.0000

These values were computed using a personal computer and spreadsheet.

Annuity Compound Factors $(C_{n,r})$

$$C_{n,r} = \frac{(1+r)^n - 1}{r}$$

Interest Rate

Period	0.50	0.83	1.0	3.0	4.0	5.0	6.0	7.0	8.0	9.0	10.0	11.0	12.0	15.0	20.0
1	0.9950	0.9917	0.9901	0.9709	0.9615	0.9524	0.9434	0.9346	0.9259	0.9174	0.9091	0.9009	0.8929	0.8696	0.8333
2	1.9851	1.9753	1.9704	1.9135	1.8861	1.8594	1.8334	1.8080	1.7833	1.7591	1.7355	1.7125	1.6901	1.6257	1.5278
3	2.9702	2.9507	2.9410	2.8286	2.7751	2.7232	2.6730	2.6243	2.5771	2.5313	2.4869	2.4437	2.4018	2.2832	2.1065
4	3.9505	3.9181	3.9020	3.7171	3.6299	3.5460	3.4651	3.3872	3.3121	3.2397	3.1699	3.1024	3.0373	2.8550	2.5887
5	4.9259	4.8774	4.8534	4.5797	4.4518	4.3295	4.2124	4.1002	3.9927	3.8897	3.7908	3.6959	3.6048	3.3522	2.9906
6	5.8964	5.8289	5.7955	5.4172	5.2421	5.0757	4.9173	4.7665	4.6229	4.4859	4.3553	4.2305	4.1114	3.7845	3.3255
7	6.8621	6.7725	6.7282	6.2303	6.0021	5.7864	5.5824	5.3893	5.2064	5.0330	4.8684	4.7122	4.5638	4.1604	3.6046
8	7.8230	7.7083	7.6517	7.0197	6.7327	6.4632	6.2098	5.9713	5.7466	5.5348	5.3349	5.1461	4.9676	4.4873	3.8372
9	8.7791	8.6363	8.5660	7.7861	7.4353	7.1078	6.8017	6.5152	6.2469	5.9952	5.7590	5.5370	5.3282	4.7716	4.0310
10	9.7304	9.5567	9.4713	8.5302	8.1109	7.7217	7.3601	7.0236	6.7101	6.4177	6.1446	5.8892	5.6502	5.0188	4.1925
11	10.677	10.470	10.368	9.2526	8.7605	8.3064	7.8869	7.4987	7.1390	6.8052	6.4951	6.2065	5.9377	5.2337	4.3271
12	11.619	11.375	11.255	9.9540	9.3851	8.8633	8.3838	7.9427	7.5361	7.1607	6.8137	6.4924	6.1944	5.4206	4.4392
13	12.556	12.273	12.134	10.635	9.9856	9.3936	8.8527	8.3577	7.9038	7.4869	7.1034	6.7499	6.4235	5.5831	4.5327
14	13.489	13.163	13.004	11.296	10.563	9.8986	9.2950	8.7455	8.2442	7.7862	7.3667	6.9819	6.6282	5.7245	4.6106
15	14.417	14.046	13.865	11.938	11.118	10.380	9.7122	9.1079	8.5595	8.0607	7.6061	7.1909	6.8109	5.8474	4.6755
16	15.340	14.922	14.718	12.561	11.652	10.838	10.106	9.4466	8.8514	8.3126	7.8237	7.3792	6.9740	5.9542	4.7296
17	16.259	15.790	15.562	13.166	12.166	11.274	10.477	9.7632	9.1216	8.5436	8.0216	7.5488	7.1196	6.0472	4.7746
18	17.173	16.651	16.398	13.754	12.659	11.690	10.828	10.059	9.3719	8.7556	8.2014	7.7016	7.2497	6.1280	4.8122
19	18.082	17.506	17.226	14.324	13.134	12.085	11.158	10.336	9.6036	8.9501	8.3649	7.8393	7.3658	6.1982	4.8435
20	18.987	18.353	18.046	14.877	13.590	12.462	11.470	10.594	9.8181	9.1285	8.5136	7.9633	7.4694	6.2593	4.8696
21	19.888	19.193	18.857	15.415	14.029	12.821	11.764	10.836	10.017	9.2922	8.6487	8.0751	7.5620	6.3125	4.8913
22	20.784	20.026	19.660	15.937	14.451	13.163	12.042	11.061	10.201	9.4424	8.7715	8.1757	7.6446	6.3587	4.9094
23	21.676	20.852	20.456	16.444	14.857	13.489	12.303	11.272	10.371	9.5802	8.8832	8.2664	7.7184	6.3988	4.9245
24	22.563	21.672	21.243	16.936	15.247	13.799	12.550	11.469	10.529	9.7066	8.9847	8.3481	7.7843	6.4338	4.9371
25	23.446	22.484	22.023	17.413	15.622	14.094	12.783	11.654	10.675	9.823	9.077	8.422	7.843	6.464	4.948
26	24.324	23.290	22.795	17.877	15.983	14.375	13.003	11.826	10.810	9.929	9.161	8.488	7.896	6.491	4.956
27	25.198	24.090	23.560	18.327	16.330	14.643	13.211	11.987	10.935	10.027	9.237	8.548	7.943	6.514	4.964
28	26.068	24.882	24.316	18.764	16.663	14.898	13.406	12.137	11.051	10.116	9.307	8.602	7.984	6.534	4.970
29	26.933	25.669	25.066	19.188	16.984	15.141	13.591	12.278	11.158	10.198	9.370	8.650	8.022	6.551	4.975
30	27.794	26.448	25.808	19.600	17.292	15.372	13.765	12.409	11.258	10.274	9.427	8.694	8.055	6.566	4.979
31	28.651	27.222	26.542	20.000	17.588	15.593	13.929	12.532	11.350	10.343	9.479	8.733	8.085	6.579	4.982
32	29.503	27.988	27.270	20.389	17.874	15.803	14.084	12.647	11.435	10.406	9.526	8.769	8.112	6.591	4.985
33	30.352	28.749	27.990	20.766	18.148	16.003	14.230	12.754	11.514	10.464	9.569	8.801	8.135	6.600	4.988
34	31.196	29.503	28.703	21.132	18.411	16.193	14.368	12.854	11.587	10.518	9.609	8.829	8.157	6.609	4.990
35	32.035	30.251	29.409	21.487	18.665	16.374	14.498	12.948	11.655	10.567	9.644	8.855	8.176	6.617	4.992
36	32.871	30.993	30.108	21.832	18.908	16.547	14.621	13.035	11.717	10.612	9.6765	8.8786	8.1924	6.6231	4.9929
48	42.580	39.431	37.974	25.267	21.195	18.077	15.650	13.730	12.189	10.934	9.8969	9.0302	8.2972	6.6585	4.9992
60	51.726	47.070	44.955	27.676	22.623	18.929	16.161	14.039	12.377	11.048	9.9672	9.0736	8.3240	6.6651	4.9999
120	90.073	75.684	69.701	32.373	24.774	19.943	16.651	14.281	12.499	11.111	9.9999	9.0909	8.3333	6.6667	5.0000
360	106.79	113.99	97.218	33.333	25.000	20.000	16.667	14.286	12.500	11.111	10.000	9.0909	8.3333	6.6667	5.0000

These values were computed using a personal computer and spreadsheet.

Present Value of Annuity Factors ($A_{n,r}$)

$$A_{n,r} \equiv \frac{1-(1+r)^n}{r}$$

Interest Rate

Period	0.50	0.83	1.0	3.0	4.0	5.0	6.0	7.0	8.0	9.0	10.0	11.0	12.0	15.0	20.0
1	1.0000	1.0000	1.0000	1.0000	1.0000	1.0000	1.0000	1.0000	1.0000	1.0000	1.0000	1.0000	1.0000	1.0000	1.0000
2	2.0050	2.0083	2.0100	2.0300	2.0400	2.0500	2.0600	2.0700	2.0800	2.0900	2.1000	2.1100	2.1200	2.1500	2.2000
3	3.0150	3.0251	3.0301	3.0909	3.1216	3.1525	3.1836	3.2149	3.2464	3.2781	3.3100	3.3421	3.3744	3.4725	3.6400
4	4.0301	4.0503	4.0604	4.1836	4.2465	4.3101	4.3746	4.4399	4.5061	4.5731	4.6410	4.7097	4.7793	4.9934	5.3680
5	5.0503	5.0840	5.1010	5.3091	5.4163	5.5256	5.6371	5.7507	5.8666	5.9847	6.1051	6.2278	6.3528	6.7424	7.4416
6	6.0755	6.1263	6.1520	6.4684	6.6330	6.8019	6.9753	7.1533	7.3359	7.5233	7.7156	7.9129	8.1152	8.7537	9.9299
7	7.1059	7.1774	7.2135	7.6625	7.8983	8.1420	8.3938	8.6540	8.9228	9.2004	9.4872	9.7833	10.089	11.067	12.916
8	8.1414	8.2372	8.2857	8.8923	9.2142	9.5491	9.8975	10.260	10.637	11.028	11.436	11.859	12.300	13.727	16.499
9	9.1821	9.3058	9.3685	10.159	10.583	11.027	11.491	11.978	12.488	13.021	13.579	14.164	14.776	16.786	20.799
10	10.228	10.383	10.462	11.464	12.006	12.578	13.181	13.816	14.487	15.193	15.937	16.722	17.549	20.304	25.959
11	11.279	11.470	11.567	12.808	13.486	14.207	14.972	15.784	16.645	17.560	18.531	19.561	20.655	24.349	32.150
12	12.336	12.565	12.683	14.192	15.026	15.917	16.870	17.888	18.977	20.141	21.384	22.713	24.133	29.002	39.581
13	13.397	13.670	13.809	15.618	16.627	17.713	18.882	20.141	21.495	22.953	24.523	26.212	28.029	34.352	48.497
14	14.464	14.784	14.947	17.086	18.292	19.599	21.015	22.550	24.215	26.019	27.975	30.095	32.393	40.505	59.196
15	15.537	15.907	16.097	18.599	20.024	21.579	23.276	25.129	27.152	29.361	31.772	34.405	37.280	47.580	72.035
16	16.614	17.040	17.258	20.157	21.825	23.657	25.673	27.888	30.324	33.003	35.950	39.190	42.753	55.717	87.442
17	17.697	18.181	18.430	21.762	23.698	25.840	28.213	30.840	33.750	36.974	40.545	44.501	48.884	65.075	105.93
18	18.786	19.333	19.615	23.414	25.645	28.132	30.906	33.999	37.450	41.301	45.599	50.396	55.750	75.836	128.12
19	19.880	20.494	20.811	25.117	27.671	30.539	33.760	37.379	41.446	46.018	51.159	56.939	63.440	88.212	154.74
20	20.979	21.665	22.019	26.870	29.778	33.066	36.786	40.995	45.762	51.160	57.275	64.203	72.052	102.44	186.69
21	22.084	22.845	23.239	28.676	31.969	35.719	39.993	44.865	50.423	56.765	64.002	72.265	81.699	118.81	225.03
22	23.194	24.035	24.472	30.537	34.248	38.505	43.392	49.006	55.457	62.873	71.403	81.214	92.503	137.63	271.03
23	24.310	25.236	25.716	32.453	36.618	41.430	46.996	53.436	60.893	69.532	79.543	91.148	104.60	159.28	326.24
24	25.432	26.446	26.973	34.426	39.083	44.502	50.816	58.177	66.765	76.790	88.497	102.17	118.16	184.17	392.48
25	26.559	27.666	28.243	36.459	41.646	47.727	54.865	63.249	73.106	84.701	98.347	114.41	133.33	212.79	471.98
26	27.692	28.897	29.526	38.553	44.312	51.113	59.156	68.676	79.954	93.324	109.18	128.00	150.33	245.71	567.38
27	28.830	30.137	30.821	40.710	47.084	54.669	63.706	74.484	87.351	102.72	121.10	143.08	169.37	283.57	681.85
28	29.975	31.388	32.129	42.931	49.968	58.403	68.528	80.698	95.339	112.97	134.21	159.82	190.70	327.10	819.22
29	31.124	32.650	33.450	45.219	52.966	62.323	73.640	87.347	103.97	124.14	148.63	178.40	214.58	377.17	984.07
30	32.280	33.922	34.785	47.575	56.085	66.439	79.058	94.461	113.28	136.31	164.49	199.02	241.33	434.75	1181.90
31	33.441	35.204	36.133	50.003	59.328	70.761	84.802	102.07	123.35	149.58	181.94	221.91	271.29	500.96	1419.30
32	34.609	36.498	37.494	52.503	62.701	75.299	90.890	110.22	134.21	164.04	201.14	247.32	304.85	577.10	1704.10
33	35.782	37.802	38.869	55.078	66.210	80.064	97.343	118.93	145.95	179.80	222.25	275.53	342.43	664.67	2045.90
34	36.961	39.117	40.258	57.730	69.858	85.067	104.18	128.26	158.63	196.98	245.48	306.84	384.52	765.37	2456.10
35	38.145	40.442	41.660	60.462	73.652	90.320	111.43	138.24	172.32	215.71	271.02	341.59	431.66	881.17	2948.30
36	39.336	41.779	43.077	63.276	77.598	95.836	119.12	148.91	187.10	236.12	299.13	380.16	484.46	1014.30	3539.00
48	54.098	58.718	61.223	104.41	139.26	188.03	256.56	353.27	490.10	684.30	960.20	1352.70	1911.60	5456.0	31594
60	69.770	77.429	81.670	163.05	237.99	353.58	533.13	813.52	1253.20	1944.80	3034.80	4755.10	7471.60	29220	281733
120	163.88	204.80	230.04	1123.7	2741.6	6958.2	18120	47954	128150	344289	927081				
360	1004.52	2241.29	3494.96	1394021											

These values were computed using a personal computer and spreadsheet.

Compound Factors ($F_{n,r}$).
$$F_{n,r} = (1+r)^n$$

INTEREST RATE

PERIOD	0.50	0.83	1.0	3.0	4.0	5.0	6.0	7.0	8.0	9.0	10.0	11.0	12.0	15.0	20.0
1	1.0050	1.0083	1.0100	1.0300	1.0400	1.0500	1.0600	1.0700	1.0800	1.0900	1.1000	1.1100	1.1200	1.1500	1.2000
2	1.0100	1.0167	1.0201	1.0609	1.0816	1.1025	1.1236	1.1449	1.1664	1.1881	1.2100	1.2321	1.2544	1.3225	1.4400
3	1.0151	1.0252	1.0303	1.0927	1.1249	1.1576	1.1910	1.2250	1.2597	1.2950	1.3310	1.3676	1.4049	1.5209	1.7280
4	1.0202	1.0337	1.0406	1.1255	1.1699	1.2155	1.2625	1.3108	1.3605	1.4116	1.4641	1.5181	1.5735	1.7490	2.0736
5	1.0253	1.0423	1.0510	1.1593	1.2167	1.2763	1.3382	1.4026	1.4693	1.5386	1.6105	1.6851	1.7623	2.0114	2.4883
6	1.0304	1.0510	1.0615	1.1941	1.2653	1.3401	1.4185	1.5007	1.5869	1.6771	1.7716	1.8704	1.9738	2.3131	2.9860
7	1.0355	1.0598	1.0721	1.2299	1.3159	1.4071	1.5036	1.6058	1.7138	1.8280	1.9487	2.0762	2.2107	2.6600	3.5832
8	1.0407	1.0686	1.0829	1.2668	1.3686	1.4775	1.5938	1.7182	1.8509	1.9926	2.1436	2.3045	2.4760	3.0590	4.2998
9	1.0459	1.0775	1.0937	1.3048	1.4233	1.5513	1.6895	1.8385	1.9990	2.1719	2.3579	2.5580	2.7731	3.5179	5.1598
10	1.0511	1.0865	1.1046	1.3439	1.4802	1.6289	1.7908	1.9672	2.1589	2.3674	2.5937	2.8394	3.1058	4.0456	6.1917
11	1.0564	1.0955	1.1157	1.3842	1.5395	1.7103	1.8983	2.1049	2.3316	2.5804	2.8531	3.1518	3.4785	4.6524	7.4301
12	1.0617	1.1047	1.1268	1.4258	1.6010	1.7959	2.0122	2.2522	2.5182	2.8127	3.1384	3.4985	3.8960	5.3503	8.9161
13	1.0670	1.1139	1.1381	1.4685	1.6651	1.8856	2.1329	2.4098	2.7196	3.0658	3.4523	3.8833	4.3635	6.1528	10.699
14	1.0723	1.1231	1.1495	1.5126	1.7317	1.9799	2.2609	2.5785	2.9372	3.3417	3.7975	4.3104	4.8871	7.0757	12.839
15	1.0777	1.1325	1.1610	1.5580	1.8009	2.0789	2.3966	2.7590	3.1722	3.6425	4.1772	4.7846	5.4736	8.1371	15.407
16	1.0831	1.1419	1.1726	1.6047	1.8730	2.1829	2.5404	2.9522	3.4259	3.9703	4.5950	5.3109	6.1304	9.3576	18.488
17	1.0885	1.1515	1.1843	1.6528	1.9479	2.2920	2.6928	3.1588	3.7000	4.3276	5.0545	5.8951	6.8660	10.761	22.186
18	1.0939	1.1610	1.1961	1.7024	2.0258	2.4066	2.8543	3.3799	3.9960	4.7171	5.5599	6.5436	7.6900	12.375	26.623
19	1.0994	1.1707	1.2081	1.7535	2.1068	2.5270	3.0256	3.6165	4.3157	5.1417	6.1159	7.2633	8.6128	14.232	31.948
20	1.1049	1.1805	1.2202	1.8061	2.1911	2.6533	3.2071	3.8697	4.6610	5.6044	6.7275	8.0623	9.6463	16.367	38.338
21	1.1104	1.1903	1.2324	1.8603	2.2788	2.7860	3.3996	4.1406	5.0338	6.1088	7.4002	8.9492	10.804	18.822	46.005
22	1.1160	1.2002	1.2447	1.9161	2.3699	2.9253	3.6035	4.4304	5.4365	6.6586	8.1403	9.9336	12.100	21.645	55.206
23	1.1216	1.2102	1.2572	1.9736	2.4647	3.0715	3.8197	4.7405	5.8715	7.2579	8.9543	11.026	13.552	24.891	66.247
24	1.1272	1.2203	1.2697	2.0328	2.5633	3.2251	4.0489	5.0724	6.3412	7.9111	9.8497	12.239	15.179	28.625	79.497
36	1.1967	1.3480	1.4308	2.8983	4.1039	5.7918	8.1473	11.424	15.968	22.251	30.913	42.818	59.136	153.15	708.80
48	1.2705	1.4891	1.6122	4.1323	6.5705	10.401	16.394	25.729	40.211	62.585	97.017	149.80	230.39	819.40	6319.70
60	1.3489	1.6450	1.8167	5.8916	10.520	18.679	32.988	57.946	101.26	176.03	304.48	524.06	897.60	4384.00	56348
120	1.8194	2.7060	3.3004	34.711	110.660	348.910	1088.200	3357.800	10253	30987	92709	274636	805680		

These values were computed using a personal computer and spreadsheet.

CHAPTER

6

THE NEOCLASSICAL THEORY OF PRODUCTION AND COST

- Introduction
- The Firm
- Cost Minimization and Profit Maximization
- Production Functions
- Short-Run Cost
- Long-Run Cost
- Economies of Scale
- On the Estimation of Production Functions
- The Firm's Response to an Input Price Change
- Derived Demand
- Learning, Rate, Volume, Intermittent Production, and the Multiproduct Firm
- The Assignment of Joint Cost
- The Multiplant Firm
- Topics to Review
- Study Problems
- Suggested Readings
- Suggested Solutions to Selected Study Problems
- Appendix—On the Estimation of Input Demand Functions

INTRODUCTION

This chapter begins a new section in this textbook. Its central focus is the firm. We examine both the internal workings of the firm and its external relations with input suppliers and buyers. You will see that there are two distinctly different ways to analyze the firm. The first method treats the firm as though it were a living, breathing thing. This abstraction allows us to analyze the important issues of what the firm produces, how it is produced, and the price of this output. We examine the nature of production and cost in this chapter, the firm in competition in Chapter 7, and imperfect markets, including the monopoly firm in Chapters 8, 9, and 10. The material in this section is often referred to as **neoclassical analysis of the firm**. We switch gears in Chapters 12 and 13 to examine the inner workings of the firm. This is sometimes referred to as **property rights analysis**. The analysis of property rights pierces the veil of the firm to explore the contractual relations between the various input suppliers that constitute what we commonly call the company.

Neoclassical analysis concerns the operation of the classical economic firm and its external relations with suppliers, customers, markets, and competitors. It is designed to acquaint you with the essential elements of profit maximization, cost minimization, and the nature of cost itself. The concept of the production function, borrowed from engineering principles, is introduced as background for economic analysis. A set of short- and long-run cost curves for the firm is developed from the production function. This section of material also includes some analysis of the effect of learning on cost. After this, the impact of changing input prices is explored. We also explore the fundamental questions of how much output the firm produces and how it will produce that output. The demand for inputs is analyzed.

In this chapter, we start by differentiating between the firm as a unit of analysis, as though it were a person making decisions, and the alternative, property rights approach, which explores the inner workings of organizations. The principles of cost minimization and profit maximization are presented. The concepts of the short and long run are introduced along with the production function. These are used to develop the analytical tools of cost curves and economies of scale. Input demand, learning, and related topics complete the chapter.

THE FIRM

The firm is a legal fiction. In the strictest sense of reality, no such thing exists except in our minds. Since firms do not exist, they cannot make decisions. Only people can make decisions. For instance, a firm does not decide the compensation package for its employees. Instead, officials of the firm make this choice. This may sound like a semantic distinction without substance, but as we explore the matter more fully, you will begin to respect the difference. Nevertheless, in spite of this fact, there are a large number of wide-ranging problems for which it is economical to treat the firm as a behavioral unit. In essence, we assume away the complex decision-making process within the firm and only analyze the outcome of that process without trying to understand the motives or means that created the decision. In this chapter and the next four, the problems that present themselves are best addressed by assuming that firms make decisions. Chapters 12 and 13 look at the other side of the coin, the one where managers, not firms, make decisions. In essence, there are many ways to examine the firm, and the appropriate set of assumptions is dictated by the particular problem at hand. At the outset, we are interested in issues concerning cost, production, and price. In effect, we assume that the firm maximizes profit or net present value. In later chapters, we explore the question of how it is that the firm comes to maximize the wealth of its owners.

In many respects, the fundamental building blocks of the theory of the firm are the same as those that comprise the theory of the consumer. That is, the firm is rational, but instead of maximizing an abstract utility function, the firm attempts to maximize profits or the capital value of its assets. In that sense, the firm has no morals or social conscience. Whether that is good or bad is left to the moralist; here the purpose is to analyze and predict the behavior of firms, not to judge them. The principles of utility maximization are essentially the same as the fundamentals of profit maximization. This makes a basic understanding of the firm come quickly and without the necessity of learning a wide range of new techniques.

COST MINIMIZATION AND PROFIT MAXIMIZATION

The classical economic firm is built upon a foundation of several important assumptions. One of the most important is the presumption that firms maximize profit. This implies that the firm will attempt to exploit all opportunities to make more money and avoid any project that is not expected to make the firm richer. The firm does not want to be in a position in which there is something it can do to make more money. Strictly speaking, in a multiperiod framework, we assume that the firm maximizes **value**, the present discounted value of all future net cash flows, but since virtually all of the instruction here involves one period, the profit maximization assumption is sufficient. Material in Chapter 5 and Chapters 12 and 13 covers multiple periods, and the value maximizing objective is investigated.

Students sometimes get confused about profit maximization and cost minimization. **Profit maximization** requires that the firm capitalize on all opportunities to improve the bottom line; it follows from this that the firm must produce its output as cheaply as possible—**cost minimization**. This implies that firms minimize their costs of production at the chosen output rate. However, strictly speaking, the firm does not minimize costs. This would imply that the firm simply produces nothing at all. If in fact the firm maximizes profits, then it necessarily minimizes costs for a chosen output level, but the reverse is not true. Simply minimizing costs does not imply that profits are maximized. For instance, stopping production can reduce costs to zero, and obviously, there would be no profits at that point.

Does the firm actually have other goals besides profit maximization? Well surely it might, but we can only touch on them briefly. When the owners of a firm receive their income, they can choose to spend it in many ways. One avenue is to use the resources of the company to further their own personal tastes and preferences. For instance, a wealthy owner of a business forms company who happens to have a keen and abiding interest in soccer might choose to support a local amateur team by hiring some good players, under the condition that they play for his favorite team. Another owner might choose to spend some of the company's resources under his control to protect the South American rain forests. The owners of another company might use some of their earnings to support the cause of liberty and responsibility in a free society. There are many ways to spend money. When the managers or shareholders of a company want to spend their dividends or wages to foster their own personal tastes and preferences, it sometimes appears that the profit maximizing objective has been lost for some other goal. Perhaps sadly, this is a topic that because of its complexity must wait for further discussion in other courses and books.

PRODUCTION FUNCTIONS

Production is characterized by the relation between inputs and outputs. This link is called the **production function,** and mathematically it takes the following form:

$$q = q(x_1, x_2, x_3, x_4, \ldots, x_n)$$

where q is the output rate per unit time and x_i is the ith input. The inputs encompass all things required for production, including raw materials, machines, employees, automobiles, typewriters, managers, computer programs, computers, buildings, carpeting, electricity, and so forth. The function that describes the amount of output obtained for specified amounts of the inputs is called the production function. It embodies the existing state of technology. In essence, it is the recipe that describes the amounts and timing of inputs that yield outputs. Cookbooks are full of production functions. Assembly instructions on children's toys are another good example.

Suppose a construction company is building a large office complex employing a 45-story crane, large bulldozers, backhoes, and the like. Across town there is another company building a one-story house using a backhoe and laborers with shovels. Are they using the same technology? Yes. Technology describes the state of the physical sciences at any point in time that, in turn, dictates the physical relation between inputs and outputs. Although the nature of technology may influence the choice of inputs, the actual decision with regard to inputs by one company versus another must not be confused with the state of technology per se. Just because one person is using backhoes and another person is using shovels does not mean they are employing different technologies, only different input bundles. The technology available to them is the same.[1]

---

[1] To be sure, they may face different prices for inputs.

The Long and the Short Run

It is sometimes convenient to talk about a short run and a long run. This distinction is an analytical convenience, not something that describes the real world. The short run is a set of assumptions, not a particular amount of time. The **short run** is that analytical period when the firm cannot choose all of its inputs. By contrast, the **long run** is an analytical framework in which the firm has options over all of its inputs.[2] The dichotomy is created to increase the predictive capacity of the models. Suppose a rich donor gave your university $275 million. As a consequence of that gift, an abnormally large number of students attempted to enroll the subsequent semester, say, an extra 10,000 applicants. Unless the gift was well anticipated, school officials do not have the physical capacity to deal with the extra enrollment immediately. That is, in all probability, the administrators would have to take as given their physical plant, at least for a while. For better or worse, they are stuck with the current buildings, for some time. For a variety of problems, it might be useful to discuss how the officials would respond to the donation when, in fact, it is difficult to change the stock of physical capital, the buildings, and such. We call this situation, where the capital stock (or any other asset) is fixed, the short run. By contrast, in the long-run framework, the university can add new buildings and dormitories. Quite often the appropriate decisions under the two disparate scenarios will be very different. Diagnosing decisions that the firm must make without the ability to alter all inputs is called short-run analysis. By contrast, in the long run, analytically speaking, the firm can choose the amounts of all its inputs.

The appropriate length of time embodied in the long and short run varies considerably across classes of firms. An electric utility company usually takes 5 to 15 years to alter its productive generating capacity, while a construction company can, via rental, change all of its inputs daily. In the first case, the short run lasts for years, in the second, hours.

The Short-Run Production Function

For simplicity, assume there are only two inputs, labor and capital. Then the production function between the two inputs, l and k, and output, q, is

$$q = q(l,k).$$

Further assume that the amount of capital is fixed at some amount k_0, and hence, the analysis is short run. Then the short-run production function is written as

$$q = q(l,k_0).$$

---

[2] In other branches of economics, particularly macroeconomics, the distinction between the long and short run is more directly tied to the passage of time. Most of you have heard the expression by the famous English economist, John M. Keynes, "In the long run we are all dead." Clearly, Professor Keynes was referring to the ticking of clocks and not the analytical period where the firm can choose all of its inputs.

Labor varies as the firm hires more or fewer workers. Under these circumstances, the relation between inputs and outputs is similar to the one described in the upper panel of Figure 6.1. Given a fixed stock of capital, k_0, output increases as labor input increases, but the impact of extra labor declines as additional labor is hired. At point A, the firm employs l_1 labor; output is q_1 units per time period. After point A, additional workers add to output, but each adds less than the previous one. Eventually, at point C, there are so many workers that the facility is crowded and additional workers get in the way; output actually declines if more

FIGURE 6.1
The Short-Run Production Function

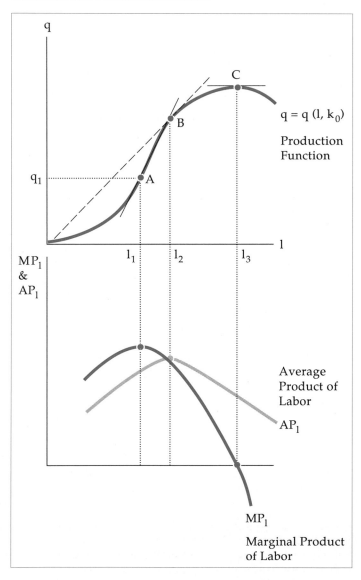

people are hired. The facility after some point has too much labor relative to the stock of capital.

The derivative of the production function with respect to the amount of labor input is called the **marginal product of labor**; we can abbreviate this to MP_l.[3] The slope of the short-run production function at any amount of labor depicts the marginal product of labor. The MP_l is drawn in the lower panel of Figure 6.1. Notice that MP_l peaks at point A and is zero at point C. The marginal product of labor is the change in output that results from a change in the amount of labor employed.

The **average product** of an input such as labor is total output, q, divided by total input, l. Graphically, this is the slope of a ray drawn from the origin to the production function. The dashed line that passes through the origin and point B is one such ray, which happens to be the steepest ray possible and hence defines the amount of labor input that maximizes the average product of labor. Since this ray is tangent to the production function, it happens to also be the marginal product of labor at this point. At point B, the average product of labor and the marginal product of labor are equal. Notice the lower panel of the figure at this point.

Suppose there is a small pizza delivery store. Inside the store are an oven, telephone, cash register, refrigerator, and all the other fixings to make pizza for take out. The store owns a fleet of delivery vehicles. We call all this stuff capital, and it is not variable in the short run. Think of the problem this way. When the pizza store manager arrives at work to open the store, she finds the building in place, the ovens are there, the phone is installed, the property taxes have been paid, all the insurance is up to date, the counters are in place, and all the ingredients for making pizzas are in the cooler. The only factor of production missing is labor. If the manager decides to close the shop that day and not to bake any pizzas, all the fixed costs will persist. The rent on the building and the bank loan on the ovens must still be paid, whether the store operates or not. Economists call assets in place that cannot be altered in the short run, *fixed assets,* and the manager simply accepts them as a given. Of course, the manager can cancel the lease, sell the ovens, let the insurance lapse, and have the phone removed, but we call those long-run decisions. In the short run, the capital in place and the expenditures on it are beyond control of the manager and are determined by decisions made in the past. For this reason, the expenditures on fixed assets are sometimes called unavoidable expenditures.

Consider the hypothetical example portrayed in Table 6.1. If the firm has 1 employee, she must take orders, cook pizzas, and make deliveries. Presume that she could produce and deliver 1 pizza per hour. Add a second worker. Together the two of them can specialize a bit, he to cooking and she to delivery, and imagine that pizza deliveries could now total 3 per hour on average. The marginal product of the second worker (whomever it is) is 2 pizzas. The average product of labor when there are 2 workers is 1.5 pizzas. Similarly, the marginal product of the

---

[3] This generalizes to any input. The derivative of the production function with respect to the stock of capital input is called the marginal product of capital, and so forth.

TABLE 6.1   PIZZA PRODUCTION

NUMBER OF WORKERS	TOTAL NUMBER OF PIZZAS DELIVERED	INCREMENTAL NUMBER OF PIZZAS DELIVERED	MARGINAL PRODUCT OF LABOR	AVERAGE PRODUCT OF LABOR
0	0			
1	1	1	1	1.0
2	3	2	2	1.5
3	6	3	3	2.0
4	9	3	3	2.25
5	11	2	2	2.2
6	12	1	1	2.0
7	12	0	0	1.71
8	10	−2	−2	1.25

fifth worker is 2 pizzas delivered and the average product is 2.2. If the pizza store hires 6 workers, the total output will be 12 pizzas delivered per hour. Hiring a seventh worker overloads the store, and output does not increase. Seven workers are too much for the amount of floor space available. Consequently, there is no additional output produced when 7 workers are hired. The marginal product of the seventh worker is nil. When the store is hiring just a few workers, the capital stock is large relative to the amount of labor, and the marginal product of labor increases with additional workers. However, when there are a lot of workers relative to the size of the facility, additional workers add very little to output. Indeed, an eighth worker would actually cause total output to decline. When a firm attempts to expand production by engaging more of one factor without adjusting all inputs, the result is inevitable that at some point, additional units of the variable factor will have little impact on output. We call this the **law of diminishing marginal productivity**. It is important to recognize that this phenomenon is the result of mixing additional amounts of one factor with fixed amounts of other factors. When all factors are adjusted—what we call the long run—the law of diminishing returns need not hold, and in general, it does not. Additional labor, when combined with additional capital and the other essential inputs, need not experience declining marginal productivity.

Table 6.1 is a short-run production function. Figure 6.2 is a graphical presentation of this short-run production function. Notice that output peaks at 6 and 7 workers. Figure 6.3 plots the marginal and average products of labor. Notice that the average product of labor increases so long as the marginal contribution of an extra worker exceeds the average, and that the average product declines when the marginal product is less than the average. The marginal product is negative for the eighth worker. The short-run production function described in Table 6.1 and graphed in Figures 6.2 and 6.3 is a specific case of the general function represented in Figure 6.1. It turns out that the short-run production functions of most business applications have this classic shape, and importantly, the short- run production function provides the cornerstone for understanding the nature of the costs of production.

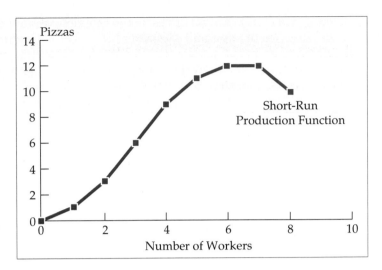

FIGURE 6.2
Total Production of Pizzas

SHORT-RUN COST

There is a one-to-one correspondence between the production function and the cost function for the firm. Given a set of input prices and a production technology, a **cost function** describes the cheapest way to produce any particular level of output:

$$C = C(q, w_i)$$

FIGURE 6.3
Marginal and Average Product of Labor

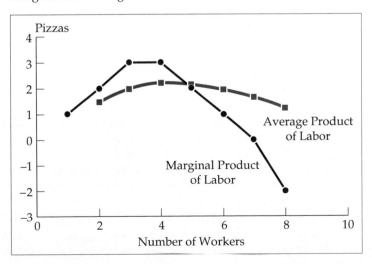

where w_i is a vector of input prices. In the simple two-input case, the cost function maps the price of labor and capital and the level of output into the total cost of production under the assumption that the firm buys inputs in the cost minimizing proportions. The derivative of the cost function with respect to output rate, dC/dq, is called **marginal cost**. It is the extra or incremental cost of producing one additional unit of output per unit time. **Average cost** of output is total cost divided by total output, C/q.

The production functions depicted in Figure 6.1 are used to create a set of short-run cost curves of the firm. Let capital cost w_k per unit. Therefore, total expenditures on capital are the fixed stock, k_0, times the price per unit, or $k_0 \cdot w_k = F$. Average cost of capital per unit of output is F/q, which declines monotonically with q since F does not change. See Figure 6.4.

Variable costs are the amount of labor input employed, l, times the wage rate, w_l. Call this cost V; then $V = l \cdot w_l$. Consider the short-run production function graphed in Figure 6.1 that describes the relation between l and q (given k), $q = q(l,k_0)$. Convert the l-axis from physical units of labor into labor costs by multiplying that axis by the wage rate of labor, w_l. Then the new axis is denominated in dollars and measures the variable cost of production; the point that was l_1 in Figure 6.1 is now $l_1 \cdot w_l$ in Figure 6.4; the point l_2 becomes $l_2 \cdot w_l$; and so forth. The form or shape of the curve originally labeled q in Figure 6.1 is unchanged when mapped into Figure 6.4. It is simply stretched or compacted by the scale change in the l-axis. Now rotate the axis so that the l-axis is vertical and the q-axis is horizontal. See Figure 6.4 where V is drawn.

Total costs, T, are simply capital costs, F, plus labor costs, V. Therefore, the vertical addition of F and V gives T.[4] In the lower panel, average capital, average variable (or average labor), and average total costs are drawn. Each is the slope of a ray from the origin to the respective function.

Marginal cost is the change in total cost for a change in output, dC/dq, the slope of T. Hence, at point B, since the ray from the origin (average cost) is just tangent to T, marginal and average cost are equal.

To the economist, cost is opportunity cost. In that sense, the expenditure of capital, F, is not a cost in the short run; it is an unavoidable expenditure: money that is contractually obligated, but money that *does not affect decisions*. Since the firm cannot alter the stock of capital in any way—it cannot buy more or sell some it owns—capital, the fixed input, represents a sunk cost. The firm has no option, no alternatives. In this view, fixed costs are sunk costs, and for the purpose of making decisions in the short run, they are not costs in the economic sense. According to this line of reasoning, since fixed costs are unavoidable, they do not have opportunity costs. The firm is obligated to make the fixed payments, and it has no legal choice but to do so. Consequently, it is common to leave the curve F/q

---

[4] The variable and total cost functions bend backward at the maximum attainable output. If the firm would (foolishly?) purchase additional units of labor past this point, cost would rise, but output would decline. In some important economic sense, the backward bending portions of the variable cost and total cost functions are irrelevant. No reasonable firm would ever continue production past the point where additional units of inputs actually caused output to *decrease*. For this reason, some economists prefer to delete the backward bending portions of variable and total costs.

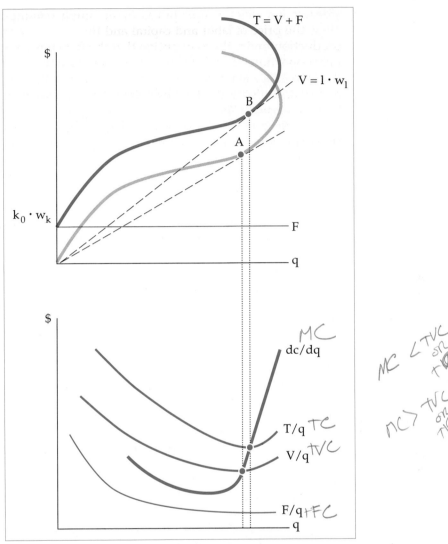

FIGURE 6.4
Short-Run Cost

off the diagram. The remaining three curves, marginal cost, average total cost, and average variable cost comprise a set of short-run cost curves useful in a wide variety of analytical situations. You might reasonably ask, "If the fixed cost function is left off the diagram, why is the average total cost function not also removed?" The answer lies in the fact that the minimum of the average total cost function carries important information that helps us understand industry equilibrium. This will become obvious as we progress.

Marginal cost intersects average cost from below at the minimum of average cost. Marginal cost is the change in total cost associated with producing an additional unit of output. If marginal cost is currently less than average cost, then average cost must be declining. On the other hand, if the incremental cost of producing one more unit exceeds the current average cost of production, then producing that additional unit must increase average cost. To wit, when marginal cost is below average cost, average cost is falling; and when marginal cost is above average cost, average cost is rising. Therefore, marginal cost must intersect average cost at its minimum. Moreover, by the same logic, marginal cost is more inelastic than average cost after the minimum of marginal cost.

The minimum of average cost is frequently called the **engineering efficient production rate** or the design capacity of the plant. The average unit is produced most cheaply here, and from a technological point of view, efficiency is attained. Do not be confused; this does not mean that profits are maximized, that the plant is properly managed from an economics point of view, or that the managers' jobs are not in jeopardy, only that the machines are built and designed to run most cheaply at this rate of output.

Let's continue with the example of the pizza delivery store summarized in Table 6.1. Imagine that labor costs $5 per hour. Further assume that building expense is $2000 per month, telephone expense is $50 per month, and taxes and insurance add an additional $1000 per month to short-run fixed cost. Delivery car rental payments add up to $1500 per month, and other similar sundry fixed expenditures including the pizza material total $1450 per month. The total short-run fixed cost of this enterprise is $6000 per month. Table 6.2 depicts the short-run cost structure for this enterprise.

To construct Table 6.2, the following assumptions were employed: The store is open 40 hours per week and 4 weeks per month. Thus, each worker costs $5 times 40 hours times 4 weeks per month or $800 per month. Similarly, we know from Table 6.1 that 3 workers can produce 6 pizzas per hour. So, these same 3 workers can produce 3 times 40 times 4 or 960 pizzas per month. Total cost of this business is total labor cost plus total fixed cost. Average cost per pizza is computed by dividing total cost by the number of pizzas per month. For example, when 6

| TABLE 6.2   SHORT-RUN COST OF PIZZA DELIVERY |||||||
NUMBER OF WORKERS	TOTAL LABOR COST/MONTH	FIXED COST PER MONTH	TOTAL COST PER MONTH	TOTAL NUMBER OF PIZZAS DELIVERED PER MONTH	AVERAGE COST OF PIZZAS	MARGINAL COST OF PIZZAS
0	$ 0	$6000	$ 6000	0	—	—
1	800	6000	6800	160	$42.50	$5.00
2	1600	6000	7600	480	15.83	2.50
3	2400	6000	8400	960	8.75	1.67
4	3200	6000	9200	1440	6.39	1.67
5	4000	6000	10000	1760	5.68	2.50
6	4800	6000	10800	1920	5.62	5.00
7	5600	6000	11600	1920	6.04	—

people are employed, 1920 pizzas are made each month, and total cost is $10,800. Therefore, average cost per pizza is $10,800/1920 = $5.62 per pizza. The computation of marginal cost is straightforward. When 3 workers are employed, an additional 480 pizzas are made each month. The incremental or extra cost of these pizzas is the extra cost of the third worker or $800 per month.[5] Thus the marginal cost of pizzas produced by the third worker is $800/480 or $1.67, and so forth for all the other rows in Table 6.2 except the last one. Since employment of the seventh worker yields no additional output but imposes costs, marginal cost cannot be computed mathematically; it is $800/0. Logically we say it is infinite. Notice that average cost is minimized at 6 workers and 1920 pizzas per month. Note also that marginal cost is increasing after the addition of the fourth worker. The scenario in Table 6.2 creates a situation very much like the general graphs described earlier in Figure 6.4. For practical and analytical purposes, they are the same.

LONG-RUN COST

The long run is the analytical period in which all inputs are variable. For heuristic purposes, think of the firm as having a choice among various plant sizes. A different short-run cost curve is associated with each particular plant or plant size. In Figure 6.5, the first set of short-run cost curves in the upper left describes

FIGURE 6.5
Long-Run Cost

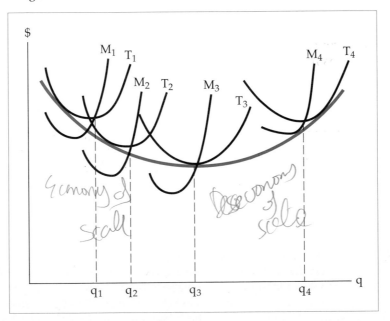

[5] We are obviously ignoring the cost of the extra or incremental cost of the materials used in these pizzas. These could be added to the analysis, but, at this point, it only serves to complicate the analysis.

plant size #1. A couple of points are worthy of note here. Associated with plant #1 is marginal cost M_1, average total cost T_1, and the engineering efficient production rate, q_1 (the design or cost minimizing rate). Consider a larger plant, plant #2, and assume that the plant is more technically efficient than the first plant because it is larger. We discuss what this means in the next section. This plant has average cost T_2 and marginal cost M_2. In this plant, q_2 is the output that minimizes average cost—that is, the engineering efficient rate of production in this plant is q_2. Consider another plant, #3, which is more efficient than #2 because it is still larger. Its engineering efficient rate of production is q_3. Or put another way, in this particular plant, the average cost is minimized if the output rate is q_3. Consider one last plant, #4. It is too large from an efficiency point of view; in general, its cost of production is higher than that for plant #3.

Long-run average cost (LRAC) is the **envelope** of short-run average cost—the lowest average cost achievable allowing all inputs to vary. In the case depicted in Figure 6.5, long-run average cost declines at low levels of output. It is minimized at plant size #3 and increases thereafter. The long-run curve is a **planning curve**; it describes the change in average cost as the firm anticipates ever larger plants. In essence, the long-run average cost or planning curve describes the firm's options for expansion, showing the myriad of short-run situations available to the firm, from which, of course, only one can be selected at any point in time. Once a plant is built, the firm's options are delimited in the short run, but inspection of the long-run average cost curve reveals alternatives the firm could employ. The actual shape of the long-run cost curve depends on economies of scale.

ECONOMIES OF SCALE

Economies of scale is an engineering principle, not an economic concept. This is easy to see using the concept of homogeneous functions. Consider a homogeneous production function:

$$q = q(x_1, x_2, x_3, \ldots, x_n).$$

A function is homogeneous of degree r if and only if

$$q \bullet \lambda^r = q(\lambda \bullet x_1, \lambda \bullet x_2, \lambda \bullet x_3, \ldots, \lambda \bullet x_n).$$

What does this mean? If we multiply each input by some amount, λ, then the homogeneity of the function describes how much the dependent variable will change as a consequence. Suppose production is homogeneous of degree 1. Then, when the firm buys 25 percent more of *each* input, output increases by 25 percent also. Under these circumstances (and holding constant the prices of all inputs), average cost is constant; costs increase by 25 percent, but total output rises by the same amount. Let C_0 and q_0 be the initial total costs and output. Then, when production is homogeneous of degree 1,

$$C_0/q_0 = (1.25 \bullet C_0)/(1.25 \bullet q_0) = C_0/q_0.$$

If production is homogeneous of degree *less* than 1, then when the firm purchases an additional portion of all inputs, total output increases *but less than the increase in input usage.* Hence, average cost increases because total cost rises more than output. This time, suppose the firm purchases an incremental 10 percent of each input; overall costs increase by 10 percent as a consequence. But when production is homogeneous of degree less than 1, output increases, *but less than 10 percent.* Let C_1 and q_1 be costs and output after the increase in input use. Then,

$C_1 = 1.1 \cdot C_0$ and

$q_1 < 1.1 \cdot q_0.$

Therefore,

$C_0/q_0 < C_1/q_1;$

average cost after the use of additional inputs is *greater.* Average cost has risen.

On the other hand, if production is homogeneous of degree *greater* than 1, when the firm buys an additional amount of each input, output increases more than the increase in inputs, and average cost declines. Again let input use rise by 10 percent. In this case,

$C_1 = 1.1 \cdot C_0,$ and

$q_1 > 1.1 \cdot q_0.$

Therefore,

$C_0/q_0 > C_1/q_1;$

average cost *falls* after the use of additional inputs.

For the class of homogeneous functions we say that **economies of scale** exist, or that there are **returns to scale**, if production is homogeneous of degree greater than 1. **Diseconomies of scales** are present if production is homogeneous of degree less than 1. If production is homogeneous of degree 1, we say there are **constant returns to scale**. Hence, in Figure 6.5, there are production economies of scale up to plant size #3. After that, there are diseconomies of scale. Homogeneous functions make the concept of economies of scale easy to visualize, but decreasing or increasing cost can arise with nonhomogeneous functions too.

In general, technical laws of nature determine whether economies of scale exist or not, and, of course, these vary across production processes. Most industrial operations exhibit the U-shaped configuration of first declining, then constant, and then increasing average cost, but there are exceptions.

A U-shaped long-run average cost curve such as the one drawn in Figure 6.5 implies a unique plant that is the best to build given a price of output, technology, and the costs of inputs. A different plant is associated with every point on the long-run average cost curve. If the firm picks the cheapest way to produce in the long run and builds a plant associated with that level of output, it must have chosen the minimum of long-run cost, which must also be the minimum of some short-run average cost. In other words, if the long-run average cost curve is U-shaped, there will be at least one plant that has short-run average cost equal to the minimum of the long-run average cost; economic efficiency implies engineering efficiency. Moreover, that plant is the one that minimizes average cost in the short run. Any other plant size must have higher cost of production in the long and short run. This means that if the production process for some good is characterized by a U-shaped average cost curve, there is a unique plant that minimizes cost. If the firm does not build that plant, it will face higher cost than its competition.

Be careful of several things. In the preceding discussion, we were talking about a *firm*, not an industry. The particular production process within a particular firm gives no clue to the structure of industry cost. Extra care must be taken to distinguish between the individual firm that might have one type of costs, say constant average costs, and an industry that can have a completely unrelated cost structure, say increasing costs. The two concepts are basically unrelated, and serious errors in analysis are made if the two are confused. For example, in the next chapter, we demonstrate that it is possible for a firm to have constant average cost of production while, for the industry, costs of production increase with output.

ON THE ESTIMATION OF PRODUCTION FUNCTIONS

It is possible to use statistical methods similar to those discussed in Chapter 4 to estimate production and cost functions. The techniques of regression analysis can be employed to estimate the parameters of a production function and to uncover the relation between inputs and outputs. The process begins with the specification of some functional form. A number of different forms are available. Let's start with the most simple one, the two-input, linear production function:

$$q = \beta_0 + \beta_1 x_1 + \beta_2 x_2$$

where q is the output of the process, x_1 and x_2 are the inputs, and β_0, β_1, and β_2 are the unknown, technological production parameters that need to be estimated. When a linear production function is assumed, there are no diminishing marginal returns to the inputs. The marginal products of the inputs are constant. That is, the marginal product of the input does not change as the level of the input use is altered. Thus, the linear, constant marginal product, production function has limited use over narrow ranges. As we have discussed in the previous sections, holding constant one input and applying various amounts of a second input, we almost always find that the variable input is eventually subject to diminishing marginal returns. As a consequence, the linear production function is only used in limited circumstances when the range of input use does not vary much.

A second function form that incorporates the potential for diminishing marginal returns is the quadratic form:

$$q = \beta_0 + \beta_1 x_1 + \beta_2 (x_1)^2 + \beta_3 x_2 + \beta_4 (x_2)^2$$

which, of course, can be generalized to even higher level polynomial forms. In the quadratic production function, when the inputs are subject to diminishing marginal returns, the coefficients on the squared terms, β_2 and β_4, have negative signs. At low levels of input use, when an additional amount of either input is used, say x_1, output grows because the linear term dominates the squared effect. However, as the use of x_1 increases, with a negative coefficient on the squared term, the marginal returns to x_1 are forever declining. When input use increases, output grows at a decreasing rate; this is what we call *diminishing marginal returns*. This form can also be modified to include dependence between the inputs:

$$q = \beta_0 + \beta_1 x_1 + \beta_2(x_1)^2 + \beta_3 x_2 + \beta_4(x_2)^2 + \beta_5(x_1 \bullet x_2).$$

One of the most commonly used models for production functions is the **Cobb-Douglas functional form**, which is an exponential form. In the Cobb-Douglas functional form, each input is raised to its own respective power. In the two-input case, the Cobb-Douglas production function takes the form

$$q = \beta_0 x_1^{\beta_1} x_2^{\beta_2},$$

where β_0–β_2 are all positive numbers.

THE POINT OF ZERO MARGINAL PRODUCT

The simple quadratic production function is given by

$$q = \beta_0 + \beta_1 x_1 + \beta_2(x_1)^2 + \beta_3 x_2 + \beta_4(x_2)^2.$$

To find the point where the marginal product of the first input, x_1, is zero, we take the partial derivative of the production function with respect to x_1, set it equal to zero, and solve for x_1. The partial derivative of the production function with respect to x_1 is

$$\partial q/\partial x_1 = \beta_1 + 2\bullet\beta_2\bullet x_1.$$

We set this equal to zero:

$$\beta_1 + 2\bullet\beta_2\bullet x_1 = 0,$$

and solve for x_1:

$$x_1 = -\beta_1/(2\bullet\beta_2).$$

In the quadratic form, the marginal product of an input, x_1, is equal to zero at the point found by taking minus the linear parameter and dividing by twice the quadratic parameter.

If we take the logarithms of both sides of this equation, the production function reduces to a linear relation in the logs of the variables:

$$\ln q = \ln \beta_0 + \beta_1 \cdot \ln x_1 + \beta_2 \cdot \ln x_2.$$

This transformation of the production function makes for simple estimation of the parameters, β_0–β_2.

To explore these functional forms further, consider the data reported in Table 6.3 for the electric power industry in the United States. Steam generation is the total amount of electricity produced in each state in 1983 using conventional steam powered methods. This excludes nuclear- and hydro-generated electricity. Nuclear- and hydro-generation technologies are sufficiently different that it seems appropriate to model them separately. Also listed in the table are the levels of the main inputs to the generation process, the fuels and generators. Labor is omitted for two reasons. First, in the case of electricity production, the dynamos and fuel are the main inputs, and second, the data on labor are not publicly available.

The data in Table 6.3 are used to estimate several different forms of the production of electricity. First, the linear model is estimated. The ordinary-least-squares estimates of the linear parameters are reported in Table 6.4. A quadratic specification is reported next, followed by a cubic form. The Cobb-Douglas form is presented last in the table.

In the linear form, we see that each input is positive and significant. The estimated slope coefficients are the marginal products of the inputs. By construction, they are all constant. The quadratic and cubic forms allow for diminishing marginal returns. However, in this case, two of the coefficient estimates on the squared terms are positive, the ones for coal and natural gas. This implies increasing marginal returns, an unlikely prospect in general. However, in the cubic form, we find negative coefficients on the cubic terms for coal, fuel oil, and natural gas. The squared term on generating capacity remains negative. Moreover, the cubic term on capacity is statistically insignificant. The Cobb-Douglas specification has diminishing marginal productivity for each input as each estimated coefficient is less than unity.[6]

Each of these specifications maps inputs into output. Which one is the best? That is not an easy question to answer. Each functional form has its own merits. The linear form is simple and easy to use. Yet it does not allow for diminishing

---

[6] To see why this is true, consider the two-input Cobb-Douglas production function. Take the second derivative of the production function with respect to the first input, x_1:

$$\partial^2 q / \partial (x_1)^2 = (\beta_1 - 1) \cdot \beta_0 \cdot \beta_1 \cdot (x_1)^{\beta_1 - 2} \cdot (x_2)^{\beta_2}.$$

Since β_0 is positive, this expression is negative whenever β_1 is less than one. The first partial derivative is the marginal product of the input. The second partial derivative is the rate of change in the marginal product of the input. When the second partial derivative is negative, we have a declining marginal product of the input. Whenever the exponent of the input is less than one, the input is subject to diminishing marginal returns.

marginal returns. Even so, unless we desire to forecast production far outside the existing ranges of data, this is probably not a serious flaw. The quadratic and cubic forms are more complex and difficult to interpret, and some of the quadratic estimates do not suggest that the fuel inputs are subject to diminishing returns. This is compounded by the statistical insignificance of several coefficient estimates. In this light, the exponential, Cobb-Douglas specification may be the most useful. An alternative, arguably superior way to assess the quality of the various specifications is to collect data from additional years and reestimate the equations to resolve these problems.

THE FIRM'S RESPONSE TO AN INPUT PRICE CHANGE

Input price changes affect average and marginal cost but in different ways. As a general but not universal principle, input price increases raise marginal and average cost while input price declines cause marginal and average cost to shift down. The amount by which these curves shift depends on the relation between the input in question and output. Inputs fall into three classes, inferior, normal, and superior, and the classification of the input determines the way that marginal and average cost shift when the input price changes. We will define and explain these classifications, but first we explore the problem of cost minimization, which provides the basic understanding of the relation between input prices and cost.

Cost Minimization—The Efficient Use of Inputs

Whatever output the firm chooses, it must produce that output as cheaply as possible if profit is to be maximized. This means that the firm must choose the inputs it uses in the proper proportions depending on their prices and productivity. The analysis is made easy by reference to the problem of utility maximization. Recall the section Maximizing Utility in Chapter 3 where we discussed the concept of a utility function. The principles of cost minimization are analytically analogous. On the one hand, the consumer's utility increases the more goods are consumed. By parallel, the output of the firm grows the more inputs it uses. The consumer climbs utility mountain; the firm climbs production mountain.

Examine Figure 6.6. A two-input production function is graphed there where output is determined by the amount of capital, K, and labor, L, used. As more of either capital or labor is used, holding the stock of the other constant, output is greater; the height of the production function at any combination of capital and labor measures the amount of output produced. For instance, using K_1 of capital and L_1 of labor, output is measured by the height at point A in the figure. The *same* amount of output could be produced by using less capital, K_2, but more labor, L_2. The height of the production function at point B is the same as at A, and hence the output is the same. In fact, these two points trace out what we call an **isoquant**. Decompose the word to grasp its meaning. The first part of the word is *iso* meaning equal. The second part, *quant*, is a shortening of quantity—equal quantity. Despite subtle and important differences, isoquants are to production analysis what indifference curves are to utility analysis.

Isoquants farther from the origin represent higher levels of production. For

TABLE 6.3	ELECTRICITY PRODUCTION AND INPUTS				
STATE	CONVENTIONAL STEAM POWER PRODUCED (MILLIONS OF KWHS)	COAL USED (THOUSAND TONS)	FUEL OIL USED (THOUSAND BARRELS)	NATURAL GAS USED (MILLION CU. FT.)	CONVENTIONAL STEAM GENERATING CAPACITY (KWHS)
Alabama	39886	17164	128	554	11235
Alaska	2844	321	934	31348	861
Arizona	26902	12464	747	19209	8746
Arkansas	19111	9628	97	33275	5815
California	55216	0	11185	465066	27167
Colorado	22605	12193	194	4526	5492
Connecticut	11939	0	19736	0	3789
Delaware	9472	—	—	—	2022
District of Columbia	221	—	—	—	868
Florida	76159	12435	50302	174813	27448
Georgia	54740	22778	280	1633	13781
Hawaii	6210	0	10876	0	1444
Idaho	0	0	0	9	50
Illinois	70920	34265	6349	11948	23783
Indiana	70437	33526	356	2877	18478
Iowa	19013	11921	155	3249	7592
Kansas	23408	12814	530	47226	9047
Kentucky	54439	24236	246	1196	15195
Louisiana	37025	5804	672	296490	15393
Maine	2043	0	3516	0	1104
Maryland	19120	—	—	—	7390
Massachusetts	28363	3413	27574	24396	7405
Michigan	53329	22872	1397	12618	16767
Minnesota	17277	10703	93	2861	6448
Mississippi	13359	3802	206	49773	6122
Missouri	50924	24614	455	2806	14340

TABLE 6.3 (continued)

State	Conventional Steam Power Produced (Millions of KWHs)	Coal Used (Thousand Tons)	Fuel Oil Used (Thousand Barrels)	Natural Gas Used (Million Cu. Ft.)	Conventional Steam Generating Capacity (KWHS)
Montana	3535	2356	31	335	1108
Nebraska	9586	5656	80	1581	4146
Nevada	13280	6115	68	9562	3787
New Hampshire	4090	1019	2680	20	1147
New Jersey	21214	3132	8593	96886	10501
New Mexico	26998	14359	234	30626	5297
New York	62358	6711	57964	135811	22725
North Carolina	56189	21913	464	163	13533
North Dakota	17224	15386	98	11	3290
Ohio	100807	44017	626	1046	26659
Oklahoma	43139	12042	51	236950	11299
Oregon	446	358	25	1	1347
Pennsylvania	107708	40046	19231	1654	26894
Rhode Island	574	0	713	3079	243
South Carolina	17336	6989	140	942	6619
South Dakota	2286	2201	42	45	862
Tennessee	45438	18672	291	107	12054
Texas	205009	64007	3850	1190648	56661
Utah	11029	5223	79	1259	2794
Vermont	109	28	16	220	164
Virginia	17855	6577	2724	3330	6967
Washington	6170	4298	23	30	2040
West Virginia	72057	28970	418	115	14979
Wisconsin	27749	15094	251	3514	8650
Wyoming	25107	16135	81	136	5591

Source: Statistical Yearbook of the Electric Utility Industry 1983. (Washington, DC: Edison Electric Institute, 1984), pp. 10, 24, 33.

TABLE 6.4   ESTIMATES OF THE ELECTRICITY PRODUCTION FUNCTION

Dependent Variable: Total Power Produced Using Conventional Steam Methods

LINEAR SPECIFICATION

F Ratio	Prob > F	R^2	Sample Size
888.017	0.0001	0.9880	48

VARIABLE	PARAMETER ESTIMATE	STANDARD ERROR	t RATIO	PROB > $|t|$
Intercept	−2037.9268	935.2292	−2.179	0.0349
Coal Used	1.4448	0.1193	12.102	0.0001
Fuel Oil Used	0.3770	0.0807	4.667	0.0001
Natural Gas Used	0.0298	0.0063	4.699	0.0001
Generating Capacity	1.3799	0.2184	6.317	0.0001

QUADRATIC SPECIFICATION

F Ratio	Prob > F	R^2	Sample Size
466.319	0.0001	0.9897	48

VARIABLE	PARAMETER ESTIMATE	STANDARD ERROR	t RATIO	PROB > $|t|$
Intercept	−2063.7435	1336.9832	−1.544	0.1308
Coal Used	1.0483	0.2915	3.596	0.0009
(Coal Used)^2	1.5E−5	7.2E−6	2.015	0.0508
Fuel Oil Used	0.5025	0.1998	2.515	0.0161
(Fuel Oil Used)^2	−8.9E−7	3.7E−6	−0.239	0.8120
Natural Gas Used	0.0400	0.0211	1.891	0.0661
(Natural Gas Used)^2	7.8E−9	3.0E−8	0.291	0.7725
Generating Capacity	1.7825	0.4834	3.688	0.0007
(Generating Capacity)^2	−2.5E−5	1.7E−5	−1.490	0.1443

TABLE 6.4 (continued)

Cubic Specification

	F Ratio	Prob > F	R²	Sample Size
	344.429	0.0001	0.9916	48
Intercept		−563.2180	−0.351	0.7276
Coal Used		−0.1105	−0.120	0.9048
(Coal Used)²		8.5E−5	1.557	0.1285
(Coal Used)³		−1.0E−9	−1.214	0.2330
Fuel Oil Used		−0.5025	−1.084	0.2859
(Fuel Oil Used)²		5.5E−5	2.190	0.0353
(Fuel Oil Used)³		−6.4E−10	−1.965	0.0574
Natural Gas Used		0.0087	0.252	0.8023
(Natural Gas Used)²		2.0E−7	1.148	0.2586
(Natural Gas Used)³		−1.8E−13	−0.756	0.4547
Generating Capacity		2.9399	1.802	0.0802
(Generating Capacity)²		−0.0001	−0.852	0.4002
(Generating Capacity)³		2.2E−9	0.597	0.5542

Dependent Variable: Log of Total Power Produced Using Conventional Steam Methods

Cobb-Douglas Specification

	F Ratio	Prob > F	R²	Sample Size
	322.483	0.0001	0.9721	42
Intercept		0.4961	1.476	0.1485
Log of Coal Used		0.6344	9.107	0.0001
Log of Oil Used		0.1135	4.047	0.0003
Log of Gas Used		0.0504	3.039	0.0043
Log of Generating Capacity		0.2994	2.773	0.0087

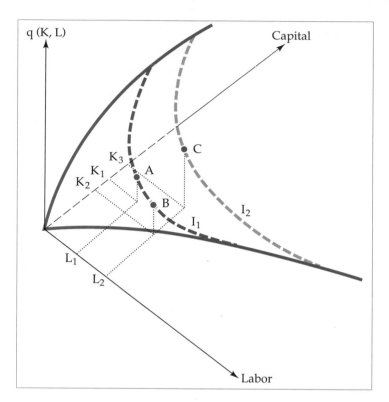

FIGURE 6.6
Production Mountain

instance, at point B in Figure 6.6, K_2 capital and L_2 labor are used to produce I_1 level of output. Suppose the *same* amount of labor were used, but more capital was employed, say K_3. Then production would be higher at point C on isoquant I_2. Isoquant I_2 is farther up production mountain, representing a higher level of production.

Figure 6.7 uses isoquants displayed in two dimensional space to describe the cost minimizing strategy. Let the prices of our two inputs, capital and labor, be r and w respectively to stand for interest and wages. Suppose q_0 is the desired level of output and is represented by the isoquant I_0 in Figure 6.7. The objective of the firm is to produce this level of output as cheaply as possible. Thus the decision the firm must make is, What quantity of capital and labor will minimize the cost of producing q_0?

There are many different ways to produce this particular level of output, but three of them have been depicted in the figure. Point A uses K_A of capital and L_A of labor. Point B uses less capital, K_B, and more labor, L_B. These two points were chosen in a special way. The line connecting them has a slope equal to the negative of the relative prices of the two inputs. This line is important for it represents the combination of inputs where cost is constant. It is an isocost line; each point on it represents a constant level of cost. Moreover, the farther the line

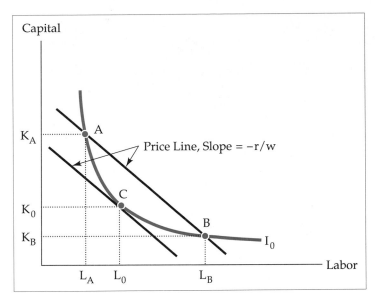

FIGURE 6.7
The Optimal Input Mix

lies from the origin, the higher is the level of cost. The closer the line is to the origin, the lower is the level of cost.

At either point A or B, although the desired level of production would be obtained, it is overly costly. At point A, if the firm would use less capital and more labor, moving to point C, the price line would shift in, indicating that less total money is spent to produce the *same* level of output. Similarly, at point B, if the firm used less labor and more capital, cost could be lowered without reducing output. Thus, for the firm to minimize cost, the price line must be as close to the origin as possible. Conceptually then, the optimal input mix for any given level of output is found by moving the price line in toward the origin until it is just tangent to the relevant isoquant. This condition is found at point C with the firm using K_0 units of capital and L_0 units of labor.

It bears noting that the slope of an isoquant is the negative of the ratios of the marginal products of the two inputs, what we call the **marginal rate of transformation**. At the point of tangency this slope equals the slope of the price line. This equality defines the cost minimizing input use (where the minus signs on both sides of the equality have been dropped):

$$\frac{MP_K}{MP_L} = \frac{r}{w}.$$

The marginal rate of transformation must equal the ratio of the input prices. Another way to write this condition is to rearrange terms:

$$\frac{MP_K}{r} = \frac{MP_L}{w}.$$

COST MINIMIZATION—A MATHEMATICAL PRESENTATION

Total cost, C, is the quantity of each input, x_i, times its price, w_i:

$$C = x_1 w_1 + x_2 w_2 + {}_{x3} w_3 + \ldots {}_{xn} w_n,$$

where n is the number of inputs used in the production process. Output, q, is determined by the quantity of inputs employed, x_1, x_2, x_3, through x_n, and the state of technology, the functional relational q:

$$q = q(x_1, x_2, x_3, \ldots, x_n).$$

Cost minimization, given some level of output, q_0, is achieved by minimizing cost subject to the constraint that output, for a given set of inputs, is maximized. Mathematically this means we minimize cost (the sum of the expenditures on the inputs), $\Sigma x_i \bullet w_i$, subject to the constraint that $q_0 = q(x_1, x_2, \ldots, x_n)$ or that $q(x_1, x_2, \ldots, x_n) - q_0 = 0$. Forming the Lagrangian function of constrained optimization and letting λ be the unknown Lagrangian multiplier, we see that costs are minimized only if

$$\mathscr{L} = \Sigma x_i \bullet w_i - \lambda[q(x_1, x_2, \ldots, x_n) - q_0]$$

is minimized. In this formulation of the problem, the firm can only choose the appropriate amount of each input, and as a consequence, the first order conditions necessary to minimize $\mathscr{L}$ and therefore costs are

$$\partial \mathscr{L} / \partial x_i = 0 \text{ for } i = 1, n, \text{ and} \tag{i}$$

$$\partial \mathscr{L} / \partial \lambda = 0. \tag{ii}$$

Taking the appropriate derivatives, equations (i) and (ii) imply

$$w_i = \lambda \partial q / \partial x_i \tag{iii}$$

for each of the ith inputs, and

$$q_0 = q(x_1, x_2, x_3, \ldots, x_n). \tag{iv}$$

Equation (iii) says that the firm hires each input until its marginal product equals the cost of the input at the margin, and equation (iv) says that the firm produces as much output as it can, given that it has hired $x_1 - x_n$ inputs. Equations (i) and (ii) imply a set of simultaneous equations in $(n + 1)$ unknowns, one for each of the x_i's plus one for λ. These $(n + 1)$ equations can be solved for each of the x_i's, and the solution creates a set of input demand functions of the form:

$$x_i = x_i(w, q_0) \tag{v}$$

where x_i is the demand for the ith input, w is a vector of input prices, and q_0 is the chosen level of output. Intuitively, the demand equation identified in equation (v) implies that the amount of each input the firm buys is a function of the input prices and the volume of output the firm wants to produce, presuming, of course, that the firm produces this output as cheaply as possible. It is a simple matter to show that the firm buys less of any input when its price increases. Not surprisingly, $\partial x_i/\partial w_i < 0$ for each input; the first law of demand holds for inputs. For each of the n inputs, when its input price decreases, the firm uses more of that particular input.

This condition generalizes. When costs are minimized, the ratio of the marginal product of each input divided by its price is equal for all inputs. In other words,

$$\frac{MP_1}{p_1} = \frac{MP_2}{p_2} = \cdots = \frac{MP_n}{p_n},$$

where MP_i is the marginal product of the ith input, p_i is the price of the ith input, and n is the number of inputs in the production process.

This result is full of economic intuition. The marginal product of an input divided by its price is the (marginal) benefit-cost ratio for the input. When this ratio is unequal across inputs, some input has a higher marginal net benefit than the others. A profit opportunity exists. By using more of the input that has the high benefit-cost ratio (and less of the others), the firm can reduce its costs of production without reducing output.

Classes of Inputs

Inputs are divisible into three categories: inferior, normal, and superior. For the **inferior input**, $\partial x_i/\partial q < 0$; the firm uses less of the input as output increases, holding constant all prices. It is widely believed that inferior inputs are quite rare in most business situations. But for the sake of example, imagine a small family restaurant. Each evening the place is swept by the staff after closing. The restaurant is popular and expands. Now, instead of sweeping, a large vacuum cleaner is used, even though the prices of brooms and vacuum cleaners are unchanged. In this case, brooms are inferior inputs; larger output leads to less sweeping. It is easy to imagine circumstances in which hand calculators are inferior inputs as well. Business expansion leads to the purchase of personal computers and abandonment of the calculators, prices being constant.

Inputs that are used more as output expands are called **normal inputs**; for these inputs, $\partial x_i/\partial q > 0$. A special case of the normal input is the **superior input**. For superior inputs, the increased demand for the input exceeds the increase in output in percentage terms. That is, the output elasticity of the input demand is greater than one. Thus some people strictly define an input as normal if the output elasticity of input use is greater than zero but less than one.

For the normal input, an increase in output, say 10 percent, leads the firm to

---

CLASSES OF INPUTS

Inferior Input: $(\partial x_i/\partial q)\bullet(q/x_i) < 0$.   The output elasticity is negative.
Normal Input: $0 < (\partial x_i/\partial q)\bullet(q/x_i) < 1$.   The output elasticity is positive, but less than 1.
Superior Input: $(\partial x_i/\partial q)\bullet(q/x_i) > 1$.   The output elasticity is greater than 1.

Inferior Inputs—output expansion leads to less input use
Normal and Superior Inputs—output expansion leads to greater input use

---

use more of the input, but less than 10 percent more. For the superior input, the firm uses *more* than 10 percent more of the input, and of course, for the inferior input, the firm actually uses less of the input as output expands.[7]

Changes in Marginal and Average Cost

As noted earlier, the impact of an input price change on marginal and average cost depends on the class of input. For all inputs, price increases cause average cost to rise, but in distinctly different ways. Consider Figure 6.8. Three different scenarios are presented there—increasing cost for the normal, superior, and inferior input. Average cost shifts in a different but predictable way in each case.

When the price of an inferior input increases, the new average cost curve shifts up, and *the minimum of the new average cost curve lies to the right of the old marginal cost curve.* This means that marginal cost actually declines. Increases in the price of an input that the firm uses less of when the firm expands production cause the marginal cost of producing to go down; average cost increases. Optimal firm size increases. To repeat, the new minimum of average cost lies to the right of the old minimum but *below* the old marginal cost. This zone is lightly tinted in Figure 6.8.[8] It bears repeating that production economists and cost engineers have not found many inferior inputs in actual use. As an empirical matter, most inputs are normal or superior, and we have a hard time locating inputs that are used less as output expands.

For the normal input, both average and marginal cost increase. The minimum of the new average cost lies to the right of the old minimum, but above the old marginal cost curve. That is, average cost increases relatively more than marginal cost. Optimal firm size gets bigger. This is the uncolored center zone in Figure 6.8.

---

[7] It is worth emphasizing that the labels—inferior, normal, and superior—bear no relation to the intrinsic quality of the actual inputs. The definitions strictly describe whether input use declines or rises with output expansion.

[8] The proof of these propositions is contained in Richard D. Portes, "Long-Run Scale Adjustments of a Perfectly Competitive Firm and Industry: An Alternative Approach," *American Economic Review*, June 1971, 430–34. He provides a mathematical and graphical exposition.

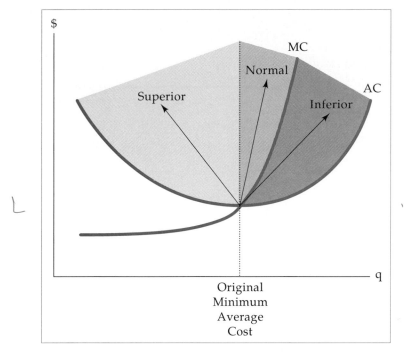

FIGURE 6.8
Input Price Changes

For the superior input, both marginal and average cost increase, but the increase in marginal cost dominates the increase in average cost. Hence, minimum efficient firm size declines. If the price of an input with an output elasticity greater than one increases, the optimally sized firm gets smaller, and the minimum of average cost shifts to the left and above the old minimum. This is the darkly colored zone marked on the left in Figure 6.8.

DERIVED DEMAND

The firm's demand for inputs is a **derived demand**. The firm has no intrinsic use for things; it only buys goods that can be used to make money. Take a simple case. The technology to produce some product, say cotton fabric, is well known. It is a relatively simple matter for the firm to estimate the marginal cost of fabric production given the prices of labor, machines, and land. What the firm must decide is how much it is willing to pay for the raw cotton to use in the plant. Put another way, given the marginal cost of production, how much is the firm willing to pay for cotton fiber—what is the firm's demand for raw cotton fiber? Consider Figure 6.9. The price of a given quality cotton greige goods is determined by the market. It is p_g. The marginal cost of production, *not including raw cotton*, is MC_1, a function of output, q.

Assume for simplicity that there is a fixed relation between the use of cotton input and the greige output. That is, the production of x pounds of cotton greige

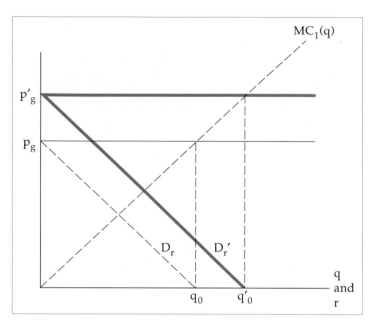

FIGURE 6.9

The Derived Demand for Inputs (Fixed Proportions)

fabric requires $\alpha \cdot x$ pounds of raw cotton where α is the fixed proportion coefficient. In simple terms, each unit of cloth manufactured uses the same amount of raw cotton input. This is called **fixed proportions production**. The firm's willingness to buy cotton is determined by the difference between the price of cotton greige goods and the marginal cost of all other inputs. The most the firm is willing to pay for an additional unit of raw cotton at any given volume of cotton is $p_g - MC_1(q)$. The horizontal axis can be measured in terms of output, q, or input of raw cotton, r. Because of fixed proportions, there is a one-to-one correspondence between output and cotton use, $q = \alpha \cdot r$. The firm's demand for raw cotton is D_r, the vertical difference between p_g and $MC_1(q)$.

When the price of output increases to p'_g, the firm's demand for raw cotton increases to D'_r. Similarly, if the marginal cost of producing, exclusive of cotton, declines, the firm's demand for raw cotton fiber increases. In the first case, when output is more valuable, the firm is willing to pay more for each unit of greige goods input, and in the second case, when the costs of other factors of production fall, the firm finds it profitable to buy more raw cotton to go along with the other, cheaper inputs.

Consider a numerical example. Let cotton greige goods sell for $5 per yard; p_g = 5. Suppose the cost of weaving cotton is a linear function of output, say c_w = $0.1 \cdot g$, where c_w is the marginal cost of weaving cloth per yard and g is the number of yards woven. Further, there is a fixed relation between the pounds of raw cotton used and the number of yards that can be woven. Assume this relation is g = $5 \cdot f$, where f is the pounds of raw cotton fiber used. How much is the firm willing to pay for raw cotton fiber? What is the firm's demand for the cotton input? Well, the output can be sold for $5 per yard, but each yard costs $0.10 to manufacture (leaving aside the cost of the cotton fiber). How much does that leave over to pay for raw cotton fiber? What is the firm's demand price, p_f, for raw cotton fiber? The answer is $p_g - 0.1 \bullet g$, but g is determined by the amount of cotton used, f. Therefore, the derived demand for raw cotton fiber, the firm's willingness to pay for raw cotton, is $p_g - 0.1 \bullet (5 \bullet f)$ or

$$p_f = p_g - 0.1 \bullet (5 \bullet f) = 5 - 0.5 \bullet f.$$

This function can be inverted, solving for f,

$$f = 10 - (p_f / 0.5),$$

which maps the price of raw fiber, p_f, into the firm's quantity demanded of raw fiber. For example, if $p_f = \$0.10$, then the firm purchases $f = 10 - 0.1/0.5 = 9.8$ units of raw cotton and similarly for other prices. When the price of raw cotton equals the price of the finished product, the firm is unwilling to buy any of the input. There is nothing to be gained. Table 6.5 reports the quantities demanded for fiber at various fiber prices.

Fixed proportions is just a special case of derived demand. Functions similar to D_r exist in the variable proportions case as well. They are determined by input prices and the state of technology. Recall the input demand functions derived earlier: $x_i = x_i(w, q)$. The graphical presentation in Figure 6.9 for fixed proportions is a special case, but nevertheless an informative one. The only substantive difference between fixed and variable proportions is a matter of degree. In the fixed proportions case, when the price of raw cotton increases, the firm buys less raw cotton, it produces less, and it uses less of all inputs; but it uses the same proportion of all inputs at the lower output level. In the variable proportions case, the results are the same except that the firm also adjusts by substituting out of the higher priced input into more of the now relatively cheaper inputs. Its input mix shifts away from the higher priced input. This, of course, is not possible in the fixed proportions case.

TABLE 6.5 THE DERIVED DEMAND FOR FIBER	
FIBER PRICES	FABRIC PURCHASES
$p_f = \$0.20$	$f = 9.6$
$= 0.50$	$= 9.0$
$= 1.00$	$= 8.0$
$= 1.50$	$= 7.0$
$= 5.00$	$= 0.0$

LEARNING, RATE, VOLUME, INTERMITTENT PRODUCTION, AND THE MULTIPRODUCT FIRM

Learning

Learning is the ability to reduce costs through experience, and obviously it is most important for the young firm or the firm introducing a new product. Other good examples include made-for-order products that can be unique. Firms in the construction industry often never build exactly the same building twice. Yet, at any one particular site, the same general process is repeated—the second floor repeats itself numerous times as the building grows taller. In this situation, learning often takes place; average and marginal costs decline as output increases. That is, it is cheaper *per floor* to build a unique structure six stories high than the same structure four stories tall.

The introduction of such new products as transistors, color televisions, microwave ovens, semiconductors, personal computers, compact disks, and the like is typically associated with a learning period as the producing firms discover new techniques for reducing cost. Generally, this effect tapers off as the industry exhausts the possibilities for cost reduction.

Rate and Volume

Rate and **volume** are different concepts, especially in the made-for-order business. Consider the construction of airplanes. Large producers such as Boeing, McDonald Douglas, and Lockheed produce many of their aircraft on order. A buyer places an order for, say, 150 units, to be delivered on or before a certain date (generally with a reorder option). Under such circumstances, certain principles apply:

1. Increasing the rate of production, holding constant the total planned volume, increases the cost of production. The faster output must be produced, the more it costs.

2. As the rate of production increases, holding constant the total planned volume, cost increases at an increasing rate. The faster output is produced, the more it costs, and this cost increases at an increasing rate.

3. Holding constant the rate of production, total cost increases as the planned volume of output increases, *but at a decreasing rate*. Hence, the average cost per unit declines as the total planned volume of production increases.

4. The longer the firm has to produce any given planned volume of output, the lower is cost.[9]

It is important that these principles are independent of any learning that

---

[9] For a more complete discussion on the rate-volume question, consult the classic by Armen Alchian, "Costs and Outputs," in M. Abramovitz et al., *The Allocation of Economic Resources* (Stanford, CA: Stanford University Press, 1959).

might take place. The structure of costs just characterized is due to transactions costs and economies of scale. If Boeing is only planning to build 10 planes of a certain type, it may not pay to build a new plant, purchase certain large machines, or investigate new lightweight metal alloys. On the other hand, if Boeing plans to build 100 aircraft, then the new, modern plant; the expensive, efficient machinery; and the research and development expenditures may now be worthwhile. These investments can reduce cost per unit, but they are only cost effective if they can be amortized over a relatively large volume of production.[10]

Intermittent Production and the Multiproduct Firm

In some production situations, rate cannot be altered easily. Examples include pipelines, assembly lines, airplanes, trucks, many chemical processes, and most agricultural commodities. Driving these machines at rates different from the engineering efficient rate, their design rates, can impose large costs on the firm. However, these costs can be avoided by **intermittent production**. For example, transportation firms adjust to slack demand by stopping their vehicles rather than slowing them. Similarly, automobile manufacturers often shut down entire plants while they sell off accumulated stocks.

Consider Figure 6.10. Suppose the firm's costs are given by the average and marginal cost curves A_1 and M_1 respectively. Imagine that demand is insufficient

FIGURE 6.10
Intermittent Production

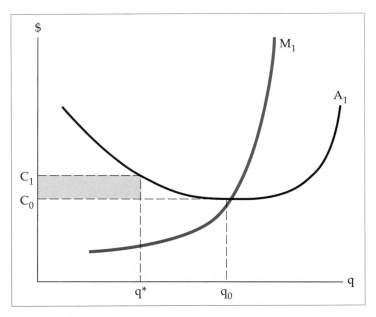

---

[10] Of course, if the machinery can be rented, then the propositions are empirically irrelevant. But it is precisely the transactions costs of rental that create the cost principles.

to allow the company to sell all its output if it produces continuously at the average cost minimizing rate, q_0. In order to deal with this problem, the firm produces at a slower rate, q^*, for the entire time period. The cost per unit of output at this rate is C_1. Total output is q^* times the length of time the facility operates. Let's call this amount of output, s, to represent total sales over the period. There may be a strategy that is superior to continuous production.

Suppose we ignore transactions costs for a moment. When the market will not purchase enough of a firm's output to allow the continuous use of all inputs at their most efficient rate, one option that the firm might explore is to manufacture intensively at the average cost minimizing rate, accumulating inventories in excess of sales, until the appropriate volume of output is reached. The firm stops *production* at this point, but sales continue. This depletes inventories. When sales can no longer be made from inventories, the production machinery is restarted. The firm stops and starts to accommodate demand, but it always produces at the cost minimizing rate when it is running. Intermittent production, combined with inventory accumulation, allows the company to ignore the rate of sales when it plans its rate of production. This can lead to a substantial savings in cost.

To consider the problem formally, remember that s is the total amount of output produced over some time period, t_0. Let's call it a month, although it could be an hour, or a day, or any other period. The variables q^* and q_0 are the continuous rate of production and the cost minimizing rate of production, respectively. Let α be the fraction of the month that the firm must operate if it is to produce s *at the cost minimizing rate*, q_0. This means that $0 < \alpha < 1$ and that $\alpha = q^*/q_0$. Then, the firm produces at the rate q_0 for an α fraction of the month ($\alpha q_0 \cdot t_0 = s$), but goods are sold for the whole month at a rate determined by demand conditions in the market, s/t_0, which is just q^*. Let C_0 be the cost per unit when output is produced at the cheapest rate, q_0. During the first part of the month when the facility is operating (from time 0 until time αt_0), production exceeds sales and inventories accumulate. See Figure 6.11. When sufficient output has been manufactured, the plant shuts down. At this point, inventories are at their maximum, $[1-(q^*/q_0)]\cdot s$. Sales continue out of inventories for the rest of the month. Once the facility is shut down, sales continue; but there is no production. Once the stock of inventories is depleted, the facility is reopened, and the cycle begins anew.

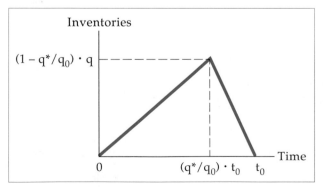

FIGURE 6.11

Inventories with Intermittent Production

Figure 6.11

This intermittent production strategy saves money. The total costs of producing continuously are $(t_0 \cdot C_1 \cdot q^*)$. Producing intermittently only costs $\{[(q^*/q_0) \cdot t_0] \cdot C_0 \cdot q_0\}$, which is less, $t_0 \cdot C_1 \cdot q^*$, by the amount $(C_1 - C_0) \cdot t_0 \cdot q^*$. This is the area tinted in Figure 6.10. Depending upon the structure of average cost, these cost savings can be substantial.

Consider the accompanying box which relates a story about plant consolidation in the automobile industry. Two items are especially worthy of note. First, the General Motor's plan is designed to match plant capacity to demand, and second, the plan will increase capacity utilization. Given the enormous costs of constructing an automobile assembly line, it is easy to understand the company's desire to keep the capital working as often as possible. If idle hands are the devil's workshop, then inactive machines are the stockholder's nightmare.

In actual practice, a firm using this strategy faces a number of costs. One is the opportunity cost of the resources idled when production is interrupted. The company has a plant at its disposal, but it is producing no output. The perfect solution to this problem is to produce another output during the idle time. A good example of this phenomenon is laundry detergent production. For technical reasons, powdered soap can only be produced at one specific rate. If demand is not large enough to warrant building the average cost minimizing size of plant, the single product firm is faced with the choice of producing continuously in a

---

ASSEMBLY LINES IN THE AUTOMOBILE INDUSTRY

The General Motors Corporation and a local chapter of the United Automobile Workers union have tentatively agreed to begin near-nonstop assembly operations at G.M.'s Lordstown, Ohio, plant starting next summer. The step would enable G.M. to effectively produce as many cars at one plant as the company can now assemble in two.

The move represents a growing trend among American auto makers to cut costs by wringing more use from existing plants. The Chrysler Corporation, for example, has an agreement with the U.A.W. to step up mini-van production, if needed, by using three shifts instead of the usual two.

Robert C. Stempel, G.M.'s chairman, has vowed to operate the No. 1 auto maker's plants at 100 percent capacity by the end of 1992. But he also aims to do so profitably, and that means matching capacity more closely to . . . demand. . . .

G.M. currently also makes a van at the Lordstown plant, but its production is being consolidated at a plant in Flint, Mich. The 1,500 hourly workers who now assemble vans in Lordstown will get an opportunity to be part of the expanded production of cars there.

G.M. operates a few European assembly plants almost nonstop, and G.M. executives say they wish to use the practice more widely in the company's American and Canadian plants. Auto assembly plants in the United States normally operate one or two eight-hour shifts daily.

Doron P. Levin, "G.M.'s Plan for a Nearly Nonstop Auto Plant," *New York Times,* July 3, 1991, p. D1. Copyright © 1991 by The New York Times Company. Reprinted by permission.

smaller but more expensively operated facility or idling the average cost minimizing facility from time to time.[11] However, if the firm can find another product to produce in the idle periods, then the firm can afford to build the larger and more efficient facility. The average cost of soap is lowered to its minimum by running the facility continuously, alternating between products. These are the facts surrounding Procter & Gamble's soap products Tide and Cheer. They are produced in the same facility, and when the plant is switched from running Tide, a white soap, to Cheer, a blue soap, the mixed product is boxed and marketed as Oxydol.

Those processes in which physical laws dictate certain narrow limits of production rate are obvious candidates for intermittent production diversification and product line expansion. Examples that immediately come to mind are trucks, trains, and airplanes, all of which must travel at more or less constant speeds. Hence, it is no surprise that many companies employ their own trucking and motor pools. The firm keeps vehicles employed at many different jobs using a variety of drivers, avoiding the transactions costs of periodically leasing cars and trucks. Chemical processes must often proceed at precise rates without regard to economic forces, and, of course, most agricultural products grow at rates not easily adjusted by farmers. Thus, firms manufacturing in these lines of business are inclined to produce more than one product. The ability to switch the assets of the firm from one product line to another allows the firm to produce each of its varied products using the least-cost methodology. The extra product lines then are a way of avoiding the costs of idle resources.

Consider the following story from the *Wall Street Journal:*

> Almost a year after Procter & Gamble Co. bought Richardson-Vicks, Inc., the consumer products giant yesterday announced some substantial steps toward integrating the two companies.
>
> Among other changes, William I. Bergman, 55 years old, currently executive vice president of the Richardson-Vicks, Inc. subsidiary, will become president of the Richardson-Vicks USA division of the subsidiary. He will report to the P&G group vice president for health and beauty care. Currently, Mr. Bergman reports to John S. Scott, 60, who had reported directly to John Pepper, P&G president.
>
> Mr. Scott, who headed Richardson-Vicks, Inc. when it was acquired, will remain chairman of the subsidiary but will relinquish his posts as president and chief executive officer of the subsidiary. He will continue to report to Mr. Pepper. However, the operations that Mr. Scott and other Richardson-Vicks executives had supervised, including Vicks's domestic and foreign operations, will report directly to P&G top management in Cincinnati. All changes are effective Jan. 1.
>
> Todd A. Garrett, 45, currently president and general manager of Richardson-Vicks's Americas/Far East division, will move to Cincinnati as division manager of a new Asia/Pacific division of P&G, handling both companies' Asian operations. John R. Markely, 52, currently executive vice president, Richardson-Vicks, will become president, Richardson-Vicks Europe, and will move to Europe from

---

[11] In a lot of situations, the firm finds it valuable to employ a mixed strategy of intermittent production. The firm produces at a rate greater than that indicated by the intersection of marginal cost and marginal revenue but less than the average cost minimizing rate. It accumulates inventories and then shuts down while the inventories are sold off.

Richardson-Vicks headquarters in Wilton, Conn. Richardson-Vicks's Latin American and Canadian operations will be merged into P&G's operations in those areas.

In line with P&G's insistence since the acquisition that Vicks would remain an independent subsidiary, the changes are evolutionary, "a blending of contours. In the year 2020, Richardson-Vicks will be integrated," said Hugh Zurkuhlen, of Salomon Brothers, Inc. Though some analysts have looked for P&G to get some efficiencies earlier by melding the two faster, Mr. Zurkuhlen says P&G is still "learning" by watching Vicks, as it often does after an acquisition. "They just have a longer time horizon than Wall Street," he said.

Analysts saw Vicks's international expertise as a particular boon to P&G. Vicks products have garnered substantial market shares, while P&G "is not an international powerhouse; it never has been," says Joseph Kozloff of Paine-Webber, Inc. But it isn't simply a matter of folding P&G operations into Vicks's because neither the products nor the distribution systems overlap. In Europe, for example, where the two companies' operations will remain separate, Vicks has personal care products, sold through pharmacies, while P&G has primarily diapers and detergents, sold through groceries.

Despite the merged Asian operations, P&G and Vicks will also remain separate in Japan, where P&G is trying to reverse large setbacks in its diaper business.

There are other signs of the expanding cooperation. This spring, P&G eliminated some duplication by transferring marketing responsibilities. Research for Vicks's products is now handled under four new groups that are responsible for both Vicks's and the parent's research. The companies are also buying media time together, television ads for P&G products, such as Scope, run with those for Vicks products.[12]

As this story highlights, consolidation of managerial talent can be an important force behind product line expansion via merger. Note that there was an integration of operations and that executives of the target company took positions overseeing integrated operations. Indeed, market analysts had anticipated that the two companies would combine operations; the merger plan was no surprise. Apparently, one of the forces motivating merger was P&G's desire to expand its European activities, a strong point in the R-V line. Even so, duplication of services was eliminated by the consolidation of marketing and research responsibilities of both companies. This case represents an excellent example of an intermittent production merger, in which managerial capital and organization are the underutilized resources prompting consolidation.

The new expanded product line company has several options for disposing of or using the resources leftover from consolidation. Liquidation is an obvious alternative, as is physical depreciation. The resources may also be internally converted for use in other product lines.

It is important to note that this consolidation does not erase the cyclical inventory pattern in each product line, even though it increases overall capacity

---

[12] Jolie Solomon, "P&G Takes Steps Toward Integrating Operations of Vicks Unit with Parent's," *Wall Street Journal,* October 16, 1986, p. 38. Reprinted by permission of *The Wall Street Journal,* © 1986 Dow Jones & Company, Inc. All Rights Reserved Worldwide.

utilization. After expansion, the firm still accumulates inventories in each product line, but instead of simply shutting down to draw off these stocks, it takes up production of other goods. Inventories do not decline to zero, although they may decline in all product lines. Because there is consolidation of resources after expansion, the new firm does not have the same production options that the old firm had. Specifically, the new, multiproduct firm has higher overall resource utilization. This means that the new firm is restricted in its ability to increase production when demand unexpectedly increases, and it is buffered from unexpected demand declines.

THE ASSIGNMENT OF JOINT COST

Most firms produce more than one product. Consider the simple example of a meat packing plant. Live cattle are purchased for slaughter, producing meat and hides. Is it possible to calculate profits separately for meat and hides? The answer is no. Slaughtering an animal necessarily produces meat and hides; it is not possible to have one without the other. Therefore, it is not possible to discuss the opportunity cost of just hides or just beef. Some might be inclined to say that having killed the animal and obtained the meat, the hide is free, but the reverse could be true as well. Having butchered and skinned to get the hide, the meat is free. Which version is correct? The answer is neither. Since beef and hides come together, it only makes economic sense to talk about the cost of the entire package, the meat and the hides. So, profits can be made or lost on the slaughter of animals, producing meat and hides, but it defies the principle of opportunity cost to discuss the profits from the sale of meat or hides separately.

Many inputs produce joint products. For example, in a single factory, many different types of toys might be produced, or in a retail store that does a lot of local advertising, many different items are offered for sale. In the first case, it is not logically possible, in the context of opportunity cost, to allocate the costs of the building construction, maintenance, insurance, and security among the various toys manufactured. Strictly speaking, then, profits cannot be assigned to the separate product lines. In the second case, if the advertising addresses the whole store, the entire line of goods for sale, the promotional budget is not apportionable. No one knows, or could ever know, whether McDonald's makes more money on its French fries or Big Macs. It is only possible to compute whether the restaurant is profitable or not.

THE MULTIPLANT FIRM

It is common for firms to produce the same output in several plants, but the costs of production are usually not the same in each plant. What does the firm do in this situation? Consider Figure 6.12. M_1 and A_1 are the marginal and average costs at the first plant. M_2 and A_2 are the costs in plant #2. The horizontal summation of the marginal costs gives the firm's marginal cost. If the industry is competitive, then the profit maximizing rule is to equate marginal cost to the price of output, p, and produce q_t total output. How is this output to be apportioned between the plants? If costs are to be minimized, then the cost of the marginal or most

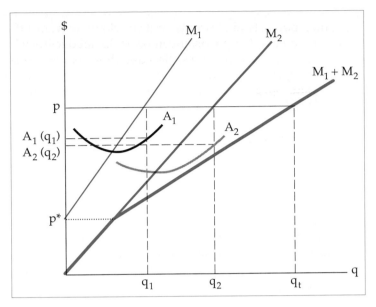

FIGURE 6.12
The Multiplant Firm

expensive unit produced must be the same in each plant. Therefore, production in plant #1 is q_1 and q_2 in plant #2. Note that average cost is higher in plant #1, $A_1(q_1)$, than in plant #2, $A_2(q_2)$. Both plants are currently making profits, but plant #2 is more efficient than #1.[13] Nevertheless, marginal cost has to be the same across plants or there is a profit opportunity. If the marginal cost of production were cheaper in plant #2 than #1, it would pay to shift production into plant #2 and away from #1. Only when the two respective marginal costs are equal is total cost of any given output minimized.

Consider the problem mathematically. Suppose a company manufactures a homogeneous product in two different plants; output at the first plant is q_1 and q_2 is produced at the second facility. Costs at each plant are

$$c_1 = c_1(q_1) \text{ and} \tag{6.1}$$

$$c_2 = c_2(q_2), \tag{6.2}$$

respectively. Assume all output is sold at price p. Then profits are revenues minus costs:

$$\Pi = p \bullet (q_1 + q_2) - c_1(q_1) - c_2(q_2). \tag{6.3}$$

---

[13] The rule of equal marginal costs holds whether price is greater than average cost or not. So long as price exceeds variable costs in each plant, it pays to operate both plants.

The first order conditions necessary to maximize profits are found by taking the partial derivative of equation 6.3 with respect to the two choice variables, output at each plant, q_1 and q_2. These conditions are

$$\partial \Pi / \partial q_1 = p - \partial c_1 / \partial q_1 = 0 \text{ and} \tag{6.4}$$

$$\partial \Pi / \partial q_2 = p - \partial c_2 / \partial q_2 = 0. \tag{6.5}$$

Equations 6.4 and 6.5 say that output at each plant must be selected so that marginal cost in the plant is equal to the price of output. In turn, this implies that

$$\partial c_1 / \partial q_1 = \partial c_2 / \partial q_2. \tag{6.6}$$

Marginal cost of production must be equal across the two plants. This theorem generalizes to any number of plants, *and it holds regardless of whether average cost at the plant is above or below product price* (so long as price exceeds average variable cost).

Last, reexamine Figure 6.12. If market price falls below p^*, the price where even variable costs cannot be recovered in plant #1, then production is consolidated solely in plant #2. At prices above p^*, production is split between the plants, keeping marginal cost equal across plants. $M_1 + M_2$ is the firm's short-run marginal cost curve.

TOPICS TO REVIEW

These are topics that you should feel comfortable with before you leave this chapter. If you cannot write out a clear and concise sentence or paragraph explaining the topic after you have worked on the study problems, you should reread the relevant section of the text.

Classical Analysis of the Firm

Property Rights Analysis of the Firm

Profit Maximization and Cost Minimization

Production Function

Short Run and the Long Run

Marginal and Average Product

Marginal and Average Cost

Fixed or Unavoidable Cost

Variable Cost

Cost Function

Long-Run Cost

Marginal Rate of Transformation

Efficient Input Use

Normal, Inferior, and Superior Inputs

Input Price Changes

Demand for Inputs—Derived Demand

Learning

Rate

Volume

Intermittent Production

Joint Cost

Multiplant Firm

STUDY QUESTIONS

1. Consider the following production function for a firm:

    $$q = 100L - L^2 + 200K - 0.5K^2.$$

    The current price of output is $2. The current price of L is $100 per day, and the price of K is $200 per day. Assume that the firm is a price taker in all markets.

    a. How much K and L does the firm employ?
    b. How much output does the firm produce daily?
    c. What are revenues, costs, and profit per day?

2. Suppose you have just been hired as the new production manager of ABC Steel Enterprises. There are three plants currently producing ½-inch sheet steel of identical quality. Total cost of production in plant #1 is

    $$C_1 = 1 + 10q_1,$$ *2 tons*

    where q is measured in tons and C is in dollars. The total cost function in plant #2 is

    $$C_2 = 10 + 0.5(q_2)^2 + 2q_2.$$ *4 tons*

    Cost at plant #3 is given by

    $$C_3 = 5 + (q_3)^2.$$ *4 tons*

    a. Traditionally, 10 tons of steel have been produced each period. Plant #1 has produced 2 tons, plant #2 has produced 4 tons, and plant #3 has produced 4 tons. You have been assigned the task of developing ways to reschedule production among plants to reduce costs, given that the output level remains at 10 tons per day. What changes, if any, do you suggest?
    b. You question whether output of 10 tons per day is profit maximizing. Suppose the current market price is $6 per ton, and the market is competitive. Would you change total output? If so, how?
    c. If your suggestions are implemented, what will profits be?

3. Suppose production is characterized by the following function:

    $$q = 12L - 0.01 \cdot L^2 + 0.1L \cdot K$$

where q is output, L is the amount of labor employed, and K is the stock of capital machines in use. Suppose the stock of capital is currently fixed at 10 machines and each costs $500 per day. Workers cost $125 per day.

   a. Derive and make a table of the average total, average variable, and marginal cost functions over the range of 10 to 500 workers.
   b. Graph each of these three functions.
   c. What is the minimum of average total cost?

4. Suppose production is characterized by the following function:

$$q = 100 \bullet (L)^{0.4} \bullet (K)^{0.6}$$

where q is output, L is the amount of labor employed, and K is the stock of capital machines in use.

   a. If there are 100 workers and 100 units of machinery, how much output is produced?
   b. If the number of workers is doubled, but the stock of machinery is held fixed, how much output is produced?
   c. If the number of workers is 100, the original level, but the stock of machinery is doubled, how much output is now produced?
   d. If the number of workers and the stock of capital are doubled from the original level, how much output is produced?
   e. What is the relation between output and average cost of production?

5. A company produces according to the following production function:

$$q = 500L - 0.5L^2 + 1000K - 0.25K^2 + 100E - 0.1E^2,$$

where q is output per month, L is number of workers employed per month, K is machines used per month, and E is electricity. All output is sold at $10 per unit. L costs $2000 per month, machines cost $9000, electricity costs $0.10 per kilowatt hour.

   a. What is the profit maximizing level of output?
   b. What are total revenues, total costs, and total profits per month?

6. Suppose cut flowers are grown according to the following production function:

$$q = 15000L - 0.5L^2 + 10000M - M^2 + 2000F - 0.1F^2,$$

where q is the quantity of flowers produced, L is the number of workers in the field, M is the quantity of planting and harvesting machinery, and F is the acres of land devoted to planting. Suppose the flowers are sold competitively at $0.50 a bunch. Workers earn $5000 per growing season, machines rent for $4000 per growing season, and land rents for $100 per acre per growing season.

   a. What is the profit maximizing level of land, labor, and capital?
   b. How much output does the firm produce per season?
   c. What are gross revenues and costs per growing season?
   d. How much profit does this firm make per growing season?
   e. How much output would the firm produce if the price for flowers increased to $0.60 per bunch?

7. Examine the regression output in Table 6.4 where several functional forms for the production of electricity were estimated. Using the cubic specification, determine the levels of coal, fuel oil, natural gas, and generating capacity where the marginal product of each input is equal to zero.

8. If a firm has two plants, one of which has diminishing marginal cost of production, it will always pay to concentrate production of a given volume of output in that one plant. True or false?

SUGGESTED READINGS

Alchian, Armen A. "Costs and Outputs." In M. Abramovitz et al., *The Allocation of Economic Resources.* Stanford, CA: Stanford University Press, 1959.

Breit, William, Hochman, Harold, and Saueracker, Edward, eds. *Readings in Microeconomics.* St. Louis: Times Mirror/Mosby College Pub., 1986.

Christensen, Laurits, Jorgenson, Dale, and Lau, Lawrence. "Transcendental Logarithmic Production Frontiers." *Review of Economics and Statistics* 55 (February 1973):28–45.

Hirshleifer, Jack and Glazer, Amihai. *Price Theory and Applications,* 5th ed. Englewood Cliffs, NJ: Prentice Hall, 1992.

Maloney, Michael T. and McCormick, Robert E. "Excess Capacity, Cyclical Production, and Merger Motives: Some Evidence from the Capital Markets." *The Journal of Law and Economics,* October 1988, pp. 321–50.

Portes, Richard D. "Long-Run Scale Adjustments of a Perfectly Competitive Firm and Industry: An Alternative Approach." *American Economic Review,* June 1971, pp. 430–34.

Silberberg, Eugene. *The Structure of Economics: A Mathematical Analysis,* 2d ed. New York: McGraw-Hill, 1990.

Stigler, George. *The Theory of Price,* 4th ed. New York: Macmillan, 1987.

SUGGESTED SOLUTIONS TO SELECTED STUDY PROBLEMS

The following are only *suggested* solutions to the study problems presented at the end of this chapter. In all cases, the suggestions here put heavy emphasis on analysis rather than a single correct answer. Since most managerial problems do not fall into neat little boxes, the individual characteristics of the problems that you will encounter on the job will typically mandate a solution using the principles developed here and in other courses. Memorizing these solutions will not make you a good manager; learning the *principles* detailed here will help make you a better manager.

1. There are many ways to solve this problem. Two of them are presented here. The long way is presented first. It has several steps.

   a. First derive the profit function. Profit is revenue minus costs, or

   $$\Pi = R - C.$$

   Revenue is price times quantity. In this case price of output is $2 and quantity is given by the production function. Therefore we have

   $$R = \$2\cdot(100L - L^2 + 200K - 0.5K^2).$$

Costs of production are the price of labor times the units of labor employed plus the price of machines times the number of machines used, or

$C = \$100L + \$200K.$

Therefore, by substitution of the revenue and costs equations into the profit function, we have

$\Pi = 2 \cdot (100L - L^2 + 200K - 0.5K^2) - 100L - 200K$, or

$\Pi = 100L - 2L^2 + 200K - K^2.$

The firm can choose the amount of labor and capital it wants. Mathematically, this means that we maximize the profit function by selecting the appropriate L and K. Call these L^* and K^*. That is, L^* and K^* are the values of labor and capital that maximize the profit function. These are found by taking the partial derivatives of the profit function with respect to the two choice variables, L and K, and setting them both equal to zero. These two partial derivatives are

$\partial\Pi/\partial L = 100 - 4L$, and

$\partial\Pi/\partial K = 200 - 2K.$

We set these two equations to zero and solve for L^* and K^*. This provides the optimal or profit maximizing level of the two inputs. These are

$L^* = 25$ and $K^* = 100.$

This solution can be found indirectly by noting that the necessary condition for profit maximization is that the marginal revenue product of each input must equal its price. The marginal revenue product of the input is its marginal product times the price of the output. In the case of labor the marginal product is the derivative of the production function with respect to labor, or

$MP_L = \partial q/\partial L = 100 - 2L.$

First we multiply this marginal product times the price of output, $2, and then by setting the result equal to the price of labor, $100, we also have the profit maximizing level of labor to use.

$200 - 4L = \$100$, or

$L^* = 25.$

Using the same technique we compute the marginal revenue product of capital. The marginal product is the derivative of the production function with respect to K, or

$MP_K = \partial q/\partial K = 200 - K^2.$

We multiply this times the price of output, $2, and set it equal to the price of capital, $200.

$400 - 2K2 = 200$, or

$K^* = 100$.

Either way, we get the same result.

b. To determine the amount of output produced, we simply insert the values of L and K that we have just determined into the production function. Call the profit maximizing level of output q^*. Then,

$q^* = 100 \bullet 25 - 25^2 + 200 \bullet 100 - 0.5 \bullet 100^2 = 28{,}125$.

c. Revenues are price, $2, times quantity, q^*, or

$R^* = \$2 \bullet 28{,}125 = \$56{,}250$.

Costs are

$\$100 \bullet L^* + \$200 \bullet K^* = \$100 \bullet 25 + \$200 \bullet 100 = \$22{,}500$.

Profits per day are revenues minus costs, or

$\$56{,}250 - \$22{,}500 = \$33{,}750$.

2. Let's work this problem using calculus.

a. First let's compute the marginal cost at each plant. What are the respective marginal cost functions in each plant? We take the derivative of the total cost function with respect to output to determine the marginal cost function in each plant. This yields

Plant #1: $MC_1 = 10$

Plant #2: $MC_2 = q_2 + 2$

Plant #3: $MC_3 = 2q_3$

At the current levels of output the respective marginal costs are $10 in plant #1, $6 in plant #2, and $8 in plant #3. The marginal costs are not equal. Hence, costs are not minimized. It is better to increase output in the second and third plants because marginal cost is lower there. Cost will only be minimized if output is apportioned across plants so that marginal cost is equal in each plant. Therefore, we must ensure that

$MC_1 = MC_2 = MC_3$, or

that

$10 = q_2 + 2 = 2q_3$.

Moreover, $q_1 + q_2 + q_3 = 10$. Since marginal cost in plant #1 is constant at $10 and exceeds marginal cost at the other two plants, we do not want to produce there at all unless marginal costs at either of the other two plants exceed $10 when we concentrate production there. So for the two plants we have two equations

$q_2 + 2 = 2q_3$ and

$q_2 + q_3 = 10$.

Solving for the two unknowns, q_2 and q_3, we have

$q_2 = 6$ and

$q_3 = 4$.

If we produce 6 units at plant #2 then marginal cost there is $8. If we produce 4 units at plant #3 then marginal cost there is also $8. Since marginal cost at plant #1 is $10, we should shut down that plant and produce the 10 units in the second and third plants only.

3. a.   Examine Table 6.6.[14] The first column is the number of workers from 10 to 500. The second column is output determined by the production function assuming that there are 10 machines used. The third column multiplies the number of workers times $125 to compute the variable costs of production. The fourth column adds the fixed costs (10 times $500) to the variable costs. The fifth column is variable cost divided by output. The sixth column is average total cost. This is computed by dividing column four, total costs, by column two, output. Marginal cost is the last column, and it is computed by taking the change in total cost and dividing by the change in output. For instance, when the firm goes from 10 workers to 20 workers, total costs increase from $6250 to $7500 while output increases from 129 to 256. Therefore, marginal cost is ($7500 − $6250)/(256 − 129) = $1250/127 = $9.84. Other rows are computed in the same fashion.
    b.   See Figure 6.13.
    c.   According to the table and the figure, average cost equals marginal cost between 190 and 200 units of output. Average cost is falling up to this point and rising afterwards. Therefore, the minimum is in the range between 190 and 200 units of output.

4. a.   Inserting the values of 100 for both L and K into the production function yields an output of 10,000 units.
    b.   Inserting the values of 200 for L and 100 for K into the production function yields an output of 13,195.08 units.
    c.   Inserting the values of 100 for L and 200 for K into the production function yields an output of 15,157.17.
    d.   Output is 20,000.
    e.   There are constant returns to scale in this production function. Thus, average cost is constant as output increases.

5.   First we determine the profit function, which is revenues minus costs. Revenues are price times quantity, and quantity is determined by the production function:

$R = pq = \$10 \bullet (500L - 0.5L^2 + 1000K - 0.25K^2 + 100E - 0.1E^2)$.

Costs are the sum of the inputs used times their prices:

$C = \sum_{i=1}^{3} w_i x_i = 2000L + 9000K + 0.10E$.

---

[14] The table was created using the spreadsheet by Borland, Quattro Pro.

TABLE 6.6 STUDY PROBLEM 6.3						
LABOR	OUTPUT	VARIABLE COST	TOTAL COST	AVERAGE VARIABLE COST	AVERAGE TOTAL COST	MARGINAL COST
10	129	$ 1,250.00	$ 6,250.00	$ 9.69	$48.45	—
20	256	2,500.00	7,500.00	9.77	29.30	9.84
30	381	3,750.00	8,750.00	9.84	22.97	10.00
40	504	5,000.00	10,000.00	9.92	19.84	10.16
50	625	6,250.00	11,250.00	10.00	18.00	10.33
60	744	7,500.00	12,500.00	10.08	16.80	10.50
70	861	8,750.00	13,750.00	10.16	15.97	10.68
80	976	10,000.00	15,000.00	10.25	15.37	10.87
90	1089	11,250.00	16,250.00	10.33	14.92	11.06
100	1200	12,500.00	17,500.00	10.42	14.58	11.26
110	1309	13,750.00	18,750.00	10.50	14.32	11.47
120	1416	15,000.00	20,000.00	10.59	14.12	11.68
130	1521	16,250.00	21,250.00	10.68	13.97	11.90
140	1624	17,500.00	22,500.00	10.78	13.85	12.14
150	1725	18,750.00	23,750.00	10.87	13.77	12.38
160	1824	20,000.00	25,000.00	10.96	13.71	12.63
170	1921	21,250.00	26,250.00	11.06	13.66	12.89
180	2016	22,500.00	27,500.00	11.16	13.64	13.16
190	2109	23.750.00	28,750.00	11.26	13.63	13.44
200	2200	25,000.00	30,000.00	11.36	13.64	13.74
210	2289	26,250.00	31,250.00	11.47	13.65	14.04
220	2376	27,500.00	32,500.00	11.57	13.68	14.37
230	2461	28,750.00	33,750.00	11.68	13.71	14.71
240	2544	30,000.00	35,000.00	11.79	13.76	15.06
250	2625	31,250.00	36,250.00	11.90	13.81	15.43
260	2704	32,500.00	37,500.00	12.02	13.87	15.82
270	2781	33,750.00	38,750.00	12.14	13.93	16.23
280	2856	35,000.00	40,000.00	12.25	14.01	16.67
290	2929	36,250.00	41,250.00	12.38	14.08	17.12
300	3000	37,500.00	42,500.00	12.50	14.17	17.61
310	3069	38,750.00	43,750.00	12.63	14.26	18.12
320	3136	40,000.00	45,000.00	12.76	14.35	18.66
330	3201	41,250.00	46,250.00	12.89	14.45	19.23
340	3264	42,500.00	47,500.00	13.02	14.55	19.84
350	3325	43,750.00	48,750.00	13.16	14.66	20.49
360	3384	45,000.00	50,000.00	13.30	14.78	21.19
370	3441	46,250.00	51,250.00	13.44	14.89	21.93
380	3496	47,500.00	52,500.00	13.59	15.02	22.73
390	3549	48,750.00	53,750.00	13.74	15.15	23.58
400	3600	50,000.00	55,000.00	13.89	15.28	24.51
410	3649	51,250.00	56,250.00	14.04	15.42	25.51
420	3696	52,500.00	57,500.00	14.20	15.56	26.60
430	3741	53,750.00	58,750.00	14.37	15.70	27.78
440	3784	55,000.00	60,000.00	14.53	15.86	29.07
450	3825	56,250.00	61,250.00	14.71	16.01	30.49
460	3864	57,500.00	62,500.00	14.88	16.17	32.05
470	3901	58,750.00	63,750.00	15.06	16.34	33.78
480	3936	60,000.00	65,000.00	15.24	16.51	35.71
490	3969	61,250.00	66,250.00	15.43	16.69	37.88
500	4000	62,500.00	67,500.00	15.63	16.88	40.32

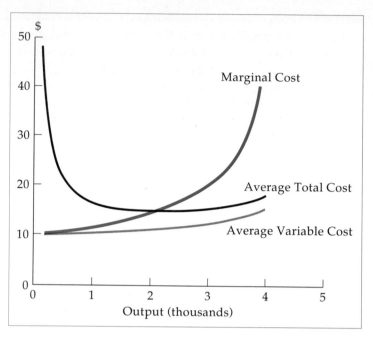

FIGURE 6.13
Study Problem 6.3

Therefore, profit is

$$\Pi = 10(500L - 0.5L^2 + 1000K - 0.25K^2 + 100E - 0.1E^2) - 2000L - 9000K - 0.10E.$$

To maximize profit, we employ each input to the point where the change in profit associated with hiring an additional unit of the input is zero. That is, we set the partial derivatives of the profit function with respect to each input equal to zero and solve for the optimal input use. There are three inputs, and, thus, there are three equations, one for each input. For labor,

Labor: $\partial\Pi/\partial L = 10(500 - L) - 2000 = 0$

which implies that $L = 300$. In the case of capital,

Machines: $\partial\Pi/\partial K = 10(1000 - 0.5K) - 9000 = 0$

which implies that $K = 200$. For electricity,

Electricity: $\partial\Pi/\partial E = 10(100 - 0.2E) - 0.10 = 0$

which implies that $E = 499.95$. Insert these three values for the optimal level of input use into the production function to determine the profit maximizing level of output:

a. $q = 500 \cdot 300 - 0.5 \cdot 300^2 + 1000 \cdot 200 - 0.25 \cdot 200^2 + 100 \cdot 499.95 - 0.1 \cdot 499.94^2 = 320{,}000$ units.

b.   Total revenue is price times quantity: $10•320,000 = $3,200,000 per month. Total cost is the sum of the input prices times their levels of use.

Labor: $2000•300 = $600,000 per month
Capital: $9000•200 = $1,800,000 per month
Electricity: $0.10•499.95 = $50 per month
Total Cost: $2,400,050 per month

c.   Profit is revenue minus cost, or $3,200,000 − $2,400,050 = $799,950 per month.

On the Estimation of Input Demand Functions

- Introduction
- Production Function
- Cost Minimization
- Input Demand Functions
- Cobb-Douglas Functional Form
- Joint Estimation

To better understand the relation between inputs and outputs and the impact of inputs on cost, let us reconsider the production of electricity. Recall that we have estimated the production function for conventional steam powered electricity using the fuel inputs and generators. These estimates were reported in Table 6.4. The data on production and input use for each of the states were reported in Table 6.3. Figure A6.1 plots one of the inputs, coal consumption in each state, as a function of the output produced in that state (total conventional steam generation).

It is possible from the data in Table 6.3 to estimate the demand functions for some of the inputs used in the production of electricity. Of course, each observation listed in the table is for an entire state, not a firm, but in this case, since there are but a few producers of electricity in each state, the problem is not likely to be serious. It is also important to control for any regional or firm differences in the prices of inputs. The data on input prices as reported in Table A6.1 were collected from *The Statistical Yearbook of the Electric Power Industry* published by the Edison Electric Institute. These data are self-explanatory except for the price of capital. The Edison Electric Institute does not report this information. As a substitute, the state regulatory allowed rate of return on capital was used to construct a proxy for the price of capital.[1] The price of capital is measured by one minus the allowed

FIGURE A6.1
The Consumption of Coal

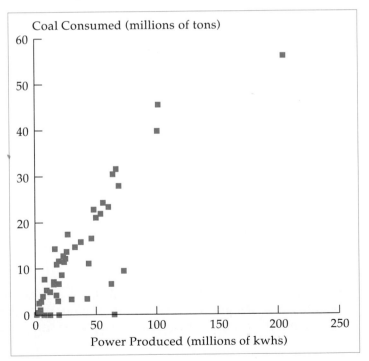

---

[1] The data on allowed rate of return were collected from Salomon Brothers.

TABLE A6.1   INPUT PRICES

STATE	COAL $/TON	FUEL OIL $/BBL.	GAS $/100000 CU.FT.	CAPITAL (1-RETURN)
Alabama	$52.25	$22.85	$337.69	0.875
Alaska	20.30	27.64	79.20	—
Arizona	21.77	28.67	407.21	0.85
Arkansas	30.92	33.41	306.02	0.862
California	19.65	44.61	526.47	0.85
Colorado	23.21	38.90	348.67	0.845
Connecticut	63.56	29.93	425.05	0.849
Delaware	48.37	30.52	421.76	0.85
DC	48.37	30.52	421.76	—
Florida	54.45	27.33	212.07	0.855
Georgia	45.42	29.11	380.88	0.856
Hawaii	—	41.53	—	0.852
Idaho	20.49	21.07	586.00	0.851
Illinois	42.85	45.97	480.08	0.857
Indiana	34.32	40.60	355.80	0.862
Iowa	28.94	32.35	355.54	0.875
Kansas	24.19	21.54	245.13	0.861
Kentucky	37.14	37.81	315.41	0.861
Louisiana	38.33	36.30	321.58	0.86
Maine	63.56	30.84	425.05	0.862
Maryland	48.37	30.52	421.76	0.86
Massachusetts	68.15	28.42	425.61	0.858
Michigan	46.99	35.79	252.24	0.865
Minnesota	23.22	21.65	288.90	0.865
Mississippi	57.10	35.69	301.98	0.86
Missouri	30.59	30.77	367.76	0.862

rate of return. The higher the regulatory allowed rate of return on capital, the lower is the cost of using capital. Thus, the proxy seems reasonable absent better information.[2]

Consider the general production function for electricity:

$$q = q(x_c, x_g, x_o, x_d)$$

where q is the total state conventional steam generation of electricity, x_c is the quantity of coal input, x_g is the volume of natural gas input, x_o is the amount of fuel oil input, and x_d is conventional steam generating capacity input (dynamos).

---

[2] From alternative sources, it might be possible to obtain data on the interest rate paid on debt by the various utility companies in each state. Arguably this would be a better measure of the cost of capital.

| TABLE A6.1 (continued) | | | | |
STATE	COAL $/TON	FUEL OIL $/BBL.	GAS $/100000 CU.FT.	CAPITAL (1-RETURN)
Montana	17.36	29.53	313.45	0.865
Nebraska	21.32	37.62	294.07	—
Nevada	27.05	27.23	435.80	0.85
New Hampshire	51.86	26.34	425.05	0.841
New Jersey	59.46	33.05	442.72	0.862
New Mexico	15.90	24.92	339.81	0.845
New York	47.03	30.20	435.46	0.859
North Carolina	47.29	37.13	400.85	0.858
North Dakota	9.44	34.27	335.29	0.867
Ohio	40.03	38.15	447.17	0.854
Oklahoma	26.97	20.22	212.81	0.847
Oregon	31.33	34.33	2382.35	0.848
Pennsylvania	41.05	34.41	442.77	0.842
Rhode Island	63.56	29.04	394.60	0.862
South Carolina	48.10	28.17	405.22	0.875
South Dakota	14.93	33.11	330.00	0.87
Tennessee	43.52	22.91	394.74	—
Texas	22.75	21.39	322.17	0.845
Utah	32.87	37.15	225.06	0.832
Vermont	29.14	40.55	568.22	0.855
Virginia	50.97	29.45	420.00	0.865
Washington	17.46	47.70	1390.90	0.847
West Virginia	42.48	42.50	410.00	0.855
Wisconsin	35.67	38.90	353.16	0.867
Wyoming	14.63	41.47	436.09	0.87

Source: Statistical Yearbook of the Electric Utility Industry 1983.

As discussed earlier, labor, an obviously important input, is omitted, and these data are not publicly available. From the cost minimization problem discussed earlier in the chapter, we theoretically obtain the demand curves for the fuel inputs and capital, respectively:

Coal: $x_c = x_c(q, w_i)$

Gas: $x_g = x_g(q, w_i)$

Oil: $x_o = x_o(q, w_i)$

Capital: $x_c = x_c(q, w_i)$

The w_i's are the prices of the inputs, and q is the total output produced. A question arises as to the appropriate form of the production function, which, in turn, implies a form for the demand functions. Theory is weak help here; the best guide is experience. The appropriate methodology is to investigate alternatives, using the data to tell us which form best describes the relation between inputs and outputs. Earlier, we estimated several different production functions for electricity. Table 6.4 reported these estimates. Arguably, the Cobb-Douglas exponential form is the best, and it is one of the most commonly used models for production functions. In the Cobb-Douglas functional form, each explanatory variable is raised to its own respective power. The demand functions obtained from applying the cost minimization technique with a two-variable, Cobb-Douglas production take the form:

$$x_i = x_i(w_1, w_2, q) = \beta_0^{-\frac{1}{\beta_1 + \beta_2}} \times \left(\frac{\beta_1 w_2}{\beta_2 w_1}\right)^{-\frac{\beta_1}{\beta_1 + \beta_2}} \times q^{\frac{1}{\beta_1 + \beta_2}}. \tag{A.1}$$

Assuming that electricity is produced according to the Cobb-Douglas functional form, the electricity firm's demand for inputs takes the form shown in equation A.1. If we take the logs of both sides of equation A.1, we have a linear relation between the log of the input and the log of all input prices that we can estimate with ordinary-least-squares. There is a demand equation for each of the inputs in which the amount of each input used is a function of the prices of all inputs and the level of output produced. We can estimate these demand functions using the econometric techniques outlined in Chapter 4.

Ordinary-least-squares (OLS) estimation of the input demand equations is almost surely statistically inefficient because, in all likelihood, the error terms across the demand equations are correlated with each other. For instance, a company that buys an abnormally large quantity of coal definitionally has a positive residual in the demand for coal. In this case, we do not expect that the error terms in the other fuel demand equations are zero. In all probability, the firm will buy less of one or more of the other fuels than the model predicts; one or more of the other error terms in the fuel demand equations will be negative. If this is true, then OLS estimation of the equations is statistically inefficient, and it may be important to take into account the across equation correlation. One way to reduce this problem is to employ the regression method of seemingly unrelated regressions. In addition, since there is a relation between the use of coal and the amount of electricity generated, the inputs are endogenous; that is, they are not independent of the level of production. Note that in the input demand functions, the level of output is an argument. This suggests that the input demand functions should be estimated jointly along with the production function. In this case, there is a bias induced into the ordinary-least-squares estimates of the parameters, and the appropriate correction technique is called three-stage-least-squares.[3] For all these reasons, the more sophisticated methodology is employed. It is not essential that you master the more complex technique here. This can be

---

[3] In actuality, the problem is even more serious than this, but the topic is beyond the scope of this text. See Laurits Christensen, Dale Jorgenson, and Lawrence Lau, "Transcendental Logarithmic Production Frontiers," *Review of Economics and Statistics*, 55, February 1973, 28–45, and Laurits Christensen and William Greene, "Economies of Scale in U.S. Electric Power Generation," *Journal of Political Economy*, 84, 1976, 655–76.

done in other courses and classes where sufficient time is allotted to cover the issues in detail. For our purposes however, the problems associated with ordinary-least-squares are sufficiently large that the technique of three-stage-least-squares (3SLS) is used and reported.

Table A6.2 reports the three-stage-least-squares estimates of the input demand equations for fuel and capital; the simultaneous, three-stage estimates of the production function are also reported there. You may wish to compare the parameter estimates of the production function with the OLS estimates reported earlier in Table 6.4.[4] First, note the own price elasticities of demand for each of the fuel inputs: coal, -0.8848; oil, -1.3649; and gas, -2.4662. The coefficients on coal and gas are statistically significant at the 1 percent level. The coefficients on oil and capital are not. Next, note the output elasticities (the coefficients on output): coal, 1.0026; oil, 0.7715; gas, 0.6696; and capital, 0.7942. According to these estimates, all the fuel inputs and capital are normal inputs. The output elasticities for each input are greater than zero but less than one. The coefficient in the coal equation is almost exactly one.

These results have some unpleasing characteristics. Several of the cross elasticities of demand are not estimated to be the same across equations; they should be. This may be due to the fact that the model is misspecified by the absence of an important input, labor. It could also be due to inappropriate specification of the form of the production function. Clearly, more work is required here before making any important managerial decisions. For instance, the cross elasticity of demand between coal and gas is negative in the coal equation but positive in the gas equation; the two coefficients, theoretically, should be the same. There is an important lesson here in addition to learning the skills of demand estimation; the wise manager does not blindly accept numbers or data thrown at a problem. Before trudging through reams of data with sophisticated computer software, the prudent analyst constructs a *theory* to guide her through the research project. Theory provides a bench mark when data yield apparently conflicting results; plus, theory can help identify inconsistencies in empirical results that require additional inquiry.

---

[4] In addition to differences due to estimation technique, there is one small additional difference in these results. Data are missing for some fuel prices for some states. In three-stage-least-squares estimation any state with any missing data is completely deleted from the analysis. In OLS, the observation is only deleted from the equation that has missing data. Thus the sample sizes are slightly different across the two techniques.

TABLE A6.2   THREE-STAGE ESTIMATION OF INPUT DEMAND EQUATIONS AND PRODUCTION FUNCTION—LOGS

INPUT DEMAND FUNCTIONS

DEPENDENT VARIABLE: LOG OF COAL CONSUMPTION

VARIABLE	PARAMETER ESTIMATE	STANDARD ERROR	t RATIO	APPROXIMATE PROB $> \lvert t \rvert$
Intercept	1.3371	1.2501	1.0696	0.2933
Log of Output	1.0026	0.0495	20.2178	0.0001
Log of the Price of Coal	−0.8848	0.1348	−6.5619	0.0001
Log of the Price of Natural Gas	0.1567	0.1369	1.1444	0.2615
Log of Price of Oil	0.2371	0.2819	0.8409	0.4070
Log of (1 − Allowed Rate of Return)	6.1483	4.9347	1.2459	0.2224

Dependent Variable: Log of Oil Consumption

Intercept	−7.5753	5.7892	−1.3085	0.2006
Log of Output	0.7715	0.2135	3.6132	0.0011
Log of the Price of Coal	2.2275	0.6202	3.5914	0.0012
Log of the Price of Natural Gas	−0.1445	0.6407	−0.2256	0.8231
Log of Price of Oil	−1.3649	1.3233	−1.0314	0.3106
Log of the Interest Rate on Debt	−23.5974	23.1093	−1.0211	0.3154

Dependent Variable: Log of Natural Gas Consumption

Intercept	−0.0782	7.6431	−0.0102	0.9919
Log of Output	0.6696	0.2830	2.3656	0.0247
Log of the Price of Coal	2.0793	0.8191	2.5384	0.0166
Log of the Price of Natural Gas	−2.4662	0.8455	−2.9169	0.0066
Log of Price of Oil	−0.4671	1.7459	−0.2675	0.7909
Log of the Interest Rate on Debt	−70.6326	30.4923	−2.3164	0.0275

Dependent Variable: Log of Generating Capacity

Intercept	−0.1612	0.5670	−0.2850	0.7776
Log of Output	0.7942	0.0251	31.5469	0.0001
Log of the Price of Coal	0.4235	0.0619	6.8403	0.0001
Log of the Price of Natural Gas	−0.0404	0.0609	−0.6633	0.5122
Log of Price of Oil	−0.0676	0.1246	−0.5425	0.5915
Log of the Interest Rate on Debt	−0.5839	2.1909	−0.2665	0.7917

PRODUCTION FUNCTION

DEPENDENT VARIABLE: LOG OF TOTAL POWER PRODUCED USING CONVENTIONAL STEAM METHODS

Intercept	−0.1113	0.2311	−0.4815	0.6336
Log of Coal Used	0.4502	0.0304	14.7958	0.0001
Log of Oil Used	0.0449	0.0075	5.9614	0.0001
Log of Gas Used	0.0150	0.0065	2.2905	0.0290
Log of Generating Capacity	0.6338	0.0460	13.7544	0.0001

CHAPTER

7

THE THEORY OF THE FIRM IN COMPETITION

INTRODUCTION

Chapter 6 opened a new section of material focusing on the neoclassical theory of the firm by introducing the concepts of production and cost. This chapter explores that material in more detail and introduces you to one of the bedrocks of economic thinking, the competitive firm. We start with some discussion of opportunity cost. We then apply the concept of profit maximization to the problem of output determination. After that the discussion is opened to include rivalry between firms. We begin with a problem for you to consider.

OPPORTUNITY COST

Hypothetical Business Problem 7.1

The following is an excerpt from an interview with the president of CBS Sports, Neal Pilson:

A growing problem for all networks, he said, is that rather than being spent with the networks, some money is being spent on signs in stadiums and arenas, bought because they will show up during TV sports coverage.

"The people who buy signs are clocking the time they're on TV and telling their clients," he said.

It really hurts, he continued, when one beer is sponsoring a game, but the camera follows a play right into the foam of another's sign saying "This one's for you" in letters 10 feet high (*Greenville News*, April 2, 1987, p. D1).

How much are the signs in the arenas costing CBS and the other networks? What can be done about this problem?

Cost is opportunity cost. The economic model contends that managers and other rational agents make decisions on the basis of the current alternatives, not accounting costs, sunk costs, the historical costs, or any other values. To put it simply, things are worth what you can sell them for, not what you paid for them. This paradigm is sometimes hard for people to grasp. Note the anger that many a shopper feels as he or she peels a price sticker off some good to find a lower price marked underneath. Some states have even gone so far as to consider laws that prevent retail stores from marking up goods already priced. The principle is easier for consumers to understand when they put a home they have owned for many years on the market. The price is set based on the current value of real estate, not the purchase price of the house.

Suppose Kodak, a very large consumer of silver, accidentally discovers a large silver deposit on some land it owns in Colorado. Silver is one of the most expensive inputs in the production of film. Will Kodak's discovery affect the price of film, the quantity of film produced, or the use of other inputs? By the reasoning of some, the price of film will fall because Kodak's cost of business has gone down, but this line of thought is flawed by the fact that Kodak could sell the silver it extracts from the mine for the current market price of silver. Hence, any time

Kodak uses silver in its plants, it forgoes the revenue it could get from selling the silver. The use of silver costs its price, even if the silver is cheaply obtained.[1]

Let's explore opportunity cost a bit more. Imagine a thought experiment. There are two nearly identical fast food restaurants. The first one, call it *A*, buys potatoes in the spot market. That is, the managers of this store buy potatoes straight off the delivery truck, paying whatever the prevailing market price is at the time. The current price of potatoes is $15 per bushel. Given this price for potatoes, the prices for all other inputs, and the demand conditions in their market, the managers have decided to sell a large order of French fries for $1.09. Suppose for the sake of our example that this is the profit maximizing price. No other price for French fries, given the current situation, will make more money for store *A*.

The second store, *B*, is otherwise identical, except that the managers here have entered into a long-term contract for the delivery of potatoes. Suppose that the price agreed to is $15. Since everything else is the same at this store, by construction of the example, the profit maximizing price for French fries must be the same as at store *A*. All demand and cost conditions are the same, and therefore, the profit maximizing price of French fries at store *B* is $1.09.

Imagine that the market or spot price of potatoes increases to $20 per bushel. This cost increase necessitates an increase in the price of French fries. Suppose the new profit maximizing price for French fries at store *A* is $1.14. What price will the managers of store *B* set for their French fries?

According to the principle of opportunity cost, any potatoes used in the production of French fries by the employees of store *B* cost $20. Why is this true? Under the assumption that potatoes are marketable, the use of them as inputs for French fries forgoes their sale, which is worth $20. Think of the problem this way. When the delivery truck pulls up at the back door of store *B*, the managers could say to the driver, "Leave my potatoes on the truck, and tell your supervisor to give us credit for the order." How much credit will store *B* get? Potatoes are currently selling for $20 per bushel and the wholesaler is just as glad to buy them from store *B* as from the farmer. In fact, given the long-term relation that the wholesaler has with store *B*, it would be foolish not to give a $20 credit. In all events, if the credit is not $20, the managers of store *B* simply pull the potatoes off the truck and sell them privately to some other establishment, a grocery store for instance, at the price of $20. In either event, the use of the potatoes prevents the store from putting $20 in its cash register, and in that sense, the cost of the potatoes for decision-making purposes is $20, regardless of the fact that the managers agreed to purchase them some time ago for $15.

It is worth noting that store *B* is better off under this scenario than store *A*. It is richer because it bought potatoes for $15 that turn out to be worth $20. But the fact remains, that even though store *B* is better off than store *A* when the price of potatoes increases, they will both charge the same price for French fries, at least according to the economic principle of opportunity cost.

---

[1] For an interesting and detailed look at how some firms react when input prices are volatile, see "Some Fuel Users Hedge Against Price Run-Up," *Wall Street Journal*, August 29, 1990, pp. B1, B5.

Let's put the principle of opportunity cost into practice. Reexamine Hypothetical Business Problem 7.1 and consider the following approach to that problem.

Suggested Solution to Problem 7.1

Mr. Pilson is arguing that the sale of advertising by arenas is hurting his advertising revenues, and surely it is, but that does not mean that CBS is harmed by the arena advertising. CBS must purchase the rights to broadcast sports events from the teams that play in the arenas, and the teams either own or rent the right to play there. Hence, if the arena owner is selling advertising and the advertising is hurting broadcast advertising, CBS simply deducts the cost from what it is willing to pay the sports team, which, in turn, deducts from its rental payment the amount that CBS subtracted. Put another way, viewers are the ultimate recipients of the advertising, and advertisers do not care whether they pay CBS or arena owners. The amount they are willing to pay is unaffected by who gets the money, and most important, the arena owners do not care whether their revenues come from CBS or directly from advertisers. So if advertising contracts and broadcast contracts are freely negotiable, then CBS simply reduces its payments to the arena (through the team) by an amount equal to its lost advertising revenues. Nothing real changes.

The arena advertising could be a problem for CBS if and only if it has a long-term contract with the sports team and pays a fixed sum regardless of its advertising revenues. Then, after negotiating a contract with a sports team and presuming that the contract does not contain a provision limiting the number of signs in the arena, the team can sell advertising space in the arena detracting from CBS's ability to sell over-the-air advertising. Of course, this is only a problem if the events were unanticipated by CBS, which even if they were in the past, they will not be in the future, according to Mr. Pilson.

In a nutshell, CBS owns the broadcast rights to the sporting events. They can charge advertisers directly, or they can charge them indirectly through the arena owners by paying less for the rights to telecast. Except for the long-term contracting problem, CBS should be indifferent.

OUTPUT DECISIONS

This section is designed to help you understand the basic theory behind output determination. Just how does a firm decide how much output to produce? Let's start by assuming that the firm seeks to maximize profits. Profit, abbreviated by the letter II, is the difference between revenue and cost.[2] Revenue is the price of output times the quantity sold, and cost is some function of output. Initially, we restrict ourselves to the case in which the firm sells all output at the same price.

---

[2] The abbreviation II is just a convenience and bears no relation to the mathematical constant 3.1416.

Formally,

$$\Pi = R - C,$$

$$R = p \bullet q,$$

and

$$C = C(q).$$

For the moment, let's consider the case in which the firm has no choice over the price of output. This is the case of competition. (In later chapters, we explore the situation in which the firm can raise price and not lose all of its sales.) The competitive firm can sell all the output it manufactures at the prevailing market price. It can sell none at a higher price. Let the firm be an agricultural producer of corn or wheat or a trader in foreign exchange. The firm must decide the output level to produce, but it need not concern itself with a pricing strategy. The condition necessary to maximize the objective function (profits) is that the derivative of the profit function with respect to q must be equal to zero. Mathematically, this means that

$$d\Pi/dq = p - dC/dq = 0,$$

or

$$p = dC/dq.$$

The **profit maximization rule** follows: Choose an output rate so that marginal cost equals price. What is the intuition of this rule? The owner sits at his plant—a cash register on one side and a production process on the other. Selling an additional unit of output yields the market price, p, in revenues. Manufacturing an extra unit puts an additional p dollars, say $2, into the cash register. Suppose current production is low; the incremental cost of the last unit that comes off the line is low, say $1. From the sale of that unit there is an extra $2 in the cash register, but only one additional dollar must be paid to the people and machines working in the plant. On net, $1 is left over. Even so, profits are not maximized. There is an excess of price over and above marginal cost. A profit opportunity exists; if one more unit could be sold, profit would rise by (approximately) $2 − $1 = $1.

Suppose more units are manufactured. In the short run, since marginal cost increases, it will cost more than $1 per unit to increase output. Suppose the firm produces 10 extra units. Now, the revenue from 1 more additional unit is still p, or $2; but marginal cost has risen to say $1.75 for the tenth unit. The firm now makes more money than before. However, even now a profit opportunity exists. But first note how much better off the company is by producing the extra 11 units. Each one generates revenue in excess of its own marginal cost. The surplus is profit. Therein lies the intuition of the profit maximizing rule; the firm expands until there is no profit potential left. The opportunities are exhausted when producing additional output costs just as much as the revenue from selling it.

Consider Figure 7.1. Suppose price is p_1. Assume the firm follows the profit maximizing rule and produces so that price is equal to marginal cost, q_1 output. Imagine that output was for some reason reduced to q_2. Even though average cost declines slightly from c_1 to c_2, the decision is not wise. At q_2 output, the extra or marginal cost of producing one more unit is m_2, but the extra revenue from selling one additional unit, **marginal revenue**, is equal to price, p_1. At output level q_2, price, p_1, is greater than marginal cost, m_2; a profit opportunity is forgone if the firm does not produce the extra units between q_2 and q_1. Similarly, if the firm produces more output than q_1, marginal cost exceeds marginal revenue, and it will have undertaken a losing proposition. Unless the firm produces where marginal cost equals price, there is something the firm can do to make more money, and anytime that is true, profits are not at a maximum.

There is one other situation to consider. In Figure 7.1, let price be p_2. According to the profit maximizing rule, q_3 is the optimal output, but in this situation the firm is losing money. Average cost of production, c_3, is greater than average revenue, p_2. (Price and average revenue are the same because each unit sells at the same price, p_2.) In this case, profits are maximized, but at a level less than zero; the firm is losing money on every unit sold. The firm continues to operate even though this situation is bad because, given price and cost, there is nothing better to do. Notice that price exceeds average variable costs; there is a surplus of revenue over avoidable cost. After paying the variable costs, some money remains to service the unavoidable or fixed costs of debt service, rental, maintenance, and

FIGURE 7.1
The Output Decision

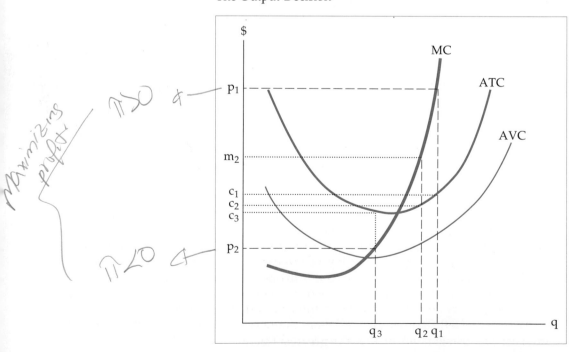

the like. In the short run, the firm experiences losses, but it operates; and in the long run, the firm must decide to close or wait for higher prices (or lower costs). The decision is based on expectations about future price changes.

The preceding analysis makes it possible to define the individual firm's short-run supply curve. The profit maximizing rule mandates that output be chosen to equate marginal cost to price. Therefore, at any given price, the level of marginal cost dictates the output of the firm; the **short-run supply** curve of the firm is its short-run marginal cost function.

Shutdown

The preceding discussion suggests that in the short run, if price is less than average *variable* cost, the firm shuts down. When price is so low that there are not even enough revenues to cover avoidable expenses, it is wise to temporarily (permanently?) cease operation. Consider seasonal businesses. During slack periods, revenues are inadequate to pay the workers and purchase the raw materials of production. In this case the firm shuts down, waiting for the return of higher revenues. Other examples include retail establishments that close at night or on the weekend.

Consider an example of two different types of firms. Suppose there are two mutually consistent ways to weave rugs; one is relatively labor intensive and the other uses predominately capital. Specifically, the first technique uses $20 worth of labor and an equal dollar amount of machinery time, while the second process uses different and more modern machinery. This mode uses $30 worth of machine time, not because it takes longer, but because the machines cost more, and $10 worth of labor. So, both processes can produce rugs at an average total cost of $40. Imagine that each process is capable of producing four rugs per hour.

Is one of these plants more likely to operate at night and during the weekend? The answer is yes. Suppose that sales during daylight hours amount to $160 per hour. Four rugs per hour cost $160 to make. Revenues equal costs; each plant breaks even. However, suppose that at night or on weekends, sales and hence revenues are much smaller. Say they are only $60 per hour. Since each process manufactures four rugs per hour, the labor intensive firm can only earn $15 per rug per hour operating at night or on the weekend. This is not enough to cover the avoidable costs of labor, and hence, the profit maximizing solution is to send the workers home at this time. The plant shuts down at night and on weekends. By contrast, the capital intensive firm, which can also earn $15 for each rug it produces at night or on the weekend, only expends $10 worth of labor during these hours. The $30 capital costs are unavoidable at this company, but the $10 of labor costs are avoidable. However, it is not wise to shut down; the $15 of revenues more than cover the labor expense. Spending $10 for labor generates $15 worth of revenues, leaving $5 to pay a portion of the costs of machinery that cannot be avoided in any event. This plant continues to operate at nights and on weekends, recovering a portion of its unavoidable fixed expenses at this time even though total revenues are insufficient to cover total costs fully.

We can make the generalization, then, that when differing production methods exist side-by-side, those using the greatest fraction of avoidable expenses will operate the least number of hours per day, week, or month, other things being the same. See if you can apply this lesson to the following problem: Suppose there are two universities. Their costs of operation are about the same, but one is better than the other because it has a superior, more highly paid faculty. Then, relatively speaking, the better school is labor intensive. Other things being the same, which school is more likely to have afternoon and night classes?

BREAKEVEN ANALYSIS

Breakeven analysis is the economist's trial-and-error method of estimating a firm's cost, revenue, and profit functions. It closely corresponds to the now common computer spreadsheet technique of what-if analysis. It is routine in a computer-generated spreadsheet to insert different parameter values into a formula and observe what happens to the equation: What if sales were 100,000 units this year? What would our profits be? Breakeven analysis incorporates revenue and cost projections to forecast profits based on various levels of output. The technique has its merits and its demerits.

Linear Revenue and Cost Functions

Breakeven analysis usually starts from the presumption that the firm can market its output at a given, constant price. This makes the procedure simple, but reality sometimes has other visions of a firm's sales potential. This weakness can be overcome by **sensitivity analysis**, the act of varying the price and observing the resulting changes, but nevertheless the problem persists because managers rarely know for sure what price their product will command in the marketplace. Moreover, some firms find it necessary to lower price in order to increase sales.[3] This further weakens the value of breakeven analysis. In spite of these problems, the technique can be used to provide crude clues about the relation between production, costs, revenues, and profits.

When we assume that the firm can sell all of its output at a constant price, the firm's revenue is a linear function of its output:

$$R = p \cdot q$$

where R is revenue, p is product price, and q is quantity. On the cost side, there are two components, fixed and variable costs. By their very nature, fixed costs do not change as output varies, but variable costs are tied to the level of production. Let C be total costs, F be fixed costs, and V be variable costs. Then,

$$C = F + V.$$

---

[3] These firms are sometimes labeled monopolists and are the topic of discussion in Chapters 8, 9, and 10.

Again assuming linearity, suppose that the variable cost is the same for each unit produced, v. Then, variable costs are given by the function

$$V = v \bullet q.$$

Profit is the residual of revenue minus costs:

$$\Pi = R - C,$$

or by substitution

$$\Pi = \overset{R}{p \bullet q} - \overset{\mathcal{E}}{v \bullet q} - F.$$

Examine Figure 7.2. Notice that the revenue function is a straight line (constant slope), indicating that revenues increase at a constant rate with output. The slope of the revenue function is the price of output. Similarly, variable costs are a linear function of output with a constant slope equal to the variable cost per unit. Fixed costs are constant. Variable costs added to fixed costs yield total cost, and they too increase linearly with output. Total costs are simply variable costs shifted vertically by the amount of the constant fixed costs. Suppose output were q_1. Revenues would be R_1, variable costs would be V_1, fixed costs would be F, and

FIGURE 7.2
Linear Breakeven Analysis

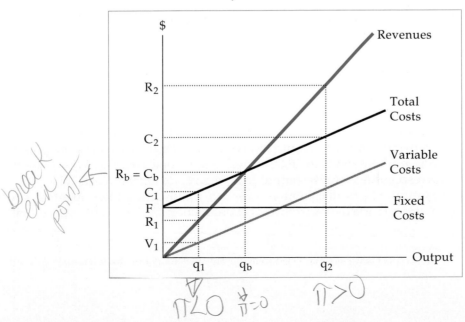

total costs would be C_1. At this level of output, total costs exceed revenues, and the firm is losing money. If output were increased to q_2 then revenues would be R_2, total costs would be C_2, and revenues would exceed costs. The firm would now be making money. The output level q_b defines the breakeven point, the level of production where revenues are just sufficient to cover all costs, fixed and variable. Unless the firm can sustain this level of output, positive profits cannot be earned.

At this point in the analysis it is easy to see the natural relation between breakeven analysis and computer spreadsheets. Armed with cost data on fixed and variable costs and a price for output, it is a relatively simple project to construct a spreadsheet that details the level of profits across a wide range of output choices. At the same time, it is easy to alter the cost projections and price forecasts to investigate the sensitivity of the profit projections to the assigned values of the parameters of the problem.

Relaxing the Assumption of Linearity

Let's loosen the restrictions on linearity to explore the output, cost, profit relation more. Suppose a company is considering the manufacture of a new product line, designer concrete blocks. The firm has estimated that it will cost $250,000 to construct a facility for the manufacture of the blocks. This facility will last for several years, and based on prevailing interest rates, the principal and interest payments for the facility will be $10,000 per month. On top of that there are additional fixed costs for office personnel, utilities, advertising, insurance, taxes, and the like, which add $5000 per month to fixed costs. Thus, fixed costs are $15,000 per month. Cost engineers have estimated that the variable cost of producing blocks in this plant will be $0.25 each up to the point of capacity of the plant. The sales manager believes that the blocks can be sold at various prices depending on the level of sales. In order to make sales in the outlying areas where the firm is expected to have intense competition from rivals, the firm must offer discounts. In markets closer to the plant, the firm believes that it can sell its blocks for a slightly higher price. Thus, in order to boost sales in the fringe areas, the firm must lower its price. The function that describes these discounts is thought to be

$$p = \$3 - 0.0001 \cdot q.$$

Table 7.1 is a spreadsheet-like table that depicts the levels of revenues, costs, and profits at various levels of output.[4] At the outset, restrict your attention to the first six columns of the table. We will explore the last three columns momentarily. The first column lists various levels of output for the enterprise, ranging from 500 units per month up to 20,500 units. The second column is the price that each corresponding level of output can be sold for in the marketplace ($p = \$3 - 0.0001 \cdot q$). The third column is revenues, simply price times quantity. The fourth column reports the variable costs of production ($\$0.25 \cdot q$). The fifth column is total

---

[4] In fact, the table was constructed using the spreadsheet by Borland International, Quattro Pro©.

| TABLE 7.1 | BREAKEVEN ANALYSIS OF CONCRETE BLOCK SALES | | | | | | | |

			FIXED COSTS = $15,000 VARIABLE COST PER UNIT = $0.25			FIXED COSTS = $10,000 VARIABLE COST PER UNIT = $0.40		
OUTPUT	PRICE	REVENUES	VARIABLE COSTS	TOTAL COSTS	PROFIT	VARIABLE COSTS	TOTAL COSTS	PROFIT
500	$2.95	$ 1475	$ 125	$15125	$ − 13650	$ 200	$10200	$ − 8725
1000	2.90	2900	250	15250	− 12350	400	10400	− 7500
1500	2.85	4275	375	15375	− 11100	600	10600	− 6325
2000	2.80	5600	500	15500	− 9900	800	10800	− 5200
2500	2.75	6875	625	15625	− 8750	1000	11000	− 4125
3000	2.70	8100	750	15750	− 7650	1200	11200	− 3100
3500	2.65	9275	875	15875	− 6600	1400	11400	− 2125
4000	2.60	10400	1000	16000	− 5600	1600	11600	− 1200
4500	2.55	11475	1125	16125	− 4650	1800	11800	− 325
5000	2.50	12500	1250	16250	− 3750	2000	12000	500
5500	2.45	13475	1375	16375	− 2900	2200	12200	1275
6000	2.40	14400	1500	16500	− 2100	2400	12400	2000
6500	2.35	15275	1625	16625	− 1350	2600	12600	2675
7000	2.30	16100	1750	16750	− 650	2800	12800	3300
7500	2.25	16875	1875	16875	0	3000	13000	3875
8000	2.20	17600	2000	17000	600	3200	13200	4400
8500	2.15	18275	2125	17125	1150	3400	13400	4875
9000	2.10	18900	2250	17250	1650	3600	13600	5300
9500	2.05	19475	2375	17375	2100	3800	13800	5675
10000	2.00	20000	2500	17500	2500	4000	14000	6000
10500	1.95	20475	2625	17625	2850	4200	14200	6275
11000	1.90	20900	2750	17750	3150	4400	14400	6500
11500	1.85	21275	2875	17875	3400	4600	14600	6675
12000	1.80	21600	3000	18000	3600	4800	14800	6800
12500	1.75	21875	3125	18125	3750	5000	15000	6875
13000	1.70	22100	3250	18250	3850	5200	15200	6900
13500	1.65	22275	3375	18375	3900	5400	15400	6875
14000	1.60	22400	3500	18500	3900	5600	15600	6800
14500	1.55	22475	3625	18625	3850	5800	15800	6675
15000	1.50	22500	3750	18750	3750	6000	16000	6500
15500	1.45	22475	3875	18875	3600	6200	16200	6275
16000	1.40	22400	4000	19000	3400	6400	16400	6000
16500	1.35	22275	4125	19125	3150	6600	16600	5675
17000	1.30	22100	4250	19250	2850	6800	16800	5300
17500	1.25	21875	4375	19375	2500	7000	17000	4875
18000	1.20	21600	4500	19500	2100	7200	17200	4400
18500	1.15	21275	4625	19625	1650	7400	17400	3875
19000	1.10	20900	4750	19750	1150	7600	17600	3300
19500	1.05	20475	4875	19875	600	7800	17800	2675
20000	1.00	20000	5000	20000	0	8000	18000	2000
20500	0.95	19475	5125	20125	− 650	8200	18200	1275

costs, which is variable costs plus the $15,000 of fixed costs. Profit is reported in the sixth column and is computed by subtracting total costs from revenues. Each of these functions is graphed in Figure 7.3. From the table and the figure you can observe that the breakeven point occurs at 7500 blocks per month. Revenues increase with output until sales reach a level of 15,000 blocks. After that, the effect of lower prices overwhelms the impact of larger volume. Maximum profit is achieved between 13,500 and 14,000 blocks per month, implying a price between $1.60 and $1.65 apiece. At this point revenues are approximately $22,300. Variable costs are about $3400. Fixed costs are $15,000, leaving a profit of approximately $3900 per month.

Let's run an experiment. Suppose a smaller plant could be built that would only cost $6000 per month in principal and interest payments. The smaller plant would require less staff, insurance, and taxes. Therefore, the other component of fixed costs would also be lower, say $4000. In this new scenario, fixed costs are only $10,000 instead of the original $15,000. However, the smaller plant has a higher variable cost of producing blocks; more labor is used. Suppose the new variable cost is $0.40 per block. How do these changes affect the analysis? The last three columns of Table 7.1 show the computations. First, note that revenues do not change. Revenues and costs are independent in this example. Variable costs are higher at each level of output, but total costs of the smaller plant are always lower (at least over the ranges of output reported in the table). The breakeven point occurs at a lower level of output. In the second case with the smaller plant, the firm can cover all costs at an output level between 4500 and 5000 blocks. With the smaller plant, maximum profit is higher, $6900 versus $3900, and it occurs at a slightly lower level of output. Of course, this does not mean that a smaller plant is always better than a larger plant.[5] As a general proposition, the optimal size depends on the trade-off between fixed and variable costs. In this example, the smaller plant saves $5000 per month on fixed costs but adds $0.15 more per unit in variable costs. If the savings in fixed costs had been less or the increase in variable costs more, then the larger plant could be the more attractive alternative. This ambiguity points out the value of having accurate cost estimates and the widespread use of spreadsheets to examine the options.

Breakeven analysis demonstrates the relation between production, costs, revenues, and profits. It can be used by managers to help understand the complexities of output determination. However, caution is in order. A number of simplifying assumptions make the procedure appear more scientific than it might actually be. For instance, the manager must assign cost and price data to the problem. Any analysis of this type is no more reliable than the accuracy of those assignments.

---

[5] Indeed, the analysis does not even mean that the smaller plant is better in this situation. We have not taken into account the possibility that demand might change in the future. When demand can fluctuate or grow, the investment of the larger plant might be worthwhile even though it does not perform as well at the moment.

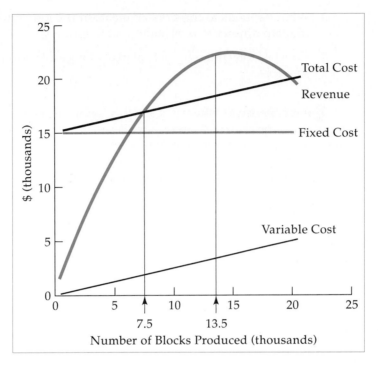

Breaк
even ⇒
TC = R

FIGURE 7.3
The Sale of Concrete Blocks

THE COMPETITIVE INDUSTRY

Hypothetical Business Problem 7.2

Consider two distinctly different tax plans for raising revenues by state government. The first places a business tax of $10,000 per year on all fast food restaurants in the state irrespective of sales at the restaurant. There are 1500 taxable establishments in the state. Total tax collections are (approximately) $10,000•1500 = $15,000,000. The second tax plan places a tax of $0.03 *per meal sold* at each restaurant. The tax on meals, $0.03, has been computed in order to raise exactly the same total tax as the first plan, $15,000,000 per year; each restaurant serves 333,333 meals per year, 6410 per week.

1. In the long and short run, does either plan affect the number of restaurants in the state? If so, does one plan have a bigger impact than the other?

2. In the long and short run, does either plan affect the output of the representative firm in the industry?

3. What happens to the price of meals in the long and short run under the two different tax plans?

4. Contrast total industry output in the long and short run under the two schemes.

The **competitive industry** is a collection of firms in which each firm has no control over the price of the product sold. In the eyes of some, the model is sterile: The firms are homogeneous; output is homogeneous; there are no transportation costs or information costs; and the model is static. However, the competitive paradigm stands as a bench mark for understanding numerous problems, such as the one that introduced this section, and moreover, it has predictive capacity in its own right. The model of the competitive industry is one of the most useful in all economic analysis. One would have to go back to a time before Adam Smith to find an economist who has not studied it in considerable detail. It is only through a thorough understanding of long-run competitive equilibrium that the student can analyze the problems of advertising, locational advantage, vertical integration, price discrimination, and the like.

For the firm in the short run, something is fixed. Typically it is the capital stock, the number of machines, and plant size. Additionally, when considering the industry, the number of firms is also fixed. The short run for the industry is that period of analysis where the number of firms does not change, and the firms cannot change all of their inputs—the capital stock is fixed for the firm and the industry. The firms cannot get any bigger or smaller physically, and the industry cannot increase or reduce the number of firms. For the firm in the short run, the amount of output supplied is determined by its marginal cost of production. Remember the profit maximizing rule—equate marginal cost to price so long as price is sufficient to cover average variable cost. Thus, in the short run, since firm size and the number of firms are fixed, industry output is determined by the short-run marginal cost of the existing firms that make it up.

In the competitive industry, all firms are **price takers**. This means that the price of output is beyond control of the seller. For the industry in the short run, total output produced is the sum of the individual firms' outputs. Correspondingly, then, since the marginal cost curve of the firm is its short-run supply curve, the horizontal sum of all the firms' short-run cost curves is the industry short-run supply curve. Hence, the industry adjustment to a higher price is simply the sum of the individual firms' responses to the price increase, given by the short-run marginal cost curves of each. To make this come alive, let's consider an example. Begin with the assumption that the marginal cost of the representative firm, m_i, is the square of its output. In other words, marginal cost of the ith firm is

$$m_i = q_i^2. \tag{7.1}$$

This marginal cost function can be stated in the reverse by inverting equation 7.1 and solving for q_i. When we do this the result is

$$q_i = \sqrt{m_i}. \tag{7.2}$$

The profit-maximizing rule says that marginal cost must equal marginal revenue or price. Therefore, if the firm maximizes profit, it follows that

$$m_i = p. \qquad (7.3)$$

The combination of these two equations (7.2 and 7.3) yields the representative firm's short-run supply curve,

$$q_i = \sqrt{p}. \qquad (7.4)$$

Table 7.2 describes the firm's output at several prices. The first column is price, and the second is the output as characterized by equation 7.4.

Of course, in the competitive industry, there are many firms. For the sake of this example, suppose there are 100 producers just like our representative firm. Then industry output is 100 times the output of the individual firm. This allows us to create the industry short-run supply curve. Mathematically, all we have to do is sum the supply curves of the individual firms. Thus, if we let Q represent the total industry output, then by the summation of equation 7.4 over all the firms, we have

$$Q = \sum_{i=1}^{100} q_i = \sqrt{p} + \sqrt{p} + \sqrt{p} + \ldots + \sqrt{p} = 100 \times \sqrt{p}.$$

Industry short-run supply is simply the horizontal summation of the individual firms' short-run marginal cost curves.

Let us generalize the problem to the situation where marginal cost is MC_i for the individual firms. For the moment, we assume that all firms are the same. Let n represent the number of firms in the industry, and let AC_i be the average cost of production for each of them. Figure 7.4 shows the costs at the firm level and the market at the industry level. Consumers value the good being produced by these firms. Let their demand for the output of the industry be the function labeled D_1. The market short-run supply is the sum of the individual firms' marginal cost curves. Since we have assumed that all firms are the same, the industry short-run supply curve is simply n times MC_i. This summation is labeled S_1 in the figure,

TABLE 7.2 SHORT-RUN SUPPLY	
PRICE OF OUTPUT, p	OUTPUT OF THE FIRM, q_i
$ 0	0.0
1	1.0
2	1.4
4	2.0
25	5.0
100	10.0

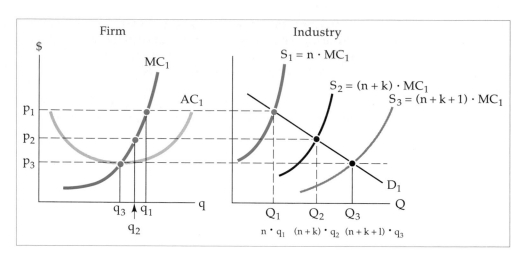

FIGURE 7.4
The Competitive Industry

and it is the market short-run supply curve. For this market to clear in the short run, the price must be determined by the intersection of the demand and supply curves. If price is not determined by this intersection, a surplus or a shortage will exist. Thus, the initial, short-run market price, determined by the intersection of D_1 and S_1, is p_1.

At this price, the representative firm maximizes profit by producing the level of output such that price equals marginal cost. In this case it is q_1. The market or industry output is the sum of the individual firms' outputs, Q_1. This sum is $n \cdot q_1$. Note that the industry elasticity of supply is the same as the firm's elasticity of marginal cost.[6]

As the situation is drawn, each firm is making a profit because price exceeds average cost at q_1 level of output. This industry is not in long-run equilibrium unless it is impossible for new firms to enter this line of business. The extra high returns available to the existing firms in this industry attract rivals, who, in quest of the above normal profits, desire to enter the industry themselves and set up shop.

Let us suppose that the industry is unregulated. This means that entry is not legally barred or controlled by the government. Further suppose that violence is not used by the existing firms to deter the entry of new rivals. If both these conditions hold, and if demand is expected to remain at D_1 or higher, then new firms will eventually enter the industry. When price exceeds average cost, investors outside this industry can make more money here than elsewhere, by definition, and entry occurs over time. As this transpires, the industry short-run

---

[6] The individual firm's elasticity of marginal cost is $(\partial m_i/\partial p)\Sigma(p/m_i)$. The industry elasticity of supply is $(\partial Q/\partial p)\Sigma(p/Q)$. The first term in the industry elasticity is just n times the first term in the firm's elasticity, and Q is simply n times m_i. The two n's cancel in the industry elasticity formula leaving the firm's elasticity of marginal cost. *Q.E.D.*

supply shifts out to the right. For instance, when k new firms have joined the industry, the new industry short-run supply curve becomes $(n+k) \cdot MC_i$. The new industry short-run supply curve is now S_2, and $S_2 = (n+k) \cdot MC_i$.

At this point, it is wise to pause and reflect on a couple of points. First, the introduction of new firms expands industry output from Q_1 $(=n \cdot q_1)$ to Q_2 $[=(n+k) \cdot q_2]$. The expansion of the industry by the entrance of new firms has led to greater output overall. But notice that individual firm output has fallen from q_1 to q_2. We know this because market price is lower, and when price is lower, output *at the firm level* will be less. How then do we know that industry output is actually higher? Again, it is because price is lower. According to the first law of demand, the customers will only purchase a larger quantity if price is lower, and thus a lower price must mean that a larger quantity is being consumed (and produced). The second point concerns profits. Why are profits present? The answer is that price exceeds average cost. We can readily see that profits, and hence entry, will continue until price equals average cost. If price were higher than average cost, there would be a profit opportunity for outside investors. The only situation in which price can equal average cost is at the minimum of average cost. Why is this true? Remember that the firm produces where price equals marginal cost, and for price to equal average cost, average cost must also equal marginal cost. This only occurs at the minimum of average cost. This simple result has a number of important implications. First, it is the free entry (and exit) of firms that makes a competitive market work. Second, entry (and exit) occurs by natural forces until all supranormal profits (or losses) at the firm level are erased. Third, when the excess profits (losses) are gone, each firm produces at the minimum of its average cost, at the engineering efficient level.

The following story from *The Economist* offers a sobering look at the entry and exit of firms and suggests that corporate survivability is far more fragile than normally thought to be true.

At about $22 billion, the market value of Microsoft, a 17-year-old computer-software firm, is now as great as that of General Motors, the world's biggest manufacturer. Many will dismiss this as a freak of the stockmarket. How can a firm peddling shrink-wrapped computer discs, with only 10,000 employees and sales of just $1.8 billion, be worth as much as the mighty GM, whose 766,000 employees produced cars and thousands of other goods that sold for $124 billion last year?

The answer is simple, but has uncomfortable implications. The value of both firms reflects the best guess of millions of investors about how much profit each firm will earn in the future. Even millions of investors could be wrong, and they might suddenly change their minds if new information comes along. Yet neither valuation is a freak. GM is still big, but no longer mighty. Its future looks bleak. Though Microsoft's shares were not even quoted on the stockmarket until 1986, its future looks dazzling. Many investors are betting that it is the brash software firm without a single factory to call its own, not the vast manufacturing empire of GM, which has the best chance of surviving into the next millennium.

This is not as outlandish as it might seem. Big companies assume the trappings of solidarity and permanence. Corporate headquarters, glorious or appalling, are always among the most ostentatious buildings in any city. Big firms spend lavishly on anniversaries, preach tradition to employees, proudly publish their own histories and generally behave as if they have been around since time began. Most people crave some kind of stability, so this is understandable. It is also something of a sham. The most remarkable thing about big companies is not their longevity, but their transience.

Most of the company names which now seem like immutable fixtures either did not exist or were still obscure when our grandfathers were children. GM itself dates back only to 1908. Britain's biggest manufacturer, Imperial Chemical Industries, was born in 1926, when a group of smaller chemical companies merged. . . .

Many firms which are now ubiquitous began even more recently. Sony, Honda, and Xerox are post-war creations. Before the war Toyota was a textile-machinery company. Even most firms that can claim a longer heritage—General Electric, Coca-Cola, Nestlé, Unilever, Mitsubishi, Philips, Daimler Benz—are not much more than a century old. They have managed to survive that long only by snapping up other companies and turning themselves inside out. RCA and Pan Am, once synonyms for innovation and business acumen, are gone.

Of the 100 firms heading *Fortune's* first list of American's 500 biggest companies, published in 1956, only 29 can still be found in the top 100 list, published on April 1st [1992]. Of the 100 biggest non-American firms listed in 1956, only 27 were still there in 1989, the last time the magazine published such a list. Within the span of one working life, well over two-thirds of the world's biggest companies were jostled out of the way by faster-growing firms. Many lost their place after being acquired by a more successful firm. Some simply fell behind. Others disappeared altogether. A clue to the future: in *Fortune's* latest list, three of the top four places ranked by sales are taken by GM, Ford, and IBM. Ranked by profits, their places are numbers 474, 472 and 473 respectively.

A future measured in months

The disconcerting truth is that, in business, history counts for little. No matter what a firm's past triumphs, no matter what its size, its future is assured only by an order book usually measured in months, sometimes just in weeks. If customers stop buying even briefly, the grandest of corporate edifices quickly begins to crumble. A good reputation and established brand names can help insulate a company from sudden shocks. But a new rival or a new technology can rapidly shift the ground beneath the best-known and most respected of firms.

In an apt phrase, Joseph Shumpeter described this as the "creative destruction" of capitalism. He was right to identify a propensity for continual change as capitalism's greatest virtue. Every GM in its death throes releases talent and cash for an upstart like Microsoft, which can make better use of them. The decline and fall of a corporate empire disrupts the lives of thousands. But propping up ailing giants, as governments everywhere are constantly asked to do, only delays the final deathbed scene, as well as the birth of the new. Companies are not enduring institutions. Nor should they be.[7]

---

[7] "Capitalism's Creative Destruction: All Companies Are Mortal, And Most Have Not Been Around As Long As You Think," *The Economist,* April 4th–10th, 1992, p.15. © 1992 The Economist Newspaper Ltd. Reprinted with permission.

Another point worth noting concerns the impact of new firms on the cost structure of the existing firms. When the k new firms come into the industry, they consume additional quantities of the inputs used in the production process. This increase in demand for inputs can cause the price of one or more of them to change. For the moment we ignore this complication, assuming instead that industry expansion does not affect the prices of any inputs used by the firms. (In the next section we discuss the second case in which industry growth changes input prices.) This constant cost assumption is important because it means that an industry can grow by the addition of new firms without altering the cost of production of any firm already in the market. In turn, we will soon see how, in the long run, this means that an industry can accommodate an increase in demand for its product without affecting the price of its goods.

Recall where we are in this analysis. We started with demand D_1 and n firms each producing with marginal cost MC_i and average cost AC_i. Under these conditions, price was higher than average cost, and k new firms came into the market. This pushed the industry short-run supply curve out to S_2, causing price to decline to p_2. This new lower price leads each firm to produce a little less output, q_2, but the total output of the industry, Q_2, is higher because there are more firms. This process of entry continues until the short-run supply curve is pushed out far enough to cause price to be p_3. At this new low level, price is now equal to average cost, and the industry is in long-run equilibrium. The new long-run equilibrium, industry short-run supply curve is S_3, and $S_3 = (n+k+l) \cdot MC_i$ where l represents the additional new firms that have come into the market. Now, because price equals average cost, there are no abnormal profits in the industry. No existing firm wants to leave the industry, and no new firms want to enter.

Several points are so important that they are worth repeating. First, if industry expansion affects the price of any input, then the firm's marginal and average cost functions will shift when other firms enter the industry. Second, if government or guns are used to prevent the entry of new firms, the short-run supply curves will *not* shift out in the fashion just described, price will *not* fall, industry output will *not* rise to Q_3, and the existing firms will make profits equal to the difference between price and average cost, minus any costs they incur preventing entry. Third, in long-run equilibrium, each individual firm produces at minimum average cost, and hence the industry produces at minimum cost. Consumers get their goods as cheaply as input prices and technology allow.

It also bears noting that this process of entry works in the reverse. If price were too low for the existing firms to make a normal rate of return on their investments, then some will ultimately exit. This departure reduces the industry short-run supply curve causing price to rise. The higher price increases the output of the individual firms, even while market output declines. This process continues until the remaining firms make sufficient money to warrant their continued existence. At this point we have a condition in which market price equals marginal cost equals average cost, the same result we obtained via entry. Entry and exit are the lifeblood and the engine of the competitive industry.

We have just developed the long-run supply curve of the competitive industry. Under the special circumstance when industry expansion and contraction do not affect the prices of any inputs, the long-run supply curve is horizontal at the same price level as the minimum of the firm's short-run average cost curve. When demand changes, price moves along the industry short-run supply curve, but the market eventually adjusts through the entry or exit of firms. This correction modifies the short-run supply curve. Ultimately, in the long run, a constant cost competitive industry adjusts to changes in demand, not by the expansion and contraction of existing firms in the industry, but rather by the entry and exit of new producers into the market.

To put this into perspective, consider a community or part of a city with a couple of fast food restaurants. Suppose demand grows. What will happen? In the short run, each restaurant will produce a slightly higher volume; the prices of hamburgers, shakes, and French fries will be higher. Typically the existing stores do not remodel larger. Instead, these higher than normal prices will attract rivals. New restaurants, remarkably similar in size to the existing ones, are erected in the neighborhood. The increase in demand has been accommodated by the construction of new firms, not the expansion of existing ones. Let us demonstrate this result more formally in the next section.

The Constant Cost Industry

Examine Figure 7.5. Demand is D_1. The short-run supply curve, labeled S_1, is the sum of the marginal cost curves, MC_i, of the n firms in the industry. The current price is p_1, and the total industry output is Q_1. Suppose this is a point of long-run equilibrium. Then we know that average cost for the firms in the industry is equal to price, p_1. The point (p_1, Q_1) in Figure 7.5 represents long-run industry equilibrium. Excess profits are zero. No firm wants to leave or enter the industry given the state of technology, input prices, and demand. Price is equal to average cost. The profits are just sufficient to keep the existing firms in business and not high enough to attract new firms into the market. We are assuming here that there

FIGURE 7.5

The Constant Cost Industry

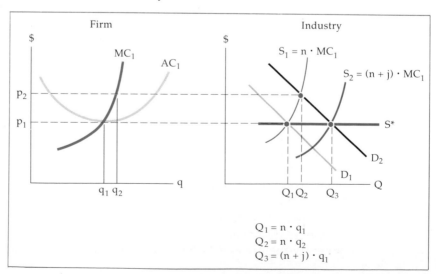

were *no* specialized inputs in this industry. The industry buys a small fraction of the output produced by the suppliers of its inputs; when the industry expands, the input suppliers can provide all the extra inputs necessary without resorting to price increases. This is called a **constant cost industry**.

Starting from the initial point of long-run equilibrium, (p_1, Q_1), suppose demand unexpectedly and permanently increases to D_2. In the short run, price is bid up along the short-run supply curve to p_2 where D_2 intersects S_1. The output of the individual firm increases to q_2, and industry output increases to $Q_2 = n \cdot q_2$. At this point, price exceeds the average cost of production; excess profits (actually quasi-rents, see next section) exist temporarily for the firms in the industry. However, these profits attract rivals. As these new firms enter the market, industry output expands, and the industry short-run marginal cost curve shifts rightward reflecting the additional competition. This process continues until the supranormal profits are erased, which occurs when price is again equal to average cost, p_1. Because there are no specialized inputs (by assumption), all this was accomplished without any changes in input prices. The original firms are right back where they started. In the interim they earned above normal profits, and they produced above normal levels of output. The industry started out with n firms; an additional j firms have joined them. The new industry short-run supply curve, S_2, is the sum of the marginal costs of the $(n + j)$ firms in the industry. The big difference now is the sum is larger because of the j new firms.

This means that point (p_1, Q_3) is *another* point of long-run industry equilibrium. The connection between the first point, (p_1, Q_1), and the second, (p_1, Q_3), traces the industry long-run supply curve, which, in this case, is perfectly flat, S^*.

In sum, when an industry is small relative to its input suppliers and when it uses no specialized inputs, the industry can expand without imposing additional costs on the existing firms simply by adding new firms identical in structure to the ones already in place. As we noted earlier, fast food restaurants seem to be a good example. They purchase advertising, meat, bread, electricity, bricks, potatoes, and labor. Intuition suggests that none of these is better suited for the production of cheeseburgers and French fries (or even chocolate milk shakes) than it is for a wide variety of other products. Consequently, all firms gravitate to a unique size (the minimum of average cost). Nonstandard firms are driven out of business because they have higher costs of production. Expansion of the industry is accomplished not by the restaurants' getting bigger, but rather by the addition of clone firms. In the long run, price is unaffected by demand. Demand determines industry output, not price. Minimum average cost of production determines price and firm output.

Specialized Inputs and Economic Rent

The preceding discussion is predicated on the assumption that industry expansion and contraction have no impact on the prices of the inputs used in production. When this is true, we say the inputs used by this industry are not specialized. That is, the inputs are equally effective at many other occupations outside this industry. Pencils are a good example. They are no more useful in banks than they are at accounting firms or universities. Electricity is another good illustration. It is used to produce light, heat, and air conditioning and to turn motors. Generally speaking, it is no more effective cooling retail stores than office buildings. In sum, many things like pencils and electricity are no better suited to one use than another. By contrast, some individuals are much better equipped to perform certain tasks than others. Jose Canseco is almost certainly a better baseball player than concert pianist, and surely the talents of Steven Spielberg are more valuable as a movie producer than as a certified public accountant. Certain types of land can produce some crops in greater abundance (cheaper) than other crops. The examples of grapes for wine and land containing underground oil immediately come to mind. Resources better suited for certain activities rather than others are said to be **specialized**.

Consider a simple pedagogical example. There is a town. Around the town, farms arranged in concentric circles grow agricultural produce for the people in the village. The land has no alternative uses. It is cultivated to the point where the cost of production plus the cost of transportation to the village equal the price of the vegetables in the town. Land farther away lies idle. Note Figure 7.6. Formally,

$$p_v = c_1 + k \cdot d_m \tag{7.5}$$

where p_v is the price per unit of vegetables, c_1 is the cost per unit of cultivating vegetables, k is transportation charge per unit of vegetables per unit of distance,

FIGURE 7.6
Specialized Resources

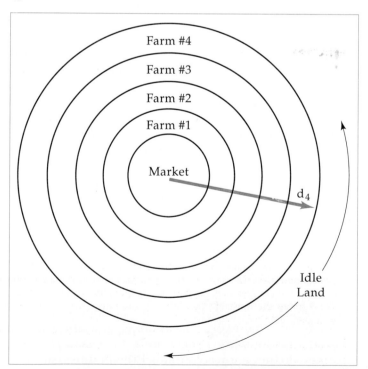

and d_m is the distance from the marginal farm to the market. Farmers cultivate the land so long as all costs are covered. The distance from the market to the ith farm is d_i. Therefore, on farms closer to the market than the marginal farm (farm 4 in the figure), p_v exceeds outlays on production and transportation. This surplus is called **economic rent**, or simply rent (purists call it quasi-rent in some applications). The rent per unit of production for the ith farm is:

$$R = (d_m - d_i) \bullet k$$

where d_m is the distance to the no-rent farm, the marginal farm.[8] Land is one of the best examples of a specialized resource, and it is easy to see how different pieces of land are better suited to one type of production than others. Indeed, often nothing more than location gives rise to the cost advantage and the rents. Of course, location need not be the only source of rents. Some land can be naturally endowed with more fertilizer, more rain, and so on than others, creating the rents.

What happens to the cost of land when the demand for vegetables grows? First, price increases. Suppose the existing land is being cultivated as intensively as possible. Then the extra demand will be accommodated through the cultivation of land currently idle. But in order for these farms to cover all their costs, the price of vegetables must remain high. Recall equation 7.5. Because the new farm lies farther from the market than the existing farms, the cost of production is higher. In situations like this, we say that land is specialized in production, and greater volumes of output cause price to rise permanently.

The Increasing Cost Industry

The basic difference between the increasing and constant cost industries is that one or more inputs are specialized to the **increasing cost industry**. When the increasing cost industry attempts to expand, it must purchase additional quantities of the specialized input; typically, larger quantities of the input will be less productive or more costly than the units currently in use. Consider petroleum refining. Presumably, crude oil is a specialized input to this industry. Imagine that the demand for refined petroleum products increases. In the short run, individual firms try to expand along their marginal cost curves. In the long run, the industry gets larger via the entry of new refiners. In both cases, additional crude is required (assuming that crude is also a normal input). But production of

---

[8] Actually, the problem is slightly more complicated. The inframarginal farms are induced to produce more output than the no-rent farm(s). This is called working the intensive margin. They work more laborers and employ more fertilizer to exploit their locational advantage. This principle generalizes. Think about the most talented athletes and musicians. They are the analytical equivalent to the inframarginal farms. While we expect the best land to be the recipient of the best seed, fertilizer, and irrigation, we also expect the best musicians and athletes to employ the best equipment and to practice the most. When an asset naturally has abnormal productivity, it usually pays to cultivate it intensively.

additional crude requires the use of lower quality crude (high-sulphur crude for example), crude more difficult to get out of the ground, crude from the North Sea or the North slope in Alaska, or crude in shale. Increased demand for crude oil puts upward pressure on its price because the supply of crude is upward sloping. Producers with high-quality crude or crude close to the surface earn increased economic rent as the price is bid up.

Higher prices for crude shift the cost curves of all firms in the industry. Again assuming that crude is a normal input, marginal and average costs shift up, but average cost shifts more than marginal cost. The new *minimum* of average cost lies to the right of the old minimum; efficient firm size has increased.

Consider Figure 7.7. Demand is D_1; marginal and average cost at the firm level are M and A. The original equilibrium has price p_1 and industry output Q_1. The representative firm produces q_1 output at minimum average cost. Imagine that demand increases unexpectedly to D_2. The individual firms attempt to expand along their respective marginal cost curves. Additional demand raises marginal and average costs of the firms to M' and A', respectively. These curves both shift up because the specialized input has increased in price. This means that the industry does not expand along its existing marginal cost curve, S_1, but rather along S_2, the sum of the new and higher marginal costs. Output of the individual firms increases but less than predicted by the original marginal cost, M. Each firm anticipates being able to expand along M, but, as they all attempt it, M shifts up.

So long as demand remains at D_2, the price of the specialized input will remain elevated. Even though this higher cost situation is permanent, the industry is not in long-run equilibrium. Notice the left panel of Figure 7.7. Price p_2 exceeds average cost, c_2, at output q_2. Excess profits are positive. Entry of new firms is invited. This has two effects. First, it shifts the short-run supply out to the right, reducing price and expanding industry output. Second, it puts additional upward pressure on the price of the specialized input, pushing a firm's marginal

FIGURE 7.7

The Increasing Cost Industry

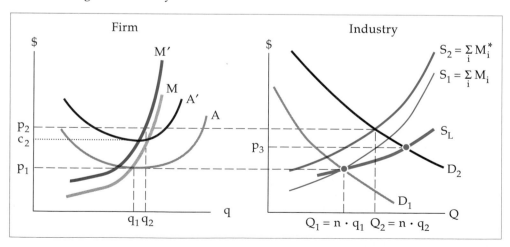

and average costs upward even more. These two forces work jointly until excess profits are erased, until the price of output equals the marginal cost and average cost of production. The eventual solution is a new point of long-run industry equilibrium which lies to the *right* of Q_2 at a price *below* p_2. The curve labeled S_L is the industry long-run supply curve, and it is upward sloping.

In sum, when one or more inputs are specialized to a particular production process, the industry that employs the input is an increasing cost industry. Growth in demand for output leads to long-run higher costs of production and output prices. It also leads to the growth of the individual firms (when the specialized input is also a normal input). Note that the *minimum* of the new average cost, A', lies to the right of the minimum of the original, A. Increased demand has attracted more firms into the industry, but less than the comparable constant cost industry.[9]

Follow the path of price over time when demand changes. It starts at long-run equilibrium of p_1. Demand grows, and in the short run, price goes up to p_2. In the long run, as additional firms enter the industry, price declines to p_3, but it remains above the original long-run equilibrium price. The original point and the subsequent long-run equilibrium define the industry long-run supply curve, S_L.

One additional scenario is worthy of consideration. Suppose the specialized input is superior; the output elasticity of demand is greater than one. In this case, the preceding steps repeat themselves with the following corrections. Now, marginal cost shifts more than average cost. The short-run price effect is more dramatic than before. Moreover, the minimum of average cost shifts to the left. Hence, once the new long-run equilibrium is achieved, the individual firms produce less output. Industry output still goes up because of the demand shift; the expansion is accomplished by the entry of new firms. Compared to the normal input case, there are more new firms when the input is superior. In sum, as the output elasticity of a specialized input increases, any demand change is associated with (1) decreasing optimal firm size and (2) declining industry concentration; there are more firms.

The Decreasing Cost Industry

The **decreasing cost industry** is analytically similar to the increasing cost industry except that one or more input prices decline as the industry expands. The reduction in input prices can come about in several ways. First, suppose there is an inferior, specialized input. Expansion of the industry reduces the demand for the input. Reduced demand for the input lowers its price. This reduces the average cost of all firms in the industry, and in the long run, the industry produces at lower price.

---

[9] The problem is slightly more complicated. The short- and long-run output elasticities of demand for the specialized input do not have to be equal. For example, suppose the specialized input is fixed in the short run. Then the individual firms *do* expand along their original short-run marginal cost curves because no additional amount of the specialized input is employed. In this case, it is only the entry of new firms that raises input price and shifts the curves up. In either case, the long-run conclusions are the same.

Second, if one of the inputs is immature in the sense that it has not been on the market for a long time, then, as learning takes place in the industry producing the input, its cost may decline to the others employing this good as an input—the downstream user. Hence, as the industry expands, more learning occurs in the production of the upstream input, and costs decrease for the downstream industry.

Third, a volume effect may exist. That is, as the industry buys larger quantities of an input, the input suppliers can adopt advanced (capital intensive) technology not efficient at lower levels of output. This lowers prices for inputs.

In all cases, if an input price declines as an industry expands, average cost decreases at the firm level. Marginal cost increases or decreases depend on the class of input in question. For the normal and superior input, marginal cost decreases, so the expansion leads to both short-run and long-run price declines for the output of the upstream industry.

The Heterogeneous Industry

Sometimes there is more than one way to skin a cat. That is, two different production processes may yield the same output. Over a wide range of input prices, different methodologies may coexist. For example, in the production of electricity, some plants use coal-fired generators, some employ nuclear-powered generators, and others use hydro-powered dynamos. Glass can be hand or machine blown. Tomatoes can be grown in a greenhouse or outdoors. Underground coal can be mined using massive grinding machines and relatively few miners, or with many miners and small machines.

Typically, the choice is dictated by some act of nature or a locational advantage in prices; it is difficult to build hydro-electric generators where there are no rivers or little rainfall. Relative prices at the time capital was purchased can dictate different input mixes. One firm builds its plants in 1970 when the price of labor relative to machinery is inexpensive—it is relatively labor intensive. A newer firm builds its plant in 1990 when the price of labor is relatively more expensive. The second firm uses different machines, those requiring less oversight and maintenance than the first firm uses. Overall it is capital intensive compared to the first firm. Yet both survive. Consider Figure 7.8. For simplicity, let there be just two production strategies, capital intensive, K, and labor intensive, L, but let there be many firms employing each method. The procedures have different marginal and average costs due to input price changes that have taken place since the original placement of capital. In this case we have here, the costs are higher for the labor intensive producers.

How is price determined in this environment? Demand is D. Short-run supply, S, is the sum of all the firms' marginal cost curves, M_L and M_K. The intersection of S and D determines price, p. Each firm produces the output rate where p equals marginal cost. The labor intensive producers each produce q_L, and the capital intensive firms produce q_K each. Total output for the industry is Q^*.

The lower cost firms earn economic profits or rents equal to the difference between price and average cost. What is the source of these rents or profits? It depends on the reason why their costs are lower than those of the labor intensive

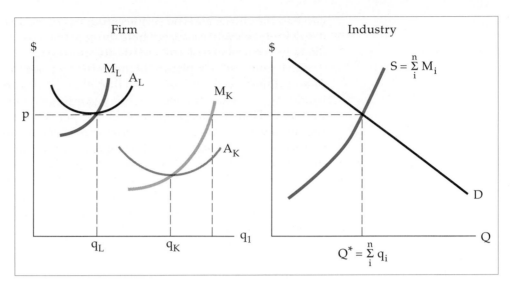

FIGURE 7.8
Heterogeneous Firms

firms. If there is a perfectly elastic supply of the inputs employed by the capital intensive firms, new firms will enter the industry employing this input mix in quest of the above normal rates of return available here. This will ultimately drive the labor intensive firms out of business as price falls to the minimum of A_K. At the other extreme, if there is a fixed supply of one or more inputs to the capital intensive industry, clone entry is not possible. The fixed input is responsible for the lower cost of production, and ultimately its price will be bid up by firms seeking to use it. Costs for the capital intensive firms will rise to equal costs for the labor intensive firms.[10]

Take a simple case as an example: One set of firms has access to a patent that some other firms have chosen not to purchase. Using the patent, costs are low (A_K); without the patent, costs are high (A_L). If the patent owner is wise, the price of the patent will nearly reflect the cost difference, and the firms will be almost indifferent between using the patent and not.

You have now been exposed to a number of important principles relating the firm in competition with its rivals. Recall Hypothetical Business Problem 7.2 and consider the following approach to that problem.

Suggested Solution to Problem 7.2

First construct the industry situation before any tax is levied. An assumption must be made about the structure of the industry. Is the industry increasing, constant, or decreasing cost? The analysis is not overly sen-

---

[10] In this example, there is competition within both classes of firms. In a different case, there are but a few, even just one, of the lower cost firms. This model, the dominant firm, is examined in Chapter 10.

sitive to the choice and the serious student will construct answers to the empirically relevant cases, but here the constant cost case is deemed most likely in the absence of any facts to the contrary.

See Figure 7.9 for a picture of the industry prior to taxation. The price of an average meal is p^*. Assume that $p^* = \$3$. The representative firm produces q^* meals per week (6410 according to the statement of the problem). That is, total revenue is $19,230 per week per restaurant. Since the industry is assumed to be in long-run equilibrium, average cost and marginal cost are each $3 per meal also. Total industry output is the number of firms times $6410 = 9,615,000$ meals per week.

Tax Plan #1: This plan imposes a fixed charge on each firm irrespective of output. Average cost per meal increases by the amount of the tax divided by the number of meals produced. Average cost at the representative firm i increases from A_i to $(A_i + T/q_i)$ where T is the amount of the tax ($10,000). *Marginal cost does not increase.* There is no change in the cost of delivering an extra meal. Hence, in the short run, there is *no* impact on market price; the short-run supply is unaffected by the first tax proposal. The firms lose money in the short run, and eventually, if the tax is permanent, some will go out of business. The reduction in the number of firms shifts the short-run supply backward to the left. This process continues until price equals average cost, at some price, let it be $3.05, and output of q_i'.[11] Total industry output is $(1500 - k) \cdot q_i'$ where k is the number of firms that left the industry.

Tax Plan #2: This plan places a three-cent tax on each meal served. This

FIGURE 7.9
Suggested Solution to Problem 7.2

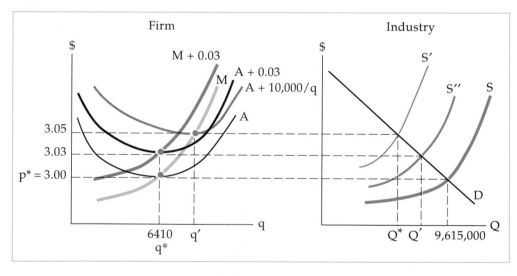

---

[11] The actual price is determined by the elasticities of marginal and average cost, plus the price elasticity of demand.

causes both marginal and average cost to shift vertically by the amount of the tax. In the short run, price increases *less than* three cents. For the price to remain constant, the industry would have to sell the same output as before the price increase; this violates the first law of demand. Output must decline as price increases, and since the number of firms is constant in the short run, it must be the case that the short-run price increase is less than three cents. This means that firms are losing money; price is less than average cost. If the tax is expected to remain, some firms will exit, and this continues until price equals average cost; l firms have gone out of business. In the long run, price is $3.03, and individual firm output is exactly the same as before the tax, 6410 meals per week. Total industry output is $(1500 - l) \cdot 6410$ meals per week (l is the number of firms that left the market).

What makes the two tax plans different? The first distorts the relative prices of inputs. The tax here is on firms, and hence the individual firms know that if they expand, the amount of the tax per meal served will be smaller. Put another way, the relative price of labor and meat, compared to taxes, has declined. The second plan does not distort factor or input prices. The amount of the tax, per meal, is the same regardless of firm size.

TOPICS TO REVIEW

These are topics that you should feel comfortable with before you leave this chapter. If you cannot write out a clear and concise sentence or paragraph explaining the topic after you have worked on the study problems, you should reread the relevant section of the text.

Profit Maximizing Rule

Marginal Revenue

Shut Down

Long-Run Equilibrium in the Competitive Industry

Breakeven Analysis

Production, Revenue, Cost, and Profit Relations

Constant Cost Competitive Industry

Decreasing Cost Industry

Increasing Cost Competitive Industry

Price Takers

Entry and Exit

Specialized Inputs

Economic Rent (Quasi-Rent)

Heterogeneous Industry

Capital Intensive

Labor Intensive

STUDY PROBLEMS

1. Several years ago Congress raised the tax on cigarettes from $4/1000 to $8/1000. Suppose that tobacco land is a specialized input to the production of cigarettes. What impact did the tax increase have on

    a. The quantity of cigarettes bought and sold
    b. The price of cigarettes
    c. The output per firm in the cigarette producing industry
    d. The price of tobacco

2. Crude oil is a normal input to the petrochemical refining industry. Assume that crude oil is produced with constant returns to scale but that increased output requires drilling deeper. That is, drilling costs for an additional foot are the same at 100 feet as they are at 10,000 feet. The current price of crude is p per barrel. Suppose the federal government imposes a tax of $\$b$ per barrel on the production of crude oil. Assume that gasoline is the only output of the petrochemical refining industry. What will happen to the price of *gas*, the output per firm, and the number of petrochemical refiners in the long and short run?

3. Two alternative proposals for protecting current producers of good X are being debated in city hall. Proposal A is simply to bar entry of new firms completely. Proposal B calls for (1) a tax on new entrants of $\$k$ per unit produced and (2) a subsidy of $\$s$ per unit of X consumed to all demanders of X. Current producers are evaluating these alternative proposals in light of reliable forecasts that the market demand for X will increase over the next few years. Optimistic producers expect this demand increase to be substantial while pessimists expect the increase to be trivial. Can you predict which proposal the optimists prefer and which one the pessimists prefer?

4. Suppose your firm has the opportunity to purchase either of two drugstores. One is the only drugstore in a small town and the building inspector there has guaranteed that no additional drugstores will be permitted. The second is a drugstore in a large city where there are hundreds of competitors. Is the purchase of the monopoly store the better decision?

5. Over the past decade, the state of Georgia has extensively renovated the highway system in and around Atlanta. This has considerably reduced the time necessary to travel from the suburbs to downtown. Who benefits from this construction?

6. You are the manager of a large corporate farm. You have farms located throughout several midwestern states. You have a production quota assigned from your boss. If you produce a given volume of wheat in such a way that the average cost of wheat per bushel is $4.50 at each farm under your control, will you have minimized the total cost of wheat production?

7. Throughout Europe, banks and stores convert currencies from one to another. Most of these establishments post the prices of various currencies in terms of the local currency. Rates change frequently. For example, in June 1987, in Venice, Italy, one store devoted exclusively to currency conversion

offered to sell 1280 lire for 1 $U.S. during the day (10 A.M.–5 P.M.), when other change stores and commercial banks were open and in competition. However, when the other change stores and banks closed for the evening, this particular change store increased the price of lire to 1240 per 1 $U.S. A similar phenomenon existed in Interlaken, Switzerland. There a commercial bank offered to sell 1.48 Swiss francs for 1 $U.S. during regular business hours, but when other banks closed, this bank (Credit Suisse) kept one window open for currency exchange purposes only, and it increased the price of francs, only offering 1.42 for 1 $U.S. In both cases, a similar phenomenon exists for other currencies: During the evening hours a purchaser of the local currency gets less money than a purchaser during the daytime. Why do these currency exchange establishments change the price of converting into the local currency during the evening hours?

8. Midwest Media Inc. is a broadcasting firm that owns and operates radio and television stations in the Midwest. The firm is currently considering the purchase of a proximate fast food chain that is experiencing financial difficulty. One group of Midwest's managers strongly supports the proposed acquisition on two grounds. First, they assert that radio and television advertising is crucial to the profitable operation of a fast food chain, and all managers responsible for the ultimate decision agree with this assertion. Second, the group in favor argues that since Midwest owns radio and television stations, it can purchase advertising for the fast food restaurants at cost rather than the regular retail price charged the current owners of the hamburger joints. Since this crucial input can be purchased for less, the group supporting acquisition argues the chain could be operated profitably under Midwest supervision. Critically evaluate the arguments in favor of acquisition.

9. Suppose a local company has a patent on a certain type of petroleum refining. It uses the process itself to produce several specialty oils. It also licenses other firms to use the process for a fixed annual fee of F. Since the other companies must pay the extra charge for the license, relative to the patent owner, their costs of production are higher. Hence, the local company will sell its product for a lower price than its rivals. True or false?

10. Imagine there are 100 firms in a competitive industry. Each produces an output, q, using labor, L, and capital, K, according to the following short-run production function:

$q = 5 + 4L - 0.25L^2 + K.$

Each firm currently has five units of K. The price of each worker is $50 per day. The price of capital, K, is $100 per day. Suppose the industry is in long- and short-run equilibrium.

a. How much output does each individual firm produce?
b. How much output does the entire industry produce?
c. What is the price of output in this industry?

11. Suppose a constant cost, competitive industry is in short- and long-run

equilibrium. Consider two different scenarios. In the first case a normal, variable input to the production process increases in price.

a.   What happens to industry price and output in the short run?
b.   What happens to output per firm in the short run?
c.   What happens to industry price and output in the long run?
d.   What happens to firm output in the long run?
e.   What happens to the number of firms in the industry in the long run? Now, as the second part of the problem, suppose a normal, *fixed* input increases in price. Are the answers to questions a–e different? If so, how and in what direction?

12. Many Latin American countries are having financial difficulties at this time. For instance, the Guatemalan government is running short of money and is thinking of ways to increase its revenues. Two slightly different proposals are being debated to accomplish this goal. The first plan imposes a Q1 (a Q is a Quetzal, the Guatemalan currency, and is currently worth about $0.25 U.S.) tax on each gallon of gasoline sold in the country. Since there are about 5 million gallons of gasoline sold each day in Guatemala, this plan will raise about 4 million Quetzals (accounting for the decrease in consumption caused by the higher price). The second plan is designed to raise *exactly* the same amount of revenue by placing a tax on stations that sell gasoline without placing any additional tax on gas itself. At present there are approximately 4000 stations selling gasoline in the country, and consequently the proposed tax on stations is to be 4,000,000/4000 or Q1000 per station per day. *In the short run,*

a.   Which plan will have the greater impact on the price of gasoline?
b.   Which plan will have the greater impact on the amount of gasoline sold per station?

13. Arguably, Michael Jordan is currently the most talented basketball player in the world. On his team, and others around the National Basketball Association, there are a number of players who get very little playing time. They are similar to bench warmers in major league baseball who play part of the season in the big leagues and part in the minors, never quite reaching greatness. Typically speaking, Who practices more? Jordan or the bench warmer? Who lifts weights more intensively?

14. Suppose labor is a normal, but not superior, input to the production of education.

a.   In the short run, what do professorial wage rate increases do to tuition?
b.   In the short run, what do professorial wage rate increases do to the number of colleges in the land?
c.   In the long run, what do professorial wage rate increases do to tuition and the number of colleges?
d.   In the long run, what do professorial wage rate increases do the average enrollment at colleges?
e.   If professors were a superior input to education, how would your answers to a–c be changed?

SUGGESTED READINGS

Breit, William, Hochman, Harold, and Saueracker, Edward, eds. *Readings in Microeconomics.* St. Louis: Times Mirror/Mosby College Pub., 1986.

Hirshleifer, Jack and Glazer, Amihai. *Price Theory and Applications*, 5th ed. Englewood Cliffs, NJ: Prentice Hall, 1992.

Patinkin, Don. "Multiple-Plant Firms, Cartels, and Imperfect Competition." *Quarterly Journal of Economics* (February 1947):173–205.

Silberberg, Eugene. *The Structure of Economics: A Mathematical Analysis*, 2d ed. New York: McGraw Hill, 1990.

Stigler, George. *The Theory of Price*, 4th ed. New York: Macmillan, 1987.

SUGGESTED SOLUTIONS TO SELECTED STUDY PROBLEMS

The following are only *suggested* solutions to the study problems presented at the end of this chapter. In all cases, the suggestions here put heavy emphasis on analysis rather than a single correct answer. Since most managerial problems do not fall into neat little boxes, the individual characteristics of the problems that you will encounter on the job will typically mandate a solution using the principles developed here and in other courses. Memorizing these solutions will not make you a good manager; learning the *principles* detailed here will help make you a better manager.

1. a,b. An increase in the tax on cigarettes increases the cost of production. As a consequence, the supply of cigarettes falls (shifts to the left). A reduction in supply causes the equilibrium price of cigarettes to rise (but less than the increase in the tax). Also, the quantity bought and sold decreases (price increases, *ceteris paribus*, cause quantity demanded to decrease).

   c. The correct answer here depends on the structure of the cigarette producing industry. If the industry is constant cost, then there is no impact on the output per firm. Marginal and average cost of production shift vertically by the amount of the tax increase. Therefore, the optimal output per firm, the average cost minimizing level of output per firm is unaltered by the tax. The total reduction of output in the industry in this case is accomplished by a reduction in the number of producers. Some sellers exit the market. By contrast, it is more likely that there are specialized inputs to the production of cigarettes, specifically, land on which tobacco is grown. Hence, since total industry output decreases because of the tax, the price of the specialized input, tobacco (and land on which tobacco is grown) decreases. Thus, part of the tax shifts from cigarette producers to the sellers and producers of the specialized input tobacco. But now, with the price of tobacco falling, we must know whether tobacco is a normal, inferior, or superior input to the production of cigarettes before we can answer the ultimate question of what happens to output per firm in the cigarette producing industry. If tobacco is a normal or superior input (and given the nature of the product, almost surely it is), then the decline in the price of tobacco reduces the marginal and average cost of producing cigarettes. Thus, optimal firm size, the level of output that minimizes average cost is now *greater* than before. In the case where tobacco is a specialized input and it is either normal or superior in the production of cigarettes, the firms that remain in the production of cigarettes are actually larger than they were before the tax increases. Of course, since overall industry output has to decline in the face of the higher price, this implies that there must be fewer producers in the industry.

3. First analyze the case in which demand does not increase by any substantial portion. In this case, there are not likely to be any new producers regardless of the tax situation, so the tax on new producers does not affect the current sellers of the good. Thus, the pessimists, those who anticipate a trivial increase in demand over the next few years, are inclined to favor the subsidy on the buyer's side. A subsidy to buyers increases demand for the good being sold, and hence, if there are any specialized inputs earning rents or quasi-rents in the industry, the increase in demand occasioned by the subsidy will drive up the price of the specialized factors of production, making the owners richer. For static demand situations, the subsidy to buyers is preferred. Of course, if there are no specialized inputs and the industry is constant cost, the subsidy will not increase profits, but instead it will only cause extra firms to enter the industry. Short-run rents can be earned by the incumbent sellers, but these excess returns are only transitory (unless, of course, the city government uses zoning or other laws to prevent the entry of new firms).

   Optimistic producers, those who think demand will grow in large measure over the next few years are more inclined to support the tax on new producers. As demand increases, in the short run, price increases along the short run supply curve (the sum of the short run marginal cost curves of the firms currently in the industry). In the long run and with free entry, new firms come into the market driving price back down toward the zero-profit price, the minimum of average cost. However, if entry of new firms is impeded by the tax, fewer firms will enter. Zero profits for the entering firms occurs where the average cost of production *plus the tax* equals the market price. Since the old producers, the grandfathers as they are known, do not have to pay the tax, for them, price is always higher than average cost by the amount of the tax. They earn economic profits on what are more properly costed as rents for the right to produce without having to pay a tax. Presumably this rental payment is a reward for lobbying, bribes, and political action. In this sense the profits are simply a return on that political investment.

4. The purchase of the monopoly store is only a better buy if the sellers are fools. If the current owners of the monopoly store show good judgment, they will include in the selling price the current discounted value of all future monopoly rents. Thus, any buyer should expect to only earn a normal rate of return. Put another way, the prospective buyer must pay *up-front* for the monopoly profits. The current owner has the monopoly and will charge a price to include the future stream of excess profits.

5. This question concerns the issue of economic rents. The beneficiaries will be those individuals whose assets are made more valuable by the highway construction. They are too many to list, but the primary recipients will be land owners with proximate access to the new highways. People in the outlying regions who can now develop their land for homes and businesses because people can reasonably get to their property from the city are one group. Others include inner city land owners who now can rent or sell their property for higher prices because the new highways make it cheaper to travel to their location.

6. To minimize the total cost of producing a given volume of output, the *marginal* cost of production must be the same in each farm. Unless the farms all have the same cost structure, minimizing the average cost of production will not equate the marginal cost of production across farms.

7. The cheap, but sadly incorrect, answer to this question is to say the absence of competition in the night causes the higher prices. This cannot be right. If profits were above normal during the night, the businesses that are open during the day would remain open at night too. The rate of profit at night must be the same as during the day or the day stores would open at night too. Therefore, since price is higher at night, but profits are not, costs of production must be higher in the evening. There might be many reasons for this. Security may be more expensive at night; labor may cost more during the evening. The only way that the price is higher at night due to the absence of competition would be if there are regulations requiring banks to close at night, leaving the market to foreign exchange specialists.

8. Using the concept of opportunity cost, the cost of running ads on TV stations is not affected by the ownership of a fast food chain. An ad costs the revenues that could have been earned by running another ad.

9. False. The company that owns the patent and uses the process to manufacture must include the opportunity cost of the patent in its cost calculations. If the patent costs are properly included in the owner's cost of production, then its costs are the same as all its rivals. The patent cost of production should be included because there is an opportunity cost. If the parent company, the company that owns the patent, did *not* use the patent rights itself, they could be sold to another company. Or put another way, the price the patent-owning company can charge for the patent surely depends on the number it sells. Hence, by using the patent itself, it forgoes higher revenues from all the firms who do purchase the patent, who would be willing to pay more for the patent if the parent company would agree not to use the process. When the parent company uses the patented process, it renders the patent less valuable to its rivals because there is increased competition. In all cases, the patent-owning company faces a cost when it uses the patented production process. Including these costs into its own cost calculations raises its average cost of production to the same level of its rivals. To be sure, since the company pays itself for the use of the patent, it makes more profits. After all it owns the patent. The company is richer and more profitable in the accounting sense, but it does not sell its output at a lower price on this count.

10. There are a number of ways to solve this problem, but they all start from a basic understanding of the fact that in a competitive industry, price equals marginal cost equals average cost. In turn, this implies that the firms produce at the minimum of average cost. This is the only place where marginal cost and average cost are equal. Profit maximization requires that price equal marginal cost. Entry and exit of firms ensures that price equals average cost. Thus, in long-run equilibrium, the minimum point on the average cost function determines both the output per firm and the price of output. We can find that minimum of average cost using calculus, or we can develop a spreadsheet. Each is adequate and the choice depends upon whether you are more comfortable with math or computers. Let's use the spreadsheet method this time.

   a. Examine Table 7.3. The first column is the number of workers from 0 to 8. The second column is the output that each level of labor would produce computed from the production function, assuming that there are five units of capital. The third column is total cost, which is just $500 plus $50 times the number of workers. The fourth column is average cost, which is total cost divided by output. Notice that average cost is minimized at 23.75 units of output at a cost of $31.58 per unit. Figure 7.10 graphs average cost. Again, notice that the minimum occurs at 23.75 units and a cost of $31.58.

   b. There are 100 firms and each produces 23.75 units. The industry output is 100•23.75 or 2375 units per day.

   c. The price is determined by the minimum of average cost, $31.58. The entry and exit of firms ensures that the firms in the industry earn a normal profit, where price equals average cost.

11. a. In the short run, the number of firms is fixed and the industry responds by each firm's experiencing an increase in marginal and average cost. However, the increase in average cost is greater than the increase in

TABLE 7.3   THE AVERAGE COST FUNCTION

Number of Workers	Output	Total Cost	Average Cost
0	10.00	$500.00	$50.00
1	13.75	550.00	40.00
2	17.00	600.00	35.29
3	19.75	650.00	32.91
4	22.00	700.00	31.82
5	23.75	750.00	31.58
6	25.00	800.00	32.00
7	25.75	850.00	33.01
8	26.00	900.00	34.62

marginal cost. Since marginal cost increases for each firm, the industry short-run supply, which is the sum of the marginal cost curves of the individual firms, moves up or to the left. Product price increases.

b.   Since price is higher in the market, the quantity demanded must go down. Consumers buy less. With a fixed number of firms in the market, the output per firm must decrease.

c.   Since average cost increased more than marginal cost, the firms are losing money. Some will exit. This shifts the industry supply curve to the left as there are fewer firms in the industry. This raises product price even higher. There is an initial short-run price increase because marginal cost has increased. There is a second, long-run price increase as firms exit the market. This process continues until price rises sufficiently high for the remaining firms to cover costs, and the industry is again in long-run equilibrium. Thus, in the long run, price increases over and above the beginning short-run price rise. And, according to the first law of demand, this second price increase is also accompanied by a further decrease in consumption. Thus, industry output also falls in the long run.

d.   Since the input whose price increased is normal, the minimum of average cost shifts up and to the right. Recall the discussion surrounding Figure 6.8 in Chapter 6. This means that the output per firm increases in the long run.

FIGURE 7.10
Average Cost

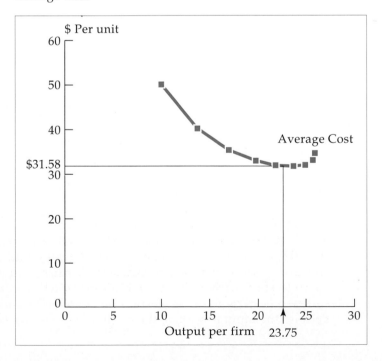

e. The number of firms decreases in the long run. After the initial price shock, all firms are losing money, and eventually some exit. In addition, optimal firm size is bigger now because the minimum of average cost has shifted up and to the right. This increase in minimum efficient firm size puts additional pressure on some firms to exit.

If a fixed input increases in price, there is *no* short-run adjustment. Marginal cost does *not* increase when a fixed input increases in cost. Average cost rises along the marginal cost function, but the marginal cost curve does not shift. This means that the short-run industry supply curve does not move. There is no price change in the short run. In the long run, the increase in average cost makes profits negative. As a consequence, some firms will eventually exit causing the industry short-run supply curve to shift leftward. This exit of firms will cause the long-run price to rise until the firms left in the market can cover costs.

12. a. The per unit tax on each gallon of gasoline will have the greater impact in the short run. The tax increase shifts the marginal cost of production up by the amount of the tax. For the industry, this amounts to a leftward shift of the short-run supply curve. Market price will increase, but less than the amount of the tax. By contrast, the second tax plan has *no* impact on marginal cost. The incremental cost of supplying gasoline has not changed. The average cost of selling gasoline has increased but not the marginal cost. Thus, in the short run, the second plan only taxes stations and not consumers. The price is unaffected.

b. By the same argument, there is no impact on gasoline sales in the short run. Marginal cost is unaffected. Price is unaffected, and hence, the quantity demanded is also constant.

13. According to the theory of economic rent, the inframarginal producers are expected to cultivate their assets more intensively. Farms close to the market will be used more often, with the best seeds and fertilizers. They will be irrigated more often, and they will have the highest quality labor used on them. By the same argument, the most talented players are the inframarginal producers of basketball. Thus, we expect that they wear the best equipment, get the best coaching, and work out on the most advanced equipment. In most all dimensions, they too cultivate their talents the most intensively, more so than the marginal bench warmers.

14. Labor is a normal input. When its price increases, marginal and average cost increase, but average cost increases more. The minimum of average cost moves up and to the right. Since marginal cost increases, the industry short run supply will shift up or to the left. This will cause market price to rise, but less than the increase in average cost. Schools will lose money in the short run. By definition, the number of schools cannot adjust in the short run. However, in the long run some schools will exit, causing the short-run supply curve to shift further left. This raises price, which continues until price is sufficiently high to cover costs. The number of colleges has decreased. Because the input is normal, the minimum of average cost has shifted to the

right, and therefore, the remaining schools have a larger minimum efficient firm size. Enrollment grows at the representative school. If professors were a superior input (which they do not appear to be), then the only difference would be that the new minimum of average cost moves to the left when wages increase. This makes the representative school get smaller in the long run.

CHAPTER

8

MONOPOLY, SEARCHING FOR THE BEST PRICE

INTRODUCTION

This chapter, like Chapters 6 and 7, is about the firm's external relations with input suppliers and customers. However, the primary focus here is on firms with some command over the price at which they sell. Many economists like to call these firms **monopolists** or price searchers. Control over price creates an interesting economic problem that the competitive seller does not have to worry about— that is, finding the best price. Since the competitive firm cannot affect price, it simply treats it parametrically and indifferently. The monopoly firm, by definition, must choose the price at which it sells, creating an extra managerial responsibility. We begin this chapter with an analysis of marginal revenue. Next, attention is devoted to the situations that create the ability to control price, the sources of monopoly. Last, we explore the concept of monopoly profits, where they come from and where they go.

After we explore the pure world of monopoly, we extend the analysis to other imperfectly competitive environments, primarily oligopoly and monopolistic competition. These market structures are variations on the theme of monopoly in which the firms involved have control over price but face rivals at the same time.

Some people bristle when the term *monopoly* is used. This probably results from the unsavory reputations held by many monopolists. In this material we are using the term *monopoly* less to mean nasty treatment of customers and more to refer to the price elasticity of demand facing the firm. Consider a simple example. You are shopping in the grocery store and a clerk is marking up some items on your list. Do you automatically leave the store to buy these items elsewhere? Typically no. Given the time you have spent driving to the store, parking, and walking in, the small cost of the price markup will not usually lead you to shop elsewhere for the necessary items. In the very short term, your demand curve is less than perfectly elastic. You are willing to pay a higher price for some goods. The store will not lose your sales because it has marked up some prices. To be sure, you may not return or you may buy fewer of the higher priced items *on your next trip,* but that makes the point. The price elasticity of demand facing virtually all firms is less than perfectly elastic in the immediate time period. As the length of time is expanded, demand becomes more elastic. The analysis presented in this chapter is called monopoly, but it is intended to help you understand all pricing and output decisions when the firm faces a less than perfectly elastic demand for its products. If you have trouble thinking this way when the term monopoly is used, simply substitute the phrase, price searcher. A price searcher is a firm that faces a downward sloping demand curve for its product, and a price searcher must decide for itself what price to charge its customers.

THE MONOPOLIST

The competitive firm must take price as determined in the market. A competitive firm that raises price above its rivals loses all its sales. By contrast, the monopolist does not lose all its customers by raising price; the monopolist determines price. Demanders then choose the quantity they wish to purchase. Alternatively, the monopolist produces the output it would like, and competition among numerous demanders forces them to reveal the price they are willing to pay for the limited quantity.[1] Regardless of the way we might pose the problem analytically, the monopolist can choose either the selling price or the level of output. Buyers choose the other. It is useful to think of the competitive firm as a **price taker**; the firm has no choice over the price of its output. But the monopolist is a **price maker** or a **price searcher**, looking for the best price, the profit maximizing price. Formally, the monopolist faces a downward sloping demand:

$$p = p(q),$$

with the first law of demand dictating that price is lower when quantity is higher—$dp/dq < 0$. Think of the monopolist as a firm that faces a less than perfectly elastic demand curve for its product. The monopolist faces the problem of finding the price that induces consumers to purchase a quantity that maximizes profits.

Marginal Revenue

Marginal revenue is the contribution of additional sales to revenue. For the competitive firm, marginal revenue always equals the price of output; the firm can sell as much output as it chooses at the prevailing market price. This means that for the competitive firm, the extra revenue it receives from selling an additional unit of output is the price of the output. However, for the monopoly firm that sells all of its units at the same price, the so-called **single-price monopolist**, price must be reduced to sell additional units. The price searching firm faces a downward sloping demand function for its output, and, therefore, additional sales require a lower price as the firm produces more output and moves down the demand curve for its product. A monopolist reduces price on all units when it decides to sell more output. The price of all output falls to the new lower level, and, hence, price is always greater than marginal revenue. If the firm can sell additional units at the existing price, it is not, by the definition used here, a monopolist or a price searcher. Since the monopolist can increase sales only if it lowers price, increasing output imposes a cost in that *all* output must be sold at a lower price. Hence, the net contribution to revenues from making additional sales will always be less than the selling price of the extra units.

Consider a numerical example. Hypothetically, let demand be

$$q = 1000 - 25p.$$

---

[1] A few years back Cadillac introduced a new model, the Allanté. According to local dealers, only 4500 of these cars were scheduled to be produced in 1987. Similarly, Chevrolet routinely limits production of its Corvette. In both cases, the seller sets the level of output; typically, price is then negotiated at the final point of sale. Notice, however, neither firm restricts the number of the mass-produced cars such as Seville or Monte Carlo.

MARGINAL REVENUE—A MATHEMATICAL PRESENTATION

Revenue is price times quantity,

$$R = p \cdot q.$$

Substituting the demand function for p, we have

$$R = p(q) \cdot q. \tag{i}$$

Marginal revenue is the change in revenue occasioned by a change in output—that is, the derivative of R with respect to q, or

$$dR/dq = (dp/dq) \cdot q + p(q). \tag{ii}$$

By the first law of demand, dp/dq is less than zero; as quantity increases, price declines. Since price is positive, $p(q)$ is greater than zero, it follows from equation (ii) that

$$p(q) > (dp/dq) \cdot q + p(q) = dR/dq. \tag{iii}$$

This mathematical result implies that price is always greater than marginal revenue. Note the first term on the right-hand side of the inequality, $(dp/dq) \cdot q$. This is revenue on original units sold that the monopolist loses when price is reduced to the market. The change in price is dp/dq, and q is the original units sold. Since the monopolist faces a downward sloping demand for its product, lowering price to raise sales has a cost. The volume currently being sold will be marketed in the future at a lower price. Hence, the net contribution to revenues from making additional sales will always be less than the selling price of the extra units.

In many problems, it is useful to state the demand curve in the **inverse.** This is derived by solving the demand function for the price the customer is willing to pay for each specified quantity. Inverting our hypothetical demand function yields

$$p = 40 - q/25.$$

Stating demand this way—price offered by consumers is a function of quantity—is sometimes referred to as specifying a Marshallian demand curve.[2] Revenue is price multiplied by quantity, or, from the inverted demand function,

---

[2] Mathematically, a function, $y = f(x)$, can be inverted if the mapping from x to y is one-to-one, that is, if $f'(x) \neq 0$. This way of stating demand, price is a function of quantity, is the epistemological or historical reason that economists usually draw demand curves with price on the vertical axis and quantity on the horizontal axis.

$$R = p \bullet q = (40 - q/25) \bullet q.$$

Therefore, by taking the first derivative of revenue with respect to quantity, we determine that marginal revenue is

$$dR/dq = 40 - 2q/25. \quad \triangleleft \text{ Marginal Revenue}$$

Table 8.1 reports the quantity demanded and marginal revenue for a variety of prices. Figure 8.1 graphs price, quantity, and marginal revenue using the numbers in the table. As price falls, quantity demanded increases, and marginal revenue

TABLE 8.1 PRICE AND MARGINAL REVENUE

PRICE	QUANTITY	MARGINAL REVENUE
$40	0	$40
39	25	38
38	50	36
37	75	34
36	100	32
35	125	30
34	150	28
33	175	26
32	200	24
31	225	22
30	250	20
29	275	18
28	300	16
27	325	14
26	350	12
25	375	10
24	400	8
23	425	6
22	450	4
21	475	2
20	500	0
19	525	−2
18	550	−4
17	575	−6
16	600	−8
15	625	−10
14	650	−12
13	675	−14
12	700	−16
11	725	−18
10	750	−20

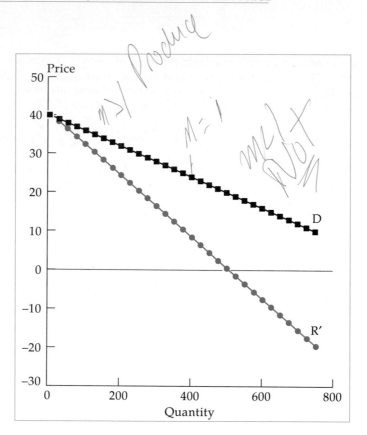

FIGURE 8.1
Price and Marginal Revenue

declines. Note that marginal revenue is always lower than price, that marginal revenue has the same intercept on the price axis as the demand function (at $q = 0$, both p and $dR/dq = 0$), and that the slope of marginal revenue is one-half as large (twice as large in absolute value terms) as the slope of the demand function. Also note that marginal revenue equals zero at 500 units of output. Let us compute the own price elasticity of demand at this point.

The formula for elasticity is $\eta = (dq/dp) \cdot (p/q)$. The first term in the formula is the slope of the demand curve, dq/dp. In this example, since $q = 1000 - 25p$, the slope, dq/dp, is -25. From Table 8.1, we observe that marginal revenue is zero when price is $20, and at this price the quantity demanded is 500 units; therefore, substituting these values the elasticity of demand is computed as

$$\eta = (dq/dp) \cdot (p/q) = -25 \cdot (20/500) = -1.$$

When marginal revenue is zero, the price elasticity of demand is -1, and one important managerial rule emerges: The firm would never willingly and knowingly sell more than 500 units (if all units are sold at the same price) since marginal revenue is negative after 500 units, sales larger than this actually cause total revenue, and thus profits, to decline. And this is true even if the costs of production are zero. (We cannot determine the optimal output unless we have cost data; the profit maximizing level of output depends on the cost of production.) This result generalizes to all demand curves, not just the one we are using as an example. Any firm that can control its price would never willingly sell where marginal revenue is negative or where demand is inelastic.

Determining Maximum Profits

To determine the best or profit maximizing level of output, we must incorporate the costs of production. The intuition of the profit maximizing rule is simple and straightforward: Exploit all opportunities to make more money. If some action will increase net revenues, that is, if revenues will increase more than costs or if revenues will decline less than costs, then take the action. By definition, marginal revenue is the change in revenue from changing sales. Similarly, marginal cost is the change in cost from producing extra units. When these two are equal, there is no remaining profit opportunity. When marginal revenue is the same as marginal cost, any action will cause revenues to either fall more than costs or rise less than

---

MARGINAL REVENUE IN ELASTICITY TERMS

It is possible to state marginal revenue in terms of the price elasticity of demand facing the firm. Consider the function for marginal revenue:

$$dR/dq = (dp/dq) \bullet q + p(q). \tag{i}$$

First, multiply it by q/p. This yields

$$(dR/dq) \bullet (q/p) = (dp/dq) \bullet q \bullet (q/p) + p(q) \bullet (q/p). \tag{ii}$$

Now multiply by p/q, yielding

$$dR/dq = [(dp/dq) \bullet (q/p) + 1] \bullet p. \tag{iii}$$

The first term on the right-hand side of equation (iii) is simply the inverse of the price elasticity of demand:

$$(dp/dq) \bullet (q/p) \equiv 1/\eta. \tag{iv}$$

Therefore, marginal revenue can also be expressed as

$$dR/dq = p \bullet [1 + (1/\eta)]. \tag{v}$$

Marginal revenue equals the current price times one plus the inverse of the price elasticity of demand.

costs. Thus, when marginal revenue is equal to marginal cost, all profit opportunities have been taken, and profit is at a maximum.

Figure 8.2 presents the theory graphically. A is average cost; M is marginal cost; demand is D; and marginal revenue is R'. The profit maximizing output, determined by the intersection of marginal revenue and marginal cost, is q_0. Consumers are willing to pay price p_0 for q_0 output. Average cost is A_0 for this level of output. Net profit, actually a rent to the asset that creates or is responsible for the monopoly in the first place, is the area of the tinted rectangle, $q_0 \bullet (p_0 - A_0)$.[3] So long as entry does not occur, this is long-run equilibrium.[4]

The marginal revenue equals marginal cost rule is full of economic intuition. Suppose that marginal revenue is greater than marginal cost. Then the incremental revenue from selling an extra unit exceeds the increase in cost of producing it. Thus, a profit opportunity exists. By producing and selling extra units, net revenues go up because marginal revenue exceeds marginal cost. Conversely, when marginal cost is greater than marginal revenue, the change in cost of production from manufacturing extra units is greater than the supplementary income received from selling them; reducing production will lower costs more than revenue. Here, profits will increase if the firm produces less. Only when marginal revenue equals marginal cost have all profit increasing opportunities

---

[3] Recall the discussion of economic rent in Chapter 6. Literally speaking, a monopolist does not make profit in the long run even if average cost is less than average revenue. Some state of affairs, to be discussed later in this chapter, creates monopoly. Whoever owns or is responsible for the monopoly condition gains the rewards from price exceeding average cost. Properly accounted, this payment to the responsible factor increases average cost to price, extracting all profits. A detailed discussion follows in the section Accounting for Monopoly Profits.

[4] To be sure that profit is a maximum and not a minimum at the point where marginal revenue equals marginal cost, the marginal cost curve must intersect the marginal revenue schedule *from below* (note the intersection of marginal cost and marginal revenue in Figure 8.2). If marginal cost equals marginal revenue, but marginal cost is falling faster than marginal revenue, marginal cost intersects marginal revenue from above, and *profits are minimized,* not maximized. Mathematically, the second order condition sufficient to ensure profit maximization is identified by taking the second derivative of the profit function with respect to q. This derivative, $d^2\Pi/dq^2$, is

$$d^2\Pi/dq^2 = (d^2p/dp^2) \bullet q + dp/dq - d^2C/dq^2.$$

For profits to be at maximum, this second derivative must be less than zero. Therefore, if

$$(d^2p/dp^2) \bullet q + dp/dq - d^2C/dq^2 < 0,$$

or if

$$(d^2p/dp^2) \bullet q + dp/dq < d^2C/dq^2,$$

then the marginal revenue equals marginal cost rule produces maximum, not minimum, profits. What is the intuition of the second order condition? The left-hand side of the equation is the rate of change in marginal revenue—that is, the slope of the marginal revenue curve; the right-hand side is the slope of the marginal cost function. The equation says that for profits to be at maximum, the slope of the marginal revenue curve must be less than the slope of the marginal cost curve. From the previous discussion on marginal revenue, we know that the slope of marginal revenue is negative. Thus, marginal cost must intersect marginal revenue from below.

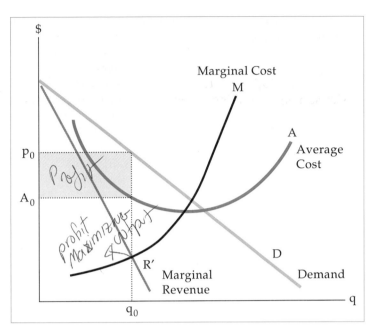

FIGURE 8.2
Monopoly Price Determination

been eliminated. A skilled manager will always exhaust all chances to make more money. Only when there is no more money to be made is it time to go home.

The profit maximizing solution can also be stated in terms of the price elasticity of demand. Recall the formulation of marginal revenue in terms of the price elasticity of demand: $dR/dq \equiv R' = p\bullet[1 + (1/\eta)]$. The profit maximizing rule that marginal cost must equal marginal revenue allows us to substitute marginal cost for marginal revenue in the elasticity formula for marginal cost. Thus, the profit maximizing rule can also be written

$$dC/dq = p\bullet[1 + (1/\eta)]. \tag{8.1}$$

In words, the monopolist charges a price (or chooses an output level) so that marginal cost is equal to price times one plus the inverse of the own price elasticity of demand. Since the price elasticity of demand is always negative, the term in brackets is less than one. Therefore, marginal cost is price times a number less than one; marginal cost will always be less than price for the profit maximizing monopolist.

The Level of Profits

The monopolist does not necessarily make positive profits. Consider Figure 8.3. Suppose demand is D, then marginal revenue is R'. Let marginal cost be M, but for the sake of analysis, average cost can take one of three different scenarios,

MAXIMUM PROFITS—A MATHEMATICAL PRESENTATION

By definition, profit, Π, is revenue minus cost,

$$\Pi = R - C. \tag{i}$$

Revenue is price times quantity, but price is determined by the level of output. Therefore,

$$R = p(q) \bullet q. \tag{ii}$$

Cost is also determined by the level of output. Generally speaking, costs are higher when output is greater:

$$C = C(q). \tag{iii}$$

Therefore, by the substitution of equations (ii) and (iii) into the profit equation (i), profit can be expressed in terms of output:

$$\Pi = p(q) \bullet q - C(q). \tag{iv}$$

The problem faced by the monopolist is to choose the right amount of output in order to maximize profit. We can determine this level of output in a number of ways. One of the quickest is by the use of the principle of mathematical optimization.[a] This approach has two conditions that must be met for profit to be at maximum. These are called the first and second order conditions. The first order condition necessary to maximize equation (iv) is found by taking the first derivative of the profit function with respect to the choice variable, which in this case is output or q, setting this derivative equal to zero, and solving for q. The first derivative of Π with respect to q is

$$d\Pi/dq = (dp/dq) \bullet q + p - dC/dq. \tag{v}$$

Setting equation (v) equal to zero and rearranging terms implies that

$$(dp/dq) \bullet q + p = dC/dq. \tag{vi}$$

The left-hand side of equation (vi) is **marginal revenue,** the change in total revenue from selling one additional unit of output. The right-hand side is **marginal cost,** the change in cost from producing one additional unit. The rule identified in equation (vi) makes intuitive sense. Exhaust all profit opportunities; produce until the increase in revenue from selling additional units is just offset by the increased costs of producing the extra unit.

[a] See the appendix to Chapter 2 for details on this technique.

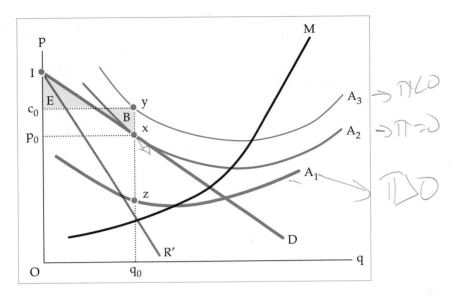

Figure 8.3
Monopoly Profitability

either A_1, A_2, or A_3. Regardless of the level of average cost, profits are at maximum when output is q_0 and price is p_0; here marginal revenue equals marginal cost. In the first case of average cost, A_1, average cost (the height of point z in Figure 8.3) is less than price at the profit maximizing level of output, q_0; profits (actually rents to the monopoly creating asset) are positive. In the second case, A_2, average cost (x) happens to equal price at the profit maximizing level of output; profits are zero, and the firm just breaks even. In the third case, A_3, average cost (y) is greater than price at q_0; the firm loses money.

The last case is most interesting in the context of the multidivisional firm. Suppose a company has a computer division, a motor pool, an airplane, or a similar enterprise that serves other divisions within the company. Heuristically, call it the support division. The entire company uses the services of the support division. The derived demand for the services of the support division is D in Figure 8.3 (recall the discussion of derived demand in Chapter 6). The average and marginal cost of supplying support are given by A_3 and M respectively. Note that there is *no* single price that exceeds average cost. If the support staff produces q_0 output for the other divisions, the average value of each unit is p_0, but the average cost is c_0; $c_0 > p_0$. This suggests that the support division is not paying its way and should be shut down. It seems that the other divisions within the company should provide their own support staffs or purchase the required services in the outside market. For example, they can fly commercial airlines rather than use the company plane. But is this the right choice?[5]

---

[5] In Chapter 12, we discuss a case very much like this involving a support division at Bellcore, a spinoff of AT&T.

Consider the problem in a different light. The area under the demand curve (the integral of demand from 0 to q_0) is the *total* value of the support division to the company. This area sums the value to the company of every individual unit produced by the support division. In Figure 8.3, this is represented by the area of the trapezoid $0q_0xI$. If the cost of producing support services is very high, as represented by the average cost curve A_3, then the total cost of supplying the services is output times average cost or $q_0 \cdot c_0$, which is rectangle $0c_0yq_0$ in the figure. The net value of the support division to the company is the area of triangle E minus the area of triangle B. Why is this true? The area under the demand curve represents the total value of the support division—that is, the sum of the value of each unit. The area under the derived demand curve up to q_0 output is the total value of the support division to the rest of the company. The total cost of the support division is simply q_0 times its average cost of production, c_0, the height of y. Subtracting the total cost, c_0q_0, from total value, we are left with the area of E minus the area of B.

Of course, the average cost of producing support services can take many levels, depending on the particular circumstances of the situation at hand. From the figure, we see that three outcomes are possible: $E > B$, $E < B$, or $E = B$. If the average cost is relatively low and $E > B$, the support division is valuable to the company even though, on average, the support division *appears* to lose money because $p_0 < c_0$. But if $E < B$, the support division costs more than it is worth, and the company would earn more money if it hired support services from the outside market, flew commercial, rented cars, or purchased computer consulting services outside the firm. The support division should be shut down. The third case, when $E = B$, is a wash. The support division just pays its way, and the company is indifferent between producing the services internally versus purchasing them on the outside.[6]

SOURCES OF MONOPOLY

For the firm selling its wares in a market under the circumstances characterized in Figure 8.2, the equilibrium may not be stable. It all depends on the circumstances surrounding the creation of monopoly. There are a number of situations that can create monopoly.

---

[6] The problem of pricing within the vertically integrated, multidivisional enterprise is considerably more complicated than indicated here. Indeed, rarely is it the case that the value of the whole firm is maximized when one of the divisions monopolizes, charges a price greater than marginal cost, to another division within the same company. Typically, goods must be transferred, intradivisionally, at marginal cost. Chapter 12 has a section on transfer pricing that briefly discusses this issue. This means the monopoly solution portrayed in Figure 8.2 is inappropriate *within* the corporation. The example is chosen to illustrate the perplexing situation in which the total value of production is positive, but there is no price greater than average cost that can be sustained in a market environment.

Patent

Patents are government enforced rights to prevent the entry of rivals. Patents are generally assigned for 17 years and give the owner an exclusive, alienable right to prevent others from using the patented product, idea, invention, or process.[7] In this case, the monopoly profits are actually a rent payment to the patent. The monopolist can sell the patent for the expected present value of the rent over the next 17 years at the appropriate discount rate. If the exclusive production technology or idea is not government enforced but just a trade secret, then the rent is a payment to the owner of the secret and to those with the ability and resources to keep it secret; the formula for Coca-Cola comes to mind. The decision to sell the patent or produce internally using the process covered by the patent is an important managerial decision, one that receives considerable attention in later sections.

Exclusive or Unique Asset

Sometimes a firm buys, discovers, steals, invents, or otherwise obtains a unique or unusual input. A hot spring or a mineral spring that spews water might be a good example. The spring, irrespective of the fact that it flows for free thanks to nature, is not reproducible given the current state of technology. In this case, the owner of the spring faces the market demand for spring water; there is no other supplier, nor could there be any save for new discoveries of springs.

Many human skills seem to fit into this category. Extraordinary intelligence, athletic ability, endurance, cunning, artistic creativity, and musical talent can be enhanced, but certain people have more than others based on accidents of birth. People endowed with these rare talents need not take wage rates as given, as most of us must. These people shop for the best price and negotiate their wages, unlike the bulk of workers who can either work or not at the posted price but have little bargaining power otherwise.

Locational Advantage

A firm's spatial location often gives it a competitive advantage and can give rise to monopoly power, the ability to set price. Candy counters inside motion picture theaters are a good example, restaurants in airports another. These sellers do not strictly face the rigors of competition. To be sure, patrons can refuse to visit, they can sneak popcorn into the theater, or they can take a cab to restaurants surrounding the airport; but in all cases, these alternatives pose costs. These costs give rise to some monopoly power. Since the consumer must bear expenses to find options, the captive seller has a locational advantage. Put another way, a

---

[7] Legally speaking, an alienable right can be rented, sold, destroyed, or otherwise alienated from the owner, hence the term. Chapter 12 develops this concept in more detail.

competitive firm faces a perfectly elastic demand for its output. The locational monopolist faces a demand curve that is less than perfectly elastic depending upon the customers' costs of traveling to alternative sellers.

Consider your local pharmacy. Suppose the owner raised all prices by 25 percent. Do you think the store would lose all of its sales? Perhaps in the long term, some other people would build a store in the neighborhood, lower prices, and capture the sales of the first store. But in the near term, until the new store is built, we do not expect that higher prices will eliminate all sales. Given the costs of finding other sellers and the time it takes competitors to respond, almost all firms have some (temporary) discretion over their prices.

Regulation

Government creates monopoly privileges besides patent, copyright, and trademark protection. Electric utilities and local telephone companies have exclusive franchise privileges sanctioned by state and local governments. Taxicabs in many American cities have exclusive operating privileges via licenses created by local governments. The list is long: truck regulation by the ICC, (former) airline regulation through the CAB, cable television by city governments, liquor store licensing, zoning ordinances, and many more. In each of these cases, the police power of the state is used to restrict the entry of rivals, protect existing businesses from competition, and give them monopoly privileges. The modern theory of economic regulation holds that these monopolies are sought by the regulated companies as a means of raising profits above the competitive level.[8]

Collusion

Monopoly power can arise through agreement among competitors. If most or all competitors agree to behave according to a set of rules, then competition may fail. Of course, prospective competitors must also be kept at bay. A general discussion of collusion is in Chapter 10 under the heading of cartels.

Economies of Scale—Natural Monopoly

In Chapter 6 we discussed the principle of economies of scale. When a firm produces with economies of scale, using more of all inputs (in the same proportions) causes output to increase more than the increase in inputs. Naturally, then, the average cost of production decreases. Suppose a firm uses 10 percent more of each input, but output increases by 12 percent. Total costs will increase by 10 percent, but output increases more. Average cost will be lower. When this situation is present, we call it economies of scale.

When average cost is declining, there is a tendency for the firm to expand; costs will be lower. In this circumstance, only the largest firms can survive. This

---

[8] Chapter 15 discusses the economic theory of regulation in some detail.

trend makes it natural for one large firm to dominate the market via a cost advantage. Economists sometimes call this situation a **natural monopoly** for obvious reasons. For many years, economists took the position that most utilities were natural monopolies. Recent empirical investigation casts some doubt on this issue, but the theoretical proposition remains valid. When economies of scale exist in production, the potential exists for one firm to control the market and face the entire product demand curve.

Imagine a small town. The village has a single hardware store. Why doesn't it have two? Minimum efficient firm size considerations dictate one large store as opposed to two small ones. That means that average cost is declining over the relevant range of output. If, in fact, there were two small stores in town, some smart, enterprising person could build a large store that would operate at lower average cost and drive the two small stores out of business by offering lower prices. In fact some people believe that this is the logic behind the phenomenal success of the Wal-Mart retailing chain. Once in place, however, the large store would be isolated from the competition that each of the two small stores faced from each other. Therein lies the essence of monopoly created by economies of scale. This is not meant to suggest that the large store would have no competition. There are always mail order stores and stores in the next town. But, compared to the two small stores scenario, the one large store faces a *more inelastic* demand curve for the wares on its shelves. It is a price searcher to some extent.

ACCOUNTING FOR MONOPOLY PROFITS

The economist and the accountant treat profits differently and for good reasons. Primarily, the accountant attempts to describe or replicate or paint a picture of the happenings within an organization *without putting words into the mouths of the people looking at the picture.* Accounting characterizes the past.[9] Economic principles are also used to see the past, but the purpose is different. In accounting, the *emphasis* is on what the facts are; in economics, the main concern is what made the facts transpire as they did. Interpreted in this context, there is no conflict between accounting principles and economic theory. They are simply different. This is best seen in connection with cost. Accountants usually cost inputs at purchase price, concentrating on whether the first or the last unit of input was used to produce the most recent unit of output, FIFO versus LIFO. Furthermore, there is an occasional discussion about using replacement cost as the measure of value. To the economist, cost is only replacement cost, and the FIFO, LIFO distinction is basically meaningless. Since the economic paradigm presumes that managers base decisions only on the basis of opportunity cost, who cares what the inputs cost originally? But, of course, the economist is not generally charged with making a report to absentee owners about the behavior of managers. Therein lies

---

[9] This description clearly shortchanges the services of accounting, especially in the areas of managerial and cost accounting. There are a multitude of accounting devices that managers use to affect behavior, to preclude malfeasance, to motivate employees, and the like. But for our purposes here, it is useful to think of these as reporting devices even when they have incentive effects.

one difference. Accounting is essentially designed to make a historical record; in the bulk, economics is used to interpret that account.

The profits, if any, of monopoly are a case in point. Consider Polaroid film. The process was invented by Polaroid's founder, Mr. Edwin Land, in the 1940s. The process of instant film development was patented by the company. The invention was a big success. The question is, Did Polaroid make large profits over the period covered by the patent? According to accounting reports, the answer is a resounding yes. However, imagine that Mr. Land had organized his company slightly differently. In this fictional account, he created two companies: Polaroid, more or less the same as it is now, and IFP Inc. (an acronym for Instant Film Patent). IFP was assigned the exclusive patent rights to the instant film process, *and Mr. Land forced Polaroid to pay IFP royalties on each unit of film sold corresponding to the market value of the patent.* It is no simple matter to compute this royalty payment. We must take into account the future cash flows earned by the company, the costs of production, and other issues concerning quality and longevity of the product. To avoid these complications, let's just assume that he allowed Fuji, Kodak, and BASF to bid for the rights to use the formula and, in turn, used the highest bid to determine the royalty payment between his two companies: Polaroid and IFP. Now under this fictional account, do you expect that Polaroid's profits were significantly different from those of most other companies over the same period? The answer is no! The accounting profits from the invention of instant film are captured by IFP. It was the access to the patent that caused the high profits at Polaroid. If the patent owner had been properly rewarded, then Polaroid's profits would have been considerably lower. That is one difference between the accountant's and the economist's use of the word **profits**.

What economic theory does is treat the Polaroid case as if the fictional account just rendered did indeed occur. We assign the extra profits due to the instant film invention to a **rental payment**; we do not call these excesses profits. Instead, they are a payment to the factor creating the riches in the first place—in this case, Mr. Land's ingenious invention. Similarly, if a company skillfully lobbies the state legislature for protection from its competitors, as most electric utilities have done, creates monopoly power, and causes price to diverge from marginal cost, the extra money that accountants would assign to profits are, in the economic approach, called a rental payment to skillful political action. In this way, each input gets costed, and average cost is *forced* to equal price. Any apparent divergence between the price and the economist's version of average cost can only be a temporary phenomenon due either to short-run conditions in the marketplace—that is, changes in demand that have not been adjusted for by entry or exit of firms—or the absence of assignment of rents to factors of production creating monopoly power.

THE STUDY OF MONOPOLY IN A WORLD OF COMPETITION

Many people have difficulty when the subject of monopoly comes up. This natural reaction probably stems from three sources. Morally speaking, in the eyes of some, monopoly connotes ruthless behavior, callous treatment of customers, and other unsavory behavior. Moreover, under the antitrust laws in the United

States, many monopoly practices are illegal. Finally, many people believe that monopoly is quite rare in actual practice and therefore not especially useful for analysis. Those taking this view see competition on every front. The study of monopoly presented in this chapter has no quarrel with any of these arguments. On the first count, the normative issue of whether monopoly is good or bad, the analysis presented here is benign. The reader must make this judgment. The author does not wish to influence the student's moral vision, only his or her analytical skills. On the second count, knowing the legal environment of business is a prerequisite for high-quality managerial decision making; and with respect to the third point, it is an empirical issue whether the theory of monopoly is relevant. The view taken here is that there are too many institutions and practices that cannot be explained solely with a model of competition—advertising and brand names to pick two. This is not meant to imply that the theory of monopoly applies to all firms in all circumstances, but rather, there are *some* problems that cannot be addressed in an environment in which price equals marginal revenue. Indeed, it is argued here that it is only through a thorough understanding of monopoly that we come to appreciate the breadth and vigor of competition.

In sum, the theory of monopoly can be used to understand a number of important managerial problems. In all cases, whether a firm possesses monopoly power depends on the price elasticity of demand for its product. In this sense, all firms are monopolists to some degree. As we shorten the time period of analysis, the elasticity of demand decreases (in absolute value), reflecting the second law of demand. The shorter the time period analyzed, the more empirically relevant is the theory of monopoly.

TOPICS TO REVIEW

These are topics that you should feel comfortable with before you leave this chapter. If you cannot write out a clear and concise sentence or paragraph explaining the topic after you have worked on the study problems, you should reread the relevant section of the text.

Monopolist, Price Searcher, and Price Maker

Marginal Revenue

Single-Price Profit Maximizing Rule

Marshallian or Inverted Demand Function

Sources of Monopoly—Patent, Exclusive or Unique Asset, Locational Advantage, and Collusion

Natural Monopoly

Profit, Rent, Quasi-Rent, and Cost of Production

STUDY PROBLEMS

1. It is commonplace for a firm accused of being a monopolist in violation of the antitrust laws to claim it is innocent on the basis of the fact that the price elasticity of demand for its product is inelastic. Does this claim make any economic sense?

2. Suppose the production of bolts is given by the following function:

$$q = 500{\cdot}L - L^2 + 5000{\cdot}K - K^2 + 100{\cdot}K{\cdot}L + 200{\cdot}M - 0.1M^2$$

where q is the number of bolts produced per day, L is the number of workers, K is the number of machines, and M is the pounds of metal used. Suppose that labor costs $100 per day, machines rent for $200 per day, and metal costs $1 per pound. The demand curve facing this firm is given by

$$q = 10,000 - 16.5{\cdot}p$$

where p is the price of the bolts. Suppose 10 laborers, 10 machines, and 1000 pounds of metal are used per day.

a. What is the appropriate price for these bolts?
b. How much output will this firm produce?
c. What is the daily wage bill?
d. What is the daily payment for capital?
e. What is the daily expenditure on metal?
f. How much profit does the firm make per day?
g. Is this the profit maximizing level of price and input use?

3. A store has collected the following facts: A loaf of bread costs $0.69 from the wholesaler. It costs the store an additional $0.11 to price the bread, shelve it, and sell it. Overhead adds $0.05 more per loaf to the cost. It has estimated the demand for bread in its store as

$$q = 220 - 120{\cdot}p.$$

The current price is $1.19 per loaf. Is this the profit maximizing price?

4. Why do beer, hot dogs, pizza, and sodas usually cost more inside a baseball stadium than they do in your local restaurant or tavern?

5. In the early 1980s long-distance telephone service was deregulated. Prior to that AT&T had a legal monopoly in the supply of that service. Today, there are a relatively large number of producers in the market. Competition is the order of the day. Recall the Alchian and Allen Theorem. In the context of that theorem, describe the level of quality demanded by consumers when the industry was monopolized and compare it to the level now that the industry is competitive.

6. Suppose one of the inputs a monopolist uses in production unexpectedly decreases in price. What happens to the amount of output produced by the monopolist? What happens to the price of this output?

SUGGESTED READINGS

Lerner, Abba P. "The Concept of Monopoly and the Measurement of Monopoly Power." *Review of Economic Studies* (June 1943):157–75.

McGee, John S. "Predatory Pricing Revisited." *The Journal of Law and Economics* 23 (October 1980):289–330.

Stigler, George J. "The Division of Labor Is Limited by the Extent of the Market." *Journal of Political Economy* 59(3) (June 1951):185–93.

SUGGESTED SOLUTIONS TO SELECTED STUDY PROBLEMS

The following are only *suggested* solutions to the study problems presented at the end of this chapter. In all cases, the suggestions here put heavy emphasis on analysis rather than a single correct answer. Since most managerial problems do not fall into neat little boxes, the individual characteristics of the problems that you will encounter on the job will typically mandate a solution using the principles developed here and in other courses. Memorizing these solutions will not make you a good manager; learning the *principles* detailed here will help make you a better manager.

1. If a firm has the power to set price, then it is not wise to let price be in the inelastic portion of the product demand curve. If price is set in the inelastic portion of the demand curve, then higher prices will raise revenues and reduce output which almost surely will cut costs. On both counts, profits should rise. Thus, a firm with control over the price of its product is not maximizing profit if price is set in the inelastic portion of demand. If, in fact, then, demand is inelastic, it suggests that the firm does not control the price of the product. This constitutes a defense against a charge of monopoly by the antitrust authorities.

3. The profit maximizing rule requires that marginal revenue equal marginal cost. In this case, marginal cost is the cost of another loaf of bread, $0.69 from the wholesaler, plus the costs of pricing, shelving, and selling, $0.11, for a total of $0.80. Overhead is not a marginal cost. It is a fixed cost. Selling additional units of bread, does *not* add to overhead expenses, and thus, they are excluded from marginal cost. Marginal revenue is determined from the demand function. Demand is

$q = 220 - 120 \cdot p.$

Invert this demand equation to state it in terms of price:

$p = (220 - q)/120 = 1.833 - q/120.$

Revenue is price times quantity, or

$R = p \cdot q = 1.833 \cdot q - q^2/120.$

Marginal revenue is the derivative of revenue with respect to quantity, or dR/dq:

$dR/dq = 1.833 - q/60.$

Set this formula for marginal revenue equal to the marginal cost of $0.80 per loaf and solve for q:

$1.833 - q/60 = 0.80,$

implies that

$q = 61.98$ or 62 loaves.

The firm maximizes profit by selling 62 loaves, and the price is determined by the demand function:

$$p = 1.833 - q/120 = 1.833 - 61.98/120 = \$1.32.$$

Accordingly, the profit maximizing price is $1.32 per loaf, and the current price charged by the store, $1.19, is too low. The average cost per loaf is $0.69, plus $0.11, plus $0.05 for a total of $0.85. This means that the store makes $1.32 − $0.85 = $0.47 of profit (which is actually a quasi-rent) on each loaf. Using the methods of accounting, we would subtract the fixed costs of overhead to report profits.

An alternative way to work this problem is with a spreadsheet and personal computer. Examine Table 8.2. The first column is a list of prices ranging from $0.59 to $1.59 per loaf. The second column is the quantity that would be sold at each price. The third column is the variable costs of selling each quantity (overhead costs are excluded as they are unavoidable). The fourth column is total revenue (price times quantity), and the last column is the difference between revenue and variable costs. Using the spreadsheet method, we see that profit is maximized at a price of $1.32 per loaf, the same answer we obtained using the methods of calculus.

5. Regulation implies high prices, competition low ones. The higher prices of regulation are, under the appropriate assumptions, the analogue to the fixed transportation charges in the Alchian and Allen Theorem. That is, monopolists charges higher prices for the same goods. These higher prices apply to both high and low quality goods, but for the same increment in price, the *relative* price of the high quality good does not rise as much. Thus, today, with competition and lower prices for long distance telephone service, the relative price of high quality is higher than it used to be under regulation and monopoly. Thus, demanders seek lower quality under competition than they desired under regulation because the relative price of low quality is now lower.

TABLE 8.2   STUDY PROBLEM 8.3

PRICE	QUANTITY	VARIABLE COSTS	REVENUE	PROFIT (QUASI-RENT)
$0.59	149.2	$119.36	$88.03	($31.33)
0.64	143.2	114.56	91.65	(22.91)
0.69	137.2	109.76	94.67	(15.09)
0.74	131.2	104.96	97.09	(7.87)
0.79	125.2	100.16	98.91	(1.25)
0.84	119.2	95.36	100.13	4.77
0.89	113.2	90.56	100.75	10.19
0.94	107.2	85.76	100.77	15.01
0.99	101.2	80.96	100.19	19.23
1.04	95.2	76.16	99.01	22.85
1.09	89.2	71.36	97.23	25.87
1.14	83.2	66.56	94.85	28.29
1.19	77.2	61.76	91.87	30.11
1.24	71.2	56.96	88.29	31.33
1.29	65.2	52.16	84.11	31.95
1.32	61.6	49.28	81.31	32.03
1.34	59.2	47.36	79.33	31.97
1.39	53.2	42.56	73.95	31.39
1.44	47.2	37.76	67.97	30.21
1.49	41.2	32.96	61.39	28.43
1.54	35.2	28.16	54.21	26.05
1.59	29.2	23.36	46.43	23.07

CHAPTER

9

PRICING AND PRICE DISCRIMINATION

INTRODUCTION

This chapter discusses pricing practices. A firm that faces a downward sloping demand curve for its product can, under certain conditions, increase its profits by selling various units of its output at different prices. In economics, this practice is known as price discrimination. In virtually all situations, some demanders value a good more than others. When this is true, a firm that can charge a high price to those who value the good the most and a lower price to those who value it less will make more money than a firm selling all of its output at the same price to everyone. There are many ways to price discriminate. These include market segmentation, block pricing, all-or- nothing pricing, and multipart pricing. Good business practices demand that a firm exploit the legal opportunities to make money. Taking advantage of differences among consumers is one of these. Choosing the best price is a most important managerial responsibility. Careers are made and lost here.

PRICE DISCRIMINATION

Hypothetical Business Problem 9.1

Suppose a firm sells a good in two markets, domestic and international. The international market is perfectly competitive, but the firm has an exclusive franchise to sell in the domestic market. If the firm is forced to sell at one price in both markets, what price will it charge? If the firm can charge different prices in the two markets, what price(s) will it charge?

Given that a price searcher can raise its price without losing all its customers, there are many situations when it is not wise to charge the same price to all buyers. This chapter is devoted to alternative pricing schemes designed to raise profits. The first section deals with price discrimination. It is followed by a discussion of more complicated pricing schemes: two- and three-part pricing and demand revealing mechanisms. **Price discrimination** is the art of charging more than one price to customers for the same (or nearly the same) product. Strictly speaking, to qualify as price discrimination, the price differential cannot be cost based. For example, if shipping charges are based on distance and cost is determined by miles shipped, charging local customers and distant buyers different rates would be, prima facia, not price discrimination.

MARKET SEGMENTATION

When a monopolist can divide a single market into two or more separate submarkets, domestic and international, catalog and showroom, male and female, adult and child, and the like, it can be profitable to charge different prices in the submarkets. In order for this strategy to be successful, several conditions must be met. First and obviously, *the markets must be separable*. Second, *the price elasticities of demand must be different across the markets*. Third, the firm must be able to *prevent resale* across the markets by the consumers. Fourth, the company must be able to *avoid antitrust prosecution* under the Robinson-Pattman Act of 1946.[1]

Consider the two demand curves represented in Figure 9.1 for entrance into a nightclub. In order to make the problem tractable, let us concentrate on the selection of the appropriate cover charge or entry fee and ignore the appropriate

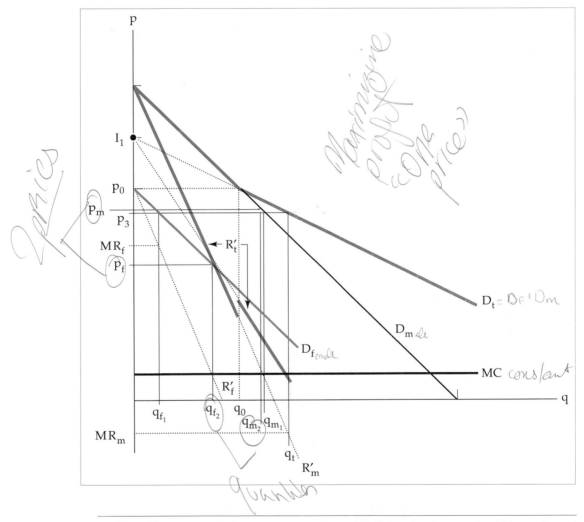

FIGURE 9.1
Market Segmentation

---

[1] Robinson-Pattman disallows charging customers different prices for "goods of like grade and quality" if the effect "may be substantially to lessen competition or tend to create monopoly in any line of commerce, or to injure, destroy, or prevent competition with any person who either grants or knowingly receives the benefit of such discrimination, or with customers of either of them." In 1960, the Federal Trade Commission prosecuted 560 cases. Of these, 166 or 29.6 percent were violations of the Robinson-Pattman Act. In 1980, the FTC processed 63 cases in total and 2 (3.2%) were Robinson-Pattman violations. Thus, avoiding Robinson-Pattman is increasingly less of a problem.

price of drinks inside of the club. The demand by women is D_f, and male demand is D_m. The marginal cost of letting people in the club is small: the extra cost of wear and tear on the carpet, the wrath of the fire and building inspectors, the wages of the bouncers at the door, and the marginal cost of cleaning up after the customers. Let these marginal costs be constant over the relevant range at MC. Total demand to visit the club is D_t, the horizontal sum of D_f and D_m. If all customers pay the same price, total marginal revenue is the marginal revenue schedule derived from total demand, the sum of male and female demand. The appropriate construction of marginal revenue begins with the addition of the two separate demand functions. D_t is found by horizontally summing the quantities specified by D_f and D_m at various prices. At prices above p_0, no females enter, and total demand is just D_m. When price is below p_0, both females and males consume, and, therefore, total demand, D_t, the sum of D_m and D_f, is kinked at the price women are first willing to attend, p_0. Marginal revenue is discontinuous at this quantity, q_0; both its slope and intercept change here. At quantities less than q_0, no females enter (price is too high for them), and as a consequence, marginal revenue is tied to male demand, D_m, only. Over the range of output 0 to q_0, marginal revenue has the same intercept and half the slope (twice the slope in absolute value) as *the male demand curve*, D_m. When price falls below p_0, females enter, demand is the sum of D_f and D_m, and marginal revenue is constructed from D_t. At quantities to the right of q_0, marginal revenue has the same intercept as the sum of male and female demand, I_1, and one-half the slope as D_t; hence the discontinuity at q_0.[2]

If the club charges a *single* price, the profit maximizing quantity is determined by the intersection of (total) marginal revenue and marginal cost, MC. This is q_t. The corresponding price from the total demand curve is p_3. At that price q_{m_1} males and q_{f_1} females visit the club. These quantities are found in the figure by noting the intersection of the price p_3 with the two demand curves, D_m and D_f, respectively. Total visits are $q_t = q_{m_1} + q_{f_1}$. In the figure, total quantity, q_t, is determined at the intersection of p_3 and total demand D_t. However, suppose the club separates this market into two classes, men and women, and charges them *different* prices, say p_m for males and p_f for females. At these new prices q_{f_2} females and q_{m_2} males now frequent the business. How are these prices computed and what happens to profit with this type price discrimination?

Suppose there is but one price for all visitors, p_3. What is the marginal revenue from one additional male compared to the marginal revenue from an extra female? When q_{f_1} females call on the club, one additional female customer would add MR_f dollars to revenue. When q_{m_1} males visit, one more male would add MR_m dollars. Indeed, the extra revenue from males is actually negative; the price to them is so comparatively low that revenues are being lost on the marginal male customer. Moreover, even though the marginal revenues are substantially different, the extra cost of serving one more person is the same, MC, regardless of sex. At a single price, p_3, additional females add more to revenue (and thus profit) than males. Hence, it is in the interest of the club to let more women and fewer

---

[2] In the special case where the two demand curves have the same price axis intercept but different slopes, total demand has no kink and marginal revenue is continuous.

Market Segmentation Price Discrimination

With two markets, total revenue is the sum of price times quantity in each of the two submarkets,

$$R_1 \;=\; p_1(q_1) \bullet q_1,$$

and

$$R_2 \;=\; p_2(q_2) \bullet q_2.$$

Since output is homogeneous, cost is determined by the sum of output in the two markets,

$$C \;=\; C(q_1 + q_2).$$

Profit, Π, is total revenue minus costs,

$$\Pi \;=\; R_1 + R_2 - C(q_1 + q_2) \;=\; p_1(q_1) \bullet q_1 + p_2(q_2) \bullet q_2 - C(q_1 + q_2).$$

Of course this formulation generalizes to the case where there are many markets by simply taking the appropriate sums. The profit maximizing solution to this price discrimination problem is found by taking the partial derivatives of the profit function with respect to the two choice variables (the sales in each submarket), q_1 and q_2, setting both derivatives equal to zero, and solving. The two partial derivatives of Π are

$$\partial\Pi/q_1 \;=\; \partial R_1 - \partial C/\partial q_1$$

and

$$\partial\Pi/q_2 \;=\; \partial R_2 - \partial C/\partial q_2.$$

Both of these must equal zero, and since output is homogeneous

$$\partial C/\partial q_1 \;=\; \partial C/\partial q_2 \equiv MC,$$

it follows that

$$MC \;=\; (dq_1/dp_1) \bullet q_1 + p_1 \;=\; (dq_2/dp_2) \bullet q_2 + p_2$$

where MC is the marginal cost of an extra person in the club and q_1 and p_1 are the quantities and prices in each of the two markets. The new rule is: Marginal cost must equal marginal revenue in *each* market.

men in, but not to admit additional customers in total; total marginal revenue is equal to marginal cost. The way to discourage male customers is to raise the price to them. Additional females are attracted by lowering the cover charge to them. The profit opportunity is only exhausted when the marginal revenues across the two classes of customers are equal, when $R'_f = R'_m$, and when both are equal to the marginal cost of additional customers, MC.

This analysis yields the conclusion that price discrimination leads to higher profits. To better see why this is true, recall the profit maximizing rule: Marginal cost equals marginal revenue [$MC = (dp/dq) \cdot q + p$]. This is the rule for the single-price monopolist, but it can be modified to accommodate market separation. Market separation takes a single market and divides it into two or more sub-markets, artificially creating additional markets for the purpose of charging different prices and raising profits.

In each market the profit maximizing rule is employed: Equate marginal revenue to marginal cost. Since the output destined for each market is the same, the marginal cost of production is the joint or total marginal cost of producing all units. The intuition of the rule is straightforward. Make sure that the units sold in *each* market have a marginal revenue equal to the marginal cost of producing the units.

As an example, let the two demands be

Male: $q_m = 100 - p$,

and

Female: $q_f = 80 - 1.5p$.

Let the marginal cost in terms of cleaning and so on be constant over the relevant range of output at $0.50 per person. What single price maximizes profit? How many men and women visit the club at this price? If the markets are separated, what are the two prices? What happens to attendance in the two classes of customers, and what happens to net revenue when the single-price solution is abandoned in favor of two separate prices?

First, let's compute the price assuming that all customers pay the same cover charge. This is called the single-price solution. After that we will compute the separate prices for the two classes of customers. Total demand is the sum of the male and female demands, but when the price is greater than $53.33, the quantity demanded by females is zero. This means that at prices greater than $53.33, the total demand is the same as the male demand:

$q_t = q_m = 100 - p$ for $p > = \$53.33$.

At prices less than $53.33, total demand is the horizontal sum of the demand by males and demand by females:

$q_t = q_m + q_f = (100 - p) + (80 - 1.5p) = 180 - 2.5p$ for $p < = \$53.33$,

or stated inversely,

$p = 72 - q_t/2.5$ for $p < = \$53.33$.

How do we determine these equations graphically? Male demand is $q_m = 100 - p$. Therefore, if $p = 0$, 100 males will enter; if price is $100, no males will enter. Similarly for the women, if there is no cover charge (the price is zero), 80 will go in. If the price is $53.33 [= (80/1.5)]$, no women will enter. The slope of the total demand curve at prices less than $53.33, namely -2.5, is determined by observing that 180 total visitors will enter if the cover charge is $0, and 46.67 men and 0 women will visit if the price is $53.33. Connecting the latter point with the former yields a slope of -2.5 and an intercept of 180. Hence, $q_t = 180 - 2.5p$. This is an exercise that you might want to construct for yourself on a piece of graph paper or with your personal computer.

Consult Figure 9.2. At prices above $53.33, only males enter the club. Below that, as price is reduced, females choose to visit. Thus, at prices greater than $53.33, total demand is identical to male demand. At prices less than $53.33, total demand is the horizontal summation of D_f and D_m.

If the club owner sets a single price, profit is maximized by equating marginal revenue to marginal cost. At this point there are two ways to proceed. There is the numerical approach and the method of calculus. The numerical technique is better for some students and some applications; the tools of calculus are preferred in others. Both methods are offered here. See the accompanying box for the analytical solution.

Table 9.1 reports the quantities demanded by females and males at prices ranging from $30 to $40.[3] The quantities are rounded to the nearest integer. At each level the total quantity demanded is the sum of the female and male demand. Total revenue is price times quantity. Cost is marginal cost, $0.50, times quantity. Profit is revenue minus cost. As we computed earlier, maximum profit

FIGURE 9.2
Market Segmentation Example

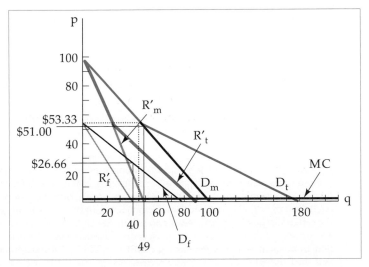

---

[3] The table was created using the spreadsheet by Borland, Quattro Pro.

THE SINGLE-PRICE SOLUTION—ANALYTICAL METHOD

Marginal revenue, dR/dq, is the change in revenue for a change in output. Revenue is price times quantity. Therefore,

$$dR/dp = d(p \cdot q)/dq.$$

Price is given by the inverse demand function, $p = 72 - q/2.5$. Therefore,

$$dR/dq = d[(72 - q/2.5) \cdot q_1]/dq = 72 - 2 \cdot (q_1/2.5) = 72 - 0.8 \cdot q_1,$$

and marginal cost is \$0.50. Therefore, maximum profit is determined by equating marginal revenue to \$0.50. This exercise yields

$$72 - 0.8 \cdot q_1 = 0.5,$$

and solving for the optimal total quantity, we have

$$q_1 = 89.375.$$

To attract these (approximately) 90 people, the club owner sets price determined by the total demand curve:

$$p = 72 - q_1/2.5 = 72 - 90/2.5 = \$36.$$

occurs at a price of \$36 per patron (a club for jet setters?). Total revenue at the door is \$36•90 = \$3240, and variable costs are \$0.50•90 = \$45. Therefore, revenues at the door each evening return \$3240 − \$45 = \$3195 over variable cost. Economists call this a **quasi-rent** that the owner uses to pay the unavoidable costs—the electricity, the heating, the bribes to local officials, the property and business taxes, and the bank note on the building and furnishings.[4] If there is any money left over, it is profit for the owners of the business (there may be additional profits or losses from the operation of the bar and restaurant inside the club).

---

[4] A quasi-rent is very similar to profit, taking into account sunk costs. If there are unavoidable expenditures associated with operating a business, in this case the rent on the building and so forth, there is profit only after subtracting these expenses. However, since these monies must be paid regardless of output at the bar, they are not a cost, in the opportunity sense of the word. Therefore, the difference between quasi-rents and profits depends on the level of sunk costs. Profit includes an accounting of sunk costs while quasi-rents exclude them. For a more complete discussion, see Benjamin Klein, Robert Crawford, and Armen Alchian, "Vertical Integration, Appropriable Rents, and the Competitive Contracting Process," *The Journal of Law and Economics*, 21, October 1978, 299. They explain the difference between a quasi-rent and a monopoly rent. Basically, a quasi-rent exists due to costs of moving and installing resources.

TABLE 9.1 THE SINGLE-PRICE SOLUTION—NUMERICAL METHOD

PRICE	FEMALE DEMAND[a]	MALE DEMAND	TOTAL DEMAND	TOTAL REVENUE	TOTAL COST	PROFIT (QUASI-RENT)
$30.00	35	70	105	$3150.00	$52.50	$3097.50
30.50	34	70	104	3164.38	51.88	3112.50
31.00	34	69	102	3177.50	51.25	3126.25
31.50	33	69	101	3189.38	50.63	3138.75
32.00	32	68	100	3200.00	50.00	3150.00
32.50	31	68	99	3209.38	49.38	3160.00
33.00	31	67	97	3217.50	48.75	3168.76
33.50	30	67	96	3224.38	48.13	3176.25
34.00	29	66	95	3230.00	47.50	3182.50
34.50	28	66	94	3234.38	46.88	3187.50
35.00	28	65	92	3237.50	46.25	3191.25
35.50	27	65	91	3239.38	45.63	3193.75
36.00	**26**	**64**	**90**	**3240.00**	**45.00**	**3195.00**
36.50	25	64	89	3239.38	44.38	3195.00
37.00	25	63	87	3237.50	43.75	3193.75
37.50	24	63	86	3234.38	43.13	3191.25
38.00	23	62	85	3230.00	42.50	3187.50
38.50	22	62	84	3224.38	41.88	3182.50
39.00	22	61	82	3217.50	41.25	3176.25
39.50	21	61	81	3209.38	40.63	3168.75
40.00	20	60	80	3200.00	40.00	3160.00

[a] Figures are approximate due to rounding.

At a uniform price of $36, 90 customers visit. We can separate these by gender using the respective demand functions. Males number $q_m = 100 - 36 = 64$, and there are $q_f = 80 - 1.5 \cdot 36 = 26$ females. These numbers are also shown in Table 9.1. For the sake of comparison, let's now compute the appropriate prices assuming that the market is separated into females and males. Call this the two-price solution. Then we can compare the profits or quasi-rents under this scheme with the quasi-rent of $3195 earned in the single-price situation to determine if market segmentation increases profits.

We start by examining marginal revenue under the two-price scheme. Examine Figure 9.2 again. Marginal revenue is R'_m at prices above $53.33, and R'_t below that. Notice the change in the slope of the total demand curve at the maximum price women are willing to pay to purchase, $53.33. Marginal revenue is only discontinuous in the single-price case. The discontinuity in the single-price case occurs at the output level where females first enter the market, at prices above $53.33. Intuitively, females are excluded at prices above $53.33 because none of them is willing to pay more than that to gain entrance. But, in the two-price case, females are allowed to enter when their *extra revenue*, not their price, is equal to the extra revenue from another male. In the two-price, market separation case, females are only excluded when the marginal revenue from male customers exceeds the maximum price women are willing to pay, $53.33. Thus, in the two-price situation, marginal revenue is *kinked but not discontinuous* at the maximum price women are willing to pay to enter the club, $53.33. Note R'_t in Figure 9.2.

Now let's compute the appropriate prices. In the two-price case, profit is maximized if marginal revenues from female customers equal marginal revenues from male customers and both are equal to marginal cost—if $R'_f = R'_m = MC$. Therefore, for women, since $q_f = 80 - 1.5 \bullet p_f$, price to females is found by inverting the demand function and solving for p_f:

$$p_f = (80 - q_f)/1.5 = 53.33 - q_f/1.5.$$

Revenue is price times quantity or

$$R_f = q_f \bullet p_f = q_f \bullet (53.33 - q_f/1.5).$$

Marginal revenue from female customers, R'_f, is the derivative of R_f with respect to q_f:

$$dR_f/dq_f = 53.33 - (q_f/1.5) - (q_f/1.5) = 53.33 - q_f/1.33.$$

Setting this equation for marginal revenue equal to marginal cost, $0.50, yields the appropriate number of women and their cover charge:

$$53.33 - q_f/1.33 = 0.50,$$

or

$$q_f = 39.72.$$

The price females are willing to pay has been found by inverting the female demand function, and we can insert the appropriate quantity, 39.72, into this function to determine the profit maximizing price:[5]

$$p_f = 53.33 - q_f/1.5 = \$26.85.$$

The price to women must be $26.85, which we can round off to $27, and approximately 40 of them will enter.

Revenue from male customers is q_m times p_m, and the profit maximizing values of p_m and q_m are found in the same manner used for females. The male demand function is

$$q_m = 100 - p_m,$$

and therefore the male price equation is,

$$p_m = 100 - q_m.$$

---

[5] Since people usually only enter in integers, we round up to give $q_f = 40$.

Revenue from males is

$$R_m = p_m \bullet q_m = (100 - q_m) \bullet q_m.$$

Male marginal revenue, R'_m, is

$$dR_m/dq_m = 100 - q_m - q_m = 100 - 2\,q_m.$$

Marginal cost must also equal marginal revenue in this submarket as well, and thus,

$$0.50 = 100 - 2q_m.$$

Therefore, the optimal number of male customers is

$$q_m = (0.50 - 100)/(-2) = 49.75.$$

Again, dealing with integers, we round up to the nearest whole number letting

$$q_m = 50.$$

The appropriate price is

$$p_m = 100 - q_m = 100 - 50 = \$50.$$

Therefore, using the profit maximizing rule, $q_m = 50$ and $p_m = \$50$.

As before, we can obtain this solution numerically by inserting different prices into the demand function and observing the change in revenue and cost. Examine Table 9.2. Males and females are separated in the table because their prices are determined separately. The prices are determined individually because marginal cost is constant at \$0.50. If marginal cost were a function of output, that is, if marginal cost increased with sales, we would have to sum the individual quantities demanded to determine the appropriate prices. In this case, however, we are spared this complication. The first column in the spreadsheet-like table lists various prices. The second column is the quantity demanded. The third column is revenue, price times quantity. The last column is profit or quasi-rent from each class.[6] Echoing the analytical solution, we see that the prices are \$27 for females and \$50 for males.

Refer again to Figure 9.2 which presents the analytics of the problem graphically, while Table 9.3 summarizes the preceding calculations. Several things are noteworthy. Under the two-price scheme, the price to females is reduced, and more of them attend. The price to males is increased, and fewer of them enter. Total revenue is higher under the two-price scheme, \$3566.50 versus \$3240, a

---

[6] Profit is revenue minus cost. Cost is 0.50 times quantity. The cost column is omitted from the table for the sake of compactness.

| TABLE 9.2   THE TWO-PRICE SOLUTION—NUMERICAL METHOD |

PRICE	FEMALE DEMAND[a]	REVENUE FROM FEMALES	PROFIT FROM FEMALES
$26.00	41	$1066.00	$1045.50
26.25	40.625	$1066.41	$1046.09
26.50	40.25	$1066.63	$1046.50
26.75	39.875	$1066.66	$1046.72
27.00	**39.5**	**$1066.50**	**$1046.75**
27.25	39.125	$1066.16	$1046.59
27.50	38.75	$1065.63	$1046.25

PRICE	MALE DEMAND	REVENUE FROM MALES	PROFIT FROM MALES
$47.00	53	$2491.00	$2464.50
48.00	52	$2496.00	$2470.00
49.00	51	$2499.00	$2473.50
50.00	**50**	**$2500.00**	**$2475.00**
51.00	49	$2499.00	$2474.50
52.00	48	$2496.00	$2472.00
53.00	47	$2491.00	$2467.50

[a] These numbers are not rounded to allow precision in the computation of revenues and profits.

difference of $326.50, and costs are unchanged because the total number of customers is unaltered.[7] Profit is higher with market separation.

Using Elasticities to Determine Prices

An alternative way to examine this problem is with elasticity tools. At the profit maximizing single price, $36, the female elasticity of demand, η_f, is

$$(dq_f/dp_f) \bullet (p_f/q_f) \ = \ -1.5 \bullet (36/26) \ = \ -2.07,$$

and the male price elasticity, η_m, is

$$-1 \bullet (36/64) \ = \ -0.56.$$

---

[7] This result, that quantity is the same under market segmentation, is tied to the particular (linear) demand functions of this example. In other situations, output of the two-price monopolist does not necessarily equal output of the single-price monopolist. It can be higher or lower. Nevertheless, the conclusion that profits are higher with market segmentation is *not* tied to the hypothetical demand functions of this example. For a detailed discussion, consult Joan Robinson, *The Economics of Imperfect Competition* (London: Macmillan, 1933).

TABLE 9.3 PRICE COMPARISON					
	MALE		FEMALE		TOTAL
	QUANTITY	PRICE	QUANTITY[a]	PRICE[a]	QUANTITY[a]	REVENUE[b]
Single Price	64	$36	26	$36	90	$3240
Two Prices	50	$50	40	$27	90	f = $1066.50 m = $2500.00 t = $3566.50

[a] These numbers are rounded to the closest whole number.
[b] These numbers are exact. See Table 9.2.

Male demand is relatively inelastic compared to female demand, $|\eta_m| < |\eta_f|$. Hence, raising price to the men and lowering it to the women, holding total quantity constant, must raise revenue. According to these relative elasticities, raising price to males reduces their quantity, but not very much compared to the increase in females when their price is lowered. Thus, the existing level of output is made more valuable by shifting sales from men to women. Profit is necessarily increased (so long as men impose no less marginal cost than women in the club). How do we know forcing the price elasticities of demand toward equality makes profit go up? Recall the relation between marginal revenue and elasticity,

$$dR/dq = p \bullet (1 + 1/\eta).$$

Of course, this holds for males or females separately as well. In the single-price case, $p = p_f = p_m$, and since the demand elasticities are different, the marginal revenues must also be unequal. As the marginal costs of males and females are the same, a profit opportunity exists; raise price to the buyer with the relatively inelastic demand, the one with the low marginal revenue. At the profit maximizing solution, the two elasticities are equal:

$$\eta_f = (dq_f/dp_f) \bullet (p_f/q_f) = -1.5 \bullet (27/40) = -1.0125,$$

and

$$\eta_m = (dq_m/dp_m) \bullet (p_m/q_m) = -1 \bullet (50/50) = -1.0.[8]$$

Through market segmentation, one profit opportunity has been eliminated; marginal cost now equals marginal revenue in both submarkets.[9]

---

[8] This solution is approximate and obtains because of the vagaries of this hypothetical problem, specifically rounding error, which has two sources—humans come in integers and marginal cost is almost zero.

[9] The owner could, of course, employ multiple market segmentation rules if the demand conditions (elasticity conditions) warrant: males under and over 40 years old, local females and females from out of town, for examples.

A simple managerial policy emerges. When markets are separable, when resale across markets is preventable, when the scrutiny of Robinson-Pattman is not an issue, adjust prices across markets until the price elasticities of demand are equal in all the markets, ensuring that the marginal cost of additional sales in any market is not different from marginal revenue in that market.

There are different ways to skin this cat. Perhaps the manager can separate the market by cheaply making the product particularly unattractive to one class of buyers in some superficial way that does not affect quality. Consider disposable razors. Suppose for some unknown reason men do not like to shave with pink razors, but women do not care what color razor they use. Further suppose that the male elasticity of demand for this company's disposable razors is relatively low compared to the female elasticity. Then a profit opportunity exists. The firm produces two identical razors except one is coated pink and the other is blue or yellow or black. The razors are packaged in see-through plastic. The prices are marked the same, say $0.99, but there are seven pink razors in a bag and only six blue, yellow, or black ones. The market has been separated by color (but really by gender), the elasticities of demand are different, resale is prevented, and it is doubtful that any court would hear a complaint from male shavers that they are the victim of price discrimination. Profits are increased.

Services are a general class of products for which it is relatively easy to price discriminate. Here there is usually a face-to-face personal relationship between the buyer and the seller. In some cases, this makes it easier for the seller to estimate the price elasticity of demand by the buyer, and in almost all cases resale is prevented. For example, in the days before health insurance paid most doctors' fees, physicians were in a classic position to price discriminate. They typically charged different prices to rich and poor customers because their rich customers usually had a more inelastic demand for the care of health professionals. This is one reason doctors routinely inquired the occupational status of their patients, so they could estimate income and the elasticity of demand for their services. Price discrimination seems to be declining in American medicine, perhaps because there is an increasing trend to only one class of patron, the insured customer.

In sum, the price discrimination game is played by finding demand curves for different classes of customers with unequal price elasticities of demand. If, in any two groups of customers, the demand elasticities are not the same, one will be relatively inelastic compared to the other. If this is the case, the firm always makes more money, even if it produces the same output, by rerouting sales within customer classes. It sells less to the customers with relatively inelastic demands, raising the price to them, and sells more to the people with the relatively elastic demands, cutting their price. The increase in revenue from higher prices to the price inelastic demanders more than compensates for any loss in revenues to the price elastic demanders. Total revenue goes up simply by redistributing output among the two classes of customers.

Examples of Market Segmentation Price Discrimination

It is a common practice for motion picture theater operators to charge adults and children different prices. Presumably, children have a more elastic demand for attendance probably because, on average, their incomes are lower. Therefore, survival requires that the manager separate the markets and charge the customers with the relatively inelastic demands (the adults) a higher price. Resale is prevented by the color coding of tickets. Another example of price discrimination involves the common practice of offering discounts to senior citizens. Hotels frequently use this tactic. Why is it that senior citizens typically have more elastic demands for hotel rooms than the average traveler? Several reasons come to mind. First, being older, they tire more easily, and hence, they travel fewer miles per day. They stop sooner and are less in a hurry to find a room; they search more. Being retired, their time is worth less, and being experienced travelers, they are skilled shoppers. On all counts they are more likely to browse around for a room. Hence they are more sensitive to price changes than the general traveling public.

Newspapers commonly charge prices for want ads based on the value of the item being sold. The price for an ad to sell a $10,000 car is typically two or three times the price to sell a $100 baby bed. Presumably, the seller of the baby bed has a relatively elastic demand for the want ad because the net gain from selling is small compared to the used car seller. The relative cost of the ad, compared to the gain, is markedly different in the two cases, yielding on average a more inelastic demand by the used car seller. Publishers who jointly produce a morning and an afternoon edition can subtly price discriminate by charging all classified ad buyers the same price per line, but allowing the low-valued item sellers (the elastic demanders) the right to have their ad run in both papers while charging the high-valued item sellers for each edition.

It bears emphasizing that, in all cases, the price discriminating firm must be a monopolist. Otherwise, if the firm starts charging men and women different prices, the higher price class of customers will desert to purchase from other sellers, and the firm will be left with only the lower price buyers.

We have explored price discrimination in sufficient detail for you to construct a solution to Hypothetical Business Problem 9.1. Consider the following analysis.

Suggested Solution to Problem 9.1

The international market is perfectly competitive. If the firm sells in this market, it must sell at the international price. At any higher price, there will be no sales. With a competitive international market, international buyers need only pay the competitive price. Thus, if the domestic firm must sell at one price, such that the domestic price equals the competitive price, then the firm must sell domestically at the international price.[10] If the firm can charge two prices, and the conditions for market segmentation are met, then it will pay to charge a high price in the domestic market and the world price in the international market.

Examine Figure 9.3. The demand curve, D_d, is the domestic demand for the output of this firm. The price line, p_w, is the world or international competitive price and is in effect the international demand function. The

---

[10] Depending upon the rules in place, the domestic firm might be able to sell at one price, the domestic monopoly price, offering its goods for sale in the international market at a price above the competitive level. Naturally, all foreigners will eschew the higher price in favor of the competitive price from other sellers, but the firm might be able to comply with the law by this trick.

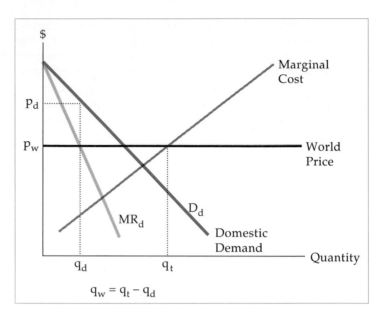

FIGURE 9.3
Suggested Solution to Problem 9.1

firm equates marginal revenue in each market to marginal cost to deter-mine the appropriate levels of output. Since the international price is constant, marginal revenue in that market is equal to price. So the firm produces where marginal cost equals the international price. The firm apportions that amount of output between the domestic and interna-tional by setting the marginal revenues equal in the two markets. Thus, domestic output is q_D and the remainder of the total is sold in the international market, $q_t - q_d = q_w$ where q_w is the amount of output sold in the world market.

The price of domestic output is determined by the domestic demand function. This is price p_d in the figure. Of course, the price of the output sold in the international market is p_w. When the firm can separate the markets, profits increase by the amount $(p_d - p_w) \cdot q_d$, which is the in-crement in price when the firm separates the markets, times the quan-tity sold domestically.

A Digression on Consumer's Surplus

To fully appreciate most price discrimination schemes, it is important to under-stand consumer's surplus, a topic we discussed in Chapter 3. In general terms, consumer's surplus is the area between the consumer's demand price of a good and the price paid for the item. Consult Figure 9.4. Suppose consumer demand is D and the current price is p^*. At this price, the buyer purchases five units. Notice that this person would be willing to pay a much higher amount, p_1, for the first unit, and if the price were p_1, the consumer would buy just one unit. Similarly, for the second unit, *having bought the first*, the consumer is willing to pay p_2, and so on

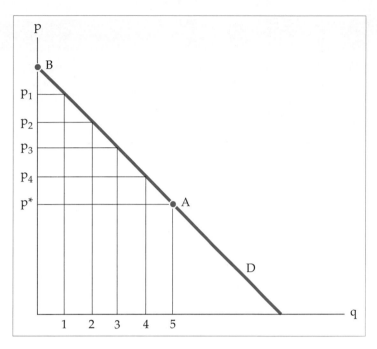

FIGURE 9.4
A Digression on Consumer's Surplus

for the third and fourth units. Note, however, that even though the consumer is willing to pay p_1, p_2, p_3, and p_4 for the first four units, he is only required to pay p^*. This divergence creates a consumer's surplus that is estimated by the area of the triangle, p^*AB, the difference between the consumer's demand prices and the actual price paid.[11] The consumer values the first four units more than he must pay for them and leaves the store happy and smiling. From a seller's perspective, this is a sad state of affairs. In the limit, the manager would prefer to extract all that happiness, leaving the customer just barely willing to purchase each unit of the product. Ideally, the customer is made almost, but not quite, indifferent between purchasing each unit and leaving it on the shelf.

BLOCK PRICING

It is a common practice in public utilities to charge **block prices,** which means that the first segment of consumption costs one rate and subsequent blocks are offered at lower rates, much akin to quantity discounts. Table 9.4 lists sample long-distance telephone rates using Southern Bell service as reported in the December

---

[11] You will recall from the discussion in Chapter 3 that this estimate is *not* unique. There are multiple ways to measure consumer's surplus. Practically speaking, however, the area under the so-called ordinary demand curve above price is most relevant when it comes to managerial pricing decisions. The consumer's demand price is given by the Marshallian, or inverse, demand function.

TABLE 9.4 TELEPHONE PRICING					
SAMPLE RATES FROM ATLANTA TO	WEEK DAY (D)		EVENING (E)		NIGHT AND WEEKEND (N)	
	FIRST MINUTE	EACH ADDITIONAL MINUTE	FIRST MINUTE	EACH ADDITIONAL MINUTE	FIRST MINUTE	EACH ADDITIONAL MINUTE
Athens, GA	$0.50	$0.32	$0.37	$0.24	$0.25	$0.16
Columbus, GA	0.52	0.35	0.39	0.27	0.26	0.18
Madison, GA	0.48	0.30	0.36	0.23	0.24	0.15

1986 Atlanta phone book. In addition, there is a minimum charge of one minute for any call, day or night. The various rates for a call from Atlanta to Athens are plotted in Figure 9.5. Notice that each rate schedule, D, E, and N, looks suspiciously like a demand curve. That is no accident. Ideally from a management point of view, the block pricing schedule mimics consumer demand for the good or service.[12]

To better understand this pricing scheme, consider Figure 9.6. A hypothetical demand function,

$$p = 100 - q,$$

is plotted there for a single buyer. For simplicity, let marginal cost of production be zero. For the single-price seller, the profit maximizing price is determined by the rule that marginal revenue equal marginal cost. Alternatively, we can use the formula that marginal cost must equal price times one plus the inverse of the elasticity of demand:

$$dC/dq = p \cdot (1 + 1/\eta).$$

The price elasticity of demand, η, is $(dq/dp) \cdot (q/p)$. For the demand curve $p = 100 - q$, the slope is -1, and therefore the first portion of the elasticity formula, dq/dp, is also -1. Therefore, in this case, $\eta = -1 \cdot (q/p)$. Making this substitution, we have

$$dC/dq = p \times (1 + \frac{1}{-q/p}).$$

---

[12] There is an old debate in economics, somewhat normative in nature, carried out by a number of people, Frank W. Taussig and A. C. Pigou to name two, as to whether utility pricing was price discrimination or simply the recovery of costs associated with the large volume of fixed assets put in place by utilities and railroads. For a vision of this, see Harold Hotelling, "The General Welfare in Relation to Problems of Taxation and of Railway and Utility Rates," *Econometrica*, 6, 1938, 242–69 or the related discussion in Robert B. Ekelund and Robert F. Hebert, *A History of Economic Theory and Method*, 2d ed. (New York: McGraw-Hill, 1983).

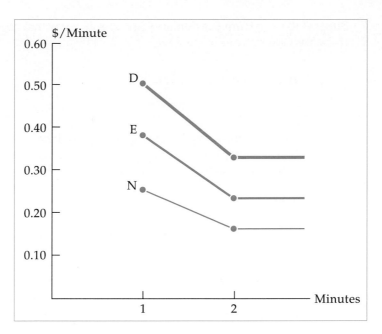

FIGURE 9.5
Atlanta-Athens Long-Distance Rates

FIGURE 9.6
Block Pricing

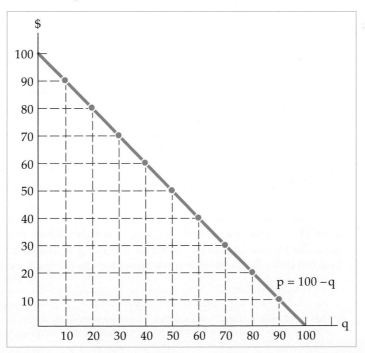

But $p = 100 - q$ from the demand curve, and, marginal cost is zero. Therefore, by these two substitutions we have

$$0 = (100 - q) \times (1 + \frac{1}{-\frac{q}{100-q}}).$$

Solving for q, the profit maximizing quantity, we have $q = 50$.[13] If the firm sells all units to this one buyer at a single price, the profit maximizing price is found by inserting the profit maximizing quantity into the price equation:

$$p = 100 - q = 100 - 50 = \$50.$$

Revenues are simply $p \bullet q = \$50 \bullet 50 = \$2500$. Since marginal costs are 0, all \$2500 of the revenues are quasi-rents, or profits, if there are no fixed or sunk costs of operation.

Now consider a block pricing scheme instead of a single price. This procedure charges the buyer \$90 for the first 10 units purchased, \$80 for the next 10, \$70 for the subsequent 10, and so on, down to \$10 for any units purchased in excess of 90. Several things are noteworthy. First, output increases from 50 to 100 units because marginal revenue has increased. We are still pricing where marginal revenue equals marginal cost, but now marginal revenue is higher because the firm does *not* cut price on the first units sold when it increases output. Since marginal cost is constant at zero, there is no change in the costs of production, a fact that has little bearing on the outcome of this example. Total revenue, R, increases dramatically. Under this hypothetical block scheme, revenue is

$$R = \$90 \bullet 10 + 80 \bullet 10 + 70 \bullet 10 + \ldots + 20 \bullet 10 + 10 \bullet 10 = \$4500,$$

an increase of \$4500 − 2500 = \$2000, or 80 percent, over the single-price solution. It is no wonder public utilities relish the declining block rate schedule.

Two questions remain. First, what determines the optimal number of blocks, and second, what conditions must prevail for this strategy to be viable? The preceding simple example ignores several complexities of demand. First, multiple demanders can easily complicate the solution in two ways. Suppose there were many buyers, each with the demand function $p = 100 - q$. According to the preceding analysis, each of the buyers purchases 100 units paying a total of \$4500 for them. But, *if communication and transactions costs are low among the buyers,* if they are neighbors or friends for example, then a contract among the buyers is possible, creating a potential disaster for the seller. Suppose five of the buyers agree to let one of their number be a buying agent, who, in turn, purchases not just 100 units for herself, but 500 units for the whole group. Notice what happens

---

[13] This solution is verified by noting that the price elasticity of demand is −1 where marginal revenue is 0, and the price elasticity of demand for a linear demand curve is the midpoint, in this case, where $q = 50$.

to the seller's revenues. They are $4500 for the first 100 units sold, but only 400•$10 = $4000 for the remaining 400 units. Total revenue with block pricing is $4500 + $4000 = $8500. Contrast this outcome to the single monopoly price of $50 per unit for all units. In the single-price case, revenue is $50•500 = $25,000, a tremendous increase in revenues and profits over the block schedule. Declining block tariffs may not pay if buyers act collectively, reselling the good among themselves. This state of affairs forces the firm to (1) reduce the number of blocks, raising the price of the last block, (2) limit the quantity purchased by any one buyer, (3) discover ways to prevent product resale among buyers, or (4) resort to some other pricing scheme.

The second complexity of demand creating a barrier to block pricing is the heterogeneity of buyers. The preceding example artificially assumed that all buyers had the same demand. This is clearly atypical. When buyers are not homogeneous, the appropriate block schedule varies among them. For example, suppose only one buyer had demand $p = 100 - q$, while numerous others had demand $p = 60 - q$. In this case, the declining block schedule identified previously is inferior to a single price of $30 per unit. Consider why. At a single price of $30 per unit, the first buyer purchases 70 units, and all other consumers buy 30 units. In the single-price case, total revenue is $30•70 + $n•$30•30 where n is the number of demanders save the first one. In the declining block case, *only the first buyer purchases any of the product at all.* The most any of the secondary buyers is willing to pay for even a single unit is $60, and according to the block plan, buyers must purchase 30 units at prices of $90, $80, and $70, to even have the right to buy at $60. Clearly revenues and profits are less under the block scheme here; the firm only sells to one buyer. But all is not lost; this just means a block scheme with lower prices must be adopted. Of course, by necessity it will have fewer gradations or levels; the $90, $80, $70, and $60 prices are gone. A principle emerges: The more heterogeneous the collection of buyers, the fewer is the appropriate number of block prices.

In all cases, the seller must be able to prevent large-scale resale of the product. Of course, this is precisely why public utilities are ripe for block pricing. Electricity, water, and telephone services are, at best, technically difficult and economically costly to resell.

Finally, it bears noting that probably the most prevalent form of block pricing is simply volume discounting. A local bakery sells a dozen glazed doughnuts for $0.99 (a substantial discount) with the purchase of a dozen at the regular price of $2. US Sprint offers a discount on long-distance telephone service if the buyer purchases more than $25 of service in any one month. Many grocery items are offered for sale at say $0.39 apiece or 3 for $1.

Block pricing captures consumer's surplus for the seller. In the original and simple case of one price, $50, and one demander purchasing 50 units, the consumer's surplus is the area under the demand curve from zero units up to the level of consumption, 50 units, less the price paid, $50. For a linear demand curve this area is simply the area of the triangle starting at a price of $50 and moving over to the demand curve, and from there moving up the demand curve to the price intercept of $100. The area of this triangle is 0.5•(50)•(100 − 50) = $1250. For nonlinear demand curves, we must integrate the demand function to compute the area under the curve. This more general approach applied to our example reveals the same answer:

$$\int_{0}^{50} [(100 - q) - 50] \, dq = \int_{0}^{50} (50 - q) dq = 50 \times 50 - 50^2/2 = \$1250.$$

In the declining block tariff, the consumer's surplus on the comparable quantity, the first 50 units purchased, can be computed using triangles or via integration. Using integration the solution is

$$\int_{0}^{10} [(100 - q) - 90] dq + \int_{11}^{20} [(100 - q) - 80] dq + \int_{21}^{30} [(100 - q) - 70] dq +$$

$$\int_{31}^{40} [(100 - 1) - 60] dq + \int_{41}^{50} [(100 - q) - 50] dq = \$250.$$

As this example is constructed, consumer's surplus under a single price is \$1250, and on the same units it falls to \$250 with block pricing. Block pricing extracts \$1000 of the consumer's surplus, converting it into revenues for the seller. Managers are remiss in their fiduciary responsibilities to company owners if they do not pursue all legal avenues to capture this wealth from their customers. Faint-hearted employees, those incapable or unwilling to devise and implement value-enhancing strategies such as block pricing, are doomed to mediocrity or the unemployment lines.

PERFECT PRICE DISCRIMINATION: ALL-OR-NOTHING PRICING

Perfect price discrimination is the limiting case of block pricing; all consumer's surplus is appropriated by the seller. That is, the seller charges the buyer the prices indicated by the demand curve, leaving the consumer indifferent between purchase or not. Practically speaking, although from a seller's point of view this is nirvana, perfect price discrimination is difficult to implement. Indeed, in actual practice, probably the only way to accomplish total dissipation of consumer's surplus is through all-or-nothing pricing. Again, consider the demand curve

$$p = 100 - q,$$

and, for simplicity, let marginal cost of production be zero.[14] Again, the single-

---

[14] This assumption is not as analytically remote as you might first imagine. Conceptually, just reorient your mind. If marginal cost is \$10, and demand is $p = \$110 - q$, simply reconstruct the figure with the origin shifted to the point (0, 10) rather than the natural origin (0, 0). This realignment effectively shifts the demand curve down by the amount of marginal cost. That is, construct a net of marginal cost demand curve. All analytical principles hold here that apply to the original problem, and the exercise is greatly simplified.

price solution is to sell 50 units at $50 returning revenues (profits or quasi-rents as the case may be) of $2500. But now consider the practice of not offering the customer a choice over price or quantity—that is, make him a take-it-or-leave-it offer in *price and quantity*. This is called an **all-or-nothing pricing** strategy. We have now abandoned the idea that the monopolist chooses either price or quantity and the buyer chooses the other. Now the seller selects both price and quantity. What is the appropriate price and quantity? The goal is total extraction of consumer's surplus. This suggests a solution. The total consumer happiness achieved from buying 100 units is the area under the demand curve. Since the demand curve in question is linear, this can be computed as the area of the triangle under the demand curve from zero units up to 100 units, or by integration of the demand curve over the same range. The area of the triangle is 0.5•(100)•(100) = $5000. Using the general technique of integration, this is

$$\int_{0}^{100} (100 - q)\, dq = \$5000.$$

A simple strategy emerges: Charge the buyer $5000 for the right to buy 100 units, or say to the buyer, "You may buy 100 units at $500 per unit." Of course, the buyer is indifferent between (1) buying the 100 units for a total of $5000 and (2) leaving the store without purchasing anything. Consequently, the seller must sweeten the offer ever so slightly, say 100 units for $4995. The customer then accepts the all-or-nothing offer, buys the 100 units, and leaves the store with $5 of consumer's surplus. Profit or value maximization requires that the inducement to buy, $5 in this case, be as small as possible. Generosity of this type is unrewarding to the firm. The offer must be sufficiently large to entice purchase, but no larger. Competition among managers and other firms makes survival a tenuous proposition at best. Managers of firms who have the ability to perfectly price discriminate but fail to exercise that power are slowly but surely replaced by rivals.

Price Determination under All-or-Nothing Pricing

Under perfect price discrimination, all-or-nothing pricing, the demand curve becomes the marginal revenue function. Each additional unit of output sold commands the buyer's demand price. In essence, all-or-nothing pricing perfectly price discriminates, extracting all the consumer's surplus from the buyer. Profit maximizing output is determined by the intersection of demand and marginal cost. The average price per unit is computed by integrating the demand function to the optimal output (calculating the total willingness to pay), yielding total revenue, and simply dividing by output. All consumer's surplus is appropriated. This **average revenue function** lies above (to the right) of the demand function; the all-or-nothing price is greater than marginal revenue. See Figure 9.7. A product demand schedule is drawn. By the previous analysis, this demand schedule is the firm's marginal revenue function. Average revenue lies above the demand curve. The profit maximizing quantity is determined at the intersection

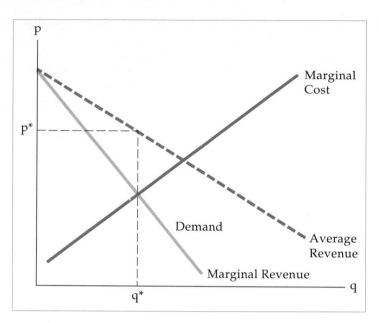

Figure 9.7
All-or-Nothing Pricing

of demand (marginal revenue) and marginal cost. The all-or-nothing price is read from the average revenue function.[15]

The problem of all-or-nothing pricing is now greatly simplified. The firm equates marginal revenue to marginal cost and prices off the all-or-nothing demand function. *This is the same algorithm employed in the case of the simple, single-price monopolist.* The only alteration is that here the product demand curve is the marginal revenue function. Marginal cost equals marginal revenue at q^* output; the all-or-nothing price is p^*. The buyer is offered q^* units at a price of p^* per unit. One last observation is worth noting: Since marginal revenue under all-or-nothing pricing lies to the right of marginal cost in the simple, single-price case, *the perfect price discriminating firm produces more output* than the single-price seller.[16]

For a general solution to the problem of all-or-nothing pricing consider the problem mathematically. The appropriate all-or-nothing price extracts the entire consumer's surplus. Demand is

$p = p(q)$.

Revenues are the area under the demand curve,

---

[15] For a linear demand curve, the average revenue function has the same price axis intercept and one-half the slope.

[16] Indeed output is the same as it would be under competition. Only the price differs.

$$R = \int_0^q p(q) \, dq.$$

Costs are determined by output,

$$C = C(q),$$

and therefore profit is

$$\Pi = \int_0^q p(q) \, dq - C(q).$$

Maximum profits occur where marginal revenue equals marginal costs or where

$$d[\int_0^q p(q) \, dq]/dq = dC/dq,$$

but by the rules of integration and differentiation, marginal revenue in the all-or-nothing case is simply the demand function,

$$d[\int_0^q p(q) \, dq]/dq = p(q).$$

Therefore, profit is at maximum where $p(q) = dC/dq$. From this we see that when the firm uses an all-or-nothing pricing strategy, the demand curve becomes the marginal revenue function. The profit maximizing output is determined by the intersection of the demand function with marginal cost.

Examples of All-or-Nothing Pricing

Have you ever noticed that candy bars in theaters are typically much larger than the ones offered in grocery stores and vending machines? Why? Once a person has purchased a ticket into a theater, competition from candy sellers is delimited. The theater faces the market demand for candy, presuming the movie goer has not smuggled in sweets. To exploit this situation, the theater offers only large candy bars for sale, putting you, the buyer, in an all-or- nothing situation. You are not allowed to purchase one, two, or three small candy bars; instead, you can buy a single very large bar, or none at all. Faced with this choice, some buyers opt for the large purchase even though many, if not most, would have chosen a smaller quantity (at the prevailing price per unit) if that option were available. If the theater has properly chosen the size of the candy bar and the price, the consumer is virtually indifferent between a big box of candy and none at all. The only solution, short of buying candy outside and sneaking it in, is to go to the movies with a friend and share, a common practice in fact. Remember the rule: *A customer who leaves your store happy is a customer with your money in her pocket.*

In many resort towns during special occasions, say in New Orleans during the Sugar Bowl or Mardi Gras or in Calgary during the 1988 Winter Olympic Games, hotels only book rooms for a minimum of three days. So-called two-for-one sales are another example of all-or-nothing pricing. Here, rather than cutting the price in half for each good, the seller effectively cuts the price in half, but only if the buyer purchases two or more units.

MULTIPART PRICING

Hypothetical Business Problem 9.2

A community theater produces 12 different plays per year. Each play is performed three nights per week for a month. There are two types of demanders, high and low. The high demander's willingness to pay to see plays is given by the function

$$q_h = 40 - p.$$

The low demander's function is

$$q_l = 30 - p.$$

The marginal cost of selling an extra ticket is practically zero, and for simplicity we assume it is:

$$MC = 0.$$

The community has 100 low demanders and 100 high demanders. If a single price is charged all viewers, what price maximizes profit? Is it profitable to employ a multipart tariff in this situation? If so, what are the appropriate prices?

Multipart tariffs present the solution to many pricing problems. Country clubs often charge two-part prices. Members pay monthly or annual dues for the right to play golf and tennis, to swim, or to eat in the restaurant. Each of these services also commands a separate price for each use. The total charge has two parts—a fixed fee irrespective of consumption, and a second price dependent on the actual quantity used by the buyer. Two- (and three-) part pricing strategies can be used to implement market segmentation and perfect price discrimination when neither would otherwise be possible. For example, if there are differences in the price elasticity of demand across buyers, but not in ways discernible to the seller, market segmentation is not possible. In the right circumstances, two-part pricing forces the buyers to reveal their price elasticity of demand.

Each segment of a two-part tariff has its purpose and effects. The fixed fee, F, is designed to capture consumer's surplus *without affecting the quantity demanded.* Hence, it is not tied or related to the amount purchased. The second component, the per unit charge, restricts the amount taken by the buyer. Without this charge, the buyer would consume virtually limitless quantities up to the point where the marginal value of additional service was nil (unless of course there are transportation or other transactions costs borne by the purchaser). Naturally, both charges add to revenues.

Start with the simple case presented in Figure 9.8. Here there is *one* demander for the good in question. His demand is D. Let marginal cost be constant at MC. In this simple case, the profit maximizing two-part tariff is easy to calculate. The goal is complete expropriation of consumer's surplus. This is accomplished by charging a fixed fee equal to the area below demand but above marginal cost, shown by the tinted area in Figure 9.8. In addition, there is a per unit price, p^*, equal to marginal cost. Given this price the demander purchases q^* units of the good. Revenue to the seller is

$$F + p^* \cdot q^*.$$

What is the logic of this strategy? In general, the producer does not want to induce the buyer to purchase units that she or he values less than the marginal cost of production; on net, this only detracts from profits. Since the demander values units past q^* less than they cost to produce, if forced to purchase them at marginal cost, his consumer's surplus from earlier units bought is diminished. This reduces the consumer's surplus available for capture by the seller. To repeat, in general, forcing the buyer to take units that he values less than their marginal cost of production is not attractive.[17]

FIGURE 9.8
Two-Part Tariff, One Demander

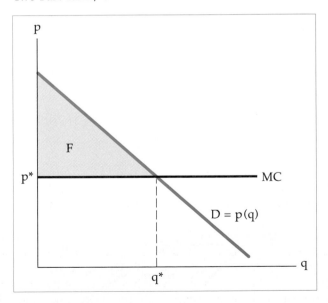

---

[17] This proposition is predicated on the condition that the buyer may purchase whatever volume she chooses. As we have previously discussed, there are situations, such as all-or-nothing–style offers, where this condition does not hold.

In sum, the per unit tariff is set to marginal cost, $p^* = MC$, and the fixed fee extracts all consumer's surplus,

$$F = \int_0^{q^*} [p(q) - p^*]dq.$$

The effect of perfect price discrimination is replicated; price equals marginal cost, and the seller gets all the consumer's surplus. Adding additional *but identical* buyers does not affect the solution. Each demander pays a fixed fee of F for the right to purchase unlimited quantities and a price of $MC = p^*$ per unit for each unit bought. With multiple buyers, total revenue is

$$n \bullet F + n \bullet p^* q^*,$$

where n is the number of identical buyers.

Of course, the buyers are not usually homogeneous. Consult Figure 9.9. Two demands are represented, D_1, which is $q_1 = q_1(p)$, and D_2, $q_2 = q_2(p)$. We have set the problem up here so the seller sets price and the buyer purchases as much as he likes at that price. In the ideal case, the seller charges each demander marginal cost per unit consumed, extracting the individual consumer's surpluses with two separate fixed fees. This strategy breaks down if the seller cannot identify the buyers or if resale between the buyer is possible. Hence and in general, the seller

FIGURE 9.9
Two-Part Tariff, Nonidentical Buyers

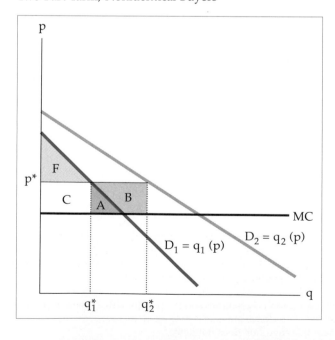

charges each buyer the same fixed fee.[18] At this point, a decision must be made whether to sell to both buyers or forsake the lesser demander, D_1 in this case, and address only the larger demander, D_2, and perfectly discriminate against him. So, at all points in the case of multiple potential buyers with different demands, the seller must compare the profits from having n buyers versus the profits from $n - 1$ demanders. What is profit in the two-demand case? It is twice the fixed fee plus the difference between price and cost times sales:

$$\Pi = 2 \bullet F + (p - MC) \bullet [q_1(p) + q_2(p)].$$

The seller selects F and p, but F cannot exceed the consumer's surplus of the smaller demander. Therefore, F is constrained to be

$$F = \int_{p}^{\infty} q_1(p)dp.$$

Substituting this expression for F into the profit function yields the constrained profit function:

$$\mathscr{L} = 2F + (p - MC)[q_1(p) + q_2(p)] + \lambda[F - \int_{p}^{\infty} q_1(p)dp].$$

The first order conditions necessary to maximize profit are found by taking the partial derivatives of $\mathscr{L}$ with respect to the two prices, F and p, and the multiplier, λ, setting them all to zero, and solving.[19] In reverse order, these are

$$\partial \mathscr{L}/\partial \lambda = F - \int_{p}^{\infty} q_1(p_1)dp = 0, \tag{9.1}$$

$$\partial \mathscr{L}/\partial p = (p - MC) \bullet [q'_1(p) + q'_2(p)] + [q_1(p) + q_2(p)] - \lambda \bullet [q_1(p)] = 0, \tag{9.2}$$

and

$$\partial \mathscr{L}/\partial F = 2 - \lambda = 0, \tag{9.3}$$

where q'_i is the slope of the ith demand function; that is, $q'_i \equiv \partial q_i/\partial p$. Equation 9.3 implies that $\lambda = 2$, the number of demanders. Substituting this equality into

---

[18] It is noted that some sellers can charge different fees. Examples include the American Economic Association, which charges dues based on faculty rank, and the Faculty Club at the University of Rochester, which employs the same strategy.

[19] See the appendix to Chapter 2 for a discussion of the method of Lagrange multipliers applied to the problem of maximizing a function.

equation 9.1 for λ yields the solution to the profit maximizing problem in two equations:

$$F = \int_{p}^{\infty} q_1(p_1)dp \tag{9.4}$$

and

$$(p - MC) = [q_1(p) - q_2(p)]/[q_1'(p) + q_2'(p)]. \tag{9.5}$$

Since both demands are assumed to obey the first law, then $q_i' < 0$ for the two of them, and since the second demand is greater than the first at every price, $q_2(p) > q_1(p)$, it follows that the expression on the right-hand side of equation 9.5 is positive. We conclude that $(p - MC) > 0$ or $p > MC$. Price is greater than marginal cost, but the differential is smaller than in the case of the single-price seller.[20]

Refer again to Figure 9.9. The profit maximizing price, labeled p^*, is plotted. The optimal fixed charge, labeled F, equals the area of the consumer's surplus to the smaller demander, which is the tinted area in the diagram. The seller gets this fee from *both* buyers. The first buyer purchases q_1^* output, and the second chooses q_2^*. Revenues from fixed fees are $2 \cdot F$. Net revenues from quantity sales—that is, revenues minus avoidable costs, are two times the area of C in the figure plus the area $A + B$. Thus, total net revenues can be expressed as $F + C$ (from the first buyer) plus $(F + C + A + B)$ from the second buyer, or $(2 \cdot F + 2 \cdot C + A + B)$. Raising the price per unit (and lowering F) reduces $F + C$ and increases A to the first buyer. Since the seller does not capture the area of A from the first buyer, on net, the change in A marks the decrement in revenue to the first buyer. Raising the per unit charge, p^*, to the second buyer also reduces $F + C$ and raises A, but here the seller captures the area A from the second or smaller buyer. The area of B, captured by the seller, also changes when price per unit is raised. Hence, the strategy can be summarized as follows: Choose a price per unit, p^*, to maximize the area $B - A$, and charge a fixed fee to capture the entire consumer's surplus of the smaller demander. In cases where the two-part tariff is tractable, this pricing policy improves profits over the single-price strategy. However, there may exist an even better policy. Consider the three-part price.

---

[20] For the single-price seller, the profit maximizing price, p_s, is determined by the condition

$$(p_s - MC) = -[q_1(p_s) + q_2(p_s)]/[q_1'(p_s) + q_2'(p_s)].$$

In all cases,

$$-[q_1(p_s) + q_2(p_s)]/[q_1'(p) + q_2'(p)] > -[q_1(p) - q_2(p)]/[q_1'(p) + q_2'(p)]$$

because

$$q_1(p_s) + q_2(p_s) > q_1(p) - q_2(p);$$

the sum of the quantities sold to both buyers under a single price exceeds the difference between the quantities sold to the two buyers under a two-part tariff.

The Three-Part Price

Consult Figure 9.10, and consider the problem through the eyes of the second buyer. At price p^*, she chooses to buy q_2^* units. But notice that the value to her of some additional units exceeds marginal cost. At q_2^*, her demand price lies above the marginal cost curve. Suppose the seller makes an amendment to the status quo ante, offering to sell any units in excess of, say m, at a price equal to marginal cost, MC. If m is sufficiently close to q_2^*, the buyer may choose to buy more output. Specifically, if the area of triangle d in Figure 9.10 is less than the area of triangle e in the same drawing, then the buyer's total consumer's surplus increases by her purchase of an extra set of units, those between q_2^* and q_2^{**}. To ensure profit maximization, m must be chosen by the seller to equate the areas of triangles d and e.

In the two-part tariff case, the second buyer pays a fixed fee F and price p^* for q_2^* units of output. If faced with the right to buy *more* units at a price of MC, the buyer chooses an extra $(q_2^{**} - q_2^*)$ units when $d < e$; that is, the opportunity to buy more units yields positive net utility. In practice, for example, a golf club may charge annual dues per member of $1000. Green fees per 18-hole session are $15 until the member has played six 18-hole sessions in the month, and then the green fee is $7.50 per round for all additional rounds.

FIGURE 9.10
The Three-Part Tariff

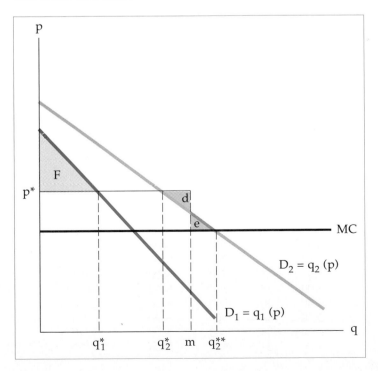

This section on multipart pricing was introduced with a hypothetical business problem. We have developed the theory in sufficient detail for you to solve that problem. Consider the following analysis as one approach.

Suggested Solution to Problem 9.2

To solve problem 9.2, observe that since marginal cost is zero, the marginal cost equals marginal revenue rule mandates that marginal revenue, R', also equal zero. But what is marginal revenue? Compute total demand first. Consider Table 9.5 where the demand schedules are computed.

TABLE 9.5   THEATER DEMAND

PRICE PER TICKET	q_h	q_l	TOTAL QUANTITY DEMANDED	TOTAL REVENUE	MARGINAL REVENUE
$30.00	1000	0	1000	$30000	$25.00
29.00	1100	100	1200	34800	23.00
28.00	1200	200	1400	39200	21.00
27.00	1300	300	1600	43200	19.00
26.00	1400	400	1800	46800	17.00
25.00	1500	500	2000	50000	15.00
24.00	1600	600	2200	52800	13.00
23.00	1700	700	2400	55200	11.00
22.00	1800	800	2600	57200	9.00
21.00	1900	900	2800	58800	7.00
20.00	2000	1000	3000	60000	5.00
19.00	2100	1100	3200	60800	3.00
18.00	2200	1200	3400	61200	1.00
17.50	2250	1250	3500	61250	0.00
17.00	2300	1300	3600	61200	−1.00
16.00	2400	1400	3800	60800	−3.00
15.00	2500	1500	4000	60000	−5.00
14.00	2600	1600	4200	58800	−7.00
13.00	2700	1700	4400	57200	−9.00
12.00	2800	1800	4600	55200	−11.00
11.00	2900	1900	4800	52800	−13.00
10.00	3000	2000	5000	50000	−15.00
9.00	3100	2100	5200	46800	−17.00
8.00	3200	2200	5400	43200	−19.00
7.00	3300	2300	5600	39200	−21.00
6.00	3400	2400	5800	34800	−23.00
5.00	3500	2500	6000	30000	−25.00
4.00	3600	2600	6200	24800	−27.00
3.00	3700	2700	6400	19200	−29.00
2.00	3800	2800	6600	13200	−31.00
1.00	3900	2900	6800	6800	−33.00

The computation of marginal revenue is straightforward. Total demand, q_t, is the sum of the individual demands,

$$q_t = 100 \cdot q_h + 100 \cdot q_l =$$
$$100 \cdot (40 - p) + 100 \cdot (30 - p) = 7000 - 200 \cdot p.$$

The inverse demand function is

$$p = 35 - q_t/200,$$

and total revenue is this price times total quantity:

$$R = p \cdot q = (35 - q_t/200) \cdot q_t.$$

Marginal revenue is the derivative of the revenue function with respect to quantity:

$$R' = 35 - q_t/100.$$

Setting this equal to marginal cost, zero, and solving for q_t, yields the profit maximizing number of tickets to sell,

$$q_t = 3500.$$

From the price formula, the profit maximizing price is

$$p = 35 - 3500/200 = \$17.50.$$

Note in Table 9.5 that marginal revenue is zero at a price of $17.50 per ticket. The theater charging one price sells 3500 tickets per year at $17.50 apiece. Total sales can be split between the two demand classes by inserting the price into the respective demand functions. High demanders purchase 22.5 each per year, for a total of 2250 [$100 \cdot (40 - 17.50)$]. Low demanders purchase the remaining 1250 [$100 \cdot (30 - 17.50)$]. Total revenue is $17.50 \cdot 3500 = \$ 61,250$ per year. Contrast this outcome with a plan to require each patron to pay an annual membership fee for the right to buy tickets.

What is the profit maximizing membership fee and price per ticket here? Recall the solution computed in the last section—that is, equations 9.4 and 9.5, and applied to this problem:

$$F = \int_{p}^{\infty} Q_1(p_1)dp, \qquad (9.6)$$

$$(p - MC) = [Q_1(p) - Q_2(p)]/[q_1'(p) + Q_2'(p)] \qquad (9.7)$$

where Q_1 is the total small demand and Q_2 is the total large demand. In this example, the total small demand is 100 times the individual small demand, q_l; $Q_1(p)$ is $100 \cdot q_l(p)$. Therefore,

$$Q_1 = 100 \cdot [q_l(p)] = 100 \cdot (30 - p) = 3000 - 100 \cdot p,$$

and similarly, the total large demand, $Q_2(p)$, is 100 times the individual large demand, q_h:

$$Q_2 = 100 \cdot [q_h(p)] = 100 \cdot (40 - p) = 4000 - 100 \cdot p.$$

Consequently, the slopes of the two aggregate demand functions are

$$Q'_1 = -100,$$

and

$$Q'_2 = -100.$$

Inserting all these values into equation 9.7 (recall that marginal cost is zero) and solving for p yields the profit maximizing price per ticket,

$$p = [(3000 - 100 \cdot p) - (4000 - 1000 \cdot p)]/(-100 - 100),$$

or

$$p = \$10.00.$$

Note that this is quite a bit less, $7.50 or 43 percent, than the profit maximizing single price of $17.50 computed in the first case.

What is the appropriate annual fee? It must extract all the consumer's surplus from each of the lesser demanders. To do this, we must find the area under the small demand curve above the per unit price. The per unit price is $10 per ticket, and the maximum price any small demander is willing to pay for a ticket is $30. Therefore, integration of the smaller demand function from the price per ticket, $10, to the upper limit of the buyer's willingness to pay, $30, yields the consumer's surplus for the representative small demander and, hence, the optimal lump sum fee, F. From equation 9.6,

$$F = \int_{10}^{30} q_1(p)dp,$$

or

$$F = \int_{10}^{30} (30 - 10)dp = \$200.$$

The two-part pricing solution involves an annual fee of $200 per patron, and each ticket to a play costs $10. Figure 9.11 also demonstrates calcula-

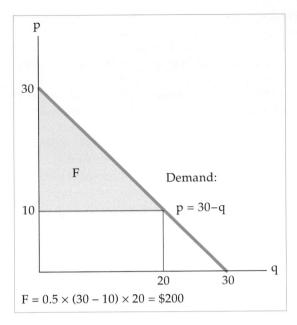

$F = 0.5 \times (30 - 10) \times 20 = \$200$

FIGURE 9.11
Annual Fee Computation

tion of the profit maximizing annual fee. Demand for a representative small demander is drawn there. Note that the maximum price this person is willing to pay for a ticket is $30, the upper limit of integration. At the price per ticket of $10, 20 tickets are purchased per person per year. The annual fee that extracts all consumer's surplus is the area of the tinted triangle, F [$= 0.5 \bullet 20 \bullet (30 - 10) = 200$].

Compute total revenue and compare it to the revenues under a single regime. Revenues from annual fees, R_F, are the sum from the two classes of demanders,

$$R_F = F \bullet 100 + F \bullet 100 = \$200 \bullet (200) = \$40,000,$$

and revenues from tickets sales, R_t, are

$$R_t = \$10 \bullet 100 \bullet (40 - 10) + \$10 \bullet 100 \bullet (30 - 10) = \$30,000 + \$20,000 = \$50,000.$$

Total revenues are $40,000 + $50,000 = $90,000.[21] Compared to a single price, revenues with a two-part price, are

---

[21] The prudent manager must ensure that profits here are not less than they would be if the theater only sold to the high demanders. The appropriate strategy there is to charge marginal cost, nothing, to each of the high demanders and extract all their consumer's surplus with a lump-sum, fixed fee. Individually their demands are $q_h = 40 - p$. Therefore, at a price of 0, consumer's surplus is $800, which is extractable through a fixed annual fee. Summed over the 100 buyers, this strategy yields a total revenue of $80,000, but this is inferior to the scheme selling to both classes of demanders. Therefore, the theater sells to both classes.

$$\$90,000 - \$61,250 = \$28,750$$

higher, an increase of 46.9 percent. Since the marginal cost of patrons is zero, profits are also higher by $28,750. Also observe the change in attendance summarized in Table 9.6.

Total attendance is considerably higher under the two-part pricing strategy; 5000 total tickets are bought compared to 3500 under the single price. Moreover, the *average* revenue per ticket sold has actually increased slightly from $17.50 to $18.00 ($90,000/5000 = $18), and since more people purchase tickets, *revenues and profits are higher.*

Given the discussion about three-part prices, there may be an even better strategy yet. Consider Figure 9.12, where the demand schedule for a representative high demander is drawn. At a price of $10, this demander buys 30 tickets per year. Her consumer's surplus, net of the annual membership fee, is the area of triangle *ABC* minus the fixed fee, or 0.5•30•(40 − 10) − $200 = $250. There is additional consumer's surplus equal to the area of triangle *BDE* that can be captured by the appropriate three-part pricing rule. Suppose the theater offers patrons as many tickets as they would like for free after they have bought 35 tickets during the year. Then the customer thinks, "At the current price, I am buying 30 tickets. However, I can get additional consumer's surplus equal to the area of triangle *BDE,* $50 in monetary terms, if I buy five more tickets for $10 each, and then get five more tickets for free. On net I am no worse off."[22] So the high demander buys the extra five tickets for $10 apiece and gets another five additional tickets for free.[23] Revenues and profits increase by

TABLE 9.6   THE IMPACT OF TWO-PART PRICING

	HIGH DEMANDER'S QUANTITY	LOW DEMANDER'S QUANTITY	REVENUE
Single Price $17.50	2250	1250	$61,250
Two-Part Price p = $10.00 F = $20.00	3000	2000	$90,000

[22] The theater might throw in a canvas gym bag with its logo on the side in order to make the three-part price attractive to the high demander. Remember the theater would like to extract most of the consumer's surplus but not all. This leaves the buyer indifferent. We must leave the buyer some residual surplus or he or she will not take the third part of the pricing scheme.

[23] Obviously, the theater must somehow prevent the buyer from taking an unlimited number of tickets and reselling them. One way to stop this is to supply a membership card that must be shown for admission. Another way is to print the buyer's name on the ticket. Yet another scheme simply puts the person's name on a list which allows free entry.

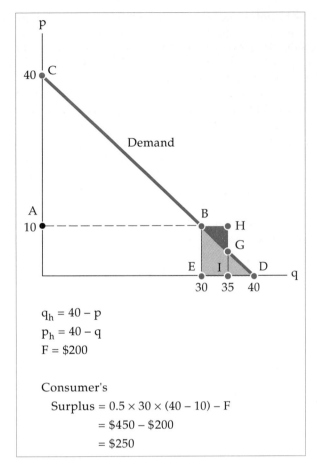

$q_h = 40 - p$

$p_h = 40 - q$

$F = \$200$

Consumer's
Surplus $= 0.5 \times 30 \times (40 - 10) - F$
$= \$450 - \$200$
$= \$250$

FIGURE 9.12
The Three-Part Price

$50 per high demander, or 100•$50 = $5000. Under three-part pricing, total revenue is $90,000 + $5000 or $95,000.

From the consumer's point of view, the extra cost of the additional 10 units is the area of the rectangle *BHIE* or $10•5 = $50. The value of the extra units is given by the area under the demand curve from point *E* to point *D* (0.5•$10•10 = $50). The net gain to the buyer is the area of the rectangle minus the area of the triangle. Therefore, the consumer is better off accepting the third part of the offer as long as the area of the triangle *GDI* exceeds the area of the triangle *BGH*. In this case, they are equal, making the consumer indifferent.

In sum, the three-part pricing strategy requires each patron to make an annual membership contribution of $200. The first 35 tickets a person buys are $10 each, and, after that, entry is free and unrestricted. It is worth noting that this strategy does not require the theater manager to classify individual patrons into the high or low demand class; they reveal themselves through their purchasing pattern. Perhaps this is the most important feature of the multipart pricing scheme.

PEAK LOAD PRICING

Many companies must cope with fluctuating demand. The post office is a good example. Restaurants are another. During the lunch hour, say 12:00 to 2:00, demand in a restaurant is one level, but during the dinner period, say 7:00 to 11:00, demand is considerably higher. Parking lots face one demand schedule during weekdays, quite another on weekends. Electric utilities have much larger demand for their output during daylight hours than during the early hours of morning, say 2:00 A.M. to 5:00 A.M. Similarly, telephone companies encounter the highest demand for their services during the day and the lowest demand late at night. For some establishments, demand is so small in some periods, they simply shut down. Economists call these consistent and predictable demand shifts, **peak loads** or **peak demand**.

Analysis of peak load problems is rather straightforward, seemingly similar to price discrimination, yet different. Almost by definition, products that have peaking demand characteristics are unstorable and not resalable by the purchaser. Recall the examples. Lunches are not easily changed to dinners by the customer. Most food requires refrigeration, and the very nature of serving lunch precludes its resale or storage by either buyer or seller.[24]

Strictly speaking, peak load pricing is not a monopoly problem, although it may be. Many competitive firms, those with perfectly elastic demand for their services, encounter consistent, predictable demand shifts. Again, the restaurant comes to mind immediately. Whether monopoly or competitor, the analytics of peak load pricing are the same. The following story, an open letter from the CEO of American Airlines to his passengers, reports on the peak load problems faced by airlines.

> One of the questions lots of customers ask, often, is "Why can't you put a few less seats on your airplanes and give us more space?"
>
> The answer is that our customers don't put enough value on more space to enable us to do so.
>
> Now obviously, every airline passenger would like to have more space. Moreover, we'd like to provide it. However, like every other company, we must offer products our customers—and those who purchase travel for them— are willing to *buy*, and more space isn't high on the list of things that influence a traveler's choice of airlines. When your customers vote as they do with their pocketbooks every day, there are many more votes for low fares and frequent flights than there are for fewer seats with more space between them.

---

[24] It is interesting to note that the so-called fast foods are made more storable and resalable by their very nature of construction. The inputs are stored until you arrive in the restaurant, muting the peak load problem for these establishments. Perhaps this helps explain the absence of time-of-day pricing in many hamburger restaurants.

Here's how the tradeoff works. Let's assume that Open Airways puts 100 seats on a particular kind of airplane and that Cozy Airlines puts 120 seats on the same airplane. While travelers like the greater comfort Open offers, Cozy can carry more passengers. Thus, at peak flying times—on Friday afternoons, for instance, and around major holidays—Cozy Airlines does a lot better than Open. Open can make up the difference only if it gets far more than its share of travelers during off-peak periods, when flights are *not* full.

To cast a meaningful vote and make Open's investment in added space pay off, passengers would have to seek out Open's flights even if that were moderately inconvenient. Let's say a business traveler finishes a meeting earlier than expected, arrives at the airport for the trip back home at 3:30 P.M. and has a choice between a Cozy flight at 4:00, on an airplane with more seats, or an Open flight on an airplane with fewer seats—45 minutes later. The only way he or she could vote for Open would be to wait for its flight at 4:45.

But that is not the choice most passengers make. Years of experience and lots of research have taught us that our customers prefer two things above all else: first, low prices, and second, frequent service and lots of time-of-day choices. Unhappily, greater comfort does not seem to be as important as other product features in attracting preferential patronage. That is, most people are not willing to make an effort to find a seat on Open just because it has more space and that, in turn, creates a real problem for any airline that would like to offer its customers more comfortable accommodations.

To quantify the problem, let's consider the impact of taking out a single row of seats. At American, 77 percent of our aircraft are narrowbodied planes with an average of 146 seats, either five or six to a row in the coach cabin. Taking out just one row of coach seats would cause us to forgo more than $50 million a year of revenue. Removing two or three rows, depending on the aircraft type, would allow us to offer as much room between each row of coach seats as there is in first class on those aircraft—and would cost upwards of $150 million per year!

At American, we have tried several "more space" experiments over the years. While our customers are always complimentary about the improved comfort, they have never thought it significant enough to give us the off-peak market-share premium we would need to balance the losses we would suffer by turning away customers at peak times.

What this means, in effect, is that there isn't more space because our customers don't value it highly enough. Given that fact, we work hard at making everyone on board as comfortable as possible—a goal to which every one of us is dedicated.[25]

To better understand the problem of peak demand, two different demands for a restaurant are drawn in Figure 9.13. Lunch demand is D_l; dinner demand is several times as large, D_d. The marginal cost of supplying meals is given by MC. Because of the nature of meals, it is inappropriate to sum the demand schedules and charge a price based on the marginal revenue function associated with this total demand. Moreover, it is not wise to attempt price discrimination based on total demand. Instead, since lunch meals can be produced separately and inde-

[25] Robert L. Crandall, "Why Not More Space? To our Customers from the Chairman of American Airlines," Reprinted from *American Way,* the inflight magazine of American Airlines, September 1, 1991, p. 10.

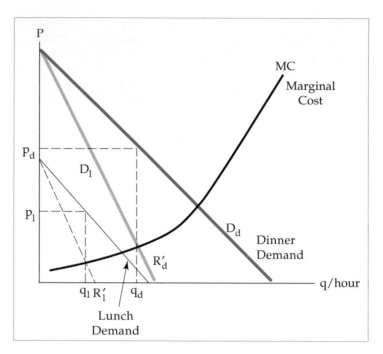

FIGURE 9.13
Peak Load Pricing

pendently from dinner meals, the firm bifurcates production and prices each product without regard to the other. Specifically, in Figure 9.13, marginal revenue from lunches, R'_l, intersects marginal cost at q_l meals. These are priced at p_l apiece. Similarly, profit maximization produces q_d dinners at a price of p_d each. During the peak period, dinner in this example, price is higher to the customer partly because demand is greater but also because, in the example chosen, marginal cost increases with output.

Peak load pricing is a topic separate from price discrimination; it is discussed here because in practice it resembles price discrimination. When a firm faces different demand at different times of the day, week, month, or year, and when production in these separate times is independent, the appropriate strategy is to segregate demand, treating each component separately. To be sure, nothing prevents a firm from employing price discrimination or multipart tariffs *within* a demand classification, but the firm is ill-advised to merge demands for pricing purposes under these circumstances. In the case of a restaurant, it is generally not prudent to add the lunch and dinner demands together, compute the total marginal revenue, and equate it to marginal cost. Rather, this calculation should be done for lunch and dinner separately. Some electric utilities charge different prices during day and night, but they still price discriminate between residential and commercial customers.

Table 9.7 reports the fees charged by one large yacht rental service for one

TABLE 9.7   WEEKLY YACHT RENTAL RATES

BOAT[a]	PEAK SEASON 12/16–4/14	MID-SEASON 4/15–7/31	LOW SEASON 8/1–11/15 11/16–12/15
Tartan 33	$1495	$1250	$1000
Beneteau 35	1686	1375	1150
Morgan 38	1888	1375	1200
Morgan 41	2110	1540	1332
Endeavour 40	2296	1642	1480
Endeavour 42	2597	1768	1642
Morgan 44	2495	1723	1587
Irwin 44	2595	1723	1587
Hirsh 45	2595	1723	1587

[a] The number after the brand name of each boat is its length in feet.

week-long rental in the U.S. Virgin Islands.[26] Like many seasonal or peak businesses, price is higher when demand is greater.

In addition, the company offered a special in mid- and low season. (Is this price discrimination or peak load pricing?) In mid-season, the renter could use the boat for nine days in lieu of a week; and during the low season, the boat was available for 11 days. Thus we have peak load pricing coupled with all-or-nothing pricing. One is designed to accommodate regular and anticipated seasonal shifts in demand, the other to exploit the elasticity of demand.

Examine Table 9.8, which reports the prices charged in 1988 at a large resort hotel in North Carolina.[27]

The first feature to note is the peak load pricing scheme. The interesting thing here is the peak load pricing scheme *within* a peak load bracket. The resort charges higher rates during the summer months of July and August than the spring and fall months; demand is the highest in the summer. But throughout the year, the rates are lower for guests arriving on Sunday or Monday, the days of the week when demand is lowest regardless of season. Next note the all-or-nothing style pricing approach of offering packages for golf and tennis. A room by itself costs $53 per person per day or $371 per week. The same room with all the golf you care to play is $404. If the person plans to play $404 − $371 = $33 or more of golf (more than two days since the greens fee is $15 per day for guests not on the golf package), then he is better off choosing the package, *but this choice must be made in advance.* This strategy takes advantage of the consumer's uncertainty about the

[26] Hirsh Yacht Charters, 3655 Cortez, Bradenton, FL, 1987. Hirsh is no longer in business.

[27] The High Hampton Inn & Country Club, Cashiers, NC 28717.

TABLE 9.8   RESORT HOTEL PRICING

All Rates are per Person including 3 Meals
and a service charge in lieu of tipping

	APRIL 1 THROUGH JUNE 30 SEPT. 1 THROUGH OCT. 31			JULY 1 THROUGH AUG. 31		
	7 DAYS	4 DAYS	4 DAYS[a]	7 DAYS	4 DAYS	4 DAYS[a]
Golf Package (unlimited golf and tennis)						
2 Persons–1 Room	$404	$230	$207[a]	$425	$240	$216[a]
1 Person–1 Room	471	263	237[a]	484	269	242[a]
Tennis Package (unlimited tennis)						
2 Persons–1 Room	$384	$210	$187[a]	$405	$220	$196[a]
1 Person–1 Room	451	243	217	464	249	222[a]

REGULAR RATES
RATES PER PERSON PER DAY FOR A 7 DAY STAY

	APRIL 1 THROUGH JUNE 30 SEPT. 1 THROUGH OCT. 31	JULY 1 THROUGH AUG. 31
2 Persons–1 Room	$53	$56
1 Person–1 Room	63	65

(For stays of less than 7 days, add $3 per person per day)
(For stays of 4 weeks or longer, subtract 5%)
(Double Rooms are rented to one person at a single rate before July 1 and after August 31)

GREENS FEES FOR GUESTS NOT ON GOLF PACKAGE

Day	$15
Week	55
2 Weeks	102
3 Weeks	140
Month	175 for 1 person
	110 for additional family members

TENNIS

$4 per person per hour

all [a] rates only apply to stays beginning on Sunday or Monday

A policy is noted on the pricing schedule in bold face: If you wish to be on the Golf or Tennis package, you must advise us at the time of reservation or arrival. Because of accounting procedures, it is not possible to change rate schedules during or at the end of your visit.

number of golf games or tennis matches she might like to play.[28] The buyer is locked in from the start. Next observe the market segmentation pricing scheme. People who stay less than one week pay a higher price per day than people staying for a week. Visitors remaining for a month or more receive an additional discount. Observe that a second person always costs less than the first person, be it in the room or on the golf course. Note that tennis is charged by the hour not the court. A doubles match is charged twice as much as a singles match for the same court time.

Higher rates are charged for rooms with one person. This represents a classic example of market segmentation price discrimination. Presumably couples have a more inelastic demand for rooms than single visitors, and, of course, the market segmentation problem is resolved simply by observing the number of people in a room. This result may seem strange at first. After all, two people are consuming rather than one, but keep in mind what is being sold—a hotel room. And regardless of how many people sleep there, only one room is rented. It bears noting that this hotel includes meals with rooms, and hence all of the extra charge for a second person is *not* due to differences in the elasticity of demand across single and couple visitors. The restaurant sells meals to nonguests for $28 per day. However, this daily meal fee is less than the price difference for the room. The residual difference is the price discrimination wedge. Consider the regular spring or fall room rates; a single person pays $63 per day of which $28 is for meals, leaving a charge of $35 for the room and bed. At the same time, a couple pays twice $53 less two times $28, or $50, for the same room. So couples rent a double room for $50, while a single person rents a similar room with one bed for $36. We presume that part of this extra cost for the couple is due to the additional services used by the second person—more hot water, towels, and cleaning—but the remainder is due to the couple's more inelastic demand.

Is there a theoretical basis for believing that couples have a more inelastic demand for the hotel room? Well, if resort vacations are an income elastic good, a reasonable assumption, and if couples are richer than single renters, then a couple's demand may be more inelastic. It may be more difficult for a couple to impose on friends, sleep in a car, or find alternative accommodations; the substitutes are delimited, making demand more inelastic for them. It is also likely that couples are less willing to search the alternatives—they have already found someone to share vacation time with, while a single traveler may be more inclined to peruse the options in search of companionship. In addition, travel is more expensive for a couple than a single person, giving the loner more options. Additional search by the single vacationer makes demand more elastic for her or him; the choices are better known.

The main purpose of this example is to point out the myriad ways a firm might exploit the price elasticity of demand it faces. Not all hotels or motels encounter demand sufficiently inelastic to warrant the costs of such detail in

---

[28] The rate policy notes that "Because of accounting policies . . . " plans cannot be changed. What they might mean is, "Because the managers must *account* to the owners, we must make as much profit as possible. Therefore, you cannot change plans in midstream." If guests were allowed to change plans, no one would choose the golf plan until she was about to play the third day of golf.

pricing, and it would be a mistake to conclude that hotels not employing a strategy similar to the one outlined here are poorly managed. The circumstances of demand may be different. However, when the situation dictates, the forces of competition require the firm to exploit its position. Competition from other would-be managers usually leads to the replacement of managers who are armed with the ability to price discriminate but have no compunction to do so.

Public utilities face regular and predictable peak load demand shifts. Consider electric utilities. Early in the morning as people awake, industries start their facilities, and businesses open, the demand for electricity jumps. In the summer late in the afternoon, hot weather places a large demand on capacity as air conditioners run virtually nonstop. The producers of electric power must cope with this shift by having sufficient capacity to supply the extra demand. However, this creates the economic problem that during the late night and early morning hours their plants have excess capacity; they have idle capital. This means that they have idle resources that do not earn much money. Are there alternative ways of dealing with this problem? In a word, yes. Electric power producers have developed a notion they call **demand management**, which refers to the problem of coping with shifting demand.

They use a number of tools to contend with demand fluctuations. For instance, they construct pump storage facilities. In these situations a nuclear- or coal-powered plant is constructed near two lakes, one above the other in altitude. On the weekends and in the early morning hours, the power plant runs at full capacity, some electricity is sold, but the remainder is used to pump water uphill from the lower lake into the upper pool. Then, in the morning or other peak load period, the water runs back downhill turning hydro-generators to produce electricity. This technique effectively smooths the demand for electricity in the same way that regular firms produce for inventory.[29] In addition, some utilities cut the price of electricity in the low demand periods, say late at night and early in the morning, the same way the telephone company changes the rates for long distance during different hours of the day. Moreover, some companies have experimented with sophisticated devices that allow the power company to actually turn off a customer's hot water heater, air conditioner, or other device for a certain number of minutes each hour during the highest demand periods. Many industrial and commercial users of electricity pay an extra fee whenever their instantaneous demand exceeds a certain level. This is sometimes called a "demand charge."

We close this section by noting two time-of-day pricing schemes used by Domino's Pizza. The first involved a gambit called "Beat the Clock." In this 1988 pricing practice, Domino's had a special on Monday through Wednesday from 4:00 P.M. until 6:30 P.M. The caller paid the time of day as the price for a 16" one-topping pizza. This strategy charged an ever higher price as the time of day approached the peak period, beginning about the dinner hour, 6:30 P.M. in this case. We presume that demand was less in the late afternoon than it was at dinner time, and hence Domino's charged a lower price. In addition, we imagine that

---

[29] See the section in Chapter 7 on intermittent production for a more elaborate discussion.

each restaurant had some idle capacity during this period, making the costs of production lower in the 4:00–6:30 P.M. window.

Similarly, at another time in 1988, Domino's offered a "Late Night Special." On Sunday through Thursday nights, *after* 10 P.M., the buyer could purchase a 12" one-topping pizza for only $5. Again, we conjecture that demand was less after the primary dinner hour, and costs were lower because production capacity was less strained. Note that in both these examples, the "Beat the Clock" and the "Late Night Special," the discounts were not offered on the weekend. This suggests that pizza demand is higher (or the costs of production are higher) on Friday and Saturday than during the other days of the week.

TOPICS TO REVIEW

These are topics that you should feel comfortable with before you leave this chapter. If you cannot write out a clear and concise sentence or paragraph explaining the topic after you have worked on the study problems, you should reread the relevant section of the text.

Price Discrimination

Market Segmentation

Rules for Market Segmentation Price Discrimination

Block Pricing

All-or-Nothing Pricing

Multipart Pricing—Two-Part Pricing and Three-Part Pricing

Computation of Fixed Fees

Peak Loads and Peak Load Pricing

STUDY PROBLEMS

1. Purchase a soft drink from a vending machine close to your class. Now buy the same drink from a convenience store. Now buy the same soda from a large grocery store. Are the prices different? If so, why?

2. Return to the discussion of the pricing policies at the resort hotel. Observe that couples pay a higher price for a room than a single person renting the same room. Most motels and hotels do not employ this practice; two people can rent a room for the same price as a single person. Explain this difference. Is the resort hotel making a mistake, or are the rest of the motels and hotels in the world bypassing a profit opportunity? Or, do the circumstances merit the different pricing strategies? Before you answer, be aware that the resort hotel discussed is in the North Carolina mountains, isolated from comparable establishments and somewhat difficult to reach by car or plane. The nearest airport is more than an hour's drive away.

3. Recall the male-female bar pricing problem from the section on price discrimination and summarized in Table 9.3. Suppose the state passes a tax on all bar customers of $2 per person. What happens to the profit maximizing prices for

males and females? Further imagine the law prohibits price discrimination between males and females; the bar must charge one price. What is the new price with the $2 tax?

4. Most of you have access to some sort of a charge card. Consider the ones offered by American Express, Visa, and Mastercard. When a customer uses one of these in a store, the merchant pays a small fee, usually about 5 percent, of the charge to the credit card company. A customer who pays cash is rarely offered this discount. By contrast, some gasoline retailers who offer their own charge cards sell their gas at two prices, one for credit card users and a lower price for cash customers. Why don't other retailers routinely offer a discount to cash customers?

5. Many firms have patents giving them monopoly power; yet, many do not price discriminate across state boundaries. Almost surely there are differences in the price elasticity of demand across states. Why don't most manufacturers take advantage of this opportunity?

6. Many large mail order companies also have stores; Sears and L. L. Bean come to mind. Do you expect mail order prices (ignoring shipping costs) to be higher, lower, or the same as prices in the store?

7. At the Final Four of the 1987 NCAA Division I Soccer Championships, tickets were sold in two ways. A tournament pass was available for $11, allowing entry to the two semifinal games on Saturday plus entrance to the championship on Sunday. Alternatively, tickets to the Sunday game could be purchased for $9. In your opinion, is this an example of price discrimination or peak load pricing? Construct a *refutable* explanation of this pricing strategy.

8. In Seneca, South Carolina, on the corner of Townville St. and N. First Ave., is a pleasant little Mexican restaurant, Arturo's. In addition to the regular fare, the menu contains several different plates for children under 12 years of age. Interestingly, all the items on the menu are available for take-out *except* the food on the children's menu. Why do you think Arturo's does not sell children's plates for take-out?

9. For many years, AT&T was a legal monopolist providing telephone service. It charged a fee for each home phone that was tied to the system. Moreover, AT&T imposed the rule that only AT&T equipment could be attached to its lines. AT&T contended that nonstandard phones might not work properly and, worse, would foul up its network. Given the presence of so many non–AT&T phones today, one is inclined to challenge AT&T's argument. What other reason might AT&T have had for requiring customers to use AT&T phones? Does your explanation incorporate the fact that the phone company no longer charges a fee based on the number of telephones connected to a single line?

10. Before the practice was declared illegal in a famous antitrust case [*International Business Machines* v. *United States*, 298 U.S. 131 (1936)], IBM used to market its mainframe computers on a rental basis, charging all users the same rental rate per month. However, IBM required computer users to purchase all key-punch cards from IBM. This was back in the days when cards were the

primary means of communicating with a computer, and the extent of use of the computer was, as a general rule, a function of the number of cards used. IBM priced the key-punch cards quite a bit above cost, and the court argued this practice was illegal on grounds that IBM had "extended its monopoly" in computers to cards. Economic theory destroys the court's argument; any monopoly power IBM had, it could extract through the rental on the machine, no more. Therefore, the practice of requiring cards to be purchased from IBM and overcharging for them must have another explanation. Can you provide it?

11. Consider telephone charge cards. Many if not most of them are activated electronically. That is, no operator is required. The caller simply punches in his or her credit card number at the appropriate time. This billing system is nearly the same as the one used to charge for long-distance calls from a local residence or business phone. However, the rates charged for credit card calls are somewhat higher than the rates charged from an installed phone billed directly to its number. Why do the rates differ between credit card calls and direct dialed calls?

SUGGESTED READINGS

Barro, Robert J., and Romer, Paul M. "Ski-Lift Pricing, with Applications to Labor and Other Markets." *American Economic Review* 77(5) (December 1987):875–90.

Gerstner, Eitan. "Peak Load Pricing in Competitive Markets." *Economic Inquiry* 24 (April 1986):349–61.

Levedahl, J. William. "Profit Maximizing Pricing of Cents Off Coupons: Promotion or Price Discrimination?" *Quarterly Journal of Business and Economics* 25(4) (August 1986):56–70.

Murphy, Michael M. "Price Discrimination, Market Separation, and the Multi-Part Tariff." *Economic Inquiry* 15(4) (October 1977):587–99.

Oi, Walter. "A Disneyland Dilemma: Two-Part Tariffs for a Mickey Mouse Monopoly." *Quarterly Journal of Economics* 85 (February 1971):77–96.

Robinson, Joan. *The Economics of Imperfect Competition.* London: Macmillan, 1933.

SUGGESTED SOLUTIONS TO SELECTED STUDY PROBLEMS

The following are only *suggested* solutions to the study problems presented at the end of this chapter. In all cases, the suggestions here put heavy emphasis on analysis rather than a single correct answer. Since most managerial problems do not fall into neat little boxes, the individual characteristics of the problems that you will encounter on the job will typically mandate a solution using the principles developed here and in other courses. Memorizing these solutions will not make you a good manager; learning the *principles* detailed here will help make you a better manager.

2. The resort hotel in question is large. In addition, it is located in a somewhat remote area of the North Carolina mountains, and although there are other hotels in the area, they are not perfect substitutes. This hotel offers a full package of services. Based on the fact that it is in a remote area and there are few close substitutes for the hotel in question, it is reasonable to assume that

PRICING AND PRICE DISCRIMINATION

CHAPTER 9 PRICING AND PRICE DISCRIMINATIONPRICING AND PRICE DISCRIMINATION

the demand for the services of the hotel is downward sloping, giving the hotel the ability to price discriminate. Casual observation suggests that other hotels in similar situations, dude ranches in Montana for one example, Club Med type resorts in the Caribbean for another, all being remote, have the same type pricing strategy. Moreover, in a resort hotel, guests have a higher marginal cost than in a large city hotel. In a city hotel, the marginal cost of a second guest in a room is quite low. By contrast, in the resort hotel, the second guest uses the pool, tennis courts, golf course, and other recreational facilities more often, driving up the marginal cost and making it more likely that the resort hotel will charge per person rather than per room.

5.   The main reason is probably that resale across state lines is very difficult to prevent. For instance, if Kodak tried to charge a higher price for film in Kansas City, Missouri, than it did in Kansas City, Kansas, many customers will simply buy their film in Kansas and defeat the price discrimination scheme. States with substantially different liquor taxes face this problem routinely. For instance, the liquor tax in Arkansas is lower than in Tennessee, and so many residents of Memphis (illegally) try to buy alcohol in Arkansas that special police are sometimes used at the Mississippi River crossing to catch those trying to buy at the lower Arkansas prices.

8.   One explanation is based on the assumption that the children's plates are priced lower than comparable adult plates, a classic case of price discrimination. Resale is prevented in the restaurant by the simple observation of the child's age. Since this is impossible for take-out orders, the store has to preclude the take-out of the lower priced plates.

CHAPTER

10

OTHER MARKET STRUCTURES— BETWEEN MONOPOLY AND COMPETITIÓN

INTRODUCTION

In this chapter we explore a number of market structures that lie somewhere between competition and monopoly. These include monopolistic competition, which is really competition with product differentiation; oligopoly, which is competition with only a few firms; the dominant firm, which is a monopoly market leader with a fringe of competition; and the cartel, which is a collusive agreement among competitors to act like a monopolist. In each of these cases, the price elasticity of demand facing the firm(s) is less than perfectly elastic. In that sense, each firm has some monopoly power or control over price. This means that the firm must search for the best or profit maximizing price. Thus, the analysis from the last two chapters is applicable here. What this chapter does is explore how and why some firms, those with rivals, might still face a downward sloping demand curve.

MONOPOLISTIC COMPETITION

As its name implies, **monopolistic competition** is a hybrid market structure capturing elements of competition and monopoly. A monopolistically competitive market has a number of firms producing a similar product in rivalry with each other. Competition is not perfect for a number of reasons. Primarily, the products are differentiated; they are not identical. Different brands of computers, cigarettes, food products, electronic equipment, and the like come to mind. Services by their very nature have many of the characteristics of monopolistic competition. Haircuts differ from stylist to stylist. Yet the prospective buyer faces a wide range of choices. Because the products are not identical, advertising plays a role in the model. It is used by producers to inform customers about the characteristics of their good relative to the others in the marketplace.

Monopolistic competition is subsumed into the theory of monopoly in the sense that the firms face a less than perfectly elastic demand curve; product differentiation ensures this. Since consumers do not see the output of each firm in the industry as the same, the demand curve facing each firm slopes downward. The more different the products are in the eyes of the customers, the less elastic is each firm's demand curve. Given that the monopolistically competitive firm faces a downward sloping demand curve for its products, it can raise price without losing all its sales. Therefore, it must search for the best price.

The output decision is based on the same analysis as the pure monopoly: Produce where marginal revenue equals marginal cost. However, in monopolistic competition entry is unrestricted, and therefore, firms will enter or exit until profits are zero. In monopolistic competition, in long-run equilibrium, the firms earn a normal rate of return on their investments.

Consider the world of computer software. Back in the early days of personal computers, in the late 1970s, spreadsheet software was developed. The first notable package was named VisiCalc and was used on machines running the CP/M operating system. With the introduction of the IBM PC and DOS as an operating system, Lotus introduced its spreadsheet, 1•2•3. Since that time, a large number of companies have begun to offer spreadsheets, Borland with Quattro,

Microsoft with Excel, and many others. Each product offers its own particular advantages and conveniences. Some are powerful but slow. Others are simple but quick. Others specialize in graphics presentations, while even others conserve memory. The buyer faces a wide variety of choices. As time has passed, the entry of firms into the market erodes the sales of existing firms, dividing the market among more and more firms. In the limit, the firms in the industry make zero excess or monopoly profits. All the while, the demand curve facing the firms in the industry becomes more elastic.

In the world of monopolistic competition, the more rivals a firm faces, the more elastic is the demand for its product, and in the limit, of course, we have the competitive environment. Similarly, the more different is a product, the fewer rivals there are, and the less elastic is the demand for the good.

OLIGOPOLY

Oligopoly is a market structure with a few firms. The automobile industry comes to mind immediately. In oligopoly, a firm must actively concern itself with the behavior of its rivals, and as Professor Stigler has pointed out, this is a difficult problem: "The theory of price formation with oligopoly is, and for more than a century has been, one of the less successful areas of economic analysis, in spite of the fact that almost every major economist has thought about the problem, and a large number have written on it."[1] The wise words of Professor Stigler ring as true today as the day he wrote them. There is no general theory of oligopoly.

When an industry is comprised of just a few firms producing a similar, even identical product, each must take into account in its decisions the expected response by its rivals. Economists have tried several different approaches to this problem, each with its strengths and weaknesses. The various models of oligopoly typically make some assumption about the behavior of rivals. For instance, there is the Cournot model, which attempts to model two firms selling water from a well.[2] Each of the two firms assumes that the other's production is fixed. The firm then bases its pricing decision on the market demand less the output of the other firm.

Suppose firm A changes its output. Firm B recognizes this and responds, assuming that A will not react to its adjustment. Of course, in turn, A responds to B's adjustment, and a sequence of reactions is put in place.

The model is illogical in the sense that the firms never learn to anticipate the responses of their rivals. Relying on competitors to act passively to your own actions seems a trifle foolhardy in most business situations. As a consequence, alternative models of oligopoly have developed over time. These include the kinked demand curve model, the price constant model, the dominant firm

---

[1] George J. Stigler, *The Theory of Price*, 3d ed. (New York: Macmillan, 1966), p. 216.

[2] See Augustin Cournot, *Researches into the Mathematical Principles of the Theory of Wealth*, trans. Nathaniel T. Bacon (New York: Macmillan, 1927). The original work was published by Cournot in French in 1838.

model, and most recently, game theory models that have been applied to the problem of rivalry with a small number of participants. We explore the dominant firm in some detail later. The game theory approach and the model of the dominant firm now receive the most attention from economists. Game theory and some applications of it are studied briefly in Chapter 12, but the topic is far more intriguing and complicated than the discussion there might suggest. However, the breadth and depth of the subject require that it be left for other courses and books.

To repeat, there is no general theoretical framework for oligopoly. Virtually all of the attempts to model the small numbers problem have proven weak in one area or another, and we are left with few general conclusions. However, and this point is examined in more detail in the section on the dominant firm, in oligopoly situations, price will tend to be higher than the competitive level, but lower than the monopoly level, while output is greater than with monopoly but less than with competition. The extent to which output and price diverge from the competitive level seems to depend on a number of factors: the cost of entering and exiting the market and the size of the market relative to the minimum efficient firm size.

Perhaps the most useful area of study of oligopoly focuses on cartels or collusive behavior. An oligopolistic industry has the incentive to collude, to act in concert, to behave as though all the firms in the industry were one. When this collusion is successful, the industry is a monopoly and can reap the rewards of pricing above cost. However, tremendous pressures to cheat are put in place by any collusion to raise price. These forces are the study of the next section.

CARTELS

A **cartel** is a collective agreement among a group of buyers or sellers to restrict competition. Extra care must be taken when analyzing cartels for two reasons: First, many agreements among firms look like cartels but are in fact contractual arrangements designed to improve, not impede, competition; second, many cartel arrangements are illegal in the United States under the antitrust laws—the Sherman Act of 1890, the Clayton Act of 1914, the Federal Trade Commission Act of 1914, and the Robinson-Pattman Act of 1936. In the first case, trade associations set standards of conduct that look considerably like restrictions on competition, and indeed competition may suffer in some cases. But the possibility also exists that quality standards can improve the operation of markets by reducing information costs and improving consumer certainty. Consider the case of the Underwriters Laboratory (UL) seal of approval often attached to products. According to one point of view, the UL label restricts access to the market for nonlabeled goods, reducing overall output, raising price, and restricting competition—characteristics of the classic cartel. But in this case, the UL seal probably helps competition more than it hurts. New companies, companies without brand names or reputations, can enter the market with goods if they bear the UL seal and expect to find a degree of consumer acceptance above what they might expect absent the UL seal. The seal actually eases entry for new producers and unfamiliar products, acting as a sort of guarantee to customers. Arguably then, this arrangement whereby producers must meet certain quality standards in order to get the UL seal of approval is not the classic, competition-reducing cartel, but instead competition is enhanced as firms find it easier to get their wares to customers. For the time being, we leave this class of contractual arrangements and analyze the classic cartel where the goal of the conspirators is simply to restrict competition and raise profits.

Cartels can be taxonomically divided into two types, private and government. Private cartels must enforce their agreements without the aid of a single, powerful government. For example, OPEC, the Organization of Petroleum Exporting Countries, meets occasionally to establish production quotas for the member countries. The goal of OPEC is to delimit production, raise price, and increase profits. However, there is no central government with the legal authority to enforce the arrangement, and hence there is constant bickering among the member countries about the appropriate shares of output. More important, no legal enforcement mechanism exists to ensure compliance. Of course, one or more countries can try to enforce obedience—note the attack on refineries and pipelines in the war between Iraq and Iran and the destruction of oil fields when Iraq invaded Kuwait—but this is not a legally constituted authority in the normal sense of the word. The cartel is frequently troubled by outbreaks of cheating and noncompliance with the terms of the agreement, which collectively lower the wealth of OPEC member nations. Of course, all multinational cartels encounter this problem, while intranational cartels face a similar predicament unless the central government steps in to mandate compliance.

Governmental agencies often come to the aid of cartels, enforcing production or sales quotas on the members. In the United States, it is common for the Department of Agriculture to establish and maintain production limits on crops such as tobacco, milk, peanuts, as well as many others.[3] Public utilities are

---

AN EDUCATIONAL CARTEL?

For more than two decades the eight universities that make up the Ivy League, along with the Massachusetts Institute of Technology, have gotten together and matched one another's financial-aid offers to students. It was an attempt, they say, to avoid bidding wars for the most desirable prospects. But Attorney General Dick Thornburgh charged the schools with price fixing, a violation of the Sherman Antitrust Act.

"This collegiate cartel [has] denied [students] the right to compare prices and discounts among schools," he said, "just as they would in shopping for any other service."

The schools protested that they had done nothing wrong. Last week, however, the Ivies—but not M.I.T.—signed a consent agreement ending their arrangement.

"Cracking the Ivy Cartel," *Time*, June 3, 1991, p. 25. Copyright 1991 The Time Inc. Magazine Company. Reprinted by permission.

---

[3] The USDA's authority to cartelize many areas of American agriculture was established in the Agricultural Adjustment Act of 1933 and has been amended many times since.

another good example of government-enforced cartels. Exclusive territories for public utilities are created by state governments, and competition is nonexistent between companies. To be sure, natural gas companies compete with electricity producers, but electricity producers do not compete with each other, thanks to the powerful enforcement authority of government. The point of all this is that the success of any cartel hinges on the strength and quality of the enforcing body.

Apportioning Output across Firms

By their very nature, cartels produce less output than a comparable competitive industry. This creates a problem, for some method must be devised for lowering production. Typically, each member firm in the coalition wants all the others to reduce production, but that defeats the purpose. As a general principle, some rules must be agreed upon or the cartel will be unsuccessful. The major problem faced by cartels trying to allot output in a way that will maximize the total cartel profits is that the member firms do not necessarily have the same, homogeneous costs of production.

When costs are heterogeneous across member firms in a cartel, conflicts are created. On the one hand, the cartel goal is overall profit maximization—that is, cartel profit maximization—without regard to the distribution of profits. But the individual members do not care about cartel profits per se; they care about their own. So each member firm fights to get as large a share of the pie as possible, and this fight can cause the overall profits of the cartel to diminish. Two examples should suffice to make the point. It is often argued that most of the problems faced by OPEC arise from arguments over the distribution of output. The member nations do not each face the same costs of drilling, exploration, and recovery of oil. Therefore, joint profit maximization requires different output quotas across countries, creating room for much gerrymandering and argument. Some analysts believe this inherent problem has had more to do with OPEC's instability than any other factor. For a second example, consider the NCAA college sports cartel. Until 1984, the NCAA negotiated television broadcast rights to college football games for all member colleges. As is the case with OPEC, member institutions do not have uniform costs of production. Some schools have much higher costs of production than others. This incompatibility put in motion a number of conflicts in the 1970s and 1980s. At each annual meeting, the so-called big football schools called for increased participation in the television pool; they wanted to be on TV more often. The smaller schools consistently voted them down, imposing the rule that a school could not be on national television more than four times in a two-year period and requiring that at least 82 different schools appear on television in a two-year period. These rules apparently did not properly assign production across schools; the Universities of Georgia and Oklahoma brought suit against the cartel. Ultimately they won, and today each member school of the NCAA is free to negotiate its own television contract for football broadcasts.[4] In sum, although we

---

[4] The case was resolved by the U.S. Supreme Court in *NCAA* v. *Board of Regents of University of Oklahoma*, 468 U.S. 85, 104 S. Ct. 2948 (1984).

initially model cartels assuming they wish to maximize total or joint profits, we recognize this creates its own set of problems. Having said all this, let us first create a model of joint profit maximization. This model assumes that the firms in the cartel desire to maximize cartel profits without regard for their distribution.

The problem facing a cartel mirrors the situation of the multiplant producer.[5] Output must be apportioned across the producing units in a way that equalizes the marginal cost of production, ignoring average cost at each unit. Suppose there are a number of firms producing a homogeneous product. Joint profits are the sum of revenues minus the sum of costs. The strategy is presented graphically in Figure 10.1. The demand for the output of the cartel is D. Marginal revenue is R'. In this example, let the cartel have four firms, each with its own marginal cost, MC_1–MC_4. To maximize joint profits of the cartel, marginal cost must be equal across firms and equal to cartel marginal revenue. The horizontal summation of the firms' marginal costs intersects marginal revenue, R', at the profit maximizing level of output for the cartel, Q^*. This output is apportioned across firms, ensuring that marginal cost is the same at each firm. Thus, output of the first producer is q_1; the second produces q_2, and so forth, so that $Q^* = q_1 + q_2 + q_3 + q_4$. Cartel price is determined by demand. In this case, the profit maximizing price is p^*. Knowing the average cost of an individual producer allows us to determine its particular profits. For the first firm, output is q_1, price is p^*, average cost is AC_1, and profits are the area of the tinted rectangle, $(p^* - AC_1) \cdot q_1$.

FIGURE 10.1
Cartel Production

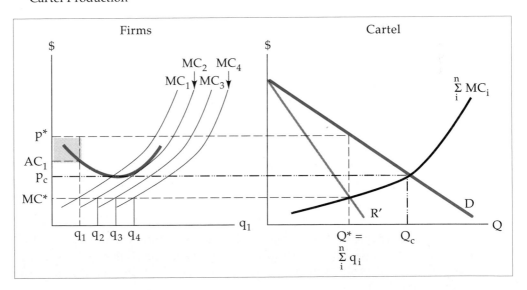

---

[5] See The Multiplant Firm in Chapter 6.

CARTEL PROFIT MAXIMIZATION—A MATHEMATICAL PRESENTATION

There are a number of firms, n, producing a homogeneous product, q. Joint profits are the sum of revenues minus the sum of costs,

$$\Pi = \sum_{i=1}^{n} pq_i - \sum_{i=1}^{n} C_i(q_i).$$

Demand for industry output is

$$p = p(Q),$$

where Q is total industry output,

$$Q = \sum_{i=1}^{n} q_i.$$

Therefore, cartel revenues are

$$p{\bullet}Q,$$

but since the cartel faces the entire demand curve, $p = p(Q)$, revenues are a function of total output,

$$p(Q){\bullet}Q,$$

or

$$p(\sum_{i=1}^{n} q_i) \times (\sum_{i=1}^{n} q_i).$$

Substituting this expression into the profit equation yields the cartel objective function,

$$\Pi = p(\sum_{i=1}^{n} q_i) \times (\sum_{i=1}^{n} q_i) - \sum_{i=1}^{n} c_i(q_i). \tag{i}$$

The cartel manager selects output for each individual firm in order to maximize joint profits, equation (i). Mathematically, we represent this choice by taking the partial derivatives of the joint profit function with respect to each of the q_i's. This procedure produces n different equations of the form

$$\partial\Pi/\partial q_i = [(\partial p/\partial q_i){\bullet}q_i + p] - \partial c_i/\partial q_i.$$

For maximum profits, each of these equations must be set to zero to determine the optimality conditions,

$$[(\partial p/\partial q_i) \cdot q_i + p] = \partial c_i/\partial q_i \text{ for } i = 1 \text{ to } n \tag{ii}$$

where n is the number of members in the cartel. The rule identified in equation (ii) says that each firm must produce where *cartel* marginal revenue, the left-hand side of equation (i), equals its *own* marginal cost, the right-hand side of the expression.

The Advantage of Cartelization

Cooperation with one's rivals generally pays rewards, at least for a while. Suppose the cartel solution just derived and demonstrated in Figure 10.1 was voided, and the firms in the industry behaved competitively. Contrast the competitive outcome with the cartel solution. Under competition, price is determined by the intersection of demand and the horizontal summation of the individual marginal cost curves. Competitive output would be Q_c, and price would correspondingly be p_c. Notice what happens to profits of the first firm. Under the cartel, profits are positive, $(p^* - AC_1) \cdot q_1 > 0$, but with competition, price equals average cost, and profits are erased. In all cases, profits fall for each firm in the cartel.

Cartel Stability

Consider Figure 10.1 one more time. For the first firm (and all the rest as well), price is greater than marginal cost, $p^* > MC^*$. The firm would prefer, in isolation, to expand production, because a profit opportunity exists; the extra revenue from selling more output exceeds the marginal cost. If the first firm produced, say, three additional units of output, the other cartel members would jointly have to produce three fewer units or price would have to fall. Suppose each of the other three firms produced one less unit apiece. Notice what happens to the distribution of profits. Profit for the first firm increases by (approximately) $3 \cdot (p^* - AC_1)$, while profit for each of the other three firms falls by (approximately) $p^* - AC_i$ respectively.[6] When price exceeds marginal cost, increasing sales will increase profits, unless the increase in output lowers its price. This creates an enormous conflict. *Each* firm wants to produce more, but if even one does, price must fall or others must produce less. To put it mildly, cartel management is tricky business. Analysis of cartel cheating is interesting and important but complex. The concept of game theory is useful here. This topic is discussed briefly in the section in Chapter 12 called Gaming Behavior and the Prisoner's Dilemma.

Faced with the serious problem of preventing cheating, the nonadherence to

---

[6] The solution is approximate because changes in output effect small changes in average cost for each firm. Since these adjustments are typically small, they are ignored here for ease of exposition.

the collective agreement, cartels frequently resort to unusual measures. Agreeing on standard hours of operation is one technique employed to prevent over-production by individual firms. For example, a collection of bars in a resort or college town might (secretly?) agree to close on Sunday, to only open after 1 P.M. on Sunday, or to close at 1 A.M. or some other hour earlier than some owners might otherwise freely choose. This collusion would make it more difficult for any bar to sell more beer than mandated by the original agreement.

Posted prices also make it easier to detect noncompliance. Suppose a number of local gasoline service stations have mutually agreed to set a price above the competitive level, say $1.09 per gallon, with allowances made for individual stations. To monitor obedience, each member of the group also agrees to post a large sign (say at least 18″ by 30″) curbside detailing its prices. The owner of any one station can now cheaply observe the behavior of her rivals simply driving home or on the way to the gym. Any such public dissemination of information about prices or output serves to facilitate cartel management.[7]

In certain cases, it may prove useful for a cartel to monitor *input use* rather than meter output production.[8] This technique will prove especially useful when there is close to a fixed relation between one or more inputs and output; if there is substitutability between the inputs, then consumption of large quantities of one particular input need not imply large volumes of output. If news media reports are to be trusted, Iran's attack on Iraq's Persian Gulf oil shipments in the early 1980s would seem to qualify as an example of metering inputs to restrict output. In this case, ocean transportation of oil was monitored and sanctioned when deemed appropriate by the Iranians. Apparently, the Ayatollah found it too expensive to sanction the production of output (bombing wells and refineries) directly, and consequently he resorted to restricting the use of Iraq's inputs, the ships.

As we pointed out, one of the most successful cartels in the United States is the National Collegiate Athletic Association, the NCAA. See the accompanying story from the *Wall Street Journal* where the NCAA was chosen by a collection of Harvard economists as the "clear and deserving winner of the first annual prize for best monopoly in America." This organization regulates intercollegiate athletic competition among member institutions. Many rules address play on the field of competition, such as the length of a football game, 60 minutes, and the number of players per team, 11 per side. However, the organization also acts as a cartel manager for the member schools in several dimensions. Until declared illegal in the Supreme Court case, the *NCAA* v. *Board of Regents of University of*

---

[7] This discussion is *not* meant to imply that the dissemination of information about prices is economically inefficient (a normative concept) or noncompetitive, only that it *can* aid in the maintenance of a collusive price agreement.

[8] It turns out that measuring inputs is a very useful managerial tool in a variety of applications, especially when output is abstract, produced jointly, or otherwise difficult to quantify. The section in Chapter 13 on Team Production presents a detailed discussion of input metering in a number of applications.

Oklahoma, the NCAA restricted the number of football television broadcasts, sharply reducing the number of games available to networks and viewers.[9] Since the Supreme Court decision voided the cartel limitations, open bidding for telecast rights—conferences and universities now cut their own deals—has increased the number of televised games and reduced the price per game. For example, in 1983 the Michigan-Iowa game cost CBS $1.2 million; in 1986, the price was $575,000. In 1983, the NCAA received $74 million from the major networks and cable carriers for the rights to broadcast college football games. In 1984, the

---

THE BEST MONOPOLY IN AMERICA

It's almost the end of summer and time for the first annual contest to choose the best operating monopoly in America. The contestants, selected by a panel of Harvard economists, are as follows:

1. The U.S. Postal Service.
2. OPEC.
3. Almost any cable TV company.
4. The Ivy League universities (for administering financial aid to students).
5. The NCAA (for administering payments to student-athletes).

Some other worthy candidates, which just missed the cut, are the National Football League, the American Medical Association, and the U.S. Departments of Agriculture and Defense. . . .

Each contestant exhibits fine monopolistic characteristics and is worthy of serious consideration for the award. . . .

[The first four nominees fail for one reason or another. However, . . .]

When the NCAA maintains its cartel by punishing schools that violate the rules (by paying too much), almost no one doubts that the evil entities are the schools or people who paid the athletes, rather than the cartel enforcers who prevented the athletes from getting paid. Given this extraordinary balancing act, the decision of the panelists was straightforward and the NCAA is the clear and deserving winner of the first annual prize for best monopoly in America.

Robert Barro, "Let's Play Monopoly," *Wall Street Journal*, August 27, 1991, p. A12. Reprinted by permission of *The Wall Street Journal*, © 1991 Dow Jones & Company, Inc. All Rights Reserved Worldwide.

---

[9] Enforcement of the cartel agreement is cheap here. It is hard to imagine an unsanctioned game, say Oklahoma versus Nebraska, being telecast without most NCAA officials' knowledge. Of course, Boise State could probably play South Dakota School of Mines live on the local station in Rapid City without incurring the wrath of NCAA officials, but the rewards are commensurately low. Again, there is little incentive to cheat on the cartel.

value of contracts with game suppliers dropped to $42 million, although revenues were enhanced somewhat by nonnetwork regional telecasts.[10]

The NCAA also cartelizes the purchase of an important input to the production of intercollegiate athletic competition—the athletes themselves. In this case, the cartel is designed not to restrict output and raise price, but to restrict the use of an input and *lower* its price; nevertheless, the basic principle of cooperation remains the same. NCAA rules restrict payments to players to nothing more than an NCAA approved scholarship—tuition, room and board, and books. *Nothing* else is allowed. However, an enormous conflict is put in place by this cartel restriction. Many schools want the best athletes, and some are willing to exceed the bounds of the cartel regulations in search of higher profits resulting from the play of high-quality athletes. If a school can attract a player whose skills exceed the value of his or her scholarship, room, board, and books, the school will make higher profits in its athletic and academic programs. This bonus prompts some schools to offer extra inducements to players, as most of you are aware.[11] Apparently unable to perfectly scrutinize the recruitment and participation of each particular student-athlete to ensure compliance with cartel regulations, the syndicate typically uses two indirect enforcement techniques. Folklore has it that member institutions police their own ranks. Schools, alumni, and coaches who offer cash payments to prospective student-athletes to attract them or those who pay players for their performances are sometimes reported to cartel authorities by other schools and coaches.

It is argued that this input cartel is also enforced by monitoring output. Schools that suddenly become victorious, surprisingly defeat opponents, and rise in national prominence are likely candidates for in-depth investigation by the NCAA enforcement staff on the grounds that something is amiss.[12] Presumably a similar phenomenon exists in more traditional cartels. Publicly traded firms experiencing large and unexpected increases in the price of their common stock would be the subject of extra scrutiny by peers with whom they had made a collusive compact to raise profits by restricting competition. Of course, cartelization is designed to pay—to raise profits—so some increase in stock prices is anticipated when an agreement is reached, but it is the abnormal increase in stock prices that attracts attention, especially after an unexpectedly large earnings

---

[10] In the winter of 1991, the Federal Trade Commission announced that it was investigating the compact between a segment of the NCAA football schools, the College Football Association, and ABC, over the potential anticompetitive effects of its television contract.

[11] Recently, Oklahoma University, Texas A&M University, the University of Kentucky, Southern Methodist University, the University of Florida, the University of Georgia, Clemson University, the University of South Carolina, Louisiana State University, the University of Southern California, the University of California at Los Angeles, Virginia Polytechnic and State University, Cleveland State University, the University of Illinois, and *many* more were sanctioned by the NCAA for operating outside the bounds of the cartel agreement.

[12] See Fleisher, Goff, Shughart, and Tollison, "Crime or Punishment?: Enforcement of the NCAA Football Cartel," *Journal of Economic Organization & Behavior*, 10(4), December 1988, 433–51 for more discussion on this point.

The NCAA Cartel

"[The] NCAA [is] the biggest problem in college sports." . . .

The fundamental problem is that universities, in collusion with professional teams, have created a *monopoly*. . . . [C]olleges have conspired with one another to stifle competition for labor by setting players' salaries at roughly zero. . . .

Thus, scandal is inevitable. Universities, *like members of any cartel*, have an incentive to cheat.

Doug Bandow, "The Real NCAA Scandal," *Wall Street Journal*, June 21, 1991, p. A10. Italics added. Reprinted by permission of *The Wall Street Journal*, © 1991 Dow Jones & Company, Inc. All Rights Reserved Worldwide.

announcement that might be signaling an increase in sales (an indication of cheating).

It is interesting to note that some buyers create institutions that appear to facilitate cartelization *against* themselves. Consider the common practice of opening and revealing sealed bids. Suppose a group of highway construction firms has secretly agreed not to compete on a collection of state contracts for highway paving. The act of revealing all bids notifies the conspirators whether there is cheating on the agreement. Notably, bid revelation is practiced almost exclusively by government agencies; most private firms soliciting construction bids do not reveal the offers of the winning or losing bidder.

Labor cartels are, for the most part, legal in the United States.[13] In some cases, police power of the federal and state governments is used to enforce the collusion, but not in all circumstances. It is sometimes left to the members of the cartel to enforce the agreement among themselves, most notably in the so-called right to work states where union membership cannot be required for employment. Enforcement here often takes extreme measures, including harassment, violence, and bodily injury. Recall the 1987 NFL players strike. Peer pressure was used; silent treatment, name-calling, and other attacks were employed to force non-members of the labor cartel, called scabs, to abide by the cartel agreement. Even when detection is possible—it was hard for Tony Dorsett and Danny White to pretend they were on strike when they dressed and played on television for the Dallas Cowboys—preventing cheating is not easy.

All told, as the last example points out, cartel enforcement is troublesome business. Tremendous pressures exist, noted in Figure 10.1, enticing firms to void the cartel agreement in pursuit of their single interest and making it difficult for cartels to survive over time. It usually takes the strong arm of the law or other threats of force to persuade compliance, and even then success is limited, as the

---

[13] Authority is established in the Clayton and Norris-LaGuardia acts.

(apocryphal?) often reported wars among drug traffickers would seem to attest. The accompanying story about the Soviet state cartel in caviar points out how difficult it is to maintain a cartel without the strong arm of the law.

Nonprice Competition

The price enhancing features of a successful cartel put in motion powerful competitive pressures to lower price, and in general, any law, contract, or agreement that restricts a firm's ability to cut price in the face of competition puts tension on the firm to compete on grounds other than price. Consider the case of airlines under CAB regulation. The Civil Aeronautics Board regulated airfares at prices above average cost, as the decline in airfares after deregulation attests. To make their own airline more attractive to the flying public, many carriers engaged in a myriad of schemes that substituted making themselves prettier for charging lower prices. These schemes included offering meals, drinks, and flight attendants above and beyond what they might otherwise have tendered. In addition, many airlines offered more flights between cities than they would have if price had been negotiable. That is, they increased service and quality since price was fixed.[14] Naturally, in the current deregulated environment, firms now compete on all these grounds and price as well. Consequently, fewer flights are offered between existing cities in any given time period (adjusting for the number of

---

CHEAP CAVIAR

But the Soviet Union's dissolution may prove the bane of beluga, say those who profit from its high price now. Competition is already beginning to break the state's monopoly, which in turn could bring the world a nightmarishly unchic new product: cheap caviar.

The autonomy movement among the former Soviet Union's separate states is wreaking havoc in the old system. The two largest Soviet fisheries now fall under the jurisdiction of different autonomous republics, each of which wants to own and operate its own lucrative caviar production business. . . .

The cumulative effect of all of these new sources of caviar, according to the Soviet news agency Interfax, is a 20% drop in the official caviar export price from last year. "We don't need this kind of competition," laments Sergei Dolya, who works for Sovrybflot, which used to hold the monopoly over caviar exports. "All of these small rivals mean that the price will fall and the market will be ripped apart. This is a delicacy—we need to keep it elite."

Jane Mayer, "Horrors! Fine Caviar Now Could Become Cheap as Fish Eggs," *Wall Street Journal*, November 18, 1991, p. A12. Reprinted by permission of *The Wall Street Journal*, © 1991 Dow Jones & Company, Inc. All Rights Reserved Worldwide.

---

[14] See George W. Douglas and James C. Miller, III, *Economic Regulation of Domestic Air Transport* (Washington, DC: Brookings Institution, 1974) for additional theory and facts on this issue.

travelers), and planes are more crowded as a result. In addition, we expect lower quality service in terms of delays and cancellations.

Nonprice competition is used by some manufacturers to get retailers to offer complementary services to their products. Suppose you make a product requiring some training to operate. Many new consumer products have this characteristic. Videocassette recorders, personal computers, and many other so-called high tech devices come to mind. One way to make retailers spend time with customers, educating them about the proper use of the item, is to set a minimum retail price. If you set this price sufficiently high, above the average cost of selling, competing retailers will vie for customers on nonprice terms, one of which is just the service you wish, namely advice and training. Naturally, as the product infiltrates the market and consumer awareness grows, the manufacturer is less inclined to impose the minimum retail price; most consumers have learned how to use the product, or they learn from friends and comrades. Eventually, price becomes the only means of competing.

THE DOMINANT FIRM

In many production situations, one relatively large firm dominates the marketplace, competing with many smaller, so-called fringe producers. Examples that immediately come to mind include Kodak in film, Xerox in photocopying, IBM in computers, and 3M in plastic tape. Typically the **dominant firm** has patents, access to superior technology (secrets), or some other cost advantage. The fringe firms survive by offering unusual services or because the dominant firm's cost advantage is not absolute. In all cases, the dominant firm faces a less than perfectly elastic demand curve, while each fringe firm must compete with the others, taking price as given.

Figure 10.2 presents a model of the dominant firm. Market demand for output is given by the function D_t. Potentially, there are an unlimited number of fringe firms, but initially suppose there are n of them. The sum of their marginal cost curves is fringe supply, S_f; the number of firms adjust as price exceeds or falls short of the fringe firms' average cost of production. The demand curve faced by the dominant firm, D_d, is the residual of the total market demand minus the supply by the fringe firms, D_t less S_f. Notice how we construct this. At the point where S_f crosses the market demand curve, price p_0, there is no residual demand. Since the fringe firms supply all the output the market will consume, there is no room for the dominant firm; its demand is nil at this price. Notice the vertical intersection of the dominant demand, D_d. At the other extreme at the price where fringe supply is zero, p_1, the dominant firm has the whole market; market demand and dominant demand are the same.

The dominant firm employs the profit maximizing rule and equates its marginal cost to its marginal revenue. Marginal revenue to the dominant firm is R'_d, and it equals marginal cost at price p^*. The dominant firm produces q_d. The fringe firms produce the remainder of the market demand, q_f, and the total, q_t, is the sum of q_d and q_f. If the current price, p^*, is less than the average cost of production for the fringe firms, some of them exit, shifting S_f to the left, D_d and R'_d to the right and raising price until the remaining fringe firms cover their costs.

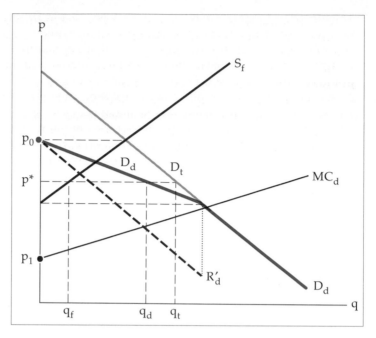

Figure 10.2
The Dominant Firm

The opposite happens if p^* is greater than the fringe firms' average cost of production. Firms enter, driving price down. The entry or exit of fringe firms ceases when market price equals their average cost of production.

By necessity, the dominant firm has lower costs than its fringe rivals, but not sufficiently low to capture the whole market. In essence, the firm dominates because it has access to superior technology, cheaper inputs, or some other cost advantage that allows it slightly lower costs.

INDUSTRIAL ORGANIZATION

In the lexicon of economics, **industrial organization** means many things to many people. Traditionally, it refers to the analysis of industry structure, competition, monopoly, oligopoly, and concentration. Newer research topics include contract and organizational structures within and across firms. This is a big and burgeoning area of interest. In this section, a brief overview of the traditional issues is presented. In some respects, the rest of this text addresses a few of the newer topics. Be cautioned, we are only skimming the surface here, and those of you who find this material enlightening should consult one of the many good texts in the field or even take a course. Virtually all business curricula include one or more.

One of the central issues in classical industrial organization is the notion of concentration. **Concentration** refers to the size distribution of firms. In practice, concentration is usually represented by two-, four-, and eight-firm concentration ratios. A concentration ratio simply computes the percentage of total industry output produced by the two, four, or eight largest firms in the industry. For example, Table 10.1 reports some concentration ratios for various industries. From the table, the eight largest manufacturers of glass containers produced 75 percent of all glass containers in 1977. Many people use these types of numbers to draw inferences about the extent of competition and monopoly in a particular industry. Antitrust authorities employ such statistics routinely. There is considerable debate about the appropriateness of concentration ratios as measures of market power. But, for our purposes as managers, it suffices to know the definition.

Herfindahl indexes are also used to characterize an industry. The **Herfindahl index** of concentration is the sum of squared relative sizes of all firms in an industry. Examine Table 10.2, which reports sales data for five hypothetical firms in one year.

The Herfindahl index is

$$0.1^2 + 0.2^2 + 0.25^2 + 0.35^2 + 0.1^2 = 0.225.$$

For contrast, just suppose the five firms in Table 10.2 had all been the same size, each producing 20 percent of the total output. Compute the Herfindahl Index here. It is

$$0.2^2 + 0.2^2 + 0.2^2 + 0.2^2 + 0.2^2 = 5 \bullet 0.04 = 0.20.$$

TABLE 10.1 INDUSTRY CONCENTRATION RATIOS—1977		
INDUSTRY	4-FIRM RATIO	8-FIRM RATIO
Pharmaceuticals	24	43
Cotton Weaving	39	58
Glass Containers	54	75
Chewing Gum	93	99

TABLE 10.2 RELATIVE SIZES OF FIRMS IN AN INDUSTRY	
FIRM	PROPORTION OF TOTAL OUTPUT
A	0.10
B	0.20
C	0.25
D	0.35
E	0.10

As firm size becomes more equal, the Herfindahl index declines. Large indexes imply disparate firm sizes and a concentrated industry, small indexes the opposite.

Another common measure of size dispersion is the **Gini coefficient**. Suppose we rank the firms in an industry from smallest to largest; reorder the hypothetical firms in Table 10.2 as A, E, B, C, and then D. Now suppose the industry output was uniformly distributed across all firms in the industry. Then each firm's output would be 0.20 of the total. Accumulate the fractions of output as we progress down the number of firms. That is, the first firm, if uniformly distributed, would produce 20 percent, the first two firms 40 percent, and so forth. Now, to compute the Gini coefficient, subtract the actual proportions of output from the hypothetical uniform distribution and sum the differences. This is the Gini coefficient. See Table 10.3. The Gini coefficient ranges from a low of zero, where output is actually uniformly distributed, to a maximum of one, where a single firm produces all the output.

In industrial organization, industries are classified by **Standard Industrial Classifications**, or SIC codes, as they are commonly called. These classifications were created and are updated by the Department of Labor of the U.S. government. The codes come in levels much like the Dewey decimal system employed by librarians to classify books. The first level has two digits, and hence is called the 2-digit SIC code. At the 2-digit level, there are 99 levels. Manufacturing enterprises comprise 20 of these, codes 20–39. See Table 10.4. Within each of these classifications, there is further gradation. For example, within the 2-digit code 37, transportation equipment, there are several 3-digit classifications: 372, aircrafts and parts; and 373, ships and boats, to name two. Each of these 3-digit codes is further broken down into 4-digit levels. In aircrafts and parts, the gradations are aircrafts, 3721; aircraft engines and parts, 3724; and miscellaneous parts, not elsewhere classified, 3728.

These codes can be used and misused. It is important to recognize that the classification is often based on the similarity of inputs, not outputs. The particular managerial problem at hand dictates the usefulness of SIC codes. A sales staff might employ SIC codes to restrict its search for potential customers. Every state

TABLE 10.3 COMPUTING THE GINI COEFFICIENT			
FIRM	UNIFORM DISTRIBUTION	CUMULATIVE ACTUAL DISTRIBUTION	CUMULATIVE DIFFERENCE
A	0.20	0.10	0.10
E	0.40	0.20	0.20
B	0.60	0.45	0.15
C	0.80	0.65	0.15
D	1.00	1.00	0.0
Sum—the Gini Coefficient			0.60

TABLE 10.4   2-DIGIT SIC CODES IN MANUFACTURING

CODE	INDUSTRY
20	Food and kindred products
21	Tobacco manufactures
22	Textile Mill products
23	Apparel and other finished products made from fabrics
24	Lumber and wood products, excluding furniture
25	Furniture
26	Paper and related products
27	Printing and publishing
28	Chemicals
29	Petroleum refining
30	Rubber and plastic products
31	Leather and leather products
32	Stone, clay, glass and concrete products
33	Primary metals
34	Fabricated metal products, except machinery and transportation equipment
35	Machinery, except electrical
36	Electrical and electronic equipment
37	Transportation equipment
38	Measuring, analyzing, and controlling instruments; photographic; medical; optical; watches and clocks
39	Miscellaneous manufacturing not elsewhere classified

U.S. Government, Office of Management and Budget, Standard Industrial Classification Manual (Washington, DC: GPO, 1972).

in the United States publishes an industrial directory, listing by SIC code the manufacturers in the state, their address, phone number, and the principal products bought and sold.[15] SIC cataloging facilitates buyer-seller transactions, reducing wasteful search. Probably the worst use of SIC codes is blindly viewing them as markets, examining classifications for high or low profits with the idea of locating areas where money might be made. Although SIC codes help delineate markets, they are neither necessary nor sufficient to characterize a market. As has been pointed out, products are often lumped together in a particular code because they share the same or similar inputs, regardless of how different the outputs might be. In all cases employing the use of SIC codes, an extra portion of managerial caution is advised.

---

[15] Some states use a private contractor to produce the materials, others employ an arm of a state university, and the rest do it bureaucratically. To locate these materials, search in the library under Industrial Directories.

TOPICS TO REVIEW

These are topics that you should feel comfortable with before you leave this chapter. If you cannot write out a clear and concise sentence or paragraph explaining the topic after you have worked on the study problems, you should reread the relevant section of the text.

Monopolistic Competition

Oligopoly

Cartel

Cartel Stability

Cartel Cheating

Nonprice Competition

Dominant Firm

Industrial Organization

Gini Coefficient

SIC Codes

Herfindahl Index

Concentration Ratios

STUDY PROBLEMS

1. On November 13, 1991, Sen. Alphonse D'Amato introduced a bill into the U.S. Senate that would require banks to lower the interest rates that they charge on their Mastercard, Visa, and other credit cards. The D'Amato bill did not allow banks to charge more than four percentage points above the rate that the IRS charges taxpayers for overdue taxes (currently 10 percent). As you know, in addition to interest on outstanding balances, many banks charge an annual fee for their credit cards. Moreover, most credit cards are only offered after the applicant has submitted to a credit and background check. In addition to credit, many banks offer ancillary services in conjunction with their credit cards. For example, the Visa credit card issued by Citibank offers a number of services including: (1) the card can be used to access cash through automatic teller machines around the country; (2) whenever you charge your car rentals to your Citibank card, the car is covered for collision, theft, or fire damage at no additional charge; (3) when you purchase plane, train, bus, or ship tickets using the card, you are eligible for $350,000 of travel accident insurance at no extra cost; and (4) whenever you use the card to purchase retail items, the wares are insured against loss, theft, fire, or accidental damage for 90 days from the date of purchase. Now suppose the D'Amato bill becomes law and banks are forced to lower their interest charges on credit cards. What do you predict will happen to the level and types of services offered in conjunction with credit cards?

2. Back in the dark days of 1974–1975, referred to as the time of the Arab oil embargo, the price of gasoline tried to rise quite a bit, but the government imposed ceilings. About the same time, many service stations ceased to

provide ancillary services: clean restrooms, mechanic services, underhood inspection, and the like. Today, the price of gasoline is again unregulated, and in real terms (accounting for inflation) is not far different from its pre-1974 level. Do you expect a return of the so-called full-service filling station? In other words, did the price ceiling have any impact on the supply of services at gas stations, or was the demise of full-service just another casualty of a growing customer do-it-yourself trend?

3.   Most governmental agencies are required to solicit bids for things that they buy. Highways and buildings immediately come to mind. In virtually all cases, the construction bids are sealed when they are submitted. Interestingly, the bids are opened to the public. That is, all the bids are published, the winning and losing bids. Does this policy facilitate collusion among the bidders? If so, how? If not, why not?

4.   Many stores have a pricing policy, "We will never be undersold. We will match any advertised price." What is the impact of this policy on the overall price of goods in question? Does this policy make overall prices lower or higher or is it neutral?

5.   It is widely held that there is a lot of violence in the underworld, in gangs, and in the illicit drug market. Why is there so much violence there? Assuming that this casual observation is true, why don't regular, legal industries have a similar amount of violence? What is the impact of this violence on the prices of the products sold in these illegal markets? Does it make them higher or lower? To put the question another way, suppose the full force of the police was put to use preventing violence among drug dealers. Would drug prices go up, down, or remain unchanged?

6.   Suppose the Iraqi invasion of Kuwait had been successful and unchallenged by the United States and its coalition partners. Assume that no other changes took place in the Middle East. Would the price of crude oil be different than it is now?

7.   Suppose that the U.S. Justice Department brings an action against the NCAA and charges it with price fixing in scholarships in much the same way that it did against the Ivy League schools.[16] Further suppose that the Justice Department successfully obtains an injunction against the NCAA that prevents the association from collectively setting the payments and amounts of scholarship awards to college athletes. What will happen to the number of athletes who go to college? What will happen to the price of football tickets at member schools?

SUGGESTED READINGS

Breit, William, Hochman, Harold, and Saueracker, Edward, eds. *Readings in Microeconomics.* St. Louis: Times Mirror/Mosby College Pub., 1986.

Bresnahan, Timothy F. "Competition and Collusion in the American Automobile Industry: The 1955 Price War," *Journal of Industrial Economics* 35 (June 1987):457–82.

---

[16] Recall the story from the section on Cartels, "Cracking the Ivy Cartel," *Time,* June 3, 1991, p. 25.

Chamberlain, Edward H. *The Theory of Monopolistic Competition,* 8th ed. Cambridge, MA: Harvard University Press, 1962.

McGee, John S. "Predatory Pricing Revisited." *The Journal of Law and Economics* 23 (October 1980):289–330.

Robinson, Joan. *The Economics of Imperfect Competition.* London: Macmillan, 1933.

Salop, Steven C. and Scheffman, David T. "Raising Rivals Costs." *American Economic Review* 73 (May 1983):267–71.

Shughart, William F., II. *The Organization of Industry.* Homewood, IL: Irwin, 1990.

Stigler, George J. "A Theory of Oligopoly." *Journal of Political Economy* 72 (February 1964): 44–61.

Stigler, George J. *The Theory of Price,* 4th ed. New York: Macmillan, 1987.

Sumner, Daniel A. "Measurement of Monopoly Behavior: An Application to the Cigarette Industry." *Journal of Political Economy* 89 (October 1981):1010–19.

Tirole, Jean. *The Theory of Industrial Organization.* Cambridge, MA: MIT Press, 1988.

SUGGESTED SOLUTIONS TO SELECTED STUDY PROBLEMS

The following are only *suggested* solutions to the study problems presented at the end of this chapter. In all cases, the suggestions here put heavy emphasis on analysis rather than a single correct answer. Since most managerial problems do not fall into neat little boxes, the individual characteristics of the problems that you will encounter on the job will typically mandate a solution using the principles developed here and in other courses. Memorizing these solutions will not make you a good manager; learning the *principles* detailed here will help make you a better manager.

1. Since credit cards have a two-fee structure, restricting one component of the price, the interest rate, will probably cause the other component, the annual fee, to increase. This will mean that credit card users who pay their entire bill each month will have to pay more for credit cards, while users who carry a monthly balance will pay less interest. In addition, since the cards carry a lot of services with them, such as automobile insurance when renting a car, we expect a reduction in those service-related conveniences that come bundled with credit cards.

3. The publication of all sealed bids reveals to all of the bidders the exact amount proposed by any one participant. Thus, if bidders were inclined to collude and rig their bids, the revelation of all bids makes it easier for the bidding firms to detect defection from the collusion. The collusion is bolstered by the information inherent in the bids. That is, Is everyone doing as promised?

4. This is a tough question. On the one hand, an offer to match any price is surely a competitive gesture. If any one firm cuts price, then the rival matches. On the other hand, the willingness to match any price cut may act to reduce the voluntary price reductions in the first place. Since any firm knows that its rival will automatically cut price if it cuts price, the incentive to lower price may be reduced.

CHAPTER

11

TOPICS IN INFORMATION AND INDUSTRIAL ORGANIZATION

INTRODUCTION

Information is an important commodity, and hence it should come as little surprise that it is a topic of study for economists. In this chapter we explore the fact that information is costly to produce but valuable to consume. For instance, it is routinely important for a customer to estimate the quality of a product prior to purchase; the appropriate price usually depends on the quality characteristics of the good in question. By the same argument, it is important for the seller of the product to have a good idea about the quality characteristics of the good in order to receive the appropriate price. Both buyer and seller have an interest in determining the intrinsic characteristics of the good being exchange. A simple solution is for both buyer and seller to inspect the item, but this duplicative investment in information reduces the overall value of the good. This creates an incentive for the parties to the transaction to find ways to limit the amount of effort put into the creation of information. We discuss this problem and the ways that market forces, institutions, and organizations have developed to deal with the situation. It turns out that brand names and advertising are two devices that serve this purpose.

In addition, some goods last for a considerable amount of time. These are called **durable goods**. Economic investigation of durable goods takes into account that their value is generated across time. Analysis of durable goods is important in many business situations because when a durable good is put onto the market, it might return for sale in the secondary or used good market, and of course, used goods are often reasonable substitutes for new goods in the eyes of many buyers. Wise sellers will account for this effect when they put their durable commodities up for sale.

MEASUREMENT COSTS AND BLOCK BOOKING

Product quality is seldom perfectly observed by the buyer prior to purchase. When you buy oranges or apples in the store, even though you have a good idea what the taste will be, the proof is in the eating. As the old saying goes, "a bird in the hand is worth two in the bush." Uncertainty about the actual quality at consumption induces consumers to invest resources in trying to assess value prior to purchase. These investments are closely akin to a tax, reducing the consumer's demand price and willingness to pay for the good. Here is a case in which the interests of the buyer and seller coincide. For a given level of quality, both would prefer to avoid the consumer's investment in information, and symmetrically, seller expenditures for quality calculations increase the cost of production, which the consumer would prefer to avoid. Ideally, the consumer purchases the product with some stated level of quality, takes the good home, uses it, and if the product yields less than the mutually agreed level of quality, it is returned and the price is renegotiated. Of course, this sets in motion a number of incentives posing costs of their own. The consumer is inclined to complain after the fact that the product was less than the prespecified quality, especially when it is expensive for the seller to confirm this complaint; even if quality is discernible ex post, someone, either the buyer, the seller, or a hired arbitrator, must spend resources detecting the truth. What course is then available? Performance bonds are one device, but they do not necessarily erase the ex post measurement requirement. Strangely enough, brand names can provide assurances as to quality. These are discussed in detail in the next section.

Let us first turn our attention to bundling as a remedy to the problem of measurement cost. Consider an example. Say Large Grade A eggs are worth $1.80 per dozen to you, and Large Grade B eggs are worth $1.20 a dozen to you. That is, they are valued at 15 cents and 10 cents apiece respectively. Suppose the cost to you or the grocery store of determining quality is 5 cents per egg; it takes time and some expertise.[1] Then, you are willing to pay 15 cents minus the inspection cost of 5 cents, that is, 10 cents for each Grade A egg, and 5 cents (10 - 5 cents) for each Grade B egg. The problem is compounded by the fact that the store does not want to sell you Grade A eggs for Grade B prices. Therefore, they too have an interest in determining quality, grading the eggs.

Now from the start, Grade A eggs are worth $1.80 a dozen or 15 cents apiece to the buyer. That is, the store can sell them for 15 cents apiece. Suppose *no one* investigates the grade of eggs, and magically, only Grade A eggs are bought and sold. Then the net gain to the buyer and seller jointly is 15 cents per egg (of course, in all cases the farmer and the chicken must be compensated, but this is an irrelevancy for the problem at hand and so we ignore it for now). However, if the seller grades the eggs, then the joint net gain to the buyer and seller falls by 5 cents to 10 cents per egg. And, if the *buyer* also spends time grading each egg, the net gain falls by an additional 5 cents to a lowly 5 cents per egg. In this second case, 10 cents out of the total 15 have been consumed in the evaluation process. If some method can be uncovered to prevent the duplication of grading, the buyer and seller can jointly be made better off by 5 cents, the cost of reproducing the information on quality.[2]

In general, when the seller finds it expedient to grade goods, to determine their quality before offering them for sale, he also has an incentive to prevent the buyer from duplicating the same investment in information. It is important to note that this mutuality of interest between the buyer and seller only coincides when both parties have the same rankings over quality of goods. Most of us agree about what constitutes a high-quality diamond, in terms of color, clarity, and weight. Similarly, we all have much the same preferences over lumber and building materials. We all prefer 2×4s that are straight and knot-free. When there is widespread agreement as to what constitutes good characteristics, then duplicative investigation of the quality parameters reduces the overall gain available from ultimately consuming the good; buyer and seller alike have incentives to reduce this duplicative investigation. By contrast, people's tastes may differ considerably on what constitutes an attractive car, a decent apartment, or an artistic picture. In such cases, inspection of quality by the buyer does not neces-

---

[1] The example works just as well if, instead of Grade A quality versus Grade B quality, you value large eggs at $1.20 per dozen and medium eggs at $0.90 per dozen, and you cannot freely determine the size of eggs.

[2] For a more complete discussion of this phenomenon, see Yoram Barzel, "Measurement Cost and the Organization of Markets," *The Journal of Law and Economics*, 25, April 1982, 27–48.

sarily parallel the original examination by the seller; each has her own preferences. Here the buyer's and seller's interests may diverge, and the buyer is much more likely to insist on a personal or disinterested evaluation of quality. But let us now concern ourselves with the former case, where buyer and seller have homogeneous preferences over quality.

The mutual goal of buyer and seller is simply to determine quality with the minimum investment. **Bundling** helps serve this purpose. Consider a bin of eggs or oranges of various qualities, free for the choosing with different prices posted for different qualities. The buyer makes his selection, but then the store must also inspect the goods in order to price the sale properly. Instead, as an alternative method of selling, suppose the store bags oranges and apples in five- or ten-pound sacks and puts some label on the outside that the store attests represents the *average* quality of the fruit inside. If schemes develop so that consumers believe the store's written assertion about the quality of the fruit, then a second and repetitious quality investigation is precluded by the bundling of fruit in bags. Indeed, if some way can be found to mix the products with a minimum of variation, even the store does not have to measure each bundle. This technique eliminates measurement costs altogether.

Indeed, many valuable commodities are sold bundled, in a fashion that strongly suggests the purpose is to eliminate redundant investment in information. Two prominent examples include the block booking of movie films from producer to movie theater and the sale of diamonds by De Beers.

> The details of the CSO [the Central Selling Organization of the De Beers group] marketing arrangement are important for understanding our analysis. Several million rough diamonds from all sources pass through the CSO's selling office each year. The CSO sorts these stones first by shape (six categories), then by quality (about seven categories), by color (about eight categories), and, finally, by weight, resulting in more than two thousand categories. The variance in the value of stones within each category is nonetheless substantial. Independent producers are paid according to the number of stones of each category they provide, with the price of the stones in each category determined by the actual selling price received by the CSO during a representative period. The long-term exclusive sales requirement, in addition to controlling total supply, prevents mines from searching through their output and selecting the best stones within each category for sale on the open market rather than through De Beers.
>
> The CSO's customers consist of approximately three hundred invited diamond traders and cutters. These customers are of two types: manufacturers who have their own cutting and polishing facilities and a few dealers in each cutting center in the world who supply small manufacturers. Each customer is expected to buy regularly and, since average annual sales per customer are approximately $10 million, is screened to be financially sound.
>
> Each of the CSO's customers periodically informs the CSO of the kinds and quantities of diamonds it wishes to purchase. The CSO then assembles a single box (or "sight") of diamonds for the customer. Each box contains a number of folded, envelope-like packets called papers. The gems within each paper are similar and correspond to one of the CSO's classifications. The composition of any sight may differ slightly from that specified by the buyer because the supply of diamonds in each category is limited.
>
> Once every five weeks, primarily at the CSO's offices in London, the diamond

buyers are invited to inspect their sights. Each box is marked with the buyer's name and a price. A single box may carry a price of up to several million pounds. Each buyer examines his sight before deciding whether to buy. Each buyer may spend as long as he wishes, examining his sight to see that each stone is graded correctly (that is, fits the description marked on each parcel). There is no negotiation over the price or composition of the sight. In rare cases when a buyer claims that a stone has been miscategorized by the CSO, and the sales staff agrees, the sight will be adjusted. If a buyer rejects a sight, he is offered no alternative box. Rejection is extremely rare, however, because buyers who reject the diamonds offered them are deleted from the list of invited customers.

Thus stones (1) are sorted by De Beers into imperfectly homogeneous categories, (2) to be sold in preselected blocks, (3) to preselected buyers, (4) at nonnegotiable prices, with (5) buyers' rejection of the sales offer leading to the withdrawal by De Beers of future invitations to purchase stones.[3]

Arguably, this represents the quintessential example of bundling. Were it not for this sales technique, just imagine how much additional time and effort buyers would expend inspecting and evaluating all the rough diamonds sold through De Beers. The point here is that once De Beers has made a quality evaluation, additional inspection simply eats away at the monetary worth of the stones. Presumably De Beers has a sufficient reputation that no one expects that it would market many diamonds of less than stated quality. Of course, this means that some other method must have existed for selling diamonds prior to De Beers's attaining an unchallenged reputation. This example demonstrates the importance of reputations. Imagine that De Beers began to cheat on this arrangement, systematically overstating the quality of its stones. Over time, buyers would detect this malfeasance and refuse to buy from De Beers unless they brought along an independent appraiser. And, of course, the wages of the appraiser would be deducted from the price buyers would pay De Beers. In other words, De Beers's reputation for honesty saves the firm from indirectly having to pay the wages of a second set of appraisers for all the diamonds it sells. Reputations and brand names can be very valuable to buyers and sellers.

In all cases, the firm selling bundled products must be able to convince the buyer that the affirmation on the label is genuine. A variety of mechanisms exist to mollify this problem in information. We turn our attention to them at this point.

BRAND NAMES AND ADVERTISING AS QUALITY ASSURING DEVICES

Consider a simple artificial example. Abner sells custom-made leather shoes. Simplistically, let all buyers be homogeneous. If the shoes last for one year, they are worth $100 per pair; were they to last two years, the buyers would be willing to

---

[3] Roy Kenney and Benjamin W. Klein, "The Economics of Block Booking," *The Journal of Law and Economics,* 26(3), October 1983, 501–502. See the article, pp. 497–540 for a detailed discussion of both practices. The U.S. Supreme Court has outlawed the practice of block booking in movies in two cases, *United States* v. *Paramount Pictures, Inc.* 334 U.S. 131 (1948) and *United States* v. *Loew's Inc.* 371 U.S. 38 (1962).

pay $175 per pair; and if the shoes would retain their luster, shape, comfort, and soles for three years, the demand price would be $225 per pair. Looking at the shoes in the store, most buyers simply cannot tell whether the shoes are the one-, two-, or three-year variety. Abner has made the shoes to last three years (and they will in normal use); therefore, he wants to get $225 for each pair. How can he convince his customers about the quality of his shoes? There are many ways to skin this cat, including offering a money back guarantee if the shoes do not last the appropriate time.[4] This technique has costs. Records of date of purchase must be kept, the shoes and the buyer must be marked and identified, and there is always the customer's concern that Abner might refuse to pay up if the shoes wear out in six months. To eliminate this possibility, suppose Abner posts a surety bond. A surety bond is a promise by some disinterested third party to pay if Abner does not live up to his commitment. For example, Abner could put a sum of money in an escrow account at the bank. An escrow account does not allow Abner, by himself, to withdraw the money. Presumably, the bank would have to inspect the shoes and make restitution, if in its opinion the shoes had not lasted the full three years. The bank account now guarantees the quality of Abner's shoes, muting the ability to pay problem. Surety or performance bonds can aid in the resolution of uncertainty about product quality, raising profits and consumer's surplus. But note, the bond must be *irrevocable* by the seller of the goods, so long as customers are at risk. From the seller's perspective, the bond is an investment paying dividends only if people buy the shoes. For example, if the money held by the bank were earning interest and could be withdrawn at any time by the seller, no assurance is provided the buyer that reparations will be made in the case of poor quality. Therefore, from the point of view of the seller posting the bond, the money must be irretrievably lost. To repeat, it is an investment, a sunk cost. The inaccessibility of the funds used to assure quality is essential to the process. It is not sufficient for customers to be made aware that the money has been drawn from the bank, because buyers will rationally anticipate that Abner might withdraw the money at any time, leaving them holding the bag (or worthless shoes as the case may be).

It is possible to generalize that many forms of sunk investment expenditures may carry features similar to money deposited in a bank escrow account. In practice, there are many ways to post what amounts to a surety bond. Suppose Abner purchases a full-page advertisement in the local newspaper, or a 30-second spot on the radio. There is no way he can retrieve the money invested in advertising unless he continues to sell shoes. If his shoe business fails, the advertising expenditures become worthless. The business *can* fail if people, consistently relying on Abner's promises, purchase his shoes, only to discover the shoes wear out after six months' use. Suppose word of mouth spreads the news about the shoes, or the bulk of Abner's business is repeat customers. In either case, shoes of lower than stated quality eventually come back to haunt Abner and ultimately boot him out of business. Repeat customers do not return. Prospective customers warned by friends and friends of friends shop elsewhere. Abner's sales

---

[4] Many tire manufacturers offer this guarantee regarding tread wear and mileage.

decline and his sunk investment in advertising is gone, *paying him no dividends.* Advertising expenses, once made, offer the seller incentive to represent the quality of his wares honestly.

It is very important to note just exactly how advertising can act to assure quality. *It is the money spent on advertising* that creates the incentive to produce a quality product, not the ad itself or its specific content. The rate of return on the advertising investment is earned only if sales are maintained, which they will not be if quality is lower than expected by the customers. The more money spent on the advertisement, the greater is the sunk expenditure and the more profound the firm's desire to maintain product quality. Have you ever noticed the great publicity surrounding the television advertising costs for commercials during the NFL's Super Bowl? It appears that the advertisers themselves (and thus the networks indirectly) want this information made public. For the expenditure to be worthwhile, the consumers must know of the large dollar amounts spent on advertising. Buyers are more assured of future quality the greater the amount of the sunk investment by the advertiser. This also helps explain why celebrities are often used in ads. Presumably, the public can easily identify these people, but more important, celebrities by their very nature are most often rich. Their wealth makes it expensive to hire them for commercials. If there is a link between notoriety and wage rates, then using public figures in ads indirectly creates quality assurance in the mind of buyers; the buyer sees the high wages of the celebrity as a bond, a sunk investment. The use of celebrities is a practical way for the advertiser to communicate the cost of the ad without having to reveal the actual accounting data. Of course, this means there is a link between the content of an ad and the extent of quality assurance. The content of an ad must convince the viewer (the consumer) that expenditures have been made that are totally unrecoverable unless the producer maintains the specified quality. Anything the seller presents in the ad that suggests expense is likely to convey this message. This helps us understand why some ads offer unusual or spectacular views—mountain tops in the Himalayas, beaches in the South Pacific, the South Pole, and other places expensive to reach or locations where it is costly to produce films.

Naturally there are limitless ways to create sunk investments that may offer insight concerning future quality to buyers. The Goodyear blimp comes to mind. Suppose there is a thin market in blimps. That is, it would be very difficult and time-consuming for Goodyear to try and sell its blimps. Goodyear, in all like-lihood, could not sell its blimps for nearly as much as it paid for them, since blimps are rare and must be constructed by special order. Therefore, there is a gap between the purchase price and the resale price of blimps (at least let us suppose there is). The extent of this gap creates a quality assuring incentive for Goodyear, *if consumers believe or can be convinced that there is a differential between purchase and resale prices.* According to this argument, a blimp offers customers considerably more quality than a comparably priced airplane with the Goodyear name painted all across it, flying over many a sporting event. Since the airplane is much more easily marketed at a figure near its purchase price, less quality assurance is offered by the fly over.

Logos and architecturally unique buildings offer similar assurances to pro-spective buyers. Facades on buildings and firm-specific logos mimic surety or performance bonds; they are sunk investments paying no return unless the company survives. The expenditure on architectural services to create a *unique* building has many of the features of the Goodyear blimp, *so long as the building cannot be sold for its cost of construction.* Again, the differential between cost and resale value creates assurance in the minds of the buyer. Notice Transamerica's advertisements. They frequently show pictures of its headquarters in San Francisco, an unusual building. Presumably, the cost of construction for the pyramid far exceeds the average cost of construction for comparable office space. Therein lies the potential for quality assurance. Of course, the expense of creating and advertising a logo may provide similar services.

In general, what accountants call **goodwill** and what economists call **brand names** are financial assets at risk that mute the firm's incentive to adulterate its products for a short-term gain. Research in this area has documented a strong and negative relation between the value of a firm and declines in the quality of its goods. Unexpected declines in quality have resulted in unexpected reductions of the firm's common stock, mirroring the decline in goodwill and brand names.[5] For example, consider the case of fatalities in airline crashes. A crash signifies the worst kind of quality, most often taking the life of the consumer. Naturally, some crashes are beyond the control of the carrier, but in many cases, airline employees—pilots and maintenance crews especially—are at fault. Economists Mark Mitchell and Mike Maloney have documented the loss of goodwill associated with the carrier-at-fault accidents and find a dramatic impact. On average over the last 10 years, airline carriers sustaining crashes for which the pilot or crew were responsible lost $3.8 million per crash, *above and beyond* the costs of the lost airplane, higher insurance premiums, and tort damages.[6] The accompanying story surrounding the admissions in the summer of 1991 by executives at Salomon Brothers, a large bond trading and investment banking concern, that they had improperly purchased U.S. Treasury securities using accounts of their clients without permission also highlights the hazards of treading on brand names.

---

[5] For a sample of the scientific evidence on this matter, consult Michael T. Maloney and Mark L. Mitchell, "Crisis in the Cockpit? The Role of Market Forces in Promoting Air Travel Safety," *The Journal of Law and Economics,* 32(2), October 1989, 329–55; Andrew J. Chalk, "Market Forces and Aircraft Safety: The Case of the DC-10," *Economic Inquiry,* 24 January 1986, 43–60; Andrew J. Chalk, "Market Forces and Commercial Aircraft Safety," *Journal of Industrial Economics,* 36(1), September 1987, 61–81; Severin Borenstein and Martin Zimmerman, "Market Incentives for Safe Commercial Airline Operation," *American Economic Review,* 78, December 1988, 512–36; Mark L. Mitchell, "The Impact of External Parties on Brand-Name Capital: The 1982 Tylenol Poisonings and Subsequent Cases," *Economic Inquiry,* 27, October 1989, 601–18; and Gregg Jarrell and Sam Peltzman, "The Impact of Product Recalls on the Wealth of Sellers," *Journal of Political Economy,* 93, June 1985, 512–36. An entire issue of *The Journal of Law and Economics,* volume 24, number 3, dated December 1981, is tangentially devoted to this topic.

[6] Creating and ensuring product quality is obviously far more detailed and complicated than simply designing an effective advertising campaign. For instance, see John R. Hauser and Don Clausing, "The House of Quality," *Harvard Business Review,* 88(3), May–June 1988, 63–74 for one example. Nevertheless, the point here remains true: Advertising and sunk expenditures can be an important motivating and quality assuring device.

According to the story, Salomon Brothers has lost a lot of business and receives lower prices for the clients it has retained, seemingly swift punishment for attempting to exploit its market situation.

Designing the Correct Marketing/Advertising Program

The preceding argument says that advertising expenditures convey information to customers about the expected quality of the products offered for sale. Mistakes of two types can be made when trying to convey this information properly. First, the patrons can believe that the product is not as good as it actually is. When this is true, the advertising program needs to convey its expense to the public better. When ads look like they are inexpensive, either by their design or the media that carries them, the viewer will incorrectly impute too low a quality assurance to the product in question. Thus, ads that appear cheaper than their cost are ineffective. They mislead the public to undervalue the product for sale.

Similarly, ads that appear to cost more than the actual expense deceive the public into believing the product is of higher quality than it truly is. At first this might seem like a plus, that ad departments should be coerced into making the ads look deceitfully grandiose. However, closer examination reveals that this might not be good at all. Suppose by careful design, viewers see an ad that costs $100,000 to produce and air, but they think it actually costs $1 million. As a general proposition, the customers will then be inclined to believe that the product being advertised is more durable or of higher quality than it really is. The reason for this is simple. The company spent only $100,000 on the ads. That is, it only has $100,000 of sunk investment at risk, but the viewers think the company has $1 million of sunk investment. The public has been fooled into believing that the

---

The Value of Brand Names

NEW YORK—Salomon Brothers Inc.'s share of Wall Street's underwriting business has slumped in the wake of the firm's Treasury-bidding scandal.

The Salomon Inc. unit's market share of new stock and bond underwritings sagged to 7.9% during the weeks since the scandal surfaced in early August, down from the big investment bank's 10.2% share in the first seven months of 1991, according to IDD Information Services Inc.

More important, Salomon's underwriting fees—which it earns by buying new securities from corporate issuers and reselling them to the public—plunged to $19.4 million, or 4.6% of the overall market, in the five weeks since the scandal broke. That is down sharply from Salomon's 12% share of Wall Street's underwriting fees for the seven months, IDD says.

Michael Siconolfi, "Salomon's Underwriting Market Share and Fees Have Tumbled Since Treasury-Bidding Scandal," *Wall Street Journal*, September 17, 1991, p. C1. Reprinted by permission of *The Wall Street Journal*, © 1991 Dow Jones & Company, Inc. All Rights Reserved Worldwide.

company has a greater incentive than it actually does to produce a quality product. Then, when the product fails to live up to the customer's expectations, he or she will be disappointed. This disillusionment will hurt future sales.[7] The company must make the decision whether the cost savings of $900,000 is worth the loss of brand name and goodwill in this and *other* product lines, as customers are likely to link the quality of one of a company's products with many of its other goods. The customer will say to friends and cohorts, "That product didn't do the job I thought it was going to do." That kind of word-of-mouth advertising will ultimately prove detrimental to sales, as the *Wall Street Journal* story on Salomon Brothers attests, and the loss may transfer to other product lines. The multi-product company has to be careful in this situation that it does not overrepresent the quality of any one of its goods on the grounds that other innocent product lines are adversely affected. In this case it may not serve the long-term interests of the company to misrepresent the quality of its products unless the customers are dolts. Most are not.

An effective advertising campaign designed to convey the idea that the company has a lot of confidence in its products has to be carefully conceived. The information being conveyed by the campaign is the extent of the sunk investment in the program, the money spent on advertising. Deceptive or poorly composed operations will cause the public to have a distorted estimate of the expenditures that buttress the campaign. And, after all, it is the money spent that creates the incentive to maintain quality. Here we have the age-old situation in which veracity is critical to ensure the absence of confusion in the customer's mind.

Dressing for the Job

There is an old saying, "Clothes make the man," which if it were written today would surely be, "Clothes make the person." Let it be so. The question then becomes, Why? In the context of the previous discussion and since used clothes have virtually no resale market, a substantial investment in wardrobe pays for itself only if the worker maintains his or her job. An expensive coat, tie, dress, or suit can act to bond an employee's services to her employer, but if and only if the clothes cannot be liquidated for their purchase price. By contrast, an expensive car is fairly useless in this dimension unless it has been customized. This is especially true as it is so easy to rent an expensive motorcar for a brief time. Hence, expensive labels on clothes can help employees, especially young ones, certify the quality of their work into the future.[8] This feature of clothes is, of course, most important when the quality of the work is most in doubt. If quality is ascertained more or less immediately at the point of production, then quality assurance is moot. Perhaps this helps explain the relative dressing habits of some professionals, for

---

[7] This type of advertising might work if the company realizes that customers *think* the ad cost $1 million. The company then would be in a position to raise the quality of the goods to the expectations of the customers, saving $900,000 of advertising in the process. But note, it will be essential even here for the goods to have the quality level expected by the customers, never mind if it is different than the company planned.

[8] Arguably, an expensively obtained diploma may offer similar surety.

example, those in the entertainment business. The quality of movies and music is more easily known as they are produced than the quality of an accounting report that may contain errors undiscovered for years. Similarly, lawyers often sell their services to clients, say in the preparation of wills, and it is more than difficult for the buyer to ever know whether the job was done correctly. Employees who meet with the public and employees whose work is not immediately measurable are inclined to offer some assurances as to quality: Expensive, fashionable, and new clothes are one way to skin this cat. This helps us understand standards of dress required by some companies, especially when employees frequently meet with the public and quality is debatable. A hamburger restaurant is more likely to impose a dress code on its salespeople than a record store. Since hamburger quality is inherently more fungible than the quality of recorded music (here we mean fungible by the retail sales staff), buyers prefer relatively more guarantees. The record seller cannot do much to adulterate a sealed record that cannot be easily observed by the prospective buyer, while a French fry cook could use old oil, have dirty hands, or use rotten potatoes with high bacteria counts. Hence, dress codes in the hamburger restaurant impose costs on the seller, offering an implicit warranty not required by the record buyer.

Some companies impose a dress code. Is that consistent with the line of reasoning offered here? Well, junior employees are actually selling themselves to their supervisors, who must inspect or otherwise confirm the quality of the subordinate's job performance. In other words, employees may use surety bonds, advertising, and fixed unrecoverable investments, if you will, to assure the quality of their own work. A dress code forces an expenditure on the juniors that pays dividends only if their future job performance is adequate. To have the proper incentive effect, the work clothes that managers are required to buy must not, at best, be salvageable, or, at least, their value in alternative uses must be less than their purchase price.[9] Hence, it makes sense for a company to require its managers to wear white shirts, blue suits, and the like, which, in general, are not fashionable in nonwork activities. A ban on pastel shirts, which might be worn to parties, bars, or other social functions, creates a sunk investment for the manager, inducing higher quality work. Many companies are known to require white dress shirts from their male employees and similar clothes from their female employees. It is widely held that this requirement is some sort of stupid, old, conservative idea whose time surely will pass when the boss eventually becomes enlightened. The argument presented here says this view may be shallow and lacking in merit.

Initiations

Many college fraternities, sororities, and other organizations have elaborate initiations. These often border on the gruesome. Some require initiates to wear ridiculous clothes; others mandate some humiliating experiences, such as eating

---

[9] This helps us understand why retail stores requiring their employees to wear uniforms do not buy the uniforms for the employees. The employee must have something at risk for the incentive effect to operate.

live fish, chewing tobacco, or worse. Similarly, many clubs have hefty initiation fees to new members. Do these initiation rites serve any purpose? Clubs are unusual organizations because most accept members for long periods of time, often a lifetime, and importantly, the value of a club is strongly linked to the behavior and character of its members. Existing members of a club have a strong incentive to protect their investment, their initiation rites. The more horrible or costly the initiation, the more strongly current members are inclined to insist on careful management of the club, especially when it comes to selecting new members. If a club or fraternity is not properly cared for, the initiation experience pays no dividends, whether it be a large cash payment or a tortuous mental and physical ordeal. Like other sunk investments, initiations create an incentive to maintain quality.

Hence, high initiation fees are more than a screening device; they also serve to motivate members, to ensure the desired behavior, and to help create a legacy of future conduct. Without such fees, clubs and fraternities would have a difficult time keeping out incompatible members. If Alfred has paid only $100 to join the local country club, he is more inclined to sponsor his brash, crude, and unkempt business associate Oscar for membership, weighing the business gains against the trivial $100 initiation fee, than if he had invested $10,000 to join the club. In the latter case, the business interests will have to be much more substantial to overcome Oscar's undesirable social graces.

Sunk investments, like surety bonds, can have profound incentive effects. Reputations are more than just words. They are costly to acquire, but extremely useful when it comes to convincing a skeptical buyer about the quality of products being sold. The more it costs to ascertain quality, the more important advertising, surety bonds, sunk investments, and reputations become.

DURABLE GOODS

Hypothetical Business Problem 11.1

Your company sells college textbooks. Typically, the books become dated in about three years, and a new and updated edition is released. You are concerned that used books seriously hurt your sales of new books. You are considering alternative plans to reduce the incidence of used book sales. One plan prints the books on cheap paper and binds the books loosely, so that at the end of one semester, the books are worn out and unusable; they are not resold. Another plan prints a new edition each year, updating the old book and making it obsolete and virtually unsalable. Does either of these plans offer a profit opportunity? Put another way, what is the impact of secondary or used book sales on the sales of new books?

In a number of important respects, **durable consumer items** are markedly different from one-time consumable goods. Durable consumer goods are kin to capital goods; they provide a flow of services across time. Unlike a candy bar which once eaten is gone, a car provides transportation today and tomorrow (unless the owner is a very bad driver or the car breaks down). As with a capital good, the value of a consumer durable commodity is the present value of the net future subjective utilities. Indeed, if we transform utility into a money equivalent, the value of a consumer durable good—a car, a refrigerator, a home, a lamp, a set of encyclopedias, or a bicycle—is computed the same way we value a capital item. Actually, a consumer durable good is just a different moniker for a particular type of capital good—one that applies to things used directly by consumers.

This product durability makes the consumer demand for enduring goods somewhat different from the demand for one-time consumable goods. The demand for regular goods derives directly from the utility they provide when purchased. By contrast, the demand for a durable good includes the current utility, but also the future utility as the product is used in days to come. On the surface, this appears to make the demand for consumer durables greater than that for regular goods, and based on this effect, it is. However, there is an important countervailing effect that terribly complicates the analysis. Once a durable good has been sold onto the market, used versions (being close substitutes for the original version) are available for sale by the original buyer. This creates competition for the original seller, reducing the demand for new goods. Sellers of computer software are acutely aware of this potentiality and many have gone to great lengths to protect their products from being copied as a means of preventing buyers of the original good from selling duplicates. VCR movie sellers have encountered similar problems, resorting to not so subtle warnings about the FBI's investigating cases of unauthorized duplication of tapes. You may recall the uproar among sports fans in the fall of 1990 when CBS and NBC decided to encrypt the satellite feeds of NFL football games to stations, depriving patrons of sports bars of the opportunity to view games other than the ones being broadcast locally over the airwaves. And, of course, if the original buyer bases his purchase on some expected resale price, then the seller is in position to reduce the resale value simply by expanding production in the future and lowering the price of new items. All told, these myriad forces create quite a number of dilemmas for the monopoly producer of durable goods: (1) the original selling price, (2) the actual longevity of the product, its durability, and (3) whether to impede or facilitate the resale market in used goods. Let us consider a simple example.

Suppose you have a vacation planned for Europe next summer. Your first choice is to purchase a bicycle and tour from Amsterdam to Paris to the Riviera, on to Venice, and from there to Zurich from where you will fly home. Suppose, given your budget and itinerary, a Raleigh 10-speed touring bicycle is worth $500 to you as transportation for this great excursion. Table 11.1 reports the computation of your demand price for the bike based on your ability to market the used bike after your vacation. Suppose your vacation will last three months, and the annual interest rate is 12 percent (making the quarterly discount rate 4 percent). We can then map the future resale price into its current value. The sum of your $500 consumption value and the present value of the resale price is your total willingness to pay for the bike. Suppose you can sell your used bike for $100 once you finish your vacation. The present value of $100 in three months is $100/1.04 or $96.15. Given that the bike is worth $500 in consumption, the resale potential raises your demand price to $596.15. Your demand price is your consumption

---

TABLE 11.1   THE DEMAND FOR DURABLE GOODS

CONSUMPTION VALUE	POTENTIAL RESALE PRICE	PRESENT VALUE OF RESALE VALUE	DEMAND PRICE
$500	$ 0	$ 0	$500.00
500	100	100/1.04	596.15
500	200	200/1.04	692.31
500	300	300/1.04	788.46
500	400	400/1.04	884.62

value plus the present discounted value of the future resale price ($500 + $96.15 = $596.15). The right-hand column of Table 11.1 represents your demand price for the bicycle at various resale prices.

Two things are noteworthy about the resale value. First, as the resale price of the bike increases, your demand price increases. Second, as the interest rate rises or as the length of time you expect to keep the bike grows (holding constant your consumption value), your demand price falls. Why is this true? In the third column, where we divide the resale price by discount factor, if the interest rate were higher, the present value, and hence, the potential demand price, would be lower.

Now consider a number of situations you might face after you have purchased your bike. Suppose your trip is scheduled to start at the beginning of May. Along with you, there are multitudes of Americans traveling to Europe at this time, contemplating a similar excursion. Most of you plan to complete your trip in late August or early September. The market for used bikes will then be flooded with sellers, and most buyers of used bikes expect to hold them for sale next spring to another crop of tourists. As a consequence, the expected resale price is relatively low, say $100. This means the most you are willing to pay for the new bike is $596.15. Worse yet, you fear that Raleigh may cut the price of *new* bikes over the summer, further reducing your ability to sell the bike at the end of the summer. To help alleviate this problem, suppose Raleigh agrees to repurchase the bike subject to inspection for damages, or alternatively, imagine Raleigh just rents you the bike. Either arrangement mutes the problem you the buyer face in determining the value of the new bike to you. In either case, the use value of the bike is $500, which, absent competition or other similar complications, the seller can charge you up front, agreeing to repurchase it for a sum exceeding what you expect the bike is worth in the resale market. The seller must buy it back at a price higher than you expect to face in the used market or the problem is not eliminated; you must still estimate the resale price. Of course, in terms of uncertainty, a repurchase promise reduces the *variance* in your expected selling price, and hence, the buy-back price need not be markedly above the expected resale price. Naturally, rental eliminates all these problems but, as we see in Chapter 12, it introduces difficulties of its own. Specifically, the renter has a muted incentive to maintain the bike properly. Naturally, guaranteed repurchase carries the same maintenance problem.

The point of this example is straightforward. The demand price for a durable good has two components—the original buyer's intrinsic use value plus the ultimate resale value. Producers routinely lament the existence of a second hand or resale market, for they feel that the sale of those used goods represents lost sales of new products to themselves. Although the problem of durability is quite complicated, this simple-minded approach ignores the fact that some buyers may only purchase a good the first time if they can reasonably expect to peddle it second hand before its useful life is completed. Thus, sellers of bicycles in London, Amsterdam, and Brussels—places where many Americans arrive planning to purchase bikes—may actually go to great lengths to *foster* a resale market in used bikes. We can note that many retailers of automobiles establish used car lots adjacent to their new car showrooms.

The seller has other options that must be considered. In almost all cases, the producer can affect the life of the good in question. In the case of a bicycle, the quality and thickness of the seat, the type of metal employed, and the extent of rust proofing applied can all be varied. Refrigerators can be made to last as little as one year or as many as 20. The same logic applies to automobiles, hand tools, houses, and personal computers. The grade of materials and quality control used in the production process can vary and ultimately impact the life span of the article in question. In the limit, the seller can contractually or otherwise eliminate the resale market. Some computer software manufacturers have written programs that can only be used on one machine.[10] Without breaking the code, there is no way the original purchaser can enter the used market with the program, even when she has no further use for it. The original versions of Disk Technician are an example.[11] Virtually all car manufacturers offer a warranty on their vehicles to the original purchaser, commonly for 12 months or 12,000 miles. Some manufacturers allow the transfer of this warranty to used car purchasers; most do not. This points out the intrigue of the problem. There are circumstances in which the original seller benefits from a secondary market, but there are also cases in which an active resale market in used goods is perceived by sellers to negatively affect sales of their new goods.

The preceding analysis puts you in position to construct a solution to Problem 11.1. Consider the following approach. First we adopt a formal, mathematical technique, and then we offer an intuitive approach.

Suggested Solution to Problem 11.1

We are now in position to tackle the problem of college textbooks posed at the beginning of this section and the general problem of durability and secondary or resale markets. Let us construct a formal model. For

---

[10] SAS, Statistical Analysis System, a copyrighted computer software program of the SAS Institute, Box 8000, Cary, NC, dies inside your computer annually. On the day after the purchase anniversary, the software, having checked with the internal clock in the computer, refuses to operate. The owner is required to manually alter the date in the computer or update the site license in order to use the program thereafter.

[11] Disk Technician is a copyrighted program of Prime Solutions, Inc., 1940 Garnet Avenue, San Diego, CA.

simplicity, let there be just two periods, the first and the second—a new textbook is coming out, and due to the nature of the material, it will be in use for only two years. The firm chooses the volume of new books it would like to sell in each period; call these N_1 and N_2 respectively. N_1 is sales of new books in the first year, and N_2 is sales of new books in the second year. The price consumers are willing to pay for the new books in the first period, P_1, is partly determined by their own personal use of the book throughout the first period (a function of the quantity produced, N_1); since they may wish to sell the book after they are finished with the course, the discounted value of the expected price for *used* books in the second year must also be included:

$$P_1 = P_1(N_1) + \text{Expected}(P_u \bullet D) \tag{11.1}$$

where P_u is the used price of books in the second year; D is the discount factor, $1/(1 + r)$; and r is the appropriate discount rate. The price the buyer is willing to pay for the new book is the personal use value plus the present discounted value of the used book. By the first law of demand, higher prices for new books in the first period reduce sales of new books in the first year, $\partial P_1/\partial N_1 < 0$; increasing the output of new books lowers the price the market will pay for them. But higher expected future prices for used books increase the current willingness to pay for new books.[12] The price consumers are willing to pay for the *new* books in the second period, P_2, is determined by the quantity of the new books made available, N_2, and the relative substitutability of the used books for the new ones—that is, the price of used books. In other words, the price buyers are willing to pay for new books in the second year is a function of the number of new books produced in the second year and the price of used books:

$$P_2 = P_2(N_2, P_u). \tag{11.2}$$

Again, by the first law of demand, more new books in the second year reduces their price, $\partial P_2/\partial N_2 < 0$, and lower used book prices reduce the price people will pay for new ones, $\partial P_2/\partial P_u < 0$.[13]

The price of used books is determined by the stock available in the second period, U:

$$P_u = P_u(U). \tag{11.3}$$

---

[12] We could complicate the analysis by including the expected value of the price of new books in the demand equation as well. Some people might be willing to wait to buy (take the course later) if the future price, relative to the current price, is sufficiently low. However, omitting this twist has few consequences on the problem at hand and significantly facilitates the analysis.

[13] We might also consider the possibility that some first period consumers purchase the good simply to resell it *new* in the second period when they believe that $P_1 < D \bullet P_2$. For now we ignore this arbitrage complication.

The stock of used books, U, is determined by the rate of depreciation, α, and the volume of new books sold in the first period, N_1:

$$U = (1 - \alpha) \bullet N_1. \tag{11.4}$$

Initially, we make two simplifying assumptions that are relaxed later. We presume that neither the firm nor the buyer can affect the rate of depreciation. That is, only forces in nature determine the physical rate of deterioration. Substituting equation 11.4 into equation 11.3 yields the formula for the price of used books as determined by the depreciation rate and the stock of new books in the first period:

$$P_u = P_u[(1 - \alpha) \bullet N_1]. \tag{11.5}$$

For a person buying a new book in the first year, the resale price he *expects* to receive is one minus the rate of depreciation, $1 - \alpha$ (the probability that the book can be sold in the used market), times the price of used books, P_u, and discounted to the present. Therefore, the expected present value of selling a used book is

$$\text{Expected}(P_u \bullet D) = (1 - \alpha) \bullet D \bullet P_u[(1 - \alpha) \bullet N_1].$$

The first term, $1 - \alpha$, is the probability that the new book will last and be available for resale. The second term, D, is the discount factor. The last term, $P_u[(1 - \alpha) \bullet N_1]$, is the price of used books in the second year. Therefore, by substitution, the full demand price for new books, equation 11.1, is rewritten as

$$P_1 = P_1(N_1) + (1 - \alpha) \bullet D \bullet P_u[(1 - \alpha) \bullet N_1]. \tag{11.6}$$

Similarly, from equations 11.2 and 11.5, we obtain the price of new books in the second year:

$$P_2 = P_2\{N_2, \ P_u[(1 - \alpha) \bullet N_1]\}. \tag{11.7}$$

The value of the firm, V, is the net present value of the two cash flows. It is the revenue from sales of new books in the first year plus the present discounted value of the revenues from sales of new books in year two:

$$V = N_1 \bullet P_1 + D \bullet N_2 \bullet P_2 - C(N_1) - D \bullet C(N_2) \tag{11.8}$$

where $C(N)$ is the cost of producing new books. Substituting the appropriate expressions for P_1 and P_2 (equations 11.6 and 11.7) into equation 11.8 yields

$$V = N_1 \bullet \{P_1(N_1) + (1 - \alpha) \bullet D \bullet P_u[(1 - \alpha) \bullet N_1]\} + D \bullet N_2 \bullet P_2\{N_2,$$
$$P_u[(1 - \alpha) \bullet N_1]\} - C(N_1) - D \bullet C(N_2). \tag{11.9}$$

To maximize V, the value of the firm, the firm must choose the appropriate number of new books to sell in each year, N_1 and N_2. Mathematically, this is determined by setting the partial derivatives of V with respect to N_1 and N_2 equal to zero. These (somewhat messy) first order conditions are

$$\partial V/\partial N_1 = P_1(N_1) + (1 - \alpha)\bullet D\bullet P_u + N_1\bullet\partial P_1/\partial N_1 + N_1\bullet D\bullet(\partial P_u/\partial U)\bullet$$
$$(1 - \alpha) + D\bullet N_2\bullet(\partial P_2/\partial P_u)\bullet(\partial P_u/\partial U)\bullet(1 - \alpha) = \partial C/\partial N_1, \quad (11.10)$$

and

$$\partial V/\partial N_2 = D\bullet[P_2 + N_2\bullet(\partial P_2/\partial N_2 + \partial P_2/\partial P_u)] = D\bullet\partial C/\partial N_2. \quad (11.11)$$

These two equations can be solved, at least conceptually, for the optimal values of N_1 and N_2. When we do this, we obtain the value maximizing level of production of new books in the first and second years. Call these quantities, N_1^* and N_2^*. If we take these two values and insert them into the value equation, equation 11.9, we obtain what economists call the **indirect value function**, and we label it V^* to represent the fact that the maximizing values of the choice variables have been employed. It is called the indirect value function because it represents the maximum quantity obtainable for the value function. When the company sells the optimal quantities, N_1^* and N_2^* then the value of the firm is V^*. This function can be used to answer a host of interesting questions using the **envelope theorem**.[14]

Of central importance is the relation between the rate of depreciation and the value of the firm. Of course, books decay naturally. But, in addition, some consumers take poor care of books bought in the first period—they lose them or otherwise keep them out of the resale market. We have already discussed some ways the producer can alter the rate of depreciation: using less durable materials and lower quality control to name two. If we let N_1^* and N_2^* be the values of N_1 and N_2 that maximize V, and we let V^* be the maximum value of V given the conditions of the model, then the derivative of V^* with respect to α, the rate of depreciation, predicts the relation between changes in depreciation and the value of the firm, given that the firm optimally chooses the number of books to sell in each period.[15] The indirect value function is obtained by inserting the solutions to equations 11.10 and 11.11 into the V^* equation, equation 11.9. When we make this substitution and take the derivative with respect to the rate of depreciation, α, we discover that

---

[14] Consult the mathematical appendix to Chapter 2 for a discussion on indirect functions in general and the use of the envelope theorem.

[15] Again, this mathematical conclusion involves an understanding of the envelope theorem. This theorem, although powerful, requires some training to be put through its paces, and some of you may not find the investment worthwhile.

$$\partial V^*/\partial \alpha = N_1^* (1 - \alpha) \bullet D \bullet (\partial P_u/\partial U) \bullet N_1^* \bullet (-1) + N_1^* \bullet D \bullet P_u \bullet (-1) +$$
$$D \bullet N_2^* \bullet (\partial P_2/\partial P_u) \bullet N_1^* \bullet (-1),$$

or

$$\partial V^*/\partial \alpha = - (N_1^* \bullet D) \bullet [P_u + (1 - \alpha) \bullet N_1^* \bullet \partial P_u/\partial U + N_2^* \bullet \partial P_2/\partial P_u]. \quad (11.12)$$

This expression can be positive or negative, and that is the whole point of this exercise. The specific conditions of the situation determine the impact of the resale market on the profits of the seller. It is imprudent management to blindly and dogmatically declare that the used book market definitively hurts sales of new books. According to the theory laid out here, it can go either way, and the appropriate way to treat the used book market hinges on two countervailing forces. To understand this result, break the right-hand portion of equation 11.12 into two parts (note that we have placed the minus sign before the second term):

(1) $N_1^* \bullet D$, and

(2) $- [P_u + (1 - \alpha) \bullet N_1^* \bullet \partial P_u/\partial U + N_2^* \bullet \partial P_2/\partial P_u].$

What is the important aspect of this overall problem? What are we really trying to uncover here? The issue is, When does it pay a company to make its goods more durable, to cause the depreciation rate to be lower? In the context of the mathematical model presented here, we are asking, Under what conditions does a reduction in α cause V^* to go up? So what we want to know is, When is $\partial V^*/\partial \alpha < 0$? That is, when is equation 11.12 negative? Since the first part of the determining expression, part (1) of equation 11.12, $N_1^* \bullet D$, is positive, then the product of the two parts, (1) and (2), will be negative and value will increase when depreciation declines only if the second part is negative. That is, $\partial V^*/\partial \alpha < 0$ when

$$- [P_u + (1 - \alpha) \bullet N_1^* \bullet \partial P_u/\partial U + N_2^* \bullet \partial P_2/\partial P_u] < 0. \quad (11.13)$$

One easy substitution begins to make this expression intuitively pleasing. Observe that $(1 - \alpha) \bullet N_1^*$ is simply the volume of used books sold in the second period, U. With this substitution and the multiplication of both sides by -1, which reverses the sense of the inequality, we have an expression describing the relation between book depreciation and the profits of book sellers. The circumstances under which an increase in book depreciation leads to higher profits is

$$P_u + U \bullet \partial P_u/\partial U + N_2^* \bullet \partial P_2/\partial P_u > 0, \quad (11.14)$$

or when

$$P_u + U \bullet \partial P_u/\partial U > - N_2^* \bullet \partial P_2/\partial P_u. \quad (11.15)$$

Let us try to make some sense of this mathematical condition. First, note a weak condition. Since new and used books are substitutes, $\partial P_2/\partial P_u > 0$; higher used book prices increase the consumer's willingness to pay for new books. Since the term N_2^* is simply the optimal number of new books to sell in the second period, it is positive (or zero). This means that the right-hand side of equation 11.15 is negative (or zero). Therefore, if the left-hand side of the inequality is positive, then we have the condition under which a reduction in the decay rate of durable goods will increase profits and value. The left-hand side of the expression is positive when $P_u + U{\cdot}\partial P_u/\partial U$ is positive. This condition has a congenial interpretation. $P_u + U{\cdot}\partial P_u/\partial U$ is simply marginal revenue to used book sellers. If this is anticipated to be positive, then anything the firm can do to make its product more durable will raise its net income. When the price of used books causes the marginal revenue to be greater than zero, it pays new book sellers to reduce the rate of depreciation on new books. We can state this result in terms of the price elasticity of demand for used books. We know that the demand is elastic when marginal revenue is positive, and therefore, increasing durability will increase sales, profits, and value when the price elasticity of demand for used books is anticipated to be elastic.

More precisely, after some manipulation, the condition identified in equation 11.15 is restated in terms of the own price elasticity of demand for used books, η_u,

$$P_u{\cdot}(1 + 1/\eta_u) > - N_2^*{\cdot}\partial P_2/\partial P_u. \tag{11.16}$$

Again, since the right-hand side is not positive, a sufficient *but not necessary* condition for profits to increase when depreciation declines is that the own price elasticity of demand for used books must be elastic ($\eta_u < -1$).

Let us explore the substitution term, $\partial P_2/\partial P_u$. If the goods were perfect substitutes, then the two prices, P_2 and P_u, would have to be the same; arbitrage by consumers and producers would ensure it. As the quality of used books declines vis-à-vis new books, the substitution term gets larger. For example, if the price of used books increases by \$1, the price of new books must increase *more* than \$1; $\partial P_2/\partial P_u > 1$. In sum,

$$1 < \partial P_2/\partial P_u < \infty.$$

Employing the strong condition identified in equation 11.14, we see that as the two goods become closer substitutes, as $\partial P_2/\partial P_u$ falls toward one, the right-hand side becomes less negative, closer to zero, and this increases the necessity for the own price elasticity of demand for used books to be elastic. Put another way, if consumers do not view new and used books as good substitutes, it always pays the seller to make the goods more durable. Why is this true? When new and used books are not good substitutes in the eyes of the buyers, then $\partial P_2/\partial P_u$ is quite large, making the right-hand side of equation 11.14 very negative. In turn, this means that regardless of the price elasticity of demand for used books, the expression on the left of equation 11.14 will be greater than the right-hand side, and then we know that profits will be higher when depreciation decreases.

To avoid being swamped in a sea of mathematics, let us review the solution to problem 11.1 verbally. Durable goods require extra analysis in order to price them properly. Once durable goods are sold, a market develops in used goods. Some potential buyers of new goods in subsequent time periods then have the option of purchasing from alternative sellers who are beyond control of the firm. This prospect can have a deleterious impact on future sales and profits. However, the prospect of a market for used goods in the future makes consumers willing to pay more for new goods at the outset. The option of selling in the future raises their estimation of the worth of the good beyond their own direct utility in use. We have a two-edged sword. If the firm makes its products very durable, then they are good substitutes for its *new* products in the future, but current buyers cognizant of just this prospect are willing to pay more at the beginning. Balancing these two effects requires extra managerial precision. We have noted one important result. When the price elasticity of demand for used goods is elastic, it will always pay the producer to raise product durability.[16] Likewise, facilitating the operation of used markets will enhance profitability. For example, many new car dealers go to great lengths to help their customers sell their used cars. They have large used car lots, they run ads, and they certify quality. All of these are ways of making used markets work more efficiently and, in the bargain, raise the value of new cars to prospective buyers. Notice the unending stream of Mercedes's or Volvo's advertisements claiming how its product holds its resale value. We presume that this is designed to make the new car buyer acutely aware of the resale market so that he or she will be willing to pay *more* for the new car than it is worth directly to him or her.

If the demand for used goods is inelastic, the seller of new durable goods must be keenly aware of the substitutability of new for used goods. As the goods become ever closer substitutes, the likelihood increases that greater durability of new goods adversely affects profits.[17]

We close this section with two stories that demonstrate how important the secondary market is to some sellers. The first account, from *The Economist*, illustrates the important relation between the new and used-car markets.

---

[16] Up to this point in the discussion, we have totally ignored the cost of changing durability. Of course, it is not free to make books, cars, hammers, toys, houses, or most any other good more durable. Naturally, the marginal cost of increased durability must be accounted for, and any changes in durability based on principles presented here must be balanced against changes in costs of production.

[17] Those of you interested in pursuing this inquiry further are referred to papers by Ronald Coase, "Durability and Monopoly," *The Journal of Law and Economics,* 15(1), April 1972, 143–50; and Daniel K. Benjamin and Roger C. Kormendi, "The Interrelationship Between Markets for New and Used Durable Goods," *The Journal of Law and Economics,* 17, October 1974, 381–402 among others.

> This winter, with the Japanese economy slowing down sharply, [used car] prices are lower than ever. A year-old Toyota Mark II (the trade's benchmark model) is currently going for 10% less than the equivalent model did a year ago.
>
> Dismal days for used-car dealers spell disaster for the new car trade. As elsewhere, Japanese motorists tend to hang on to their existing models when they see their trade-in values fall, hoping to sell privately instead.[18]

The second story involves the entertainment business. Apparently, a large part of the revenues earned from independent television producers comes from the so-called rerun or syndicated market. Consider the following story from *The Wall Street Journal:*

> Producer Stephen J. Cannell hasn't turned down many chances to do an action series for network television.
>
> But for the first time, the creator of "Hunter," "Wiseguy" and "The A-Team" recently walked away from an offer to do a series that he and a writer had dreamed up. The show called for boats and on-the-water shots, helicopters and other budget-busters. NBC, however, wouldn't raise its fee—and Mr. Cannell was unwilling to take a loss of $200,000 to $300,000 on each episode, as he might have done previously on an action show.
>
> "Two years ago we probably would have gone forward with it," says Mr. Cannell. But the rerun syndication business is in trouble these days, particularly for one-hour dramas. Mr. Cannell and other producers are no longer confident that they can recoup such losses by selling reruns to local TV stations.
>
> **Balking at Big Losses**
>
> Syndication is critical to the financing of a network series. NBC, ABC and CBS pay only part of the cost, generally $500,000 to $800,000, for a one-hour action episode that can cost the producers $1 million or more to make. In the past, studios and producers have willingly swallowed losses of as much as $600,000 an episode, betting that they later would rake in big money on sales of reruns to dozens of local stations.
>
> But stations have quit buying action-series reruns as the shows have faltered in the ratings. And many stations no longer have room for the shows in their schedules or their budgets anyway—they've spent too much on a few pricey hits.
>
> The syndication slump has forced producers to focus more sharply on costs. Many are seeking new customers overseas. And more series are detouring to cable, albeit usually at much lower prices. "Murder She Wrote" and "Miami Vice" will air on the cable USA Network, and "Cagney & Lacey" will be on Lifetime.
>
> Some producers are turning down new network shows rather than take the risk that they won't be able to recoup their costs. A few current shows may even be canceled by their own studios because of the poor outlook for later return sales.
>
> To cut costs, some studios are changing the scripts—dropping a helicopter from a scene or playing up bedroom-and-boardroom melodrama, which is cheaper to shoot than a car chase. For "Tour of Duty," a costly series about soldiers

---

[18] "Used Cars in Japan: Young Bangers" *The Economist*, December 21, 1991–January 3, 1992, p. 85. © 1991 The Economist Newspaper Ltd. Reprinted with permission.

in Vietnam, New World Pictures stages only a few big battle scenes and instead focuses on character interplay.

Mr. Cannell, for one, now operates as if there were no U.S. rerun market at all. He won't take on a new series unless he can hold his loss to $100,000 an episode after getting paid by the network and selling the show overseas. He bases his budget on getting nothing in the U.S.

The market for action series peaked two years ago with "Magnum P.I.," sold to local stations for almost $2 million per episode. Two other series went for $1 million-plus. "Then that was it. It was like Black Monday, prices crashed," as stations stopped buying when ratings fell, says producer Jay Bernstein, creator of "Mike Hammer" and "Houston Nights." The action series that followed sold for $300,000 an episode.

Now, Mr. Bernstein can't get studio financing for a new series he wants to make. "There isn't a major studio out there looking to deficit-finance a hard-action show," he says. He also worries the rerun slump will kill "Houston Nights."

Some producers, though, are convinced that the market for one-hour action shows will make a comeback. Local stations may overdose on the half-hour situation comedies—33 network comedies will be up for syndication in the next three years, says John von Soosten of Katz Television, who advises stations on programming.

Adds Michael Mann, producer of "Miami Vice": "Now is the best time in the world to do one-hour dramas, because there's going to be a glut in sitcoms that everybody has raced to produce."

"We all want to believe that," says Mr. Cannell, but he's doubtful. To reduce his losses on "Wiseguy," a slick and seedy drama about a cop who infiltrates the mob, Mr. Cannell films in Vancouver and edits on videotape rather than film. But he still isn't meeting his target of holding losses to $100,000 an episode.

Because of the shrinking syndication market, Mr. Cannell says the industry needs a new budget formula in which the networks pay a higher share of the costs. In "Sonny Spoon," Mr. Cannell's newest series for NBC, the network takes all of the financial risks, pays all production costs and pays the producer a per-episode fee comparable to what he gets on the shows that he owns. NBC conceived the show and owns it, but Mr. Cannell shares rerun profits if the show survives.

NBC is quick to quash any talk that the budget arrangement for "Spoon" is a breakthrough. The vice president who negotiated the deal, John Agoglia, says NBC has owned shows before.

The networks are crying poor and saying they can't afford to pay more. Raising the fees that networks pay "isn't merited," says Kim LeMasters, CBS Entertainment president. "It's always been a gamble producers take at their choice."

"Bigger-Sucker Theory"

Networks also are convinced they will still have enough shows. "The networks operate on the bigger-sucker theory," says Mr. Cannell: When one maker walks away, "the network seeks out a bigger sucker who will take it." When MCA Inc.'s Universal studio turned down rights to "Crime Story," about Las Vegas in the 1960s, New World picked it up, initially taking losses of as much as $500,000 an episode to get into TV production. New World now is running up losses of $300,000 per episode on the show.

Meanwhile, the studio also is said to be losing $300,000 or more on each episode of "Tour of Duty." Harry Evans Sloan, co-chairman of New World, insists he can at least break even with network fees, foreign sales and cable sales, and that he'll eventually make a profit on the show by selling reruns to U.S. stations.

Esther Shapiro, a creator and producer of the glitzy soap "Dynasty," calls such losses "dumb business. I would never go into a show with a $200,000 to $600,000 deficit per episode. That's done by people who don't know what they're doing."

But Ms. Shapiro, too, has had to adjust. Nighttime soaps do badly in daily reruns because plot lines take weeks to unravel. Her next show, "Private Practice," about a group of women running a medical center, will have shorter stories that wind up with each episode.

Too many action shows have "lousy stories," she says. "Everybody forgets and puts money into the wrong things. It's the story, guys, it's the story."[19]

One of the main things this article points out is the importance of the resale market. If we are to believe the facts reported, most independently produced shows are sold to networks at a loss, only making money in the second period, when the programs are sold as used goods to the nonnetwork, local stations. As the article notes, "Syndication is critical to the financing of a network series. NBC, ABC and CBS pay only a part of the cost." At this point the inquisitive student might say, "This isn't really like the other cases of durable goods discussed here, because the original producer retains the resale rights, selling the program to the local stations rather than the buyer—NBC, CBS, ABC—selling the show." But does that fact really affect the analysis? Would the pricing strategy be any different if, say, producer Stephen J. Cannell sold all the rights, including syndication, to the networks and they, in turn, sold them to the local stations? Of course not. Mr. Cannell would simply include the expected syndication fees in the price he charges the network. The network would then recover the difference upon syndication. Why the particular market structure has developed (where the original producer retains syndication rights) is an important and interesting managerial question in its own right, but it does not affect the analysis of the proper pricing of durable goods. At this point, we can only speculate about the reasons for the existing arrangement. The large networks may fear antitrust prosecution if they retained the rights, independent producers may have a comparative advantage negotiating with local TV stations, FCC regulations may disallow the networks from syndication, or perhaps the incentives to produce a sequence of high-quality programs are greater when the original producer retains rights to the residuals. This last prospect is one of the main topics discussed throughout Chapters 12 and 13.

Returning to the main point of this section, pricing durable goods presents a formidable managerial challenge. There is a knee-jerk reaction on the part of some people to disdain the secondary market for their goods, believing that the presence of used goods hurts the sale of new goods in later periods. Of course, this is true, but the analysis presented here demonstrates that it is precisely the

---

[19] Dennis Kneale, "TV Producers Turn More Cautious as the Syndication Market Shrinks," *Wall Street Journal*, March 1, 1988, p. 41. Reprinted by permission of *Wall Street Journal*, © 1988 Dow Jones & Company, Inc. All Rights Reserved Worldwide.

ability of the buyer to resell the good later that makes it worthwhile purchasing in the first place. Losing sight of this effect can cost stockholders money and managers their titles and salaries.

TOPICS TO REVIEW

These are topics that you should feel comfortable with before you leave this chapter. If you cannot write out a clear and concise sentence or paragraph explaining the topic after you have worked on the study problems, you should reread the relevant section of the text.

Measurement Costs

Bundling

Brand Names

Surety Bonds

Quality Assuring Devices

Advertising and Product Quality

Durable Goods

Block Booking

STUDY PROBLEMS

1. Used cars are basically sold in three ways: through ads in the newspaper, at franchised new car dealers, and at used car lots. At which place do you expect to find the lowest price? Why? Where do you imagine the best cars are found, the cars with least repairs required after purchase?

2. In the grocery store, oranges are often sold loose or already packaged.
   a. Which oranges cost more by the pound?
   b. If I were to give you one pound of either loose or packaged oranges, which would you choose?

3. When it comes to cars, some sellers offer long-term warranties, while others provide a relatively short-term guarantee. Other things being the same, where do you expect the greatest number of product failures, where the warranty is long and durable or where it is short and sweet?

4. The Masters Golf Tournament is held each spring in Augusta, Georgia. To attend, a fan must acquire a badge to be worn at all times while on the grounds of the golf club. Suppose technology developed so that managers of the tournament could very cheaply affix a picture of the buyer to the badge, effectively eliminating the possibility of resale. What would happen to the price of badges and the number sold?

5. Suppose a restaurant goes out of business in a particular location. A new owner takes over the facility and reopens the establishment without extensive renovation. The only major difference between the old and the new

restaurant is a change in ownership and management. Alternatively, suppose the new owner completely remodels the facility inside and out, spending a large sum in the process. Assume the menus are the same in the two scenarios. First, in which case is the new owner more likely to change the name of the establishment. Second, do you expect that the menu prices differ between the two situations?

6. Rolls Royce has made cars that last a long time. Sometimes it seems they last forever (except for those involved in accidents). By contrast, the average Chevy stays on the road about eight years. Suppose you were to lease one of each for a one-year period. In which case do you expect that you would pay as rent a greater fraction of the selling price? That is, take the annual rent that you pay and divide it by the new selling price of the car. In which case is that fraction greater and why is it so?

SUGGESTED READINGS

Akerlof, George A. "The Market for 'Lemons': Quality Uncertainty and the Market Mechanism." *Quarterly Journal of Economics* (1970):488–500.

Barzel, Yoram. "Measurement Cost and the Organization of Markets." *The Journal of Law and Economics* 25 (April 1982):27–48.

Benjamin, Daniel K. and Kormendi, Roger C. "The Interrelationship between Markets for New and Used Durable Goods." *The Journal of Law and Economics* 17 (October 1974): 381–402.

Coase, Ronald. "Durability and Monopoly." *The Journal of Law and Economics* 15(1) (April 1972):143–50.

Hauser, John R. and Clausing, Don. "The House of Quality." *Harvard Business Review* 88(3) (May–June 1988):63–74.

Jarrell, Gregg and Peltzman, Sam. "The Impact of Product Recalls on the Wealth of Sellers." *Journal of Political Economy* 93 (June 1985):512–36.

Kenney, Roy W. and Klein, Benjamin W. "The Economics of Block Booking." *The Journal of Law and Economics* 26(3) (October 1983):497–540.

Kihlstrom, Richard E. and Riordan, Michael H. "Advertising as a Signal." *Journal of Political Economy* 92 (June 1984):427–50.

Klein, Benjamin W. and Leffler, Keith. "The Role of Market Forces in Assuring Contractual Performance." *Journal of Political Economy* 89(4) (August 1981):615–41.

Marvel, Howard P. and McCafferty, Stephen. "Resale Price Maintenance and Quality Certification." *Rand Journal of Economics* 15 (Autumn 1984):346–59.

Mertens, Yves and Ginsburgh, Victor. "Product Differentiation and Price Discrimination in the European Community: The Case of Automobiles." *Journal of Industrial Economics* 34 (December 1985):151–66.

Milgrom, Paul and Roberts, John. *Economics, Organization, and Management.* Englewood Cliffs: Prentice Hall, 1992.

Nelson, Philip. "Advertising as Information." *Journal of Political Economy* 82 (July–August 1974):729–54.

Shapiro, Carl. "Premiums for High Quality Products as Returns to Reputations." *Quarterly Journal of Economics* (November 1983):659–79.

SUGGESTED SOLUTIONS TO SELECTED STUDY PROBLEMS

The following are only *suggested* solutions to the study problems presented at the end of this chapter. In all cases, the suggestions here put heavy emphasis on analysis rather than a single correct answer. Since most managerial problems do not fall into neat little boxes, the individual characteristics of the problems that you will encounter on the job will typically mandate a solution using the principles developed here and in other courses. Memorizing these solutions will not make you a good manager; learning the *principles* detailed here will help make you a better manager.

1.   A problem of asymmetric information exists whenever a used car is sold. The seller almost surely has information about the characteristics of the car that are not cheaply observed or easily determined by the prospective buyer. Indeed, the seller is in the unique position of being able to bring the car to market when she estimates that the car is worth *less* than the expected market price. Similarly, she is inclined to keep the car off the market when she thinks the car is worth *more* than the current or expected market price. Thus we have the problem of the lemons; only the bad cars come to market. Of course, both buyer and seller are aware of this problem and are inclined to seek ways to deal with it. When a new car seller offers used cars for sale at the same time, he puts the value of his reputation selling new cars at risk with the sale of used cars. If a used car buyer is taken advantage of by the car dealer who also sells new cars, then it seems likely that future sales of new and used cars will be hurt when the reputation of the dealer is tarnished. Thus, new car dealers have a reputation and brand name that they put at risk when they sell used cars. These act as a bonding device to the prospective buyer offering assurance that the used car has the stated characteristics. When a new car seller with a brand name and reputation at risk sells used cars from the new car establishment, we expect that the cars are relatively high quality and defect free, *at least compared to cars sold through the newspaper.* Cars sold through the newspaper are not backed by the brand name or reputation of an established dealer and hence are more likely to suffer the lemon problem. The prices (and quality) should be the lowest in the newspaper case, highest at the new car dealer, and somewhere in between at the car dealer who only sells used cars.

   Two other points are worthy of note. The longer a new car dealer has been in business, the more brand name reputation and goodwill she has. Thus well-established new car dealers will probably have the highest priced used cars. New car dealerships that have recently gone into business only have the brand name and reputation associated with the parent company.

   Second, suppose a person has just been transferred abroad by his employer. He cannot economically take his car. This person would like to put his car on the used market, but prospective buyers are inclined to worry that the car was brought to the market because the seller suspects that it is worth less than the expected market price; the buyer does not want to be victimized by the problem of asymmetric information. This puts the seller in a predicament. What can he do? His options are limited, but he might try to market his car to a friend, family member, or colleague at work—*someone with whom he has a reputation at risk.* Sellers in situations like this are known to advertise "Must Sell" as a way of signaling that they are not bringing the product to market to exploit an informational advantage. In many cases, he will simply have to live with the situation and accept the capital loss as a cost of moving. Some companies seem to be aware of this problem when the stakes are large, a home for instance, and deal with it by buying the house from the employee or making up any financial loss that the transferred worker incurs from having to sell.

3.   This is a complex problem and a number of different answers, analyses, and perspectives are reasonable. However, in addition to the obvious, consider the following line of reasoning. When a buyer purchases a good with a long-term warranty, she need not worry much about whether the product will perform as implied. If the product fails, she can seek redress from the seller through the warranty process. In this case she will only need to be concerned about the willingness and financial ability of the seller to perform the required warranty work. On the other hand, and by direct contrast, when a person buys a good from a seller *without* this explicit long-term product warranty, the question arises as to whether the good will deliver the expected flow of services. In this case, only brand names, reputations, goodwill, and detailed inspection of the product will assure the buyer that the good will deliver as promised. Thus, to the extent that products with a short-term warranty are expected to last for a long time, only the reputation of the seller implies the warranty. When the warranty is long term, the buyer need only return it to the seller for repair. This suggests that products with a long-term warranty may in fact not be as reliable as similar goods with a short-term explicit guarantee.

According to this line of argument, there are two options. A buyer can purchase a good with a long-term warranty and when it fails to perform she can return it for repairs. Alternatively, the reputation of the seller combined with the high quality of the product in question removes the necessity of offering a long-term guarantee.[20]

---

[20] For more on this point, consult Yoram Barzel, "Measurement Cost and the Organization of Markets," *The Journal of Law and Economics*, 25, April 1982, 27–48.

CHAPTER 12

AN INTRODUCTION TO PUBLIC GOODS, PRIVATE GOODS, AND COMMON ACCESS GOODS

INTRODUCTION

All the previous chapters in this book have dealt with the firm and its external relations with input suppliers, customers, and rivals. This chapter departs from this framework to explore the internal organizational structure of the firm. To accomplish this goal effectively, it is important to provide some background material, beginning with a study of team production, public goods, private goods, and common access goods. This emphasis on the structure of property rights naturally flows into an analysis of some specific problems—the incentive problem, the horizon problem, and the inalienability problem. During this discussion, an important result is established, the Coase Theorem. At this point, the background material is used to study a number of important managerial issues—the not-for-profit enterprise, opportunism, and vertical relationships. The chapter closes with several sections on various incentive-related topics.

Throughout this chapter, it is important for you to appreciate the fact that the firm is a fiction. The managerial problems addressed here simply cannot be understood under the assumption that General Motors is a real thing with a life of its own. In this framework, companies do not make decisions; managers do. This should not be interpreted to mean that you can forget all the lessons on demand, cost, and pricing that we have previously discussed. Instead, it means there is another class of problems best approached by removing the shroud called the firm and examining the **contractual relations** and **organizational structure** inside the firm.

Consider the following selection of problems, none of which can effectively be examined without piercing the veil of the firm:

Just imagine that two major institutions in the United States are hiring new presidents. Let them be AT&T and Harvard University. Do you suppose the average length of the contract offered the prospective new presidents systematically differs between the two institutions, and if so, why?

McDonald's owns many hamburger restaurants. However, it also franchises its name, under a complicated contract, to other individuals to operate and manage restaurants. Why does McDonald's franchise in some situations, but manage other stores itself?

Many companies assign office space to their employees, often providing local telephone service at no charge. Yet, for long-distance service, many companies budget their workers. Similarly, some companies reimburse their employees for approved travel, while others assign a budget for travel. In the latter case, travel often does not require a supervisor's blessing. Which method is better?

The U.S. Post Office is the object of much criticism, so much so there is a movement to privatize the postal system. Suppose the organization were turned over to its employees without restriction. That is, suppose the U.S. Post Office was converted to a private corporation with the current employees owning all the shares, but each individual worker had the right to sell any or all of his or her shares. What would happen to the price of postal service, the quality and timeliness of service, and the wealth of the current employees of the postal service?

Some companies have many large, decentralized divisions acting much like separate private businesses inside the parent company. The Chevrolet and Delco divisions of General Motors come to mind. Yet some other large companies such as U.S. Steel do not create such divisions, choosing instead to centralize operation of the company with senior managers and the CEO. Which system makes for higher profits? Why do companies pick one method over the other?

Your university, the Salvation Army, the United Auto Workers, and the Tennessee Valley Authority do not have an owner in the classic sense of the word. What this means is that if any one of these organizations suddenly had a financial windfall, no one *currently* knows who would get the money. By contrast, if your individually owned business or partnership experiences an increase in earnings, we know now who would benefit, you and your part- ners. If Exxon makes money this year, it accrues to the stockholders of record, *who can be identified ex ante.* Does this distinction matter? If it does, why? More important, if one system is better, why don't the other organizations switch?

For years in Yugoslavia, most companies were managed by the workers. The practice was so common that the expression *the Yugoslavian firm* came to generically mean any organization managed by the employees. In essence, workers organized as teams belong to counsels that vote on important decisions for the firm. By contrast, other worker teams such as the Dallas Cowboys, the L.A. Lakers, the Montreal Canadians, and the N.Y. Yankees, teams of some long-standing repute in their respective sports, do not, as a general rule, allow players to vote on important decisions. In a football huddle, the play is called by the quarterback or signaled in from the bench. Just imagine that sports leagues were organized as Yugoslavian firms. There would be no owners in the common sense, players would vote on coaches and maybe even on important decisions during games. What would happen to the quality and popularity of professional football, basketball, hockey, and baseball? Put differently, suppose the Australians put together a 12-meter yacht crew to try and recover the America's Cup and instead of having a captain who dictates decisions, each member of the crew used electronic devices to signal his or her opinion of the appropriate strategy to the pilot who, using a sophisticated computer program, did what the overall wisdom of the crew suggested. Putting aside the question of yacht design, do you think this Australian boat would have much chance of recapturing the prize?

Your company has a large legal staff in-house for advice and counsel. Yet, the company often hires outside legal counsel to litigate. Construction com- panies are known to employ subcontractors for one job and use their own laborers at the next. Most daily newspapers own their own printing presses. Yet, the publisher of this text, Prentice Hall, like most publishers of hardback books, subcontracts the actual printing process. In the middle, some soft- cover and magazine publishers print their own material, while others hire the printing done. When is it wise to subcontract work outside the firm, and when is it preferred to "do it yourself"?

In the late summer of 1989, United Airlines was negotiating with its pilots' union to purchase a large share of the company. If the deal had gone through, a small portion of the company, 15 percent, would have been purchased by British Airways, existing management would have acquired 10 percent, while the remaining 75 percent was to be owned and controlled by the union. Putting aside the interest of British Airways, the pilots could have chosen to run the company by a vote of the employees, since such a large segment of the workers now owns the company. Instead the plan was to keep the company corporate, that means keep the stock form of organization. Also, the blueprint called for the existing chairman, Stephen Wolf, and chief financial officer, John Pope, to continue running the company. Why weren't the pilots going to run the airline themselves as a worker-managed enterprise? The deal never actually came to pass; the pilots were unable to arrange the necessary financing. Had it been successful, UAL would have become the nation's largest employee-owned firm. But would this have really been a worker-managed firm?

It should be obvious that none of the answers to these queries can be adequately addressed without casting aside the concept of the firm. All these questions concern the inner workings of the firm, and hence, the real questions here concern organizational structure and rights and responsibilities within the company. So, for a deep and abiding understanding of the complicated set of relations that exists inside what we often rather casually refer to as the firm, we now consider the single individual worker or asset owner as the unit of analysis. The thing that binds these people together is the **contract.** Here we have the current operating definition of the firm borrowed from one of the economists who has researched this field extensively, Michael Jensen of Harvard University: A **firm** is a nexus of contracts between individuals and resource owners. Or as another famous contributor to this field, Oliver Williamson, has put it, a firm "is usefully regarded as an instrument for mitigating frictions that are associated with the operation of labor, intermediate product, and capital markets."[1]

To facilitate our understanding of this beast, the firm, we begin at ground zero, the fundamentals of any organization, and build ourselves up from there. We start with what is perhaps the single most important issue in this whole arena, the concept of **property rights**. After that follows a theoretical examination of team production. Then we try to meld the theories of joint production and

---

[1] Oliver E. Williamson, "The Modern Corporation as an Efficiency Instrument," in Svetozar Pejovich (ed.), *Governmental Controls and the Free Market: The U.S. Economy in the 1970's* (College Station, TX: Texas A&M University, 1976), p. 164. Consult the Suggested Readings at the end of this chapter for additional references on Professor Williamson's contributions to the understanding of markets and hierarchies.

property rights to yield a cogent and thorough understanding of the theory of the firm. In the end, if all goes well, you will possess the rudiments for analyzing organizational behavior from an economic perspective.

AN INTRODUCTION TO PUBLIC AND PRIVATE GOODS

This section introduces a new concept in this text, the so-called **public good**. In economics, public goods have a very precise definition: those commodities whose consumption by one party does *not* diminish the consumption opportunities of others. By contrast, consumption of a **private good** by one person eliminates the possibility that anyone else might enjoy the particular object in question. A loaf of bread is a private good. If I eat it, you cannot also eat it. By contrast, when I view a play, a public good, my attendance does not preclude your seeing and enjoying the play *simultaneously*. Of course, as the theater crowds, the play converts from a purely public good into a purely private good once the last seat is taken. For private goods, consumption is mutually exclusive; but for public goods, consumption is joint and simultaneous. A play is a public good; each and every seat in a theater is a private good.

Aggregating Demand for Public Goods

Imagine that two families have recently moved into a new suburban subdivision. Near the rear of their properties is an old junk car that both families find offensive. The first family is willing to pay $50 to have the car towed, and the second is prepared to pay $25. Because having the car removed is a public good, the total demand for towing is not one car were the price $50 and two cars were it $25; instead, total demand is the sum of the parties' willingness to pay to have *this one junk car towed*, $75. There is no demand to have two cars removed.

Calculation of the market demand for a public good differs from that of a private good. For a private good, total demand is the (horizontal) sum of the individual quantities each person consumes at various prices. However, for the public good, since individual demanders can simultaneously consume the same unit of output, total demand is the (vertical) sum of each individual's willingness to pay for specified quantities. Recall the example of the play in Chapter 7, Hypothetical Business Problem 7.2. High demanders' willingness to pay to see plays is

$$q_h = 40 - p,$$

and the low demanders' function is

$$q_l = 30 - p.$$

Let there be 100 of each type demander. Suppose only one play were offered per year. The high demanders would be willing to pay

$$1 = 40 - p_h \quad \text{or}$$
$$p_h = \$40$$

each to view the play. Total demand or willingness to pay for one performance (so long as the theater will hold all 100 demanders) is the vertical sum of all 100 demanders' willingness to pay; specifically, $100 \cdot p = 100 \cdot \$40 = \$4000$ for one performance. Similarly, the 100 low demanders would be willing to pay $30 apiece or $3000 in total. The play could receive total receipts of $7000 for one performance.

The point is very simple. If a firm sells each individual unit to more than one buyer as in a theater, an airplane with some empty seats, a football game, a concert, a pretty view, or the like, its demand is computed by vertically summing the individual buyers' willingness to pay for each unit, not by adding the quantity each would like to purchase at various prices. Naturally, marginal revenue is the vertical sum of the individual marginal revenues, not the horizontal (quantity) summation. For private goods, total demand is the horizontal sum of the individual demand curves; but for public goods, total demand is the vertical price summation of the individual demand schedules.

Public goods are sometimes confused with **common access goods**. Common access goods are not necessarily public goods, although they may be. When a good is **common access**, no one person has the authority to exclude others from using the good, and this is true whether the good is a public or a private good. Consider a number of examples. In general, city parks are common access, but Disneyland is private property. The high seas are common access, but your hot tub is not. Interstate highway I-5 is common access, the driveway at your house is not. Books in the public library are common access, this particular textbook is not. The coffee pot in the office may be common access, depending on the rules at hand, but your coffee pot at home is your private property. The university computer, which anyone can use, is common access property, but the personal computer on your desk at home is private property. Indeed, the personal computers in the business school study room may be common access. The point of all these examples is simple: Property is not innately common or private access. The rules created and enforced by individuals in positions of power make this determination. By marked contrast, a good is either public or private depending on its physical characteristics. The latter distinction is not malleable by human forces, while the former most certainly is. This chapter is devoted to an analysis of these institutional distinctions, their effects, and the implications for managerial decisions. In many respects, this is the most important chapter in this text, if for no other reason than the material presented here is missing from almost any other course you may take in your curriculum. Most schools offer specialized courses in topics covered throughout the other chapters of this text—the many courses in econometrics that expand on the material in Chapter 4 are one example—but rare is the curriculum that includes a detailed discussion of the role of property rights. This should not be taken as a slight against the other material here, but rather as an indication that this new area in economics is quickly advancing into the classroom.

Consider the following business problems:

Several years ago a hotel was constructed next to the hotel Fontainebleau in Miami Beach, Florida, by the Forty-Five Twenty-Five Corporation. The new hotel cast an afternoon shadow, shading the Fontainebleau's beach. The owners of the Fontainebleau sued the proprietors of the new hotel and won damages. What impact did the ruling have on (1) tourist trade in the two hotels, (2) room prices in the two hotels, and (3) the value of each of the two hotels?

In his book *Ecology and Economics,* Marshall Goodman argues that "rapid advances in industrial technology have influenced the seriousness of the pollution problem."[2] The interesting question is in what direction—is the problem more or less serious?

The U.S. government gives away licenses through the Federal Communications Commission to broadcast radio and television signals over the air. State governments sell hunting licenses. First, why are the two licenses treated differently? Second, suppose the FCC started selling broadcast licenses to the highest bidder. What would happen to the rates radio and television stations charge for commercials?

Shopping mall owners perform a variety of tasks in and around their malls. Generally they plant trees around the mall, furnish and clean the mall, and in areas of snowfall, plow the parking lots. By contrast, most individual shops along the roadside are responsible for supplying these services themselves. Why do mall developers and managers not leave maintenance up to the individual store owners?

In many professional sports, a draft of college players is common. It is frequently argued that a draft is necessary to ensure competitive balance among teams. "Without a draft, rich teams like the N.Y. Yankees or the Dallas Cowboys would buy up all the good players and ruin the sport." What impact does a draft have on the allocation of player talent across teams? Does free agency, the opposite of a draft, have an impact on ticket prices to professional sporting events?

These examples are chosen to show the breadth of problems that can be analyzed with an understanding of property rights, and they only touch the surface. Before we tackle some of these issues, let us go through some basic analysis of property rights.

The Tragedy of the Commons

Many years ago, writing in *Science,* Garrett Hardin coined the phrase, the **tragedy of the commons**.[3]

---

[2] Marshall I. Goldman, *Ecology and Economics: Controlling Pollution in the 70s* (Englewood Cliffs, NJ: Prentice Hall, 1972), p. 9.

[3] Garrett Hardin, "The Tragedy of the Commons," *Science,* 162, December 13, 1968, 1243–48. Copyright 1968 by the AAAS.

The tragedy of the commons develops in this way. Picture a pasture open to all. It is to be expected that each herdsman will try to keep as many cattle as possible on the commons. Such an arrangement may work reasonably satisfactorily for centuries because tribal wars, poaching, and disease keep the numbers of both man and beast below the carrying capacity of the land. Finally, however, comes the day of reckoning, that is, the day when the long-desired goal of social stability becomes a reality. At this point, the inherent logic of the commons remorselessly generates tragedy.

As a rational being, each herdsman seeks to maximize his gain. Explicitly or implicitly, more or less consciously, he asks, "What is the utility to me of adding one more animal to my herd?" This utility has one negative and one positive component.

1. The positive component is a function of the increment of one animal. Since the herdsman receives all the proceeds from the sale of the additional animal, the positive utility is nearly $+1$.

2. The negative component is a function of the additional overgrazing created by one more animal. Since, however, the effects of overgrazing are shared by all the herdsmen, the negative utility for any particular decision-making herdsman is only a fraction of -1.

Adding together the component partial utilities, the rational herdsman concludes that the only sensible course for him to pursue is to add another animal to his herd. And another; and another. . . . But this is the conclusion reached by each and every rational herdsman sharing a commons. Therein is the tragedy. Each man is locked into a system that compels him to increase his herd without limit—in a world that is limited. Ruin is the destination toward which all men rush, each pursuing his own best interest in a society that believes in the freedom of the commons. Freedom in a commons brings ruin to all. (p. 1244)

What is the point of the story by Hardin? It is quite simple. When valuable property is freely accessible to a host of users, its value is destroyed by overuse. Suppose there is a lake with many fish, call it Lake Great. Initially, suppose only one person fishes the lake; let's say he is the only one who knows where it is. But for the sake of analysis, let us say that, legally, anyone who might like to fish Lake Great may. This means that no one has the right to exclude anybody from fishing the lake. The lake and the fish in it are common access, but for the moment there is only one fisherman. *The fish in the lake are not a public good; the rights to fish the lake are common access.* This difference is much more than a semantic one.

When our fisherman spends time fishing on the lake, he catches fish according to the following fish production function:

$$f = 6.6 \bullet L - 0.1 \bullet L^2 \tag{12.1}$$

where f is the pounds of fish caught per hour, and L is the number of hours he spends fishing on the lake. The production function has the characteristic that at the outset (when L is low) as more time is spent fishing, more fish are caught, but the output of fish increases at a decreasing rate—$df/dL = 6.6 - 0.2L$ (which is greater than zero so long as L is less than 33) and $df^2/d^2L = -0.2$.

Imagine that fish caught on Lake Great are worth \$1 per pound in the marketplace. Then the revenue earned by our fisherman, R, is $1 times the pounds of fish he catches, which is determined by the amount of time he spends fishing:

$$R = \$1 \bullet f = \$1 \bullet (6.6 \bullet L - 0.1 \bullet L^2). \tag{12.2}$$

If our lone fisherman can earn $5 per hour in town working at the factory, how many hours does he choose to work? How much fish does he catch? To maximize his overall profit, he equates the marginal revenue from fishing with the marginal cost. We can compute this from the fishing production function, equation 12.2. Marginal revenue is the change in revenue for a change in the amount of labor supplied, or the derivative of revenue with respect to labor:

$$dR/dL = \$1 \bullet (6.6 - 0.2 \bullet L). \tag{12.3}$$

The opportunity cost of fishing on Lake Great is the wages that might be earned otherwise, in this case $5 per hour. Setting marginal revenue equal to marginal cost of $5 per hour yields the income maximizing number of hours of labor to supply fishing, L^*:

$$6.6 - 0.2 \bullet L^* = 5 \quad \text{or}$$

$$L^* = 8. \tag{12.4}$$

In other words, this fisherman efficiently allocates his time if he spends eight hours per day fishing Lake Great. We can determine the total catch in pounds from the production function, equation 12.1, by evaluating the function at eight hours. The catch is $6.6 \bullet 8 - 0.1 \bullet 8^2 = 46.4$ pounds; or, since fish sell for $1, his revenue is $46.40 per day. However, his time spent fishing only costs him eight hours times $5 per hour or $40 in total. By fishing, he earns $6.40 more than he might by working in the factory for the same amount of labor supplied. Economists call this extra revenue a **rent** to the lake.[4] Since in actuality it is the lake that is responsible for the extra earnings of the fisherman, we say the excess revenues accrue to the lake. Under this scenario, Lake Great is worth $6.40 per day to our fisherman and hence to society.

Table 12.1 summarizes the single fisherman's production on Lake Great.

The average and marginal products of fishing on Lake Great are plotted in Figure 12.1. Notice that the marginal product of fishing equals the wage rate at eight hours per day; this confirms the optimality of fishing eight hours per day. When eight hours are spent fishing, the average catch per hour is 5.8 pounds or $5.80 per hour. Also note that the *average* catch per hour declines as more effort is spent fishing the lake; it is harder to catch fish as fish are caught. The single fisherman opts to supply eight hours fishing on the lake. In general, the single fisherman works on the lake until *his* marginal reward equals his marginal

---

[4] Recall the discussion of economic rent in Chapter 6.

LABOR INPUT	FISH CAUGHT (POUNDS AND DOLLARS)	AVERAGE PRODUCT OF LABOR	MARGINAL PRODUCT OF LABOR	WAGE RATE
1	6.5	6.5	6.4	5
2	12.8	6.4	6.2	5
3	18.9	6.3	6.0	5
4	24.8	6.2	5.8	5
5	30.5	6.1	5.6	5
6	36.0	6.0	5.4	5
7	41.3	5.9	5.2	5
8	46.4	5.8	5.0	5
9	51.3	5.7	4.8	5
10	56.0	5.6	4.6	5
11	60.5	5.5	4.4	5
12	64.8	5.4	4.2	5
13	68.9	5.3	4.0	5
14	72.8	5.2	3.8	5
15	76.5	5.1	3.6	5
16	80.0	5.0	3.4	5
17	83.3	4.9	3.2	5
18	86.4	4.8	3.0	5
19	89.3	4.7	2.8	5
20	92.0	4.6	2.6	5

TABLE 12.1   FISHING ON LAKE GREAT

opportunity cost. This scenario persists so long as no one else chooses to fish the lake. The difference between the fisherman's opportunity cost of effort, his wage rate (w), and the average return to his effort at the optimal level, A^* ($= \$5.80$), is actually the value of the lake to him. Indeed he would be willing to pay that amount, ($\$5.80 - \$5.00) \cdot 8 = \$6.40$ to have the right to fish the lake each day (so long as he is the only person fishing). This extra revenue is the marginal product of the lake, and it is the rental value of the lake. The present value of this rental payment, $[(A^* - w) \cdot L^*]/r$ (r is the discount rate), is the net worth of the lake, *under the stipulation that only one person fishes.* Put differently, the sole fisherman would be willing to pay $[(A^* - w) \cdot L^*]/r$ for the exclusive rights to the lake in perpetuity. In this example, with an interest rate of 10 percent per year, this amounts to $[(\$5.80 - \$5.00) \cdot 8]/(0.1/365) = \$23,360.$[5]

But recall, the lake is actually common access. Anyone who chooses may legally fish. What will happen? Common access to the value of the lake puts in motion forces that ultimately totally destroy the value of the asset. Suppose a wash woman who works independently at the edge of town earning $5 per hour

---

[5] This calculation presumes that no prices are expected to change in the future, specifically, the price of fish and labor.

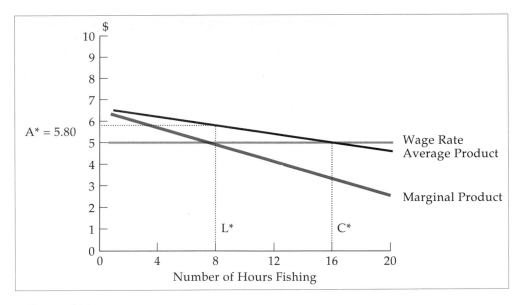

FIGURE 12.1
The Tragedy of the Commons

observes our fisherman going and coming back from the lake with his catch each day. One rainy day she follows him to Lake Great and discovers its location. She also sees that he only works eight hours and catches, on average, $5.80 worth of fish every hour, a total of $46.40 per day. She sees a profit opportunity (putting aside the cost of a boat and fishing tackle), because the eight hours fishing only cost her $5 per hour or $40 per day in lost wages from washing. So, the next day she too fishes the lake. How much will she fish? The answer is complicated and depends on just exactly what the original fisherman does. But we can make a primitive guess. Suppose they both start fishing at the same time. At the end of the first hour in the day, two hours have been worked; therefore, we see from Table 12.1 that 12.8 pounds of fish are caught instead of the usual 6.5 with the sole fisherman. Assume that each person is equally proficient; he has caught 6.4 pounds and she the same. She can sell these fish for $6.40 and the hour only costs her the lost wages from washing clothes, which we have presumed to be $5. The wash woman is now a fisherwoman. She can make more money fishing in water than washing clothes in it. Indeed she can make more money fishing than washing so long as the total catch divided in half is greater than or equal to five pounds per hour. As we can see from the table, this means she also fishes eight hours per day. When she does, her catch is one-half the total or 0.5•80 = 40 pounds, which she can sell for $40. Therein lies the tragedy of the commons. She makes the same amount of money fishing as washing, $40 per eight-hour day, *but the original fisherman now also makes only $40 per eight-hour day.* When he fished alone, he made $46.40 per day, but free entry onto the common access lake has drowned his supranormal earnings. Of course, the extra earnings were actually the marginal value of the lake, which means that free or common access has totally destroyed the value of the lake as a fishery. *No one would now be willing to pay to have the right to fish on the lake.* The rental value of the lake is $0, and its value to people who would fish is likewise. As a fishery, the lake has no value to society. To reiterate Hardin, "Freedom on the commons brings ruin to all."[6]

Managing the Problem of the Commons

The wealth-destroying features of the commons have led people to develop institutions to undo its consequences. Prominent among these are cooperation, regulation, and privatization. Each has its own place and time, but as a general rule, privatization is the most prevalent and arguably, under most circumstances, has the most desirable features. We discuss each in turn.

Cooperation   Obviously, cooperation between the man and the woman can ameliorate the dissipation of the lake's wealth created by common access. Realizing that two people fishing makes him $6.40 worse off per day, he approaches her with a suggestion. Realizing that the bountiful catch she imagined is not any better than washing clothes for a living, she listens. He proposes that they only fish a *total* of eight hours per day on the lake, splitting the net value of the catch in half. Each agrees, and, since the factory does not hire part-time workers, she agrees to return to full-time washing, leaving him to fish the lake eight hours. But now, at the end of each day, he stops by her home and delivers one-half of the difference between the value of the catch ($46.40) and his opportunity cost ($40), or $3.20. The lake is again worth $6.40 per day to the pair even though it is split between two persons. The tragedy of the commons is erased by a mutual agreement not to overindulge in its riches.

Obviously, cooperation between two parties is a relatively cheap vehicle to solve the tragedy, but when the number of people involved is large, cooperation is problematic. Suppose friends, neighbors, and relations of our two characters begin to fish Lake Great. Cooperation becomes more expensive. A meeting must take place, someone must be selected to do the fishing and disburse the funds. Cynics or skeptics are likely to demand an accounting of the proceeds. To make matters worse, as the number of fishers grows, the total rental value of the lake, $6.40 per day, is divided into ever smaller pieces. This creates its own set of problems. In sum, cooperation as a solution to the problem of common access property is viable, but only when the number of participants is relatively small.

---

[6] For additional reading, you may wish to consult John S. McGee, *Industrial Organization* (Englewood Cliffs, NJ: Prentice Hall, 1988), pp. 398–411.

Mr. Reynolds and His Exciting Value Machine

If rapid development threatens supplies in a given area, [Mr. Reynolds] simply decrees the existence of a water basin, and by the act brings all its waters under his control. Those who have established their rights through prior use are largely unaffected, but new water seekers and existing ones who want to increase their use must line up before Mr. Reynolds. He decides how much, if any, they can have. This often makes him unpopular. He doesn't care. . . .

Mr. Reynolds makes friends as well as enemies, however, because by declaring a basin *he creates wealth.* Water is worth *nothing* in unregulated areas because it's there for the taking; when he slams the lid on, rights to use it, established by prior use, can become worth up to $12,000 for the equivalent of one acre filled to one foot. "An engineer who undeclared the Rio Grande Basin now would get himself shot. Value established over 25 years would be destroyed," he says.

And under New Mexico law, water flows uphill to money as easily as it slips downhill by gravity. In sharp contrast to most Western states, water here is an open market commodity for sale to the highest bidder, and rights can be *transferred* around a basin, with the engineer's approval, as long as this doesn't damage the rights of others. This lets the water supply shift quickly to meet changes in the state's economic mix.

"Hot Spot, In New Mexico, Water Is Valuable Resource—And So Is Water Boss." *The Wall Street Journal,* May 1, 1980, pp. 1 & 22. Reprinted by permission of *The Wall Street Journal,* © 1980 Dow Jones & Company, Inc. All Rights Reserved Worldwide. (emphasis added)

EXAMPLES OF COOPERATION   As just stated, cooperation by mutual agreement often solves the problem of the commons, so often in fact that we sometimes forget just how useful cooperation can be. In essence, cooperation is nothing more than the private assignment of property rights. Individuals agree that certain other people have particular rights and privileges, and in return for recognizing these, the others themselves agree to observe the individual's own rights and privileges. For instance, in a public restroom, cooperation usually resolves the problem of access to toilets. When a person observes another using a toilet, he or she is typically inclined to look elsewhere.

In an office, it is routine for two or three people to share a coffee pot or a copy machine. Each agrees, so long as the others behave properly, to follow a commonly agreed-upon set of rules. Many smokers observe the wishers of non-smokers. However, this solution is generally inadequate in elevators and restaurants. There, because of the large number of people involved and the fact that the participants are generally not familiar with each other, cooperation breaks down, and some other solution is required to alleviate the problem of the commons. In golf, it is common for slow players to allow faster players who are being held up on the course to play through. This courtesy amounts to a cooperation extended by most golfers to any and all other golfers in exchange for the reciprocal courtesy. It is expected that this gesture is most common in small clubs where most of the members know each other and where few strangers play. The courtesy is least likely in public courses where most players are not familiar with the others and large numbers of outsiders visit.

GAMING BEHAVIOR AND THE PRISONER'S DILEMMA   For cooperation to be viable, there must be the analogue of a quid pro quo. Each person who agrees not to exploit the commons must expect that the other people who might potentially exploit it will also act with restraint. In effect a trade is made, the enforcement of which is tenuous at best. Keeping cooperation alive is the subject of much research under the heading of **game theory**. Consider the famous example of the prisoner's dilemma. Two suspected bank robbers are arrested by the police. The prisoners are separated before interrogation begins. Individually, each suspect is told, "If you confess and implicate your accomplice, *but your partner does not confess,* then we will let you turn state's evidence and go free. If neither of you confesses, we will hold you over for trial without bail and you will stay in jail for at least six months. If both of you confess, you will each get three years in jail." So collectively if the crooks keep their mouths shut, they both end up spending six months in jail; but from their individual perspectives, each is better off ratting on the other. In the process, of course, they both go to jail for three years. Cooperation is better, but it fails. Examine the payout matrix in the accompanying box.

Cooperation takes a different character when we unsterilize it and allow for repeat situations. Suppose these same two crooks had previously been arrested together and both had faced the same dilemma, but magically neither had confessed. Now, on the second or repeat occasion, *based on past experience,* each is inclined to believe that the other will keep his mouth shut, and cooperation does not fail. Reputations matter, and that is precisely why cooperation is so difficult within large groups and among transients where reputations do not exist.

THE PRISONER'S DILEMMA

		First Prisoner	
		Confesses	Does Not Confess
Second Prisoner	Confesses	Both get 3 years	1–5 years 2–free
	Does Not Confess	1–free 2–5 years	Both get 6 months

So we see that cooperation is tenuous and ever subject to disintegration, but the rewards can be gigantic. Strategies in game theory have been developed to help keep cooperation intact. Prominent among these is something called TIT FOR TAT. Consider the following remarks by Douglas Hofstadter, who is discussing, in part, research done by Robert Axelrod:

There are really three aspects of the question "Can cooperation emerge in a world of egoists?" The first is: How can it get started at all? The second is: Can cooperative strategies survive better than their non-cooperative rivals? The third one is: Which cooperative strategies will do the best, and how will they come to predominate?

To make these issues vivid . . . Axelrod [commenced] a roundrobin Prisoner's Dilemma tournament, with the overall goal being to amass as many points as possible. . . .

Every program was made to engage each other program (and a clone of itself) 200 times. . . . The program that won was submitted by the old Prisoner's Dilemma hand, Anatol Rapoport, a psychologist and philosopher from the University of Toronto. His was the shortest of all programs submitted, and is called TIT FOR TAT. TIT FOR TAT uses a very simple tactic:

Cooperate on move 1;

thereafter, do whatever the other player did the previous move.

That is all. It sounds outrageously simple. How in the world could such a program defeat the complex stratagems devised by other experts? . . .

Axelrod summarizes the first tournament this way:

"A major lesson of this tournament is the importance of minimizing echo effects in an environment of mutual power. . . . [T]he real costs [of noncooperation] may be in the tertiary effects when one's own isolated defections turn into unending mutual recriminations."

In summary, the lesson of the first tournament seems to have been that it is important to be *nice* ("don't be the first to defect") and *forgiving* ("don't hold a grudge once you've vented your anger"). TIT FOR TAT possesses both these qualities, quite obviously.

TIT FOR TAT won the tournament, not by beating the other player but by eliciting behavior from the other player which allowed both to do well. TIT FOR TAT was so consistent at eliciting mutually rewarding outcomes that it attained a higher overall score than any other strategy in the tournament.

So in a non-zerosum world you do not have to do better than the other player to do well for yourself. This is especially true when you are interacting with many different players. . . . There is no point in being envious of the success of the other player, since in an iterated Prisoner's Dilemma of long duration the other's success is virtually a prerequisite of your doing well for yourself.[7]

What is the lesson here? Cooperation can work, but not cheaply. It requires discipline and the willingness of the players to behave according to certain rules. Narrow or myopic self-interest has to be put aside for long-run self interest to be

---

[7] From *The Evolution of Cooperation*, by Robert Axelrod. Copyright © 1984 by Robert Axelrod. Reprinted by permission of Basic Books, Inc., Publishers, New York.

served, and this cannot be guaranteed in all circumstances. TIT FOR TAT is a useful strategy, but participants must be able to recognize just who it is that is defecting in order to retaliate. Hence, cooperation is assured of failure in large number situations or when identities are unknown.[8]

Government Regulation or Licensing   Government regulation or licensing is another solution to the tragedy of the commons. Let us generalize the problem now to demonstrate how regulation can be effective. Efficient or rent maximizing use of the resource requires that the marginal labor effort produce a return just equal to its opportunity cost. Any effort beyond that reduces the overall value of the asset, as can be seen by the previous example of the fisherman and wash woman. Reexamine Figure 12.1. Rent or wealth maximization occurs when the marginal product of labor equals the marginal cost of labor, the wage rate, at eight hours fishing per day. A licensing or regulatory authority can be governmentally empowered to limit the use of the asset to its rent maximizing value. And if government could be magically made to work perfectly, that solution is amenable. Even when government works less than perfectly, as it always does, that solution is sometimes the least-cost alternative. We will return directly to give examples of this. But for now consider the by-products of government regulation. First, some bureaucrat must determine the optimal level of use on the asset. This is not free. Second, he or she must be properly controlled to ensure that even when armed with the correct choice on the right amount of asset use, the bureaucrat does not succumb to laziness or moral turpitude. For then the optimal or rent maximizing level of use will not attain either. In other words, an incentive problem exists. Much more will be said on this later, but for now allow as how this can be serious.

Depending on the situation at hand, regulations within the firm, which we shall call **rules**, are often used to solve the problem of the commons. Indeed, it is hard to imagine a company that does not employ some rules to this end. Most companies have canons about the use of the phone, the mail, the copying machine, the fax, and the like. And, even if apocryphal, we have all heard of the executive wash room. Here is the use of regulation or licensing to resolve the problem of the commons.

Consider the case of important company secrets that could be common access, and were they to be so, their loss would be imminent and devastating. To prevent this, only certain people are licensed to have access. Elaborate procedures are put in place to prevent uncertified access. This corresponds, for instance, to the Federal Communications Commission's licensing of television and radio stations to prevent overuse, abuse, and ultimate destruction of the electromagnetic spectrum. It is critical to note, however, that licensing or regulation is not necessary to prevent the tragedy of the commons in either case, the secrets or the spectrum. We have already discussed how cooperation might work in some cases, and later in this chapter we discuss how privatization of the access rights mutes the problem without rules, regulations, or licensing. It suffices to say for now that

[8] For additional reading see Robert Axelrod's book, *The Evolution of Cooperation* (New York: Basic Books, 1984).

rules and regulations are the best choice when (1) cooperation is not viable or (2) the cost of enforcing private rights is high relative to the benefits.

Sometimes the precision required for private rights to sufficiently solve the tragedy of the commons is difficult to achieve. This problem is most prominent when the asset in question is abstract or nebulous. For instance, the Federal Aeronautics Administration regulates the use of air corridors for airplane travel. It is difficult (but not impossible) to imagine the private assignment of these corridors. Hence, regulation is adopted, and it goes without saying that the rules are complex and expensive to enforce. It requires an army of air traffic controllers and lots of computer hardware and software plus many radars and myriad other electronic devices. It is interesting to note, however, that by distinct contrast, outside these corridors, cooperation is usually employed to resolve the problem of common access to the airways. Pilots call this VFR for visual flight rules, and each flight crew keeps its eyes open for others, all desiring to avoid using the identical air space for obvious reasons.

Pollution control is another area in which private rights have not been widely used in the United States, and regulation has been the alternative. Why this is true has been the subject of considerable debate among economists, but we can note that rules and regulations of the Environmental Protection Agency notwithstanding, many economists believe that private rights in the pollution arena would be superior to the current alternative. Others, including many biological scientists, contend that privatization is untenable and regulation is the only alternative to a dead planet. The debate goes on.[9]

Another problem avoided by regulation is the creation of rents. Privatization of assets not only creates rents, but assigns the value of these rents to the owner of the asset. Sometimes this has undesirable consequences, and sometimes, these can be avoided with regulation. In such cases, regulation is superior to privatization because of the way regulation distributes the rents associated with a valuable asset. For instance, if Joe Doe were given the key to the safe where the Coke formula was kept, *and it were truly his key,* then he could do with it whatever he liked, including selling it to Julie Pepsi, an undesirable outcome from the point of view of the shareholders of Coke. Hence, in this case, a simple company policy or rule delineating who has access to the safe where the formula is kept helps avoid this particular problem.

The problem of rent creation is even more offensive in the context of something economists call rent seeking. **Rent seeking** refers to expenditures by individuals in the pursuit of rents. A simple example will demonstrate the wasteful nature of rent seeking. Suppose the Coca-Cola Company has actually decided to assign someone control over the key to the safe with the formula in it with no rules attached. The key is to become the private property of the keyholder.

---

[9] Two of the papers that attempt to explain why regulation has been adopted instead of privatization include James M. Buchanan and Gordon Tullock, "Polluter's Profits and Political Response: Direct Controls versus Taxes," *American Economic Review,* 65, March 1975, 139–47; and Michael T. Maloney and Robert E. McCormick, "A Positive Theory of Environmental Quality Regulation," *The Journal of Law and Economics,* 25, April 1982, 99–124. Additional papers on the topic are listed in the Suggested Readings at the end of this chapter.

Further suppose that several different individuals within the company are in line to get the key. Now imagine the behavior of these people. They will begin to jockey and lobby, spending time, money, and labor in their effort to become the keyholder. The expenditure of these resources will cost the company money. Less work will get done while these people try to get the key rights, and real company resources will be wasted in the bargain. The wasteful or redundant expenditure of resources in pursuit of an existing or potential rent is called rent seeking. Nothing real is produced in the process, and the company is left permanently poorer by the exercise. Rent seeking institutions are to be avoided if at all possible.[10] To put it simply, we do not want a manager spending the *business's* resources—the telephone, the secretary, the copy machine—lobbying for rights to use the company's vacation beach home for private use.

In sum, rules and regulations can be an effective way to prevent the problems associated with common access property. This is especially true when alternative arrangements are difficult to employ, when cooperation is untenable, and when privatization is expensive. However, regulation can itself raise a host of problems that astute managers will not ignore. The following story about regulation of fishing rights in the Atlantic Ocean off New England highlights some of the practical problems associated with regulation as a solution to the tragedy of the commons.

> OFF CAPE COD, Mass.—On a brilliant, sun-splashed morning, Frank Mirarchi lowers the net from his 60-foot trawler into the gleaming blue water of the Atlantic near Stellwagen Bank, long one of America's richest fishing grounds.
>
> But when he hauls it in 2½ hours later, it holds just 350 pounds of fish—half of what he would have caught in the early 1980s. As usual, the net has swallowed almost no large codfish and flounder. Many fish have barely reached the legal minimum size for keeping. As for haddock, one of the most prized species in these once teeming waters, not a one is to be found.
>
> "I used to catch a lot of haddock, thousands of pounds a year of haddock," laments Mr. Mirarchi, 47 years old, a commercial fisherman for 28 years. "Now I catch three or four fish a year—25 pounds."
>
> Where have all the fish gone? Mostly, they have been caught—and over a period so ominously short that the future of one of America's oldest industries is threatened.
>
> ### Boat-Building Binge
>
> Only 14 years ago, the U.S. declared a 200-mile boundary around its shores, banning most foreign trawlers that had plundered America's waters. It was, proponents said, the only way to save beleaguered New England fishermen.
>
> It worked, until Americans themselves began overfishing. The region's fishermen went on a boat-building binge, encouraged in part by a federal loan program. They equipped the new trawlers with powerful fish-finding electronics.

---

[10] There is a vast literature in economics on the subject of rent seeking. Several excellent review articles exist. Among these one of the best is Robert D. Tollison, "Rent Seeking: A Review," *Kyklos*, 35, 1982, 575–602. Chapter 15 of this text also offers a section on rent seeking theory and practice.

They lobbied hard to get timid bureaucrats to remove quotas on catches. And, for a while, they caught a lot more fish.

But the trawler catch in New England peaked in 1983 and has since fallen sharply. Stocks of flounder and haddock are near record lows. The cod population is down. Bluefin tuna and swordfish have been depleted.

Many New England fishermen find themselves in dire straits, victims of a get-it-while-you-can mentality that could exhaust stocks beyond recovery. . . .

Fishermen crowd public meetings, berating bureaucrats over proposed conservation measures. They also bombard elected officials with letters opposing limits on their catches. . . .

"What are we saving fish for? For who?" asks Ed Lima, director of a fishermen's group in Gloucester, Mass., who worries about measures that might cost fishermen their jobs. "Where does conservation stop? Where does it end?"

Things weren't supposed to turn out this way. When the U.S. set the 200-mile boundary for foreigners in 1977, it was hailed as the savior of the New England fishery. But U.S. fishermen quickly filled the vacuum. Accelerating the move was a rise in prices as health-conscious Americans turned less to beef and more to fish. From 590 vessels in 1976, the New England groundfishing fleet—trawlers that fish for species that live on the ocean floor—grew by more than two-thirds, to more than 1000, in the early 1980s.

At this point, critics say, fishery managers made a fatal mistake. The New England Fishery Management Council—one of seven regional bodies made up largely of fishing industry representatives, appointed by the Department of Commerce—caved in to pressure from fishermen and lifted catch quotas and trip limits in 1982. A 1990 report by Massachusetts says the action "received considerable criticism . . . that it would lead to overfishing because it set no direct controls on fishing mortality. Those predictions of overfishing have now been borne out."

In 1983, the trawler catch reached 410 million pounds (mostly groundfish such as cod, flounder and haddock), up 66% from 1976. In 1990, though, the haul declined to 282 million pounds. While up from the low of 234 million pounds in 1989, marine scientists say the increase was achieved by catching huge numbers of juvenile fish that have just reached the minimum size. . . .

Steven Murawski, a scientist for the national Marine Fisheries Service, says . . . "We flubbed it," by not having stricter catch limits. . . .

[O]ther fishermen and conservationists insist that current measures—minimum net mesh sizes and occasional closures of overfished waters—simply aren't enough. Strict catch quotas, trip limits, even a moratorium on new boats, are needed. . . . Rep. Gerry Studds (D.-Mass.) yesterday proposed legislation to reduce the size of the New England fleet by buying out vessels with money from a tax on diesel fuel the fishing boats use.

"I used to be strongly opposed to any kind of limited entry in fisheries," says Dick Allen, vice president of the Atlantic Offshore Fish Association in Newport, R.I. "But I've come to feel we have to have some way of rationally allocating fishery resources just as we do other resources."[11]

---

[11] Lawrence Ingrassia, "Dead in the Water: Overfishing Threatens to Wipe Out Species and Crush Industry," *The Wall Street Journal,* July 16, 1991, p. A1. Reprinted by permission of *Wall Street Journal,* © 1991 Dow Jones & Company, Inc. All Rights Reserved Worldwide.

This story highlights the difficulties faced by regulators trying to solve the tragedy of the commons. In this case, they stopped one source of overfishing, only to have it replaced by another. The point is that whether we are talking about a fishery or a fax machine, rules have to be chosen with care or they will not prevent the overuse and abuse of the common access property.

Minerals under the ground, such as oil, are prone to suffer the tragedy of the commons. When oil is discovered there is generally a race by land owners on the surface to extract the oil in large quantities as quickly as possible.[12] Otherwise, it will be left for someone else to remove with another well. The oil discoveries in the early twentieth century in Texas and Oklahoma are testimony to the problems created by the common pool characteristics of underground oil. A number of important oil field discoveries were made in the early 1900s. In each case significant increases in production occurred, accompanied by substantial declines in prices. When the East Texas oil field was discovered in 1930, the pool was so large that the price of crude oil fell from roughly $2 per barrel to less than $0.25 per barrel.[13] Cooperation between oil producers, called oil field unitization, has been proposed as a solution to the tragedy of the commons in this situation, but in most cases, the strong arm of the law has been used to enforce production limits. For instance, in August 1931 the governors of Texas and Oklahoma declared martial law in oil field production and used troops to enforce production quotas.[14] Since 1931 the Texas Railroad Commission has been legally empowered to limit the output of oil wells in Texas.[15]

Privatization   Privatization is an alternative solution to the problem of common access. Delineating private, exclusive rights to use and enjoy an asset definitionally prevents the problem of common access; others are denied the oppor-

---

[12] There is a common law principle known as the rule of capture which holds that the owner of the oil in the ground is the person who brings it to the surface.

[13] See Steven N. Wiggins and Gary D. Libecap, "From Heterogeneities and Cartelization Efforts in Domestic Crude Oil," *Journal of Law, Economics, and Organization*, 3(1), Spring 1987, 1–25.

[14] For additional research in this area, consult Gary D. Liebcap and Steven N. Wiggins, "Contractual Responses to the Common Pool: Prorationing of Crude Oil Production," *The American Economic Review*, March 1984, pp. 87–98; Gary D. Liebcap, and Steven N. Wiggins, "The Influence of Private Contractual Failure on Regulation: The Case of Oil Field Unitization," *Journal of Political Economy*, 93(4), 1985, 691–714; Wallace F. Lovejoy and Paul T. Homan, *Economic Aspects of Oil Conservation Regulation* (Baltimore: Johns Hopkins University Press, 1967); Stephen L. McDonald, *Petroleum Conservation in the United States: An Economic Analysis* (Baltimore: Johns Hopkins University Press, 1971); James W. McKie and S. L. McDonald, "Petroleum Conservation in Theory and In Practice," *Quarterly Journal of Economics*, 76, February 1962, 98–121; Jacqueline Lang Weaver, *Unitization of Oil and Gas Fields in Texas: A Study of Legislative, Administrative, and Judicial Policies* (Washington, DC: Future, 1986); and Mason S. Gerety and Raymond D. Sauer, "Regulation of Oil Production," unpublished manuscript, Clemson University, Department of Economics, 1992.

[15] These attempts to regulate production should not be seen as solely an attempt to cure the tragedy of the commons. There is considerable argument and reason to believe that an additional purpose of regulation was to limit output, raise price, and cartelize production. This characterization of regulation is covered in more detail in Chapter 15.

tunity to overuse and abuse the property. For this reason, economists generally tend to view privatization as the first or best solution to the tragedy of the commons. Private rights, however, are neither perfect nor free; and they must be employed with care, for blind application can create its own set of problems that damage performance and profits. As a general proposition, for privatization to work, the rights must be **alienable**. An **alienable right** is one that can be disposed, destroyed, or transferred. To paraphrase Thomas Jefferson, some rights are alienable and others, life and liberty to name two, are inalienable. Leaving aside this issue for a moment, first let us see why privatization mitigates the problem of common access.

Suppose our Lake Great actually *belongs* to the original fisherman. That is, the lake is not common access; he has the right to exclude any and all others from fishing on the lake. This is what we mean when we say private. The owner can exclude others from using the asset. The wash woman has no legal rights or privilege to fish on the lake. We know how much the owner will fish if he fishes alone, eight hours per day. Importantly, there is no other level of labor that creates a greater rent for the lake. Moreover, he can keep the wash woman and all others like her off the lake by definition. He owns the lake. We are making a huge presumption here—namely, that when we say a person owns something, we mean that no one else can use it without permission. Of course, private rights must be maintained or enforced, sometimes with force or guns. And of course, these are not free.[16] So, the presumption of private rights has built into it some enforcement mechanism. In the case at hand, it may be something as simple as a rock wall and a locked gate. In other cases, even elaborate vaults, burglar alarms, motion detectors, and organized police forces may be inadequate.[17]

In order for privatization to resolve the common access problem, the rights to the asset must, as a general rule, be freely transferable or alienable. Let us demonstrate the consequences of inalienability. To do so, we must expand our analysis to include multiple periods. Recall Table 12.1. This is the fishing situation for one day. However, fish swim, eat, breathe, and procreate. Removing one fish today may impact the ability to catch fish tomorrow. Two possibilities are prominent. First, fish caught today may reduce the breeding pool, thereby decreasing the total volume of fish available to be caught tomorrow. The opposite is also possible. Catching today increases the food stock for the remaining fish, and thus it is conceptually possible that the school tomorrow is larger in quantity and

[16] Research by David Laband estimates the cost of enforcing private property rights in the United States. For a summary of his findings, see David N. Laband, "The Cost of Property," *Wall Street Journal,* September 18, 1991, p. A14.

[17] Converting from a system of common access to private property has its own set of problems as the recent events in Eastern Europe attest. See Barry Newman "Poland Unlocking Mysteries of Privatization," *Wall Street Journal,* December 18, 1990, p. A11. In addition, there is a considerable literature in economics on the topic of emerging property rights. Consult the Suggested Readings at the end of this chapter for some of these.

quality. Without knowing the facts of the particular situation at hand, we cannot make a definitive statement. But we can create a theoretical construct to cope with both circumstances.

OWNERSHIP IN PERPETUITY AND ALIENABILITY   Consider Table 12.2. Here we have constructed the net returns from fishing on Lake Great using the data reported in Table 12.1. Total labor cost is the wage rate per hour, $5, times the total number of hours worked. Net revenues from fishing on the lake are total revenues minus total costs. These net revenues represent the economic value of the lake to all of society. They are the residual after all other costs of production have been paid. Again, for emphasis, we call this an economic rent that accrues to the lake, or more specifically, to the person who owns the lake.

The net revenues are graphed in Figure 12.2. Note the same result we obtained before; the net return is maximized at eight hours fishing per day, and the rent or excess return is $6.40. As we just stressed, up to this point we have taken a simple view of fishing, ignoring any impact that today's catch might have on future productivity. In order to address this situation, consider two alternative scenarios. First, suppose that some of the fish captured today were fertile and would have reproduced. In this case, removing these fish from the lake lowers the

TABLE 12.2   NET REVENUES ON LAKE GREAT

Labor Input	Output	Total Labor Cost	Net Revenues
0	$ 0.0	$ 0	$0.0
1	6.5	5	1.5
2	12.8	10	2.8
3	18.9	15	3.9
4	24.8	20	4.8
5	30.5	25	5.5
6	36.0	30	6.0
7	41.3	35	6.3
8	46.4	40	6.4
9	51.3	45	6.3
10	56.0	50	6.0
11	60.55	55	5.55
12	64.8	60	4.8
13	68.9	65	3.9
14	72.8	70	2.8
15	76.5	75	1.5
16	80.0	80	0.0
17	83.3	85	−1.7
18	86.4	90	−3.6
19	89.3	95	−5.7
20	92.0	100	−8.0

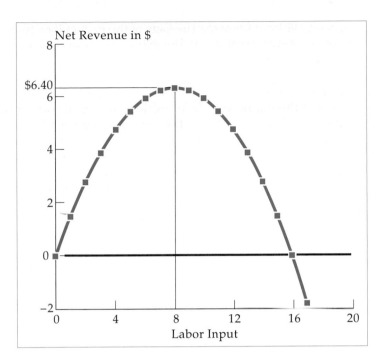

FIGURE 12.2
Net Revenues on Lake Great

stock of fish in later time periods. In plain economic terms, catching fish today imposes a cost above and beyond the simple expense of today's labor effort; in the future, labor will be less productive because fish will be more difficult to catch than they would otherwise have been. To maximize the value of the lake, the owner must take account of these future costs. We can analyze the problem several ways. First, let us do it mathematically.

Gross returns to fishing on the lake are given by the fish function, equation 12.1,

$$f = 6.6 \cdot L - 0.1 \cdot L^2. \tag{12.5}$$

Subtracting the wage rate of labor, w, times the hours of labor worked, L, from production, yields net revenues, R:

$$R = 6.6 \cdot L - 0.1 \cdot L^2 - L \cdot w. \tag{12.6}$$

However, each fish caught today reduces the school of fish in the future, thereby lowering productivity of future labor. This impact typically depends upon the stock of fish present; the more fish present, the less impact there is. When the school of fish is large, the taking of any one fish has, at most, a small detrimental impact on the future size of the school. However, as the size of the school diminishes, the taking of that same fish today is likely to have a greater impact on the school in later periods. When this is true, the extra cost in the future of catching fish today increases with the size of the catch today. Mathematically, we write,

$$E = E(f), \tag{12.7}$$

with

$$dE/df > 0. \tag{12.8}$$

To properly account for the future lost revenues of catching fish today, we subtract the $E(f)$ effect, equation 12.7, from net revenues, equation 12.6, which yields the long-run net revenues, N:

$$N = 6.6{\bullet}L - 0.1{\bullet}L^2 - L{\bullet}w - E(f). \tag{12.9}$$

For the sake of simplicity, let us assume that the future effect of fishing today is characterized by the function

$$E = 0.2{\bullet}L + .004{\bullet}L^2.$$

This E function is sometimes called an **externality** because it imposes an external cost on the operation of the enterprise. Table 12.3 expands the fish production function to incorporate the externality effect created when catching fish today reduces the size of the school in the future.

Figure 12.3 graphs (1) the single period net revenue function, which is just total revenue minus labor costs, (2) the externality cost function, and (3) the new net revenue function, which is single-period net revenue minus the externality costs. Recall that net revenues are maximized in the simple case with no externalities by working eight hours per day and producing 46.4 pounds of fish. However, if we take into account the detrimental impact catching fish today has on the productivity of labor in the future, then the value maximizing amount of labor input falls back to seven hours and 41.3 pounds of fish produced per day. This is found in either of two ways. First, in Table 12.3 observe that net revenue minus the externality cost is largest when the fisherman works seven hours and catches a total of 41.3 pounds of fish. No other level of labor effort produces as much net output. Graphically, this is found by equating the slope of the externality function, the marginal externality cost, to the slope of the net revenue function, which is marginal revenue. This too occurs at seven hours' labor. The latter approach demonstrates that the marginal net effort today must equal the incremental cost that catching fish today has on the value of the asset in the future.

What is the point of this exercise? First, recognize that the optimal use of the asset, the fishery, differs when there are long-term effects associated with production today. Of course this point generalizes to an amazing variety and volume of business activities. For instance, consider maintenance of machinery, which in many ways is the same as the externality just described for the fishery. Using a machine today without proper oiling and adjustment imposes costs in the future;

TABLE 12.3   THE INCREASING COST EXTERNALITY

LABOR INPUT	OUTPUT	LABOR COST	REVENUE MINUS COST	EXTERNALITY	NET REVENUE (REVENUE − COST − EXTERNALITY)
0	$ 0.0	$ 0.0	$0.0	$0.0	$0.0
1	6.5	5	1.5	0.204	1.296
2	12.8	10	2.8	0.416	2.384
3	18.9	15	3.9	0.636	3.264
4	24.8	20	4.8	0.864	3.936
5	30.5	25	5.5	1.1	4.4
6	36.0	30	6.0	1.344	4.656
7	41.3	35	6.3	1.596	4.704
8	46.4	40	6.4	1.856	4.544
9	51.3	45	6.3	2.124	4.176
10	56.0	50	6.0	2.4	3.6
11	60.5	55	5.5	2.684	2.816
12	64.8	60	4.8	2.976	1.824
13	68.9	65	3.9	3.276	0.624
14	72.8	70	2.8	3.584	−0.784
15	76.5	75	1.5	3.9	−2.4
16	80.0	80	0.0	4.224	−4.224
17	83.3	85	−1.7	4.556	−6.256
18	86.4	90	−3.6	4.896	−8.496
19	89.3	95	−5.7	5.244	−10.944
20	92.0	100	−8.0	5.6	−13.6

FIGURE 12.3
The Increasing Cost Externality

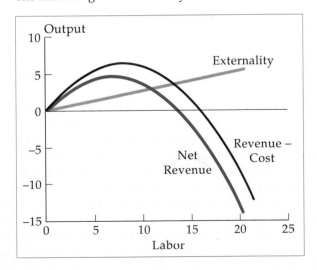

the machine will be less productive when it is worn and rusty. Thus, and most important, the amount the machine should and will be used depends on whether the owner of the machine recognizes and feels the future externality costs imposed today. That is the point.

If our fisherman had the rights to fish on Lake Great for one day or even one year and he was a **renter** instead of an owner, how much would he fish? Well, since the cost of smaller schools in the future is of no consequence to him, the lake and the fish left in it are not his, he will ignore the future repercussions of his fishing and only account for the current cost. In other words, he will fish eight hours per day, taking 46.4 pounds of fish, although we have just demonstrated that this is inefficient and wasteful. Properly accounting for all costs, present and future, he should fish seven hours per day, catching 41.3 pounds and leaving the other 5.1 pounds of fish to procreate for tomorrow.

In general, only the owner in **perpetuity** has the incentive to be concerned about the future consequences of today's actions. The temporary or ersatz owner/operator is disinterested in the future costs or benefits of behavior today as they do not enter into his revenue, cost, or profit function. This line of reasoning also points out why **alienability** of property rights is so important.

Suppose the owner of Lake Great cannot sell it. In order to capture the rents associated with fishing on the lake, he must operate it forever or as long as he lives. The consequences are grave. Since no one usually lives forever, the inalienable owner discounts or totally ignores any future costs or benefits to the lake of fishing today that accrue after his expected death. For instance, if he is 40 years old and expects to live until he is 70, any action today imposing costs or benefits in more than 30 years is likely to be discounted more than it would be to an everlasting owner. By contrast, if the owner can sell the rights to fishing on the lake, and the next owner can as well, and so on in perpetuity, then all the future costs and benefits are imputed into the present value of the rents, regardless of how long the current owner expects to possess the rights. When the rights are transferred to the next owner, they include all the future consequences of past actions. Thus, even if the current owner only expects to hold the asset for a year, he will manage the lake as if he were going to own it forever. If he does not take into account the externality effects, then the price he receives at the end of the year, when he sells the lake, will be lower because the stock of fish has been diminished. Ownership in perpetuity and alienability are critical to ensuring that ownership of the lake solves the tragedy of the commons.

Similar arguments hold when the externality leads to *lower* costs in the future. Suppose the catching of fish today reduces demand on the food supply, causing the remaining fish to be larger and healthier. Then, the multiperiod owner will rationally fish more than eight hours today because, even though the value of today's harvest at the margin is less than its opportunity cost, it pays extra dividends in the future in a larger school of fish, making labor in the future more productive than it would be otherwise. Examples of this principle in business practice are commonplace. One of the most obvious is building and machine maintenance. These endeavors impose cost today without immediate rewards, but they pay dividends in the future because the assets last longer. Naturally, the single-period owner or the residual claimant with an inalienable right has little incentive to make this sort of investment; it lowers her net revenues today, and she has no claim to the returns in the future. Car renters surely do not take the same precautions about maintenance and the like that car owners do.

We close this section by remarking on two prominent characters in American folklore, Santa Claus and Mickey Mouse. There is an important difference between these two. Santa Claus is a common access resource. Anyone can legally dress and portray the character, as you know. During the Christmas season every store has Santa, not to mention most corners and shopping malls. Santa is everywhere, so much so that the value of the character is seriously tarnished, the classic tragedy of the commons. We have all heard of the sad stories about drunk Santas fondling children on their knees. By stark contrast, the Mickey Mouse character is privately owned by the Disney Company. For this reason, visitors to Disneyland or Disney World never see multiple versions of the creature. In fact Disney goes to great lengths to protect its rights in Mickey Mouse. The amusement park is divided into regions with only one Mickey per territory, making it impossible for most kids to discern that there are multiple versions. Indoors, kids are only allowed to see Mickey in very small groups. All told, it would take an overly bright kid to realize that there is more than one reproduction of the famous mouse. Privatization creates rents and sustains them. Put another way, if you could receive the royalties currently paid for the rights to play Santa or Mickey, which would you choose?

Internalizing the Externality and the Coase Theorem

The problem of the commons is more widespread than it might appear at first blush. The smoke from your classmate's cigarette offends you. The smoke from your barbecue pit disturbs your next door neighbor. Your neighbor refuses to cut the grass or paint his dilapidated house, causing your property value to decline. Sulfuric acid falls from the sky onto your oak trees because some plant in the Midwest burns coal. For a manager, the dirty restroom in the McDonald's restaurant 25 miles away reflects poorly on his McDonald's restaurant even though his toilets are spic and span. Tanya owns a Titan muffler shop in Terra Haute. She is a crook, overcharging and using substandard parts. You own a Titan muffler shop in Indianapolis. People who have traded at Tanya's Titan muffler shop are discouraged from dealing with you because of the bad experience they had there. She has soiled your reputation with her business practices. All these examples involve a common property resource of one variety or another. And try as we might, it is sometimes hard to deal with the problem. Circumstances arise in which cooperation, private rights, and regulation are all too costly or problematic to be satisfactory. In this situation, however, all hope is not necessarily lost.

In all the cases just described, we say an **externality** exists. **Internalization** of an externality is sometimes used to rectify the situation. Internalization is the process of making one party bear all the external costs or benefits previously externalized. For instance, if the firm or firms putting sulfuric acid into the air owned all the oak trees in the world affected by acid rain, then the costs of emitting the pollution would be borne totally and completely by the coal burner. The social problem of the externality would be eliminated. Some trees might still die, but as a society, we would not have to worry whether it was worth the cost or not. The managers of the coal-burning facility would be making that decision armed with all the incentives necessary to compute the proper costs and benefits. The managerial point is actually quite simple. When a person creates external costs or benefits—that is, when she or he does not feel all the implications of the actions—problems arise that can be muted by making the party creating the situation bear all the costs and benefits. Let us elaborate.

Suppose you manage a café with an outdoor seating section. Next door is a printing company that routinely runs its presses at exactly the wrong times from your point of view. The manager of the printing press simply ignores the impact the noise has on your customers. You plead or seek redress in court; you even offer a payment to the owner to shift the noisy process away from lunchtime hours, but he ignores you. The last option might work if a suitable contract could be hammered out, but suppose enforcement is a problem. Then, the situation persists. Now imagine some large company buys *both* shops but leaves both of you as managers. Will the noise abate? In this situation, the costs of the printing noise previously felt only by you in lost soup sales are now felt by the parent company. And if the cost of the lost revenues at the café is more than the cost of shifting the printing to different hours or moving the printing shop elsewhere, the problem will be resolved. We expect the managers of the parent company to alter the hours of the printing press, move the café, or resolve the problem some other way. In economics, we say the *externality has been internalized.*

In 1960, Ronald Coase wrote what has become the most cited article in the literature of modern economics, "The Problem of Social Cost."[18] In it he identified an important economic principle that now bears his name, the **Coase Theorem**. Moreover, and more important, he identified the conditions under which the theorem does *not* apply, and it is this latter point that paves the way for us to understand a host of important issues in property rights management. To better understand this point, first let us construct the theorem.

The Coase Theorem holds that the assignment of liability does not affect the allocation of resources under a special set of circumstances: when transactions costs are free and when there are no income effects. The special circumstances are, of course, the heart of the theorem, because they point out why the assignment of liability actually matters. First let us demonstrate the theorem by continuing with the example of the noisy printing press and the café. Consider Table 12.4. Suppose that the printing press produces a net revenue, revenue above and beyond the cost of paper, ink, and labor, of $3 every minute. Also imagine that net revenue at the café is $6 per customer. That is, after all costs have been paid, the café makes a profit of $6 per customer. Observe the external costs imposed on the restaurant by the noisy printing press in total and at the margin. These too are listed in the table. For instance, when the printing press runs five minutes per hour, the noise drives away one customer from the café.

---

[18] Ronald Coase, "The Problem of Social Cost," *The Journal of Law and Economics,* October 1960, pp. 1–44. Professor Coase was awarded the Nobel Prize in Economics in 1991 for his contributions to our understanding of property rights.

TABLE 12.4 THE NOISY PRINTING PRESS AND THE CAFÉ					
	IMPACT ON CAFÉ			IMPACT ON PRINTING FIRM	
MINUTES RUN PER HOUR (PRINTING PRESS)	LOST CUSTOMERS AT THE CAFÉ	TOTAL LOST REVENUE AT THE CAFÉ	MARGINAL LOST REVENUE AT THE CAFÉ	TOTAL REVENUES	MARGINAL REVENUE
5	1	$ 6	$ 6	$15	$15
10	3	18	12	30	15
15	6	36	18	45	15
20	10	60	24	60	15
25	15	90	30	75	15

Now consider two cases. In the first situation, suppose that the printing press operator has the legal right to run at any time, and without going into the details, let us imagine that 25 minutes per hour is the optimal or profit maximizing amount of time to operate the press *ignoring the impact of the noise on the neighboring café*. Thus, on any random day, the press operates 25 minutes during the lunch hour, imposing a cost of 15 customers on the restaurant for a total cost of $90 in lost profits to the café owner. One day the café owner, call her Anna Marie, decides to bargain with the manager of the printing press, call him Exley, to reduce the amount of noise. Anna Marie pleads and begs, but Exley does not hear. He correctly contends that he has the legal right to operate and that running less would cost him money. So Anna Marie takes a different approach. She says, "What if you reduce the amount of time you run during lunch hour?" Exley responds, "Only if you compensate me for my losses." Can she afford to do that?

If Exley prints 5 minutes per hour less, he loses $3 per minute or $15. However, over at the café, 5 *more* customers are fed, increasing net revenues there by $6 times 5 or $30. There is a net gain of $15 to the two businesses. The café gains $30, while the printer loses only $15. Anna Marie offers Exley one-half of the difference between her gains and his losses, 0.5($30 − $15) = $7.50, plus his lost revenues, $15, for a total of $22.50. He is $7.50 better off if he does not operate, and she is also $7.50 richer. After a few days, the two managers sit down to evaluate their arrangement, and one of them suggests a further experiment. Suppose Exley runs only 15 minutes per hour instead of the 20 he is currently operating. This will cost him an additional 5 minutes running time or $15, but it will lead to an extra 4 customers in the café. The noise now only keeps 6 customers away instead of the 10 who were avoiding the 20 minutes of noise. What happens to profits at the two establishments?

Reexamine the table. If the printing press operates 15 minutes per hour, the café loses only $36 in revenue. This is $24 less than Anna Marie loses when the presses run for 20 minutes per hour. They are both made better off by this new arrangement. He loses an additional 5 minutes or $15, but she gains $24 in revenue. She can compensate him for his losses, $15, plus a little extra, say $4.50, leaving herself also $4.50 better off. She gets an additional $24 in revenue and gives $19.50 of it to the owner of the printing press for his cooperation. An additional 5 minutes less printing produces similar results. It costs $15 to the printer, but gains $18 to the café. There is still room to negotiate a reduction in noise, leaving both parties better off. At this point the printing press is running only 10 minutes per hour.

Notice that additional reductions in printing press noise *do not* increase the joint profits available to the two owners. If printing is cut back to 5 minutes per hour, $15 of printing revenues are lost. At the café, however, the gain in revenue is only $12, not enough for the owner to pay to shut down the printing presses the additional 5 minutes. Thus, in the absence of transactions costs, a negotiated equilibrium emerges. The printing press runs only 10 minutes per hour. This imposes a total cost of $18 on the café, but under the circumstances it is the best alternative. There are no gains from further adjustment in the operation of the printing press.

To further understand the Coase Theorem, now suppose the law is changed, favoring the café. The new noise abatement law requires noise nuisance to be decreased at the request of the offended party. Let us see what would happen in this case. You might be naively inclined to say, well, in this case, the printing press cannot legally operate at all because of the nuisance it creates at the café, but is this right? If the press could run just 5 minutes per hour, it would generate $15 in revenue. At the same time, it would impose a cost of only $6 in lost revenues on the café. Under the assumption of zero transactions costs, the two owners can strike a bargain. The printing press operator agrees to compensate the café owner for her losses if he is allowed to operate the 5 minutes per hour. Say he offers to cover the losses, $6, plus a little more, say $4.50 or $10.50 in total. She is better off by $4.50, and he is too by a like amount. The deal floats. Is this the equilibrium solution? No.

If he operates the presses for an additional 5 minutes, or 10 minutes in total, he imposes an extra $12 cost on her, but there are sufficient net revenues created at the press shop to fully compensate the café owner and more. He can pay her $12 + $1.50 or $13.50, leaving himself $1.50 better off in the process.[19] Are further increases in printing negotiable? No, because the lost revenue at the café dominates the gain in net revenue at the printing press. So the equilibrium solution under the new law again yields 10 minutes printing per hour, and there you have the Coase Theorem. The negotiated solution to the problem of the external effect, the noise, *does not depend on who bears the cost of the offense.* Naturally, as we shall see, this powerful result strongly depends on the artificial assumption of no transactions costs, and it is this last result that is truly important. Of course, the rule of law matters, but it matters because transactions costs are not zero. The assignment of liability does affect resource allocation, but because it is often expensive or costly for parties to sit down and come to a mutual agreement.

A couple of further points are worthy of note. You may wonder what would

---

[19] Throughout this example, we have been evenly splitting the gains from trade. In fact, that is but one solution. The actual outcome depends on the relative bargaining strength of the parties involved and in all likelihood would not generally be exactly one-half for each party.

happen if the printing press or café could be relocated. Suppose it costs $50 to move the plant or café, or it costs $50 to sufficiently insulate the walls between the two properties in a way that allowed no sound to pass. Would the Coase Theorem still hold? Would it still be true that the assignment of liability had no impact on the operation of the two enterprises? The answer is yes. The only difference is which party must pay. If it is efficient for one party to pay the expense of moving or insulating, then it necessarily will be efficient for the other party if and when the law is changed.

This result helps point out the important outcomes of the reassignment of the liability. In the first scenario of the case we just examined, the café owner was responsible for reducing the noise. The printing press owner had the legal right to run. Under this rule of law, the café owner had to make the side payments to the printing press operator to adjust the minutes of operation. When the law was changed, the printing press owner had to compensate the café owner for the noise in order to operate legally, and wealth flowed in the opposite direction. The press operates the same amount of time in both cases; in the first circumstance, the printing press operator is richer, while the café owner is wealthier in the second case. Surely this matters to the two individuals concerned, so do not conclude that just because the press runs the same amount of time under both versions of the law that the two parties are indifferent between the two legal environments. They surely are not. The printing press operator favors the first law and the café owner the second. Indeed, both are willing to spend money to persuade judges or legislators to that end.

With some imagination, we can see the importance of this result. Let us suppose the two businesses, the café and the printing press, were both acquired by some third firm via merger or cash purchase. Furthermore, suppose the previous owners are hired as the new managers as part of the acquisition deal, a common situation. Moreover, each is compensated in part on the profits of the division he or she operates. In other words, the managerial incentives are some-what the same, although now some third party has oversight and ultimate control over the operation of the two enterprises. What will the upstairs manager do?

First note that the so-called externality created by the noise of the printing press has been internalized at the headquarters of the new owner (a point we briefly discussed earlier in this section). What this means is that any profits lost to the café because of noise at the printing press are felt on the bottom line of the central manager. Moreover, any lost profits that accrue because the printing press does not operate are also registered there. Therefore, the new, single owner of the two businesses has the incentive to properly account for the noise created by the printing press, but exactly so. Exactly so in the sense that there is no incentive to reduce the noise level beyond that which takes into account the problem created at the café.

Integration of the facilities paves the way for the property rights or externality problem to be alleviated. With integration, a single person feels all the gains and losses from the operation of the press. The only thing that remains is for this manager to properly motivate the two downstream managers, Anna Marie at the café and Exley at the printing press, to achieve joint profit maximization. This can be accomplished in many ways. One solution is to simply dictate the proper amount of time to run the printing press. Previously we have called this the regulatory solution. In the hypothetical example we are studying here, this implies that the overall manager dictates to the printing press manager that he operate only 10 minutes per hour during lunch time. The main problem with this solution is making sure that Exley does as he is told. Since he is being paid partly based on profit, his incentive to follow the orders exactly is muted. So the general manager has choices. He can spend a lot of time and effort monitoring the printing manager, or he can sever the link between salary and profits. Alternatively, he can allow the café manager to complain when the printing manager does not follow his instructions.

Another way to solve the problem is to pay the manager of the printing press part of the profits of the café and vice versa. Under this scheme, when the printing press operates too much, the manager's salary is lower because café profits are reduced. It also mutes complaints from the manager of the café for the same reason. When printing profits are low, her salary is reduced. Linking the two operations helps to solve the externality problem. It creates individual responsibility for the impact that the operations of one division in the company have on other production units and profits of other branches in the business. There are costs of tying managerial compensation to other divisions within a company, but these are too complicated for us to consider here. You should be aware that linking compensation like this is not perfect.

The previous discussion highlights one of the reasons why the allocation of property rights is so important in managerial decision making: In the normal world of costly transactions and negotiations, the assignment of rights affects the use of resources. In simple terms, the rules that managers create can have a big impact on the way the business operates. Organizational structure is an important part of creating an environment for profit and success.

IMPLICATIONS OF PROPERTY RIGHTS ASSIGNMENT FOR MANAGERS

The preceding analysis has profound implications for managerial decision making. To better understand these ramifications, let us first summarize the findings.

1. Freedom on the commons brings ruin to all. Uncontrolled access to a valuable resource leads to overuse and abuse of the asset, effectively destroying its worth in the process.

2. A number of arrangements exist to correct this situation.

    a. *Cooperation or contractual agreement* between the many people who are using the common access property can ameliorate the problem and restore value to the asset. However, questions over distribution and enforcement make this solution difficult in cases involving anything but the smallest number of participants.

    b. *Governmental regulation, licensing,* or *rules* can also solve the problem, and this solution can work in the large numbers case in some situations. Rules work best when the expense of monitoring private ownership rights is high. Rules can also be cost effective when the value of use is more or less homogeneous across users. However, rules and regulation suffer their own set of problems. These include bureaucratic incentive problems and the question of who gets to determine the rules themselves.

   c.   *Private rights* to the valuable asset are often the most cost effective way to maximize the value of the asset in question. Necessarily, these rights must be defined and enforced. In addition, in most applications for the rights to be most effective, they must be established in perpetuity and must be tradeable or transferable.

PROPERTY RIGHTS TO INTANGIBLE ASSETS

A battle is brewing over property rights to creative assets such as films, television shows, and music. For instance, with the growth of the home satellite television market, most broadcasters scramble their signals to prevent their unlicensed interception. Naturally, this is understandable for stations such as ESPN and HBO where the rights to view the programs are sold to cable TV systems and home satellite owners, but it is harder to fathom when network broadcasters such as CBS, ABC, and NBC also encrypt the signals they send to the station affiliates. In the latter case, viewers are not charged. Instead revenues are earned via advertisers. Just what is going on here?

Consider the following story reported in the *Wall Street Journal.*

It seems that just about everybody is mad at the cable industry these days. For composers trying to get paid when their music is heard on cable television, irritation has escalated into a war with some of cable's biggest powers.

If the composers win, cable companies will have to pay millions more for the music used in their programs. Those increases could well be passed on in subscriber charges, leaving consumers singing the blues as well.

The battle is tangled and extensive, with at least half a dozen suits and countersuits already filed between the groups that collect fees for composers and various cable companies. A judge is scheduled today to issue a ruling in one of the cases that could hamper cable powerhouse HBO's ability to operate.

The critical issue isn't just how much the societies want to charge cable for music rights—a lot more—but whom they charge. Observing that the biggest share of money in cable flows from subscribers to local cable franchises, the composer groups want to charge performance fees to local operators in addition to the cable channels. The cable industry is fighting that plan on every possible front.

Protecting Composers

Now, the average guy watching a movie in his living room may only notice the sound track in passing. But someone has to make sure that John Williams gets paid when "Indiana Jones and the Last Crusade" is shown on HBO. In that case, the someone is Broadcast Music Inc., known as BMI, which represents some 100,000 composers and publishers, from the estate of Charles Ives to Michael Jackson. The other major performing-rights society, Ascap, the American Society of Composers, Authors, and Publishers, monitors performances for its 45,000 members.

Both BMI and Ascap have been collecting money for years from bars, skating rinks, and radio and television networks, with each new field they enter sparking a major battle. These days the two are even going after shopping malls and convention planners for music fees, but cable television is a much vaster new territory. "Composers can't collect these fees themselves, and it's our responsibility to protect them as new technologies arise," says Frances Preston, BMI's president.

. . . Currently, an average HBO subscriber pays between $100 and $125 a year to watch the channel: From that, HBO's fee amounts to 27 cents per subscriber to BMI and Ascap combined to cover a year's worth of music performances.

Still, HBO contends that if BMI gets the rate increase it wants, the group's revenue from cable will leap to $130 million a year from about $10 million now.[20]

This article poses an interesting problem in property rights and pricing. BMI and Ascap represent the original producers of music, and their job is to charge whoever uses their clients' merchandise. There is a tendency to say, "Since there is no marginal cost to the music producer from the use of the product, the optimal or correct price is zero." There are two problems with this view. We first discuss these two problems, and then we return to explore the solution to the music licensing problem.

First, as we have seen, when a resource such as a song is made common access, the tragedy of the commons ruins its value to society. What does that mean in this context? Overuse and abuse of a song mean that it gets played so many times in so many different settings that people get sick of hearing it, rendering it valueless. Many radio stations are acutely aware of this problem and have what they call "No repeat workdays," during which they do not repeat a song between the hours of 9–5. Pricing is one way for the individual or group who owns a song to reduce the number of times it gets played on radio or television, or in a shopping mall, dentist's office, or elevator.

Second, if BMI and Ascap are successful and they get the rights to charge local cable TV operators a fee for each use of their products, will the cost of cable service actually increase? The property rights approach says no. Why so? And if not, why is HBO so upset?

Think of the problem this way. Viewers are already being charged the price that extracts the profit maximizing amount of revenues from them. Owners and managers of cable systems see to that. Thus, if the cable operators must pay an additional royalty fee to BMI and Ascap, then HBO will have to cut the rates it charges the cable operators. According to this view, HBO will reduce its rates by an amount that offsets the additional royalties, or the cable operators will have to eat the losses.[21] To see why this is true, let us construct an example using major league baseball as a guide.

---

[20] Meg Cox, "Composers' Groups Try to Call the Tune in Battle over Cable-Television Payments," *The Wall Street Journal,* September 5, 1990, p. B1. Reprinted by permission of *Wall Street Journal,* © 1990 Dow Jones & Company, Inc. All Rights Reserved Worldwide.

[21] On August 18, 1991, Judge Joyce Green of the federal court in Washington dismissed an antitrust suit filed by cable TV groups against BMI, saying that the blanket license covering BMI composers is not illegal. At the same time the judge ruled that a 1966 consent decree signed by BMI prevents it from charging according to split licenses. In other words, the judge ruled that BMI can charge cable companies but not each cable user separately. For a more complete version of the story, see Meg Cox, "Federal Judge Dismisses Antitrust Suit Filed by Cable-TV Groups Against BMI, *Wall Street Journal,* August 19, 1991, p. B6.

The Reserve Clause in Major League Baseball

Recall the days before free agency in professional major league baseball, when baseball players were not free to sell their services to the highest bidding team. There was a contract feature called the **reserve clause** that basically said that once a player signed on with one team, he could not negotiate with any other major league team. The original signing team reserved the right to renew the contract, and no other team could negotiate without the permission of the original team.

This contractual feature reduced a player's options and lessened competition for his services. The net effect was lower player salaries.[22] However, and importantly, players could be traded by the owner of the team. Thus, any player signed by the N.Y. Yankees could be traded to any other team without the player's permission. Suppose a player is worth $1 million a year to the Yankees, but $1.4 million to the L.A. Dodgers and even more, $1.5 million a year to the Oakland Athletics. Imagine that the player is paid $250,000 a year, which more than covers his next best alternative occupation. Under the old system, the reserve clause setup, there was little competition between teams once a player was signed, and hence players were routinely paid less than the value of their contribution to the team. But leaving that issue aside, since the Athletics value this player more than the Yankees, a trade develops, sending the player to Oakland from New York. The Yankees send the player to Oakland, the highest bidder, in exchange for players worth the difference between his salary of $250,000 and the bid by Oakland. In order for Oakland to outbid L.A., the offer must be just a bit more than $1.4 million, say $1.45 million. Thus the Yankees get players from Oakland worth $1.45 million minus $250,000 or $1.2 million worth of player assets in exchange for their star.

Once the player is traded, his salary remains at the contracted $250,000, *but his cost to Oakland is his opportunity cost,* not his salary. Just what is his opportunity cost? The Dodgers stand ready, willing, and able to pay $1.4 million. Thus, and this is important, when the Oakland manager says to the player, "Put on that uniform and get out there to batting practice," the Athletics have just given up $1.4 million that they could have had by trading the player to the Dodgers. The opportunity cost of the player is his value to the other teams in the league, not his salary.

To see the importance of this type of analysis, let us erase the reserve clause from the contract, something that began to happen in the mid-1970s with the Curt Flood case. Curt Flood was a major league player for the St. Louis Cardinals who sued over the reserve clause in his contract. What impact does elimination of the reserve clause have on major league baseball?

Consider our player who was traded from the Yankees to the Athletics. Without the reserve clause, this player is now free to peddle his talents to any and all teams.[23] When this player goes into the so-called free agent market, we know

---

[22] For those of you who demand to see the evidence on this point, you are recommended to the paper by Gerald W. Scully, "Pay and Performance in Major League Baseball," *American Economic Review,* 64, December 1974, 915–30.

[23] Actually the player-owner agreement has some restrictions on movement, and they are important. But for the sake of analysis here, let us ignore them.

that the Dodgers will bid something close to $1.4 million for his talents. In fact, they will offer the player the same amount they would have offered the Athletics in trade for the rights to the player under the old system. Thus, and this is the important result, Oakland will now have to compensate the player in wages the *same* amount as his previous opportunity cost in trade. In other words, from the point of view of decisions, *the player does not cost any more, in the opportunity sense, than he used to under the reserve system.* Under the reserve system, the cost of using a player was a forgone opportunity, the money or players the Dodgers would have offered in exchange. Under the free agency system, the opportunity cost of the player is his salary. Thus we have established the result that from an opportunity cost point of view, there is *no* impact of the change in regimes. Given that costs are the same, there will be no change in ticket prices, location of players, or other aspects of the game. The only difference is that now the players get paid more. Owners are poorer, players are richer, but the game goes on. Ticket prices are unaffected, the price of hot dogs is unaltered, and the allocation of player talent around the league is not altered.[24] In the context of opportunity cost, not getting players in trade under the first system, and paying a player a high salary equal to the value of those players under the second regime does not represent a change.

With this framework in mind, let us return to the *Wall Street Journal* story about charges for music aired on cable TV. If the preceding story applies, and it seems that it does, then cable TV charges to HBO and similar movie channels will not change when the new fee system is installed. Rather, HBO and cable TV operators will simply have to live with less income, just as baseball owners now have to survive with higher player salaries. In sum, the question involves the distribution of wealth, not the allocation of resources, at least that would seem to be the case here. In July 1991 U.S. Magistrate Michael H. Dolinger ruled in New York's federal court that Ascap must issue "direct-to-the-viewer licenses to the cable networks."[25] It is expected that Ascap will appeal the ruling limiting its right to charge each cable TV viewer.

PROPERTY RIGHTS INSIDE THE FAMILY: A BRIEF CASE STUDY

We close this chapter with a lesson learned on the job. The following case history is both enlightening and entertaining as it points out how valuable the issue of property rights can be to managers of all types.

---

[24] One caveat is in order here. Given that players are now richer—they are being paid higher wages— some players may have consumption-based wealth or income effects that alter their choices of playing location. Thus some richer players may offer to work in different towns at different wages than they would have under the old, reserve clause system, but leaving aside this income effect, there is no impact of a change in rules on the apportionment of player talent around the league.

[25] See Meg Cox and Stephanie Simon, "Cable-TV Industry Wins a Round in Battle With Ascap," *Wall Street Journal,* July 22, 1991, p. B2.

When I was a young mother, arguments over property rights became a big problem at our house. Things have improved over the years, and our eight children, whose current ages range from 9 to 21 years, have fewer of these arguments now. Part of it is that they are older and that I am a seasoned parent. However, I credit much of this harmony to having followed some advice I received in those early years that helped me deal with ownership quarrels and helped me teach my children to share. I have forgotten the source but not the advice. It went like this:

Never bring anything into the house without designating clear ownership.
The owner is not required to share.

Initially, these suggestions ran counter to my understanding of cooperative living. However, we already had three small sons, and ownership quarrels occurred all too frequently. Whenever two of the boys would present themselves for my judgement, each came with an ironclad case.

"Phil put the bat down and left," Peter would argue. "You said if someone quits playing with something, the other person can have it."

"But Mom," Phil would object, "I only put it down because *you* called me to put on my jacket!"

Making firm rulings in these cases was difficult. Also, I suspected that much of the drama often centered less on who got the item in dispute and more on whom Mom would side with. I was being out-maneuvered, and I was ready to try a new technique.

To begin with, I realized I needed to be more attentive about assigning ownership. I loved to go to garage sales and would often bring home games and toys for the children. However, I rarely matched a particular item with a particular child. Upon reflection, I could see how the fuzziness of ownership easily led to arguments. If everything belonged to everyone, then each child felt he had a right to use anything. A lot of confusion was cleared up when I began making the effort to designate ownership when new items entered the house.

Dealing with possessions through ownership rights soon became standard procedure. As the family grew larger, the rule became more valuable. The basic premise was and is: The owner always wins. When Stephen complained that he had just spent 15 minutes fixing the chain on a bicycle, only to have his brother Marcus ride off on the bike, the question "Whose bike is it?" settled the matter. There could be no argument when ownership had been established beforehand.

When someone received a new toy, he could choose to share or not to share. Of course, this made things easier for me, as the children began coming to me less often with their arguments. Each one already knew who would win—and whoever won knew it was not because he or she was "Mom's favorite," but because he or she happened to be the owner.

I enjoyed the way things were working out but still felt a little guilty about teaching my children to be selfish. However, it was not long before I discovered that, rather than being selfish, the children were becoming more relaxed about others using their things. Once they realized that no one could take their property without their permission and that they could have their things back whenever they liked, they became tolerant of sharing. It also did not take them long to realize that in a large family there were a lot of things around that belonged to the other people with whom they lived. If anyone developed a reputation for not lending his possessions, he quickly found that his siblings were less than anxious to let him use *their* things. More importantly, though, the children seemed to enjoy sharing. It gave each of them a sense of satisfaction to grant someone permission to use his things. It raised their self-esteem to see themselves as generous persons.

Sometimes it was difficult for me to remain consistent. I had a tendency to want to make the older ones give in to the younger ones, but I knew things always went more smoothly when the rule *The owner is not required to share* was followed. I was also a little embarrassed when friends brought their children over to play, since with the ownership rule in operation, my children had the right to refuse to let the visitors play with their things. I could tell by the other mothers' faces that this was an unpopular position to take. I remained firm, though, because I had come to realize that when a mother took a toy from her child to give to his playmate, that child was *not* sharing. Only the owner can share. Often, but not always, my children became unconcerned about other children playing with their toys once they felt certain that unless they chose to share them, their possessions were safely theirs.

The real surprise, however, has come now, years later, because a totally unexpected benefit has resulted from this policy: Our children have a deep respect for other people's property. Having developed a strong sense of the right they have to rule over their own things, they award that same right to other people and their possessions. Rarely do our children use each other's things without asking first, and they respect a "No" when they get one. Best of all, when someone who has every right to say "No" to a request says "Yes," the borrower sees the gift for what it is and says "Thanks" more often than not.

Recently our 20-year-old son, Matt, was getting ready to go to the airport to catch a plane to France for a college study program. He could not find his watch and did not want to leave without some means of keeping track of time. I suggested that he ask his brother, Marcus, if he could borrow his watch for a month.

"Good idea," said Matt, and called Marcus's school and asked to speak with his 14-year-old brother.

"Thanks a lot," I heard Matt say into the phone and could easily imagine with what pride Marcus would reenter his eighth-grade classroom and casually whisper to a friend, "Oh, that was just my brother, Matt. He wanted to ask me if he could take my watch to France."

Never bring anything into the home without designating clear ownership.

The owner is not required to share.

At first glance, these simple guidelines may seem illogical and unworkable to a parent struggling with complex issues of quarrels and ownership. But surprisingly, they become a valuable means for instilling the joy and self-esteem that a child enjoys who has truly learned to share.[26]

TOPICS TO REVIEW

These are topics that you should feel comfortable with before you leave this chapter. If you cannot write out a clear and concise sentence or paragraph explaining the topic after you have worked on the study problems, you should reread the relevant section of the text.

Property Rights Theory of the Firm

Team Production

---

[26] Katherine Hussman Klemp, "Give and Take: A Mother Teaches Her Children That Sharing Means Caring," *Sesame Street Parent's Guide*, December 1989, pp. 36–38. © 1989 Children's Television Workshop (New York, New York). All rights reserved.

Nexus of Contracts

Yugoslavian Firm

Public Good

Private Good

Common Access Good

Aggregating the Demand for a Public Good

Tragedy of the Commons

Solutions to the Tragedy of the Commons—Cooperation, Regulation, and Privatization

Prisoner's Dilemma

TIT FOR TAT

Alienability, Long Run, and Managerial Myopia

Externality

Coase Theorem

STUDY PROBLEMS

1. Not long after the Iranian revolution ousted the long-time dictator, the Shah, the following story appeared in *Newsweek*. Can you explain what is going on?

   Cavalier about Caviar in Iran

   Moscow fears that Ayatollah Khomeini's Iranian regime could disrupt the international market in an important Russian export: caviar. In the past, by agreement, Iran and the Soviet Union limited the sturgeon catch in the Caspian Sea to assure a stable supply of caviar, which consists of sturgeon eggs. But reports from Russian observers suggest that Iran, for unknown reasons, no longer strictly enforces the sturgeon limit. So much caviar is flooding the Iranian market that fishermen in Caspian ports are retailing it at just over $5 a pound—barely 10% of the government-controlled price under the Shah a year ago.[27]

2. For the period 1973–1981, there were price controls on crude and refined petroleum products sold in the United States. Two aspects of those regulations were the so-called entitlement program and the creation of two different classes of oil, *old* and *new*.

   It is an oversimplification, but essentially the regulations said that all oil discovered prior to 1973 was *old* and its price was frozen at $5.75 per barrel. Purchasers (mostly refiners) of *old oil* prior to 1973 received an entitlement giving them the right to buy roughly the same quantity as they had in the past

---

[27] See *Newsweek*, October 1, 1979, p. 17. Also see Jane Mayer, "Horrors! Fine Caviar Now Could Become Cheap as Fish Eggs," *Wall Street Journal*, November 18, 1991, p. A1, for a more recent update on the plight of sturgeon eggs after the fall of the Communist government in the Soviet Union.

at the old price of $5.75. Newly discovered crude oil was essentially unregulated and commanded a considerably higher free-market price. What effect did this entitlement program have on

    a.   The price of refined petroleum products

    b.   The quantity bought and sold of refined petroleum products

    c.   The wealth of crude oil producers, petroleum refiners, and the consumers of refined petroleum products

3. One famous story in the economics literature concerns the incentive to collect information. According to this story, if one person or firm collects information about another company or financial asset in order to see if there is a profit opportunity, then other firms can free-ride on that information. As a consequence, there is a reduced incentive to obtain such information.

    Consider an open auction. Suppose there is a buyer with an excellent track record of selecting the best bargains. For example, she astutely and repeatedly selects the best and fastest horses out of the group being sold. Free-riders can simply observe the bidding pattern of the person with the superior skill, and hence there is a reduced incentive for the skillful bidder to even go to the trouble to collect the information and bid. Some people make a similar argument to explain why the financial tender offer market is inefficient. In essence, information is a common property resource.

    Suppose this argument were true. What do you expect would happen? First explain who suffers by the existing circumstances. Then detail the evolution of institutions that could or would mitigate the problem.

4. In the late 1970s and early 1980s many of New York State's independent school districts successfully drilled for natural gas on their property. The school administrators at these institutions universally expressed delight at the prospect of using this gas to reduce the cost of education, as the wells often produced more gas than had previously been used for cooking and heating. Explain how these energy discoveries affected

    a.   The amount of energy consumed by the schools

    b.   The amount of other inputs, such as teachers, desks, and computers, used by the schools

    c.   The economic cost of educating students

5. For a number of reasons, people generally decorate the interior and exterior of their homes differently. When building a large number of homes in a tract, however, developers usually do most if not all of the landscaping. They grade the lots, plant grass, and place shrubbery and even trees. By distinct contrast, they do not usually install draperies or furniture, and they often leave wall and carpet color selections to the buyer. Since the builder cannot perfectly predict the consumer's preferences, it is obvious why the entire choice is left to the buyer. But the same argument falls on hard times explaining the exterior finishing. Why do we observe the difference between internal and external decorating?

6. There is a great deal of controversy over the proliferation of nuclear power plants. Many people are concerned over the potentially devastating effect of large-scale accidents at these plants. Some plants have been forced to close.

The ordinary negligence law currently covers damages that might result from such accidents, except that the U.S. Congress passed a law in 1957 limiting the liability of any one plant operator to $560 million per accident.

    a.   What effect do you expect the passage of that law had on the number of nuclear plants planned for construction?

    b.   Who stands to gain and lose from such a law?

    c.   The Nuclear Energy Regulatory Commission regulates the operation of nuclear power plants. Do you predict that NERC had to impose tougher and more stringent safety rules after the law was passed? Do you expect that NERC altered its fine structure and the size of its enforcement staff after the law was passed?

7. Read the accompanying story about cable TV taken from the *Wall Street Journal.* Pay particular attention to the paragraph that argues that "monthly cable bill[s] could increase by as much as $5" if cable TV companies are forced to make payment to television broadcasting networks and the counter claim by broadcasters that "cable operators don't have to raise prices if the so-called retransmission fee passes." Analyze these contradictory claims. Who do you think is right?[28]

CHARGING FOR FREE TV?

Viewers who have suffered through lackluster shows on ABC, CBS or NBC and rolled their eyes and said, "Well, at least we didn't have to pay for that one" may have a new thing coming.

The three major networks, their local affiliates and independents are urging Congress to pass new legislation that would enable them to charge cable operators for the right to carry their programming. Currently, cable operators must pay cable channels for programs but can blithely pull down broadcasters' signals and retransmit them at no charge.

The cable industry argues that a viewer's monthly cable bill could increase by as much as $5 if cable companies suddenly are forced to fork over payments to broadcasters. . . .

Broadcasters insist cable operators don't have to raise prices if the so-called retransmission fee passes. . . .

The cable industry scoffs at such a suggestion. . . .

"Isn't my signal worth something?" asks David Lane, president of WFAA, the ABC affiliate in Dallas. "Right now, it's being treated like nothing because it's given away," he says.

Kevin Goldman, "Networks Seek Law Permitting Charges to Cable Concerns," *Wall Street Journal,* July 8, 1991, p. B3. (emphasis added) Reprinted by permission of *The Wall Street Journal,* © 1991 Dow Jones & Company, Inc. All Rights Reserved Worldwide.

---

[28] Broadcast television and cable TV have squared off in a fight over this issue. The struggle involves TV and newspaper advertisements, plus lobbying before Congress. For an in-depth discussion of this ongoing struggle see Kevin Goldman, "Advertising: Local TV Stations and Cable Clash in Ads Aimed at Swaying Congress," *Wall Street Journal,* August 29, 1991, p. B3.

8. Both coal and whales are scarce resources. However, there is a limited supply of coal in the world. Someday we will run out of it. By contrast, whales procreate, and it is entirely conceivable that whales will exist on the earth for millennia to come. Interestingly, there are groups such as Greenpeace that are devoted almost entirely to the preservation of whales. Again by contrast, there are few groups of any size or stature, certainly not in the league of Greenpeace, Ducks Unlimited, or the Sierra Club, devoted to saving the coal. Why is it that conservation groups are focused on the renewable resources and not the nonrenewable ones such as coal and oil?

9. Consider the production of nuclear power. There is potential there for serious devastation as the events at Hiroshima, Nagasaki, and Chernobyl attest. How is it that the owners of nuclear power plants in the United States get their operators to act responsibly and carefully enough for the rest of society to be willing to bear the risk of a nuclear accident? Consider two different types of nuclear plants. One is cooled by a large lake built on land owned almost exclusively by the power company that owns and operates the plant. The other facility uses cooling towers or a giant natural lake for cooling purposes.[29] Do you expect the method of cooling has any impact on the safety of the nuclear plant? Similarly, suppose that the homes and families of the employees of a nuclear plant live in close proximity to the plant. Do you expect that the plant will be operated more safely than the average nuclear plant or one where the bulk of the employees commute a substantial distance to work?

10. Suppose it were true that a great deal of the heavy industry in Pittsburgh was closely owned by families who live in the city. By contrast, imagine that the ownership of most of the heavy industry in Houston was widely dispersed to shareholders around the world. Other things being the same, which town do you expect has the greater pollution problem, Pittsburgh or Houston?

11. Grandparents are often observed to give cake, cookies, and candy to their grandchildren in larger quantities and with greater frequency than offered by the parents of the children. Why do you think this is so?

12. Do students ask more questions in large or small classes?

13. Many companies have a rule that the families of their senior executives must move and live with the executive when he or she is reassigned. Can you provide an economic rationale for this rule?

SUGGESTED READINGS

This is a long list. I have marked with an asterisk a few of the articles that most managerial economists would call classics or those that provide especially cogent summaries of a particular area.

---

[29] Duke Power Company has a large nuclear facility on Lake Keowee in South Carolina which was built almost exclusively for the cooling of the nuclear generator. Duke owns a great deal of land around the lake. By contrast, Niagara-Mohawk Power Company operates a nuclear facility at Oswego, New York, on the shores of Lake Ontario which if uses for cooling.

Anderson, Terry L. and Hill, Peter J. "The Role of Private Property in the History of American Agriculture." *American Journal of Agricultural Economics* (December 1976):937–45.

Anderson, Terry L. and Hill, Peter J. "Privatizing the Commons: An Improvement?" *Southern Economic Journal* 50 (October 1983):438–50.

Barzel, Yoram. *Economic Analysis of Property Rights.* Cambridge: Cambridge University Press, 1989.

Block, Walter, ed. *Economics and the Environment: A Reconciliation.* Vancouver: Fraser Institute, 1990.

Cheung, Steven N. S. "The Contractual Nature of the Firm." *The Journal of Law and Economics* 26(1) (April 1983):1–22.

*Coase, Ronald. "The Nature of the Firm." *Economica* 4 (November 1937):386–405.

*Coase, Ronald. "The Problem of Social Cost." *The Journal of Law and Economics* 3 (October 1960):1–44.

*Furubotn, Eirik and Pejovich, Svetozar. *The Economics of Property Rights.* Cambridge, MA: Ballenger Press, 1974.

*Gordon, H. Scott. "The Economic Theory of a Common-Property Resource: The Fishery." *Journal of Political Economy* 62 (April 1954):124–42.

*Hardin, Garrett. "The Tragedy of the Commons." *Science* 162 (December 13, 1968):1243–48.

Helm, Dieter and Pearce, David W. "Assessment: Economic Policy Towards the Environment." *Oxford Review of Economic Policy* 6(1) (Spring 1990):1–16.

*Jensen, Michael C. and Meckling, William H. "Theory of the Firm: Managerial Behavior, Agency Cost and Ownership Structure." *Journal of Financial Economics* 3(4) (October 1976):305–60.

Jensen, Michael C. and Ruback, Richard, eds. *Symposium on the Structure and Governance of Enterprise. Journal of Financial Economics* 27(2) Parts I and II (October 1990).

McCormick, Robert E. and Meiners, Roger E. "University Governance: A Property Rights Perspective." *The Journal of Law and Economics* 31(2) (October 1988):423–42.

*Manne, Henry G. *Economics of Legal Relationships.* New York: West Publishing Co., 1975.

*Scott, Anthony. "The Fishery: The Objectives of Sole Ownership." *Journal of Political Economy* 63 (April 1955):116–24.

Williamson, Oliver E. *Markets and Hierarchies: Analysis and Antitrust Implications.* New York: The Free Press, 1975.

Williamson, Oliver E. "Organization Form, Residual Claimants, and Corporate Control." *The Journal of Law and Economics* 26(2) (June 1983):351–66.

*Williamson, Oliver E. *The Economic Institutions of Capitalism.* New York: The Free Press, 1985.

Williamson, Oliver E. *Economic Organization: Firms, Markets and Policy Control.* New York: New York University Press, 1986.

Williamson, Oliver E. "Transaction Cost Economics: The Comparative Contracting Perspective." *Journal of Economic Behavior and Organization* 8(4) (December 1987):617–25.

Zerbe, Richard O., ed. *Research in Law and Economics,* Vol. 12. Greenwich, CT: JAI Press, 1989.

SUGGESTED SOLUTIONS TO SELECTED STUDY PROBLEMS

The following are only *suggested* solutions to the study problems presented at the end of this chapter. In all cases, the suggestions here put heavy emphasis on analysis rather than a single correct answer. Since most managerial problems do not fall into neat little boxes, the individual characteristics of the problems that you encounter on the job will typically mandate a solution using the principles developed here and in other courses. Memorizing these solutions will not make you a good manager; learning the *principles* detailed here will help make you a better manager.

1. Presumably, when the Shah was deposed, fisherman took a more myopic approach to the harvest not knowing what the future political situation would be. Since a pound of roe in the hand is worth two in the future, it might be better to harvest now rather than wait and see that some other person or even country has obtained the rights to fish the Caspian Sea.

2. The creation of a distinction between old and new oil has no impact on the cost of producing refined petroleum products. Oil used in production costs is lost opportunity. The cost of using an old barrel of oil is a new barrel of oil, as they are perfect substitutes in production. The owners of rights to purchase oil at less than its replacement cost are made richer by the law, but the value of the output of their chemical plants is the same whether they used old or new oil. The argument that old oil costs less is equivalent to pricing products based on their accounting value rather than their replacement costs, a mistake few managers will make. The impact of the law is to reduce the wealth of old oil sellers and to make the income of refiners who own rights to purchase these entitlements as they were called richer. There is no impact on consumers. For a more detailed look at the actual, more complicated regulations, see Mike Bradley, Gregg Jarrell, and Rodney Smith, "Studying Firm-Specific Effects of Regulation with Stock Market Data: An Application to Oil Price Regulation," *Rand Journal of Economics,* 17, Winter 1986, 467–89.

3. The point of this question is that information, without proper controls, can be a common access good. Now many people often confuse a public good with a common access good. The publicness of information is basically irrelevant. However, if one party collects information and it freely becomes available to another, the tragedy of the commons is present. In the face of this situation, the incentive to invest in the production of information is muted if not eliminated. However, since information can be valuable, an incentive exists to collect it. Thus, we expect entrepreneurs will develop tricks, tools, and institutions that prevent common access to the information they develop. For instance, in the case of an auction, an astute bidder may use signals, such as a touch to the ear, or a cough or some other secret method of bidding to prevent others from expropriating the information he has collected. You may wish to examine a story in the *Wall Street Journal,* "Pressing Mexico to Protect Intellectual Property," by Joe W. Pitts, January 25, 1991, page A13.

6. a. The law limited the liability of the nuclear power operators. However, according to the Coase Theorem, this shifting of the liability will only have an impact on resource allocation if there are transactions costs or income effects. In this case, it is easy to believe that it would be quite costly for the land owners surrounding a nuclear power plant to organize to bargain with the plant operator. If this in fact is the case, then shifting the law of liability will reduce the costs of nuclear plant operation. Therefore we expect there was an enhanced incentive to build nuclear facilities after the law was passed.

b. Again by the Coase Theorem, shifting the law of liability redistributes wealth, in this case from land owners near power plants to the owners and operators of the plants. The land owners proximate to the plant now must either bear the costs of the threat of disaster or compensate the nuclear plant operators to reduce or eliminate the risk.

c. Before the law was passed, nuclear plant operators faced unlimited liability by the common law of nuisance. After the law limited their legal exposure and assuming that the transactions costs were too high for the neighboring land owners to effectively bargain with the nuclear plant operators, then safety is less of a concern to the operators. If this is true, it seems reasonable to conclude that the political process responds by forcing more stringent standards on the nuclear plant operators than they would choose voluntarily.

7. It does not seem reasonable to conclude that cable television companies will increase their rates if they have to start paying for over-the-air television broadcasts. Think of the problem this way. Does the current cable service include the over-the-air signals? Of course, the answer is yes. Do you think that the cable TV companies are giving this service away? Since the current signal arriving over cable already includes the over-the-air broadcasts, then presumably the fees charged for that service reflect its value. Basic cable TV service already includes over-the-air telecasts, and unless the owners and managers of cable TV companies are fools, an unlikely prospect in general, their fees reflect the value of their service *regardless of whether the cable TV company has to pay for the signal or not.* Remember the Coase Theorem: The assignment of property rights does not affect resource allocation. Based on this logic, we do not expect cable TV companies to increase their rates if they are forced to compensate over-the-air broadcasters for their signals. The value of those signals is already reflected in the cable TV subscription rates.

8. Most coal has a well-defined owner. Whales do not. With private ownership of coal, the asset is extracted efficiently. By contrast, no one owns a whale until it is killed and possession is taken aboard a ship. Whales swimming in the ocean are a common access resource and without some form of regulation or cooperation, subject to the tragedy of the commons. Therefore, it seems to make quite good sense for conservationist groups to focus on whales, fish, fowl, and other animals that do not have well-defined owners.

CHAPTER

13

TEAM PRODUCTION, COORDINATION, AND CONTROL

INTRODUCTION

This chapter expands on the discussion of property rights that began in the last chapter. The basic concepts of common access property and the tragedy of the commons are extended to address a number of organizational problems inside the firm. We start with an introduction to the notion of team production. Team production, as its name suggests, refers to situations in which a collection of individuals can do more acting in concert than they can do all acting separately. When team production exists in a business situation, as it often does, a number of property rights problems emerge that astute managers will not ignore. Notable among these is the incentive for workers to shirk. A number of techniques are used to control shirking, sometimes called the incentive problem, and some of these are discussed. After this, we discuss the horizon and alienability problems that are present in most organizations.

TEAM PRODUCTION

[B]oats are pulled upstream by a team of coolies prodded by an overseer with a whip. . . . an American lady, horrified at the sight of the overseer whipping the men as they strained at their harness, demanded that something be done about the brutality. She was quickly informed . . . "Those men own the rights to draw boats over this stretch of water and they have hired the overseer and given him his duties."[1]

Team production is a relatively simple concept. When a collection of individuals can produce more jointly than each can separately, then we say there is team or joint production. When team production is present, the productivity of any one individual worker depends on the output or productivity of all the other workers on the team. This means the marginal productivity of each worker is higher when her peers work harder, and lower when they supply less labor or are less productive. Formally, consider the production function

$$q = q(x_1, x_2, x_3, \ldots, x_n),$$

where x_1 is the amount of effort supplied by the first worker and so forth. If team production is present, then the marginal product of each worker depends on the level of effort supplied by all the other workers:

$$\partial q/\partial x_i = q_i(x_1, x_2, x_3, \ldots, x_n)$$

for each of the i workers. Although simple, the implication of this result is profound: *The marginal productivity of any worker can only be determined by observing the input of all the other workers.* In this situation, we sometimes say there is **synergy** in production. The whole is more than the sum of its parts.

---

[1] See John McManus, "The Costs of Alternative Economic Organizations," *Canadian Journal of Economics*, August 1975, p. 341.

Consider two different examples. First, suppose four people are mountain climbing, tethered to each other. The harder each pulls on the person below, the easier it is to climb; the marginal productivity of each climber depends on the effort exerted by the other three climbers. We say there is team production here. By contrast, let the same four people be running a marathon together. No matter how hard any one person races, the time to finish of any other runner depends solely on his or her own efforts.[2] No team production exists in this case. Hereafter, when we say team or joint production, we mean a situation in which the output of one worker depends on the output of the other workers. It necessarily follows that observation of any one worker's marginal productivity is not a simple matter; the effort level of all team members must be known. The problem is profound. If the marginal productivity of individual workers is not easily observed, how then are they to divide the rewards of effort?

Consider the case of the mountain climbing team. Suppose a foundation has posted a bounty for the first human to reach the summit of some particular mountain. When our hypothetical team gets to the top and receives the reward, how do they allocate the money? The choices include equally or proportionately on the basis of height or age or weight or some other criterion. This problem vanishes in the race case; there is no jointness in production. The money goes to the individual runner who reaches the finish line first, but that algorithm fails for the mountain climbing team, since four people are necessary for any one person to reach the summit. Some sharing rule must be devised to preclude serious negotiation problems, such as jockeying for position, as the climbing team nears the summit. Ideally, to perfectly assign rewards to effort, the team members would get paid on the basis of their own respective contributions. But, this is impossible—the individual contributions are inherently immeasurable.

The inability of the team members to cheaply and objectively quantify the contributions of the other team members creates a variety of organizational problems. First, as we have just noted, some scheme must be devised to allocate the proceeds of the team's effort; wages must be determined. Second, membership in the team must be apportioned; some method for allocating slots on the team must be determined. Third, some scheme must be conceived for dealing with suppliers of other inputs. The most efficient solution to each of these difficult problems is likely to vary across industries and team production processes. At the one extreme, there is the classic Yugoslavian firm where team members vote democratically on many of these issues. At the opposite end of the spectrum is the boat rowed by the Chinese coolies referred to in the opening of this section where the coxswain dictates behavior with the whip. Universities are typically managed in part by the faculty who often determine curriculum, hours of operation, and the like through democratic voting schemes, although the extent of faculty governance differs considerably across schools.[3] By contrast, rare

---

[2] We put aside any psychological or drafting effects for the moment.

[3] See Robert E. McCormick and Roger E. Meiners, "University Governance: A Property Rights Perspective," *The Journal of Law and Economics,* October 1988, pp. 423–42.

562 CHAPTER 13 TEAM PRODUCTION, COORDINATION, AND CONTROL

is the modern U.S. corporation that allows its employees to vote on similar important decisions. Why the difference?

For the moment, let us leave aside the question of why some organizations make managerial decisions by voting and concentrate our attention on those enterprises in which choices are made by single individuals, not groups collectively. Returning to the basic team production problem, we see that the inherent immeasurability of individual marginal output creates problems. Primarily, the incentive to **shirk**, to supply less than the appropriate effort, exists. Just exactly what is shirking? Here we do not mean laziness in the normal sense. If a doctor in private practice decides to close the office every Wednesday and play golf, there is no shirking according to the definition posited here. **Shirking** is the undersupply of effort relative to some contractually specified amount. The problem with the team production process is that it is impossible to determine with precision just how much effort each member supplies, and, hence, it is impossible for anyone other than an individual team member to know whether he or she is living up to the terms of the contract.

Why do team workers shirk? First, work is not fun. Definitionally, people have to be paid to engage in what we call work. Things that people do for fun, even if sweaty and laborious, are not called work in economics. An exercise class may be a terrible physical ordeal to all the people in it, but it is only work to the instructor who is paid to supervise; to the students who paid tuition, it is consumption, not work in the economic lexicon. Obviously, physical training, weight lifting, and the like are work to professional athletes. Put differently, at the margin and in general, people will supply less work if they are paid less. So even though Michael Jordan might play some basketball if he were unpaid, he would not participate with the same vigor he did in 82 regular season games, playing 3281 minutes for the Chicago Bulls during the 1986–1987 NBA season and similar amounts in seasons since. Because work is not fun, if people can be paid and not work, many will choose to exercise this option. But, of course, not working has its costs. Specifically, team production is lower, but *the costs are distributed across all team members.*

As an example, imagine a restaurant with 25 waiters, bartenders, and other people who bus tables. Clearly, the overall quality of service in the restaurant jointly depends on the individual work efforts of many people. Suppose one person does a poor job. Let it be the bartender who, instead of quickly mixing drinks, is very casual, often watching television or flirting with customers. Patrons in the restaurant who do not receive their drinks in a timely fashion cannot cheaply determine whether slow service is due to a lackadaisical waiter or bartender. In the bargain, both are likely to suffer when tip time transpires. Now suppose the restaurant has a rule that tips are pooled and shared equally by the 25 workers, and further imagine that the substandard performance by the bartender costs the tip pool $5 per meal. For the sake of the example, suppose the diner leaves a $10 tip in lieu of $15 because the drink service was slow. In this example, the bartender only loses 1/25 of the lost tip, $5, or $0.20, seriously muting the incentive to do a competent job. From the selfish, single-minded point of view of the bartender, if conversing with patrons or watching television is worth 20 cents or more, he or she is better off to shirk and supply what is to the overall team a substandard performance. Suppose that shirking is not worth the full $5 in lost tips to the bartender that it costs the restaurant team—some alternative arrangement might exist that *makes everybody including the bartender better off.* This last result may not be obvious, so let's explore it in more detail.

Suppose the bartender is willing to pay $0.50 per patron to watch television and cavort with customers. *To him,* the cost of working slowly, under the equal sharing rule, is only $0.20, and thus, being a rational, self-interested individual, he shirks; the benefits, $0.50, exceed the costs, $0.20. But, in total, the costs to all, $5.00, far outweigh the benefits, only $0.50; the gain from supplying quality service is $5.00, while the costs are only $0.50 of forgone frivolity. There would be a net gain to all concerned of $4.50 if the bartender could be assuaged from shirking. The bartender would lose $0.50 in fun, but the waiter pool would pick up an extra $5.00 in tip money. Thus, a potential profit opportunity exists.

The other employees could hire someone to watch over the bartender and prevent malfeasance, affording to pay as much as $4.50 per patron for the services of the overseer. Alternatively, the bartender could be persuaded with a cash payment to shirk less. Just suppose the bartender were allotted not a 1/25 share of the tips, but 1/5 of all the tips. Now, *if he works hard,* he receives 1/5 of $15 or $3 instead of 1/25 of $15, which is $0.60. The value of shirking is unaltered; it is $0.50. Now compare the margins with regard to working or shirking. Shirking now costs him $1 in lost tips. When he shirks, he gets 1/5 of $10 or $2; when he works hard he gets $3. Shirking is only worth $0.50; therefore, he is dissuaded from shirking. The $1 in extra tips he gets from working dominates the $0.50 of fun he enjoys from shirking. In this contrived example, the bartender is better off not shirking when he gets 20 percent of the entire tip.

What happens to the other 24 members of the group? When the bartender shirks, they get 1/25 of the original tip or $10/25 (= $0.40). With the modified sharing rule, the bartender does not shirk, and consequently the tip is now $15. Each of the 24 waiters now gets 1/24 of 4/5 of the total tip or 1/24 of 4/5 of $15, a share of $0.50 per person. On the whole, the bartender is better off; he gets an extra $1 and no cavorting, a net gain of $0.50. Each of the other 24 people now gets $0.50 instead of the original $0.40. *Everyone is better off.* Of course, different tip amounts could change this outcome, but this example was constructed to prove a point: An equal sharing rule often has incentive effects that make all members of a team suffer, and when this is true, it is frequently possible to devise an alternative payment or sharing rule that voids or mutes the problem.

COORDINATION AND CONTROL IN PROCESSES IN WHICH TEAM PRODUCTION EXISTS

In this section, we discuss three prominent and important managerial problems that are present in virtually all companies, regardless of their line of business or orientation. These are the incentive problem, the horizon problem, and the inalienability problem.

The Incentive Problem

In any business enterprise, selfish individuals find that it serves their own narrow self-interest to work less than they would individually and alone because they only bear some portion of the cost.[4] When team production exists, it is virtually impossible to precisely determine which individuals are shirking; hence, it behooves all the people involved to shirk some. Call this the **incentive problem**. All businesses, partnerships, corporations, sole proprietorships with more than one employee, not-for-profit firms, Yugoslavian firms, and pure communist organizations must deal with the reality of this problem. They do so in many different ways.

In general, there are two basic approaches to combating the incentive problem: the stick and the carrot. Consider the example of people who sell for a living. Imagine a furniture store with 20 sellers, half men, half women. A customer walks in the door. If the sales staff is paid hourly or is on salary, who rushes to greet this customer? The point here is that no single individual seller has any monetary incentive to react to the new customer. In order to solve this problem, the manager or owner of the store must create rules of conduct or employ some other method of motivation that we can call the **stick method**. The potential to be fired, coupled with the stick method, can motivate the sales staff to try and serve the new customer. What rules will be used in the stick method? Many qualify, but a few examples should suffice to demonstrate the point. Coffee breaks will have time limitations on them. Bathroom breaks may be similarly limited. Personal time on the phone will have to be restricted. A dress code may be mandated. If the sales staff is paid on salary, then it might be necessary to have rules and punishments about tardiness or early departure from work. Screaming and hollering have been known to motivate workers in this situation. Most certainly, the general manager or owner will have to spend a great deal of time watching and monitoring the employees to detect, prevent, and punish recalcitrants.

An alternative to monthly or hourly wages is a system of individual responsibility. There are many ways to create such a system, but a common technique is to pay a portion or all of the wages as commission on sales. Commissions serve many functions. They make the salesperson a residual claimant to her behavior. A **residual claimant** is someone who gets to keep what is left over after some action has been taken—that is, to claim the residuals. In this case, the salesperson gets to claim some portion of the sales, if any, that result from the service rendered.[5] This is the **carrot**. The commission is a carrot that acts as an incentive to keep the employee out of the restroom, off break, properly dressed, and on time. As the proportion of salary taken as commission increases, the incentive effect goes up;

---

[4] Refer to the beginning sections of this chapter for more on the incentive to shirk.

[5] In the example of the printing press and the café in Chapter 12, a profit sharing arrangement between the two enterprises makes the managers of both enterprises residual claimants to the other's operation and thus has the effect of internalizing or muting the externality problem created by the noise pollution.

TEAM PRODUCTION AND INCENTIVES

Entrepreneurial incentives that give teams a piece of the action are highly appropriate in collaborative companies. . . . Innovative companies are experimenting with incentives like phantom stock for development of new ventures and other strategic achievements, equity participation in project returns, and bonuses pegged to key performance targets. Given the cross-functional (i.e., team production) nature of many projects today, rewards of this kind must sometimes be systemwide, but individual managers can also ask for a bonus pool for their own areas, contingent, of course, on meeting performance goals.

Rosabeth M. Kanter, "The New Managerial Work," *Harvard Business Review,* November-December 1989, pp. 85–92.

---

the incentive problem declines. The optimal commission level depends on a number of factors. We only briefly consider them here.

Many different conditions in the world other than the salesperson's effort determine the actual volume of furniture sold. We can note several. Weather conditions influence the number of people shopping. General economic conditions affect the demand for furniture. The opening or closing of neighboring stores can affect sales. In each of these cases, the change in sales is beyond control of the salesperson. Thus, when remuneration includes commission on sales, factors outside the sphere of influence of the salesperson will affect the salary of the employee, and as a general principle, this is not good for at least two reasons. It makes the employees worry, fret, or otherwise expend resources trying to forecast these extra events. Second, it introduces variance into the income stream of the employees, and in general, people will pay to avoid such disturbances. This

---

PAY FOR PERFORMANCE

Pay for performance seems like one of the simplest ideas around: Pay diligent workers more than goof-offs and pay more for success than for failure. Most big companies already base some part of their top officers' pay on corporate performance. . . .

According to a survey by consultants Hewitt Associates, 51% of companies are practicing some form of pay for performance for more than top management, up from 44% in 1989. . . . The average grant: less than 7% of pay, compared with one-half to two-thirds of most CEO's compensation.

Amanda Bennett, "Paying Workers to Meet Goals Spreads, But Gauging Performance Proves Tough," *Wall Street Journal,* September 10, 1991, p. B1. Reprinted by permission of *The Wall Street Journal,* © 1991 Dow Jones & Company, Inc. All Rights Reserved Worldwide.

latter point means that with a commission pay schedule, the employee must, on average, be paid more than he would require under straight salary. There is no free lunch. Commissions motivate, but they cost money.

Based on the preceding principles, we can make some conjectures about commissions. The greater the chance of outside influence on sales, the smaller the commission as a percentage of total compensation and the greater the reliance on sticklike rules to encourage the sales staff. The less variance there is in sales, the greater the commissions as a fraction of total wages, and the fewer rules used to inspire quality work.

The principle of commissions as a motivating factor generalizes outside sales staff to many productive activities at many levels of management. The basic point of using commissions is to link performance with compensation, thus creating individual responsibility and residual claimancy. This point helps us understand why some managers are required to hold stock in the company for which they work. The rising and falling value of the stock provides an instant feedback and reward system to those people whose decisions might affect the stock price. Naturally, this effect declines as one moves from the top of the organization, the CEO, down to the assembly line worker. It is more important for the CEO to own stock than the stock boy, but in both cases, poor job performance maps into less income or wealth. This same line of reasoning helps explain the use of **stock options** as a motivating tool. Stock options give senior managers the right to purchase blocks of shares at prespecified prices.[6]

EMPLOYEE STOCK OPTIONS

RAHWAY, N.J.—Merck & Co. is marking its centennial with an unusual one-time gift to each of its 37,000 employees: options to buy 100 shares of Merck stock at potentially hefty profit.

How hefty—and how much employees will profit—depends on how much Merck's stock rises in value over the next five to 10 years.

Under the plan, every employee on the payroll as of this past Friday [September 6, 1991] can buy the 100 shares at $127.25 each—approximately Friday's closing price—any time between Sept. 6, 1996, and Sept. 5, 2001, as long as they either still work at Merck or have retired from the company. Thus, they stand to profit from any increase in Merck's stock price over the option price. . . .

"We needed to find ways to get everyone in the work force on board in terms of our goals and objectives," said Steven M. Darien, Merck's vice president, human resources.

Gilbert Fuchsberg, "Merck & Co. Options Are Being Offered To All Employees," *Wall Street Journal,* September 12, 1991, p. A6. Reprinted by permission of *The Wall Street Journal,* © 1991 Dow Jones & Company, Inc. All Rights Reserved Worldwide.

---

[6] Rules made by the Securities and Exchange Commission govern stock options. For instance, managers must hold stocks for at least a six-month period, beginning from the day the option is offered.

Consider a simple example. Eunice is hired by ABC Software as CEO in the spring of 1989. She is given 10,000 shares of common stock as a signing bonus, plus she is offered the option to purchase an additional 10,000 shares at $10 ($10 is called the **strike price**). The current price of the common stock is $10. The option has value initially because the stock might someday rise above $10, and it has more value the higher the stock price rises, no matter what the level of the stock price is. Computing the value of options is a complicated and tricky business, but leaving aside the question of the variance in the stock price (which affects the value of the option in important ways), then the option increases in value $1 for every $1 increase in the stock price. The stock option provides a bunch of carrots. For every $1 increase in stock price, the value of each option increases by a like amount. As a general principle, CEOs are in especially strong positions to make decisions that affect the value of the company. Thus, a firm run by a person holding both stock and stock options is, other things being the same, expected to be better managed than its counterparts, where some other mechanism must be used to motivate the senior officer in the company.

One advantage of stock options over outright stock ownership is that the managers do not have to have large wealth holdings to be given stock options. By contrast, large holdings of stock require a substantial outlay on the part of the manager or the company. The option has a cost if it is exercised, but then the benefits in terms of the stock price are already in place. This helps us understand why stock options are a common form and large component of executive compensation.

A letter to the editor of the *Wall Street Journal* by Howard D. Sherman, vice president of Institutional Shareholder Services, points out that carrots and sticks can work together to motivate managers:

MANAGERS AND PERFORMANCE

The core principle of effective motivation is simple yet powerful: managers deliver outstanding performance when they think as owners. The opportunity to create personal wealth through equity is almost always a more compelling incentive than what even the most ingenious salary and bonus systems can provide. Thus perhaps the single most important reform an organization can make is to transform its managers into significant owners of the business—or better still, significant owners of the business units in which they work.

Making managers into owners is not just a matter of stock certificates and financial rewards. The ownership imperative should engage executives and employees at an emotional level. Pride in work, prudent risk taking, and above all, a deep sense of responsibility for the success or failure of the enterprise are critical attitudes that separate owners from hired hands.

G. Bennett Stewart, III, "Remaking the Public Corporation from Within," *Harvard Business Review*, July-August 1990, p. 127.

> Shareholders are beginning to use executive compensation as a new tool of corporate accountability. . . .
>
> Shareholders view compensation not just as a tool of accountability, but also as an incentive device. . . . If the current mix of assets is not providing as much value as it could to those who own the company and who put their money at risk—the shareholders—management is obligated to reshuffle the mix. . . .
>
> [T]here are tools for shareholders to use to motivate management to behave as real asset managers, and compensation happens to be one of the strongest.

Some companies extend the practice of stock ownership to include almost all employees. This practice is sometimes referred to as an ESOP—an employee stock-ownership plan. The principle remains the same, to establish residual claimancy within the ranks of all workers to more closely align their own personal incentives with the company's goal of profit maximization.[7]

A Case Study involving Telephone Budgets   In August 1983, the Department of Economics at Clemson University switched its method of accounting for faculty expenses. Prior to that time, faculty members were allowed to make any reasonable long-distance phone calls they deemed appropriate. The head of the department periodically checked the records to ensure that the system was not being abused. Under the old system, travel had to be approved by the department head. Faculty who wished to purchase equipment, computers, books, or other supplies had to get permission from the department head. August 1983 brought a new system. Faculty were assigned expenditure budgets depending upon rank and ability. Individual faculty were now responsible for making their own decisions with regard to long-distance telephone calls, travel, books, computers, and the like. Use of the telephone now cost the faculty the opportunity to travel or buy materials.

Under the old system, long-distance calls were the easiest thing to use among the class of items included in the new research budgets. They did not require preapproval of the department head. All other expenses did. Hence, according to the theory previously outlined, we expect that under the new system of *individual* responsibility, faculty would economize on long-distance calls in favor of other expenditures—travel and materials. Table 13.1 reports the monthly long-distance phone bills for the department under the two different regimes. The total operating budget of the department is also listed. The fraction of the total operating budget spent on long-distance calls is reported in the last column under each heading.

Casual examination suggests that long-distance expenditures declined in the period of the individual budget. In the case of long-distance telephone service, the commons has been privatized under the new system, and according to the theory, there should be less use and abuse. This means that people should have

---

[7] In the recession of 1991, an interesting event took place. Weirton Steel Corp. of Weirton, WV, a company owned exclusively by its employees, laid off some of its owner-workers. The story is recounted in Maria Mallory, "How Can We Be Laid Off If We Own the Company?" *Business Week*, September 9, 1991, p. 66.

made fewer long-distance telephone calls. The data in the table suggest this, but we can examine this question more rigorously using statistical methods.

Table 13.2 reports the test of whether the average expenditures on long-distance phone calls are different under the two systems. In the preindividual budget period, the average expenditure on long-distance calls was 20.6 percent of the total office budget. However, once individuals had to pay for their own calls, long-distance expenditures fell to only 17.5 percent of the total expenditures. Privatizing the budget led to less use of the system. Statistically, the t ratios reported in Table 13.2 suggest that this difference is significant. Under the hypothesis of either equal or unequal variances, the t test is significant at the 10 percent confidence level or better. We can conclude from this one case study that letting individual employees bear the costs of their own actions leads to lower levels of expenditures on the item that previously had been common access—namely, the long-distance telephone budget. Naturally, the point would seem to generalize to most any other resource as well, and it points the way for clever managers to eliminate wasteful spending within their company. Budgeting expenditures creates individual accountability and responsibility and induces workers to be more careful in their spending.

Harold Sirkin and George Stalk, Jr., report a case study involving the reorganization of a failing company, where a realignment of incentives was deemed crucial to the rescue of the enterprise:

> They established a bonus plan for all employees—from the mill manager to the janitors—that was pegged to improvements in individual product-line margins or volume but contingent on the mill's overall profitability. (For bonus purposes, the mill's overall financial performance would be assessed after six months and at six-month intervals thereafter.)[8]

Let us now turn our attention away from the incentive problem to a second property issue, which we have previously introduced. This is the horizon problem.

The Horizon Problem

As a general rule, people do not live or work forever. This fact creates a managerial issue that we call the **horizon problem**. Quite simply, the horizon problem arises because people are not inclined to impute into their decision calculus the costs and benefits that their actions today might have after they have left the business. Recall the theoretical discussion of Lake Great, when fishing today has implications for the size of the school in the future (recall the discussion in Chapter 12 in the section Ownership in Perpetuity and Alienability). Unless the net present value of *all* future cash flows is incorporated into the decision calculus of the owner or manager, the proper use of the asset will not be forthcoming.

---

[8] Harold Sirkin and George Stalk, Jr., "Fix the Process, Not the Problem," *Harvard Business Review*, July-August 1990, pp. 26–35. For a related discussion on incentives, see G. Bennett Stewart III, "Remaking the Public Corporation from Within," *Harvard Business Review*, July-August 1990, pp. 126–37.

TABLE 13.1 OPERATING EXPENSES

	PERIOD OF NO FACULTY BUDGETS					PERIOD OF INDIVIDUAL BUDGETS			
YEAR	MONTH	TOTAL OPERATING EXPENSES	LONG-DISTANCE PHONE EXPENSES	FRACTION OF OPERATING EXPENSES ON LD PHONE	YEAR	MONTH	TOTAL OPERATING EXPENSES	LONG-DISTANCE PHONE EXPENSES	FRACTION OF TOTAL EXPENSES ON LD PHONE
1980	7	$2251.17	$ 587	0.2608	1983	8	$4061.58	$ 870	0.2142
1980	8	2251.17	1071	0.4758	1983	9	4061.58	958	0.2359
1980	9	2251.17	446	0.1981	1983	10	4061.58	973	0.2396
1980	10	2251.17	617	0.2741	1983	11	4061.58	959	0.2361
1980	11	2251.17	684	0.3038	1983	12	4061.58	919	0.2263
1980	12	2251.17	528	0.2345	1984	1	5147.33	849	0.1649
1981	1	3974.17	444	0.1117	1984	2	5147.33	1199	0.2329
1981	2	3974.17	583	0.1467	1984	3	5147.33	1100	0.2137
1981	3	3974.17	574	0.1444	1984	4	5147.33	922	0.1791
1981	4	3974.17	679	0.1709	1984	5	5147.33	995	0.1933
1981	5	3974.17	561	0.1412	1984	6	5147.33	1323	0.2570
1981	6	3974.17	1755	0.4416	1984	7	5147.33	806	0.1566
1981	7	3974.17	676	0.1701	1984	8	5147.33	727	0.1412
1981	8	3974.17	640	0.1610	1984	9	5147.33	695	0.1350
1981	9	3974.17	639	0.1608	1984	10	5147.33	646	0.1255
1981	10	3974.17	641	0.1613	1984	11	5147.33	878	0.1706
1981	11	3974.17	849	0.2136	1984	12	5147.33	738	0.1434
1981	12	3974.17	638	0.1605	1985	1	6024.67	879	0.1459
1982	1	3575.83	556	0.1555	1985	2	6024.67	812	0.1348
1982	2	3575.83	786	0.2198	1985	3	6024.67	663	0.1100
1982	3	3575.83	681	0.1904	1985	4	6024.67	951	0.1579
1982	4	3575.83	670	0.1874	1985	5	6024.67	558	0.0926
1982	5	3575.83	—	—	1985	6	6024.67	819	0.1359

TABLE 13.1 (continued)

Period of No Faculty Budgets

Year	Month	Total Operating Expenses	Long-Distance Phone Expenses	Fraction of Operating Expenses on LD Phone
1982	6	3575.83	593	0.1658
1982	7	3575.83	853	0.2385
1982	8	3575.83	772	0.2159
1982	9	3575.83	825	0.2307
1982	10	3575.83	664	0.1857
1982	11	3575.83	863	0.2413
1982	12	3575.83	737	0.2061
1983	1	4061.58	676	0.1664
1983	2	4061.58	748	0.1842
1983	3	4061.58	694	0.1709
1983	4	4061.58	793	0.1952
1983	5	4061.58	739	0.1819
1983	6	4061.58	662	0.1630
1983	7	4061.58	776	0.1911

Period of Individual Budgets

Year	Month	Total Operating Expenses	Long-Distance Phone Expenses	Fraction of Total Expenses on LD Phone
1985	7	6024.67	930	0.1544
1985	8	6024.67	2219	0.3683
1985	9	6024.67	2210	0.3683
1985	10	6024.67	2219	0.3683
1985	11	6024.67	868	0.1441
1985	12	6024.67	738	0.1225
1986	1	7545.83	1120	0.1492
1986	2	7545.83	900	0.1198
1986	3	7545.83	803	0.1064
1986	4	7545.83	1268	0.1680
1986	5	7545.83	898	0.1190
1986	6	7545.83	787	0.1043
1986	7	7545.83	1043	0.1382
1986	8	7545.83	1450	0.1922
1986	9	7545.83	939	0.1244
1986	10	7545.83	694	0.0920
1986	11	7545.83	1089	0.1443
1986	12	7545.83	1626	0.2155
1987	1	6941.67	1089	0.1569
1987	2	6941.67	1255	0.1808
1987	3	6941.67	1116	0.1608
1987	4	6941.67	1030	0.1484

BUDGET TYPE	N	MEAN	STD. DEV.	STD. ERROR OF THE MEAN
Department	36	0.2061	0.0740	0.0123
Individual	45	0.1753	0.0669	0.0099

VARIANCES	t STATISTIC	PROB $> \lvert t \rvert$
Unequal	1.9424	0.0560
Equal	1.9643	0.0530

TABLE 13.2   THE DIFFERENCE IN EXPENDITURES

Hypothetical Business Problem 13.1

Consider a large, integrated paper products firm. The company produces kraft paper from pine wood pulp as one of its major lines of business. For a variety of reasons, some of which we consider in the section in Chapter 14 on Vertical Integration and Opportunism, the company owns its own land on which it grows trees for future use. However, pine trees take anywhere from 15 to 25 years to mature. Suppose the CEO of our paper products company only expects to work for 10 more years. What incentive does he have to plant trees now? Let's make the problem even more interesting. Suppose by any reasonable method of computation, planting 50,000 acres in baby pine trees is a good investment given the current market conditions. What we mean is that for any discount rate within reason, the net present value of the cash flows from the trees 25 years from now is greater than the cost of planting them now, including a sum for the rental value of the land that is tied up while the trees are growing. In other words, the company will be richer if the trees are planted. The project is a good idea; let us take that as a given. Will the CEO order the trees planted?

Suggested Solution to Problem 13.1

To appreciate this problem, let's make a simple assumption. The CEO of our hypothetical paper products company is paid based on company profitability. So, the higher annual profits are, the higher is the CEO's salary. Now consider the thoughts that go through the head of the CEO as he decides whether to plant the trees or not. To plant the trees, land must first be acquired. The land that will grow these pine trees costs, say, $500 per acre. On top of this, suppose the trees themselves cost $20 per acre to plant. Thus, for 50,000 acres, the land costs $500•50,000 or $25 million, and the trees cost another $1 million to plant. In total then, this project will require an initial outlay of $26 million. Suppose the CEO receives as part of his total annual compensation 0.1 percent of corporate profits, and say profits would be $100 million without the investment in land and trees. The CEO's bonus, if the trees are *not* planted, is 0.1 percent of $100 million or $100,000. However, if he plants the trees, profits this year will decline by the costs of the tree planting investment, or $26 million, which will reduce his bonus by $26,000. Thus, in order to make the right decision from the point of view of the company, to plant the trees, he has to forgo $26,000 in salary bonus. He would have to really love the company to make that choice, and love is surely a capricious carrot to count on. From his narrow self-interested perspective, he is better off if he cancels the land purchase and tree planting, pocketing $26,000 in the bargain. However, we know the company and its shareholders are made worse off by that decision. Is there a contract or an institution they can create to resolve this problem?

A number of solutions exist to mollify this situation. First, there is a board of directors that oversees important managerial decisions like this one. Were the board members called to vote on the issue, they might be counted on to veto the CEO's recommendation not to plant. But what incentives do they have to do a competent job? We cannot cover every topic here, so let's leave this one aside, and presume for the moment that the sterling and long-standing reputations of the members of the board lead them to behave in ways that maximize the value of the company; they are *not* paid based on annual profits. Then, when the CEO recommends nonacceptance of the present value increasing project of tree planting, the board balks and, if pushed, will demand the resignation of the CEO for incompetence. So, and in general, oversight of managerial decisions by a benevolent board of directors acts to forestall bad decisions. However, the board simply cannot investigate every decision. Other techniques must be found to motive the CEO and other senior officers, many of whose chores are very important but too numerous to bring before the board.[9]

The problem is partly resolved if the CEO plans to stay with the company until the tree planting project comes to fruition. For if he does, company profits in the years the trees are harvested (and the land sold) will be enormous and sufficient to make up for the loss of income in the

---

[9] Legal redress is also a possibility. Since managers have a fiduciary responsibility to their shareholders, the latter can sue when managers do not take the value maximizing course, but like beauty, value is often seen through the eyes of the beholder. This means that if the shareholders think the managers have abridged their legal responsibilities, they may take them to court, but then the court must resolve the question. The managers are allowed to say why they did or did not take the project, and thus the law cannot always be counted on to serve the shareholders' interests. The problem is even more complicated than this. For more on this, see the interesting case involving an attempted takeover at Time, Inc., "Time-Paramount—Long-Term vs. Short-Term Value Maximization," *Securities and Federal Corporate Law Report,* September 1989, pp. 57–64. In general, the business decision rule says that stockholders who do not enjoy the decisions made by managers must fight those managers within the company structure, not the courtroom.

year the trees are planted.[10] This is why we call this situation the horizon problem. If the manager's horizon is long, then he will properly take all positive net present value projects and eschew the negative ones. Responsibility and accountability exist. But when the manager's horizon is short, when he will not be with the company for a long time, as retirement approaches for instance, then the problem is most severe. However, even in this situation, all hope is not lost.

Common stock can serve many purposes. Here it can be used to lengthen a manager's horizon. Let's see how that works. Imagine an annual net cash flow in perpetuity of $100. At 10 percent interest, this sum is worth in present value terms,

$$P = A/r = \$100/0.1 = \$1000.$$

So the current present value of the flow forever is $1000. How much money would someone pay to have the rights to the flow? The answer is $1000. Now suppose there are 100 equal shares to this flow. What is the value of each share? It is $1000/100 or $10 per share.

Now to see the point, imagine that the manager of this enterprise owns 10 percent of the stock, and let us suppose that he controls the destiny of the company by making an important decision today. If he chooses option A, then the cash flows persist forever and the company is worth $1000 in total or $10 per share. However, if he chooses option B, then the cash flows stop after five years.

Consider two cases. In the first situation, the manager is paid on commission a portion of the company's cash flows, and that is all he receives. Let the commission be 10 percent of net revenues. Then this manager is paid 10 percent of $100 per year or $10 per year *as long as he works for the company,* and to make the point obvious, suppose he plans to retire after four more years. Leaving aside all things except his salary, does this manager have a preference over option A, which pays $100 to the company forever, or option B, which also pays $100, but only for the next five years? In a narrow sense no. Under plan A, he gets $10 per year for the next four years and then retires, but under plan B he also gets $10 per year for the last four years of his employment. He gets paid the same no matter which plan of action he pursues. His wealth and income are unaffected by his decision, and thus, if it costs him anything to think about this problem, if it takes any of his time or other resources, he will simply toss a coin and guess one solution. In this case, he might just as likely take option B as A.

In case two, we make the manager a residual claimant to the impact of the actions he takes now even if they occur after he departs. We do this by giving him some stock in the company, say 10 percent or 10 shares. The value of the shares critically depends on the choice he makes. If he selects option A, then the shares are worth $10 apiece, but if he picks B then they are worth much less because the

---

[10] Can you demonstrate how we know this is true?

cash flows stop after five years. The value of the shares under option B is given by

$$V_B = \{\$100\bullet[1/(1.1) + 1/(1.1)^2 + 1/(1.1)^3 + 1/(1.1)^4 + 1/(1.1)^5]\}/100$$

$$= [\$100\bullet3.79]/100 = \$3.79.$$

Since the manager owns 10 shares, if he chooses option A his stock is worth $10\bullet\$10$ or $100, but if he chooses option B it is only worth $10\bullet\$3.79$ or $37.90. Now he has a self-interest incentive to take the time and energy to make the right choice. He will not necessarily make the right decision all the time, but at least the incentive exists to try. Stock ownership and stock options mute the managerial horizon problem.

Before we leave this discussion, consider pension plans. Under federal law, pension plans are heavily regulated, and that is important to note. Leaving the legal issues aside, however, imagine that the pension plan of some company is heavily endowed with the stock of the company. When the company does well, there are dividends and capital gains that can be used to pay pensioners. When the stock performs poorly, there is little pie to be split among the retirees. This technique of putting a portion of the company's stock in the pension fund can act to mute the managerial and worker horizon problem. Workers and managers know that if they do dumb or stupid things today, things likely to have dire consequences in the future if not now, they will suffer *even after they leave the company.* What better way is there to promote quality performance on the job than this? Allocating some portion of future annual profits to the fund has similar incentive implications.

We close this section by noting that failing to take a positive net present value project is only one managerial or worker indiscretion. Taking bad projects, ones that do not pay the freight, also reduces the wealth of shareholders or owners. The horizon problem creates an incentive for a manager or worker to ignore costs that might accrue to the company after his or her employment is terminated. All of the schemes discussed tend to lengthen the horizon and reduce myopic decision making. However, the world is not perfect, and no technique has ever been designed to flawlessly solve the horizon problem. Although they stand outside the purview of this text, several other methods for lengthening workers' horizons are noted. Some companies almost never fire their employees. Since the workers expect more or less permanent employment, saving for gross malfeasance or legal or moral indiscretions, they have a long horizon relative to companies that fire their workers with greater frequency. We know the stick method of dismissal has its own rewards. When a firm gives up the right to dismiss workers, it must get something valuable in return. Thus, companies that choose not to use dismissal as a motivator must truly have serious horizon problems that require drastic measures; hence the long tenure for employees. Japanese companies are especially noted for hiring workers for life. This system should work most effectively when its alternatives are weak. Thus we are inclined to believe that annual bonuses, be they stock or cash, outright stock ownership, and stock options are likely to be less prevalent in Japanese companies than they are in the American counterparts. The same argument holds for American companies that seldom dismiss employees, IBM for instance.

The Inalienability Problem

When the rights to the net cash flows of an enterprise cannot be sold or liquidated, we say there is **inalienability of the cash flows**. When the owners of a business cannot sell their claims to the company, certain problems will exist. In some circumstances, the advantages will outweigh the disadvantages, but even then the incentives created by inalienability persist. Organizational structure matters, and managers are remiss when they do not recognize and deal with the unusual problems associated with the absence of well-defined residual claimants.

In the section Ownership in Perpetuity and Alienability in Chapter 12, it was demonstrated that owners of assets who have the privilege to sell their holdings will behave differently from temporary owners or those who cannot free themselves from their possessions. Typically, owners who cannot sell will not have incentives to account for effects that take place after they expect to expire. For instance, if I am allowed to farm a plot of land for as long as I live, but upon my death or retirement, the rights to use the land revert to some other person or the government, then I am less likely to be worried about the long-run consequences of soil conservation or fertilization. This problem becomes more grave the closer I get to death or retirement. From my personal perspective, as my tenure approaches its end, I become a less concerned steward of the land, failing to make investments that a more long-run oriented manager would consider.

This effect manifests itself in many ways. For example, consider the incentives of renters. People who lease cars have a short-run ownership claim to the use of the automobile, and as a consequence, they are less inclined to worry about checking the oil or performing other maintenance. Apartment renters surely do not care for their rooms with the same diligence as they do when they purchase their own home. Although these two examples, strictly speaking, are not inalienability problems, they help us see how truncated ownership affects use.

An owner who cannot sell the claims to her assets has features in common with renters. Her concern about the future consequences of her actions today may not be fully reflected in her wealth. Indeed, when the repercussions are known to take place after death or retirement, they may be ignored entirely. This is not a satisfactory state of affairs. Investments that would increase value stand a chance of being passed by, and equally as bad, investments that do not cover their full costs may be undertaken when some of the costs will be borne after the current owner has departed.

For instance, we have previously discussed how brand names can be an important quality assuring mechanism. For a company managed by workers without alienable claims to the cash flows (the profits), the incentive to protect the brand name is muted and dulled. And such companies will have to resort to alternative (and presumably more expensive) means of guaranteeing the quality of their products. When the managers in charge of the enterprise, who are paid partly in annual profit bonuses, approach death or retirement, they have an incentive to cut costs. They can do this by lowering inspection and quality control and thereby increasing the current net cash flows of the business, some of which they can put in their pockets before they depart via higher profit bonuses. Current profits are higher, but the value of the company is lower for their actions will necessarily reduce the worth of the brand name of the enterprise in the future, an effect that the existing managers do not take into account since it does not affect their well-being.[11] This is sometimes called the **end-game problem**. Thus, businesses run by managers who do not have alienable rights to the cash flows will be beset by problems of quality control and the like more frequently than similar companies with alienable rights. To counter this effect, we expect such companies to spend resources above and beyond the norm to protect quality. For instance, such companies are perhaps more inclined to offer money-back guarantees on their products. Government-run businesses immediately come to mind as an example.

Other examples include companies started on the back of one person or a small group of persons who have a very large stake in the enterprise. Often it is the case that these investors form the core of the senior management team, and the value of the business is strongly tied to their continued employment with the company. For example, Steve Jobs was a founder and large shareholder in Apple Computers for many years. Sam Walton had a similar association with the retailing chain Wal-Mart. William Gates is reported to own 40 percent of the computer software giant, Microsoft.[12] In each of these cases, the value of the person's shares probably depends in part on his remaining with the company. To a certain extent, his shares are inalienable. For the market value of the shares to hold, the manager has to remain active. In each case then, we expect that the company takes extra steps to ensure that its brand name is kept sound by particular attention to quality control. These companies are also expected to take extra prudence when it comes to making long-term investment decisions to ensure that they do not pass up projects that are valuable but distant in time.[13]

Of course, the most obvious examples of inalienability are found in government-managed and not-for-profit businesses. The next section deals with this type of organizational structure.

MANAGING IN THE NOT-FOR-PROFIT ORGANIZATION

For analytical purposes, let us dichotomize companies into two types. The first we can call the **private company**, and the second the **not-for-profit company**. These distinctions are specifically *not* meant to refer to the issue of whether the company wishes to make a lot of money or not. Instead, this is an organizational lexicon designed to relate whether there are well-defined and marketable residual claims to the proceeds of the business venture. A few examples should suffice to demonstrate the distinction. Most large American corporations use the private format. Here the owners of the company are known by name and listed with the company. Shares of stock are issued denoting the particular rights of the indi-

---

[11] In Chapter 5, the section Manipulating the Price of a Capital Good contains a numerical example in which the managers manipulate the cash flows over time in this way.

[12] See "A Rare Look at the Very, Very Rich," *Fortune,* October 12, 1987, p. 127.

[13] They might also hold life insurance on these senior executives.

vidual who is the properly registered owner. Typically, these shares can be sold through well-organized markets without seeking the permission of any other person inside or outside the company. General Motors, IBM, and EXXON are prominent examples of this organizational format. The owners have *private* rights to the company.[14] It bears noting that ownership of a company is a nebulous thing.

As an aside, we have been saying that the holders of the common stock are the owners of the company. In reality they only own the common stock and whatever rights go with it—dividends and the like. The point is that in more sophisticated models of the firm than we explore here, the notion of the owner of a company is discarded, and the analysis focuses on the specific contractual rights and responsibilities among the holders of common stock, debt holders, owners of preferred stock, employees, managers, senior managers, consultants, contractors, subcontractors, and all the other individuals who make up what we so casually call the firm. Having made this point, we must leave it for other times and places. It lies outside the scope of this book. Just as physics keeps looking deeper and deeper inside the molecule, economics is forever peering deeper inside the firm.

Returning to our base discussion, in contrast to what we are calling the private organizational form or the private company, a host of companies do not have well-defined, prespecified residual claimants to the cash flows of the enterprise. These companies are called not-for-profits. Examples include most colleges and universities, virtually all government-run businesses, most charitable associations, and labor unions. Not-for-profits are typically at a distinct disadvantage when it comes to resolving the managerial problems we are talking about in this chapter, and relative to their for-profit counterparts, they must resort to unusual means to survive. Why is this so?

We have already highlighted many of the explanations in the previous discussions, but let us review and expand upon the reasons here. First, solutions to the incentive problem are fewer and more costly for the not-for-profit than they are for the stock or private company. As we have stressed, it is very hard if not impossible to use some of the carrot motivational techniques with a not-for-profit company. The use of stock bonuses, stock ownership, and stock options is precluded by definition. This means that not-for-profit companies have to use alternative and presumably more expensive methods to motive the senior managers and junior workers.

As we have discussed, myopia, or the horizon problem, can be serious in any organization, especially when actions today have repercussions in the future, as they almost always do. However, the methods using common stock to mute the problem in the private firm cannot be used by the not-for-profit businesses. They

---

[14] The reader should not confuse the headings public and private. *Private* here means the rights to the company are the private property of some individual(s). The phrase *public company* is often used to refer to companies whose stock is publicly traded. In this latter lexicon, when a company is private, its stock is not offered for sale to the public. So get this straight: The private companies we are talking about here can be publicly traded or privately traded. This dichotomy only refers to the manner of stock transactions. The one we are focusing our attention on here describes the organizational question of whether stock even exists or not.

must resort to other, presumably more costly and less effective, methods. What might these be?

As we have noted about Japanese enterprises, not-for-profit businesses can use long-term employment, tenure if you will, to give workers and managers a long-term horizon. This implies that labor union bosses will serve long terms compared to their private counterparts; the average term length of the president of the United Auto Workers should exceed the average term length of the presidents of GM, Ford, Chrysler, and the like. The union chief's lengthy sinecure works to make him consider the long-term ramifications of his decisions. The longer the leaders expect to stay in office, the longer their decision horizon. Thus, we should not be surprised when the presidents of major American unions and universities serve what seem to us mere mortals as interminable terms. Once the head of a union is empowered, the members want that person to think he will be there for an extremely long time so that he will be more inclined to take all the future consequences of his actions into account at decision time. The same argument holds for university presidents. The students, faculty, and alumni want the president to take a long-run view of the enterprise. Does this line of reasoning help explain the routine reelection and lengthy terms in office of U.S. representatives and senators? If so, what does the argument imply about the current, popular movement to restrict the terms of our congressional representatives?

By a similar line of reasoning, nepotism, especially toward children, should be fostered in not-for-profit organizations more than it is in private companies. Since most parents have strong feelings for their children, when children follow their parents in a not-for-profit enterprise such as a union, the parents' planning horizon is lengthened. Instead of just thinking about their own lifetime within the organization, the parents consider factors that might also influence the well-being of their children. Parents are more likely to consider the future consequences of their behavior today if they expect their children will be impacted by the decision in the future. Thus, myopia in decision making is reduced. College sororities and fraternities, the prototypical not-for-profit organizations, bend over backwards to admit legacies, the children of previous members. Presumably, they do this to lengthen the horizon of current members. Giving preferential treatment to legacies induces members to worry about the quality of the organization long after they cease being active.

Many colleges give preferential admission treatment to children of faculty and staff. Again, we imagine that this causes the employees to be more concerned about the long-run viability of the enterprise than they would be if their children went to some other college. In the process, the quality of decisions is superior as the faculty, staff, and administrators become increasingly concerned about the permanent health of the school, eschewing the attitude, "Why should I worry about what happens to the school after I'm gone or retired" and instead taking the position, "I should worry about the long-run consequences of the decisions we make today because they will likely affect my kid's welfare even after I have left or retired." Thus, something as simple as the institution of nepotism can have important managerial implications. It bears noting that the not-for-profit enterprise *must* resort to these nonfinancial incentive schemes, while the privately organized business only has to use them when the financial alternatives do not seem to work well or are expensive to implement. In all cases, the private firm has incentive options foreclosed to the not-for-profit organization.

Given that the not-for-profit organizational form has a harder time coping with the incentive and horizon problems, why do some firms opt for that format? Two reasons are prominent. First, in many situations it is required by law—for example, the labor union. In addition, it is hard to imagine most charitable firms being run with the private form. Since a lot of revenues to firms such as the United Way, the Salvation Army, the Catholic Church, and the NAACP come via outright donations, the private firm would suffer a distinct disadvantage. Were these concerns private, the owners could abscond with the wealth, simply paying themselves a large dividend. Naturally, donors are aware of this problem, refusing to make substantial gifts unless a system is in place to prevent such malfeasance. Thus, even though the not-for-profit enterprise is typically more costly to manage and more expensive to operate, it is better suited for some lines of business than its private counterpart.

In addition, certain types of team production require special treatment. In those unusual cases in which output is nebulous or abstract, it is extra difficult to measure the marginal product or value of individual workers. One way to deal with this problem is to let cohorts provide appraisals as a cheap by-product of their own work within the organization. Thus, in a medical professional association or an accounting firm, the value of each worker is sometimes difficult to measure. Surely hours billed or patients served are useful, but they are not perfect as they do not account for quality of service. Thus, one way that professional associations (and universities) cope with this problem is to use peer review as a means of evaluating and rewarding performance. But then it becomes important to ensure the quality of the review process, and one way to do this is to make the reviewers partial residual claimants to the business. In other words, the workers have to become partial owners of a sort.

This helps us understand, in part, why some professional associations and universities are not organized with alienable residual claims. The senior workers must have an incentive to perform high-quality peer appraisal. This can be accomplished by making the workers residual claimants to the business, but for this to work their shares or rights can not be liquidated without knowledge or permission of the other workers. Typically, this is accomplished by a partnership agreement or a simple rule that the rights cannot be sold (as it is within the university or labor union).

We close this section with a discussion of worker participation in management. In the minds of many people, there are widely and strongly held views that effective management requires worker participation. The casual argument says that when workers believe that their opinions are important, they feel more like an integral part of the team, and they respond by working harder and more carefully. This argument makes economic sense as far as it goes, but it specifically does not imply that workers have to actually vote or decide important prerogatives. What the argument says is that workers must have a voice and an input in the decision-making process. The main point of the preceding sections has been to demonstrate that responsibility is vital to ensure high-quality decisions. This does not mean that workers are stupid and their advice and counsel should be disregarded. Quite the contrary, production line workers are often in position, by the very nature of their jobs, to have access to information not cheaply or routinely known to their superiors. In this situation, it would be foolhardy to ignore the ideas and suggestions of subordinates. But, by the same token, the junior employees do not have access to other vital information that may be important in making a good decision. Worse yet, junior employees often do not face the right incentives to make them properly account for all the relevant economic factors crucial to making a quality decision. For instance, we have just gone through a long discussion of the incentive and horizon problems. Surely these become increasingly severe as one moves down the production chain to the base of the hierarchy.

In a nutshell, to say that workers should participate in management does not mean that they have to make the ultimate decision. Instead, it suggests that their voice should be heard, not only because this makes them feel more important to the company, thus more likely to work hard, but also because they often have cheap access to economically relevant information. The managerial theory being presented here suggests that astute managers will listen to their workers with a keen ear but then retire to their offices to make the final decisions. The contention of the property rights theory of the firm is that diffuse decision making dulls an individual's incentive to make good decisions. Thus, concentrating responsibility creates accountability.

It would be incorrect to conclude that the not-for-profit organizational form is always inferior to its private counterpart as an organizational structure. We have already observed how charitable organizations have an advantage being organized in the not-for-profit mold. Therefore, not-for-profits must find unusual ways to cope with team production, incentive, and horizon problems. The successful ones may provide insights useful even within private firms. Nevertheless, government and not-for-profit firms are usually less efficient with higher costs of operation and lower quality service than their private counterparts. Read the accompanying story from the *New York Times* which reports how the conversion from government production to private production has resulted in "big cost savings and better service."

THE ROLE OF MANAGERS IN TEAM PRODUCTION

Managers play a critical role in situations where team production is present.[15] Recall the story at the beginning of the section Team Production about the coolies who had *hired* an overseer to prevent malfeasance within their own ranks. As we have discussed now in some detail, when team production is present, the output of the production process is something very much like a common access good. It is difficult to know who owns what because it is hard to know who produced what. One of the roles of mangers is to help prevent the tragedy of the commons when this happens. How do managers help? Their contributions are numerous.

---

[15] You are recommended to the classic work of Armen Alchian and Harold Demsetz, "Production, Information Costs, and Economic Organization," *American Economic Review*, 62(5), June 1972, pp. 777–95 for a detailed exploration of the role of managers in team production.

MANAGEMENT IN THE NOT-FOR-PROFIT SECTOR

Twenty years ago, management was a dirty word for those involved in nonprofit organizations. It meant business, and nonprofits prided themselves on being free of the taint of commercialism and above such sordid considerations as the bottom line. Now most of them have learned that nonprofits need management even more than business does, precisely because they lack the discipline of the bottom line. The nonprofits are, of course, still dedicated to "doing good." But they also realize that good intentions are no substitute for organization and leadership, for accountability, performance, and results. Those require management and that, in turn, begins with the organization's mission. . . .

"The businesses I work with start their planning with financial returns," says one well-known CEO who sits on both business and nonprofit boards. "The nonprofits start with the performance of their mission."

Starting with the mission and its requirements may be the first lesson business can learn from successful nonprofits. It focuses the organization on action. It defines the specific strategies needed to attain the crucial goals. It creates a disciplined organization. It alone can prevent the most common degenerative disease of organizations, especially large ones: splintering their always limited resources on things that are "interesting" or look "profitable" rather than concentrating them on a very small number of productive efforts.

The best nonprofits devote a great deal of thought to defining their organization's mission. They avoid sweeping statements full of good intentions and focus, instead, on objectives that have clear-cut implications for the work their members perform—staff and volunteers both. The Salvation Army's goal, for example, is to turn society's rejects—alcoholics, criminals, derelicts—into citizens. The Girl Scouts help youngsters become confident, capable young women who respect themselves and other people. . . .

A well-defined mission serves as a constant reminder of the need to look outside the organization not only for "customers" but also for measures of success. The temptation to content oneself with the "goodness of our cause"—and thus to substitute good intentions for results—always exists in nonprofit organizations.

Reprinted by permission of Harvard Business Review. An excerpt from "What Business Can Learn from Non Profits," by Peter F. Drucker, 4(July/August 1989), 88–93.

First, managers can, by the examination of the levels of inputs of the workers, make a determination about outputs. That is, they monitor inputs and meter rewards. This is obviously not a perfect system, but it has its advantages in a host of situations, specifically those in which there is a close correspondence between observable input effort and output. When five people grab a rope in a tug of war, those groaning and sweating are likely pulling their weight. Those who look relaxed and whose muscles are not bulging need prodding. This is the role of the manager.

Second, to ensure that the managers do a competent job, they must have some incentive. One natural so-called incentive-compatible way to accomplish this is for them to supply other inputs necessary for production, such as raw

Privatizing Government Services

From Phoenix to Chicago to Newark, city administrators are inviting private companies to help provide public services—and swearing by the results: big cost savings and better service. . . .

Mayor David N. Dinkins has a group of labor and business leaders examining the issue of what is called privatization. . . . City Council Speaker Peter F. Vallone proposed turning some city services over to private enterprise. . . .

The estimates of how much can be saved by contracting with private companies . . . vary widely from 10 to 40 percent. E. S. Savas, a management professor from Baruch college . . . said the average tends to hover around 25 percent.

Examples of local governments that have turned to the private sector are plentiful. Los Angeles County recently contracted management of five small airports; Chicago is now contracting vehicle towing and parking-ticket collection; Phoenix has long fostered competition between its private and public work forces for ambulance service, street-sweeping and garbage collection.

Those who have looked at the prospects for New York say they believe the city could save between $2 billion and $4 billion a year. . . .

While the supporters and detractors of privatization often do battle in the political sphere, the reality is that New York city has already turned to the private sector for many of its services.

In fixing up Bryant Park, for instance, the city enlisted the help of private enterprise. The city has private companies operating many of its properties, like its seaplane base, through leases. And New York makes extensive use of the most classic example of privatization: contracting public services.

Private companies reconstruct all of the city's streets, light all of its street lamps and provide janitorial services to many of the city's public buildings. And a large part of the city's social services, like foster care and drug-treatment programs, are provided through contracts. . . . All told, the city directly spends about $5 billion on private contractors each year, or roughly one-sixth of its budget. . . .

The issue that divides supporters and detractors is whether contracting can be done effectively in a city as large and politically intricate as New York. As things stand now, about 60 percent of the city's contracts are in the social-services area. Yet this area is among the hardest to measure or monitor and therefore does not lend itself well to successful privatization. . . .

Sarah Bartlett, "Looking to Save in New York: City Jobs, Outside Workers," New York Times, July 7, 1991, pp. 1 and 8. Copyright © 1991 by The New York Times Company. Reprinted by permission.

materials and capital. In this approach to the firm, the workers have an incentive problem within their ranks because it is difficult to assign the marginal products of each person. Managers come to their rescue to monitor inputs, counsel shirking, and dispense the wages. They bring with them the other inputs necessary for production. Managers put their wealth at risk, which acts as a carrot to perform their monitoring function properly. This helps us understand why management and ownership often go hand in hand.

Third, managers are often left as the residual claimants to the production process. They contract with workers, paying them fixed wages, more or less. They also contract with all the other input suppliers on a fixed fee basis. They organize the production process, reducing or eliminating the team production problem along the way, selling the output when finished, and keeping any amounts left over at the end. This too acts to motivate the managers properly. In the process, they assume many of the financial risks that go with production. Typically, they pass some or all of this along to others, debtors and shareholders, via capital markets. Therein lies the essence of the property rights theory of the firm.

TOPICS TO REVIEW

These are topics that you should feel comfortable with before you leave this chapter. If you cannot write out a clear and concise sentence or paragraph explaining the topic after you have worked on the study problems, you should reread the relevant section of the text.

Team Production

Nexus of Contracts

Yugoslavian Firm

Alienability, Long Run, and Managerial Myopia

Externality

Incentive Problem

Horizon Problem

Inalienability Problem

Not-for-Profit Organizational Form

STUDY PROBLEMS

1. Some universities charge a fixed fee for a semester regardless of the number of classes taken. Others charge students based on the number of credit hours registered. Which type school is more likely to have a rule restricting the number of hours a student may take in any one semester? On average and other things being the same, at which type school do students take the larger credit loads?

2. Lease contracts in large shopping malls generally have a number of interesting characteristics. For example, the owner of the mall usually receives a specified percentage of the total sales of each of the stores in the mall as a portion of the rent. Given that it is costly to monitor this arrangement—that is, it is cheaper to specify a fixed fee per month as the rental price, there must be some economic advantage to this contractual provision. What forces might be at work to make this technique advantageous to the mall owner and/or renters? Does your answer help explain why the malls have large commons

inside and out? Expand your answer to explain why most mall operators contract for mall and parking cleaning, but they charge back the stores for this service. Why does the operator not leave cleaning and snow removal to the individual stores in the mall? Or, why, given that the operator performs these chores, does the contract have a charge back system? Why not just include the average cost of cleaning in the rental rate charged up front?

3. In most large shopping malls built today, stores are individually owned and operated. There is no legal reason why the mall developer does not run the entire operation, hiring managers for each section in the mall rather than renting space to private store owners. Similarly, the cosmetic counters in some large stores are run by private, independent operators. In some grocery stores, shelf space is rented to certain sellers. Why is production organized this way? What are the advantages of leasing shelf space, counter space, and store space, as contrasted with outright ownership?

4. The newest hotels in the United States are different from old hotels in this country. For one thing, new hotels have many shops in the facility: clothing stores, jewelry stores, flower shops, coffee shops, and the like. Old hotels often seem to rely on neighboring, unrelated firms to provide these services. Can you explain this evolution? Predict some of the features of the contracts between the hotel owner and the owner or manager of the in-house shops.

SUGGESTED READINGS

This is a long list. I have marked with an asterisk a few of the articles that most managerial economists would call classics or those that provide especially cogent summaries of a particular area.

Aoki, Nasahiko, Gustafsson, Bo, and Williamson, Oliver E., eds. *The Firm as a Nexus of Treaties.* London: Sage, 1990.

*Alchian, Armen and Demsetz, Harold. "Production, Information Costs, and Economic Organization." *American Economic Review* 62(5) (June 1972):777–95.

*Alchian, Armen A. and Woodward, Susan. "The Firm Is Dead; Long Live the Firm: A Review of Oliver E. Williamson's *Institutions of Capitalism*." *The Journal of Economic Literature* 26(1) (March 1988):365–79.

Barney, Jay B. and Ouchi, William G., eds. *Organizational Economics.* San Francisco: Jossey-Bass, 1986.

Barzel, Yoram. *Economic Analysis of Property Rights.* Cambridge: Cambridge University Press, 1989.

Berman, Katrina V. and Berman, Mathew D. "An Empirical Test of the Theory of the Labor-Managed Firm." *Journal of Comparative Economics* 13(2) (June 1989):281–300.

Caves, Douglas and Christensen, Laurits. "The Relative Efficiency of Public and Private Firms in a Competitive Environment: The Case of Canadian Railroads." *Journal of Political Economy* 88 (October 1980):958–76.

Cheung, Steven N. S. "The Contractual Nature of the Firm." *The Journal of Law and Economics* 26(1) (April 1983):1–22.

Clarkson, Kenneth. "Some Implications of Property Rights in Hospital Management." *The Journal of Law and Economics* 15(2) (October 1972):363–84.

*Coase, Ronald. "The Nature of the Firm." *Economica* 4 (November 1937):386–405.

Crain, Mark and Zardkoohi, Asghar. "A Test of the Property-Rights Theory of the Firm:

Water Utilities in the United States." *The Journal of Law and Economics* 21(2) (October 1978):395–408.

De Alessi, Louis. "The Economics of Property Rights: A Review of the Evidence." *Research in Law and Economics* 2 (1980):1–47.

DeFusco, Richard A., Johnson, Robert R., and Zorn, Thomas S. "The Effect of Executive Stock Option Plans on Stockholders and Bondholders." *Journal of Finance* 45(2) (June 1990):617–27.

Drucker, Peter F. "What Business Can Learn from Nonprofits." *Harvard Business Review* 89(4) (July-August 1989):88–93.

Easterbrook, Frank H. "Two Agency-Cost Explanations of Dividends." *American Economic Review* 74(4) (September 1984):157–86.

Fama, Eugene F. "Agency Problems and the Theory of the Firm." *Journal of Political Economy* 88(2) (April 1980):288–307.

Fama, Eugene F. and Jensen, Michael C. "Separation of Ownership and Control." *The Journal of Law and Economics* 26(2) (June 1983a):301–26.

Fama, Eugene F. and Jensen, Michael C. "Agency Problems and Residual Claims." *The Journal of Law and Economics* 26(2) (June 1983b):327–50.

Fama, Eugene F. and Jensen, Michael C. "Organizational Forms and Investment Decisions." *Journal of Financial Economics* 14 (1985):101–19.

Frech, H. E., III. "The Property Rights Theory of the Firm: Some Evidence from the U.S. Nursing Home Industry." *Zeitschrift fur die gesamte Staatswissenchaft* 141(1) (March 1985):146–66.

*Furubotn, Eirik and Pejovich, Svetozar. *The Economics of Property Rights.* Cambridge, MA: Ballenger Press, 1974.

Jensen, Michael C. "Agency Costs of Free Cash Flow, Corporate Finance and Takeovers." *American Economic Review* 76 (May 1986):323–29.

Jensen, Michael C. "Takeovers: Their Causes and Consequences." *Journal of Economic Perspectives* 2 (1988):21–48.

Jensen, Michael C. "Eclipse of the Public Corporation." *Harvard Business Review* 89(5) (September-October 1989):61–75.

*Jensen, Michael C. and Meckling, William H. "Theory of the Firm: Managerial Behavior, Agency Cost and Ownership Structure." *Journal of Financial Economics* 3(4) (October 1976):305–60.

*Jensen, Michael C. and Meckling, William H. "Rights and Production Functions: An Application to Labor-Managed Firms and Codetermination." *Journal of Business* 52(4) (1979):469–505.

Jensen, Michael C. and Murphy, Kevin. "Performance Pay and Top-Management Incentives." *Journal of Political Economy* 98(2) (April 1990):225–64.

Jensen, Michael C. and Ruback, Richard, eds. *Symposium on the Structure and Governance of Enterprise. Journal of Financial Economics* 27(2) Parts I and II (October 1990).

Kanter, Rosabeth M. "The New Managerial Work." *Harvard Business Review* 89 (November-December 1989):85–92.

Kirby, Michael G. and Albon, Robert P. "Property Rights, Regulation and Efficiency: A Further Comment on Australia's Two-Airline Policy." *Economic Record* 61 (June 1985):535–39.

Lindsay, Cotton M. "A Theory of Government Enterprise." *Journal of Political Economy* 84(5) (October 1976):1061–78.

McChesney, Fred S. "Team Production, Monitoring, and Profit Sharing in Law Firms: An Alternative Hypothesis." *Journal of Legal Studies* 11(2) (June 1982):379–93.

McCormick, Robert E. and Meiners, Roger E. "University Governance: A Property Rights Perspective." *The Journal of Law and Economics* 31(2) (October 1988):423–42.

Manne, Henry G. "The Political Economy of Modern Universities." In *Education in a Free Society,* ed. Anne H. Burleigh, pp.165–205. Indianapolis, IN: Liberty Press, 1973.

*Manne, Henry G. *Economics of Legal Relationships.* New York: West Publishing Co., 1975

Mason, Kenneth. "Four Ways to Overpay Yourself Enough." *Harvard Business Review* 88(4) (July-August 1988):69–74.

Peltzman, Sam. "Pricing in Public and Private Enterprises: Electric Utilities in the United States." *The Journal of Law and Economics* 14 (April 1971):109–47.

Rogers, T. J. "No Excuses Management." *Harvard Business Review* 90(4) (July-August 1990):84–103.

Sirkin, Harold and Stalk, George Jr. "Fix the Process, Not the Problem." *Harvard Business Review* 90(4) (July-August 1990):26–35.

Smith, Clifford W., Jr. and Warner, Jerold B. "On Financial Contracting: An Analysis of Bond Covenants." *Journal of Financial Economics* 9 (1979):117–61.

Stewart, G. Bennett, III. "Remaking the Public Corporation from Within." *Harvard Business Review* 90(4) (July-August 1990):126–37.

Williamson, Oliver, E. *Markets and Hierarchies: Analysis and Antitrust Implications.* New York: The Free Press, 1975.

Williamson, Oliver E. "Organization Form, Residual Claimants, and Corporate Control." *The Journal of Law and Economics* 26(2) (June 1983):351–66.

*Williamson, Oliver E. *The Economic Institutions of Capitalism.* New York: The Free Press, 1985.

Williamson, Oliver E. *Economic Organization: Firms, Markets and Policy Control.* New York: New York University Press, 1986.

Williamson, Oliver E. "Transaction Cost Economics: The Comparative Contracting Perspective." *Journal of Economic Behavior and Organization* 8(4) (December 1987):617–25.

Zerbe, Richard O., ed. *Research in Law and Economics, Volume 12.* Greenwich, CT: JAI Press, 1989.

SUGGESTED SOLUTIONS TO SELECTED STUDY PROBLEMS

The following is only a *suggested* solution to the study problem presented at the end of this chapter. The suggestion here puts heavy emphasis on analysis rather than a single correct answer. Since most managerial problems do not fall into neat little boxes, the individual characteristics of the problems that you encounter on the job will typically mandate a solution using the principles developed here and in other courses. Memorizing this solution will not make you a good manager; learning the *principles* detailed here will help make you a better manager.

4. For a variety of reasons, new hotels seem to want to offer shopping to their guests. Perhaps it is crime in the streets, or the absence of reasonable quality guaranties available to itinerant customers in neighboring shops or some other reason. But hotels are hotels, and they are not necessarily well versed in managing retail clothing, jewelry, or gift shops. Thus, we expect that they decentralize these operations by getting independent owners to rent the space and run the small shops. Having the shops inside the hotels allows for the internalization of a host of externalities via contract. For instance, with the stores inside the hotel, the problems of weather and crime are easily mitigated. Hours of operation are easier to contract because it is cheaper to observe whether the shop is living by the terms of the contract.

CHAPTER
14

ADDITIONAL TOPICS IN PROPERTY RIGHTS AND THE ECONOMICS OF INFORMATION

INTRODUCTION

This chapter explores a number of topics in property rights and information. First we consider the problem of opportunism. Opportunism is an economic problem that presents itself when an individual can exploit the position of another person to expropriate wealth. When anticipated, and it often is, opportunism can be a formidable barrier to economic exchange. We define this problem and investigate some of the solutions to this obstacle. The chapter also addresses the problem of transferring goods within divisions of a company. This is labeled transfer pricing. A number of other incentive issues in property rights are discussed along the way.

OPPORTUNISM

Opportunism is an economic expression for malevolence. It is an action by one party to exploit another party in an economic situation that, absent some relation between the parties, the first party would not contemplate. The action may be legal or illegal, and that difference, for our purposes here, is not usually important. It is especially important to understand opportunism in the context of contractual relations between business partners. The potential for opportunism creates the necessity to control it; contracting is one way, but others also exist. In this section, we set about to understand opportunism and the institutions that accomplished managers use to control it.

Consider the following example. Suppose Midwest Electric produces electricity in several states. A primary input to this process is coal. Further imagine that Midwest has decided to make a long-term contract with Illmin Coal Company to supply five plants in Wisconsin with coal. The contract is exclusive. That is, Illmin agrees to sell all the coal that it mines to Midwest, and Midwest agrees not to purchase coal for these five plants from any other mine. The contract is to last for 10 years, and the price is specified as $20 per ton. What opportunistic forces are put in motion by this business relation?

Both parties must now rely importantly on the other for success and maybe even survival. Let's create a situation to see how opportunism might really wreak havoc. Suppose the miners at two of Illmin's facilities go out on strike demanding higher wages. What course of action might the managers of Illmin take (that they would not otherwise consider), if they did not have the contract with Midwest Electric—that is, what kind of opportunism is possible? Imagine the following: Instead of negotiating in good faith with the union, the officials at Illmin Coal stall the proceedings, and after a few weeks, as coal stocks dwindle at Midwest's plants, they call the managers at Midwest and complain that the union is being very tough in its negotiation stance. Further, they tell them that in all likelihood unless Illmin grants the "exorbitant wage increases its union is demanding," Illmin will not be able to continue supplying the coal required to fuel the five Midwest plants. After some deliberations, the two agree that if Midwest were to unilaterally change the contract and agree to pay not $20 but $22 per ton, then Illmin could settle its labor dispute and keep the mines operating.

Gloating with the extra $2 per ton they will now receive, the opportunistic managers at Illmin offer the union some portion of the extra money, and the union agrees to go back to work, richer in the bargain. It does not really matter for the point to be made, but the union and the managers at Illmin could even have cooked up the whole dispute as a way of extracting a higher price from Midwest. Since this strategy is likely illegal, it behooves both parties to create a real labor disturbance and simply stand pat on their respective positions as a way of convincing the electric company of the seriousness of the problem.[1]

Under what circumstances will this opportunism actually work? First and most important, Midwest must not have an alternative—a readily available supply of coal at less than $22 per ton. Well, how can Illmin ensure that this is the case? Suppose the going spot market price for coal is $22.50 per ton, but the 10-year contract price is $21. Then, in the initial stages of the *original* contract negotiation, Illmin astutely agrees to sell at what appears to be a lower than market price, $20 instead of $21. Midwest Electric thinks this is a very good deal, but soon after the ink dries, the union at Illmin calls the work stoppage. As we have shown, this can lead to Illmin's actually getting $22 for its coal under long-term contract instead of the prevailing long-term market price of $21, and Midwest has little choice but to pay $22 because the current spot price is even higher. Naturally, Midwest could look for another long-term supplier, but for the sake of this example just imagine that negotiating such a contract takes considerable time, too long to be a viable alternative. So, we see that the exclusive supply contract that does not allow Midwest to buy from other parties creates the opportunistic situation for Illmin to exploit. Naturally, had Midwest signed long-term contracts with three or four other coal mines, the cut-off threat from Illmin would have been empty and ignored by the executives at the electricity company.

Before we leave this example, let's explore it in more detail. Note that the potential for opportunistic behavior is symmetric. This means that after they have negotiated the coal contract with Illmin Coal, Midwest Electric can also try to exploit the situation by trying to get the price lowered. How might it do this? Of course there are many ways, but consider this one. Let's say that the Environmental Protection Agency proposes some new air quality rules that might affect the operation of the five coal-fired power plants. The rules are subject to legal interpretation, but let us suppose that, arguably, Midwest Electric could claim in a court of law that the burning of coal supplied by Illmin required the installation of very expensive, high-technology cleaning devices in the smokestacks. Were this true, then Midwest managers might contact Illmin officials, saying that they were going to break the contract and not buy additional quantities of the dirty coal from Illmin unless Illmin cut the price to $19, which would allow Midwest to afford the new cleaning equipment in its smokestacks. Illmin officials might say, "If you don't buy from us as we contracted, we will take you to court for damages," but the Midwest officials respond by arguing, "We believe that compliance with the EPA standards gives us the legal right to bridge the contract." After consultation with their legal counsel, the officials at Illmin conclude that they are better off to cut the long-term price, rather than fight in court or try and

---

[1] The Clayton Act prohibits this implicit collusion between the union and management at Illmin.

find another buyer. Opportunism, once the contract is in place with Illmin Coal, pays Midwest Electric through lower coal prices.

How can Illmin avoid this situation? There are a number of ways. First, it too can avoid entering into a sole or exclusive sales arrangement. Then, when Midwest tries to renege on the contract, Illmin simply shifts its sales to other markets. This may not always be possible, but it does point out the advantage of having more than one outlet for your products. Alternatively, in situations of this type, reputations often play a very important role. What this means is that exclusive sales arrangements are often made only between business partners who have had a long-standing relationship of mutual trust and respect. Then, the reputations of the parties act to bond them from behaving opportunistically when they might. Of course, the advantage to each of having this reputation is that the buyers get to purchase more cheaply because their sellers do not fret, contract, or otherwise worry about being opportunistically exploited. Similarly, the sellers receive a higher net price because they do not spend resources trying to prevent ex post contractual opportunism.

Consider the story reported in the accompanying box about American Airlines' purchase of some computer equipment. Note that the person in charge of purchasing specifically and consciously decided to buy from three vendors even when from a technological, compatibility point of view, it would have been better to have just one. With multiple suppliers, the potential for opportunism is muffled.

An important thing to realize at this juncture is that if both parties are smart, they will be inclined to *anticipate the onset of opportunism*. If they do, then both will seek ways to preclude it from ever coming to pass. As we have just stressed, this can be done in many ways, and that is the point. Opportunism is primarily a

---

VERTICAL INTEGRATION

AMERICAN AIRLINES PURCHASES PCs

American Airlines last week said that it plans to buy more than 50,000 PC systems based on the 80386 and 80386SX, including some unannounced products from AT&T.

Selected systems include the IBM PS/2 Model 55 SX and Model 70, the Tandy 4000 SX, and as yet unannounced systems from AT&T. . . . Each of the three vendors will supply both diskless and disk-equipped SX models to American.

Hesitant to mix vendors in its widely distributed network, American tested SX workstations to be sure of interchangeable integration in offices, air terminals, and travel agencies.

"We don't want to depend on any one vendor," Bill Jewell (managing director of American's communications engineering) said. *"We chose three strong suppliers to keep competition among them and make sure they support us."*

Reported in *INFOWORLD,* a weekly PC magazine, June 26, 1989, p. 6. Emphasis added.

problem if not properly anticipated, and as we look about, we observe many arrangements and institutions and contractual provisions explicitly designed to erase the potential gains from opportunism. The next section discusses this point in more detail.

Vertical Integration and Opportunism

We saw in Chapter 12, Internalizing the Externality and the Coase Theorem, how horizontal merger can sometimes be used to internalize an externality between firms. Similarly, vertical integration can help ameliorate the opportunistic problem that exists between contract partners.[2] Let us set up another example to illustrate this. Consider the publication of daily newspapers, and for the sake of the demonstration, picture the reporting and editing of the paper being done by one company, called the publisher, that then subcontracts the actual printing of the paper to a firm we call the printer. You can see some advantages to this arrangement. The job of gathering the news is quite different from the technical job of etching the words on paper, and thus it is easy to believe that managers of one enterprise might have little expertise in the other. So this new idea emerges whereby newspapers are written and edited by one company but printed by another. To make the example easier to visualize, suppose the printing presses are located proximate to the building where the writers and editors work. Let's say they are best served by being next door to each other. Does this environment create opportunistic behavior? It might.

Assume the printer and the publisher of the paper have a written contract to print the paper for $0.10 a copy, subject to all sorts of provisions about length and color. The contract specifies timeliness and other quality dimensions such as the type of paper and ink, but the contract cannot completely eliminate the potential for opportunism. Let's say the owner of the presses calls on the publisher of the paper late one afternoon with a big pile of accounting reports and says, "Here, look at these things. I am not covering my costs, and printing your paper is costing me too much money. I don't see how I can go on much longer at this rate." Naturally, this is easy to fake even if it is not true, because the publisher most likely knows very little about printing and has little knowledge about the costs of paper, ink, or presses, much less the proper wages of the operators. So the printing press operator continues, "Unless I can get you to pay me eleven cents per paper, I'm going to have to close shop and sell my business." For the moment, suppose the publisher believes this story; it might even be true. The publisher is caught between a rock and a hard place. She has little choice but to agree to the higher price. She is the victim of opportunism or, more accurately, not anticipating opportunism.

---

[2] The diligent student is well served by a careful reading of the important contribution to managerial economics made by Benjamin Klein, Robert Crawford, and Armen Alchian in their famous article, "Vertical Integration, Appropriable Rents, and the Competitive Contracting Process," *The Journal of Law and Economics,* 21, October 1978, 297–326.

Since the daily publication of a newspaper is crucial to its long-term success, the publisher is really over a barrel, and unless she has properly prepared herself for this situation, she has almost no choice but to pay the higher printing bills. Getting the paper out on time is absolutely vital to readers and advertisers. Thus a break in production might prove devastating to a newspaper publisher. If the printer is truly smart, he will choose a price to tell the publisher that the publisher will accept. That is, he should quote a price that, in face of the alternatives, the publisher agrees to pay. In the process, the printer extracts virtually all the profits of the publisher, leaving her almost indifferent between continuing her business or quitting.

It is natural to ask, Why doesn't the publisher take the printer to court for breach of contract? The answer to that question is multifaceted. First, court action can be a viable option in some situations, but courts take time and money, and in this particular situation, time is of the essence. Second, courts must interpret contracts, which means that the publisher may not win in all cases. Third, with a skillful accountant and lawyer, the printer may appear or even actually be close to bankruptcy. There are many ways to lose money; one is to overpay certain key individuals. Thus, even when the printing business is making a good return, it can be legally siphoned by the owners to look insolvent. This makes the bankruptcy threat real, muting the court challenge. If the printing company is poor, then the publisher may not be able to recoup damages even when they are legally owed and court ordered.

Before we continue, consider the symmetry of opportunism in this particular situation.[3] Suppose when the printer pulls out his accounting reports, the publisher retorts with an even larger stack of numbers purporting to demonstrate the large sums of money she is losing on the publishing end of the newspaper business. This takes the printer by surprise, and he is nonplussed when the publisher says, "Unless you cut your printing rates to nine cents per paper, we will have to go out of business by month's end." Now, the printer is over a barrel. He has invested substantial sums in printing presses next door to the newspaper, and if the newspaper closes shop, he will have to move. This will impose significant expense and hardship. So, after much thought, the printer agrees to the price reduction. As before, court action is a possibility, but in many cases this line of redress is ineffective or too costly. Opportunism by the publisher has severely damaged the wealth of the printing business.

In an experienced world, both publisher and printer will anticipate the potential for opportunism created by their contract, and both are inclined to seek a solution that prevents the preceding stories from ever coming to pass. One way to achieve this end is for the two companies to vertically integrate. Then, instead of exploiting each other, the owner of the new business would only be robbing Peter to pay Paul. Raising the price of printing makes the printing operation

---

[3] Even though both examples so far in this text have had the potential for opportunism, this does not mean that all contracts have that characteristic. They may or may not.

appear more profitable and the publishing division look less lucrative, but the joint or sum profits are unaltered. The gain from opportunism has vanished.[4]

What is the point of this exercise? It is intended to help you understand when it is important to perform some functions inside the firm as opposed to hiring independent contractors or other separate firms. When opportunism is hard to control and when it might be potentially devastating to the bottom line, managers have to consider whether it would not be better to bring the operation in question inside their own firm so that they might better prevent the onset of opportunism. For instance, we could imagine an assembly line run not by a host of people all working for the same master but by independent contractors each selling her wares to the next person on the line after her chores are accomplished. In fact Winchester Repeating Arms Company and other large and important companies used to work more or less just like this:

> Under the system of inside contracting, the management of a firm provided floor space and machinery, supplied raw material and working capital, and arranged for the sale of the finished product. The gap between raw material and finished product, however, was filled not by paid employees arranged in the descending hierarchy so dear to the hearts of personnel experts but by contractors, to whom the production job was delegated. They hired their own employees, supervised the work process, and received a piece rate from the company for completed goods. The income of a contractor consisted of the difference between his wage bill and his sales to the company, plus the day pay he earned as an employee himself.[5]

Individualizing the assembly line has a host of factors in its favor. For instance, the incentive to shirk is erased. However, enormous chances for opportunism are created. Let's see why by exploring one of the fundamental factors behind opportunism.

Opportunism or the potential for opportunism is most prominent when there are fixed assets in place. If the potentially exploitable person has options for his products, then a contracting partner's attempt to renege and to demand more favorable trading conditions is an empty threat. Thus, the greater the extent of fixed investments in place, the more the firm needs to be concerned about the

---

[4] This is not absolutely correct. Vertical integration only creates a situation in which it is possible to erase the gains from opportunism. If the two divisions within the vertically integrated enterprise, printing and publishing, are kept separate for accounting purposes, and if the managers within the respective divisions are rewarded based on their own separate profits, the opportunistic incentive persists. The two managers are still inclined to try and extract the profits of the other division. What vertical integration does is create the incentive for one person, the owner/manager of the new, joint enterprise, to eliminate the incentive to act opportunistically. Obviously, he can accomplish this in many ways. But one plan that would have to be considered would simply pay the division managers a salary independent of profits. Of course, that creates an incentive problem that would have to be dealt with. Nevertheless, the vertically integrated firm has options for controlling opportunism that are not cheaply replicated between two independent operations.

[5] John Buttrick, "The Inside Contract System," *The Journal of Economic History*, 12, Summer 1952, 205.

problem that it might be victimized by opportunism. When resources are malleable and movable, it will be difficult for some other party to try and extort them; the owner can simply relocate and shift them into alternative production when the trading partner tries to renege after the contract is in place. For instance, in the example of the printer and the publisher that we have been studying, suppose that the printing press is mobile. It is in a large tractor trailer truck. Then it will be very difficult for the publisher to opportunistically make a credible threat to try and lower the price of printing. The printing press operator will simply take his portable press to the next town and the next job. It is the fixed investment that creates the opportunistic situation. It is only when an asset owner is tied to a particular site, either physically or economically, that he must be concerned about potential ex post contractual opportunistic behavior. Of course, this happens all the time.

For instance, let us change the printing/publishing example just a little bit. Instead of a newspaper, suppose the publisher prints textbooks or romance novels. Does this alter the potential for opportunistic behavior? Yes, in several ways. First, when it comes to printing these types of books, timeliness of production is much less important. A day or even a week here or there is not very significant, much less an hour or so. This means that there is no reason for the printing presses to be physically proximate to the publishing house. The presses can be located virtually anywhere, even out of the country if need be. Since location is not vital, printers do not have to worry about being left high and dry by any one publisher. If a publisher tries to balk at a contracted price, the printer simply refuses to go along, given that he does not have to move his presses in order to sell his services to other publishers. Thus, and this is important, the *publisher* has *less* incentive to engage in opportunistic practices because she knows the printer will simply ignore her; it does not pay the publisher to dream up schemes that she might use to get the printer to cut price. The problem is muted by the absence of site specific investments. Moreover, since there is little reason for the printer to be physically close to the publisher now, he can contract with *multiple* publishers to print books. This virtually erases the potential for opportunism on the part of the publisher. When the printer is selling to multiple publishers, the loss of any one of them is not nearly so serious a threat. Both factors work to eliminate the potential for opportunism, and thus the incentive for book publishers to vertically integrate with the printing process is much less than in the newspaper business. Book publishers may own their own printing presses, but if they do it is not for the same reasons that newspaper publishers do.

The bilateral opportunism that exists between a newspaper publisher and printer is also erased in the case of the book printing. If the book printer calls on the book publisher with a sad story about costs and profits and demands a higher price than previously negotiated, the book publisher simply ignores the plea because getting the book out instantly is typically not an issue. Sufficient time almost always exists for her to find another printer. The printer's threat is empty and not credible, and hence the printer is not inclined to waste his time making it.

Where do magazines fit into this story? Magazine printing is less timely than newspaper typesetting, but more timely than book printing. Thus the potential for opportunism between printer and publisher lies somewhere between the two.

As an empirical matter then, we should expect more magazine publishers to print their own copy than book publishers, but a smaller fraction of magazine publishers will own their own presses than newspaper publishers. External production of magazines is viable when the magazine and the printer have a long-standing relation and when timeliness is not critical. Magazines vary as to the content. *Playboy, Cosmopolitan,* and *National Geographic,* all published monthly, contain dated material, but not critically so. According to the theory presented here, these publications are not inclined to actually print their magazines themselves; instead, they rely on printing specialists to perform that function. Other more disposable publications such as *TV Guide, Newsweek,* and *Sports Illustrated* are published weekly and would face more serious problems if the printer threatened a work stoppage or slowdown. This makes it more likely that they print their publications with their own presses. Otherwise, they must find printers with long-standing reputations or some other device to prevent the onset of opportunism.

We close this section with a story from the motion picture/television industry.

> Peter Fischer is a member of Hollywood's new ruling class, and he knows it. He belongs to that cadre of about 25 top writer-producers who have proven that they can create and sustain a hit show week after week. And it's what Fischer and his colleagues do best. . . .
>
> In the process, *the studios are acceding to the writer-producers' demands to be made partners—sometimes equal owners—in the shows they create, instigating a profound restructuring in the ownership and control of prime-time series.* . . .
>
> [W]hen networks specify that certain actors are a necessary condition to picking up a series from a studio, the studio typically offers the actors as much as 10 percent of the program's net profits to sign on. . . .
>
> Consider Columbia's deal with the eccentric but brilliant Ed Weinberger. Sources say that to get Weinberger's *exclusive* services for five years, Columbia has created a new program-production and distribution company, and fueled it with a $36-million cash flow to cover production. Weinberger owns 50 percent of the company, sits on its board, and expects to take home a bare minimum of $15 million. . . . [I]f the company is successful, Columbia plans to either buy Weinberger out or take the company public, for projected proceeds of more than $300 million.
>
> *With last summer's writer's strike apparently a distant memory, the studios speak warmly of their newest business partners.*[6]

This story is interesting for a number of reasons. First, it vividly points out how real the opportunistic problem truly is. Recall the bitter television writer's strike that preceded the new arrangement between writers and producers. It lasted for months, delaying the start of the 1988 fall season by several months. This was very costly to both writers and producers, and both were inclined to seek a solution to prevent its repeat. The argument being made here is that

---

[6] Neal Koch, "TV's New Ruling Class," *Channels: The Business of Communications,* May 1989, pp. 30–36. Emphasis added.

opportunism was one of the root causes of the problem. When the writers worked as independent contractors, selling their scripts to producers under various agreements, the timeliness of production made the producers subject to opportunism as evidenced by the strike. The writers claimed they wanted more money for their scripts or else they would not enter into any new contracts for services. But no contract could be devised or written that would preclude the same situation repeating itself at the end of the existing contracts; or, worse yet, even before the end of the season, the writers might balk at some arcane event that they claim gives them cause to stop supplying scripts. So by vertically integrating the two functions, making the writers part of the production company, the problem becomes remote. The writers are now partial residual claimants to the production process, and it makes no sense for them to go on strike against themselves. It would seem that this new organizational structure would make a future writer's strike a distant possibility.[7]

This example points out just how critical the make, buy, or rent decision can be to the bottom line. Incentive or opportunistic problems play an important if not critical role in determining the proper ownership structure in a lot of cases and in helping us understand important events in U.S. economic history and their implication for managerial decision making.[8]

TRANSFER PRICING

When companies stand in a vertical relation to each other—the output of one is the input to another or a division within one company produces output for another—an interesting pricing problem arises. This pricing goes under the rubric of **transfer pricing** in managerial economics. It is easy to make decisions in this situation that on the surface appear reasonable; but upon more careful analysis, they are revealed to reduce profits. To better understand this condition, let us first demonstrate what has become known as the transfer pricing theorem.

---

[7] It is a thought-provoking and interesting question why the networks vertically integrated into writing, bringing the writers into the company and making them part owners. Why integration? Why did the producers not just pay the writers a commission based on the show's profitability? One can never know all the answers, but we can presume that the ability to distort the profits and have large unnecessary costs that would deflate the commissions is one explanation. Being on the inside, the writers would have access and control over accounting reports and wasteful expenditures that needlessly cut into their commissions, chauffeurs to take the kids of the producers to school as one example. Why qualified auditors could not be hired to resolve the contracting problem is an unanswered question.

[8] Ted Kumpe and Piet T. Bolwijn, "Manufacturing: The New Case for Vertical Integration," *Harvard Business Review*, 88(2), March-April 1988, 75–81, discuss vertical integration and the importance of ensuring a steady stream of inputs to the manufacturing process. For more on the related topic of franchising, consult Paul Rubin, "The Theory of the Firm and the Structure of the Franchise Contract," *The Journal of Law and Economics*, 21(1), April 1978, 223–34; G. Frank Mathewson and Ralph A. Winter, "The Economics of Franchise Contracts," *The Journal of Law and Economics*, 28(3), October 1985, 503–26; and Benjamin Klein and Lester F. Saft, "The Law and Economics of Franchise Tying Contracts," *The Journal of Law and Economics*, 28(2), May 1985, 345–62.

The **transfer pricing theorem** holds that when a product has a declining demand function, when increased sales come only at a lower price, the joint profits of all producers involved in the manufacturing process are maximized only if the monopoly price is charged at the final output stage, and necessarily then, the transfer price at all intermediate stages of production must be at marginal cost. Let us set up an example to make the point. Suppose Company *A* buys a specialized and patented computer chip from Company *B* to make a computer that scans newspapers and books and creates bibliographies and text. Company *A* also buys a lot of other materials, but these are readily available from myriad suppliers at the average cost of production. Competition ensures that. The demand for the special computer that converts media from printed to electronic form and organizes it comes primarily from libraries and companies that want to reduce their paper and record-keeping holdings. There are substitutes for this computer—microfiche, microfilm, and hand scanners to name three—but they are technically inferior and slower to operate, catalog, and access. Because these alternative products are not as useful, the demand for our cataloging computer is not perfectly elastic. This means that the seller can raise the price without losing all the sales. The demand for the product is downward sloping.

Because the demand slopes down, the seller must search for the best price, but the lessons of Chapter 7 have taught us that the proper price occurs where marginal revenue equals marginal cost. Now the transfer pricing problem emerges because marginal cost of manufacturing the computer is influenced by the price of its components. Normally this is not a problem, but when one or more of the inputs are patented and sold by a single seller, or otherwise under the control of a single seller, we effectively have two vertical monopolists. The input producer searches for the right price for the chip, *and* the output producer searches for the right price for the final product, the computer. In this case, if the chip seller prices the chip at higher than its marginal cost of production, the joint profits to the chip seller and the computer seller will be reduced. Why is that true?

When the chip seller raises the price of the patented, specialty chip above its marginal cost, the computer manufacturer purchases relatively fewer chips by the first law of demand. In this case, the computer manufacturer sees a high price for the chip compared to the value and price of all the other inputs. This induces the computer manufacturer to substitute alternatives for the chip in the computer because they are relatively cheaper. In the particular case at hand, substitutes are not easy to find, but they include a fancy monitor, a high-quality keyboard, perhaps an elaborate and exhaustive user's manual. Software is also an option. None of these is a perfect substitute for the scanning chip, but each serves to make the overall task of scanning more user friendly and presumably better. In that sense they are substitutes for the chip. In all events, the expensive price for the chip induces the computer maker to alter the characteristics of the computer. You may be inclined to ask, so what? Well, when the computer manufacturer does this, it increases the price of the computer and necessarily reduces sales. Naturally, reduced sales have an impact on the number of specialty chips sold. Therein lies the transfer pricing problem.

If there is more than one monopoly in a vertical chain, joint profits of all producers are maximized only if the monopoly is taken once, and then only if it is taken at the final output stage. If the downstream input suppliers charge prices above marginal cost, the upstream users do not use the proper ratios of inputs. This unnaturally raises the price of the product, cutting into sales and profits *at all levels in the vertical chain.* How can this problem be avoided?[9]

Basically there are two ways: One is to integrate the vertical chain so that the two serially related monopolies are under one roof; naturally, this raises its own set of problems, but it does allow for elimination of the transfer pricing problem. The other solution is contractual. The first monopolist can try to write a complicated contract with the second monopolist that will prevent factor use distortion. **Factor use distortion** is the shifting of inputs away from the monopoly input, the one that is priced above marginal cost, and toward others, those priced at marginal cost. In our computer example, it is the shift away from the specialty chip toward elaborate software and peripheral devices. Let's explore the solutions in order.

Vertical integration allows for the elimination of the factor distortion problem, but only if the overseer of the joint enterprise is astute. Let's continue with the specialized computer example. Suppose the two separate companies, the chip maker and the computer assembler, come together as one company, but each retains its individual identity as a division within the parent company. The proper transfer price problem persists. Since, in all likelihood, the division managers are partially compensated based on their division's profitability, they retain the incentive to improperly transfer chips to the assembler at prices above their own marginal cost of production. Hence, blind vertical integration, by itself, will not raise profits to their potential. Some scheme must be employed to make the chip division feel the cost it imposes on the joint enterprise by not pricing the chips at the pooled profit maximizing price. There are a number of ways this might be done. Each has its own costs and rewards, and in general, the individual situation will dictate the appropriate practice.

The chip division can be forced by CEO mandate to transfer the chips at marginal cost, but this requires that the CEO inspect the books and records of the division to verify the correct price. Naturally, this centralization of decision making forces the CEO to do work that might better be delegated, but nevertheless it is an option. A second method allows the computer assembly division to determine the transfer price, but this just shifts the problem from one division to another. The original problem persists. Another solution pays each division manager on overall company profits, not just on division profits. This compensation scheme makes each manager feel some of the cost she imposes on the joint enterprise by not transfer pricing at marginal cost. This list of remedies to the transfer pricing problem is far from exhaustive; it is only intended to point out how important organizational structure is to performance.

The 1991 merger of AT&T with NCR appears to be an example of the vertical

---

[9] In the special case of fixed proportions in production, the monopoly charge does not have to be taken at the final stage of production. When there are fixed proportions, it is impossible to substitute inputs, and the problem goes away. The person or company owning the unique asset that creates the monopoly in the first place can extract the monopoly rents at any stage in the production process.

integration we are talking about here, perhaps partly due to transfer pricing but probably also designed to reduce the problem of opportunistic behavior. Early accounts of the merger suggest that the computer software and hardware produced by NCR will integrate nicely with the communications network of AT&T. It bears noting that sometimes a joint venture is a substitute for vertical integration. For instance, IBM and Microsoft had such an arrangement to facilitate the vertical production of computers and software. It remains an open question as to why AT&T and NCR chose merger while IBM and Microsoft attempted a joint venture. However, we can note that if newspaper and magazine accounts are trustworthy, the IBM-Microsoft venture is contentious and problematic, and some industry experts wonder whether the relationship will survive.

As we just noted, vertical integration is not the only way that two vertically dependent companies can resolve the problem of chained monopolies. A sophisticated pricing algorithm might be used in some cases. In Chapter 9, we discussed multipart pricing schemes. A really simple way to erase the inefficiency created by transferring goods at prices above marginal cost is to transfer them at marginal cost. Naturally, this reduces profits of the first monopolist in the chain, but this is easily remedied by a lump sum licensing fee, paid once in a lifetime, annually, or by any other time period, *so long as it is not related to the quantity purchased of the good being transferred.* In our computer example, the way this would work is for the chip producer to license the computer assembler for some annual fee, the computation of which is left as another exercise, with the provision that licensed firms can buy at marginal cost. The truly beautiful thing about this arrangement is that if the chip manufacturer properly determines the lump-sum licensing fee, then it has little incentive to charge the computer assembler anything but marginal cost for the chips. This is especially true when the licensing fee is paid annually.[10]

The following story about the evolution of transfer prices at one company points out the importance of setting the correct transfer price.

> We at Bellcore first got interested in transfer pricing in 1983. That's the year before AT&T was broken up and Bellcore was being formed as the centralized organization supporting the seven regional holding companies. . . .
>
> We designed our charge-back system in 1983, it was state-of-the art. But within a few years, the system's imperfections began to manifest themselves. For one thing, we had researchers and engineers spending an increasing amount of their time typing documents and making overhead slides because they couldn't abide the high prices the word processing, graphics, technical publications, and secretarial departments were charging. . . .
>
> We eventually discovered that the main problem for certain services lay with our transfer pricing system—specifically, with the way it allocated overhead and rent. Word processing graphics, technical publications, and secretarial services were paying more than their share.
>
> The costs of . . . service were lumped into overhead and assessed to all Bellcore's internal organizations. . . . [Increasingly] a majority of Bellcore employees

---

[10] Can you figure out why this is true? Think about the incentives faced by the seller when the license fee is paid annually. Does the prospect of continued revenues act to ensure quality performance?

. . . were doing their own word processing and graphics [bypassing the service centers in the process because of the high rates being charged.] . . .

The bypassed service centers had their hands tied. They were obliged to pass their costs on to a shrinking client base, which drives costs up. At one point, typed documents were costing $50 a page. . . .

We had finally gotten to the root of the problem. Word processing, graphics, technical publications, and secretarial services were losing their corporate customers because they were charging too much. They were charging too much partly because they weren't efficient enough and partly because they were paying more than their share for overhead and rent.[11]

One of the lessons from this story, and there are many that can be learned from a complete reading of the article, is that transfer prices need to reflect marginal not average cost. When transfer prices reflect average cost, all sorts of problems develop.

Transfer pricing is an important managerial responsibility. Only the bare rudiments have been discussed here, and as it is often said, "A little learning is a dangerous thing." The wise student will be provoked to further study by the lessons here. They do not pretend to cover the whole topic, only to alert you to the situation and point the way for further study.[12]

ADDITIONAL TOPICS IN CONTRACTING

An interesting managerial problem arises that closely parallels the issue of whether the firm should contract for services outside or hire salaried employees to produce them within. This question might be labeled, Who should own the tools? Let's create an example to help us understand the problem. Suppose you own a chain of automobile repair shops, not unlike the Goodyear Tire Sales and Autoservice Centers around the country. Sears and K-Mart offer similar automobile repair services. The issue arises as to whether the car repair employees or the shop—that is, the owner/manager of the shop—should own the tools used to fix the automobiles. On the surface, it does not appear that this distinction is important, but when we approach it from a property rights perspective, we see additional issues that suggest the ownership structure may have implications for profitability. First, let's lay out the naive case that suggests why ownership structure does not matter, and then we can more easily see when and where it does.

Suppose auto mechanics can be hired at $15 per hour. For the sake of instruction, let's just say that a well-equipped tool box costs $1000 and lasts for

---

[11] Reprinted by permission of Harvard Business Review. An excerpt from "Getting Transfer Prices Right: What Bellcore Did," by Edward J. Kovac and Henry P. Troy, 5(September/October 1989), 148–57. Copyright © 1989 by the President and Fellows of Harvard College; all rights reserved.

[12] The *Economic Literature Index*, a database of articles and books published throughout the world in all areas of economics, is complied by the American Economic Association. The index lists 259 journal articles, monographs, and books on the topic of transfer pricing published over the period 1969–1990. The Suggested Readings at the end of this chapter list a few of these.

five years. Implicitly then, the annual rental rate on tools is the amount of money received each year for five years that has a present value of $1000. Suppose the interest rate is 10 percent. Then, the annual rental rate on tools, R, is found by solving the following equation:

$$\$1000 = R \bullet [1/(1.1) + 1/(1.1)^2 + 1/(1.1)^3 + 1/(1.1)^4 + 1/(1.1)^5],$$

or

$$R = \$1000/[0.9090 + 0.8264 + 0.7513 + 0.6830 + 0.6210] = \$1000/3.791,$$

or

$$R = \$264.$$

In other words, an annual flow of $264 for five years returns 10 percent on a $1000 investment. So our hypothetical auto mechanic is willing to work for $15 per hour if you supply the tools, or $15 per hour plus $264 once per year if he has to supply the tools. The employee is indifferent between buying the tools and getting reimbursed or allowing the shop to supply the tools. Similarly, the shop can buy the tools from the tool manufacturer or effectively rent them from the employee by paying him higher wages. It would appear that it does not matter who owns the tools, and insofar as this line of reasoning goes, it is correct; but what needs to be considered is, Will the tools be used the same way regardless of who owns them? It turns out that the answer is no.

Suppose the shop owns the tools and employees can check them out from a tool room. Most of the time, nothing unusual occurs, and this system works well. However, on occasion an employee will get mad and abuse a tool or use it improperly to do a task for which it was not designed. Even then, there will not be a problem unless the tool is damaged. Suppose it is. Must the employee reimburse the shop or not? Therein lies the problem. If the employee has to reimburse the shop, then he is made a residual claimant and appears to have the incentive not to abuse the tool. However, other people also use this tool, and it is easy to believe that it is only through accumulated abuse that the tool is prematurely destroyed. For instance, suppose the tool has bearings or a motor that requires regular oiling. Bubba checks the tool out of the tool shed and it breaks 10 minutes later, not because he did anything wrong, but because the last employee did not oil it properly. This creates all sorts of havoc that must be avoided. Naturally, the easiest way is for the individual employee to own his personal tools. Then, when they break, the individual responsible is known with certainty. With private ownership, accountability creates responsibility. Based on this line of reasoning, it is better—that is, cheaper—for the employee to own his own tools.

This theorem has several important caveats. The first has to do with team production. When several workers must use the same tool simultaneously, then joint ownership by the team creates a tragedy of the commons problem. Which one of them will do the maintenance? Naturally, in this situation, each is inclined to shirk some as he only bears a fraction of the total cost. Thus, joint ownership of the tool has disadvantages. Second, suppose the shop has 10 mechanics, and let us focus attention on one specific tool, say an air wrench used to remove lug nuts from tires for the quick and easy removal of car wheels. To make the situation interesting, suppose that the average job lasts two hours per car when one mechanic is assigned. Removing the lug nuts from tires only takes about one minute per tire. So on a job to repair the front brakes, the mechanic only uses the tool for a small portion of the total job time, 2/120, or less than 2 percent. In this situation, if each mechanic were to own his own tools as the preceding theorem suggests, then 10 air wrenches would be required, one per person, but each would only be employed 2 percent of the time. This creates its own waste; and in the situation at hand, it is substantial. Thus, in this case, and many more like it, it is easy to see why it is better to have the shop own the tool rather than the employee.

Naturally, the problem of misuse and abuse is present when the shop owns the air tools, but now, under the circumstances, that cost is smaller than the alternative, the idle capital. With private ownership, each employee has to own an air wrench costing, say, $200 and must be compensated by the shop for this expense. The shop has effectively spent $2000 on tools, when, if the shop buys the air wrenches for all mechanics to use, it can easily get by with only two for a cost savings of $1600. The abuse problem would have to be really serious to overcome such a sum, and it will be in some cases, but not all. As the cost of the wrench declines, the less important it is to worry about its idleness. So when the tool is inexpensive, it might pay to bear the cost of inactivity to gain the rewards of individual ownership.

Can we generalize about this problem? Perhaps a bit. When tools are often used, say a carpenter's hammer, the value of individual accountability and responsibility sways the argument, and we conclude that in most situations the value maximizing solution is employee not employer ownership. Holding constant the frequency of use, the more valuable a tool is, the more important it is to eliminate its slack periods, and thus some sharing is suggested. Consequently, as the price of a tool increases, other things being the same, it is more likely that the employer will buy it, maintain it, and allow it to be used by multiple workers one after the other. And last, as the frequency of use declines, as the idle periods of tool use increase, regardless of price, the more likely it is that the employer will supply the tool to the employees. Thus, even cheap tools that are rarely used might be supplied by the owner/manager of the enterprise.

CONTROLLING MALFEASANCE:
WHEN IS IT USEFUL TO OVERPAY EMPLOYEES?

Employee carelessness, sloppy attention to detail, misuse of company resources, misappropriation of funds, and outright theft can hurt the operation of almost any firm. Finding ways to minimize these misbehaviors is an important managerial prerogative. It is foolhardy to think that one text could cover all the possible mechanisms that managers use to cope with employee malfeasance, but one trick that often goes unnoticed is the overpayment of employees. Why does overcompensation help to motivate workers? First, it gives them a property right. The value of this right is the present value of the excess of their wages over their income in alternative employment, and the longer the employee expects to work, the larger the value. Moreover, if an employee is dismissed, he must find work elsewhere, and by definition, he will be paid less there. This can be a tremendous incentive to an employee, and under the right circumstances, it can work to control malfeasance.

What are the situations in which this technique works best? To properly answer this question, we must first understand something called **risk aversion**. Risk aversion is a human characteristic. Most, but not all, people possess it, but even those who do have it do not always act in a risk averse fashion. Nevertheless, risk aversion is a common human trait. A **risk averse** individual is willing to pay less to play a game than the game is worth on average. That is, for a risk averse person, the value of a game with uncertain outcomes is less than the average value of the game. Consider a simple example. Suppose Emilia is offered the chance to play a card game. The deck has 52 cards; one of them is the ace of spades. To play the game, she blindly selects a card from the deck face down, any card she wishes. If she picks the ace of spades, she wins a prize of $520. If she chooses any other card, she wins nothing. What is the expected value of playing this game? There is a 1/52 chance of winning $520, so on average the payoff is $520/52 = $10. Were Emilia to play this game 52 times, she expects to win, on average, once. Thus, the expected winnings are $10 per play. Quite simply, a risk averse person would not pay as much as $10 to play this game; to her, the uncertain outcome of playing the game is worth less than the certain value of $10 in her hand. She might play if the price were less then $10, but only then. As a matter of note, we say a person is risk neutral if she is willing to pay up to $10 for the right to play the game, and we call a person a risk lover who is willing to pay more than $10 to play the game. It turns out that most people are risk averse, and the following discussion is predicated on that presumption. The argument applies only to such people.

There are ways to motivate besides money; we have already talked about some of them, and courses outside economics often deal with the subject. Careful selection of employees based on job history, references, character, and (until recently) lie-detector tests could be used to locate honestly inclined workers. However, there is hardly any job that does not require a variety of schemes to properly control subordinates. What we are discussing here is a technique to be used in concert with other motivating mechanisms. With that in mind, suppose Emilia works as a security guard, receptionist, bank teller, a black jack dealer in a casino, or some other job for which it is difficult to motivate her with a commission on sales or effort. We already know she is risk averse; we can use that fact to motivate her without constant supervision.

At her job, Emilia has certain responsibilities. She can perform them or not as she sees fit. Naturally, it would be nice to know when she does not execute her obligations, but that is a costly task. In many cases, it would require constant supervision to prevent the misappropriation of funds. Perhaps the most obvious example is the black jack dealer in the casino. To those unfamiliar with the game, cards are dealt to players and the dealer after bets are placed by the players. Each person plays against the dealer, not the other players. The person closer to 21 points (comparing each hand to the dealer's) but not over 21 wins. Hence, it is possible for one person at a table to win while another loses on the same hand; more than one player at a table can win on the same deal so long as each one has more points than the dealer but less than 21. When the hand is over, the dealer pays the winners and collects the bets of the losers. Great sums of money can change hands in a short period of time. Now, in this situation, it would be a simple matter for the dealer to (1) make a mistake and pay a loser or (2) intentionally defraud the casino owners by working in concert with a friend to systematically cheat by overpaying on winning hands or failing to collect on losing ones. The casino owner could watch over the shoulder of the dealer, but that would take almost as much time as dealing. Not only would this leave little time for other chores, but it would make for a very small casino. Other ways of dealing with this potential problem must be uncovered. Lieutenants can be hired to watch over dealers, but two problems surface here. How can the lieutenants be trusted? Longevity, character, and other means might work, but probably not perfectly. Notice the glass over the tables in most casinos; cameras and individuals inspect many dealers at once. Even then, the problem is not erased.

Suppose the dealers are paid more than they might earn at their next best occupational endeavor. Imagine that the average dealer could earn $10 per hour. Then, suppose the casino pays its dealers not the $10 they are worth, but $12 per hour. Each person receives $2 more per hour than she could earn outside the profession. No one wants to go to the alternative employment; it does not pay as well. How much would it cost the average dealer to lose her job and find a job in some other sector of the economy? Consult Table 14.1. There we have computed the value, to one dealer, of the extra $2 per hour paid above and beyond the opportunity cost of employment. There we assume that the discount rate is 10 percent and the black jack dealer will work for 50 weeks per year and 15 years. The present value of the extra $2 per hour is $30,424.31. This sum can be used to prevent the dealer from cheating.

As we said, she is risk averse. This means she would rather have the $30,424 with certainty than the opportunity to play a game with the same payoff. In other words, if she gets caught making mistakes, she is fired, and the $30,424 goes out the window. Thus, any scam she tries has to have an expected payout *higher* than $30,000 or she will not participate. One way to make the payoff to her of cheating or working inefficiently unattractive is to randomly and intermittently inspect her work, *when she cannot reasonably expect to be watched*. If she is obeying the rules, fine;

TABLE 14.1 EMILIA'S COST OF BEING FIRED	
Wages per year:	50•40•$12 = $24,000
Opportunity cost:	50•40•$10 = $20,000
Difference:	$24,000 − $20,000 = $4000
Present value of $4000 at 10 percent for 15 years:	**$30,424.31**

if not, she is summarily dismissed. Since she is carefully taught this is the way of life in the casino, she expects to be treated this way; and the overpayment of $2 per hour motivates her to do a proficient job.

The combination of risk aversion, overpayment, and random and unexpected inspections creates an organizational environment that fosters adherence to rules and work instructions. It reduces the need for supervision and inspection, while retaining obedience. Like all systems, this one is not perfect or suited for all situations. We close by noting a couple of problems with this managerial tool. Naturally, the extra $2 per hour paid each dealer is a cost worth noting.

In addition, if the employee can get another job dealing after being dismissed for cheating or malfeasance, then the opportunity cost of work is not the $10 that could be earned in another profession, but the $12 wages paid to dealers. This means that fired dealers must not reasonably expect to be able to get similar work, or they will not view the threat of firing as imposing serious sanctions. What can be done to ensure that firing will not lead to rehiring? Two techniques come to mind. First, be careful when hiring. Only hire people who are worth $10 per hour. There's an old expression that usually seems to make little sense, "So and so is overqualified for this job." In this case, that remark carries more weight. Over-qualified employees have high opportunity costs. When a job comes along, it will be at a relatively high salary. This implies that the $30,000 extra pay is not really present for this overqualified person. Dealing is just a temporary employment for this person, and the additional pay incentive is not nearly as effective a carrot. He can make more money somewhere else when the situation presents itself, and he will not be nearly as concerned about being dismissed as will the lower opportunity cost individual.

The second method that makes firing a real threat involves references. The expression "You'll never work in this town again" carries extra weight in this situation. If the boss can prevent alternative employment, through a network of friends, acquaintances, or references, then the opportunity cost of dismissal is a real threat and the overpayment money acts as a carrot to prevent malfeasance.

RULES OF CONDUCT VERSUS DISCRETIONARY BEHAVIOR

In virtually any enterprise, there is a hierarchy of tasks. We start with the people and machines involved in the baseline production process. Middle managers oversee these people and machines. On top of the managers are the senior officials who not only inspect and manage the day-to-day operations of the firm but also engage in long-run strategy decisions. That is, they make investment decisions and product line choices, and they determine the organizational structure of the enterprise. Each level in this hierarchy has information available to it that is not cheaply known or communicated to the other levels. This fact creates a managerial dilemma worthy of note.

Consider the example of a large orange grove in Florida or Texas. In either place, freezing weather is occasionally a serious problem. To appreciate the nature of the problem, let's set up a situation. The workers and managers at the grove have ways of dealing with a potentially damaging frost. They can light smudge pots, engage large propeller fans, or sprinkle water to warm the fruit trees. The workers and managers in the field have access to critical information, the night-time temperature. At the other end of the hierarchy, the owners of the business also possess superior information of their own. They know the price of citrus, smudge, electricity, and water, all of which are essential to make an efficient decision about properly protecting the investment. Moreover, the managers at the top of the hierarchy know better whether the loss of the crop would be devastating. They know if long-term contracts or reputations are at stake. In addition to the information they possess, the senior officials are more likely to be aware of the long-run consequences of bad weather. That is, schemes exist to make senior managers attune to the incentive and horizon problems we have discussed.

In sum then, each level of the hierarchy has some superior information, but typically not all of it, and, hence, communication among the parties is almost surely required to achieve an efficient outcome. Consider the following ways of dealing with the potential for frost: Numerous thermometers are placed throughout the orchard. Each is electronically connected via satellite to the company's main headquarters in New York. When the temperature reaches the critical value, the order is issued from on high to light the pots and turn on the fans and sprinklers.[13] Naturally, some scheme must be in place to ensure that the instructions are carried out; there is an incentive problem at the end of the chain. In addition to this problem, this method requires the senior officials to constantly monitor the thermometers. In general, it means they must keep their eyes on the production line, a chore that requires time, energy, and expertise. Thus we see how taking the information to the individuals with the incentive can work, but not freely or without its consequences.

An alternative way to deal with this problem is for the workers with the temperature information to make the decision concerning the heating. Armed with the critical information about weather, they are in the right position to make the decision. Of course, there is no free lunch here either. Unless they are properly motivated, they will turn the heaters on when it is not required, imposing costs of fuel consumed. Perhaps worse, they will ignore the threatening temperature and succumb to laziness or ineptitude, leaving the heaters off when the frost is imminent.

Which choice is better? It all depends on the circumstances, but before we discuss these, consider an electronic solution. Here the heaters are connected to the thermometers. The senior officials in consultation with citrus experts set the thermostats to kick the heaters into motion at the proper temperature. This solution has many advantages and some costs. First, what will happen if the thermostats malfunction? Second, maybe frost depends on more than just temperature. Suppose humidity is also important. Then multiple gauges are required. It goes without saying that as a general management problem, the solution to the citrus freezing predicament is not easily resolved.

---

[13] We heroically presume that the senior officials know how to compute the critical temperature. In the general case, this information may only be known to engineers or other specialists at the bottom of the hierarchy.

As another example, consider the military problem of rules of engagement. The U.S. Navy has ships around the world. Senior officials at the highest military command do not have all the information available to commanders in the field. Suppose an armed aircraft threatens a ship in the Indian Ocean. Should the ship commander relay the information to the Pentagon for a decision to fire, or should he have the authority himself? The answer depends on the state of action or peace in the world. Suppose there is relative peace. That is, the United States is currently not at war. Then, the incentives that senior officials have to make the right decision probably outweigh the value of the information that the ship commander has—that is, the extent of the threat. This means that when relative peace is at hand, strict rules of engagement are in order, and ship commanders may be required to request permission to fire from their senior commanders. By contrast, when war is rampant, as it was during the recent U.S.–Iraq conflict, this strategy is likely foolhardy. When occupied in a war, the rules of engagement are more lenient because the ship commander now has the upper hand. He has the critical information. The long-run consequences of firing have already been considered by the top officials and the appropriate rules of conduct issued.

Thus, for what appears to be the same threat, a military commander is given *less* discretion when peace reigns than when war is rampant. Naturally, the more weaponry at his disposal, the less discretion any commander has, *at any level of war.* Individual soldiers are routinely given the right to fire their rifles under a wide variety of circumstances, but people with their fingers on missiles carrying nuclear warheads have all sorts of rules imposed on them even when full-scale war is in progress.

It remains one of the most difficult and time-consuming managerial chores to cope with the decision as to whether underlings should have discretion or be shackled with rules and restrictions. The discussion here is meant to point out that simple rules of thumb are hard to come by. Each and every individual situation will normally dictate the proper course of action. The best canon is: Be aware of the consequences of imposing rules or allowing discretion. Otherwise, the manager is likely to be fooled by the outcome.[14]

A FINAL WORD ON PUBLIC GOODS, BRAND NAMES, AND ACCOUNTABILITY

In previous chapters we have discussed the problem of brand names and common access goods separately. Now consider them together, in the same light. When a good is common access, there is a tendency for its value to be driven to

---

[14] For an interesting case study of the switchover of a major corporation from a centralized operation to a highly decentralized business, consult Michael Schroeder, "The Recasting of Alcoa: Its CEO Is Slashing Management in Favor of a Decentralized System," *Business Week*, September 9, 1991, pp. 62–64. The story reports that "[o]n Sept. 2 [1991, CEO O'Neill] will begin a massive overhaul of management meant to refashion Alcoa into a highly decentralized outfit. At a management powwow in Pittsburgh in early August, some 50 worldwide senior executives were stunned to learn that O'Neill planned to give Alcoa's 25 business-unit managers unprecedented leeway to run their businesses."

zero, the tragedy of the commons. But goods do not always have to be physical ones to qualify for this destruction. Consider reputations and brand names. If a university, church, country club, corporation, or any other entity has established a reputation for quality and honesty, there are people who, if they can earn access, will try to exploit the value of the intangible asset. It will then become necessary for those who created the valuable wealth to try and protect it from overuse and abuse.

For an example, consider the following story, reported in *U.S. News and World Report*, concerning Jim Bakker, the defrocked television evangelist.

> It was the ultimate irony. As fallen PTL evangelist Jim Bakker was led from a North Carolina courthouse last week to begin serving a 45-year prison term for fraud, a 2½-year saga painful and embarrassing to TV and radio preachers drew to a close. Yet, far from being mortally wounded by the suspicion and scorn surrounding Bakker's fall, the nation's $2-billion-a-year electronic church may be emerging stronger than before. In some ways, it has Bakker to thank.
>
> Since the scandal broke in early 1987, religious fund-raisers have rushed to join *self-policing* groups that demand high standards and open books. The Evangelical Council on Financial Accountability, which requires members—from big TV ministries to tiny soup kitchens—to submit to regular audits, has seen its rolls grow by 60 percent. *"Even ministries that are run by good, well-intentioned people need to do something to assure donors that their house is in order."*[15]

What we see here is a type of regulation, albeit voluntary, that is attempted to prevent some bad eggs from spoiling the whole lot. The Evangelical Council on Financial Accountability is a certifying organization, somewhat like a large accounting firm, whose brand name itself acts to convince donors that the organizations to which they give are well run and honest. Using this technique, the tragedy of the commons is muted if not avoided.

AN EXTENDED DISCUSSION ON INCENTIVES

During the 1980s a new business form emerged—the leveraged buyout association, commonly called the **LBO** association. Fewer upheavals in corporate America have been the object of such widespread discussion and disagreement as the advent of the LBO. Just what is an LBO? What does it accomplish? Who benefits? Who loses? How does it work? Is it good? And what does it have to do with property rights, managerial decisions, and incentives?

The LBO association is a new corporate form that concentrates authority and control with a few individuals. It is substantively different from the modern corporation. Some authorities think that for many managerial purposes, it is a superior organizational form, but the idea has also been widely criticized.[16] To

---

[15] *U.S. News and World Report*, November 6, 1989, p. 14. Emphasis added.

[16] Most notably, see Michael C. Jensen, "The Eclipse of the Public Corporation," *Harvard Business Review*, 89(5), September-October 1989, 61–75, the many letters to the editor that his article spawned, and Jensen's response in the November-December 1989 issue of *Harvard Business Review*, pp. 182–208.

understand how an LBO works, imagine that you are interested in buying a house. You have been out of school for two years, living in an apartment, and now you want the joys of home ownership. Typically, what do you do?

You shop for a home, usually with a realtor. When you have made your choice, you visit a bank or savings and loan to arrange for a mortgage. A mortgage is a loan that uses the house as collateral. For new homes, the financing could be as high as 95 percent, and for others as low as 75–80 percent. The debt that you acquire is backed by the value of the home. If for one reason or another you do not make the required monthly payments of principal and interest, the bank has the legal authority to repossess the dwelling and sell it to recover its loan to you. Fundamentally, an LBO is the same idea applied to a company.

In an LBO, a number of senior managers of a company, sometimes joined by outside investors, obtain loans, using investment bankers. The proceeds of the loans are used to buy up all the stock of the company, putting control of the assets of the company in the hands of the senior partners, who are sometimes called LBO partners. Just like the leveraged homeowner, the LBO partners must make regular and routine interest payments to the debt holders. The owners of this debt are sometimes banks, as with homeowners, but just as savings and loans often sell some of their debt, the debt of LBO companies is often sold by bankers in the form of bonds. When a bank sells the debt of an LBO company, it does so in the form of a **junk bond**. These bonds are sometimes called high-yield securities.

What is the point of this exercise? Again, think in terms of your home purchase. Two incentive effects are created when you purchase your home that are absent when you rent. First, being the owner, you have a greater, vested interest in its upkeep. The same is true when you are the sole or primary owner of a company. When you, as a manager, are simply working for salary, or even salary plus bonuses, you do not reap the full rewards of your stewardship; they must be shared with stockholders who get dividends and capital gains. When you are the primary investor/owner, your incentive to work hard is enhanced. When you know that you will get to keep all or almost all of the gains from staying late at night or on weekends, you are inclined to do it, more so than when shareholders will get to keep some of the fruits of your labors. On top of that, when your own money is at stake, there is a tendency to be more precise and careful at work, at least that is the theory behind the LBO as an alternative to the corporate form of organization.

A second prong of the argument says that the necessity of making regularly scheduled interest payments to banks and bondholders realigns the priorities of managers. If managers make an investment mistake using shareholders' money, they can skip a dividend payment. This is neither pleasant nor cheap. It has been known to cost managers their jobs, but still it is less onerous, at least according to the LBO theorists, than skipping an interest payment, an event that could lead to legal action and repossession of the capital assets of the company via bankruptcy. This argument also contends that investments made with borrowed money are likely to be better because banks and lenders scrutinize the investment.

When an individual borrows money to buy a house, the money lender almost always requires a certified appraisal. This assessment is used by the bank to verify the wisdom of the loan, and thus, indirectly, it helps the buyer prevent mistakes.

Some home buyers who do not borrow might not get an assessment and are more likely to make an error by paying too much for a home. In this way, debt financing offers an extra layer of control absent in all equity purchases.

Of course, this extra layer of oversight can have the opposite effect. When the buyer has a particularly keen vision of the value of a project, the necessity of convincing skeptics imposes costs that can prevent an otherwise good idea from ever being brought to fruition.[17] Put another way, debt hobbles managers. Sometimes it is worthwhile—when free-ranging managers would put the assets of their firm to wasteful uses; and sometimes it is bad—when managerial freedom to search leads to the discovery of new ideas and profitable adventures.[18]

TOPICS TO REVIEW

These are topics that you should feel comfortable with before you leave this chapter. If you cannot write out a clear and concise sentence or paragraph explaining the topic after you have worked on the study problems, you should reread the relevant section of the text.

Opportunism

Vertical Integration

Transfer Pricing

Risk Aversion

LBO

STUDY PROBLEMS

1. The coastal plains of South Carolina, Georgia, and Florida are the home of many pulp and paper mills. There are many reasons for this, but two prominent ones include an abundance of water from ground and river sources and a large stock of pine trees to be used as raw material. In the 1980s Ft. Howard Paper Company began the process of designing, locating, and building a new paper mill. This mill was to be different from most, however. It was to use recycled paper exclusively. That is, no pine trees were required. The mill imported old newspaper and other such material and converted it into new

---

[17] See Stewart C. Myers and Nicholas S. Majluf, "Corporate Financing and Investment Decisions When Firms Have Information That Investors Do Not Have," *Journal of Financial Economics*, 13, 1984, 187–221 for an elaboration on this point.

[18] This brief treatment does little justice to the important topic of managerial compensation and its incentive effects, but we must stop at some point. The interested student is directed to the article by Michael Jensen and Kevin Murphy, "Performance Pay and Top-Management Incentives," *Journal of Political Economy*, 98, April 1990, 225–64 and the article by Kenneth Mason, "Four Ways to Overpay Yourself Enough," *Harvard Business Review*, July-August 1988, pp. 69–74. The latter summarizes four theories of managerial compensation including the pay for performance system and proposes a system to tax managers when share prices decline.

paper products. For this reason, there was no particular cause to locate the plant in the southeast United States near so many other similar establishments. In fact, on the surface it would have appeared more reasonable to locate the plant near the sources of recycled paper. Nevertheless, the plant was eventually built just outside Savannah, Georgia. Can you provide a plausible explanation based on opportunistic behavior that might help explain one of the reasons the managers of Ft. Howard decided to locate their plant in the middle of the southern pine forests, even though they were not going to use the trees there as inputs?

2.   There is a growing trend among vendors of personal computer software not to copy protect their goods. First of all, why did firms copy protect, and second, why is it better now not to? Make sure your explanation is consistent with the fact that many sellers still copy protect their products.

3.   The United States 1974 Trade Act defines dumping as "selling at a price less than fully allocated costs." Using this definition explain what types of firms or industries are most likely to engage in dumping.

SUGGESTED READINGS

Barzel, Yoram. "Measurement Cost and the Organization of Markets." *The Journal of Law and Economics* 25(1) (April 1982):27–48.

Benke, Ralph L., Jr. and Edwards, James D. "Transfer Pricing: Techniques and Uses" *Management Accounting* 61(12) (June 1980):44–46.

Coate, Malcolm B. and Fratrik, Mark R. "Dual Distribution as a Vertical Control Device." *Journal of Behavioral Economics* 18(1) (Spring 1989):1–17.

DeFusco, Richard A., Johnson, Robert R., and Zorn, Thomas S. "The Effect of Executive Stock Option Plans on Stockholders and Bondholders." *Journal of Finance* 45(2) (June 1990):617–27.

Easterbrook, Frank H. "Two Agency-Cost Explanations of Dividends." *American Economic Review* 74(4) (September 1984):157–86.

Eccles, Robert G. "Transfer Pricing as a Problem of Agency." In *Principals and Agents: The Structure of Business,* John W. Pratt and Richard J. Zeckhauser, eds., pp. 151–86. Boston: Harvard Business School Press, 1985.

Feinstein, Jonathan S. and Stein, Jeremy. "Employee Opportunism and Redundancy in Firms." *Journal of Economic Behavior and Organization* 10(4) (December 1988):410–14.

Fuhr, Joseph P., Jr. "Vertical Integration and Regulation in the Electric Utility Industry." *Journal of Economic Issues* 24(1) (March 1990):173–87.

Hirshleifer, Jack. "On the Economics of Transfer Pricing." *Journal of Business* 29 (July 1956): 172–84.

Jarrell, Gregg A. and Bradley, Michael. "The Economic Effects of Federal and State Regulations of Cash Tender Offers." *The Journal of Law and Economics* 23(2) (October 1980): 317–408.

Jensen, Michael C. "Agency Costs of Free Cash Flow, Corporate Finance and Takeovers." *American Economic Review* 76 (May 1986):323–29.

Jensen, Michael C. "Takeovers: Their Causes and Consequences." *Journal of Economic Perspectives* 2 (1988):21–48.

Jensen, Michael C. "Eclipse of the Public Corporation." *Harvard Business Review* 89(5) (September-October 1989):61–75.

Jensen, Michael C. and Murphy, Kevin. "Performance Pay and Top-Management Incentives." *Journal of Political Economy* 98(2) (April 1990):225–64.

Jensen, Michael C. and Ruback, Richard, eds. *Symposium on the Structure and Governance of Enterprise. Journal of Financial Economics* 27(2) Parts I and II (October 1990).

Klein, Benjamin and Leffler, Keith. "The Role of Market Forces in Assuring Contractual Performance." *Journal of Political Economy* 89(4) (August 1981):615–41.

Klein, Benjamin W. and Murphy, Kevin M. "Vertical Restraints as Contract Enforcement Mechanisms." *The Journal of Law and Economics* 31(2) (October 1988):265–98.

Kovac, Edward J. and Troy, Henry P. "Getting Transfer Prices Right: What Bellcore Did." *Harvard Business Review* 89(5) (September-October 1989):148–57.

Kumpe, Ted and Bolwijn, Piet T. "Manufacturing: The New Case for Vertical Integration." *Harvard Business Review* 88(2) (March-April 1988):75–81.

Mason, Kenneth. "Four Ways to Overpay Yourself Enough." *Harvard Business Review* 88(4) (July-August 1988):69–74.

Myers, Stewart C. and Majluf, Nicholas S. "Corporate Financing and Investment Decisions When Firms Have Information That Investors Do Not Have." *Journal of Financial Economics* 13 (1984):187–221.

Prusa, Thomas J. "An Incentive Compatible Approach to the Transfer Pricing Problem." *Journal of International Economics* 28 (February 1990):155–72.

Rogers, T. J. "No Excuses Management." *Harvard Business Review* 90(4) (July-August 1990):84–103.

Rugman, Alan M. and Eden, Lorraine, eds. *Multinationals and Transfer Pricing.* New York: St. Martin's Press, 1985.

Smith, Clifford W., Jr. and Warner, Jerold B. "On Financial Contracting: An Analysis of Bond Covenants." *Journal of Financial Economics* 9 (1979):117–61.

Stancil, James M. "LBO's for Smaller Companies." *Harvard Business Review* 88(1) (January-February 1988):18–26.

Zupan, Mark A. "Cable Franchise Renewals: Do Incumbent Firms Behave Opportunistically?" *Rand Journal of Economics* 20(4) (Winter 1989):473–82.

SUGGESTED SOLUTIONS TO SELECTED STUDY PROBLEMS

The following are only *suggested* solutions to the study problems presented at the end of this chapter. In all cases, the suggestions here put heavy emphasis on analysis rather than a single correct answer. Since most managerial problems do not fall into neat little boxes, the individual characteristics of the problems that you encounter on the job will typically mandate a solution using the principles developed here and in other courses. Memorizing these solutions will not make you a good manager; learning the *principles* detailed here will help make you a better manager.

1. There are many reasons why Ft. Howard might choose to locate its new plant in the region, but one that sticks out prominently is the availability of inputs. Suppose that used paper increases in price or that the suppliers of paper for recycling try to renege on their commitments to Ft. Howard. By locating near the southern pine forests, Ft. Howard reserves the right to switch its production processes from old paper to raw pulp.

3. Companies that have a lot of fixed costs, that is, sunk costs such as capital expenditures on plant and machinery, or companies that have a lot of

research and development costs, have relatively low marginal costs of production, relative to the prices of their products. These companies recover their sunk investments by charging relatively high prices compared to their actual production costs (excluding the sunk costs of their large fixed investments). Now when the value of their investments in place or their research and development expenditures are reduced, these companies are most likely to cut the price of their products and to give the appearance of selling below fully allocated costs. That is, when a substantial portion of a company's costs is fixed and sunk, a greater portion of the revenues received are quasi-rents on the investment in place. Given that the previous fixed expenditures are sunk, they are not, economically speaking, a cost of production. Thus, when conditions change that reduce the value of the fixed investments, the sellers can rationally and correctly ignore the sunk costs while giving the appearance in the accounting sense of selling below costs.

INTRODUCTION

This chapter is about the relation between government and business. This is an increasingly important topic of managerial concern. In times past, business was primarily concerned with its customers, suppliers, and rivals. Today, however, the role of government is also very important. The chapter begins with a brief introduction to the different theories underlying the involvement of government with commerce. After that, your attention is focused on the new economic theory of regulation. The purpose here is a practical one. Most of the early economic theories of regulation were normative; that is, they were designed primarily to make markets and trade work more efficiently. However, more recent analysis, commonly dubbed the economic theory of regulation, has directed attention to the actual nature of regulation, blithely ignoring the normative aspects of government rules and restrictions, trying instead to identify the forces that lead to regulation—the winners, the losers, and the implications for managers. The chapter closes with a discussion of several important regulatory agencies.

From the time of Adam Smith until today, economists have struggled with the question of whether an unfettered, unregulated free market could or would operate efficiently. Early on, it was recognized that a host of real-world conditions, imperfect information, transactions costs, public goods, exclusivity, externalities, and other such afflictions, could make it difficult for the invisible hand to work its wonders. A leading proponent of this theory was the Englishman Arthur C. Pigou. Pigou broke ranks with many of his predecessors in economics, from Adam Smith to Alfred Marshall, when he advocated an activist role for the government in curing social ailments. His approach, dating from the early twentieth century, forms an important core of basic economics today. The next section details the Pigouvian approach to regulation as it is seen today. After that, a brief overview of market failures in general is presented.

THE PIGOUVIAN TAX

Suppose there is a company, let it be a chemical plant, that uses a common access resource, say a river, to carry away its wastes. For the sake of this example, let the waste product be mercury. The chemical plant is upstream from a brewery that uses the river water to make beer. This creates an economic problem.

The economic problem arises because the stream is common access, and as we learned in the previous chapter, this open access acts to reduce the value of the stream to society. In the limit, the river is worthless. Do not misunderstand, the problem is one of ownership. Since the river is common access, neither the upstream plant nor the downstream brewery can legally exclude the other's use of the river. Thus, any use by one of them that affects use by the other creates what economists call an *externality*.

In the case at hand, the externality is negative, but externalities can be positive or negative. For instance, if the chemical plant were dumping chlorine in the river instead of mercury, then the cleansing properties of the bleach could make the water *more* suitable for brewing, thus reducing the cost of water purification at the downstream facility. In this case, the externality created by the upstream chemical plant is valued by the downstream user, and we say a positive externality exists.

When problems of common access property arise, a number of solutions exist. These were discussed in detail in Chapter 12. They include internalization, privatization, regulation, and cooperation. In this chapter, we will expand on the use of regulation as a solution. We already know that bilateral bargaining can, under a certain set of circumstances, eliminate the problem without resorting to regulation. This result is termed the Coase Theorem. For instance, the chemical plant and the brewery could merge and deal with their problem internally if no other resolution were available. Be that as it may, regulation is sometimes used to deal with the problem. One of the main reasons that regulation is used in this situation is that most real-world externalities do not involve two well-defined parties. Instead, the common case of pollution involves many parties on both sides, making the bargaining solution nearly infeasible.

Returning to the original example, the disposal of mercury into the river by the chemical company imposes a cost on the brewery, and vice versa. Students sometimes tend to get confused on this point. The problem is symmetric. Both companies want to use the river, *and the use by either one to its satisfaction precludes use by the other to its satisfaction.* When the river is mercury-free, the costs of production are lower at the brewery. At the same time, when the river is used to carry away the waste mercury, the costs of production are reduced at the chemical plant. Nevertheless and in spite of this symmetry, the Pigouvian solution to the problem is typically framed in terms of a polluter, the chemical plant, and the innocent bystander affected by the negative externality, the brewery.

Consider Figure 15.1. Here we have drawn a market for some chemical produced in the upstream plant. The price of this product is P. The marginal cost of manufacturing the good when the waste mercury is simply discharged into the river is MC_P. This marginal cost is increasing. Downstream at the brewery, the

FIGURE 15.1
The Pigouvian Solution

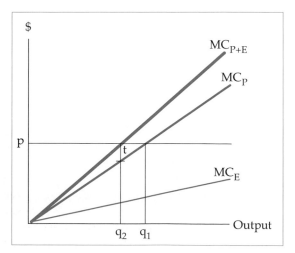

mercury has to be removed in order to use the river water in the beer, and the more mercury there is, the more expensive it is to eliminate. Thus, the curve labeled MC_E is the marginal cost of removing mercury. Since increasing output at the chemical plant discharges larger quantities of mercury into the river, the marginal cost of eliminating mercury increases with the level of production at the chemical plant. There is a correspondence between the output of the chemical plant and the cost of river water treatment at the brewery.

The Pigouvian tax solution is to charge the chemical plant a tax, t, that reflects the cost it imposes on the downstream user, the brewery. Properly administered, the tax reflects the marginal cost of mercury extraction, and hence the curve labeled MC_{P+E} is the vertical summation of MC_P, the costs of production, plus MC_E, the externality costs imposed on the downstream user. The imposition of the tax raises the cost of production at the chemical plant, inducing the company to lower its output from q_1 to q_2. Because the plant now produces less, this naturally reduces the amount of mercury in the river.[1]

In lieu of a tax, some regulatory agency could be empowered to direct the chemical plant to reduce its emissions of mercury to a level commensurate with output q_2. In either case, the externality problem is mitigated. It is important to note that there is still some mercury in the river, but less than there was before.

The implementation of either the tax or regulatory solution requires technical expertise. The taxing or regulating authority must collect information on the relevant marginal costs, MC_P and MC_E. On top of this, some way must be found to motivate them to activate the correct plan once they have uncovered it. Put another way, the Pigouvian solution is a normative theory. It is designed to describe what regulation *should do* and is not meant to be descriptive of what regulation actually does.[2] The next section expands on the rationale for government intervention in the market. After that, you are shown the other side of the coin, regulation in practice.

THE LOGIC OF GOVERNMENT INTERVENTION IN THE MARKETPLACE

Externalities are just one of a general class of problems that economists like to call market failures. A **market failure** is a situation or circumstance in which an unfettered, laissez-faire, competitive market does not generate a maximum welfare for the citizens in the economy—a market situation in which Adam Smith's invisible hand fails to work its wonders. Most of the analysis of market failures is

---

[1] Several of the states in the United States have enacted so-called bottle laws that require soft drink and other beverage sellers to impose a five- or ten-cent per bottle tax on cans and bottles that is refundable upon return of the empty container. This is the kind of tax Pigou had in mind to correct the problem of litter on the roadside.

[2] Actually the problem is more complicated than this. If the parties can bargain with each other, then the Pigouvian solution identified in Figure 15.1 is inaccurate; the tax will be too high. For a more complete discussion, see the paper by James M. Buchanan and William Stubblebine, "Externality," *Economia*, 29, November 1962, 371–84.

normative and lies outside the realm of managerial economics, but the topic is broached briefly here because government regulation is such a pervasive aspect of modern business practices not only in the United States but throughout the world.

The list of market failures studied in economics is long. We have already analyzed externalities in detail here and in Chapter 12. The proposed solutions include the Pigouvian tax, cooperation, regulation, and privatization. In addition to externalities, there are four other main categories of market failure that concern welfare economists. These are (1) public goods, (2) monopoly/monopsony, (3) informational failures, and (4) income distribution/discrimination. We briefly, very briefly, describe each of these and the proposed solution.[3]

Public Goods

We introduced the concept of public goods in Chapter 12. A public good is a joint consumption good in the sense that my consumption of it does not detract from your capacity to enjoy the same unit of the good. When I gaze at the sunset, you can bask in the light too. The presence of a public good can lead to a market failure when people act strategically to conceal their demand for it. In economics, this is called **free riding**. When a person free rides, he conceals or understates his demand for a public good, hoping others will provide the good and he can enjoy it without having to pay for it. Recall the example of the junk car we discussed in Chapter 12, An Introduction to Public and Private Goods. An old junk car rests near the backyards of two families. Each has a demand to have the car towed away. Suppose one family pretends to like the old car, and when approached by the second to discuss sharing the costs of having the heap towed away responds, "Shoot no, we ain't paying to have that old car towed away. We kind of like having it there. If you want it towed, you pay for it. I'm really sorry, but we just had to have the engine in the Olds repaired, and we are sort of short on cash right now. Maybe next time." Did you ever hear a story like that one? Now assuming that the first family truly wants the old car removed, they are lying to conceal their preferences in hopes of getting a free ride on their neighbor's tow truck.

When people try to free ride, and it often seems that they do, the total demand for the public good is understated.[4] When this happens, the normative conditions for welfare maximization are violated, and the unregulated, competitive economy produces too little of the public good and too much of all other

---

[3] There is a broad and detailed literature on market failures. The classics include Francis M. Bator, "The Anatomy of Market Failure," *Quarterly Journal of Economics,* August 1958, 351–79; Paul Samuelson, "The Pure Theory of Public Expenditure," *Review of Economics and Statistics,* 36(4), November 1954, 387–89; Paul A. Samuelson, "Diagrammatic Exposition of a Theory of Public Expenditure," *Review of Economics and Statistics,* 37(4), November 1955, 550–56; and George A. Akerloff, "The Market for 'Lemons': Quality Uncertainty and the Market Mechanism," *Quarterly Journal of Economics,* 84(3), August 1970, 488–500.

[4] Again, recall the section in Chapter 12 on the aggregation of the demands for a public good.

things.[5] In this world, it is often argued that government intervention is necessary to correct the social ailment of the free rider, especially when the number of people involved is large. The classic example is public education. In this case, when a person learns to read, write, add, subtract, and communicate verbally, it is easier for me to transact with her. Her education makes me better off. But naturally this is true of all the people with whom she interacts. I could pay her to educate herself, and I could be made better off in the bargain because my transactions costs with her would be lower. And this is true of all the people in her world. But the problem of the free rider raises its ugly head, and each of us has an incentive to pretend that we do not care if this woman can read or write or not. Thus, according to the argument, many people in our society will not receive the proper amount of education. Put another way, the marginal product of education will exceed its marginal cost. Practice calls for the government to levy a tax and provide for the public good. This does not mean that the government has to build schools— only that the government has to collect the money and contract for the schooling. The schooling can be publicly or privately produced. That is another, independent matter. An alternative to taxation is for the government to mandate that each person obtain a certain amount of education. Regulation or taxation is prescribed as the solution to the problem of public goods and the inherent free rider. Truancy laws can be justified on these grounds.

Most economists think that national defense, police and fire protection, and maintenance of the public health are categories of public goods in which the private, competitive market would underproduce these commodities relative to some hypothetical welfare maximum amount, but you should be aware that there is considerable disagreement on these issues. Economists, like most folks, seem to disagree a lot when it comes to talking about the proper role of government. Part of the problem here is that we are dealing with normative issues, issues about right and wrong or good and bad, and in situations like this, we each tend to have our own vision of the truth. In spite of this quandary, as a manager, you should be aware of this debate. Understanding tax policy and community affairs can be an important part of your job as a manager.

Monopoly/Monopsony

In Chapter 8 we analyzed monopoly in a positive way. That is, we tried to understand how monopoly firms behave. Here we will analyze monopoly in a normative framework. That is, we will attempt to investigate whether monopoly is good or bad. It turns out that under certain circumstances, monopoly is not welfare maximizing, and we prescribe some solutions to the problem.

In Chapter 8 we offered the following definition of monopoly: any firm that could raise price and not lose all of its customers. That definition will suffice here

---

[5] See Paul A. Samuelson, "The Pure Theory of Public Expenditure," *Review of Economics and Statistics*, 36(4), November 1954, 387–89 for a precise statement of the conditions.

as well. Economists like to say that a monopolist faces a downward sloping demand curve for its output; the price elasticity of demand is less than perfectly elastic. The most pernicious case of monopoly in normative economics is the natural monopoly. For the **natural monopoly** the long-run average cost curve, the planning curve, is negatively sloped, and the cost of production always decreases when output increases.[6] When this situation exists, the costs of producing any given quantity of output are minimized by concentrating that output with one firm, the so-called natural monopolist. The production of electricity or other utilities is often offered as an example of a natural monopoly, although there is considerable debate in the literature about the empirical validity of this assertion.

When the long-run average cost curve of a firm is downward sloping, there is a natural tendency for the firms in the industry to join hands via merger or consolidation to take advantage of the economies of scale in production. This natural tendency toward the dominance of one firm can create an unpleasant byproduct, a lack of competition and nonmarginal cost pricing. Left to its own devices, the monopolist will price where marginal revenue equals marginal cost, but price will be higher. When price exceeds marginal cost, the value to society of additional units of production is higher than the opportunity cost of making them. This inequality creates a deadweight loss which we discussed in some detail in Chapter 2 with reference to commodity taxes. The deadweight loss of monopoly arises out of the same circumstance as the deadweight loss of taxes; price exceeds marginal cost.

A number of remedies has been proposed to deal with this situation. One is for the government to sanction one firm as the exclusive producer and then regulate price. If this situation works perfectly, and hardly anyone suspects that it does, the price is set equal to marginal cost and the problem vanishes.[7] Alternative solutions involve competitive bidding for the rights to be a monopolist. Many cities use this strategy when awarding cable TV franchises. Some universities use this technique when they allow a private contractor to provide dormitory or food services to students. In either case, some governmental intervention is deemed necessary by those who believe that natural monopoly is a significant economic problem.

Monopoly can arise for many reasons. In Chapter 8 we listed several, including exclusive or unique asset, locational advantage, and patent protection. To that list we can add the use of force to exclude rivals. It is widely held that the purpose of the antitrust laws in the United States is to limit the excesses of monopoly in

---

[6] If you have trouble understanding the long-run average cost curve, review the sections in Chapter 6, Long-Run Cost and Economies of Scale.

[7] The astute student will recognize that when price is equal to marginal cost, that price will be below average cost. Reexamine Figure 6.5, Long-Run Cost. The properly regulated monopolist loses money. The literature has proposed a number of solutions to this problem, too many to enumerate here, but one of the most prominent involves prices discrimination that allows the seller to charge higher than average cost for the inframarginal units. Block pricing comes to mind.

our economy.[8] Ideally, government regulation is used to protect competition, to ensure the efficiency of the free market, and to limit the deadweight loss of monopoly. This is accomplished in a variety of ways, by examining mergers, by overseeing pricing practices, by scrutinizing advertising, and by supervising general business practices. The antitrust laws of the United States are interpreted and enforced by two federal agencies, the Federal Trade Commission and the Antitrust Division of the Justice Department. Later in this chapter, in the section, Some Important U.S. Government Regulatory Agencies, we explore the workings of the Federal Trade Commission in more detail.

In the normative theory of regulation, regulation of monopoly is sometimes used to cross subsidize a good. **Cross subsidization** is the shifting of resources from one line of business within an enterprise to another. For example, before the divestiture of AT&T in the early 1980s, telephone rates were regulated to cross subsidize local telephone service. Long-distance telephone calls paid higher than average cost rates and local service paid lower than average cost rates. This is attested to by the increase in local rates and the decline in long-distance fees after deregulation of long-distance service. With competition in long-distance service, cross subsidization is not possible. Competition generates average cost pricing, or nearly so, leaving no rents or profits for cross subsidization. What is the advantage of cross subsidization? There are two arguments claiming that efficiency can be enhanced by cross subsidization.

In Chapter 8, The Level of Profits, we discussed a situation in which a monopolist selling at a single price could be pricing where marginal revenue equals marginal cost and yet not be recovering all of its costs. Examine Figure 15.2. Given the demand and cost conditions that we see in the figure, the monopolist would produce q^* output and charge a price of p^* for it; marginal revenue equals marginal cost. But average cost, c^*, is higher than the optimal price, p^*. In this situation, each period the monopolist operates it loses money equal to the area of rectangle c^*abp^*, and in isolation, the firm would simply not produce or sell this product; it cannot recover its costs. But notice that the overall value of this good to society, as measured by consumer's surplus, exceeds its total cost of production.

The consumer's surplus, net of the price, is the area of the triangle p^*db. The firm's losses from producing this good are total costs minus revenues. This is represented by the area of the rectangle c^*abp^*. The net gain to society from producing this good is the area of consumer's surplus less the losses to the firm. This is measured by the area of triangle c^*dc minus the area of triangle cab, and in the case represented here, the net gain is positive. The net of consumer's surplus minus the losses to the firm is positive. Taking this approach, the economy is better off if this good is produced; yet the firm has no incentive to make the good—it is losing money on each unit sold. A variety of schemes exists to get this good to the market, including the methods of price discrimination we discussed in Chapter 9. But cross subsidization can also be used.

Suppose this firm produces another good with a downward sloping demand

[8] For an elaboration on this line of reasoning, see George J. Stigler, "The Origins of the Sherman Act," *Journal of Legal Studies*, January 14, 1985, 1–12.

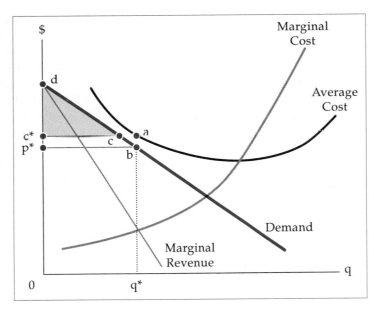

FIGURE 15.2
The Argument for Cross Subsidization

curve, and to make the problem interesting, suppose that the average costs of producing this good are sufficiently low that the monopolist makes profits, enough in fact to more than cover its losses from making the first good. In this case, regulation could be used to force the firm to make both goods and to use the excess revenues from the sale of the second good to cover its losses from the sale of the first good. According to this theory, welfare is increased by the cross subsidization. The value of cross subsidization as an economic justification for regulation depends on whether you think firms have the cunning and capacity to use multipart tariffs, price discrimination, or other schemes to survive when a single price will not cover costs.

Monopsony is the mirror image of monopoly. A firm or individual is a **monopsonist** when it purchases a sufficient quantity of a good to be able to affect the price by the amount it buys. In familiar terms, a monopsonist is a buyer who faces an upward sloping supply curve of some good. The presence of monopsony power is one of the economic justifications for labor laws. It is argued that a large firm that hires a substantial fraction of the labor force in a particular area can affect the wages of those workers; the firm faces an upward sloping supply curve of labor. When this is true, a welfare loss is generated that is similar to the deadweight loss of monopoly. In this case, firms pay workers less than the value of their marginal product. This means that if extra workers were hired the opportunity cost to society of their labors would be less than the value of the goods and services they would produce. Thus, when monopsony is present, society is not producing its output efficiently. To correct this problem, it can be argued that regulation of the workplace is necessary. At least that is the basic economic rationale for most of the labor laws in the United States.

Informational Failures

Suppose the average price of a used, 1990 Toyota Celica is $8000. Further suppose that the average one of these cars sold in your area has been driven 25,000 miles. You own a 1990 Toyota Celica with 24,850 miles on it. To make the problem interesting, further imagine that your car looks and drives about the same as those in the used car market, but your car has a serious problem with the engine. When the weather is cold, it will not usually start in the morning without the use of an extra battery and jumper cables. Sometimes even these are not enough, and you must have the car towed to the shop for a tune up. Is there anything you can do about this dilemma? Forget for a moment that you have scruples. What could you do? Well, suppose that you offered the car for sale in the summer months, or you advertised the car in the newspaper, and when someone called you about examining the car, you cranked it up in advance so that it would be warm and start easily upon inspection. The average Toyota is worth $8000, but yours is worth less because of its winter starting problem. Thus, since the average selling price is $8000 and your car is only worth approximately $7500, you offer it for sale. Economists call this situation an **informational asymmetry**. In the worst case scenario, the only cars offered for sale are the ones worth less than average, creating an ever deteriorating situation. Any buyer who does not anticipate this problem will pay too much for the used car, or worse, the used car market collapses; no used cars are bought and sold.

When an informational asymmetry exists, one party to a transaction has superior or inside information not reasonably available to the other. Since the world is not populated primarily by dunces, when a person enters into an arrangement in which an informational asymmetry might exist, he is inclined to take an extra portion of prudence. In the worst case, when a person expects that she might be the victim of asymmetric information, she simply stays out of the market. Therein lies the potential for an economic inefficiency. Two parties who might trade do not for one fears that he will be ripped off by buying (or selling) a product whose real value is different from the posted price.

Return to the used car example. You are smart. You are aware of the problem of asymmetric information. Thus, when it comes time to buy a car, you balk at the idea of a used car because you suspect that the *only* cars available will be the ones that the owner knows something that you cannot easily determine; the car is overpriced. The natural tendency is for you to stay out of the used car market. Instead you choose to buy a new car where you expect this problem to be less severe. The used car market collapses and economic efficiency goes down the drain with it. This is exactly the line of reasoning that the Federal Trade Commission used when it proposed the used car rule several years ago. The rule would have required used car sellers to post a list of known deficiencies on the window of the car. Similar laws require used car sellers to attest to the mileage on the car. There is a variety of market mechanisms that exist to deal with the lemon problem. In Chapter 11 we discussed brand names, advertising, and bundling as quality assuring devices. Whether these ploys rescue the efficiency of the free market remains an open issue because efficiency is difficult if not impossible to test, empirically speaking. We can note that many used cars are bought and sold annually.

Labeling requirements, that producers properly identify the nature and contents of the goods they sell, are sometimes justified on grounds of asymmetric information. Arguments based in the same logic are used to require motorists to wear seat belts and motorcyclists to wear helmets. The normative economic justification of regulation in these cases is that certain individuals, well-informed scientific experts or government agents, have superior information that were it in the hands of the consumers would alter their behavior to account for the information. But it is cheaper to mandate the action than to disseminate the information. Practically speaking, seat belts save lives, but convincing the public of that fact is more costly than simply requiring all of us to buckle up. At least that is the way some people in economics see the world. Whether or not you agree with that line of reasoning, you must accept the fact that many states now have laws requiring all passengers to wear seat belts, and laws are in the works to make this restriction nationwide. In a later section, An Introduction to the Reality of Regulation, we explore alternative explanations for consumer protection laws.

Income Distribution/Discrimination

There are normative economic theories arguing that regulation is necessary in a competitive market because of the existing distribution of income. In their simplest form, these theories argue that poor people would purchase larger quantities of certain goods if they had the money, and the gain in utility to these people from consuming these goods would dominate the loss in utility that richer people would lose by having to pay for them. A progressive tax structure is justified on grounds similar to this. Whether these theories are right or wrong is difficult to say because we cannot measure utility or economic efficiency. Nevertheless, some people argue that the world is better when regulation alters the distribution of income in the economy. This is the economic logic that argues for a wide variety of regulatory programs such as subsidized mass transit systems, handicapped parking zones, and nondiscrimination laws.

Discrimination, be it racial, sexual, religious, or any other type, can lead to economic inefficiency. Typically, economists frame discrimination in the context of a labor market, although the discussion generalizes to other areas. When job discrimination exists, a person is paid less than the value of his or her marginal product. Therein lies the inefficiency. A deadweight loss is created. Regulations that erase these losses, assuming they have minor side effects, can enhance the operation of the economy.

In summary, there is a vast normative literature in economics that argues what regulation should do. The guiding principle behind all of these arguments is that Adam Smith's invisible hand does not work perfectly and that government regulation can improve economic efficiency. There is considerable disagreement among economists as to whether these theories are correct or not, and to date, an empirical resolution of the argument has not been definitive. However, there does seem to be a growing agreement within the fraternity of economists that government regulation does not usually do exactly what economic theory says it should. At this point we shift gears away from the normative theories of what government should do to consider the positive question of what government regulation actually does. This is frequently called the economic theory of regulation.

AN INTRODUCTION TO THE REALITY OF REGULATION

In 1982, George Stigler was awarded the Nobel Prize in Economics. Among his many outstanding contributions to the discipline, the Nobel Committee cited his seminal work on the **economics of regulation**. Stigler is just one of many outstanding scholars who have contributed to the revolution in economic analysis that is referred to today as **public choice**. Indeed, just four years after Stigler won the prestigious Nobel award, his cohort and a major contributor to the public choice literature, Jim Buchanan, was similarly recognized. Just what is public choice and the economic theory of regulation, and what does it imply about management? In many ways, the two phrases mean much the same; they refer to previously unrecognized scientific analysis of the political marketplace by the application of economic principles to public policy making. The fundamental paradigm of public choice is quite simple to say but notably difficult to apply. It says that politicians and civil servants behave according to their own self-interest. Although this may sound naive or even heretical to some people, it forms the backbone of the modern theory of political economy. Even if you want to believe that politicians are public spirited and dedicated to making the world a better place for living things, you should be able to entertain the cynical notion that most government policy does not get formed in a public-spirited way nor does it work that way in actual practice. Let the evidence be the judge, and keep an open mind.

The public choice paradigm holds that government service is not performed for the public good. Indeed, politicians are treated no differently from other people: They must be paid to go to work; they have their own tastes and preferences; and they are no more altruistic than other people. Of course, this implies that they do not pursue the public interest any more than you or I do when we go to work. In turn this means any problems people have with government cannot be corrected by getting the so-called "right" people elected to office. Instead, the way to shape policy is through voting, making campaign contributions, lobbying, and letter writing. This approach to politics argues that the specific people in office do not determine policy; instead, it is the pressures they feel from voters and lobbyists that determine how they vote.

In this view of the world, politicians do things to garner votes and enrich themselves. They are not benevolent despots; they respond to their electorate. As we shall see, this implies that regulation is designed to **redistribute income**, not to costlessly and perfectly provide for the public good by correcting market failures. This public choice attitude is not a philosophical view. It is a hard-edged empirical approach to the world, and it is built upon 25 years of quality, interdisciplinary academic research. The purpose of the remainder of this chapter is to review and give insight into this way of thinking about and analyzing government and the political marketplace. As background, it provides a foundation to the knowledge held by many people involved in shaping the policy of federal, state, and local governments on regulation issues. Born of positive economic analysis, it seeks to be amoral and not judgmental. Whether it is good that politicians are self-interested is left to moral philosophers and political pundits. The student is cautioned against worrying about the assumptions of the model. Instead you are urged to concentrate on the conclusions of the theory and base your judgment on whether the economic theory of regulation helps you understand the world around you. You can applaud or lament the state of affairs over pizza or in other classes; that is not our focus here.

The basic point of the economic theory of regulation is quite straightforward. Government rules and restrictions can be used to prevent competition, to restrict output, and to raise price above cost, where private efforts to accomplish these goals cannot succeed. Regulation fashioned in this manner affords the regulated firms several advantages. The services of government are frequently provided at less than factor cost; often the regulated firms do not have to pay the government for the direct services tendered. Second, the monopoly police power of the state offers a unique opportunity to adjust the behavior of rivals. Just what does this mean? Most prominently, cartel enforcement or restrictions on competition are made relatively inexpensive, and the scrutiny of antitrust authorities is avoided.[9] Lobbying and other vote-getting activities are the price that must be paid by the regulated firms to the government officials in charge. This implies that whether the strategic use of regulation is profitable is a capital budgeting problem not unlike most other decisions the firm has to make about purchasing inputs. Government can be a business associate used to improve the bottom line.

When we open our model of the behavioral system to include politicians and the political market, we make regulations endogenous. This means that the laws are not assumed, taken for granted, or presumed to have come immutably and irrevocably from heaven. Instead, we analyze the passage and repeal of laws by focusing attention on the interests of the citizens in the polity. This makes it easier to understand some aspects of regulation, such as its inception and its effect on industries.

Mainly we divide the economy into two groups: consumers and producers. More sophisticated analysis recognizes the differences within both of them. These groups supply votes and campaign contributions to politicians who in turn supply regulation. The outcome of this process ultimately turns on the relative organizational costs across groups, the structure of political institutions, and the

[9] This is not always true. Whether regulation is outside the scope of antitrust enforcement depends on the type of regulation and who is doing the regulating. State regulation must meet certain procedural requirements as detailed in several Supreme Court decisions—*Parker* v. *Brown*, 317 U.S. 341 (1943) and *California Retail Liquor Dealers' Association* v. *Midcal Aluminum, Inc.*, 445 U.S. 97 (1980) among others. Moreover, certain cartel arrangements are specifically excluded from scrutiny by legislative mandate. The Federal Trade Commission cannot expend resources to investigate agricultural cooperatives and Federal Marketing Orders, and labor unions are exempt by statute in the Clayton Act and the Norris-LaGuardia Act.

extent of competition in the political market. This is the setting for the strategic use of regulation.[10]

Strategy may take the form of trying to coerce legislation, affect a bureaucratic ruling, or instigate a law suit. However, from an analytical viewpoint, these actions are all the same. In general, they serve one or more of the following purposes: to restrict the entry of rivals, to prevent nonprice competition, to differentially impose costs on members of an industry, or to restrict the production of substitute goods and services.

RENT SEEKING

Rent seeking is one of the relatively new and exciting areas of study in economics.[11] Rent seeking refers to the actions of individuals in search of wealth (or economic rents) under the control of other parties. A good example is theft. Burglars spend time learning how to pick locks, defeat security systems, and plan robberies, and then they commit crimes. All of the resources spent trying to steal money from banks are socially wasteful in that nothing *real* is produced in the bargain. There are no new buildings to occupy, no new television shows to watch, no exciting meals to eat after the robbery *that did not exist before the robbery,* and the time and energy spent trying to steal precluded the resources employed there from being used to produce the wonderful things that make life great or bearable. Even if the robbery is successful and the crooks get away with the money, society has no more wealth than it had before the robbery. That is why we say the resources spent are socially wasteful. The point of rent seeking analysis is quite simple. When a person spends effort trying to capture the *existing* wealth of another, resources are wasted. Even when rent seeking is successful, wealth is only redistributed, not created.

Robbery is but one example of rent seeking. Suppose there is no import duty into the United States on computer chips. Further imagine that there is one major producer of chips in this country, but many foreign producers in Malaysia, Korea, Japan, and other countries manufacture chips for sale in the United States. Let's say the current price of 64k of dynamic random access memory, DRAM, is $25. At that price, however, the U.S. producer, call it TELIN, is barely making money on the manufacture of the chips. Senior officials in the company devise a strategy to make additional profits. They open an office in Washington, DC, at a cost of $25,000 per month rent. Also, a senior vice president is hired at $200,000 per year with a staff budget of $500,000. This person's job is simple: Lobby Congress and the president to get a law passed restricting the importation of foreign-produced DRAM chips. To be successful, the VP gets some academic economists to write a

---

[10] For more discussion on the importance of the relation between government and business, see Martha Wagner Weinberg, "The Political Education of Bob Malott, CEO," *Harvard Business Review,* 88(3), May-June 1988, 74–81; and David B. Yoffie, "How an Industry Builds Political Advantage," *Harvard Business Review,* 88(3), May-June 1988, 82–89.

[11] See Robert D. Tollison "Rent Seeking: A Review," *Kyklos,* 35, 1982, 575–602 for a clear and concise review of rent seeking.

position paper on the strategic value of having chips produced in the United States, the deplorable current state of affairs, and the vulnerability of the United States to foreign supply shocks. This position paper is distributed to newspapers across the land, where it is published as an editorial or op-ed piece. The VP takes influential members of Congress to lunch, explaining just how the United States will be better if imports are restricted. The VP points out how many jobs will soon be lost in the representative's district unless some form of protection is granted. Similar lobbying efforts are directed at the White House, and when all is said and done, the job is effective. Congress votes a 50 percent reduction in foreign imports, and the president signs the legislation.

When this happens, the price of DRAM chips increases from $25 to $75. There is less supply available in the United States from foreign countries. It does not take a rocket scientist to figure out that TELIN is probably better off. The company has spent in one year a total sum of less than $1 million, and the result is a 300 percent increase in the price of its product. The conclusion of rent seeking analysis is, however, that the *world* is worse off. The $1 million spent by TELIN to change the price of its chips, *although it made the owners of the company better off,* did not produce any additional goods and services for the people of the world to consume. To be sure, it enriched the shareholders and employees of the company but at the expense of chip consumers throughout the United States. This contrasts markedly with the standard quid pro quo transaction between TELIN and its customers. When a free-will exchange is made between the two, *both* parties are made better off. Such is not the case with rent seeking expenditures.

The theory being presented in this chapter has important implications for the analysis of the strategic use of regulation. Transfers are typically not a zero-sum event. Forcibly taking money from one person and giving it to another imposes cost, for people will spend time and effort trying to become the lucky recipient and trying to avoid becoming the unlucky donor. Based on this line of reasoning, rent seeking analysis suggests that the economic cost of many activities is often far greater than conventionally presumed.

Consider Figure 15.3. The demand for some generic good is D; the supply is S. The competitive market price is p_c, and the quantity is q_c. Suppose the government decides to restrict output to 75 percent of the current level. In order to implement this program, the regulatory authority in charge of the program licenses 75 percent of the existing producers and forces them to maintain their current level of production. Notice what happens to price after regulation is induced. It increases to p_r. Profits increase for the lucky 75 percent of the firms that get to remain in business. For the sake of this discussion, suppose the regulatory authority bases its decision as to which firms will be allowed to stay in business on some nebulous grounds of product quality, ethical business practices, and general concern for the community. Then *all* firms in the industry will be inclined to invest resources trying to convince the agency of their worthiness. This may include hiring a public relations firm, printing slick brochures, lobbying the congressional oversight committee in charge of the regulatory agency's budget, or actually changing its business practices to conform to the new standards. How much money will the competitive firms spend in total on this sort of lobbying or positioning? Again, consider Figure 15.3. After regulation, price is

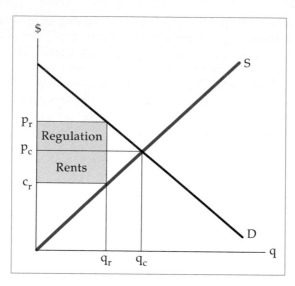

FIGURE 15.3
The Cost of Rent Seeking

higher and industry costs are lower. Price is p_r, and cost is c_r. The difference is a regulatory-induced profit or, as it is called in economics, a rent. This is free money for the firms lucky enough to be in the industry after the law takes effect. This free money puts a sequence of forces into action. Notably, competition for the money will expend resources. In the simplest form, suppose there were 100 producers before regulation, and there will be 75 after. Each firm has an equal 75 percent chance of being selected to get a license. Suppose the price under competition is $1, and the price after regulation is $1.25. Also assume that per unit costs of production decline to $0.90 (less output can be produced more cheaply). If the quantity produced under competition, q_c, is 1,000,000 units per month, then the total rents created, represented by the colored area in Figure 15.3, are 0.75•1,000,000•($1.25 − 0.90) = $262,500 per month. Suppose the regulations are expected to last forever, then the present value of the rent rectangle (at 12 percent annual interest) is $262,500/(0.12/12) = $26,250,000. This sum is free money, and we expect the 100 firms to spend large amounts of money to capture it. Indeed, it is arguable that they will collectively spend a sum equal to $26,250,000 trying to get the 75 licenses.

Think of the problem this way: $26,250,000 in total is available, which amounts to $350,000 per licensed firm. The expected payoff is 0.75 times $350,000 or $262,500 per firm currently in the market. There are 100 firms. If each one of them joins the lottery, what is the maximum that each would be willing to pay? Since the expected payoff is $262,500, if the firms are risk neutral, then each should be willing to pay the full amount of the winning prize or $262,500. If each one does that, then the total expenditure by all 100 firms trying to get the 75 licenses will be 100 times $262,500, or $26,250,000. This is an important result. The *entire* value of the rents created by regulation is consumed in the competition for the rights to receive the rents. That is why so many people say that rent seeking creates waste. Whether each company spends all $262,500 of its expected value or only a portion, the point remains. Rent seeking is wasteful.

You should be warned that there is considerable debate in economics about whether the entire rent will be wasted; and since rent seeking is a young discipline, there have been few attempts to resolve the argument empirically.[12] For our purposes the point is not critical. Any expenditures on rent seeking are wasteful.

The normative problem arises because it is impossible to differentiate rent seeking from profit seeking except in the context of a normative model. On the one hand, rent seeking refers to (wasteful) competition for rents created by gifts, grants, or government transfer activities. Profit seeking, on the other hand, refers to those activities that by definition are efficient. Research and development expenditures, piano practice, or commitment of resources to enter an industry in which price exceeds average cost are examples of behaviors that create value. By contrast, standing in line for free cheese, taking a politician to lunch in the hopes of securing her or his vote on a bill that provides a subsidy, or arguing before the ICC with an eye toward receiving a certificate of conveyance are examples of behaviors that simply consume rents artificially created by government. That is, rent seeking activities produce nothing real or consumable. They only result in a transfer. Behaviorally, rent seeking and profit seeking are indistinguishable; only with moral judgment, can they be distinguished. The point is made obvious with a simple example. Imagine two children, both of whom spend time learning to spell and write. The first uses his skills to become a successful playwright. The second uses her skills as a lobbyist for the sugar industry, obtaining quotas on imported sugar. The first is profit seeking, and the second is rent seeking, but in the classroom the two activities are identical. Rent seeking as a cost turns on the individual's definition of waste.

Rent seeking analysis has important implications because it enlightens the analysis of the strategic use of regulation. Consider the case of some vertical restraint on trade such as the prohibition on **resale price maintenance (RPM)**. Suppose that one accepts the agency cost or public good explanation for resale price maintenance. That is, RPM is a device used by manufacturers to force retailers to provide complimentary goods such as service and information at the point of sale that retailers otherwise do not rationally offer.[13] In this case, if a firm brings a lawsuit or lobbies Congress for a change in the law to allow RPM, then it can be argued that this strategic use of regulation is value increasing *even if it happens to disadvantage some rivals*. In this case, the strategic use of regulation increases the real output of society. Based on this approach, it is imperative to know the motives of a firm in order to judge its actions—a difficult chore at best.

---

[12] For a summary of the dilemma, see William R. Dougan, "The Cost of Rent Seeking: Is GNP Negative?" *Journal of Political Economy*, 99(3), April 1991, 660–64.

[13] Resale price maintenance is more complicated than this. For example, see Benjamin Klein and Kevin M. Murphy, "Vertical Restraints as Contract Enforcement Mechanisms," *The Journal of Law and Economics*, 31(2), October 1988, 265–97.

The problem is pervasive. Courts have faced it in terms of influencing the political process and made their judgment, which has been labeled the Noerr-Pennington doctrine—firms may lobby government even if it disadvantages their rivals. It is widely held that based on the Noerr-Pennington legal rulings, lobbying is legal and efficient while price conspiracy is illegal and inefficient.[14] Moreover, this doctrine extends to attempts to influence administrative agencies.[15]

The economic theory of rent seeking posits that competition for rents will drive the expected value of the rents to zero at the margin. Moreover, this competition consumes (costs) some or all of the economic value of the rents. Transfers are not free. Of course, there is also competition for profits. Therein lies the conundrum. Government action can create rents through regulation, laws, and court decisions. Firms seek these rents or profits in a variety of ways, most notably through attempts to influence government decisions. Whether this behavior is efficient or not is beyond the current state of the literature. It all depends on the nature of the regulation and whether the rents are "artificially" created by government or not.

THE ECONOMIC THEORY OF REGULATION

The first part of this section briefly reviews the economic theory of regulation. The second part focuses on the empirical literature of regulation. The last part looks at heterogeneous interest groups within an industry and across industries.

Economic Theories

It is hard to trace the evolution of the public interest model of regulation, although the late English economist Arthur C. Pigou certainly played a prominent role, as we discussed at the beginning of this chapter. The Pigouvian public interest theory argues that regulation should be used to correct market failures stemming from natural monopolies, externalities, economies of scale, public goods, informational asymmetries, or some other problem in property rights assignments. How this benevolence is accomplished through the political process is almost never addressed in the public interest theory. It is best to realize that the public interest theory of regulation was never meant to be descriptive, but instead

---

[14] *Eastern Railroad Presidents Conference* v. *Noerr Motor Freight, Inc.* 365 U.S. 127 (1965). The court concluded that there was an "essential dissimilarity" between the two activities. This position appears to have been abandoned, or at least modified, in *California Motor Transport Co.* v. *Trucking Unlimited*, 404 U.S. 508 (1972)

[15] *United Mine Workers* v. *Pennington* 381 U.S. 657 (1965). The doctrine was extended even further to include such things as boycotts in *NAACP* v. *Clairborne Hardware Co.*, 102 S. Ct. 3409 (1982). From a legal perspective, the problem is compounded by the court's indecisiveness on the antitrust character of state regulations. The Parker doctrine effectively exempts state regulations from antitrust scrutiny [*Parker* v. *Brown*, 317 U.S. 341 (1943)]. However, recent decisions have altered this course and imposed necessary guidelines for exemption. For example, see *California Retail Liquor Dealers' Association* v. *Midcal Aluminum, Inc.*, 445 U.S. 97 (1980).

prescriptive. Nevertheless, criticism of the public interest theory of regulation argues that this do-good approach to the behavior of public officials is analytically embarrassing in light of the propensity of most people to pursue their own self-interests. The theory can be partly rescued by realizing that, alternatively, *constraints* on politicians' behavior can force them to design and implement laws that have general welfare improving characteristics as part of their quest for votes and wealth.

Dissatisfaction with the paternalistic view of government implicit in the public interest theory of regulation led to the development of the economic theory of regulation. Regulation is demanded by special interest groups to limit entry, raise price, or otherwise reduce output when the private costs of cartelization are too high. For example, consider the July 1, 1991 letter to the editor of *The Wall Street Journal* from a farmer, James C. Barr, Chief Executive Officer of the National Milk Producers Federation, pleading for regulation of his industry:

> Your May 20 article about U.S. federal milk-marketing orders strongly suggests that deregulation of the market for milk be a primary goal of the Department of Agriculture. Deregulation of such industries as the airlines has proven to be a disaster. And deregulation of our financial-services industry has resulted in a bankrupt S&L system, a banking industry under severe stress, and has cost taxpayers untold billions. Now you want to add the dairy industry to the list. . . .
>
> *Most dairy farmers feel that casting milk-marketing aside would result in chaos.* Farmers would lose, processors would lose, and ultimately consumers would pay higher prices.

Regulation laws are supplied by politicians. The battle over rents is a simple struggle between consumers and producers. The theory of regulation is descriptive. It attempts to predict the effects of regulation on price and output, the onset of regulation, and the pattern of regulation and deregulation. For the most part, the theory is void of normative analysis, but there is the presumption, based on the considerable weight of the evidence, that regulation in practice bears little resemblance to the public interest vision of Pigou. That is, regulation is industry inspired and profitable. The moral connotations of this fact are usually left to the reader.

Why Regulation?

Why do firms seek regulation as a means to higher profits? There are several answers. First, government can legally use force to prevent what is nonacceptable behavior to some firms. For instance, when a private company tries to prevent the legal opening of a competitive establishment, it cannot legally use guns, threats, or violence to prevent the competition, *but government can.* If Denver Cable TV has the sole franchise to sell cable television pictures in the city limits of Denver, Colorado, then, if Colorado Cable tries to open its doors in direct competition with Denver Cable, the police powers of the state can legally be employed to prevent the sale of cable television signals by Colorado Cable. Without regulation, Denver Cable could not legally physically prevent the establishment of the competing enterprise.[16] Hence, government has a legal mandate to sanction certain activities that private individuals are precluded from exercising. This is the main benefit of regulation to a host of firms, notably and obviously electric utilities, local telephone companies, cable TV organizations, and the U.S. Post Office, none of which regularly suffers any direct competition. The absence of competition, enforced by the strong arm of government, conveys obvious benefits to the regulated firm in terms of product price, output, and profits. It bears noting that in most empirical studies of the beneficiaries of regulation, the firms are rarely the sole winners. Workers in regulated firms are often paid higher than market wages, and there is considerable evidence of cross subsidization within consumer classes. For instance, it appears that local telephone users were being subsidized by long-distance phone customers. Later in this chapter, in the section The Regulatory Triad, we discuss how regulation is used by some firms in an industry to stifle competition from their rivals.

A second reason some firms seek to be regulated is that under most circumstances in the United States, price-fixing cartels are illegal under the Sherman Act and other antitrust laws. However, under regulation, price fixing can be legally accomplished. There are many examples in American government. The Interstate Commerce Commission (ICC) regulates motor freight carriers across the states, setting rates and rules and delimiting competition by restricting the number of firms operating. Taxicab regulatory agencies perform similar tasks in a host of American cities. Without these laws and the agencies enforcing them, the price of moving goods in interstate transit would be a good bit lower. Similarly, taxicab fares would be lower without the laws governing them. Thus, in addition to less competition and less output, regulation creates higher product price than would prevail under open competition. At least that is the argument made in the economic theory of regulation.

Even when a private cartel can avoid the scrutiny of the antitrust authorities, it has to prevent cheating in its own ranks, a formidable task in many situations.[17] However, when government regulation is used to cartelize an industry, such as taxicabs in New York City, cheating is made more expensive and difficult, creating stability where it might otherwise fail. In NYC, traffic police are used to help prevent unlicensed operation of cabs, and fare negotiation is outlawed and enforced by the same authorities. Several years ago a Rochester, New York, couple began delivering what appeared to be first-class mail within the city at rates less than those charged by the U.S. Postal Service. They were arrested, tried, found guilty, and incarcerated by the U.S. Attorney for infringing on the U.S. Postal Service monopoly. Without the cooperation of the U.S. Attorney and his marshals, the post office would have had to deal with the price cutting in a different manner, by reducing its rates, increasing the quality of its services, or losing

---

[16] In June 1991, the Federal Communications Commission ruled that towns and cities that are not served by at least six over-the-air television stations may regulate local cable TV companies.

[17] See the section in Chapter 10 on cartel stability for a more detailed version of this problem.

customers. However, with the assistance of the law, the U.S. Postal Service monopoly was maintained.

It is essential for the reader to avoid judging the morals of regulation if he or she is to fully understand and appreciate its consequences. For our purposes here, it simply does not matter whether regulation is good or bad, whether there are compelling moral or economic justifications for regulation or not. The impact of regulation, how it comes to be, and what it does to price and profits are the subjects here, not the normative issue of judgment.

So here we have the economic theory of regulation in a nutshell. The next several sections are devoted to demonstrating the widespread use of regulation to constrain competition. After that, a number of the important regulatory agencies in the United States are described, including their history, organization, duties, and size.

The Empirical Evidence

One of the themes of this chapter is that regulation is often beneficial to the regulated firms. This benefit accrues in one of several fashions. In the simplest form, a regulatory agency such as the ICC acts as an imperfect cartel manager for the members of the industry—disallowing entry, apportioning and policing output, regulating price, preventing nonprice competition, and regulating the provision of substitutes. It is widely held that in their original forms, the CAB (Civil Aeronautics Board) and the ICC were operated in this way, if not designed for that purpose. It has been suggested that the ICC engages in substantial redistribution of the rents across modes of transportation. That is, some rules aid railroads at the expense of truckers and vice versa. Evidence abounds that truck drivers are cut in on the benefits of ICC regulation through higher wages. The best estimates suggest that union members get rents on the order of $1 billion. Certificate owners receive transfers totaling about $2 billion primarily because of restrictions on entry of new firms. These numbers suggest the profitability of the strategic use of regulation.

Taxicab and jitney regulation appears to fit the same mold. A jitney was a small bus used primarily to transport people to work and back on an irregular schedule. History suggests that the term *jitney* was derived from the French word for nickel, which was the fare charged, and according to research by economists Ross Eckert and George Hilton, it was not enough. According to them, jitney regulation was designed to eliminate competition with railroads in the mass-transit markets. Jitneys were a low-cost, high-quality substitute for railroad transportation, and according to these researchers, the trains "sought protection from municipal governments, which . . . proved unanimously willing to provide it."[18]

As an aside, it seems that jitneys are experiencing a renaissance in America. *The Wall Street Journal* reports that the small vans are "running circles around city buses" in New York City.

---

[18] R. D. Ross Eckert and George Hilton, "The Jitneys," *The Journal of Law and Economics,* 15, October 1972, 304.

NEW YORK—City bus driver Bill Pelletier is complaining loudly as his lumbering behemoth makes its hour-and-10-minute, eight-mile Flatbush Avenue journey from King's Plaza shopping center to downtown Brooklyn.

He says his route has become a "battle zone." Private, passenger-carrying vans speed past him on his left into oncoming traffic, pass him on his right, zip into bus stops ahead of him, and scoop up his potential passengers for $1, *15 cents less than the bus fare.* "They race to get in front of you," he says. "They break every traffic law they can."

Suddenly there is a crash. A van has plowed into the rear of Mr. Pelletier's bus. "We've been hit," he yells in exasperation.

'People's Friend'

Unbridled competition has come to the New York City transportation system. While city officials debate the abstract merits of privatizing services ranging from garbage pickup to education, the free market has sped in uninvited on steelbelted radials.

Transit officials estimate that more than 2,500 private transit vans now patrol New York City. They seem to be everywhere in the boroughs of Brooklyn and Queens, bearing names like "Knight Rider," "Island Boy" and "Leo the People's Friend." The phenomenon seems to be spreading to other cities with large Caribbean immigrant populations. In Miami, transit officials count 300 private vans, some even offering videotapes of Spanish-language soap operas to entertain riders.

At the corner of Smith and Livingston in downtown Brooklyn, a green van roars up to the curb. It bears the scars of countless minor crashes. Its chrome has been stripped in places, and none of the upholstery matches. A Jamaican flag hangs from the rear-view mirror. The front passenger seat has been removed for easier entry. "Welcome, welcome," calls out driver Donald Smith with a broad smile. "Come on in."

Several people do. "I take whatever gets to the bus stop first, and usually it's the van," says Victoria Balan, a social worker on her way home from a shopping trip. Says Beverly Dukart, another rider, "I thank God they're here."

Mr. Smith roars into traffic, reaching 45 miles per hour in a 30-mph zone. When a slower-moving city bus blocks his progress, he darts left into oncoming traffic and speeds around it. "Observe the nasty driving," he says, pointing to the bus. "He's trying to beat me to the bus stop."

Mr. Smith easily wins the race, running a red light to get to the next stop where passengers wait. *"The days of their monopoly are over,"* says the van driver, a former policeman in Jamaica. "This is the way the economy is moving, even in Russia." He arrives at the end of his run at King's Plaza in 40 minutes—a half hour less than the average bus time. . . .

The free-lance vans are illegal (though patronizing them isn't), and city police are trying to crack down. *New York state requires that all passenger-carrying vans be licensed and bars them from established bus routes.* Nearly every van now carries a CB radio to broadcast warnings of police sightings to other van drivers. Police patrols are staking out the bus stops in Brooklyn and Queens that face the heaviest van infestations.

"This is blatant highway robbery," says Ronald Contino, a Transit Authority senior vice president. He claims vans are diverting $30 million in revenue a year from the public transportation system, which is burdened by costs such as equipping

buses with pollution-control exhaust systems and hydraulic lifts for the handicapped. If the trend continues, he says, *"it will gut bus operations in the city."* . . .

Sgt. Joseph Mastromarino is a transit police officer assigned to van detail.
. . . The crackdown infuriates Mr. Smith, the driver of the battered green van on
Flatbush, who is also a sometime economics student. "The city is making a
colossal mistake," Mr. Smith says. Using the police to suppress the free-market
system will fail, he says, because it "is contrary to the thinking of Adam Smith"
(no relation).

In the past year, van drivers have been assessed fines of over $4 million. The
city has collected $150,000. Few van drivers appear at their court hearings. "They
aren't worried about losing their licenses, because they don't have licenses," says
police officer Jerry Trama.

Sgt. Mastromarino points out a decrepit van using rolled-up plastic in lieu of a
gas cap. That's a "rolling Molotov cocktail," he says. Two pedestrians were killed
on Flatbush Avenue recently when they were hit by an unlicensed, uninsured van
driver who lost control trying to speed around a traffic jam.

Still, passengers seem unfazed. Ms. Dukart, for one, contends that the vans are
safer than the city buses. Van drivers, she says, won't pick up people who are
"drunk and disorderly," and their availability means she doesn't have to wait a
long time alone at bus stops. . . .

It is 7 P.M., and traffic is easing, I am deep inside Brooklyn, facing the prospect
of a long bus ride to a subway line that will take me to Manhattan. No buses are in
sight. Suddenly a blue van materializes, emblazoned with the name "Lebanon
Valley College, Annville, Pa." Its Haitian driver smiles and beckons. Who could
resist?[19]

This story is interesting for a number of reasons. First, jitney regulation,
which must have worked in the past, now seems to be crumbling in New York
City. Why the city police and their bosses seem unwilling or unable to prevent
free and unfettered competition in this market, as the story suggests, is not easy
to understand. Note that the vans charge $1 per ride while the buses charge $1.15.
Note also that the loudest critic of the new wave of competition is the vice
president of the protected city bus line. Finally note that the illegal vans provide
higher quality, at least in the sense that they get the passengers to their destina-
tions more quickly, at least according to the story, but that they ignore some of the
niceties provided by the regulated carrier, such as lifts for wheelchairs.

CAB regulation of airlines had the same characteristics. The CAB created
rules and regulations that effectively barred entry of many air carriers into a host
of markets. At the same time, price was regulated to prevent competition from
driving down rates. It is hard to control all margins of competition, however.
Nonprice competition from within the industry eroded much of the cartel profits.
Airlines competed in scheduling and number of flights by adding capacity to the
point where expected profits were zero. It is believed that this process resulted in
average load factors equaling break-even load factors. In turn, according to

---

[19] Daniel Machalaba, "Opportunistic Vans Are Running Circles Around City Buses," *The Wall Street
Journal,* July 24, 1991, pp. A1 and A8. Emphasis added. Reprinted by permission of *The Wall Street
Journal,* © 1991 Dow Jones & Company, Inc. All Rights Reserved Worldwide.

transportation economists, this implied what economists George Douglas and James Miller called a "'ratchet effect' of regulation and reaction, in which price increases, thought by the CAB as necessary to raise profits, only resulted in a new equilibrium with greater levels of excess capacity."[20] Airlines also competed in terms of in-flight service. The CAB responded by regulating meals, flight attendants, and liquor service. What has not been adequately explained is why the CAB restricted these latter forms of nonprice competition but did not regulate the obviously more costly methods of competition through increased capacity or flights per day. One explanation is prominent. Excess capacity benefits airplane producers, pilots, engineers, and attendants. The political clout of these groups may have forestalled capacity constraints. Analysis of airline regulation within the state of California concludes that the California Public Utility Commission behaved in much the same way as the CAB, protecting intrastate airlines from competing with each other. The strategic use of regulation implies that if entry is restricted, output is reduced, and price is above cost, then nonprice competition will set in. The regulated firms will, in turn, seek ways to prevent this nonprice competition. The degree to which they are successful depends upon the impact of competition on input suppliers and diverse consumer groups.

In another area of long-standing government involvement, electric utility regulation, there is fairly strong evidence that state regulation of electricity production was sought to prevent competition where rivalry had brought *low* prices. In fact, regulation proceeded first in jurisdictions with the *lowest* prices.

It would be a mistake to think that the conventional, hands-on type of regulatory programs such as those in the electricity and transportation industries are the only ones in which the economic approach of supply and demand of political action is at work. For instance, it appears that nontariff barriers to trade implemented after the Kennedy round of tariff agreements were primarily in industries that were vulnerable to foreign competition. Similarly, the regulation of cable television looks to have been motivated primarily to protect the interests of local, over-the-air broadcast franchises. FCC Chairman Burch has said that CATV regulation could be translated "into the short-hand of protectionism for over-the-air broadcasting, but we feel that it is a public interest consideration as well."[21] Additional research supports the view that the primary beneficiaries of regulation were television stations in the top 50 markets. CATV regulations in 1966 and 1968 differentially impacted small firms and drove them out of business. A similar argument is made about antidumping laws. They are a means of preventing foreign competition. In one notable case, Outboard Marine Corporation, the sole American producer of golf carts, wanted the *American* price, its *own* price, to be used to determine whether a foreign producer was selling below

[20] George W. Douglas and James C. Miller III, *Economic Regulation of Domestic Air Transport Theory and Practice* (Washington, DC: The Brookings Institution, 1974), p. 55.

[21] Stanley M. Besen, "The Economics of the Cable Television 'Consensus,'" *The Journal of Law and Economics,* 17, April 1974, 41.

cost.[22] That is, they wanted it declared illegal for foreigners to sell below their own price—the sine qua non of the strategic use of regulation. In fact, they were unsuccessful.

These few examples are by no means the only types of regulation that are subject to strategic planning by firms. It is almost impossible to list all the research employing the economic theory of regulation, but two more examples should suffice to demonstrate the richness of the theory. First, regulations can be used to restrict the flow of information to consumers when bans are placed on advertising and, according to research by economists Lee and Alexandra Benham, "may be one of the most effective politically acceptable methods available for constraining the behavior of suppliers and consumers in the desired direction [decreased competition and higher price]."[23] Second, it is reported that the Oklahoma dry cleaning price setting board works hand-in-hand with the industry trade association to set regulations in the state. However, most of the recent research in this area stresses the diversity of interests *within* a particular industry. This is the subject of the next section.

It is important to note that not all of the empirical literature finds that regulation is profitable to the regulated firms. A study by G. William Schwert reports that the value of New York Stock Exchange seats fell in the period preceding passage of the SEC Act in 1934; regulation decreased the value of the regulated firms.[24] One explanation for this empirical anomaly is that a private cartel was already in place, but this begs the question of why regulation was ever passed in the first place.

Heterogeneous Interests

When we look at regulation in detail, we find that much of it seems to flow from the fact that most industries are heterogeneous collections of firms and factors of production whose interests often radically diverge on any particular topic. Since firms are not homogeneous, input price increases will not have symmetric effects. For example, let there be two different production technologies yielding the same minimum average cost. Let one be capital intensive and the other labor intensive. The first type uses a lot of capital and little labor; the second type uses relatively less capital and more labor. An increase in wage rates will cause average costs to increase more for the latter than the former. When this happens, some of the labor intensive firms will exit the market. Eventually, price again equals average cost,

---

[22] *Outboard Marine Corp.* v. *Pezetel*, 461 F. Supp. 384, 474, F. Supp. 168 (D. Del. 1978, 1979). See Louis B. Schwartz, "American Antitrust and Trading with State Controlled Economies," *Antitrust Bulletin*, 25, 1980, 513–55 for a more complete discussion.

[23] Lee Benham and Alexandra Benham, "Regulating through the Professions: A Perspective on Information Control," *The Journal of Law and Economics*, 18, October 1975, 423.

[24] G. William Schwert, "Public Regulation of National Securities Exchanges: A Test of the Capture Hypothesis," *Bell Journal*, 8, Spring 1977, 128–50.

but at a higher level. Since average cost for the labor intensive firms increased more than for their capital intensive rivals, it follows that price increases more than average cost for the capital intensive firms. A profit potential exists if the capital intensive firms can somehow get wage rates increased. Presumably the labor intensive firms cannot switch technologies for free. In sum, higher wages increase costs for both types of firms, but more for one than the other. On net then and perhaps remarkably, higher costs can actually make profits go up! Consult the accompanying story about regulation of computer workstations by the city of San Francisco.

Consider the simple case of an industry with specialized resources and firms of different sizes. The industry supply curve will be positively sloped. Profits are zero at the margin, but inframarginal firms (specialized factors of production) earn rents. Again, suppose regulation imposes costs on *all* firms in the industry, but not symmetrically. The supply curve will shift upward. If the costs are heaviest on the high-cost or marginal firms (factors), then supply will become more inelastic, and for some firms, price will increase more than cost because some rivals are eliminated. Therein lies the demand for regulation.

Consider Figure 15.4. Prior to regulation, industry supply is S_{pre}. Demand is D. The preregulation price is p_c, and the industry output is q_c. By construction, the firms in the industry do not all have the same costs of production. Some firms can produce more cheaply or efficiently than others. They have access to higher quality or more productive inputs at lower prices. Imagine land with natural advantages; it has more innate fertilizer, or it is physically closer to the market. The firms that own this better land can produce at lower costs than their rivals. If they own rich soil, for example, these firms purchase less fertilizer. Suppose a law is passed that increases the cost of applying fertilizer. Let's say that it can no longer be applied by airplane. The firms applying the most fertilizer have the largest

COMPUTER REGULATION IN SAN FRANCISCO

Size makes a difference. Big San Francisco companies seem to like the city's new computer comfort ordinance; small firms say the law hurts.

Starting this year, San Francisco employers must provide people who work at video-display tubes with adjustable seats, non-glare lighting, rest breaks and training in ergonomics.

Some companies anticipated the law. Last fall, **Levi Strauss** began requiring employees to attend a one-hour course in computer comfort and safety. **BankAmerica** has been buying ergonomic furniture since 1985.

But Bob Tessler, president of **DPAS Co.,** says the law is forcing the company to consider moving out of San Francisco.

John Pierson "Form + Function: San Francisco Firms Confront Computer Law," *The Wall Street Journal,* July 16, 1991, p. B1. Reprinted by permission of *The Wall Street Journal,* © 1991 Dow Jones & Company, Inc. All Rights Reserved Worldwide.

increase in costs of production, while the firms owning the highest quality land, applying the least fertilizer, experience the lowest increase in costs. This is depicted by the supply curve shift to S_{post} in Figure 15.4. Notice that price of output increases after regulation to p_r. Costs also increase for all firms, *but not by the same amount*. There are some firms, the ones applying small amounts of fertilizer, for which the cost increase is negligible. In Figure 15.4, let the cost increase, $c_r - c_c$, exactly equal the price increase, $p_r - p_c$. The firms whose costs increase by exactly this amount, $c_r - c_c$, are undisturbed by regulation; their cost increases are exactly offset by price increases. However, any firm that has a larger increase in cost than $c_r - c_c$ has lower profits because costs increase more than price. On the other hand, any firm whose costs increase *less* than $c_r - c_c$ will make *more* money; the price of its output goes up more than its cost. The firms that purchase little fertilizer can actually benefit from a regulation that increases the cost of applying fertilizer. The conditions are quite simple. There must be competing firms in the industry employing large quantities of fertilizer that experience much larger cost increases. These large cost increases affect product price and ultimately provide extra profits for the firms using little of the factor of production that increased in price.

There are many ways of achieving success this way. For instance, again suppose an industry has both labor intensive and capital intensive firms. The capital intensive firms can join with a labor union in support of an industrywide collective bargaining agreement and adopt a wage sufficiently high to exclude some rivals. The increase in the cost of labor differentially affects the industry.

FIGURE 15.4
Regulation and the Heterogeneous Industry

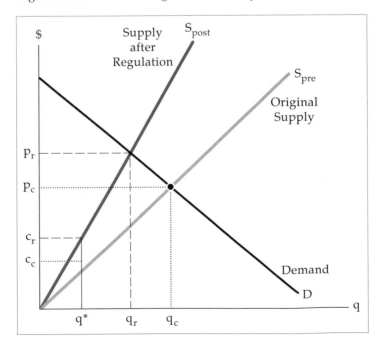

The capital intensive firms experience a small increase in costs, while the labor intensive suppliers get a big jolt to their costs of production.

Consider Table 15.1. Here we have two different types of production; let's say they are coal mines. The first uses relatively more labor than the second. From the table, when the price of labor, p_l, is $100 and the price of capital, p_k, is $100, the labor intensive firm uses 10 units of labor, L, and 5 units of capital, K, per day. Its total daily cost of operation is 10•$100 + 5•$100 = $1500.

The second type of firm uses relatively more capital and less labor; it uses more modern blasting and drilling techniques, but given the original prices, its total daily cost of production is the same as the labor intensive firms, $1500. Note what happens when unionization causes the price of labor to increase; the daily cost of production increases *more* for the labor intensive firms than for the capital intensive ones. Let's suppose that there are a large number of firms of both types. Then, in order for the firms to survive, the daily revenue to each firm must just cover costs. That is the essence of long-run competitive equilibrium. Thus, in the original situation, daily revenues to both types of firms must be $1500. What happens after unionization when the price of labor goes up?

In order for the labor intensive mines to stay in business in the long run, their daily revenues must increase enough to cover their new, higher costs, $1750. Naturally, for this to happen, the price of coal must increase. When it does, less of it will be purchased, so some of the labor intensive mines will ultimately have to close their doors. But if demand is sufficient to keep any of the remaining ones operating, then the price of coal must remain sufficiently high for them to cover their costs. This implies that the revenue to *all* coal mines, regardless of production technology, is $1750.

TABLE 15.1   DIFFERENTIAL COSTS OF PRODUCTION

LABOR INTENSIVE FIRMS	CAPITAL INTENSIVE FIRMS
ORIGINAL SITUATION	
p_l = $100	p_l = $100
p_k = $100	p_k = $100
L = 10	L = 5
K = 5	K = 10
Cost = $1500	Cost = $1500
AFTER REGULATION	
p_l = $125	p_l = $125
p_k = $100	p_k = $100
L = 10	L = 5
K = 5	K = 10
Cost = $1750	Cost = $1625

An amazing thing has happened to the income statements of the capital intensive coal mine operators. Originally, their costs and revenues were equal at $1500 per day. Their profit was $0. However, after unionization of the labor force and its concomitant wage rate increase, their costs are higher, $1625 per day, but their revenues are even higher, $1750. Their profits have increased by $125 per day.

It goes without saying that this argument works in the reverse. If regulation or other natural forces increase the cost of capital, then cost will increase more for the capital intensive producers than it will for the labor intensive ones. This is how regulation can be used by one faction in an industry to harm its rivals, not out of malevolence, but as a way of raising price and profits. Research on cotton dust regulation suggests that forces similar to these split the cotton textile industry down the middle with one group seeking regulation and the other fighting it tooth and nail.

The English Factory Laws passed in the early 1800s may be another good example of this type of struggle.[25] In early nineteenth-century England, water- and steam-powered mills had different costs of production, primarily because water-powered mills were dependent upon abundant rainfall for operation. Laws restricting child labor differentially imposed costs on these water-powered mills because it became more costly for them to operate sporadically. When there was sufficient rainfall to operate, the water-powered mills needed access to a large labor market in order to make cloth. Thus access to child workers made it feasible to operate water-powered mills. By contrast, the steam-powered mills were less variable in their demand for labor, and, even though the child labor laws imposed cost on them, the cost inflicted upon the water-powered operators was greater. That is, according to this theory, the owners of steam-powered mills sought regulation as a means of reducing output (by the water-powered mills), raising price, and increasing profits at the expense of their water-powered peers. This may be only part of the story. Additional research suggests that adult, male laborers were also involved in getting the Factory Laws implemented as a way of restricting competition within the labor force.[26] Outlawing child labor reduces the supply and raises the wage rate to those remaining in the labor market.

Environmental quality laws may also fit into this regulatory mold. The current practice of regulating environmental quality through standards rather than with emission fees is hard to explain without taking into account the interests of the regulated. Moreover, many details of environmental quality regulation are best explained by noting the potential for intraindustry transfers as described in Figure 15.4. There is evidence that some environmental quality and worker safety regulation was associated with increases in stock market value

---

[25] See Howard Marvel, "Factory Regulation: A Reinterpretation of Early English Experience," *The Journal of Law and Economics*, 23, October 1977, 379–402.

[26] Gary M. Anderson and Robert D. Tollison, "A Rent-Seeking Explanation of the British Factory Acts," in David C. Colander (ed.), *Rent-Seeking and Appropriability* (Cambridge, MA: Ballinger, 1984).

for some of the regulated firms.[27] Similarly, Bruce Yandle's research on miles-per-gallon regulation reports that in the negotiating stages, GM lobbied for a standard more stringent than was actually implemented.[28] The standard was expected to have differentially large costs on both Chrysler and American Motors, especially the latter. This implies that GM lobbied for the standard to improve its market condition relative to Chrysler and American Motors. In spite of Yandle's research, the vice president of GM in charge of congressional affairs, James D. Johnston, denies this version of the facts.

Other research suggests that regulation of accounting standards is also the focus of strategic planning.[29] After 1975, the SEC and the FASB (Federal Accounting Standards Board) required that research and development outlays be expensed instead of depreciated. Evidence is presented that large companies in high-technology industries benefited from this ruling because the small, high-tech companies reduced their research and development expenditures as a consequence of this change in tax law, and some were eventually forced to exit.

Virtually no area of economic activity seems to be free of these rent seeking forces. For example, Richard Ippolito argues that insurance regulation appears to benefit small writers at the expense of large direct writers.[30] In most cases, the large direct writers are out-of-state firms such as Allstate, whereas the smaller American Agency firms are predominately locally owned and operated. In addition, he documents that rates are tilted to effectively subsidize high-risk drivers via the assigned risk pools, raising rates to good drivers in the process. Standing in marked contrast, there is evidence that recent regulation of the California insurance industry hurt the regulated firms and helped consumers.[31]

Other researchers report that ophthalmologists and optometrists (especially the latter) have successfully used state regulation to eliminate competition from their optician rivals. The result has been higher prices for eyeglasses. Car prices

---

[27] See Michael T. Maloney and Robert McCormick, "A Positive Theory of Environment Quality Regulation," *The Journal of Law and Economics,* 25, April 1982, 99–124. John S. Hughes, Wesley A. Magat, and William E. Ricks, "The Economic Consequences of the OSHA Cotton Dust Standards: An Analysis of Stock Price Behavior," *The Journal of Law and Economics,* 29(1), April 1986, 29–59 have taken exception with their results.

[28] Bruce Yandle, "A Cost Benefit Analysis of the 1981–1984 MPG Standard," *Policy Analysis,* 6, Summer 1980, 291–304.

[29] For a general theory of the setting of accounting standards that focuses on the strategic planning of firms, see Ross L. Watts and Jerold L. Zimmerman, "Towards a Positive Theory of Accounting Standards," *Accounting Review,* 53, January 1978, 112–34, and the same authors, "The Demand for and Supply of Accounting Theories: The Market for Excuses," *Accounting Review,* 54, April 1979, 273–305. They also report evidence that large accounting firms systematically support FASB rulings that will increase the wealth of their most important clients.

[30] Richard Ippolito, "The Effects of Price Regulation in the Automobile Industry," *The Journal of Law and Economics,* 22, April 1979, 55–90.

[31] See Joseph A. Fields et al., "Wealth Effects of Regulatory Reform: The Reaction to California's Proposition 103," *Journal of Financial Economics,* 28(1/2), November/December 1990, 233–50.

are also higher because of state regulation of automobile franchises, according to Richard Smith's research.[32] He attributes the regulation to lobbying by in-state retailers who gain at the expense of out-of-state manufacturers. There is good reason for in-state regulators to try to cartelize the market for goods produced in-state. In most cases, the mass of the consumption takes place out-of-state, and the citizens there have a hard time impacting the local political process. Hence, it is reasonable to expect local regulation of production, cartelization that reduces output and raises price, especially when most of the production is under one political division and when the consumption is outside state boundaries. States such as New York, which for a long time had a big portion of the American banking industry, should, according to this theory, be heavy regulators of banking. This seems to be the case. The purpose of the banking regulations in New York is, in part, to prevent New York City banks from competing, mostly to the detriment of people living outside New York State.

Just a few more examples should suffice to demonstrate the ubiquity of the point that regulation is often beneficial to some or all of the regulated firms. There is evidence that the cigarette television advertising ban has actually increased the consumption of cigarettes (because warning ads were simultaneously dropped), and a relative price change has resulted. The cost of introducing new, low-tar brands has increased, raising the value of existing brands. Other research has found evidence that the Federal Trade Commission's ad substantiation doctrine benefits some large ad agencies while presumably harming other small ones.[33] The costs imposed by ad substantiation fall more heavily on small ad agencies because they find it more difficult to substitute ads that do not make factual claims, which are not subject to FTC review. It is reported that the large firms are vocally opposed to deregulation. Research by Paul Linneman claims that the 1973 mattress safety standard had little impact on average quality of mattresses because 80 percent of the mattresses produced already satisfied the standards. However, many small producers were adversely affected because of the increased costs of production. Some exited, and consequently as economist Linneman said, "large, significant, and predictable income redistributions from small to large producers resulted from the 1973 flammability standard."[34]

Other examples demonstrate that almost no area of regulation is free from strategic planning by firms to disadvantage rivals for higher profits. There is evidence that the large textile producers in the United States not only profited from the OSHA-imposed cotton dust standard, but they also supported its

---

[32] Richard L. Smith, II, "Franchise Regulation: An Economic Analysis of State Restriction on Automobile Distribution," *The Journal of Law and Economics,* 25, April 1982, 125–58.

[33] See Lynne Schneider, Benjamin Klein, and Kevin Murphy, "Government Regulation of Cigarette Health Information," *The Journal of Law and Economics,* 24, December 1981, 575–612. The ad substantiation doctrine requires that evidence of all factual claims exists prior to a claim's being made in an advertisement.

[34] Paul Linneman, "The Effects of Consumer Safety Standards: The 1973 Mattress Flammability Standard," *The Journal of Law and Economics,* 23, October 1980, 478.

passage. Elisabeth Landes presents evidence that laws passed in 1920 regulating maximum hours worked reduced the number of hours worked by women and their total employment.[35] Moreover, the entry of foreign-born women was deterred. Unable to work long enough hours to make the trip profitable, many foreign women chose not to immigrate into the United States. Both of these factors had the effect of raising the wages of men. Federal regulation of financial institutions differentially disadvantages thrift institutions to the advantage of commercial banks, according to J. Tucillo.[36] Consumer protection regulations at the state level are, in part, motivated by forces within industries trying to disadvantage their rivals, forcing higher prices for their own gain. Ronald Johnson and Gary Libecap discuss the conflict between inshore and offshore shrimp fishermen in the design of fishing regulations in Texas.[37] Hours-of-operation regulation in Canada benefits small stores at the expense of large ones, according to research by Steven Morrison and Robert Newman.[38] Building codes restrict the entry of foreign—that is out-of-town or out-of-state—labor and prevent use of efficient mass production techniques while increasing the demand for local labor, based on research by Sharon Oster and J. M. Quigley.[39] There is little doubt that whiskey labeling regulation has been used by certain elements in that industry, bonded producers and Scotch importers, to prevent competition from blended products. The labeling requirements in fact led customers to think that domestic blended whiskey had not been aged. At least that is the story reported by Raymond Urban and Richard Mancke.[40]

With a few exceptions, very little of this research claims or presents evidence that firms actually sought regulation to hurt their rivals, only that the effects were there. However, with all this evidence and so few contrary findings, it is hard to believe that firms do not understand the impact of regulation and how to use it to their advantage, or when to fight it because it will be detrimental—GM knew what it was doing when it lobbied for a stringent MPG standard. Burlington Industries was not stupid when it supported cotton dust standards. The eastern coal mining industry was not throwing money away when it lobbied Congress

---

[35] Elisabeth M. Landes, "The Effect of State Maximum-Hours Laws on the Employment of Women in 1920," *Journal of Political Economy,* 88, June 1980, 476–94.

[36] J. Tucillo, "Taxation by Regulation: The Case of Financial Intermediaries," *Bell Journal,* 8, Autumn 1977, 577–90.

[37] Ronald N. Johnson and Gary D. Libecap, "Contracting Problems and Regulation: The Case of the Fishery," *American Economic Review,* 72, December 1982, 1005–22.

[38] Steven A. Morrison and Robert J. Newman, "Hours of Operation Restriction and Competition Among Retail Firms," *Economic Inquiry,* 21, January 1983, 107–14.

[39] Sharon M. Oster and J. M. Quigley, "Regulatory Barriers to the Diffusion of Innovation," *Bell Journal,* 8, Autumn 1977, 361–77.

[40] Raymond Urban and Richard Mancke, "Federal Regulation of Whiskey Labelling: From the Repeal of Prohibition to the Present," *The Journal of Law and Economics,* 15, October 1972, 411–26.

and the EPA for a standards-based approach to sulphur oxide emission reductions rather than an emissions tax.

It would seem that one conclusion is inescapable. It is hard to argue that managers of firms do not anticipate some, if not most, of the effects of regulation. Rational expectations imply that they will, on average, be correct about the impact of regulation. Given the magnitude of the wealth that is estimated to be redistributed via regulation, job security implies that managers spend a substantial amount of time working a regulatory margin, not just to fight it off, but as an input to their production processes.

THE REGULATORY TRIAD

Regulation often brings together groups that have little in common. This is sometimes called the bootleggers and Baptist phenomenon, reminiscent of restrictions on the sale of alcohol in the American South. An entire industry or some subset of firms within the industry desires regulation to capture consumer wealth or disadvantage rivals through higher prices. An independent group seeks regulation to correct what it perceives is a social ailment requiring government intervention. The private interest joins the public interest, and working together with regulators they create a triad that presents a strong political force pitted against the interests of consumers or rivals. In many cases, it is only the public interest that generates sufficient political support to allow regulation to proceed.

The 1962 Drug Amendments were passed shortly after the Thalidomide incident, even though the bill had languished in committee for years. There is evidence that the amendments created a barrier to entry and raised the price of old drugs. The Food and Drug Act of 1938 was also passed following a drug accident. Elixir Sulfanilamide contained a poison that killed more than 100 people in September 1937. Similarly, the 1906 meat inspection laws were passed five months after the muckraking classic, *The Jungle,* was published. It seems the industry went to bed with the muckrakers. According to Roger Weiss, "members of the industry . . . are as ready to recall the mythology of *The Jungle* as any group has ever been."[41]

The economic theory of regulation predicts that environmental quality regulation is the product of a coalition between public interest groups and industry. This suggests the potential for a whole new way of thinking about regulation. What are the private interests behind mandatory seat belt laws or air bags? What was the role of the U.S. airline industry in limiting U.S. landings of the Concorde? Let's suppose that regulation was primarily to blame for Chrysler's financial difficulties a few years back. What was GM's role in this affair? If it is true that labor unions were a major force in the implementation of coal mine safety regulation, did they support it for the obvious reason? What if the purpose was to purge nonunion production (small mines) from the industry? Did the remaining

---

[41] Roger Weiss, "The Case for Federal Meat Inspection Examined," *The Journal of Law and Economics,* 7, October 1964, 120.

large coal-mining firms, some of which gained from the regulation, join hands with the union in support of the law? Many economists believe, and research seems to support, the conjecture that religious groups and others join forces with liquor sellers to affect regulation. The implication here is that regulation is a very important managerial responsibility, and it is simply foolhardy to automatically bemoan or rejoice at the onset of regulation. Each law and rule has to be judged on its own merits *as it pertains to the individual firm being impacted.*

ANTITRUST LAW

According to two economists, Paul Joskow and A. K. Klevorick, "The primary objective of antitrust policy is to promote full and fair market competition and to reap the benefit that competition brings with it."[42] But then there is the other side; there may be benefits to complaining that someone is preying on you. Judge Richard Posner argues that the antitrust laws can be used in this sense to harass competitors, especially those with lower costs of production.[43] Courts have recognized the problem and adopted the public posture that competition is to be protected, not competitors. It remains to be seen whether that is the case or not.

In sum, the power of antitrust law can be used by firms to limit the behavior of their rivals. It has not yet been sufficiently demonstrated whether the bulk of antitrust cases are pro- or anticompetitive, but, according to economist Janet Smith, "Mounting evidence . . . suggests that the correspondence between the stated objectives of regulatory legislation and the actual effects are sufficiently weak to lead one to seek out an alternative model of regulation that stresses the gains and losses to plural special interest groups."[44]

CONCLUSIONS

There is a major theme in this chapter: The anticompetitive or strategic use of regulation is pervasive. There is much wealth at stake, and managers would be remiss in their fiduciary responsibilities if they ignored profits available through (legal) manipulation of governmental processes. The decision to invest resources in lobbying to prevent the entry of rivals, to form a regulatory cartel, or to impose costs on existing rivals does not differ materially from all the other decisions that managers make on a daily basis.

What is the role of the politician as a regulatory entrepreneur? Does he or she function as a leader, throwing regulatory stones into the water, hoping to cast a ripple of wealth redistribution on some innocent bystanders who then surface

---

[42] Paul L. Joskow and A. K. Klevorick, "A Framework for Analyzing Predatory Pricing Policy," *Yale Law Journal*, 89, 1979, 220.

[43] See Richard A. Posner, *Antitrust Law: An Economic Perspective* (Chicago: University of Chicago Press, 1976).

[44] Janet K. Smith, "An Analysis of State Regulations Governing Liquor Store Licensees," *The Journal of Law and Economics*, 15(2), October 1982, 319.

and offer votes or other thanks? Or, by contrast, do managers and politicians work hand-in-hand developing wealth redistribution? To be specific, what has been the role of coal and oil producers and existing electricity producers in regulating the production of nuclear power? The evidence in the economics literature makes one speculate that these interest groups have not quietly watched as the NRC has slowly but surely put nuclear power on the back burner in the United States. Instead, intuition suggests that they have played an active part in eliminating their rival, especially when they have such a strong political ally as the antinuclear movement.

In sum, the economic theory of regulation and the empirical literature in its wake have one abiding theme. Real political clout is one, if not the most important, determinant of regulation. As a manager, it would not be wise to ignore this finding because the evidence is strong, some say compelling. This leaves us with room for but one conclusion: As long as there is monopoly in police power, there will be strategic use of regulation. It is common for business professionals to bemoan governmental intrusion into the marketplace. The point of this section is that many times rules and regulations can make a regulated business richer.

SOME IMPORTANT U.S. GOVERNMENT REGULATORY AGENCIES

This section gives an overview of a number of important U.S. government regulatory agencies. The potential topics that could be covered here are large in number and accumulating annually. We only discuss the ones that virtually every manager must deal with on some occasion, but this only scratches the surface.

The Occupational Safety and Health Administration

Occupational safety and health in the United States are regulated pursuant to the Occupational Safety and Health Act of 1970, sometimes called the Williams-Steigler Act, and amendments passed since then. The stated objectives of the act are to reduce employment-related personal injuries, illnesses, and deaths among workers in the United States. Labor and business lobbying interests fought over the content of the bill as it passed through Congress, but agreement was reached on the general duty clause, imminent danger clause, and priorities for inspection, investigations, and record keeping. These constitute the heart and soul of the act.

Originally, the act created three federal agencies to implement the law: the **Occupational Safety and Health Administration**, commonly called **OSHA**; the **National Institute for Occupational Safety**, often referred to as **NIOSH**; and the **Occupational Safety and Health Review Commission (OSHRC)**. Even though each agency has its own duties, the three are interrelated. OSHA performs administration and enforcement of the act, while NIOSH develops the safety and health regulations—the safety standards to be administered. OSHRC acts as adjudicator when OSHA rulings are disputed.

OSHA is a part of the Department of Commerce and is run by an assistant secretary of labor. OSHA is organized into three levels: a national office, 10 regional offices, and 54 area offices. OSHA's national office in Washington contains six directorates (health standards programs, administrative programs, federal compliance and state programs, training, education consultation and federal agency programs, and technical support) and several special offices (toxic substances; safety standards; all types of engineering, construction, and environmental standards; maritime safety standards; and the like).

On the local level, the area director answers local information requests, handles employee complaints, schedules and conducts inspections, issues citations and proposed penalties, and conducts informal conferences. OSHA compliance officers do not give advance notice of inspection, nor do they give advice during inspection. The agency does attempt to promote its objectives through nonpenalizing means as well. Compliance officers are permitted to give off-site advice to employers as requested. In addition, OSHA pays 90 percent of the costs of state safety and health agencies if the individual states enact such programs.

The Federal Trade Commission

The **Federal Trade Commission** was created as an independent administrative agency by the Federal Trade Commission Act (the FTC Act). The agency's main functions are expressed in the Federal Trade Commission Act and the Clayton Act, both of which were passed in 1914 and amended since. The FTC Act prohibits unfair competition and deceptive acts in commerce, while the Clayton Act outlaws practices that would restrict trade, such as monopoly and predatory pricing. The commission has broad powers to enforce these two laws and many others dealing with trade and commerce—for instance, the powerful Sherman Antitrust Act of 1890 and the Robinson-Pattman Act of 1936.

The commission is run by five commissioners who oversee the agency and give policy direction to its bureaus. The commissioners are appointed by the president with the consent of the Senate for terms of five years. The FTC is comprised of three divisions, each with its own director who reports to the five commissioners. The divisions are the Bureau of Competition, the Bureau of Consumer Protection, and the Bureau of Economics. Typically, lawyers head up the Bureaus of Competition and Consumer Protection, while a professional economist is usually in charge of the Bureau of Economics. The Bureaus of Competition and Consumer Protection answer complaints, investigate cases, and bring actions against law breakers. The Bureau of Economics provides support staff, aiding the other bureaus in case development while providing overall economic expertise in matters of trade and commerce.

The commission's principal functions are wide ranging, including preventing illegal trade restraints, regulating and controlling false and deceptive advertising, supervising the registration and operation of American firms engaged in export trade, regulating consumer commodity labeling and the issuing and liability of credit cards, as well as presenting data and information to Congress, the president, and the public on matters concerning economic and business conditions. Enforcement is generally accomplished through either consent decrees—that is, voluntary compliance, or mandatory orders against offenders. Through its main office in Washington or regional offices throughout the country, the FTC investigates complaints and issues cease and desist orders if the complaints are judged to violate the law. Cease and desist orders require discontinuance of the unlawful activities, and violators must verify their compliance.

The main stated missions of the FTC are to encourage economic competition and protect consumers, although many critics suggest the FTC does much more than this, as we have stressed earlier in this chapter. As Judge Posner has put it, the FTC is meant to protect the process of competition, not individual competitors. It is hard to know when a company, complaining of illegal practices by its rivals, is trying to report a law breaker or is simply using the FTC to protect itself from the ravages of its competitors.

The Consumer Credit Protection Act and a number of labeling acts, such as the Wood Products Labeling Act, the Textile Fiber Products Identification Act, and the Fur Products Identification Act, are among the major legislation regarding consumer protection. These labeling acts say they are intended to guard against deceptive labeling of consumer products, while the Credit Act establishes rules for administering credit and protects the consumer's right to privacy of credit information.

Antitrust regulation is the common term used to describe the FTC's other main area of control. Antitrust regulation has its legal roots in several legislative statutes—the Sherman Act, the Clayton Act, the FTC Act, the Webb-Pomerene Act, the Robinson-Pattman Act, and the Antimerger Act among others. The FTC competes and cooperates with the Antitrust Division of the Justice Department to enforce these laws regulating business practices. The Sherman Antitrust Act was passed in 1890, and it declares a host of practices illegal, most notably any act or conspiracy to raise price or otherwise restrict trade. Violators found guilty of Sherman Act infringements are subject to serious fines and penalties and up to three years in jail.

The Clayton Act (1914) forbids many restrictive business practices, including price discrimination, tying contracts, interlocking directorships, and intercorporate acquisitions. The FTC Act, also passed in 1914, describes a number of so-called unfair methods of competition, while the Webb-Pomerene Act of 1918 exempts some firms from antitrust scrutiny when they are engaged in foreign commerce. In addition, a number of domestic industries are similarly exempt. These include agricultural cooperatives and labor unions. The Robinson-Pattman Act (1936) strengthens the price discrimination statutes of the Clayton Act, although in recent times the FTC and the Antitrust Division have not spent many resources enforcing these statutes. For instance, in 1960 the Federal Trade Commission prosecuted a total of 560 cases. Of these, 166 or 29.6 percent were violations of the Robinson-Pattman Act. In 1980, the FTC processed 63 cases in total and two (3.2%) were Robinson-Pattman violations. The Antimerger Act, passed in 1950, expanded the prohibition of intercorporate stock acquisitions to include intercorporate acquisition of assets.

In recent years, the FTC has turned from being a reactive, antitrust enforcement agency to an active proconsumer legislative bureaucracy. The agency has devoted much of its time and budget to so-called structural cases that try to attack what are perceived as market imperfections. For instance, the FTC spent a great deal of time and energy in the late 1970s and early 1980s creating the ad substantiation doctrine that requires advertisers to know in advance whether their publicly made claims are accurate or not.[45] Such cases are held by many advocates to yield substantial economic benefits to consumers at large. Detractors argue that market forces are more than sufficient to handle any problems that arise. Notwithstanding, the FTC remains an active agency in American business, and there is little reason to think that this will change any time soon.

The Securities and Exchange Commission

The **Securities and Exchange Commission (SEC)** was created under the authority of the Securities Exchange Act of 1934. It performs legislative, judicial, and executive functions. The SEC's five commissioners are named by the president with the Senate's consent, with one of the five selected to chair the commission. The five-year term of one of the commissioners expires each year, and no more than three commissioners may be members of the same political party. The creation of the SEC followed two decades of regulation at the state level. But after the stock market crash of 1929, the Great Depression, and the ensuing Senate investigation, state laws were felt to be inadequate, resulting in federal regulation of the securities aspects of the economy. The SEC functions under the provisions of seven statutes and administers its duties in nine regional offices throughout the country.

The commission is charged in the law with protecting the interests of the public and investors against malpractice in the securities and financial markets. It also advises the U.S. district courts regarding reorganization of debtor corporations of substantial public interest. In addition, the SEC has certain responsibilities under the Bretton Woods Act of 1945 and the Internal Revenue Code of 1954. The main activities of the commission include providing full and fair disclosure and regulating securities markets, mutual funds, investment companies, public utility companies, and investment advisers. The commission is also involved with rehabilitating failing companies, representing holders of debt securities, and enforcing federal securities laws. To allow the SEC to carry out its duties, quasi-judicial functions are vested in the commission, although individuals with grievances against its decisions have rights of review by the U.S. Court of Appeal.

The concept of full and fair disclosure was laid down by the Securities Act of 1933. The act requires firms making public offerings of securities to file registration statements with the commission containing financial and other pertinent information about the issuer and the securities being offered. It is unlawful to sell unregistered securities, although there are a few exceptions. Government securities, nonpublic offerings, and offerings below a monetary value of $1.5 million are exempt. People filing false information with the commission or connected with a fraudulent public offering are at risk of fine and/or imprison-

---

[45] See Richard Higgins and Fred McChesney, "Truth and Consequences: The Federal Trade Commission's Ad Substantiation Program," *International Review of Law and Economics*, 6, 1986, 151–68 for an insider's look at the ad substantiation doctrine.

ment as well as damages due to the purchasers of the securities. Required registration does not protect purchasers against a loss in their investments; rather, it is supposed to provide information that can be used to make informed decisions about securities.

Under the Securities Exchange Act of 1934, the SEC was given broad responsibilities over the securities markets, people conducting business in securities, and self-regulatory organizations within the industry. Many provisions pertaining to the securities markets are covered by this act. The commission is directed to establish a national market system for the clearance and settlement of securities transactions and to establish the Municipal Securities Rulemaking Board to formulate rules for the municipal securities industry. The act requires securities exchanges and associations, clearing agencies, and the Rulemaking Board to adopt rules promoting just trade and protection of investors. To ensure that such rules are both in place and executed, the commission has wide-ranging authority over the activities of such organizations, as well as over individuals in the securities industry. Rules are also prescribed relating to credit extended by brokers for securities transactions, to information that must be disclosed to securities holders, and to repurchases by corporate issuers of their own securities.

Several other acts extend the SEC's jurisdiction in regulating companies and individuals. The Public Utility Holding Company Act of 1935 allows the commission to regulate purchases and sales of securities by companies in electric and gas holding company firms. The Investment Company Act of 1940 requires investment companies to register with the SEC, which regulates their activities to protect investors. Certain activities are banned by the act, unless specifically approved by the SEC. To restrict violations of the act, the commission may institute court actions to enjoin mergers and other reorganization plans, as well as plans and practices of management officials. Sanctions may also be imposed against violators. Investment advisers, as well, must register with the SEC, as their actions are subject to regulation under the Investment Advisers Act of 1940. The act prohibits advisers from deceptive practices and certain fee arrangements and requires them to disclose to clients any conflict of interest they may have.

The SEC is also responsible for some indirect regulation of companies and securities markets. Companies filing for Chapter 11 of the Bankruptcy Code must allow the SEC participation in reorganization proceedings administered in federal courts. It is the function of the commission to protect the interests of public investors in such cases and ensure their adequate representation in legal and policy issues. The commission also safeguards the interests of purchasers of publicly offered debt securities issued pursuant to trust indentures, according to provisions of the Trust Indenture Act of 1939. This act requires that certain clauses be placed in contracts to protect the debt holder and describe the duties of the indenture trustee.

Clearly the Securities and Exchange Commission has a wide range of duties. In order to perform the duties described by various acts, the SEC conducts private investigations into complaints or other evidence of securities violations. If violations are established, registration may be revoked or activities may be restrained or enjoined by federal courts. To the extent that criminal fraud is apparent, the facts are referred to the attorney general for prosecution. The commission may assist in prosecutions as well.

The Environmental Protection Agency

The **Environmental Protection Agency (EPA)** was established as an independent agency in the executive branch as a result of Reorganization Plan Number 3 of 1970. It was meant to coordinate into one organization the actions of 15 existing environmental programs managed by five different departments or councils. General consensus at the time was that an agency directed by one person with authority over many different industries would less likely be captured by any single industry or slowed by bureaucracy.

The EPA's stated mission is to control and decrease pollution in the areas of air, water, solid waste, pesticides, radiation, and toxic substances. The agency attempts to do so through assaults on environmental pollution, coordinated with the state and local government, public and private groups, and educational institutions. In its efforts to protect the environment, the agency integrates research, monitoring, standard setting, and enforcement activities. And as the EPA is intended to serve as the public's advocate for a livable environment, it is required to publish determinations of situations deemed unsatisfactory for the public health and welfare of the environment.

Specific guidelines and goals exist for each of the agency's programs. The tactics are quite similar for air, radiation, and water pollution controls. These programs represent an effort to restore the air and the nation's waters to a pollution-free condition. The agency develops national agendas, including technical policies and regulations for pollution control, along with national standards regarding safe levels. This also includes a national surveillance and inspection program for measuring radiation levels in the environment. In attempting to better enforce these standards, the EPA also gives technical directions, support, and evaluation of regional activities, while providing training in air and water pollution control.

Special offices exist for some of the agency's programs. The Office of Solid Waste and Emergency Response creates and employs policies specifically for these two programs. Its duties are the development of standards and regulations for hazardous waste treatment, storage, and disposal, as well as the enforcement of applicable laws. In addition, the office manages the Superfund toxic waste cleanup program, develops guidelines for Community Right to Know programs, and provides technical assistance in waste management programs. A special office manages pesticides and toxic substances.

The Office of Pesticides and Toxic Substances has much the same duties as the other offices of the EPA in directing and setting standards, but its entire list of duties is more extensive. It evaluates existing and new chemicals to determine what hazards exist and establishes tolerance levels for those chemicals found to be hazardous. Pesticide residue levels are monitored in food, humans, fish, wildlife, and the environment, and any pesticide accidents are investigated.

The Office of Research and Development acts as a support group to the other offices and programs of the EPA. The office heads a national research program pursuing technological controls of all forms of pollution. It directly supervises research at the agency's national laboratories and gives technical policy direction to labs affiliated with the agency's regional programs and offices. Close coordination of the various research programs exists to interpret total human and environmental needs. Demonstration results and research and development are published.

Implementing the entire EPA effort are 10 regional offices. These offices are responsible for achieving in their region the national program objectives created by the agency. They develop and execute approved regional programs for environmental protection activities. Procedures are given to them regarding how and what is to be inspected, and courses of action if violations occur. Offenders are entitled to notification of alleged violations, time to respond, hearings to determine facts of the case, and appeal. Not only do regional offices coordinate investigations, but they are also the EPA's principal representatives in other relations with federal, state, and local agencies; industry; academic institutions; and other public and private groups.

The Consumer Product Safety Commission

The consumer movement that culminated in the founding of the **Consumer Product Safety Commission** began in the mid-1960s with its most important boost coming from publicity surrounding Ralph Nader's 1965 book *Unsafe at Any Speed*. The essence of the movement, as it was expressed by President Kennedy, was the presumption that the consumer has certain rights that are being violated: the right to make intelligent choices among products and services based on accurate information, the right to have safe and healthful products of acceptable quality, and so on. As a result of this powerful movement, 21 major pieces of legislation were passed from 1965 through 1972.

The Consumer Product Safety Commission (CPSC) is an independent federal regulatory agency established by the Consumer Product Safety Act of 1972. Its stated purpose is to protect the public against unreasonable risks of injury from consumer products, to assist consumers in evaluating the comparative safety of consumer products, to develop uniform safety standards for consumer products and minimize conflicting state and local regulations, and finally to promote research and investigation into the causes and prevention of product-related death, illness, and injury. The commission is also responsible for implementing provisions of the Flammable Fabrics Act, the Poison Prevention Packaging Act, the Federal Hazardous Substances Act, and the act of August 2, 1956, which prohibits the transportation of refrigerators that do not have door safety devices.

In its quest to protect the public, the commission performs various activities. For example, it requires manufacturers to report defects in products that could create hazards and requires corrective action with respect to hazardous products already in commerce. Research is conducted on consumer product hazards, and information is gathered on product-related injuries, which is maintained in a comprehensive Injury Information Clearinghouse. The commission assists in the development of voluntary consumer product safety standards and establishes mandatory standards when necessary. Ultimately, it bans products that do not comply to its safety standards. The commission also conducts outreach programs for consumers, industry, and local government.

The Consumer Product Safety Commission headquarters is located in Bethesda, Maryland, and regional offices are in Atlanta, Chicago, Dallas, New York, and San Francisco. A five-member commission is in charge of decisions made and implemented. The commission's jurisdiction covers more than 10,000 products.

TOPICS TO REVIEW

These are topics that you should feel comfortable with before you leave this chapter. If you cannot write out a clear and concise sentence or paragraph explaining the topic after you have worked on the study problems, you should reread the relevant section of the text.

Pigouvian Tax

Externality

Public Choice

Rent Seeking

Market Failure

Informational Asymmetry

Economic Theory of Regulation

Regulation and Heterogeneous Interests

OSHA

NIOSH

FTC

Sherman Act

Clayton Act

SEC

EPA

CPSC

STUDY PROBLEMS

1. Airlines in the United States were heavily regulated by the Civil Aeronautics Board until the late 1970s and early 1980s at which time the industry was released to competition. From time to time there are renewed cries for re-regulation. Suppose regulation returns. Predict some of its features. Specifically,

   a. Will fares be regulated? If so, will they be maximum or minimum or both?
   b. What will happen to the value of the existing regulated companies when regulation returns? Will their stock prices rise or decline?
   c. Will more or fewer people travel on airlines after re-regulation?
   d. Will the salaries of airline pilots, flight attendants, and maintenance workers increase or decrease after the new regulations go into place?
   e. What will happen to bus and Amtrak fares after regulation returns?

2.   In the early 1980s, Bill Baxter and others at the Antitrust Division of the Justice Department converted long-distance telephone service in the United States from a single-seller monopoly, AT&T, to competition without disturbing the local telephone monopolies operated primarily by various Bell companies. Suppose similar deregulation occurred at the local level and the various Bell companies had to compete with Sprint, MCI, and others for local service in homes and businesses.

   a.   What do you predict would happen to the price of local telephone service?

   b.   What would be the impact of local deregulation on the number of FAX machines in individual homes?

3.   Read the accompanying story concerning new regulations for pap smears.

NEW PAP SMEAR REGULATIONS

New Federal pap smear rules will sharply increase the cost of cervical cancer tests with dire consequences for women in South Carolina, which has the nation's highest rate of the disease, an expert in the field said Friday.

The Clinical Laboratory Improvement Amendments, to be implemented in 1991, were aimed at eliminating abuses by large, state- and county-run "pap mills," which use underqualified and overworked staff, said Dr. Marshall Austin, a cytopathologist at Charleston's Roper Hospital.

But the real effect of the law will be to increase the already chronic shortage of specialists who administer the pap smear tests. It will put more of an administrative burden on them and cause a bidding war among hospitals to grab remaining specialists, Austin said.

The result will be a drastic increase in the cost of pap smears, a corresponding drop in testing and an increase in cervical cancer.

"The people that are going to pay the price for this are the low income women who already have tended to not be screened frequently," said Austin, chairman of the cytology committee of the South Carolina Pathology Society.

"Ironically, cytology experts believe that by driving up costs (the law's) regulations will increase the proportion of smears being read in large 'pap mill' labs and decrease the number going to medium-size, high quality accredited labs," he said.

In writing up the rules, federal authorities did not consult experts represented by organizations such as the American Society of Cytology, Austin said.

Those experts, he said, "have all been unanimous that it'll increase cost and impair access to testing."

Minority, rural and poor women are at the highest risk of contracting cervical cancer, which explains South Carolina's top ranking, Austin said.

Austin expressed hope that the federal pap smear law would be revoked, saying professionals nationwide have already sent 60,000 letters of complaint to the federal government.

"New Pap Smear Rules to Hike Cost of Tests," *Greenville News*, December 29, 1990, p. 1A.

According to the economic theory of regulation, which groups should be in support of this new regulation? Which groups should be opposed? What do you think the chances are that Dr. Austin's hope, that the law will be revoked, will come true?

SUGGESTED READINGS

This is a long list. I have marked with an asterisk a few of the articles that most managerial economists would call classics or those that provide especially cogent summaries of a particular area.

*Ackerman, Bruce A. and Hassler, William T. *Clean Coal/Dirty Air.* New Haven: Yale University Press, 1981.

Anderson, Gary M. and Tollison, Robert D. "A Rent-Seeking Explanation of the British Factory Acts." In David Collander (ed.), *Rent-Seeking and Appropriability.* Cambridge, MA: Ballinger Press, 1984.

Anderson, Gary M., Shughart, William F., II, and Tollison, Robert D. "Adam Smith in the Customhouse." *Journal of Political Economy* 93(4) (August 1985):740–59.

Benham, Lee and Benham, Alexandra. "Regulating Through the Professions: A Perspective on Information Control." *The Journal of Law and Economics* 18 (October 1975): 421–48.

Besen, Stanley M. "The Economics of the Cable Television 'Consensus.'" *The Journal of Law and Economics* 17 (April 1974):39–52.

Bork, Robert H. *The Antitrust Paradox.* New York: Basic Books, 1978.

Buchanan, James M. "Rent Seeking and Profit Seeking." In James M. Buchanan, Robert D. Tollison, and Gordon Tullock, eds., *Toward a Theory of the Rent-Seeking Society.* College Station: Texas A&M Press, 1980.

Caves, Richard E. "Industrial Organization, Corporate Strategy and Structure." *Journal of Economic Literature* 18 (March 1980):64–92.

Clarkson, Kenneth W., Kadlec, Charles W., and Laffer, Arthur B. "Regulating Chrysler Out of Business?" *Regulation* 3 (September/October 1979):44–49.

Clarkson, Kenneth W. and Muris, Timothy J., eds. *The Federal Trade Commission Since 1970.* New York: Cambridge University Press, 1981.

Comanor, William S. and Mitchell, Bridges M. "Cable Television and the Impact of Regulation." *Bell Journal* 2 (Spring 1971):154–212.

Dougan, William R. "The Cost of Rent Seeking: Is GNP Negative?" *Journal of Political Economy* 99(3) (June 1991):660–64.

*Douglas, George W. and Miller, James C., III. *Economic Regulation of Domestic Air Transport Theory and Practice.* Washington, DC: The Brookings Institution, 1974.

Easterbrook, Frank H. "Antitrust and the Economics of Federalism." *The Journal of Law and Economics* 26 (April 1983):23–50.

*Eckert, R. D. "On the Incentives of Regulators: The Case of Taxicabs." *Public Choice* 14 (Spring 1973):83–99.

Eckert, R. D. and Hilton, George. "The Jitneys." *The Journal of Law and Economics* 15 (October 1972):293–326.

Fischel, Daniel R. "Antitrust Liability for Attempts to Influence Government Action: The Basis and Limits of the Noerr-Pennington Doctrine." *University of California Law Review* 45 (Fall 1977):80–123.

Greenberg, Edward. "Wire Television and the FCC's Second Report and Order on CATV Systems." *The Journal of Law and Economics* 10 (October 1967):181–92.

Guttman, Joel L. "Interest Groups and the Demand for Agricultural Research." *Journal of Political Economy* 86 (June 1978):467–84.

Higgins, Richard and McChesney, Fred. "Truth and Consequences: The Federal Trade Commission's Ad Substantiation Program." *International Review of Law and Economics* 6 (1986):151–68.

Horwitz, Bertrand and Kolodny, Richard. "The FASB, the SEC, and R&D." *Bell Journal* 12 (Spring 1981):249–62.

Ippolito, Richard. "The Effects of Price Regulation in the Automobile Industry." *The Journal of Law and Economics* 22 (April 1979):55–90.

*Jarrell, Gregg A. "The Demand for State Regulation of the Electric Utility Industry." *Journal of Law and Economics* 21 (October 1978):269–98.

*Johnson, Ronald N. and Libecap, Gary D. "Contracting Problems and Regulation: The Case of the Fishery." *American Economic Review* 72 (December 1982):1005–22.

Jordon, William A. *Airline Regulation in America.* Baltimore: The Johns Hopkins Press, 1970.

Joskow, Paul L. and Klevorick, A. K. "A Framework for Analyzing Predatory Pricing Policy." *Yale Law Journal* 89 (1979):213–70.

Keeler, Theodore E. "Airline Regulation and Market Performance." *Bell Journal* 3 (Autumn 1972):399–414.

Kitch, Edmund, Issacson, Marc, and Kasper, Daniel. "The Regulation of Taxicabs in Chicago." *The Journal of Law and Economics* 14 (October 1971):285–350.

La Mond, A. M. "An Evaluation of Intrastate Airline Regulation in California." *Bell Journal* 7 (Autumn 1976):641–57.

Landes, Elisabeth M. "The Effect of State Maximum-Hours Laws on the Employment of Women in 1920." *Journal of Political Economy* 88 (June 1980):476–94.

*Landes, William and Posner, Richard. "The Independent Judiciary in an Interest-Group Perspective." *The Journal of Law and Economics* 18 (December 1975):875–901.

Linneman, Paul. "The Effects of Consumer Safety Standards: The 1973 Mattress Flammability Standard." *The Journal of Law and Economics* 23 (October 1980):461–80.

McCormick, Robert E., Shughart, William F., II, and Tollison, Robert D. "The Disinterest in Deregulation." *American Economic Review* 74 (December 1984):1075–79.

McGraw, Thomas K. "Regulation in America: A Review Article." *Business History Review* 49 (Summer 1975):159–83.

Maloney, Michael T. and McCormick, Robert E. "A Positive Theory of Environmental Quality Regulation." *The Journal of Law and Economics* 25 (April 1982):99–124.

Maloney, Michael T., McCormick, Robert E., and Tollison, Robert D. "Achieving Cartel Profits Through Unionization." *Southern Economic Journal* 46 (October 1979):628–34.

Maloney, Michael T., McCormick, Robert E., and Tollison, Robert D. "Economic Regulation, Competitive Governments, and Specialized Resources." *The Journal of Law and Economics* 27 (October 1984):329–38.

Marvel, Howard. "Factory Regulation: A Reinterpretation of Early English Experience." *Journal of Law and Economics* 20 (October 1977):379–402.

Marvel, Howard and Ray, Edward J. "The Kennedy Round: Evidence on the Regulation of International Trade in the United States." *American Economic Review* 73 (March 1983):190–97.

Maurizi, Alex, Moore, Ruth L., and Shephard, Lawrence. "Competing for Professional Control: Professional Mix in the Eyeglass Industry." *The Journal of Law and Economics* 24 (October 1981):351–64.

*Moore, Thomas G. "The Beneficiaries of Trucking Regulation." *The Journal of Law and Economics* 21 (October 1978):327–44.

Morrison, Steven A. and Newman, Robert J. "Hours of Operation Restriction and Competition Among Retail Firms." *Economic Inquiry* 21 (January 1983):107–14.

*Niskanen, William A. *Bureaucracy and Representative Government.* Chicago: Aldine-Atherton, 1971.

Noll, Roger and Owen, Bruce M. *The Political Economy of Deregulation.* Washington, DC: American Enterprise Institute, 1983.

Nuemann, George R. and Nelson, Jon P. "Safety Regulation and Firm Size: Effects of the Coal Mine Health and Safety Act of 1969." *The Journal of Law and Economics* 25 (October 1982):183–200.

Oster, Sharon M. "An Analysis of Some Causes of Interstate Differences in Consumer Regulations." *Economic Inquiry* 18 (January 1980):39–54.

Oster, Sharon M. "The Strategic Use of Regulatory Investment by Industry Subgroups." *Economic Inquiry* 20 (October 1982):604–18.

Oster, Sharon M. and Quigley, J. M. "Regulatory Barriers to the Diffusion of Innovation." *Bell Journal* 8 (Autumn 1977):361–77.

Page, William H. "Antitrust, Federalism, and the Regulatory Process: A Reconstruction and Critique of the State Action Exemption After Midcal Aluminum." *Boston University Law Review* 61 (November 1981):1099–38.

Peltzman, Sam. *Regulation of Pharmaceutical Innovation.* Washington, DC: American Enterprise Institute, 1974.

*Peltzman, Sam. "Toward a More General Theory of Regulation." *The Journal of Law and Economics* 19 (August 1976):211–40.

Pigou, Arthur C. *The Economics of Welfare.* London: Macmillan, 1932.

Pincus, Jonathan J. *Pressure Groups and Politics in Antebellum Tariffs.* New York: Columbia University Press, 1977.

Plott, Charles R. "Occupational Self-Regulation: A Case Study of the Oklahoma Dry Cleaners." *The Journal of Law and Economics* 8 (October 1965):195–222.

Posner, Richard A. "Taxation by Regulation." *Bell Journal* 2 (Spring 1971):22–50.

*Posner, Richard A. "Theories of Economic Regulation." *Bell Journal* 5 (Autumn 1974): 335–58.

Posner, Richard A. *Antitrust Law: An Economic Perspective.* Chicago: University of Chicago Press, 1976.

Posner, Richard A. "Economics, Politics, and the Reading of Statutes and the Constitution." *University of California Law Review* 49 (Spring 1982):263–91.

Salop, Steven C. and Scheffman, David T. "Raising Rivals Costs." *American Economic Review* 73 (May 1983):267–71.

Schneider, Lynne, Klein, Benjamin, and Murphy, Kevin. "Government Regulation of Cigarette Health Information." *The Journal of Law and Economics* 24 (December 1981): 575–612.

Schwartz, Louis B. "American Antitrust and Trading with State Controlled Economies." *Antitrust Bulletin* 25 (1980):513–55.

Schwert, G. William. "Public Regulation of National Securities Exchanges: A Test of the Capture Hypothesis." *Bell Journal* 8 (Spring 1977):128–50.

Shughart, William F., II and Tollison, Robert D. "The Positive Economics of Antitrust Policy: A Survey Article." *International Review of Law and Economics* 5(1) (June 1985): 39–57.

Smith, Janet K. "An Analysis of State Regulations Governing Liquor Store Licenses." *The Journal of Law and Economics* 25 (October 1982):301–20.

Smith, Richard L., II. "Franchise Regulation: An Economic Analysis of State Restriction on Automobile Distribution." *The Journal of Law and Economics* 25 (April 1982):125–58.

Spiller, Pablo T. "The Differential Impact of Airline Regulation on Individual Firms and Markets: An Empirical Analysis." *The Journal of Law and Economics* 26 (October 1983): 655–90.

Look

*Stigler, George J. "The Theory of Economic Regulation." *Bell Journal* 2 (Spring 1971):3–21.

Stigler, George J. and Friedland, Claire. "What Can Regulators Regulate? The Case of Electricity." *The Journal of Law and Economics* 5 (October 1962):1–16.

Stone, Alan. *Economic Regulation and Public Interest: The Federal Trade Commission in Theory and Practice.* Ithaca: Cornell University Press, 1977.

Temin, Peter. "The Origin of Compulsory Drug Prescriptions." *The Journal of Law and Economics* 22 (April 1979):91–106.

*Tollison, Robert D. "Rent Seeking: A Review." *Kyklos* 35 (1982):575–602.

Tucillo, J. "Taxation by Regulation: The Case of Financial Intermediaries." *Bell Journal* 8 (Autumn 1977):577–90.

*Tullock, Gordon. "The Welfare Costs of Tariffs, Monopolies, and Theft." *Western Economic Journal* 5 (June 1967):224–32.

Urban, Raymond and Mancke, Richard. "Federal Regulation of Whiskey Labelling: From the Repeal of Prohibition to the Present." *The Journal of Law and Economics* 15 (October 1972):411–26.

*Watts, Ross L. and Zimmerman, Jerold L. "Towards a Positive Theory of Accounting Standards." *Accounting Review* 53 (January 1978):112–34.

Watts, Ross L. and Zimmerman, Jerold L. "The Demand for and Supply of Accounting Theories: The Market for Excuses." *Accounting Review* 54 (April 1979):273–305.

Weinberg, Martha Wagner. "The Political Education of Bob Malott, CEO." *Harvard Business Review* 88(3) (May-June 1988):74–81.

Weiss, Roger. "The Case for Federal Meat Inspection Examined." *The Journal of Law and Economics* 7 (October 1964):107–20.

Williamson, Oliver E. "Wage Rates as a Barrier to Entry: The Pennington Case." *Quarterly Journal of Economics* 82 (February 1968):85–116.

Yandle, Bruce. "A Cost Benefit Analysis of the 1981–1984 MPG Standard." *Policy Analysis* 6 (Summer 1980):291–304.

Yandle, Bruce. "Bootleggers and Baptists." *Regulation* 7 (May/June 1983):12–16.

Yoffie, David B. "How an Industry Builds Political Advantage." *Harvard Business Review* 88(3) (May-June 1988):82–89.

SUGGESTED SOLUTIONS TO SELECTED STUDY PROBLEMS

The following are only *suggested* solutions to the study problems presented at the end of this chapter. In all cases, the suggestions here put heavy emphasis on analysis rather than a single correct answer. Since most managerial problems do not fall into neat little boxes, the individual characteristics of the problems that you encounter on the job will typically mandate a solution using the principles developed here and in other courses. Memorizing these solutions will not make you a good manager; learning the *principles* detailed here will help make you a better manager.

1. a. According to the economic theory of regulation, the purpose of regulation is to raise price and reduce output. Accordingly, if airline regulation is reintroduced, we should expect to see fare regulation. This regulation should take the form of both maximum and minimum prices. In other words, the new regulations should set price. We expect this for two reasons. First, airlines want price regulation to prevent competition among themselves. At the same time, consumers know that regulators are going to restrict entry of new firms, thus creating a monopoly-like

situation. To protect themselves against the full power of this monopoly the regulations will also cap fares. This is the effect described by Peltzman.

b. We expect the value of the existing airlines will increase with regulation. However, we do not expect that all firms will benefit the same. The industry is not homogeneous. Airlines vary in the types of planes they use and the routes they serve. We expect that the stock prices of existing airlines will increase on average.

c. We expect that fewer people will travel on airplanes after reregulation. This is due to the higher fares that will follow regulation. There may be some cross subsidization of fares so that prices are lower in some markets. If this happens, there will be an increase in air travel in the markets that get subsidized.

d. In all likelihood, the salaries of these individuals will increase. At least that is what happened with the first experience of regulation. This is probably due to many causes, but the one most frequently cited is that labor represents a powerful political force at the ballot box.

e. Since bus and train travel are almost surely substitutes for air travel, higher air fares will increase the demand for bus and train travel. When this happens, we expect higher fares for the substitutes too.

3. According to the economic theory of regulation, the demand for regulation arises from the firms in the industry. This story makes it appear as though there are basically two types of producers, the so-called "pap-mills" and the "medium-size, high quality accredited labs." The story suggests that the "pap-mills" are probably charging lower prices for their services, and thus putting pressure on price at the other establishments. In the context of the economic theory of regulation, the "medium-size" establishments seek regulatory relief from this price pressure via regulation. In all probability there is a group of well-intentioned private citizens also involved who argue that the "pap-mills" supply inferior services and should be regulated out of business.

CHAPTER

16

LINEAR PROGRAMMING

INTRODUCTION

Linear programming is a technique used by economists, managers, financial analysts, and production engineers to find the *optimal* (efficient) way to solve a well-defined production maximization or cost minimization problem. Thus, farmers might use the tools of linear programming to help them determine the appropriate amount of fertilizer and irrigation to use on a crop, or they might use the method to help them determine how much land to devote to several different crops. A plant or production manager might use linear programming routines to determine the least-cost mix of fuels to fire a boiler. An advertising firm might employ the tools of linear programming to minimize the cost across various media—radio, magazines, newspapers, and television—of reaching a specific size audience. In a nutshell, the procedures of linear programming help the manager find the least-cost way of producing, or alternatively they aid the manager in maximizing the output of a given set of inputs. Although linear programming has a strong theoretical basis, it is application oriented; it can be used to solve real business problems. Linear programming is not without its shortcomings, some of which we will identify. Nevertheless, for certain problems, it provides quick and useful solutions.

Conceptually, linear programming seeks the optimal value of a linear expression, called the objective function, while satisfying constraints that can be formulated as a system of linear inequalities. The **objective function** portrays the goal, and the linear inequalities capture the constraints. Linear programming is constrained optimization, a mathematical technique oriented toward the solution of maximization and minimization problems. Since the manager always faces at least one constraint in a linear programming problem, the analysis is inherently short run. That is, some inputs are specified and beyond control of the manager. This is frequently the case when the parent company supplies a budget, or when input supplies are not available from vendors and production must proceed out of stocks or inventories. Thus, linear programming sometimes seems artificial in the sense that the firm appears to be working without access to markets; when the firm does have access to markets, the technique has less use. This points out when linear programming is most useful—in the short run when some inputs are constrained for one reason or another.

In sum, linear programming is most useful when the choices of action available to a decision maker are limited and reduced due to one or more constraints. Moreover, the choices must be concrete and mathematically describable. The solution to a linear programming problem rests squarely on the shoulders of the specification of the objective function and the constraints. Unless these can be precisely stipulated, the technique is not very useful. Naturally, this restriction limits the use of linear programming, but even so, the procedure has many varied applications.

Production theory is one area in which linear programming is frequently used by economists and people in business. Managers can use this tool to identify the least-cost combination of inputs necessary to produce a certain level of output, or they can determine the profit maximization level of output given certain constraints, such as limited raw materials, limited skilled labor, limited high-level technology, and so on. Let us turn our attention first to the basic concepts of linear programming or **LP** as it is sometimes abbreviated.

BASIC CONCEPTS

Consider a firm producing only two goods, X_1 and X_2, that are sold at fixed prices known to the manager. Moreover, the prices are not expected to change for the duration of the problem at hand. Three different types of skilled labor are used in the production of each of the two goods. Suppose a small plant fabricates metal doors, X_1, and metal windows, X_2. Three different types of workers are used, cutters (Type 1), welders (Type 2), and finishers (Type 3). The use of the laborers is limited to 16 hours a day; the plant must close down 8 hours per day. The firm currently has the use of 6 Type 1 skilled workers, 4 Type 2 skilled workers, and 10 Type 3 skilled workers.

TYPE OF LABOR	NUMBER AVAILABLE	HOURS AVAILABLE
1—Cutters	6	$6 \cdot 16 = 96$
2—Welders	4	$4 \cdot 16 = 64$
3—Finishers	10	$10 \cdot 16 = 160$

Accordingly, a fixed quantity of labor hours is available to the firm each day. There are 96 ($6 \cdot 16$) hours of Type 1 labor available, 64 ($4 \cdot 16$) hours of Type 2, and 160 ($10 \cdot 16$) hours of Type 3 labor. This does not mean that each worker must work 16 hours per day. Rather it means that the *other* inputs, the building, raw materials, and tools, are *available* for 16 hours per day. The linear programming problem itself will determine how much each worker is used per day. The nature of linear programming is short run, and we presume that the firm cannot increase or decrease the amount of skilled labor, but it can vary the amount of the other inputs used in the production, in this case metal, welding rods, electricity, tools, and the like. Each different output and input is assumed to be infinitely divisible, and the outputs are produced according to well-defined, fixed proportions, constant returns to scale processes. The firm can purchase all inputs except the three types of skilled labor at going market prices in unlimited quantities.

The first step in the LP process is specification of the objective function. The objective function stipulates the goal of the problem. In the metal fabricating example at hand, we calculate the gross profit to be made on each product. Gross profit is determined by simply subtracting the costs of all inputs, save labor, from the market prices of the two outputs, X_1 and X_2. Suppose the market price of X_1 *net of the costs of all other inputs except labor* is \$24 per unit, and X_2 sells for \$16 per unit after paying for the other inputs used in its manufacture. Then net income from the labor we use is represented by function I:

$$I = 24X_1 + 16X_2. \tag{16.1}$$

Equation 16.1 is the objective function. The problem is to find the proper choice of labor inputs to maximize this objective. The task of the firm is to produce the output combination that maximizes total gross profit, equation 16.1.

	HOURS OF INPUT REQUIRED FOR ONE UNIT OF OUTPUT		
	TYPE 1	TYPE 2	TYPE 3
OUTPUT			
X_1	12	4	16
X_2	6	8	16

The second step in solving the LP problem is specification of the constraints. The **constraints** quantify the relation between inputs and outputs and the limits, if any, on the use of particular inputs. To find the profit maximizing combination of output, we must know the productive capacity of each type of skilled worker in each use. Suppose each unit of X_1 requires 12 hours of Type 1 skilled labor, but only 6 hours are needed to produce one unit of X_2. Similarly, suppose 4 hours of Type 2 skilled labor are required to produce one unit of X_1, and 8 hours must be used to produce a single unit of X_2. In addition, 16 hours of Type 3 labor are needed to produce one unit of X_1 or X_2. Given the constraints on labor availability identified earlier, the following expressions specify the production restrictions faced each day:

$$12X_1 + 6X_2 <= 96 \tag{16.2}$$

$$4X_1 + 8X_2 <= 64 \tag{16.3}$$

$$16X_1 + 16X_2 <= 160. \tag{16.4}$$

The three equations (16.2–16.4) reveal the possible combinations of X_1 and X_2 allowed by the total availability of the workers. For example, from the first constraint, it can be seen that if the production of X_2 is zero, the maximum amount of X_1 that can be produced each day is 8 units. Similarly from the first constraint, if all resources are devoted to the production of X_2, the maximum amount that could be produced is 16 units. The other two constraints are interpreted in the same manner. Each constraint places a restriction on the combinations of the two goods that the firm can produce in a day.

We can now specify the general linear programming problem.

Max I $= p_1X_1 + p_2X_2$

　subject to

$b_{11}X_1 + b_{12}X_2 <= r_1$

$b_{21}X_1 + b_{22}X_2 <= r_2$

$b_{31}X_1 + b_{32}X_2 <= r_3$

$X_1, X_2 >= 0$

where b_{ij} ($i=1,2,3$; $j=1,2$) is the required number of type i skilled worker hours per unit of output j; the restrictions on the program are represented by r_i—in our example, the fixed quantities of skilled worker hours available. For the specific problem at hand, we have

$$Max\ I\ =\ 24X_1\ +\ 16X_2$$

subject to

$$12X_1\ +\ 6X_2\ <=\ 96$$

$$4X_1\ +\ 8X_2\ <=\ 64$$

$$16X_1\ +\ 16X_2\ <=\ 160$$

$$X_1\ >=\ 0$$

$$X_2\ >=\ 0.$$

As we said, the first equation in the program is the total gross profit function, and it is the objective function of the linear program. The three inequalities that follow are the constraints imposed on the linear program by the limited quantity of labor available and the work force requirements for the manufacture of each good. Finally, the last two inequalities impose the restriction that negative outputs are impossible. These equations imply that there are three essential ingredients to every linear program: an objective function, a set of constraints, and a set of nonnegativity restrictions.

Since only two choice variables, X_1 and X_2, are involved in the problem, it may be solved graphically. In Figure 16.1, quantities of the first output, X_1, are plotted

FIGURE 16.1
Three Constraints, Two Choices

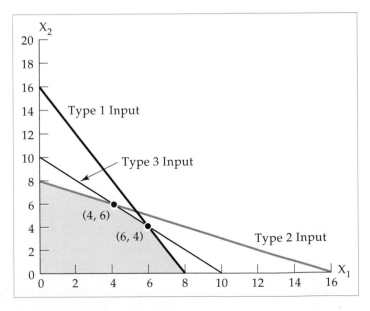

along the horizontal axis, and quantities of the second good, X_2, are drawn up the vertical axis.

The first step in the graphical solution is to draw the constraints. This is done by constructing the feasible or choice space for each input. Then the intersection of the feasible spaces of each input reveals the set of all choices available to the firm, the overall choice set. The actual solution must come from this choice set; it describes the combined effect of all the constraints imposed on the firm in the short-run problem under consideration. Examine the first constraint in Figure 16.1; it graphically represents the same constraint identified by equation 16.2. Equation 16.2 says that 12 hours of input Type 1 are required to produce one unit of output X_1; 6 hours are used in the manufacture of one unit of the second good; and 96 hours of this input are available daily. To see how the graphical constraint is constructed, first suppose that this input were used exclusively for the production of the good X_1. Given that 96 hours are available, 96/12 or 8 units would be made. So one choice available to the firm is to make 8 units of X_1 and zero units of X_2. Similarly, if all Type 1 labor is devoted to the production of the good X_2, then 96/6 or 16 units would be produced while none of the first would be made. So a second choice is $X_1 = 0$ and $X_2 = 16$. In Figure 16.1, these two points are plotted, (8, 0) and (0, 16), and they are connected with a straight line. This is the constraint labeled Type 1 in Figure 16.1. Similarly, the figure shows the other two constraints from the example and labels them Type 2 and Type 3. Since each constraint is of the so-called "less than or equal to" type, only points or (X_1, X_2) pairs lying on the line or below it satisfy the particular constraint. Since all three constraints have to be satisfied at the same time, no point lying outside *any* one of the lines can be accepted. For example, the combination $X_1 = 9$ and $X_2 = 2$ is feasible according to the constraint imposed by Type 2 and Type 3 inputs, but this combination is not attainable according to the restriction imposed by input Type 1. This can be seen in the graph. The point ($X_1 = 9$, $X_2 = 2$) lies on the Type 3 constraint and interior to the Type 2 constraint, but it lies outside the Type 1 constraint. All three constraints must be satisfied. The only feasible region of production is the intersection of the three constraints. This is the shaded area in the figure. The production choice must come from this set.

The collection of points that satisfies all three constraints simultaneously is called the **feasible region**. Examine Figure 16.2. The shaded region of the figure depicts the feasible region. From the point ($X_1 = 0$, $X_2 = 8$) to the point ($X_1 = 4$, $X_2 = 6$), the region is defined by the Type 2 constraint. From (4,6) to (6,4), the region is defined by the Type 3 constraint, and from (6,4) to (8,0), the Type 1 constraint delimits the region. The firm must choose from the set of points delineated by this area. It should be noted that the points on the boundary of the feasible set are themselves also a part of the feasible region.

Each point in the feasible region is available to the firm as a choice. However, all of the points do not represent the same level of profit. To locate the profit maximizing point (or points), the objective function must be incorporated into the analysis. This is done with the creation of isoprofit lines.

Isoprofit lines represent different production combinations of the two outputs, X_1 and X_2, that yield the same level of profit. Along any isoprofit line, profits are constant. However, each isoprofit line represents a higher level of profit the

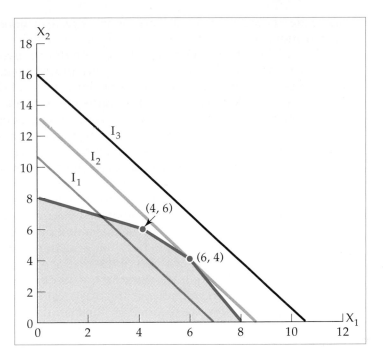

FIGURE 16.2
The Feasible Region

farther it lies from the origin. Thus, isoprofit lines are very much like indifference curves in utility theory or isoquants in production theory.

The isoprofit map is derived from the objective function. Recall the objective function from equation 16.1:

$$I = 24X_1 + 16X_2.$$

By manipulation, we can rewrite this in terms of either of the two outputs, say X_2, as

$$X_2 = (I/16) - (3/2){\bullet}X_1.$$

An isoprofit line exists for every level of I. For instance, let I be \$168. Then, if X_2 production is nil, X_1 production must be 7 units. If we arbitrarily set X_2 equal to zero, substitute \$168 for I, and solve for X_1, we get a point on the \$168 isoprofit line:

$$0 = (168/16) - (3/2)X_1$$

such that $X_1 = 7$. In other words, one way to earn \$168 net revenue is to produce 7 units of X_1 and no output of X_2. Another way is to produce no X_1 and 10.5 units of X_2. The isoprofit line graphed in Figure 3 as I_1 is all combinations of X_1 and X_2 that yield \$168 profit. Isoprofit lines I_2 and I_3 are derived similarly. In the figure we have let profit along line I_2 be \$208, and at each point on line I_3 profit is \$256.

Naturally, there is an isoprofit line for any specified level of profits; there is an infinite number of them, and they are all parallel. The slope of the isoprofit line is the ratio of the relative prices of the two outputs, X_1 and X_2.

The firm's objective is, of course, to attain the highest possible profit line while still remaining in the feasible region. From Figure 16.2, we observe that line I_2 satisfies this objective. Line I_2 achieves the highest level of profit while satisfying all constraints; it is the highest profit level that exists within the feasible set. Profit line I_3, even though it represents a higher level of profit, lies outside the feasible region and out of reach, while profit line I_1 portrays a lower and hence less attractive level of profit. Profit line I_2 intersects the feasible region at 6 units of X_1 and 4 units of X_2. Thus, the point (6,4) is the optimal solution to our linear program; it maximizes profit subject to the constraints given. Total profit for this optimal output combination can be obtained by using the values $X_1 = 6$ and $X_2 = 4$ in the objective function to yield the maximum profit, $I = \$208$ per production period. How much of each input does the firm employ? Twelve hours of Type 1 labor are used to produce one unit of the first good, and hence, at the optimal solution, 72 hours are required in total for the production of good X_1. Six hours of Type 1 labor are used to produce one unit of X_2; therefore, at the optimal solution, 24 hours of Type 1 labor are required for the manufacture of the second good. In total then, 96 hours of the first type skilled labor are used. There is no slack or surplus Type 1 labor.

The requirements for Type 2 and Type 3 labor are similarly obtained. For Type 2 labor, 4 hours per unit of X_1 are required, and 8 hours per unit of X_2. Therefore, at the optimal solution, the Type 2 labor requirements are 4•6 + 8•4 = 24 + 32 = 56 hours. Sixty-four hours are available, and so there is surplus Type 2 labor of 8 hours per day. For Type 3 labor, 16 hours are used in the production of either X_1 or X_2. Hence, at the solution, 16•6 = 96 plus 16•4 = 64 or 160 total hours are used. There is no slack in Type 3 labor.

GENERAL ALGEBRAIC SOLUTION METHOD

The easy use of the graphical method of solution is limited to the case of two choice variables, regardless of the number of constraints. When there are three choice variables, a three-dimensional graph is required, and we all know how difficult it is to draw and interpret three-dimensional figures. Therefore, in this section, a nongraphical method is presented that can be used to find the optimal solution to linear programs involving any number of choice variables. Moreover, as you might have suspected, computer algorithms to resolve linear programs are the standard solution method in most applications today, and hence we must develop numerical routines to access this cost- and time-saving technology.

The previous example is now used to illustrate the nongraphical solution. The extreme points in the graph suggest a way of finding the optimal solution when a graph is too difficult to draw or interpret. Each extreme point identifies a potential solution to the LP. Examination of each in turn reveals which is the best and points out how useful a computer is in finding solutions to linear programming problems. The general solution method is straightforward. We examine each of the extreme points and evaluate the objective function at that point. This will identify one or more maximums or minimums to the problem. In Figure 16.1, the constraints identify five extreme points. These are the (X_1, X_2) combinations (0,8), (4,6), (6,4), (8,0), and (0,0).

Each one of these extreme points falls into one of three categories: **points at intersections of constraints**, **points at the end of constraints**, and the **origin**. In the metal fabricating example, the points (6,4) and (4,6) are points at intersections of constraints. Two of the three constraints are exactly fulfilled by these points. Consider the output combination (6,4). While point (6,4) lies exactly on the Type 1 and Type 3 skilled worker constraints, it lies inside the Type 2 skilled worker constraint; we call this **slack** in the use of the Type 2 skilled worker. Type 2 skilled workers are underutilized at this point. There are additional supplies of them available at point (6,4).

The second category of points occurs at the intersection of a constraint and one of the axes. Points (0,8) and (8,0) represent such intersections in the example. These points are located on only one of the constraints, and thus, at such points, there will be slack in the two remaining constraints. At such points, two of the three types of skilled workers are underutilized. The third category consists of the origin (0,0), where slack exists in all the constraints; all three types of skilled workers are underutilized.

Slack variables are used to create an algebraic solution to the LP problem. The way to do this is to create an artificial variable, the slack variable, for each constraint. This converts the inequality constraints into equalities, thereby facilitating the algebraic solution. Whenever the number of choice variables is less than the number of constraints, at least one of the constraints will contain slack. When a particular extreme point is chosen as the optimal solution, the choice involves not only the optimal combination (X_1, X_2) but indirectly also the optimal value of the slack in at least one of the constraints. Suppose the slack in the ith constraint ($i=1,2,3$) is denoted S_i and is called the **slack factor**. The first step in the algebraic method of finding the optimal solution is to transform each of the inequality constraints into an equality by adding these slack factors, the S_i's, to the left-hand side of each of the ith constraints.

Using the earlier example and adding a slack variable to each constraint, we transform the linear program into a form tractable to an algebraic solution:

$$Max\ I = 24X_1 + 16X_2$$

subject to

$$12X_1 + 6X_2 + S_1 = 96$$

$$4X_1 + 8X_2 + S_2 = 64$$

$$16X_1 + 16X_2 + S_3 = 160$$

$$X_1, X_2, S_1, S_2, S_3 >= 0.$$

This new problem has five choice variables in all: X_1, X_2, S_1, S_2, and S_3. If there is slack in the ith constraint, then $S_i > 0$. On the other hand, when there is no slack, then $S_i = 0$, and the ith constraint is exactly fulfilled.

Using each extreme point, it is easy to determine the values of the slack factors. Starting with the origin $(0,0)$ and substituting $X_1 = 0$ and $X_2 = 0$ into the transformed constraints yields the following values for the slack variables: $S_1 = 96$, $S_2 = 64$, and $S_3 = 160$. Thus, the output combination $(0,0)$ gives the following solution vector:

$$(X_1, X_2, S_1, S_2, S_3) = (0,0,96,64,160).$$

Similarly, each extreme point is substituted into the transformed constraints (the constraints containing the slack factors). The results are presented in Table 16.1. Note that the number of nonzero entries and the number of constraints in the linear program are equal.

To determine the profit level associated with each extreme point, simply insert the values of X_1 and X_2 into the objective function. The technique for finding the solution to the linear programming problem is to locate the point that yields the maximum profit, the constrained profit maximizing output point. For instance, consider the third point in Table 16.1, point $(8,0)$. If we produce eight units of good X_1 at \$24 per unit, we earn a total of \$192, and since we are producing none of the second good at this point, this is our total profit. Similarly, Table 16.2 presents the profit contribution of the other extreme points. You will observe that this algebraic method yields the same solution as the graphical technique. The output combination $(6,4)$ is once again the profit maximization point.

We close this section by noting that the solution to a linear programming problem need not be unique. There is no theoretical reason that multiple solutions may not exist that maximize or minimize the objective function. For instance, consider Figure 16.2. Suppose the slope of the isoprofit line were equal to the slope of the line connecting the points $(4,6)$ and $(6,4)$, then *each* point in that interval would be a profit maximizing solution.

Linear programming is not limited to determining the optimal solution to maximization problems. It is also useful in finding the solution to constrained minimization problems. The next section deals with such an application.

TABLE 16.1 CALCULATING SLACK AT THE EXTREME POINTS	
OUTPUT	SOLUTION
(X_1, X_2)	$(X_1, X_2, S_1, S_2, S_3)$
$(0,0)$	$(0,0,96,64,160)$
$(0,8)$	$(0,8,48,0,32)$
$(8,0)$	$(8,0,0,32,32)$
$(6,4)$	$(6,4,0,8,0)$
$(4,6)$	$(4,6,12,0,0)$

TABLE 16.2 PROFIT AT EACH EXTREME POINT	
EXTREME POINTS	TOTAL PROFIT
(0,0)	0
(0,8)	128
(8,0)	192
(6,4)	208
(4,6)	192

THE DUAL PROGRAM

Every linear programming problem that involves maximizing or minimizing an objective function is called a **primal** problem. Each primal program has a corresponding linear programming problem called a **dual program**. For every primal maximization problem, there can be constructed a corresponding dual minimization problem; conversely, for every primal minimization problem, there can be constructed a corresponding dual maximization problem. Both the primal and the dual programs will give the same results, and the optimal value for the primal objective function will equal the optimal value for the dual objective function. This duality offers a method for solving what may appear to be extremely complicated linear programming problems.

When the original or primal LP problem is to maximize production, then the dual problem is to minimize costs, and vice versa. Maximizing production identifies the impact on revenues of obtaining additional units of restricted inputs. Solving the dual problem (minimizing costs) identifies the effect on costs of using fewer resources. Our previous metal fabricating example is put to use again. The primal problem just solved was to maximize profit subject to a set of input constraints. The dual problem in this case is to produce a given level of output as cheaply as possible, a minimization problem.

First we identify the objective function. Cost is the amount of each input times its value. Value here means opportunity cost, and hence it is measured in units of profit. Let p_i represent the opportunity cost or shadow price of each input. **Shadow prices** reveal the value of the resources used in production. Thus the dual problem is to minimize the sum of the shadow prices of each input times the quantity of each resource employed.

Recall from the problem that there are 96 hours of the Type 1 input, 64 hours of the second, and 160 hours of the Type 3 input. Each of these has a shadow price, p_i. In this case, the cost or objective function is

$$C = 96p_1 + 64p_2 + 160p_3.$$

The sum of the price of each input times its quantity is the cost to the firm of using the three inputs. The costs of the other inputs used in the production process are accounted for by subtracting their values from the selling prices of the outputs.

Thus, profit will be maximized if we minimize the shadow prices of the three remaining inputs. The question is, of course, what values do these prices, p_1, p_2, and p_3, take? The answer, once identified, reveals the cost of using additional units of each input.

The next step in the minimization problem is to identify the constraints. In the dual problem, the constraints specify that the sum of the implicit values of each unit of *input* used in the production of each unit of *output* must be at least as valuable as the unit of *output*. Shadow prices cannot be negative, but they may be zero. A zero shadow price for an input implies that the input is free, or alternatively, that it is slack. There are units of it not being used.

As to the actual specification of the constraint, notice that 12 hours of the first input are used in the manufacture of one unit of good X_1; 4 hours of the second input are used; and 16 hours of the third input are required. One unit of good X_1 contributes a net of \$24 to profit. Hence, the first constraint requires that the sum of all input requirements, multiplied by the respective input's shadow price, must be greater than or equal to the net profit contribution of the output:

$$12p_1 + 4p_2 + 16p_3 >= 24.$$

Similarly, for the second good, X_2, since 6 units of the first input are used, 8 units of the second input are employed, and 16 units of the third input are required, then the sum of the values of the inputs must be at least as much as the value of the second output, \$16. Thus, the second constraint says that

$$6p_1 + 8p_2 + 16p_3 >= 16.$$

Naturally, since the implicit value of each input cannot be negative,

$$p_1, p_2, p_3 >= 0.$$

Thus, we have the objective function and the constraints.

Both the original primal maximization problem and the dual minimization problem follow.

Primal	**Dual**
Max I $= 24X_1 + 16X_2$	*Min C* $= 96p_1 + 64p_2 + 160p_3$
subject to	*subject to*
$12X_1 + 6X_2 <= 96$	$12p_1 + 4p_2 + 16p_3 >= 24$
$4X_1 + 8X_2 <= 64$	$6p_1 + 8p_2 + 16p_3 >= 16$
$16X_1 + 16X_2 <= 160$	$p_1, p_2, p_3 >= 0$
$X_1, X_2 <= 0$	

In the primal problem, the objective function is profit; we seek to maximize it. In the dual problem, the objective function is cost; we desire to minimize it. In the primal problem, X_1 and X_2 are the output levels of the two production goods. In the cost minimization problem, p_1, p_2, and $p3$ represent **premiums** for inputs. The premium or the shadow price of the input is the implicit value to the firm of having one more unit of the input. The premium or shadow price identifies the change in cost of production that would occur if the firm employed one more unit of the input in production. Thus, in the primal problem, there are constraints on the amounts of inputs available; in the dual problem at hand, the constraints represent opportunity costs, the cost of production. The two problems mirror each other. The solution to one yields the solution to the other, and the analyst is free to choose whichever one he or she thinks is easier to conceive and solve.

In the case of the maximization problem, the constraints represent the number of hours of each type of skilled labor that can be used in the production of the two goods. In the minimization problem, the constraints represent a value that is assigned to each input, and this value cannot be less than the profit contribution provided by a unit of the two goods being manufactured. The cost minimizing constraint captures the opportunity cost of producing additional units of the two goods.

To solve the dual problem, inequalities have to be converted into equalities. This is once again accomplished by introducing slack variables. Since the constraints in this dual problem are of the "equal to or greater than" kind, the slack variables are added to the left with a negative sign. That is, the slack variables here represent costs the firm is bearing that do not contribute to profit. They must be subtracted from the net value of the inputs in use. The left-hand side of the equality captures the value of resources in use. The right-hand side measures the value of the output produced by these inputs. What the slack variables do is equate these two values. When the slack variables are included, by definition, the two sides are equal. These negative value slack variables are often called the **surplus factors**. The value of the surplus factors reveals information about production. When the surplus factor is zero, then the sum of the value of the inputs used in the process is just equal to the selling price or value of output. When the surplus factor is positive, then we know that the value of the inputs used exceeds the value of the output. Rewriting the dual program to include the surplus factors yields:

$$Min\ C = 96p_1 + 64p_2 + 160p_3$$

subject to

$$12p_1 + 4p_2 + 16p_3 - S_1 = 24$$

$$6p_1 + 8p_2 + 16p_3 - S_2 = 16$$

$$p_1, p_2, p_3, S_1, S_2 >= 0.$$

Graphical solution of this dual problem is next to impossible, simply because of the presence of three choice variables (p_1, p_2, and p_3). Therefore, we use the algebraic method. Set any three of the variables p_1, p_2, p_3, S_1, and S_2 equal to zero and then solve the constraint equations to obtain the value of the remaining two variables. A solution is outside the feasible region if it is negative and inside if it is positive. The optimal or cost minimizing solution is the one with the lowest value of the objective function. Setting p_1, p_2, and p_3 equal to zero and solving for S_1 and S_2 give the following result: $S_1 = -24$ and $S_2 = -16$. Both S_1 and S_2 lie outside the feasible region. Suppose p_2, p_3, and S_2 are equal to zero, then $p_1 = 2.67$ and $S_1 = 8$. Using these values, the value of the objective function can be calculated:

$$C = (96 \bullet 2.67) + (64 \bullet 0) + (160 \bullet 0) = 256.3.$$

Table 16.3 presents all the possible solutions and the value of the objective function at each solution. From the table, we see that some of the solutions are negative and hence not within the feasible region. The ninth solution has the lowest cost, and therefore it provides the values for the variables that minimize the objective function. At the optimal solution, $p_1 = 1.33$, $p_2 = 0$, $p_3 = 0.5$, and there is no slack in any constraint. The cost function is minimized at $208 per day. Computation of the table reveals how valuable the computer is in solving LP problems. Complex linear programs that would take hours by hand are solved in seconds with a personal or mainframe computer and the appropriate software.

This result links to the one obtained from the solution of the primal problem. The dual solution shows that the shadow price or the premium for the Type 2 skilled worker is zero. A zero premium implies that using an extra Type 2 skilled worker will leave the firm's cost unchanged. This result implies that there is slack in the second skilled labor, a fact we have already deduced from the primal problem. If additional hours of Type 2 skilled worker were available, there would *not* be any additional output of the two goods, X_1 and X_2.

Armed with the shadow prices of the inputs, it is possible to determine the optimal values of the two outputs respectively, X_1 and X_2. Since the shadow prices of the first and third types of inputs are positive, we know there is no slack in either of these two inputs. Thus, from the original production constraints, equations 16.2–16.4, we know that

$$12X_1 + 6X_2 + S_1 = 96 \tag{16.5}$$

$$4X_1 + 8X_2 + S_2 = 64 \tag{16.6}$$

$$16X_1 + 16X_2 + S_3 = 160 \tag{16.7}$$

but from the dual problem we have just deduced that there is no slack in the first or third inputs. Thus, $S_1 = 0$ and $S_3 = 0$. Substituting these into the first and third constraints, equations 16.5 and 16.7, we have two equations and two unknowns. This allows us to solve equations 16.5 and 16.7 for the optimal combination of outputs:

$$12X_1 + 6X_2 = 96,$$

and

$$16X_1 + 16X_2 = 160.$$

The solutions are $X_1 = 6$ and $X_2 = 4$. This is the same answer we obtained from the primal problem. Both methods find that the Type 2 skilled labor constraint is nonbinding, while each of the other two types of inputs is fully employed. The

TABLE 16.3 SOLUTION TO THE DUAL PROBLEM						
SOLUTION	p_1	p_2	p_3	S_1	S_2	VALUE OF THE OBJECTIVE FUNCTION
1	0	0	0	−24	−16	—
2	0	0	1	−4	0	—
3	0	0	1.5	0	4	240
4	0	2	0	−8	0	—
5	0	6	0	0	16	384
6	0	−2	2	0	0	—
7	2.67	0	0	4	0	256
8	2	0	0	0	−2	—
9	1.33	0	0.5	0	0	208
10	1.8	0.66	0	0	0	215

implication is that the firm would be better off dismissing some Type 2 workers or acquiring additional units of the other two types.

In summary, both the dual and primal problems yield the same optimal value input use and output mix. And the optimal solution obtained from the dual or primal problem provides the necessary information to obtain the optimal solution for the other. The choice of either the dual or the primal process depends upon which one is easier to solve for the problem at hand.

LINEAR PROGRAMMING AND PRODUCTION PLANNING: ONE PRODUCT

When there are multiple ways of manufacturing or producing, linear programming may be used to find the least-cost method or the maximum output technique. Suppose the task in front of the firm is to find the least-cost combination of the inputs needed to produce a particular good. Linear programming provides the solution to this problem.

Assume that a single product X can be produced by using two inputs, Land (Ln) and Labor (La), but in four different ways or using four different processes. Process 1 requires 8 units of Ln and 8 units of La to produce each unit of X. Process 2 uses 4 units of Ln and 8 units of La to produce each unit of X. Process 3 requires 3 units of Ln and 10 units of La, while Process 4 uses 2 units of Ln and 16 units of La to produce each unit of X. Furthermore, the input combinations are subject to fixed proportions and constant returns to scale. This means that by doubling or tripling the input combinations in each process, output is doubled or tripled. Consider Table 16.4. There the input requirements for one, two, three, and four units of output are reported for the four different production processes.

Figure 16.3 depicts the four production processes. Point A_1 represents one unit of output using Process 1 ($Ln=8$, $La=8$). Similarly, points B_1, C_1, and D_1 represent one unit of output using the other three processes respectively. Connecting points A_1 to B_1 to C_1 to D_1 yields an **isoquant**, the different combinations

TABLE 16.4	FOUR DIFFERENT PRODUCTION PROCESSES			

| | *PROCESS* | | | |
	1	*2*	*3*	*4*
FOR 1 unit of output:				
Ln	8	4	3	2
La	8	8	10	16
FOR 2 units of output:				
Ln	16	8	6	4
La	16	16	20	32
FOR 3 units of output:				
Ln	24	12	9	6
La	24	24	30	48
FOR 4 units of output:				
Ln	32	16	12	8
La	32	32	40	64

FIGURE 16.3
Production Isoquants

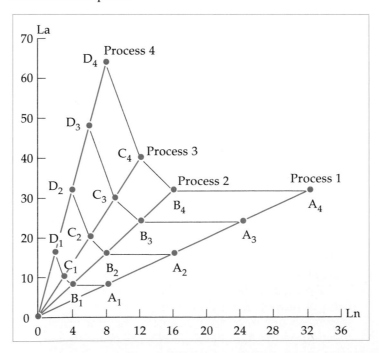

of inputs that yield an equal quantity of output, one unit in this case. The four points, A_1, B_1, C_1, and D_1, describe four different ways of obtaining one unit of output. Since there are constant returns to scale in this problem, doubling the input combination results in twice as much output production. Points A_2, B_2, C_2, and D_2 represent a doubling of all inputs. The isoquant corresponding to 2 units of output X is obtained by connecting point A_2 to D_2. Similarly, isoquants representing 3 and 4 units of output, respectively, are constructed.

Suppose a unit of labor, La, costs $8 per hour, and a unit of land, Ln, costs $16 an acre. The question is which production process is the best one to use. Suppose we would like to produce a total of 4 units of output X. The problem is to find the least-cost combination of land and labor for an output level of 4 units. This problem may be translated into a linear programming problem.

First we demonstrate a graphical solution, and then a general algebraic method is presented for solving this class of problems. Examine Figure 16.4. The isoquant for 4 units of output is reproduced. Since the price of Ln and La is known, a series of isocost curves can be drawn. The cost function is solved in terms of land in order to derive the isocost curves.

$$C = 16Ln + 8La; \tag{16.8}$$

therefore,

$$Ln = (C/16) - (1/2)La. \tag{16.9}$$

FIGURE 16.4
The Isocost Curves

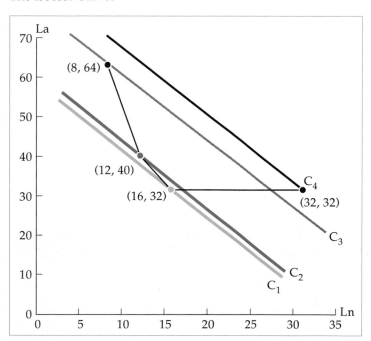

To find the least-cost combination of inputs, to determine the cost minimizing production process given a desired output of 4 units, locate the isocost curve that is nearest the origin but tangent to the production isoquant.

Four isocost cost curves (C_1, C_2, C_3, C_4) are shown in Figure 16.4. The slope of these curves is dictated by the prices of the two inputs. Each of the isocost curves represents a different level of C in equation 16.9. All four isocost curves go through the isoquant curve, but at different places indicating different levels of cost. Isocost C_1, passing through the point (16,32), is the closest to the origin. Substituting 16 units of land and 32 units of labor into the cost function gives a total cost of $512. Thus Process 2 is the least-cost way to produce 4 units of output.

Use of the algebraic method to solve the problem is even simpler. Since there is only one constraint, the isoquant, at the optimal solution there will be no slack or surplus variable. The solution can be obtained simply by substituting the extreme points into the cost functions. Each of these is shown in Table 16.5. The input combination that minimizes the total cost is picked as the proper combination. Both the graphical and the algebraic method provide the same optimal combination: A total cost of $512 is the least-cost way to produce 4 units of output, and this is accomplished by using 16 units of land and 32 units of labor in Process 2.

THE ASSUMPTION OF LINEARITY

Linear programming is true to its name. The objective function and the constraints must be linear for the solution methods discussed here to work. In a wide variety of circumstances, this presents no problem, but the reader is cautioned that broad application of LP without due regard for this presumption can lead to managerial miscues. For instance, in the dual problem we discussed, the shadow price of the first type of labor input was $1.33. This suggests that hiring additional quantities of this type labor would add $1.33 per additional unit, and this is correct over small ranges. However, after some point, diminishing returns would increase the cost of using additional Type 1 labor (holding constant the levels of the other constrained inputs). That is, the constraint, over all ranges, is not linear. Practically speaking then, LP has to be considered a local optimization problem. Generalizing any solution over a broad range of inputs or outputs will almost surely lead to inefficient conclusions.

The assumption of linearity is equivalent to presuming that production is homogeneous of degree one. When this is true, a λ percent increase in all inputs will generate a λ percent increase in output. The techniques of LP are useful and

TABLE 16.5   THE ALGEBRAIC SOLUTION

EXTREME POINTS	TOTAL COST
(8,64)	640
(12,40)	528
(16,32)	512
(32,32)	768

practical so long as this assumption holds. However, when production is subject to diminishing returns, or when some but not all inputs are increased, an extra portion of prudence is suggested.

We close this chapter by noting that linear and more complicated nonlinear programming techniques are well suited for computer solution. A wide range of computer programs exists, often custom designed or application specific, that can be used by managers rather than resorting to the manual solutions presented here. However, it bears noting that these computer solutions simply emulate the techniques presented here, and they are no more trustworthy or correct than the methods we have outlined. The manager must still specify the objective function and the constraints. The computer programs simply eliminate the drudgery of ciphering the solution.

TOPICS TO REVIEW

These are topics that you should feel comfortable with before you leave this chapter. If you cannot write out a clear and concise sentence or paragraph explaining the topic after you have worked on the study problems, you should reread the relevant section of the text.

Objective Function

Constraints

Isoprofit Line

Graphical Solution

General Algebraic Solution

Extreme Points

Slack Factor

Primal Problem

Dual Problem

Shadow Price

Premiums

Surplus Factors

Importance of the Assumption of Linearity

STUDY PROBLEMS

1. Solve the following linear programming problem graphically.

    Maximize $I = 4X_1 + 6X_2$

    subject to

    $X_1 = < 16$

    $X_2 = < 12$

    $X_1 + X_2 = < 32$

    $X_1, X_2 => 0$

2. Solve the following linear programming problem using the general solution method.

    Minimize $C = 6X_1 + 8X_2$

    subject to

    $X_1 + X_2 => 4$

    $4X_1 + 8X_2 => 10$

    $X_1, X_2 => 0$

3. A firm has budgeted $1500 for display space at a toy show. Two types of display booths are available: Preferred space costs $18 per square foot, with a minimum rental of 60 square feet; and regular space costs $12 per square foot, with a minimum rental of 30 square feet. It is estimated that there will be 120 visitors for each square foot of preferred space and 60 visitors for each square foot of regular space. How should the firm allot in its budget to maximize the number of potential clients who will visit the booths?

4. A farmer intends to plant crops A and B on all or part of a 100-acre field. Seed for crop A costs $6 per acre, and labor and equipment cost $20 per acre. For crop B, seed costs $9 per acre, and labor and equipment cost $15 per acre. The farmer cannot spend more than $810 for seed and $1800 for labor and equipment. If the income per acre is $150 for crop A and $175 for crop B, how many acres of each crop should be planted to maximize total income?

5. A lot is zoned for an apartment building to consist of no more than 40 apartments, totaling no more than 45,000 square feet. A builder is planning to construct one bedroom apartments, each of which will require 1000 square feet and will rent for $200 per month, and two bedroom apartments, each of which will utilize 1500 square feet and will rent for $280 per month. If all available apartments can be rented, how many apartments of each type should be built to maximize the builder's monthly rental revenue?

SUGGESTED READINGS

Linear programming is a vast discipline linking economics, management science, and mathematics. Hundreds of books and articles exist on a wide variety of topics within the discipline. Only a few of them are noted here.

Brickman, Louis. *Mathematical Introduction to Linear Programming and Game Theory.* New York: Springer–Verlag, 1989.

Cameron, Neil. *Introduction to Linear and Convex Programming.* New York: Cambridge University Press, 1985.

Darst, Richard B. *Introduction to Linear Programming: Applications and Extensions.* New York: M. Dekker, 1991.

Sposito, Vincent A. *Linear Programming with Statistical Applications.* Ames: Iowa State University Press, 1989.

Strayer, James K. *Linear Programming and Its Applications.* New York: Springer–Verlag, 1989.

Ozan, Turgut. *Applied Mathematical Programming for Engineering and Production Management.* Englewood Cliffs, NJ: Prentice Hall, 1986.

SUGGESTED SOLUTIONS TO SELECTED STUDY PROBLEMS

The following are only *suggested* solutions to the study problems presented at the end of this chapter. In all cases, the suggestions here put heavy emphasis on analysis rather than a single correct answer. Since most managerial problems do not fall into neat little boxes, the individual characteristics of the problems that you encounter on the job will typically mandate a solution using the principles developed here and in other courses. Memorizing these solutions will not make you a good manager; learning the *principles* detailed here will help make you a better manager.

2. *Minimize* $C = 6X_1 + 8X_2$

    subject to

    $X_1 + X_2 - S_1 = 4$

    $4X_1 + 8X_2 - S_2 = 10$

    $X_1, X_2, S_1, S_2 >= 0$

    First identify the extreme points. Let X_1 and $X_2 = 0$, then $S_1 = -4$ and $S_2 = -10$. Similarly, the other extreme points are computed. For each, the value of the objective function is computed. We observe that solution 4 is the least-cost technique where the shadow price of the first input is zero; it is slack. And the shadow price of the second input is 1.25; it is constrained. At the minimum, cost is 10.

SOLUTION NUMBER	X_1	X_2	S_1	S_2	VALUE OF THE OBJECTIVE FUNCTION
1	0	0	-4	-10	—
2	0	4	0	22	32
3	2.5	0	1.5	0	15
4	0	1.25	2.75	0	10
5	4	0	0	6	24
6	5.5	-1.5	0	0	—

3. Let X be the square footage of preferred space rented and Y amount of regular space rented. The number of visitors is 120 times X plus 60 times Y. Thus the objective function to be maximized is

    $I = 120X + 60Y.$

    Space X rents for $18 per foot while space Y costs $12. A total of $1500 is to be spent. Therefore the constraint is

    $18X + 12Y = 1500.$

    Thus the LP is to

    Maximize $I = 120X + 60Y$

    subject to

$$18X + 12Y = 1500$$

$$X >= 60$$

$$Y >= 30$$

First we identify the extreme points, and then we evaluate the objective function at those points, choosing the maximum value of the objective function as the optimal solution. To find the extreme points we first examine the origin, letting $X = 0$ and $Y = 0$. The value of the objective function here is 0. Next we let $X = 0$ and observe that if we spend all the $1500 on Y that we can purchase 125 square feet. This produces 7500 visitors. Similarly, we examine all the remaining extremes and compute the value of the objective function. A listing of all these points follows.

Output combinations	Value of objective function
(0,0)	0
(0,125)	7500
(83.3,0)	9996
(60,35)	9300
(63.3,30)	9396

From this we observe that the maximum value of the objective function is 9996 visitors, which is obtained by spending all the allotted budget on preferred space. That is, letting $X = 83.3$ and $Y = 0$.

4. First identify the objective function. Two crops are produced, A and B. Crop A is worth $150 per acre planted, and crop B produces income of $175 per acre. Therefore total income is $150A + 175B$. Thus, the objective function is

$$I = 150A + 175B.$$

Next, specify the constraints. The total acreage available is 100. Thus,

$$A + B <= 100.$$

Second, seed expenditures on crop A cost $6 per acre and $9 per acre for crop B. $810 has been budgeted for seed. Therefore,

$$6A + 9B <= 810.$$

Third, labor expenditures are budgeted to be no more than $1800. Crop A costs, in labor and land, $20 per acre while crop B expends $15 per acre. Thus the third constraint is

$$20A + 15B <= 1800.$$

Fourth, negative values of the crops are not allowed. Thus,

$$A, B >= 0.$$

These five equations create the LP:

Maximize $I = 150A + 175B$

subject to

$A + B <= 100$

$6A + 9B <= 810$

$20A + 15B <= 1800$

$A, B >= 0$

We examine the extreme points and then evaluate the objective function. If all the land budget is spent on crop A then the total acreage available is \$1800/20 = 90. Thus one extreme point is $A = 90$ and $B = 0$. Next, if all the seed budget is spent on B then \$810/9 = 90 acres can be planted. Hence, another extreme point is $A = 0$ and $B = 90$. Similarly the other extremes are determined, and in all cases the objective function is evaluated. The solutions follow.

Output space	Value of Objective Function
(90,0)	\$13,500
(0,90)	\$15,750
(30,70)	\$16,750
(60,40)	\$16,000

From this algorithm we observe that the maximum income is generated by planting 30 acres in crop A and 70 acres in crop B yielding \$16,750.

5. Identify the objective function which is the amount of each type apartment, X and Y, times the rent in each respectively:

$I = 200X + 280Y$.

Identify the constraints. The total number of apartments must not be greater than 40:

$X + Y <= 40$.

The total space is 45,000 square feet to be divided between the two types of apartments:

$1000X + 1500Y <= 45000$.

Negative apartments are not allowed:

$X, Y >= 0$.

Therefore the LP is

Maximize $I = 200X + 280Y$

subject to

$X + Y <= 40$

$1000X + 1500Y <= 45,000$

$X, Y >= 0$

Find the extreme points. The origin, $X = 0$ and $Y = 0$, provides $0 income. Putting all the space into Y type apartments allows for 45000/1500 = 30 units. Therefore, another extreme point is $X = 0$ and $Y = 30$. Putting all the space into type X apartments allows of 45000/1000 = 45 units, but that exceeds the first constraint. Therefore, another extreme is $X = 40$ and $Y = 0$. The intersection of the two constraints is the last extreme point, and it is $X = 30$ and $Y = 10$. The value of the objective function at each extreme point follows.

Output space	Value of the Objective Function
(0,0)	$0
(0,30)	$8400
(40,0)	$8000
(30,10)	$8800

The fourth solution (30,10) yields the greatest income.

CHAPTER

17

PLANT LOCATION DECISION MAKING A CASE STUDY

- Introduction
- Making Decisions in the Abstract
- General Case Description
- Summary
- Topics to Review
- Suggested Readings

INTRODUCTION

Teaching students how to apply the economic principles discussed in the previous chapters to practical management decision making is the primary objective of this book. The process of deciding where to locate a new manufacturing plant offers a good example of putting some of these economic principles to work. This example, based on an actual case study in the world of maximizing profits subject to governmental and business constraints, makes some of the principles we have been studying come alive. The facts of the case come from the files of a consulting firm hired to aid the client in making a plant location decision. We take up the managerial decision problem after the capital appropriation decision has been made by the owners of the company. Management must now decide on the profit maximizing location of a new production plant. But first we briefly discuss some fundamental concepts of decision making in order to lay the groundwork for the analytical structure to follow.

Figure 17.1 depicts the maximization problem facing the firm. In the normal order of things, the company's owners have fixed the quantity of output to be produced at the new site, and their instruction to management, once the project has been included in the capital budget, is to minimize cost. First, we simplify the problem, saying that a site consists of two site factors (or inputs) X_1 and X_2. Specific site factors or inputs are discussed later. The curve labeled I^0 is an isoquant, which gives the various combinations of X_1 and X_2 that will produce a fixed level of output. The straight line CC' is the isocost line or budget that management has to complete the project. Along I^0 there are various combinations of inputs or site factors associated with particular site locations. For instance, points M, N, and O represent specific geographic areas or cities that have various combinations of the site factors, X_1 and X_2. As discussed in Chapter 6, the optimal

FIGURE 17.1
Optimal Site Location

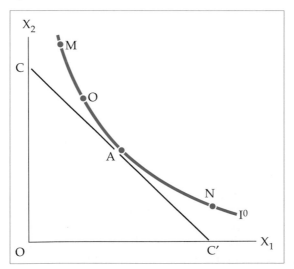

solution is at the tangency point *A*. With imperfect information, management can at best hope to come up with a few sites whose site factors, given the budget constraint, cluster around the optimal point.

Although there are a number of well-developed economic theories describing how management arrives at an optimal plant site decision, the process that actually takes place in the business world is much more murky. Managers have to have a practical method through which they can arrive at optimal site location decisions, recognizing that there are formidable constraints with which they must contend. The remainder of the chapter discusses how managers involved in an actual site location decision put the theoretical concepts to work. To see how systematic site location decisions are made, we must examine how most decisions are made in an abstract sense. Once the essential elements of decision making are exposed, we show how managers have created methods to apply these elements to the site location decision.

MAKING DECISIONS IN THE ABSTRACT

What is a decision? It is a choice among competing alternatives that best gets me what I want. Consider the professional quarterback. He takes the snap from the center and within 3.5 seconds he must decide from a host of possibilities what to do with the ball. What steps does the quarterback go through to arrive at his decision? First, he must know exactly his position on the field and his objective for that play. Second, he must have some criteria to use in judging his alternatives. For instance, is it a *must* that he make two yards or does he have the option of throwing upfield if the situation is right? Further options could be employing his running backs or throwing to his seldom used tight end as a surprise. The play called may be one to set up the play to follow. He must be able to recognize the defenses or alternative situations that confront him. If the defensive back is covering his super-fast flanker too closely, he may want to throw the bomb. If this is not enough, he must assess all the potential problems associated with his choice and determine their expected probability of occurrence. All decisions have the essential elements contained in the quarterback's choice: an objective, criteria, alternatives, and risk assessment.

It is important to see that to make a good decision in a world of imperfect information and formidable constraints, we often adopt the process of backing into the decision by eliminating alternatives. In some instances, the exact process is difficult to recognize, but the essential attributes are present. The best choice comes from applying our criteria to each alternative and judging its relative merits. As the standards become more precise and compliance is measured with greater accuracy, it is typically the case that only a small number of choices satisfy the objective.

In sum, systematic decision making involves preparing an objective statement, defining decision criteria, generating alternatives, choosing an alternative that best meets the criteria, and assessing the potential problems and risks of the choice. We now discuss each element of the decision-making process in the context of locating a new industrial plant.

GENERAL CASE DESCRIPTION

This site location decision study comes from the decision by a company to vertically integrate one of its basic product lines. The company has been in the lens manufacturing and marketing business for many years, with a distribution pattern similar to population trends in the United States. Up to this point, the company had been concerned almost exclusively with eyeglass manufacture, allowing the appurtenances, such as cleaners and solutions, to be supplied by subcontractors under their license. With the advent of hard- and soft-lens eye wear, the principal chose to reinvest some of the profits from lens sales into facilities for the production of complementary products, those items used jointly with lenses but currently supplied by third-party vendors. Demand studies suggested to management that the greatest profit potential in this area would be saline solutions. The manufacturing of saline solutions, although a necessary part of their total product, was foreign to existing management, so an outsider was brought on board with responsibility for planning the new facility.

At the outset, the project was loosely and generally defined, with details, such as plant location, to be decided at a later time. Once the new manager was hired, the project began to take shape. Senior managers decided that the plant was to be operated without an organized union, which existed at some other facilities they operated. Since the general distribution pattern of the market followed the population trends of the United States, it was decided to keep as close as possible to the geographic market center. California was excluded from the marketing region. The manufacture of saline solutions for eye care requires a clean room, sterile conditions, and a relatively high technical skill level for the production workers. This demand for well-trained technicians dictated a plant location in an area with a central city of at least 50,000 people to ensure an adequate supply of quality labor. Table 17.1 gives a rough sketch of the labor force required at the site.

TABLE 17.1   LABOR FORCE REQUIREMENTS

DAY SHIFT	SECOND SHIFT	THIRD SHIFT
73 Shift	73 Shift	73 Shift
22 Staff	1 Guard	1 Guard
12 Q.A.	6 Maintenance	6 Maintenance
5 Finished Product Warehouse		
15 Maintenance		
1 Guard		
128 Total Day Shift	80 Total Second Shift	80 Total Third Shift

	TOTAL EMPLOYMENT	
	One-shift operation = 128	
	Two-shift operation = 208	
	Three-shift operation = 288	

Objective Statement

Although at first glance it may seem trivial, an important step to making a successful site location decision is a clear statement of the objective to be achieved. Within a company, several managers will usually have the responsibility for locating a new facility, with one of them having primary responsibility. The managers would come from several areas—engineering, real estate, production, personnel, distribution, and sales to name a few.

The first step then is to state the objective. For instance, in this case the objective was: Build a new plant to manufacture saline solution to service customers jointly with existing lens products. The importance of the objective statement is that it eliminates needless distractions such as searching for an existing building to buy, purchasing an existing supplier, and other options, including doing nothing.

Decision Criteria

The next step in systematic decision making is to set some criteria to guide the decision. Decision making can be viewed as choosing the alternative that best meets the criteria *relative* to the other alternatives. Managers often see that there is no single best, perfect site, meeting all their criteria and just waiting to be discovered. Instead, the final choice is the one that emerges after ever-tightening criteria are applied to the universe of possible locations, given, in addition, search and information costs. The process is similar to that of buying a house. You rarely find one with the perfect color, floor design, size, and neighborhood. Choosing the plant location also requires some compromise on characteristics.

To enumerate the decision criteria, managers must establish any absolute *requirements* along with the less essential desirable attributes. In selecting a house, you may decide that four bedrooms and a garage are essential, while a fireplace would be nice but not critical. It is important that all the managers involved in the site choice be allowed to establish the criteria, since it is easy for one aspect of the site decision, say engineering, to dictate the final decision if other demands are not made known. Managers come to realize that the successful site choice involves both quantifiable (engineering and cost data) and nonquantifiable (livability and work ethic) criteria. A framework for balancing these different modes is developed in the rest of the chapter.

There are two levels of criteria imposed on the decision. The first is of a general nature and helps reduce the number of alternatives to a manageable level. This criterion is increasingly refined until there are between 10 and 15 site alternatives available for detailed study. The second is the site specific criterion. First, we take up the general criteria used to generate the alternative sites, and then we discuss the site specific measures.

In this case study, initial meetings to develop location criteria centered on the identification of the relevant community factors most advantageous to the company's requirements. The company desired to operate a new facility close to its geographic market center. A consultant firm was hired that submitted a questionnaire to company personnel. The responses listed 24 factors. Of these, labor

694   CHAPTER 17   PLANT LOCATION DECISION MAKING: A CASE STUDY

criteria predominated. As a result, a positive work ethic in the labor force was considered a *must,* followed by nonunion operation and adequate labor supply and skills.

Financial considerations such as comparative tax structures, area wage levels, and total freight costs between potential sites ranked second in importance.

Specific community criteria included:

- A small community (25,000–50,000) in close proximity to a large metropolitan area (defined as being within 25–30 miles of a city with 50,000 to 100,000 population)

- Availability of the amenities associated with good livability (quality school system, shopping, cultural activities, and recreational pursuits)

- Access to support services such as chemical testing labs, instrument and machinery repair, tool and die makers, catering and vending machine services, and plant protection services

- Location near an interstate highway network providing maximum efficiency in product distribution

- Proximity to a major university[1]

Availability of commercial air service was considered important in two respects. One was the occasional need to deliver the company's products on a rush order. The other was the ability to travel between the company's headquarters and the plant location in one business day.

Climatological considerations centered around the potential for warehousing liquid products without the need for a major heating or dehumidifying system. The desirability of a relatively hassle-free environment was not ignored, especially in terms of lost time due to inclement weather.

Physical site characteristics were rated next in importance. The real estate department stated a preference for a site with minimal development costs, perhaps one in an industrial park where the utilities and access routes were already developed.

The other factors can be summarized quickly. The company was interested in using tax exempt Industrial Revenue Bonds as a financing source, although this was not listed as a *must* requirement. It did not consider the availability of technical training programs to be a controlling factor. It was somewhat concerned about compliance with environmental regulations and the acquisition of the necessary permits. The primary concern here was over the amount of time required for processing applications and obtaining permit approvals. There was strong concern over FDA regulations and approval, especially in the Atlanta district. The factor considered least important was community size, although the company's staff stated a preference for a community ranging in population from 25,000–50,000.

---

[1] Since a variety of technical and quality assurance people will be employed at the plant, this would allow for continued education and/or graduate study in the biological and physical sciences as well as chemical engineering and business administration.

Generating Alternative Sites

The first objective in determining the optimum communities was to establish the geographic center of market for the company. Using marketing data, it was determined that the geographic center of market for the continental United States was in the vicinity of Springfield, Illinois. However, the company planned to supply 75 percent of the national market from the new facility, with the western 25 percent supplied under contract from California. For this reason, a second geographical center of market was plotted. This time, only distribution to the eastern section of the United States was considered. The market center for this region was located in the westernmost part of Virginia—close to Norton, Virginia.

Circles were drawn encompassing a radius of 250 miles around the centers of market. An additional circle, centered between the two geographic centers of market, was also drawn. Portions of 11 states were included in the prime areas: Ohio, Indiana, Illinois, Kentucky, Tennessee, West Virginia, Virginia, Maryland, North Carolina, South Carolina, and Georgia.

An analysis of population projection trends for the years 1978, 1985, and 2000 indicates a shift in population from the northeast and midwest to the south and west. The center of population for the continental United States has been moving steadily westward since the first census in 1790. (By 1970, this center of population was located in northwest Missouri.) The implication is that marketing trends are likely to parallel this shift in population. Projections for the states under consideration indicate a decrease in the percent of state population to total U.S. population for Ohio, West Virginia, Indiana, and Illinois. Kentucky, North Carolina, South Carolina, Virginia, Georgia, and Maryland can expect increases in their percent of population to total U.S. population by the year 2000.

In order to better define and narrow down the areas under consideration, a variety of preliminary analyses on union strength, transportation costs, and construction labor costs were performed. In terms of open shop construction, North Carolina and South Carolina are considered to be the easiest in which to operate.[2] Wage rates are the lowest in these two states as well. Virginia had some areas of union strength—especially in Newport News—but open shop construction is standard practice elsewhere in the state. Tennessee is moving away from union construction, but the urban areas such as Memphis and Nashville are still predominantly unionized. Open shop is feasible in Kentucky but must be done with care. Union strength in eastern Kentucky is substantial. Urban areas along the Ohio River remain predominantly unionized. In addition, the consultant felt that given the company's criterion, southeastern Ohio should be avoided since union strength was high.

No major nonunion industrial construction has been attempted in southern Illinois. Areas here with any industry at all are dominated by unions. Unions dominate southern Indiana, especially in and around Evansville and New

---

[2] An open shop is a legal term referring to the state of the union law and contract. When a shop is open, an employee does not have to be a member of the representing union to work in the facility.

Albany. Open shop is not considered feasible at all in Terre Haute. The entire state of West Virginia is a stronghold for union activity. As a result, communities in this state were not considered for the company's new facility.

Union activity correlates strongly with construction cost. A construction labor cost analysis for representative communities in the states under considera-tion revealed that construction in states with strong union organizations would cost from 44 percent to 62 percent more than in nonunion areas such as North Carolina and South Carolina. Both Kentucky and Tennessee ranked less than 10 percent higher than the Carolinas, while Virginia ranked 22 percent higher than North Carolina and South Carolina.

A ranking process also evaluated corporate income tax and other taxes and exemptions, right-to-work status, percentage of nonagricultural labor force in unions, and utility costs. From this exercise, 36 communities from 10 states and Puerto Rico were identified. The communities that best met the overall criteria were selected for detailed evaluation:

Fredericksburg, VA

Hendersonville, NC

Huntsville, AL

Lexington, KY, area (Danville, Harrodsburg, Nicolasville, Georgetown)

Lynchburg, VA

Puerto Rico

Raleigh, NC

Rock Hill, SC

Managers reviewed these community recommendations, and, with one excep-tion, they agreed upon the areas to be examined in more detail. Puerto Rico was eliminated from further consideration for other internal reasons. The company's headquarters were included in the analysis for financial consideration. During the initial stages of the detailed investigation, Hendersonville, NC, was dropped due to the lack of sites, and Greenville, SC, was added to the list in its place.

At this time, the company requested that the entire broad geographic area be investigated for suitable, currently available, industrial buildings. A number of potential buildings were identified. These were narrowed down to four locations:

Huntsville, AL

Lumberton, NC

Rocky Mount, NC

Savannah, GA

Subsequently, the building in Lumberton was determined to be unworkable. Since Huntsville was already being considered, the company requested that Rocky Mount and Savannah be added to the list for comparative purposes. Thus, the final community list included:

Fredericksburg, VA

Greenville, SC

Huntsville, AL

Lexington, KY, area

Lynchburg, VA

Raleigh, NC

Company Headquarters, USA (financial only)

Rock Hill, SC

Rocky Mount, NC

Savannah, GA

Site Specific Decision Criteria

The generation of alternative communities for detailed analysis was the result of applying general criteria to all possible alternatives and was done, as is usual, with publicly available information and little site specific data. Once the alternative communities are identified, the analysis becomes more structured, and measurements need to be more precise. The first step is to formulate the exact criteria for which the alternative sites will be evaluated and the level of importance each criterion should have on the overall decision.

For our case study, each manager with responsibility for some aspect of the new plant construction and operation was interviewed by the outside consultant to obtain his or her input into the factors that should be incorporated in the project. After these data were collected, a list of criteria and factor weights on a 1–10 scale was put together and submitted for the approval of senior management.

The interviews with managers involved in planning for the facility and top management of the company produced a set of criteria. These are reported in Table 17.2. The weights attached to each criterion were debated and agreed upon by the company's management team. As you can see, the site selection criteria blend both quantifiable and nonquantifiable variables. At this point, the criteria were applied to the various final sites chosen for detailed analysis. The only requirement for a consistent ranking of the alternatives is that the site that best meets the factor relative to the other sites is given a score of 10, which is then multiplied by the factor weight to arrive at the score awarded each site for that particular factor. The site that best meets the criteria relative to the other sites must get a score of 10, while the other scores can range to zero.

In the case of the labor-related variables, both quantitative and considered judgment were used to rank alternative sites. Work ethic is assessed through careful interviews of managers already established in the community. An assessment of the possibility of running a nonunion operation is determined by closely assessing the National Labor Relations Board's data detailing union organizing activity in the area and any discussions brought up in local industry interviews.

Site Evaluation and Analysis

Final site selection involves the comparisons of how well each choice matches the criteria relative to the alternatives. This involves data gathering, which requires both evaluations of measurable variables, for example, wage rates, as well as

TABLE 17.2   RELATIVE FACTOR IMPORTANCE

FACTOR	WEIGHT
Work Ethic	MUST
Nonunion Operation	10
Total Freight Cost	9
Labor Supply	8
Labor Skills	8
Support Services	8
Livability	8
Area Wage Levels	8
Interstate Highway within Designated Distance	8
Transit Time of Product (customer service)	8
Taxes	8
College or University	7
Overall Highway Network	7
Physical Site Characteristics (Topography, Configuration, Access, etc.)	7
Community Attitudes	6
Electrical Service	6
Climatological Factors	5
Proximity to Larger City	5
Technical Training	5
Industrial Revenue Bonds	5
Stated Relationship with Existing Company Plants	5
Time Required to Obtain Environmental Permits	5
Community Size	4

detailed personal interviews with business and community leaders. In any case, some of the most important considerations, such as work ethic, rely to a large degree on the subjective opinion of the person visiting and evaluating the community. This may confuse some who are used to decision making based solely on the numbers, but, as we shall see, the easily quantified factors may not carry as much weight as other factors that are difficult to measure but nevertheless important to the bottom line.

Table 17.3 compares each of the alternative sites in terms of recurring (projected total variable costs for one year) costs and nonrecurring (fixed) costs. The recurring cost figures were arrived at mostly from publicly available data and from actual surveys performed when the consultant visited the site. The nonrecurring costs are estimated using actual cost data from existing facilities with similar engineering characteristics. Savannah, GA, and the company headquarters were not considered or visited with the intention of building a new plant. From Table 17.3, it is clear, at least at this point, that there is no winner that stands out as best from the cost point of view. Management's intuition that a site at their present location would be costly was confirmed.

TABLE 17.3   COMPARISON OF RECURRING AND NONRECURRING COSTS BY SELECTED COMMUNITIES

	Fredericksburg VA	Greenville SC	Huntsville AL	Georgetown KY	Lynchburg VA	Raleigh NC	Rock Hill SC	Rocky Mt. NC	Savannah GA	Home Office	Raleigh Fuquay Varina NC	Nicholasville KY
RECURRING COSTS												
Labor	$2230	$2332	$2197	$2397	$2221	$2447	$2025	$1907	$2158	$2674	$2150	$2397
Taxes	856	735	312	812	870	878	742	925	784	1200	878	750
Electrical Power	405	215	285	274	298	265	206	265	406	242	265	274
Product Delivery to Distribution Centers	725	844	896	777	686	812	842	824	944	830	812	777
Worker's Compensation Premiums	23	30	25	48	23	17	26	13	27	81	17	48
Total	$4240	$4159	$3717	$4311	$4100	$4419	$3843	$3936	$4321	$5028	$4123	$4249
NONRECURRING COSTS												
Land	$172	$149	$230	$414	$345	$253	$115	-0-	-0-	-0-	$140	$322
Rail	-0-	-0-	-0-	-0-	-0-	-0-	-0-	-0-	-0-	-0-	-0-	-0-
Sales Tax	-0-	-0-	-0-	-0-	-0-	49	-0-	49	-0-	-0-	-0-	-0-
Utility Lines	20	100	-0-	-0-	-0-	17	-0-	-0-	-0-	-0-	-0-	-0-
Construction Labor	2493	2040	2351	2223	2314	2040	2040	2040	-0-	-0-	2040	2223
Total	$2685	$2290	$2581	$2637	$2659	$2360	$2155	$2090	-0-	-0-	$2180	$2545

(all numbers in thousands)

Table 17.4 integrates both the quantitative and nonquantitative factors to determine which sites have the best prospects for fulfilling the company's objective. The first two columns repeat the factors and their weights. Each community was visited by a consultant to collect and verify data. In each community, an initial plant site was chosen. This allows for the computation of site specific cost characteristics. Note that most criteria are communitywide, and the exact geographic location of the facility has little impact. Each community is then evaluated relative to the others, the best receiving a score of ten. The rank for each community on a particular factor is then multiplied by the respective weight to obtain the score. The total weighted score is found by adding together the scores for the individual communities. Table 17.4 reveals that there are four communities with a total score in excess of 1100 points. There is a big gap between these four, Greenville, SC, Huntsville, AL, Fuquay, NC, and Raleigh, NC, and the remaining communities.

The process of evaluating some factors requires elaboration. For instance, work ethic is evaluated through visits to existing manufacturing plants in the respective communities. Once there, an experienced consultant subjectively evaluates the attitude of persons observed in the plant and assesses information gleaned in personal interviews with plant management. Table 17.4 should not be read to imply that the work ethic in, say, Rocky Mount, NC, is low in an absolute sense. Instead this rating is relative to the other communities under evaluation. In another situation, it is quite possible for Rocky Mount to obtain the highest rating. Similar notions follow when viewing the evaluations for community attitudes, livability, and so on.

Other labor factors such as opportunity for nonunion operation, labor skills, and labor costs (as part of recurring costs) are primarily evaluated from quantitative data derived from published sources, with verification of the information done at initial visits to the community. Some of the factors such as size of community, availability of technical training, highway network, proximity to larger city, available local college or university, commercial air service, industrial revenue bonds, availability of support services, and climate yield almost clear-cut ranking among the communities. The environmental permitting factor calls for a judgment by engineers as to both the feasibility of obtaining a permit and expected time for the process.

Site Risk Analysis

There still remains the final choice of site among the four candidates with more than 1100 total points. An important part of this exercise is the identification of potential problems at each site, the possible impact, and assignment of risk associated with its occurrence. Whenever there is a final choice to be made among seemingly identical alternatives, the final decision may then rest on the severity of potential risk at each site. It is important to keep in mind that smart management realizes the economic landscape is continuously changing and its analysis to this point is a static equilibrium or a snapshot of the present conditions at each of the alternative sites. Site risk analysis helps plan for and identify where adverse consequences are most likely to occur, gives an early assessment of their importance to the project, and serves to generate some management responses to deal

TABLE 17.4   COMPARATIVE FACTOR ANALYSIS

FACTOR	WEIGHT	FREDERICKSBURG VA	GREENVILLE SC	HUNTSVILLE AL	GEORGETOWN KY	NICHOLASVILLE KY	LYNCHBURG VA	FUQUAY NC	RALEIGH NC	ROCK HILL SC	ROCKY MT. NC	SAVANNAH GA
Work Ethic	10	8/80	10/100	10/100	6/60	6/60	10/100	10/100	10/100	10/100	5/50	8/80
aTotal Nonrecurring Costs	10	7/70	10/100	8/80	5/50	5/50	7/70	10/100	7/70	10/100	-0-	-0-
Total Operating Costs	8	6/48	8/64	10/80	6/48	6/48	9/72	7/56	5/40	8/64	7/56	7/56
Nonunion Operation	10	8/80	10/100	8/80	3/30	2/20	8/80	10/100	10/100	9/90	8/80	8/80
Labor Supply	8	7/56	10/80	9/72	9/72	9/72	10/80	9/72	10/80	6/48	6/48	7/56
Labor Skills	8	8/64	8/64	10/80	10/80	10/80	10/80	8/64	10/80	6/48	5/40	6/48
Proximity to Larger City	5	10/50	9/45	8/40	9/45	9/45	6/30	9/45	10/50	9/45	3/15	7/35
Support Services	8	7/56	8/64	9/72	9/72	9/72	8/64	8/64	10/80	8/64	6/48	7/56
Livability	8	9/72	8/64	8/64	8/64	8/64	7/56	6/48	10/80	7/56	5/40	8/64
Highway Network	7	9/63	9/63	8/56	9/63	9/63	8/56	8/56	9/63	9/63	7/49	6/42
College/University	6	7/42	7/42	7/42	9/54	9/54	7/42	10/60	10/60	6/36	3/18	6/36
Commercial Air Service	7	9/63	6/42	6/42	8/56	8/56	6/42	8/56	8/56	8/56	5/35	6/42
Climatological Factors	5	6/30	8/40	8/40	6/30	6/30	9/45	8/40	8/40	8/40	8/40	8/40
Community Attitudes	6	9/54	8/48	10/60	5/30	4/24	9/54	8/48	8/48	7/42	4/24	7/42
aPhysical Site Characteristics	7	8/56	5/35	9/63	4/28	1/7	5/35	8/56	5/35	5/35	-0-	-0-
Technical Training	5	7/35	10/50	10/50	6/30	6/30	7/35	10/50	10/50	10/50	8/40	9/45
Industrial Revenue Bonds	5	9/45	9/45	10/50	9/45	9/45	9/45	6/30	6/30	9/45	6/30	9/45
Environmental Permitting	5	9/45	9/45	6/30	6/30	6/30	7/35	9/45	10/50	7/35	8/40	8/40
Community Size	4	7/28	8/32	8/32	8/32	8/32	8/32	9/32	10/40	8/32	2/8	7/28
Total Weighted Score—All Factors		1037	1123	1133	919	882	1053	1122	1152	1049	661	835
Total Weighted Score—Nonsite Factors		911	988	990	841	825	948	966	1047	914	661	835

a not included

with unexpected events if they occur. In addition, this makes it easier for management to put a monitoring system in place to identify potential problem areas. In general, risk assessment compiles a chart such as Table 17.5. In the chart, H stands for a high, M represents medium, and L is used for low seriousness or potential.

The purpose of Table 17.5 is to make the potential pitfalls in the start-up and long-run success of the project visible. Management should take care to monitor and have contingency plans in place for items that have been scored as having high potential seriousness for the project and a high chance of occurrence. For instance, the site situation in Greenville has several aspects that should cause alarm. One way to deal with this problem is to identify alternative building sites in the Greenville area as backup to the one considered in this analysis. Whether a community is eliminated at this stage is dependent on the options available to forestall or remedy any of the serious and probable adverse consequences.

Conclusion of the Site Study

In this case, the consultant recommended that the four communities with the highest composite scores be candidates for site visits by the company management:

TABLE 17.5   RISK ASSESSMENT

RISK FACTOR	SERIOUSNESS	POTENTIAL
RALEIGH		
Labor Union Election	H	L
Utility Extensions/Hookups	M	L
Environmental Permitting	H	L
Site Availability/Suitability	M	L
Skilled Labor Availability	M	M
Relocation of Skilled Personnel	L	L
FUQUAY		
Labor Union Election	H	L
Utility Extensions/Hookups	H	M
Environmental Permitting	H	L
Site Availability/Suitability	M	L
Skilled Labor Availability	M	M
Relocation of Skilled Personnel	L	M
GREENVILLE		
Labor Union Election	H	L
Utility Extensions/Hookups	H	H
Environmental Permitting	H	L
Site Availability/Suitability	M	H
Skilled Labor Availability	M	M
Relocation of Skilled Personnel	L	M

Raleigh, NC

Huntsville, AL

Greenville, SC

Fuquay, NC

Interestingly, top management at the company dismissed out of hand any possibility of the new plant locating in Huntsville, AL, for reasons not revealed to the consultant, and for this reason Huntsville is excluded from Table 17.5, the risk analysis. The company chose the final location of the manufacturing plant to be at one of the other three sites.

SUMMARY

The theoretical concepts of management decision making are well developed. They involve arriving at an optimal solution in an environment of business, informational, and political constraints. Characteristic of all systematic decision making in the business world is the development of an objective statement, criteria, alternatives, and risk assessment. The objective statement should state precisely what the management desires to accomplish. Decision criteria are developed through brainstorming about the specific requirements for success of the project and weighing the importance of each criterion. Alternatives are initially open to all possibilities remotely matching the objective statement, but they are quickly narrowed once general criteria are applied. As tighter and more precisely measured criteria are applied in successive rounds of evaluation, the field of alternatives narrows until only a few clearly meet the objective statement. Nevertheless, even the final alternatives will have flaws and pose a threat to the objective of the project, so that a risk assessment of critical elements for each of the final alternatives is also performed.

The industrial site location decision presents a good opportunity to see how the abstract concepts of systematic decision making are put to work. The managers who are to research the project and make a recommendation to the company owners are invariably faced with a fuzzy, poorly defined task. The initial chore is to write an objective statement listing the goals to be accomplished and reaching some consensus as to its contents. In our case study, challenges to the objective statement were constantly posed, ranging from leasing an existing building, moving the operations off-shore for alleged tax advantages, and placating home-town public spiritedness. The next step is to catalog the concerns and viewpoints of managers with different responsibilities within the company. This ensures that all important aspects of the optimal site are considered, whether they be engineering, real estate, production, or marketing. The next step is to transform the criteria into measurable factors and to place weights on each as to its importance in the overall scheme of the project. The objective statement and the weighted criteria make visible the assumptions and measures by which the final site selection is made.

In the case study, it was apparent that a plant to manufacture saline solutions could be sited in a number of places. This is invariably the case when a facility does not have some particular technical requirement of raw materials or environmental hazards. Since information gathering is costly, it becomes necessary to quickly pare the overwhelmingly large number of alternatives to a maximum of, say, 10, and then examine these closely. By using state right-to-work laws, community size, and market center criteria, the field of sites was quickly narrowed. The application of even more detailed criteria was necessary to arrive at the final site alternatives. Once selected, each community and possible site were visited to gather the necessary data to gauge how well each met the weighted site factors. The evaluation of a community hinges on how well it meets the standards relative to the other communities, not against some ideal standard. Out of this analysis, four final communities were selected, and the facility was finally built in one of them in the early 1980s.

TOPICS TO REVIEW

These are topics that you should feel comfortable with before you leave this chapter. If you cannot write out a clear and concise sentence or paragraph explaining the topic, you should reread the relevant section of the text.

Statement of the Objective

General Criteria

Site Specific Criteria

Relative Factor Weights

SUGGESTED READINGS

Bradfield, M. "A note on Location and Theory of Production." *Journal of Regional Science* 11 (1971):263–66.

Dorfman, John R. "Relocating a Firm Can Prove to Be Bad Sign, Some Analysts Say, but It Depends on Motive." *Wall Street Journal,* June 20, 1991, p. C2.

Emerson, D. T. "Optimum Firm Location and the Theory of Production." *Journal of Regional Science* 13 (1973):333–45.

Greenhut, M. L. *Plant Location in Theory and in Practice.* Chapel Hill: University of North Carolina Press, 1956.

Kepner, Charles H. and Tregoe, Benjamin B. *The Rational Manager.* New York: McGraw-Hill, 1965.

Kusumoto, S. I. "On the Foundation of the Economic Theory of Location—Transport Distance vs. Technological Substitution." *Journal of Regional Science* 24 (1984):249–70.

Miller, S. M. and Jensen, D. M. "Location and the Theory of Production: A Review. Summary and Critique of Recent Contributions." *Regional Science and Urban Economics* 8 (1978):117–28.

Schmener, Roger W. *Making Business Location Decisions.* Englewood Cliffs, NJ: Prentice Hall, 1982.

INDEX